D1784757

Psychological Approaches to
Crime and Its Correction

Psychological Approaches to Crime and Its Correction: Theory, Research, Practice

Irving Jacks
and
Steven G. Cox,
Editors

Nelson-Hall nh Chicago

Library of Congress Cataloging in Publication Data

Main entry under title:

Psychological approaches to crime and its correction.

Includes bibliographical references.
1. Criminal psychology—Addresses, essays, lectures.
2. Violence—Addresses, essays, lectures. 3. Deviant
behavior—Addresses, essays, lectures. 4. Rehabilitation of criminals—Addresses, essays, lectures.
5. Rehabilitation of juvenile delinquents. I. Jacks,
Irving. II. Cox, Steven G.
HV6080.P825 1984   364.3'01'9   83-17208
ISBN 0-88229-422-9
ISBN 0-88229-818-6 (pbk.)

Copyright © 1984 by Irving Jacks and Steven G. Cox

All rights reserved. No part of this book may be reproduced in any form without permission in
writing from the publisher, except by a reviewer who wishes to quote brief passages in connection with a review written for broadcast or for inclusion in a magazine or newspaper. For
information address Nelson-Hall Inc., Publishers, 111 North Canal Street, Chicago, Illinois
60606.

Manufactured in the United States of America

10 9 8 7 6 5 4 3 2 1

The paper in this book is pH neutral (acid-free).

Contents

Preface

Anyone surveying the modern scene in criminology or corrections may well be forgiven if he or she were to start wondering about the validity of a book based on the social or behavioral sciences. At the time of this writing there has been launched from several different sources a widespread attack on the entire positivistic point of view, which purports to bring scientific discipline to bear on the understanding of crime and its correction. The attack has come from a variety of sources, covering a range of special interests. Thus in 1972, at a conference entitled "Examining Psychology's Roles and Contributions in Corrections," conducted under the joint sponsorship of the National Institute of Mental Health, the Law Enforcement Assistance Administration, and the Youth Development and Delinquency Prevention Association, Judge David L. Bazelon of the U.S. Court of Appeals in Washington, D.C., voiced the fear that "the papers prepared for this conference on the role of psychology in corrections do nothing to allay my increasing doubts and uncertainties about what it is that psychologists or any other behavioralists offer."[1] Judge Bazelon's critique was particularly disturbing to the assembled psychologists because of his wide reputation among behavioral scientists as the man who paved the way for psychology in the civil court room. More recently, writing about the relationship between free-will and determinism in juvenile justice, Frederick Faust of the School of Criminology at Florida State University stated that "it is no secret that the early expectations for the administration of juvenile justice on the basis of positivistic principles have never been realized . . . the crux of the matter rests in the fact that the state of scientific knowledge about human behavior ('including anti-social behavior') is not sufficiently developed to permit accurate prediction and control."[2] In a similar vein, Robert Martinson in a recent review of correctional treatment programs, which has generated much discussion among "correctionists," summarized findings based on a total of 231 "acceptable" reports of treatment, reflecting a wide spectrum of approaches, that appeared between 1945 and 1967. He concluded rather grimly that "with few and isolated exceptions, the rehabilitative efforts that have been reported so far have had no appreciable effect on recidivism."[3]

A somewhat variant critical stance with regard to the role of psychological and social science is that of the civil libertarian who, rather than questioning the efficacy of social-psychological approaches, assumes that they are indeed capable of producing behavior change, and as such represent a potential threat to human freedom. From this standpoint, the utilization of the technology derived from social and psychological research takes on a menacing potential for control of minds and human behavior à la *Clockwork Orange*. Perhaps the best known statement of this position is the freewheeling assault on the American prison system, including its attempt at scientific approaches to rehabilitation, given by Jessica Mitford in her book *Kind and Usual Punishment*.[4]

Thus we see the wheel turn full circle from the high hopes of the late 1940s and 1950s that science, if sufficiently supported and applied, would bring about a solution to "the crime problem," to the current widespread advocacy of a return to an unvarnished "punishment model."

In the minds of some readers, recital of the bleak assessment of the contributions of social-behavioral science to crime and its correction may give rise to wonderment at an effort to compile an anthology reflecting these contributions. Yet it is just because the latest "conventional wisdom" is tending to bring into disrepute efforts to deal scientifically with criminological and correctional problems that it becomes essential to consider what possibilities for success do inhere in a scientific approach. For if, as Judge Bazelon has implied, the contributions of social-behavioral science have not had the hoped-for effect of reducing crime and especially criminal recidivism, it is nonetheless worth recalling that the turn to science was in itself a response to the failure of traditional—so-called "classical"—practices. Here, as in other fields, the student observes the ancient rivalry between the realist, who attempts to solve problems through debate and reference to abstract concepts, and the empiricist, who puts his faith in rigorously controlled experimentation as the surest source of knowledge. And if there is one observation that the history of crime and punishment enables us to make with almost as much assurance as the inevitability of death and taxes, it is that the pendulum will swing again. The nihilism represented by a pure punishment model (even when it masquerades as a justice model) is bound to emerge rapidly. As the impact of continuing increases in rates of criminality and recidivism sinks into public awareness, the public and its political leaders will again turn to the sciences of behavior and society.

In the meantime, even as the punishment model has its day, it is doubtful that criminal justice systems will entirely suspend efforts to bring about among their clients—the inmates, probationers, parolees, the violent and the larcenous, the youthful and the adult—changes in behavior that will enable them to function more productively and less destructively. These efforts, however limited they may be deemed to be, involve the employment of technologies originating in social-behavioral scientific investigations. Any improvement in their power to influence the behavior of the criminal justice clientele will depend on a cadre of professional criminal justice workers who are sufficiently knowledgeable regarding these technologies and their scientific origins to be capable of (1) knowing when, how, and with whom to use them; and (2) monitoring their effectiveness with particular clients or client-groups, so as to be in a position to modulate, modify, or shift techniques.

Lest the reader infer from the above that this, then, is a cookbook of applied techniques, we hasten to correct this impression. It may well be, in fact, that it is just such a simpleminded, uncritical, cookbook approach that is at the source of the limited successes reported for the available technologies. Even an amateur cook, slavishly following detailed instructions from a cookbook in his own kitchen, must know something of the performance properties of his oven, the quality of his ingredients, and the accuracy of his oven thermometer. The professional chef, if he takes pride in his cuisine, goes beyond this to an understanding of the biochemistry of food preparation, as well as the social and psychological requirements of his clientele.

Similarly, on the assumption that most readers of this book are preparing themselves for *professional* involvement as correctional workers (and that this is an activity with at least as much social value as the work of the professional chef), we have taken the position, in organizing this anthology, that materials dealing with those broad but basic concepts on which rest social-behavioral approaches to criminality constitute the appropriate place to begin. Having become familiar with the foundation concepts, we then turn to a consideration of major topics of concern to the preprofessional student or to the practitioner. Here the items selected represent, on the one hand, increased specificity in that all the items in a given section focus on one common topic, and on the other hand, an effort to bring together items that, in totality reveal a relationship to the foundation concepts introduced earlier. Finally, we attempt to bring the knowledge gained thus far to bear upon the central problem of the corrections professional—that is, the modification of offender behavior, or, if preferred, rehabilitation of offenders.

Obviously, one could dispute the wisdom of any particular selection of items. We would be hard put to defend either our inclusions or omissions, but the reader is entitled to know our selection criteria, at least insofar as we are capable of articulating them. Among the criteria used were the following: sound observational or research design; specificity of concepts; brevity; clear description of techniques used; availability for reproduction; minimal assumption of previous technical sophistication; relative recency of appearance. The criteria and the selections flowing from them naturally reflect our biases, which we hope we have not concealed so artfully that a discerning reader would be unable to recognize them or correct for them. Whether the criteria are appropriate and whether the selections meet the criteria, we leave to the judgment of readers.

Notes

1. Bazelon, D. L. "U.S. Judge Questions Science's Role in the Treatment of Violent Criminals" *APA Monitor* 3, no. 3 (March 1972), p. 1.
2. Faust, F. L. "A Perspective on the Dilemma of Free Will and Determinism in Juvenile Justice." *Juvenile Justice* 25, no. 1 (May 1974), pp. 54–60.
3. Martinson, R. "What works? Questions and Answers about prison reform." *Public Interest* 35, (Spring 1975), pp. 22–54.
4. Mitford, J. *Kind and Usual Punishment* (New York: Alfred A. Knopf, 1973).

Part One

Foundations for a Behavioral Approach to Criminality and Its Correction

For most categories of human behavior, modern theories of individual causation have tended to emphasize either internal or external influences. Naively, this has at times been described as the nature-nurture controversy or as heredity versus environment. Interestingly enough, both emphases can be traced back to the movement known as *positivism*, which is ascribed to the sociologist Comte and which, with respect to criminality, originated in the writings of the Italian anthropologist Lombroso and his concept of the "criminal man."

What all theories subsumed under the positivistic label have in common is a rejection of the centuries-old Judeo-Christian doctrine of free will. Known as the classical school, this doctrine, very simply stated, assumes a moral faculty in humans that enables each individual to choose either to act in conformity with morality (or, if codified, legality), or to choose to violate the code. If he or she chooses to violate, the choice can be said to reflect evil intent rationally arrived at, and as such it is subject to retaliation by society to expunge the evil. This, the reader has undoubtedly discerned, is the grand motif of the adjudicatory phase of our criminal justice system up to the present day. It determines all the processes of criminal investigation and trial, leading to a decision of the guilt or innocence of an accused. The very words *guilty* and *innocent* are redolent of choice freely taken.

Positivism, in contrast, has attempted to fit criminal or antisocial behavior into a framework of scientific determinism by emphasizing antecedent causation and denying the possibility of choice independent of conditions preceding and/or surrounding the behavior in question. As a corollary, efforts to change behavior require a change in conditions. In broad terms, such conditions can be viewed as sociological, psychological, or biological. To the extent that the focus is on identifiable individuals as tending to, or already having committed, acts of criminality, the latter two classes—psychological and biological—grow in prominence. Particularly is this the case to the extent that we may be involved in the treatment or correction of individuals previously identified as criminal or delinquent. Thus, we open this collection by affording the reader an overview of contemporary psychological and biological theories, all reflecting the positivistic approach to criminal behavior.

Shore, in addition to his review of psychological theories, offers us something of perhaps even greater long-term value. He outlines what it is that theories do for the practitioner in day-to-day encounters with clients. Shore cites three ways in which theories can help: to organize the known data, to set directions for further exploration, and—perhaps most significant for the practitioner—to plan intervention programs. To the extent that a theory can be said to satisfy these three criteria, it can be judged as useful.

Rosenthal and Kittrie emphasize concepts of biological causation. Here again, they go beyond mere restatement of particular theories to a consideration of the wider impact of such theories. Rosenthal makes it clear that the relationship between heredity and criminality is by no means a simple and direct one. One might say that instead of a simple "why" question to which the answer is "heredity," we are now forced to ask a far more sophisticated "how" question: that is, "How does heredity operate to increase the probability of criminality?" This involves a recognition that inherited potentialities interact with environmental encounters of the organism to "produce" criminal behavior. This being the case, it militates against the hopeless nihilism that a simpleminded recourse to genetic explanations frequently engenders. Instead, it encourages the practitioner to focus on environmental experiences that might interact with genetic potential to produce prosocial— or at least noncriminal—outcomes.

Kittrie takes one rather dramatic subcategory of the biological position— the XYY syndrome—to demonstrate the tension between a classical free-will position and a positivistic–deterministic one. As psychological and biological theories of criminal behavior widen their scope, it becomes increasingly difficult to justify a retaliatory posture—as distinguished from a rehabilitative one—in the disposition of convicted offenders. Just as a successful insanity defense results in an exception to the general penal disposition of convicted offenders by emphasizing the need for psychiatric care rather than ordinary imprisonment, so may we find ourselves assigning "guilty" defendants to facilities or resources tailored to the causal influences thought to be related to the criminal behavior of these defendants.

The closing selection in this section is intended to deepen the reader's perspective by introducing him to a specific psychological theory as presented by its originator. Eysenck takes the conditioning concepts of Pavlov (which have gained much prominence in the treatment of noncriminal deviance) and shows how they can be used to understand the development of criminal behavior. Besides being influential in its own right, Eysenck's concept of conditionability as an inherited attribute makes his presentation an ideal exemplar of theory-building, which draws on knowledge originating in both psychological and biological positions. What it says, in essence, is that law-abiding behavior, like most other human behavior, is learned, i.e., conditioned, through interaction with the environment; as with most other human behavior, however, some people are poorer learners, i.e., less conditionable, hence fail to learn socially acceptable behavior well enough. As we shall see later in this text, when we consider the concept of psychopathic (sociopathic) personality, Eysenck's concepts intersect with some others of contemporary vintage.

4

1

Psychological Theories of the Causes of Antisocial Behavior

Milton F. Shore

Reprinted from *Crime and Delinquency* 17 (October 1971), pp. 456–68, by permission of the author and the publisher, the National Council on Crime and Delinquency.

This paper attempts to review, organize, and evaluate the many theories that have been developed to explain the roots of antisocial behavior from a psychological perspective. Four general categories are suggested—biopsychological theories, developmental theories, psychodynamic theories, and social psychological theories. Common elements in the theories are extracted and suggestions are made for future research.

The need for a theory that can explain the causes of criminal and delinquent behavior is threefold: first, it helps organize the known data; second, it assists in setting directions for further exploration and research; and third, it aids in planning intervention programs oriented toward preventing antisocial behavior.

But evolving an adequate theory of the origins of antisocial behavior is extremely complex, largely because of the difficulty in accurately defining what is antisocial. Antisocial behavior is not a diagnostic category or unitary symptom, but a socially defined phenomenon closely tied to cultural values and often dependent on the interpretation given a behavior pattern by those agencies responsible for the regulation of social interaction. In certain communities, for example, the tolerance for deviance is lower and certain behavior may be labeled antisocial which, in another context, would not be considered deviant at all.

However, despite the cultural and social aspects of antisocial behavior, there are individuals who, given the best social opportunities, still are violent and aggressive, while others under poor social conditions do not reveal delinquent or criminal behavior. Therefore, aside from the need to understand and explain the social and cultural forces that foster criminal behavior, there is need for a theory of individual behavior that can account for individual differences and the ways in which individuals interpret and respond to social forces.

From a psychological perspective, the problem in the control of antisocial behavior can be conceived of as the question of how control over behavior is developed so that, under ordinary circumstances, antisocial behavior will not take place.[1] What are the relevant influences within the person and within his environment that foster the development of inner behavioral controls? What are the relevant variables for understanding the development of inner controls (conscience, identification, self-image, etc.)? What are the factors essential for the adequate functioning of these controls?

This paper is a review of the theories dealing with the psychological aspects of delinquent and criminal behavior. It attempts to categorize and organize the large number of psychological theories, determine their assumptions, relate them to one another, and derive the common psychological elements that need to be considered when any intervention program is planned. It is not a critical analysis or a comprehensive literature review. It aims to meet the need in the field for a broad look at the various theories so that a comprehensive theory may develop in the near future.

BIOPSYCHOLOGICAL THEORIES

Historically, the development of psychiatry and psychology from the nineteenth century's biological and medical traditions led to many early efforts to explain most antisocial behavior in biological terms. These explanations take two forms: those based on the genetic transmission of antisocial traits from generation to generation ("bad seed")[2] and those that sought to relate criminal behavior to structural constitutional characteristics such as mental capacity, neural organization, and body type. Both these approaches—the genetic and the constitutional—attempt to tie psychological characteristics such as the motor orientation, inability to delay, and low frustration tolerance, to biological roots.

One of the first attempts to correlate body structure to criminal behavior was made by Lombroso,[3] who stated that the biological structure of the criminal was biologically atavistic and that ideal social conditions had only a limited effect on criminals, for these persons could not restrain their antisocial behavior. This was confirmed, he believed, by the histological structure of the cortex.

Sheldon,[4] although he did not attribute inferior evolutionary status to the offender, related delinquent behavior to body build. The body build, he believed, was highly correlated with an inborn substratum of basic psychological traits ("temperament") which caused the person to respond in a particular way to environmental stimulation.

The interest in the biological structure and mechanisms underlying the criminal personality was continued in the work of Cleckley,[5] who believed the psychopathic personality had biological roots. Some support for his view has come from those who have found a greater number of signs of neurological disorder (tremors, exaggerated reflexes, tics, etc.) in psychopaths,[6] as well as greater physiological responsiveness to environmental changes and many more early diseases that might have damaged the brain.

At present there is great concern with the chromosomal XYY syndrome, which is believed to be associated with hyper-masculinity and poor control of aggression.

The biopsychological theories address themselves to certain known facts. There is no doubt that the antisocial behavior of certain individuals has sometimes been found to be impermeable to change by current techniques and that certain individuals have required external control within an institutional setting. Also known is that certain individuals under drugs of various kinds (e.g., alcohol) show a marked breakdown in behavioral controls. Certain neurological phenomena have also been directly related to motor control.[7] All these facts suggest that one factor that must be considered in evaluating the causes of antisocial behavior in an individual is his neurological and biochemical structure.

However, research has shown that the biological structure of the person, although contributing to lack of control under certain stimulating conditions, is in no way a prerequisite for that loss of control, nor is it often the major element in determining the antisocial dimension of the behavior.[8]

If the future directions in the field are in any way related to those of the past, many traits and tendencies which are believed to be biological in origin will most likely be found to be closely tied to experiences, perhaps to events occurring in infancy, a fact that could account for the problems in reversibility and change. For example, the current work on imprinting, where a particular event occurring during a critical period in biological maturation results in certain behavior,[9] is significant in this regard.

Recently, a close tie between experience and neurological organization has been found.[10] If certain experiences do not occur at certain ages, adequate neurological development does not take place.

These discoveries have begun to narrow the link between maturation and experience and to highlight the close ties between the two. It augurs well for eventual breakthroughs in the understanding of biological factors related to the development of behavioral controls.

DEVELOPMENTAL THEORIES: COGNITIVE DEVELOPMENT

The ability to control motor activity, to delay fulfillment of wishes and desires, to use guilt to regulate behavior, and to experience the pangs of conscience after transgression does not occur at birth but develops in a sequential order from the interaction of the maturative processes and the environment. For example, the young child who takes something belonging to another child is regarded as having an insufficient understanding of the situation and therefore is not considered to have committed an antisocial act. It is assumed that only at a certain age does awareness of the consequences of an action arise. (The concept of "legal age" implies that only at a certain chronological age can the person be assumed to understand the consequences of an act and therefore take responsibility for what he has done.) The study of the development of the understanding of morality (moral judgment) was initiated by Piaget,[11] who saw moral values as having two stages, moral realism and moral relativism. From a literal, inflexible interpretation of rules and blind obedience to a higher external authority, the child progresses to an understanding, at about age eight, of the situational and motivational elements of an act and to internalized rules.

Kohlberg[12] has studied the stages of moral development in greater detail than Piaget. True understanding of morality and justice, he believes, does not develop until adolescence.

Developmental theories assume a sequence of formal stages in the development of moral understanding. The nature of this sequence is independent of sex, intelligence, culture, social group, and biological background. However, environmental factors can delay the transition from one stage to another.

There are two important questions about cognitive theories. First, what is the relationship between the understanding of morality (a cognitive function) and moral conduct (overt behavior)? Second, what are the necessary personal and environmental conditions for the adequate development of higher moral judgment?

Studies of the relationship between moral judgment and moral behavior often show low correlations between the two.[13] Investigators in behavior modification through rewards and punishments have shown that control over overt behavior is possible without concomitant cognitive changes or generalization to other situations.[14]

Cognitive theorists have also tended to ignore the affective components in antisocial behavior. Motivation plays a minor role in their studies and often appears to lower any correlation that might exist.

However, the cognitive theorists have contributed two significant ideas to the understanding of behavioral control. They have delineated the stages in the development of controls so that one can determine how development is taking place. They have also shown why moral training and exposure to moral influences, as in Boy Scouts or religious training, are not, in themselves, adequate for developing an understanding of morality but are effective only if a certain level of conceptualization has been reached.

SOCIALIZATION

The largest group of studies on the origins of antisocial behavior deals with socialization experiences. These studies have attempted to identify the nature and the quality of the experiences necessary for the adequate development of internal controls.

ROLE OF FRUSTRATION

A major attempt to explain the social origins of aggressive behavior was the frustration-aggression hypothesis of Dollard and Miller.[15] This hypothesis has been criticized as incomplete.[16] However, there is little doubt that, although reactions to frustration may vary, under certain conditions—such as the social reinforcement of violence—aggression is a most likely response. Thus it is necessary to specify more clearly those elements or types of frustration that would lead to aggressive behavior, since even under certain stimulating conditions aggression does not always result. For example, deprivation or broken attachments may be more significant as a precursor to aggression than physical immobility at a young age.

ROLE OF FAMILY STRUCTURE AND EARLY FAMILY EXPERIENCES

The significant role of the family as the primary agent for socialization of the child cannot be denied. But what elements in family structure and functioning are essential to accomplish this socialization adequately? What factors result in inadequate socialization, producing delinquent or criminal behavior?

Many years ago, attempts to determine the most important factors in early experience related delinquency to discrete general categories of rejection, parental neglect, working mothers, and broken homes. These attempts, which represent a relatively simple effort to conceptualize the area, have been found to be too general and simplistic. Recently, efforts have been made to define the complex, subtle aspects of family interaction and family breakdown which are believed to be of particular significance in predisposing an individual to antisocial behavior.

1. Broken homes.—McCord, McCord, and Zola[17] reported that the roots of criminal behavior lie deep in early family experiences, so that only the most intensive measures, applied early in life, can ever offer hope of eradicating them. While they stated that cohesive homes produced fewer criminals, they contended that the influence of broken homes per se has been overstressed. A quarrelsome and neglectful home, whether or not it was broken, was found to be even more conducive to criminality. Toby's work[18] was consistent with these findings. Conflicts, tensions, and attitudes preceding

the actual breakdown of the family are the most important factors, he felt. But the influence of those factors depends on the age of the child. Pre-adolescents are more affected by family breakdowns than adolescents.

McCord, McCord, and Thurber[19] added another element to those listed above—namely, mothers who are working. That is, an unstable family plus a working mother shows a high correlation with delinquent behavior.

A major contribution of recent work has been to challenge the stereotype that families must have a certain specific structure with the parents playing certain specific roles. The final breakup of a family may indeed be a healthy sign if the forces that are mobilized as a result try to lead to the resolution of problems rather than their perpetuation. Likewise, mothers who choose to work may be able to better deal with their children than if they felt an obligation to remain at home seething with boredom, frustration, and guilt.

2. Influence of father.—Andry[20] has suggested that the role of the father—specifically, the physical or psychological absence of the father—has been underemphasized as an etiological factor in criminal behavior. Mischel[21] agrees, pointing out that absence of the father is highly correlated with the demand for immediate gratification (a feature found in severe delinquents) in eight- and nine-year-olds. This relationship was not present, however, in older children (eleven to fourteen years of age).

In an effort to determine what might be the reasons behind the high correlation between social class, absence of the father, and delinquency, Kvaraceus[22] concluded that aggressive behavior in lower-class male adolescents results from role anxiety. The anxiety over one's sexual role is derived from the unstable and derogatory father image presented in the home by the absence of the father or through continual devaluation of adult males by lower-class adult females.

McCord, McCord, and Zola[23] found that although the father's personality had an important bearing on antisocial behavior, it was an oversimplification to see the father and his role as the sole irreversible determining factor in delinquency. They felt that the effects of paternal neglect could be overcome if there was strong maternal love or consistent love-oriented discipline. Thus, even if the father was a criminal, maternal love and consistent discipline tended to prevent a son from identifying with the antisocial paternal model.

3. Separation and loss.—Bowlby[24] suggested still another aspect of early family experience as significant in setting the stage for later antisocial behavior. A large number of separation experiences in early life which deprived the child of a stable, close attachment to one mothering person, he felt, could lead to the development of certain basic attitudes and reactions to people which are identical to those found in delinquents and criminals. He sees this tie to a maternal figure as rooted in early biological needs.

McCord, McCord, and Zola[25] confirmed the importance of maternal love in the early years. Maternal love, even if complicated by an overprotective attitude, by anxiety, or by neurosis, was found to lead to low rates of crime. Maternal passivity, on the other hand, was significantly related to criminal behavior.

4. Other familial influences.—McCord, McCord, and Zola[26] found that boys in the middle of the birth order, especially if viewed by their parents as troublemakers, tended to be antisocial.

DISCIPLINE AND FAMILY CLIMATE

Many investigators have attempted to describe the elements of parent-child relationships most closely related to the development of antisocial behavior in an individual. One of the most obvious is discipline; it is usually believed that disciplinary measures within a family lead to the development of self-discipline.

Glueck and Glueck[27] listed discipline by the father, supervision by the mother, affection from each, and cohesiveness of the family as the factors most important for predicting future delinquent behavior (they form the items of the Glueck Prediction Scale). McCord and McCord,[28] in their review of the Cambridge Somerville Youth Study, found that consistent discipline, either punitive or love-oriented, tended to prevent criminality, while erratic punitive punishment was correlated with every type of crime except traffic violations.

The work of Sears et al.[29] sums up the findings of many studies: Discipline is necessary in child rearing, but parents of highly aggressive children have consistently been found to be more aggressive, less warm, and more inconsistent in their disciplinary techniques.

An attempt to determine the origins of the authoritarian personality[30] found that harsh, threatening discipline during childhood, in which inflexible black-and-white roles of dominance and submission were present, led not to a firmly internalized set of moral values but rather to a rigid, autocratic personality that was power-oriented and that viewed signs of weakness as dangerous.

The results of harsh discipline in child rearing are consistent with those found in experimental studies of punishment—namely, that punishment is effective in bringing about short-term conformity but does not lead to the internalization of moral values or behavioral control useful in other situations over long periods of time.

Out of these studies on discipline, three important elements emerge—consistency, intensity, and quality. Consistent discipline is more effective in producing internalization than either extreme permissiveness or lack of consistency. The more severe the punishment, the less the probability that internalization will later take place. With respect to quality, Aronfreed[31] has described two kinds of disciplinary activity. Verbal and physical attacks are sensitization techniques which make the child anticipate punishment from an external source. The opposite, which he calls induction, is where explanation and withdrawal of affection are used to try to correct the behavior. In this way independence of external factors is emphasized and the self-initiation aspects of control are in the forefront. Internalized control over behavior results.

To explain why children who have been severely punished often show highly aggressive behavior, Bandura and Walters[32] proposed a theory of the social learning of deviant behavior. The violence that is reinforced in the culture and the violence to which a child is exposed during the period of his growth when imitation and identification are important cause him to model himself after the aggressor. The importance of an adult model with whom a child could identify was noted by Rohrer and Edmonson[33] in a study of a group of Negro youths in New Orleans. Significant adults were found to be extremely important in shaping the lower-class youth's behavior; if adults were not available, individuals joined gangs in what was believed to be an effort to supply role models and values of their own. Short and Strodtbeck[34] found that lower-class gang members had lower ego ideals than a control group of non-gang members.

But identification is not a unitary process. Kohlberg[35] has suggested that there are two types of identification. In personal identification the person wishes to be like the parent. On the other hand, in positional identification family figures are seen as sources of power and the wish is to usurp the parents' sexual, authoritarian, or family roles. Research findings suggest that personal identification is related to moral learning, while positional identification is not. Personal identification clearly seems to be related to close contacts with a person whom one respects and trusts. Kohlberg sees a close tie between personal identification and the development of feelings of guilt. In identifying with another person, one assumes the role of that person in fantasy and becomes critical of transgressions, a first step in internalization and a prerequisite for experiencing guilt.

ROLE OF THE COMMUNITY

Socialization occurs not only through the family but through other community institutions as well. The relationship between the community and the family has been investigated. Maccoby et al.[36] found that communities where delinquency was high were lacking in integration, with less concern expressed by people for one another. Lander's[37] work likewise indicated that the reason juvenile delinquency was concentrated in neighborhoods where there were lower-class residents is that these areas tend to anomie; that is, there are no stable jobs, no long residences, and relatives. When upper-class areas become anomic, the rate of crime would be expected to increase.

Short[38] suggests that the significant factor is that in lower-class urban environments, there is a breakdown of norms and a "general absence of any culture." Such a condition threatens the individual with loss of individual security and produces great psychological stress and strain, resulting in personal breakdown and aberrations.

Leighton[39] felt that the frustration of sexual and aggressive impulses by socio-cultural forces was not the most important factor in precipitating antisocial behavior. Rather, the important factor was how socio-cultural disintegration produced noxious influences that then affected the achievement of love, recognition, spontaneity, and a sense of belonging to a moral order (feeling that one is right in what one does).

Psychodynamic Theories

Psychodynamic theories of antisocial behavior have addressed themselves to the complex affective elements that are significant in personality development and in leading to an antisocial act. They focus on the motivational factors, the efforts to resolve conflicts, and the unconscious aspects of the various forces behind behavior. They emphasize that the nature of a particular antisocial act is, in itself, no indication of the personality structure of an individual (neurotic, psychotic, character problem, stress reaction, or normal in a delinquent subculture) whose primary purpose is an attempt to resolve the many intrapsychic tensions in the person. The dynamic theories stress the necessity for understanding the nature of the conflict and the many motivational causes of the anxieties that lead to antisocial behavior (such as the unconscious need for punishment or the desire to punish one's parents, to prove one's masculinity, or to deny one's needs for nurturance, etc.) before attempting to bring about change or planning any intervention program.

Early formulations of the psychodynamic theories focused primarily on the needs that were being gratified by the acting-out behavior.[40] Detailed analyses were made of drive arousal, frustration, and gratification. These sources of gratification were seen not only as intrapsychic but as interpersonal as well. Johnson and Szurek,[41] for example, have shown how parents can unconsciously gain satisfaction from their children's antisocial behavior that they subtly provoke and perpetuate.

Recent formulations of psychodynamic theories have directed attention to those elements of the personality that screen, control, and direct the impulses as well as to the nature of the needs themselves. These functions (called functions of the ego) include the tolerance for frustration, the ability to delay gratification, the adequate functioning of guilt, the development of sublimations, and the evolution of self-esteem. Redl and Wineman[42] have described in some detail the ego distortions and ego defects in delinquents with severe character disorders. They elucidate the adaptive patterns of acting out where certain ego functions are well developed and serve the need for survival in an environment seen as unsatisfying and threatening.

Erikson[43] has taken these ideas a step further in his psychosocial concept of negative identity. Negative identity is defined as the ego's effort to derive stability and structure through integrating the past, present, and future into a role against society and its mores, a role seen by delinquents and criminals as preferable to the emptiness and helplessness experienced when one has no identity at all (identity diffuseness). The reinforcement of this negative identity by significant figures in the environment serves to perpetuate the antisocial behavior.[44]

The major contributions of dynamic theories lie in the highlighting of the affective elements of the personality. They are particularly valuable in pointing out the complex roots of antisocial behavior. They are also able to explain events not clearly explained by other theories, such as the differences between male and female delinquent behavior, the causes of delinquency in affluent middle-class families, and the reasons behind primitive acts of violence suddenly committed by socialized individuals.

SOCIAL-PSYCHOLOGICAL THEORIES: SOCIAL FORCES AND THE INDIVIDUAL

Social psychologists have been primarily concerned with the antisocial individual within the context of the group. They have given special emphasis to the individual's need for involvement with groups of various kinds and to gang membership as a source of gratification. They attempt to identify the social forces that are influencing the individual's behavior in social and antisocial directions.

Cohen[45] suggested that working-class males were not equipped for middle-class competition. As a result, they tend to draw together and, through their sympathetic interaction, develop social systems of their own with their own standards and status. In this delinquent subculture, virtue is seen as consisting of flouting and defying middle-class morality.

Short and Strodtbeck[46] posited a close association between school failure and joining a gang. They suggest that the school is rejected as an agent of socialization and the gang accepted because the family has not given the individual the necessary skills for coping with the middle-class educational structure. Conversely, those whose socialization confers verbal facility and achievement skills are better equipped to cope with the demands of school and other middle-class institutions.

Miller[47] felt that it was incorrect, however, to see gang membership as resulting primarily from a rejection of the majority culture. Rather it should be seen in terms of conformity to an in-group and the satisfactions obtained through conforming.

Gold[48] proposed a social psychological theory involving many variables. He hypothesized that the higher the quality of recreational facilities in a community, the greater its attractiveness to the individual and the less the likelihood of delinquency and crime. However, the role of the father is of prime importance in communicating community values to family members. Thus, the father must be seen as a successful provider, as having influence over family decisions.

ROLE OF SELF-IMAGE

Several investigations have tried to account for the nondelinquent and noncriminal within delinquent and criminal subcultures, with the hope that an understanding of these individuals might provide an explanation of vulnerability to delinquency. Reckless[49] found that most significant in this regard was the self-concept. An adequate self-concept served to protect the nondelinquent from the social and cultural pressures toward antisocial behavior. Clark,[50] in agreement, showed how, in Negroes, the loss of dignity and one's sense of self-worth leads to self-hatred and feelings of worthlessness, which in turn make the individual exceedingly susceptible to social pressures of all kinds, among them delinquency and crime.

Self-esteem continues to be seen as a significant variable in determining whether a person will be susceptible to delinquency. Bandura and Walters[51] found that children with low self-esteem more easily imitate the behavior of others. In line with their role-model theory, they suggested that criminal models would, therefore, have greater influence over these children. Sherif[52] concurred, finding that individuals who had their own personal standards were less influenced by the groups and group pressure.

Since self-image and self-esteem have been regarded as important elements in keeping a person from group influence and from delinquent behavior, Massimo and Shore[53] hypothesized that, in delinquents, changes in self-image should be highly correlated with decreases in antisocial behavior. Changes in self-image were brought about through a special program of comprehensive vocationally oriented psychotherapy.[54] This did, in fact, lead to a significant drop in delinquent behavior.

IMPLICATIONS

Research on the psychological elements believed to be related to criminal and delinquent behavior has arisen from a variety of theoretical frameworks.

Addressing itself to finding the answers to certain phenomena, each theory attempted to broaden its scope by integrating the ideas of other theoretical frameworks. Five general comments can be made about these theories.

1. Many of the theories of etiology are based on correlations between certain events. Sometimes this has led to conclusions about causal relationships. Such etiological conclusions based on correlations cannot be made even on the basis of a high relationship between two or more factors.

2. Many studies of etiology are based on the recall and reporting of past experiences rather than on direct observation. Such recall has consistently been found to be of low reliability.

3. Many studies compare large groups of delinquents and/or criminals to a large nondelinquent population. The results from such studies of large groups can be applied only with extreme caution to the individual.

4. Many studies are ex post facto. Given a known group of antisocial individuals, such studies attempt to find factors which differentiate these individuals from nondelinquents. However, to determine whether these factors are indeed of etiological significance requires the longitudinal studies, few of which have been made.

5. It is not clear why many of the factors considered to be of etiological significance lead specifically to antisocial behavior, since they are known to predispose individuals to other disturbances as well.

But despite the criticisms made of these studies, there are many areas of agreement among the psychological theorists:

1. Although the origins of antisocial behavior are very complex and although such behavior arises from many sources, plans for any program aimed at significantly reducing crime and delinquency should not ignore psychological elements. The important questions that need to be considered are as follows: What are the opportunities to identify with someone who is respected, loved, and trusted? What are the chances to develop feelings that one has control and mastery over the environment? What are the aspects of the program that offer hope for the future?

2. Most of the theorists agree that the roots of antisocial behavior most often lie in early and extremely negative interpersonal experiences with important figures, such as parents. Large-scale programs can be successful only insofar as they can assist the parental figures in bringing about the intimate, intense, positive individual attachments necessary for growth and development. Programs for prevention must be aimed at improving the emotional climate of an individual's experience with important figures and assisting families and individuals during periods of stress and crisis.

3. Because there are a complex number of causes of criminal and delinquent behavior, there must be a variety of different services available to prevent antisocial behavior. Efforts should be made to identify those who are showing early signs of disturbance, as well as to help those already involved in antisocial activities. Programs will have to differ for males and females, different socio-economic groups, and groups that have special needs (such as those with neurological disorders).

4. At times it may be necessary to institutionalize an individual. However, the rehabilitative elements in such institutions should be derived from an understanding of the psychological needs that are related to the development of internalized behavioral controls. Such controls evolve only when respect and trust are present and where discipline is not geared toward humiliation and threats. Identification with a respected and socialized individual is a precondition for control over impulsive behavior.

5. Planned courses in building character and moral training do not in themselves result in moral behavior unless translated into significant personal relationships providing socialized role models who the individual wishes to resemble and who he feels understand him. Individualized contacts should be encouraged and fostered in any program.

6. Psychological factors should not be separated from the social and cultural factors which serve to teach ways of satisfying particular personal needs. Violence within the society, as revealed in the mass media and other social institutions, presents delinquency and crime as a legitimate way of resolving personal frustrations and tensions. Those who have difficulties in controlling their primitive drives sometimes see this as a license to express their feelings directly in action.

7. No magical or simple answers for the eradication of antisocial activities can be given. Any program for crime prevention must be comprehensive and multi-dimensional, and must incorporate several disciplines. No single factor has yet been found to be most decisive in preventing crime, nor is there any indication that any such factor will ever be found. But a review of the etiological aspects of criminal and delinquent behavior gives us some direction for planning and carrying out large-scale preventive programs that are broad in scope and that can be directed toward identifying and altering many of the influences destructive to the growth of the individual.

NOTES

1. As has been shown in studies in behavior under extreme conditions, such as in concentration camps, every individual has a breaking point for control. Stealing— even cannibalism—can result under conditions of severe deprivation.
2. P. R. Newkirk, "Psychopathic traits are inheritable," *Diseases of the nervous system*, February 1957, pp. 52–54.

3. C. Lombrose, *Crime, its causes and remedies*, translated by H. P. Horton (Boston: Little, Brown, 1912).

4. W. H. Sheldon, *Varieties of delinquent youth: An introduction to constitutional psychology* (New York: Harper, 1949).

5. H. M. Cleckley, "Psychopathic states," *American handbook of psychiatry*, S. Arieti, ed. (New York: Basic Books, 1959), pp. 567–589.

6. W. McCord and Joan McCord, *Psychopathy and delinquency* (New York: Grune and Stratton, 1956).

7. N. C. Kephart, *The slow learner in the classroom* (Columbus, Ohio: C. E. Merrill, 1960).

8. P. F. Briggs and R. D. Wirt, "Prediction," *Juvenile Delinquency*, H. C. Quay, ed. (Princeton, N.J.: D. Van Nostrand, 1965).

9. W. Sluckin, *Imprinting and early learning* (Chicago: Aldine, 1965).

10. A. H. Riesen, "Stimulation as a requirement for growth and function in Behavioral Development," in Functions of varied Experience, D. W. Fiske and S. R. Maddi, eds. (Homewood, Ill.: Dorsey Press, 1961).

11. J. Piaget, *The moral judgment of the child* (Glencoe, Ill.: Free Press, 1948).

12. L. Kohlberg, "Moral development and identification," *Child Psychology: Yearbook of the National Society for the Study of Education* (Chicago: University of Chicago Press, 1963), pp. 227–333.

13. R. Havighurst and H. Taba, *Adolescent character and personality* (New York: John Wiley, 1949).

14. J. Aronfreed and A. Reber, "Internalized behavioral suppression and the timing of social punishment," *Journal of Personality and Social Psychology*, January 1965, pp. 3–16.

15. J. Dollard et al., *Frustration and aggression* (New Haven, Conn.: Yale University Press, 1939).

16. A. Bandura and R. H. Walters, "Aggression," *Child Psychology: Yearbook of the National Society for the Study of Education* (Chicago: University of Chicago Press, 1963), pp. 364–416.

17. W. McCord, Joan McCord, and I. Zola, *Origins of crime: A new evaluation of the Cambridge-Somerville youth study* (New York: Columbia University Press, 1959).

18. J. Toby, "The differential impact of family disorganization," *American Sociological Review*, October 1957, pp. 505–512.

19. Joan McCord, W. McCord, and Emily Thurber, "The effects of maternal employment on lower-class boys," *Journal of Abnormal and Social Psychology*, August 1963, pp. 177–182.

20. R. G. Andry, *Delinquency and parental pathology* (London: Methuen, 1960).

21. W. Mischel, "Father absence and delay of gratification," *Journal of Abnormal and Social Psychology*, July 1961, pp. 116–124.

22. W. C. Kvaraceus et al., *Delinquent behavior: Culture and the individual* (Washington, D.C.: National Education Association, 1959).

23. McCord, McCord, and Zola, op. cit. supra note 17.

24. J. Bowlby, *Forty-four juvenile thieves: Their characters and home life* (London: Baldiere, 1947).

25. McCord, McCord, and Zola, op. cit. supra note 17.
26. Ibid.
27. S. Glueck and E. Glueck, *Unraveling juvenile delinquency* (Cambridge, Mass.: Harvard University Press, 1950).
28. McCord and McCord, op. cit. supra note 17.
29. R. R. Sears, Eleanor E. Maccoby, and H. Levin, *Patterns of child rearing* (Evanston, Ill.: Row Peterson, 1957).
30. T. W. Adorno, E. Frenkel-Brunswick, D. J. Levinson, and R. N. Sanford, *The authoritarian personality* (New York: Harper, 1950).
31. J. Aronfreed, *Conduct and conscience* (New York: Academic Press, 1968).
32. A. Bandura and R. H. Walters, *Adolescent aggression* (New York: Ronald Press, 1959).
33. J. H. Rohrer and M. Edmonson, *The eighth generation* (New York: Harper, 1960).
34. J. F. Short and F. L. Strodtbeck, *Group process and gang delinquency* (Chicago: University of Chicago Press, 1965).
35. L. Kohlberg, "Development of moral character and moral ideology," *Review of child development research*, L. and M. Hoffman, eds. (New York: Russell Sage Foundation, 1964), pp. 383–433.
36. Eleanor E. Maccoby, J. P. Johnson, and R. M. Church, "Community integration and the social control of juvenile delinquency," *Journal of Social Issues*, No. 3, 1958, pp. 38–51.
37. B. Lander, *Towards an understanding of juvenile delinquency* (New York: Columbia University Press, 1964).
38. J. F. Short, "The sociocultural context of delinquency," *Crime and Delinquency*, October 1960, pp. 365–75.
39. D. C. Leighton, *The character of danger: Psychiatric symptoms in selected communities* (New York: Basic Books, 1963).
40. S. Freud, *Civilization and its discontents* (London: Hogarth Press, 1955 [originally published in 1930]); W. Healy and A. Bronner, *New light on delinquency and its treatment* (New Haven, Conn.: Yale University Press, 1936).
41. A. M. Johnson and S. A. Szurek, "The genesis of antisocial acting out in children and adults," *Psychoanalytic Quarterly*, July 1952, pp. 323–43.
42. F. Redl and D. Wineman, *Controls from within* (Glencoe, Ill.: Free Press, 1952).
43. E. H. Erikson, *Childhood and society* (New York: Norton, 1950).
44. E. H. Erikson and K. T. Erikson, "The confirmation of the delinquent," *Chicago Review*, Winter 1957, pp. 15–23.
45. A. K. Cohen, *Delinquent boys: The culture of the gang* (New York: Free Press, 1955).
46. Short and Strodtbeck, op. cit. supra note 34.
47. W. B. Miller, "Lower class culture as a generating milieu of gang delinquency," *Journal of Social Issues*, No. 3, 1958, pp. 5–19.
48. M. Gold, *Status forces in delinquent boys* (Ann Arbor: University of Michigan Press, 1963).
49. W. C. Reckless, S. Dintiz, and E. Murray, "Self concept as an insulator against delinquency," *American Sociological Review*, December 1956, pp. 744–46; W. C. Reckless, S. Dinitz, and B. Kay, "The self concept in potential delinquency and

potential nondelinquency," *American Sociological Review*, October 1957, pp. 566–70.

50. K. B. Clark, "Color, class, personality, and juvenile delinquency," *Journal of Negro Education*, Summer 1959, pp. 240–51.

51. A. Bandura and R. H. Walters, *Social learning and personality development* (New York: Holt, Rinehart, and Winston, 1963).

52. M. Sherif, "Group influences upon the formation of social norms and attitudes," *Basic studies in social psychology*, H. Proshansky and B. Seidenberg, eds. (New York: Holt, Rinehart, and Winston, 1965).

53. J. L. Massimo and M. F. Shore, "The effectiveness of a comprehensive vocationally oriented psychotherapeutic program for adolescent delinquent boys," *American Journal of Orthopsychiatry*, June 1963, pp. 634–42.

54. J. L. Massimo and M. F. Shore, "Comprehensive vocationally oriented psychotherapy: A new treatment technique for lower class adolescent delinquent boys," *Psychiatry*, August 1967, pp. 229–36.

2

Heredity in Criminality

David Rosenthal

Reprinted from *Criminal Justice and Behavior* 2, no. 1 (March 1975), pp. 3–21, by permission of the author and the publisher, Sage Publications, Inc.

INTRODUCTION

What makes a person a criminal is not what the person does, but what the law says he must not do. Of course, the law specifies many things that citizens must not do, and these things vary from state to state and from country to country. This, of course, is known to everyone, and I raise the point here only because the concern of my presentation is focused on *genetic factors* that may play a role in criminality. A person driving when drunk may unintentionally run over someone; a desperately hungry man may hold up a grocery to get food or money to feed himself and his family; a woman, in extreme exasperation regarding a brutal husband, may assault him with a kitchen knife; a citizen of the Soviet Union may have in his possession an underground newspaper and may thereby be sentenced to several years in Siberia; a government official may accept a bribe, or cause a rival party's office to be bugged; a young woman may be jailed for prostitution, even if she works only with high-class clientele; a reporter may be jailed for refusing to reveal his source of information; and a gangster may callously and deliberately murder someone whom the organization wants to eliminate.

From society's point of view, it may be expedient to classify such varied behaviors and many others in a single category called crime. But for purposes of evaluating the role of heredity in criminality, it is important that we know what the phenotype is that reflects the genetic factor involved, and that we define the phenotype clearly and that it be as homogeneous as possible, if we are ever going to make any sense about the possible role of heredity in regard to such behavior.

Of course, we are not talking about heredity in the same sense that Lombroso (1918) did when he talked about "stigmata of degeneration," such as a slanting forehead, long ear lobes, a large and protruding jaw, a small or receding chin, or asymmetries of the face. It is because of such outlandish notions by Lombroso, the Nazis, and people who advocate racist ideologies that any possible association that is proposed with regard to genetics and

behavior is often regarded as the devil's own handiwork. As scientists, however, we are obliged to make a reasonable effort not to put blinders on
ourselves, but rather to examine this troublesome issue thoroughly, to question its validity, and judge its implications.

Another reason why people have shied away from any association between
genetic theory and behavior has to do with the fact that many people have
always believed that if a genetic factor were implicated, the behavior at issue
would have to follow as an inevitable consequence. This notion was fostered
by Lange in 1929 when he published his research in a book entitled *Crime as
Destiny*. The clear implication of this title was that the supposedly genetically
loaded individual could not avoid his criminality, that he was constitutionally
bound to commit criminal acts. Today, of course, we know that such a view
is nonsense.

In fact, people long ago began to assign denigrating labels to people who
committed crimes, and these included names such as constitutional
psychopathic state of inferiority, psychopathic personality, or sociopathic
personality. These terms also suggested a malignant fate that was thrust
upon the individual at his conception or birth. Even the more modern and
well-intentioned World Health Organization has grouped such individuals
into four major categories:

1. Antisocial personality. Subtypes: Antisocial personality, constitutional
psychopathic state, and psychopathic personality with antisocial trend.
2. Asocial personality. Subtypes: Asocial personality, moral deficiency,
pathological liar, psychopathic personality with amoral trend.
3. Sexual deviation. Subtypes: Exhibitionism, fetishism, homosexuality,
pathological sexuality, sadism, sexual deviation.
4. Other and unspecified. Subtype: Pathological personality.

Is it possible that a single genotype can underlie so many personality
traits? Perhaps. However, let us look at what the American Psychiatric
Association has had to say about such individuals. It has stated that
sociopathic reactions are very often symptomatic of severe underlying personality disorder, neurosis, or psychosis, or occur as the result of organic
brain injury or disease. Not only that, but the Association also has said that
these individuals are ill primarily in terms of society and of conformity with
the prevailing cultural milieu; that such people are always in trouble,
profiting neither from experience nor punishment, and maintaining no real
loyalties to any person, group, or code; that they are frequently callous and
hedonistic, showing marked emotional immaturity, with lack of sense of
responsibility, lack of judgment, and an ability to rationalize their behavior
so that it appears warranted, reasonable, and justified; and that they typically

do not show significant personality deviations other than those implied by adherence to the values of their own predatory, criminal, or other social group. We know, of course, that some genes can manifest pleiotropy to a considerable extent, but to assume that a single genotype can encompass all the characteristics described above borders on the ridiculous.

Thus, from the outset of my presentation I wish to make it clear that when we talk about heredity in criminality, we are not talking about a specific gene with a specific locus and specific discernible biological defects, such as those found in diseases like phenylketonuria and sickle cell anemia.

It is important for us to recognize that not all people who commit crimes fit the definition of psychopath, and that not all people called psychopaths have committed a crime. Moreover, one of the biggest problems that we face in discussing these matters is the fact that investigators have not demonstrated convincingly that they can apply the label of psychopathy or sociopathic personality with any great consistency or reliability. For example, if we look at the epidemiological studies of the frequency of psychopathic personality disorders in different populations, we find that the highest rate reported was 15 of every 100 individuals and the lowest rate reported was 1 in every 2000 individuals. Of course, these rates are extremes, but when the variation is such that the highest is 300 times as large as the lowest rate reported, we must recognize that the investigators are basing their assessments on very different criteria. Reported crime rates also vary a great deal. A recent report (Wolfgang et al. 1972) finds that more than 1 of every 3 boys in a Philadelphia cohort of 9945 had at least one recorded police contact.

We also know that in the U.S.A. a disproportionate number of crimes are committed by individuals at the lowest socioeconomic levels of our society, and that a disproportionate number of such crimes are committed by blacks, who are overrepresented in the lowest socioeconomic class, and who tend to be disaffected and rebellious against a society that has treated them harshly and discriminatorily. Such factors strongly favor the view that crimes committed by such persons stem primarily from the social, economic, and cultural deprivations to which these individuals are subjected. If one is inclined to suppose that genetic factors might be implicated even in the criminal actions of such individuals, since not all poor blacks commit crimes, he must also try to explain why crime rates in the slum and ghetto areas can rise dramatically in a short period of time, as we have witnessed in the past ten years. No genetic explanation that I know of can make any sense of such a dramatic escalation of crime rates. It is also worth noting that in the Israeli collectives or kibbutzim, there are no courts, no police, no crime, no locked doors, and virtually no juvenile delinquency, whereas crime abounds elsewhere in Israel.

By now it may seem as though I have completely scuttled the case for any kind of genetic factor in criminality. However, bear with me a little longer. I now intend to review the literature which suggests that genes do contribute to criminality and psychopathic personality in some way.

FAMILY STUDIES

In studies of human genetics, the typical research procedure is to find individuals who manifest the trait under scrutiny, and then to examine the families of these index cases to determine the distribution and the frequency of this trait among these relatives. With respect to index cases in trouble with the law, investigators usually find all kinds of familial turbulence as well as a high frequency of criminal behavior. A well-researched sample is provided by Robins (1966), who carried out a follow-up study of children who had been referred to a psychiatric clinic for antisocial behavior. She found that most of her 524 antisocial child probands came from disrupted homes. Only 36% had both parents at home; 32% had lived in institutions or foster homes for at least six months before referral. In 50% of the cases, one or both parents had died, the parents were divorced or separated, or the mother was unmarried. Fathers showed: excessive drinking (32%), nonsupport or neglect of the home (26%), deserted (21%), cruel or physically abusive (20%), erratic worker (20%), illicit sexual behavior (18%), arrests and illegal occupations (11%), gambling, extravagance, incompetent work, coldness, and no affection (23%). Both mothers (48%) and fathers (23%) were severely nervous, mentally ill, or feeble minded. The most prominent characteristics of the mothers were nonsupport or neglect of home (20%), and illicit sexual behavior (19%).

When parents are so severely disturbed and manifest such varied psychopathological behavior themselves, it is virtually impossible to tell from the usual family studies how much of the antisocial behavior and personality difficulties in the child can be traced to either genetic or psychological influences.

For these reasons, investigators must find other ways to assess the possible genetic contribution to the criminal behavior, and they must do this by tearing apart the genetic and environmental variables. They have recourse to either of two research strategies. The first is the twin method, in which genetically identical twins are compared with same-sexed fraternal twins, who share about only half their genes in common. Since both members of each pair are reared in the same home environment, the investigator assumes that differences in concordance rates between the monozygotic (MZ) or identical twins and the dizygotic (DZ) or fraternal twins reflect the genetic contribution to the trait under study.

The second method involves a separation of the genetic family from the rearing family through the use of naturally occurring adoptions. For example, a child who has a criminal father may have been given up for adoption at an early age to a family that is highly stable and never in trouble with the law. Would such a child reveal a propensity toward criminality or would he become a pillar of the community? I will now present a summary of the salient information available to me with respect to all twin and adoption studies to date regarding criminality and psychopathic personality.

TWIN STUDIES

The basic data regarding twin studies are shown in Table 2.1.

We can see in Table 2.1 that there are nine studies spanning a period of forty years, carried out in three continents. In some studies the numbers are small. The best study of all is the one by Christiansen in Denmark, which was based on a register of all twins rather than only on twins who had been found in prisons or hospitals. Nevertheless, in every study the concordance rate for monozygotic twins is higher than the concordance rate for dizygotic twins.

Although it is not proper to compile the figures of the different studies, because of differences in sampling procedures, cultural climate, and criminal laws, nevertheless I have done so in order to obtain at least some kind of general estimate of the levels of concordance represented in these studies. As we can see, the concordance rate for MZ twins is slightly more than 50% and the concordance rate for DZ twins is slightly more than 20%. The MZ twins tend to be concordant about two and a half times more frequently than the DZ twins.

What these findings mean is quite another matter. One could claim simply that MZ twins are closer to one another than are DZ twins, that they have much stronger mutual identification patterns, that they share together more interests and activities, and that on such grounds alone one could predict that if one MZ twin were to engage in criminal activity, his co-twin would be likely either to participate with him in the same crimes, or to engage in other criminal activities to maintain the identification image. Also, if one MZ twin should be sentenced to prison, his co-twin may feel isolated, cut off, and deprived of his close association with his twin, and he might commit a crime in order to join his brother in prison. Such interpretations may seem far-fetched, but they are clearly possible and instances of such motivations could probably be documented.

Nevertheless, it is clearly not possible to rule out the potential fact that genetic factors may indeed be the primary source of the higher concordance rate in MZ as compared to DZ twins. If a genetic explanation is valid can we say anything at all about the probable mode of genetic transmission? Ordi-

Table 2.1.
Twin Studies of Psychopathy and Criminality MZ and Same-Sexed DZ Twins Only

Study	Location	Monozygotic			Dizygotic		
		Total Pairs	Pairs Concordant	% Concordant	Total Pairs	Pairs Concordant	% Concordant
Lange 1929	Bavaria	13	10	77	17	2	12
Legras 1932	Holland	4	4	100	5	1	20
Rosanoff 1934	U.S.A.	37	25	68	28	5	18
Stumpfl 1936	Germany	18	11	61	19	7	37
Kranz 1936	Prussia	32	21	66	43	23	54
Borgstrom 1939	Finland	4	3	75	5	2	40
Slater 1953*	England	2	1	50	10	3	30
Yoshimasu 1961	Japan	28	17	61	18	2	11
Christiansen 1968	Denmark	81	27	33	137	15	11
Total		219	119	54.3	282	60	21.3

*The Slater study was based on psychiatric hospital admissions only; the cases shown in the table included those in his case summaries of the psychopathic and neurotic group whom he diagnosed "psychopath" or "behavior disorder," these terms not defined. The two MZ pairs were obtained from the case history section (other cases called psychopaths, but with organic, psychotic, or primary affective diagnoses were excluded).

The other figures in the table involve criminality in convicted and incarcerated subjects.

narily, we would not expect twin studies to reveal the mode of inheritance with regard to any particular trait; we would prefer instead to examine at least two generations of proband families, but as we noted before, environmental variables are hopelessly confounded in such family studies.

Another problem regarding mode of inheritance stems from the fact that in the twin studies and in prevalence studies as well, the number of males sentenced for crime far outnumber the number of females. In the twin studies, we find that about 7 of every 8 pairs are male. To some, this may suggest the possibility that we are dealing with a sex-linked trait, and that the gene for criminality or psychopathy is a recessive allele on the X chromosome. However, we can disabuse ourselves of this possibility by examining some additional data provided us by Rosanoff and his colleagues. These data are shown in Table 2.2.

Rosanoff divided his twins according to age, and in this way generated three groups. Among the twin pairs in which at least one of the twins had a behavioral problem severe enough to have the subject called to the attention of some public agency, the number of girls at the earliest ages was approximately the same as the number of boys. However, in youth the females comprised only about 3 in 10 of juvenile delinquents, whereas in adulthood, females comprised only 1 in 5 of all adult criminals.

The data suggest that at least among twins, females begin life with propensities to behavioral disorders almost to the same extent as that found in males. Whereas the number of male twin pairs with behavioral disorders tends to

TABLE 2.2.
SEX DISTRIBUTION IN THREE GROUPS OF TWIN PAIRS
IN WHICH AT LEAST ONE TWIN HAS A BEHAVIOR PROBLEM,
ACCORDING TO AGE LEVEL
(DATA FROM ROSANOFF ET AL. 1934)

	Childhood Behavior Problems			Youth Juvenile Delinquency			Adult Criminality		
	♂	♀	N	♂	♀	N	♂	♀	N
MZ Same-Sex	25	22	47	27	15	42	33	4	37
DZ Opposite-Sex	23	37	60	16	9	25	23	5	28
DZ	26	11	37	36	12	48	22	11	33
Sum	74	70	144	79	36	115	78	20	98
%		48.6			31.3			20.4	

remain fairly constant in the three groups, the trend for females represents a sharp decline with regard to such problems. Whether the pattern of decline is as true in 1972 as it was in 1934, we cannot say. In any case, if the data of Table 2.1 do in fact reflect a genetic contribution to criminality and psychopathic personality, the data of Table 2.2 suggest that the genotype finds expression in females primarily in childhood ages, but for some reason the expected phenotype declines in manifestation over the years. One could maintain that, with the onset of puberty and its accompanying biochemical changes in females, the phenotype for criminality and psychopathy tends to become submerged in the hormonal flood. The possibility may seem strained to some. Perhaps a more plausible explanation, based on what is readily observable, is that the culture exerts great pressures on females to suppress their aggressive, hostile, rebellious, or impulsive urges. Moreover, because of male-female differences in size and strength, and the fact that it is the female who becomes pregnant, the cultural edict against female demonstration of overt aggression and "acting out" tends to be readily reinforced.

Adoption Studies

Although the findings of the twin studies are consistent with a genetic hypothesis regarding psychopathy and criminality, the data by themselves are not entirely convincing, but are mostly suggestive. In the twin studies, we see again that possible environmental factors could provide a plausible explanation of the findings. The second method of unconfounding hereditary and environmental factors is the adoption method. Fortunately, within the past year, two adoption studies have been reported, with different research strategies, one in Copenhagen and one in Iowa. Adoption studies provide a more elegant and a more precise way of separating the possible genetic and environmental variables.

The first study was reported by Schulsinger (1972) in Denmark. He began with an adoption register that included approximately 5500 people who were given up for non-family adoption at an early age, during the years 1924 to 1947. Of these adoptees, 507 had histories of admission to a psychiatric facility, or had a police record. From among these 507 subjects, Schulsinger was able to find 57 who were diagnosed as psychopaths according to his stated criteria, which included:

1. A consistent pattern of impulse-ridden or acting out behavior lasting well beyond adolescence.
2. Overreacting to provoking factors, especially in an alloplastic way.

From among the approximately 5000 adoptees who had never had any psychiatric contact, Schulsinger selected 57 controls matched for sex, age, social class, and even in many instances for neighborhood of rearing, and for age of transfer to the adopting family. He then examined case records of the biological and adoptive relatives of the 114 probands, including mothers, fathers, siblings, and half-siblings, while remaining "blind" regarding the group of relatives to which the subject belonged, and determined the frequency of psychopathic disorder in the respective groups. The main findings of the study are shown in Table 2.3.

In Table 2.3 are presented only the findings regarding the biological relatives of the index and control groups. I have not shown the data with respect to the adoptive relatives because in all instances, the frequency of the disorders in the adoptive relatives was similar to the findings in the biological relatives of the control subjects.

It can be seen that the frequency of diagnosed psychopathy in the biological relatives of the index cases is about two and a half times greater than the frequency among control relatives, the significance level for this difference falling just short of the usually accepted .05 level, probably because the number of cases so diagnosed was so small.

Schulsinger also generated what he called a "spectrum of psychopathic disorders." These cases included:

1. personality disorders in which a diagnosis of psychopathy was likely, but not all the criteria for psychopathy were available in the case record;
2. cases classified as observation for psychopathy or probable psychopathy;
3. those called character deviation or observation for character deviation;
4. and cases classified as criminality, alcoholism, or drug abuse, with no other clarifying diagnosis.

TABLE 2.3.
PSYCHOPATHY AND PSYCHOPATHIC SPECTRUM DISORDERS
IN BIOLOGICAL RELATIVES OF PSYCHOPATHS AND CONTROLS
(DATA FROM SCHULSINGER 1972)

	Core Psychopathy in Biological Relatives			Psychopathic Spectrum Disorders in Biological Relatives		
	Yes	No	%	Yes	No	%
Index	12	293	3.9	44	261	14.4
Control	4	281	1.4	19	266	6.7
	Chi-square = .065			Chi-square = .01		

It can be seen in Table 2.3 that the psychopathic spectrum disorders occur to an appreciable extent and that, so defined, they discriminate the index and control biological relatives at the .01 level of significance. The difference between the index and control relatives is comparable to the difference regarding core psychopathy in that the spectrum disorders occur again about two and a half times more frequently in the biological relatives of index cases than of controls.

It is difficult to find any environmental explanation for these findings, and indeed, I would be inclined to suggest that this is the first body of evidence to make such a compelling case for the genetic hypothesis with regard to psychopathy.

The second study to employ the adoption method was carried out by Crowe (1972), but in Crowe's study the author's concern was not with the personality disorder itself, but rather with actual arrest records. Crowe's research strategy also differed from Schulsinger's. He found a group of 41 female criminal offenders who were inmates of a women's reformatory during the years 1935 to 1956, and who had given up their babies for adoption. Of these women, 90% were felons. They had produced 52 offspring who ranged in age from 15 to 45 years at the time of the study. The author also selected a control group from the state index of adoptions. These control subjects were matched with the index subjects in regard to age, sex, race, and approximate age at the time of the adoptive decree. With the exception of the criminal mothers of the probands, little information was available on the biological parents of either the index or the control subjects.

Among the 52 index cases, 8 had arrest records as compared to 2 of the 52 controls. The difference was statistically significant. The index cases had a total of 18 arrests as compared to 2 arrests in the control group. Seven index cases had received convictions as compared to only one control, the difference again being statistically significant. Moreover, in checking traffic records with the Bureau of Motor Vehicles, the author found a rather strong tendency for the index cases to have more moving traffic violations than did the control subjects. For example, the index cases had 19 speeding convictions as compared to 8 controls. The index cases also had a total of 37 traffic convictions as compared to 21 for the controls. Crowe also compared the offense of the proband mother with the offense of the index offspring, as shown in Table 2.4.

Of course, one would not expect to find the exact same offense in the mother and the child, but there is a tendency in Table 2.4 for parent and child offenses to be of a similar nature. For example, we see instances in which both mother and child may have committed sex offenses, or offenses which involve obtaining money through deceit. Thus, Crowe's study not only provides strong evidence for the fact that a tendency to criminality is inherited, but also that the type of crime pattern may also be influenced genetically. When we combine the data of the twin studies, the Schulsinger study, and the Crowe study, it is difficult not to come to the conclusion that heredity plays some role in both psychopathy and criminality.

DISCUSSION

Even though we can conclude that hereditary factors play a role in psychopathy and criminality, we are reasonably sure that no single-gene locus can account for all criminality. The Schulsinger study, which seems to involve a continuum of personality disorder, suggests that a polygenic system may underline what we now call the antisocial personality. With regard to criminality as a separate entity, however, I am inclined to think that we are dealing with a genetic heterogeneity that not only exerts some thrust toward

TABLE 2.4.
COMPARISON OF CRIMINAL OFFENSE, MOTHERS' VS PROBANDS'
(DATA FROM CROWE 1972)

Offense of Proband's Mother*	Offense of Proband	Sex of Proband
Prostitution	Lascivious acts	♂
Desertion	Forgery†	♂
Assault	Larceny (two convictions)†	♂
Larceny	Obtaining money under false pretenses† plus six misdemeanors	♂
Forgery	Petty larceny	♀
Aiding prisoners to escape	Issuing false check (two arrests)	♀
Larceny	Delinquency	♀
Contributing to the delinquency of a minor	Delinquency, lewdness, embezzlement of auto	♀

*All felonies except the last offense.
†Indicates felonies.

criminality, but also shapes in some way the form in which the crime pattern will be expressed, as suggested by Crowe's data. I can best demonstrate this point of view by citing specific examples of very different, genetically influenced variables that are probably associated in some degree with criminality.

1. A number of studies have reported a higher incidence of EEG abnormalities in criminals than in the population at large. Such abnormalities often have a genetic origin. The EEG abnormalities may be associated with poor impulse control and with bad judgment, which lead to crime.

2. Many criminals have a low IQ. The IQ is well known to have a high heritability. Many of us know examples of low IQ individuals who, placed in an environment where they can be readily influenced by smarter individuals with criminal intentions, are easily led into crime.

3. Criminals tend to be predominately mesomorphic. Individuals with this type of body build, which clearly has a strong inherited component, tend to be strong, tough, aggressive, and relatively fearless. They seem to have a low tolerance of frustration and they are quick to fight for or take what they want. This group may comprise the bulk of individuals labelled psychopaths. It is unfortunate that Schulsinger did not present data regarding the body build of his probands and their relatives. Data taken from Glueck and Glueck (1956) give comparative data for delinquents and non-delinquents regarding body build, as shown in Table 2.5.

It can be seen in Table 2.5 that, of the four major body types evaluated, the delinquents comprise many more mesomorphs and many fewer ectomorphs than do the non-delinquents. Both body types differ in the two

TABLE 2.5.
COMPARISON OF DELINQUENTS AND NON-DELINQUENTS WITH
RESPECT TO BODY BUILD
(DATA FROM GLUECK AND GLUECK 1956)

Body Type	Delinquents	Non-Delinquents
Endomorph	59	72
Mesomorph	298	148
Ectomorph	72	191
Balanced	67	71
Total	496	482

groups at the .001 level. It is likely that mesomorphic body build and its associated temperaments may have had great utility and survival value in eons past, but often lead to trouble with legal authorities in a highly organized, controlled modern society.

4. Many crimes are committed by individuals who are psychotic or near psychotic. We now have clear evidence that the major and most common psychoses are associated with some genetic factor. Therefore, such genes can indirectly contribute as well to criminality.

5. Chromosomal aneuploidy may also contribute toward a propensity to crime. The case for XYY individuals being impelled to criminality because of the extra Y chromosome is much more in doubt than was originally thought. However, XXY individuals also manifest an increased tendency toward criminality. In a study of 50 XXY subjects (Theilgaard et al., 1971) 13 of 34 (38%) had a criminal history, as compared to 1 of 16 (6%) normal male controls. It is possible that the XXY group are driven to criminality because of the psychological distress and personality disturbance accompanying the physical deviations resulting from the additional X chromosome.

6. Many crimes are committed under the influence of alcohol, and evidence suggests an inherited factor in alcoholism.

7. Many crimes are of a sexual nature, and some findings suggest that sexual disturbances, especially homosexuality, may have an inherited basis.

8. Some investigators believe that a number of hyperactive children eventually become criminals, and some evidence suggests that the hyperkinetic syndrome is inherited.

9. It may be that most crimes in the U.S.A. today are committed by drug addicts. Who are these people who let themselves become hooked on hard drugs? Some clinicians believe that they are emotionally unstable individuals with a wide variety of personality disorders, at least some of which, such as borderline schizophrenia, are heritable.

Thus, there is good reason to believe that in crime we are indeed dealing with genetic heterogeneity, but we need a great deal more research to determine whether the nine examples of possible genetic contributors to criminality that I have described can be substantiated beyond doubt.

As I mentioned earlier, the implication of a genetic basis underlying some criminality does not mean that an individual harboring the genotype must at some time commit a crime. My own opinion is that most crime arises because of environmental and psychological influences, and that sociocultural factors in modern society primarily underlie the great current crime wave. Differently organized societies, such as the Israeli kibbutzim, can reduce the frequency of crime dramatically. Perhaps Americans must now ask themselves questions about what kind of society they want. The crime rate and the types of crime committed in a society are probably best thought of as measures that reflect the internal disparities, grievances and conflicts within it.

With respect to crime prevention in hereditarily disposed individuals, it is possible that with increased knowledge, we might be able to provide them with the kind of sociocultural environment in which criminal behavior is neither gratifying nor desirable to them, and in which provocative factors are kept to a minimum.

With respect to those who are officially concerned about crime and charged with the responsibility of dealing with criminals, I believe that they and we ourselves are impeded by a monumental lack of knowledge and understanding regarding criminality. We still classify crimes as those against person or those against property, as though we intend never to get out of the stone age of research in this field. We need to have sensible classifications of crime patterns, and these ought to be based on the psychological characteristics that are reflected in the crime patterns. We also need to classify criminals more sensibly, again focusing on their psychological make-up and the factors that underlie it. Criminals vary widely in this sense and should be assessed and treated accordingly. These are problems for the future, but I hope that our concern about them will grow now.

REFERENCES

Borgstrom, C. A. Eine Serie von Kriminellen Zwillingen, *Arch. Rass. u. Gesellschaftsbiologie*, 1939, *33*:334–343.

Christiansen, K. O. Threshold of tolerance in various population groups illustrated by results from Danish criminological twin study, in A. V. S. de Reuck, and R. Porter (eds.), *Ciba Foundation* Symposium on the Mentally Abnormal Offender, London: Churchill Ltd., 1968, 107–116.

Crowe, R. R. The adopted offspring of women criminal offenders: a study of their arrest records, *Arch. Gen. Psychiat.*, 1972, *27*:600–603.

Glueck, S., and Glueck, E. *Physique and Delinquency*, Paul B. Hoeber, Inc., New York, 1956.

Kranz, H. *Lebenschicksale krimineller Zwillinge*, Springer-Verlag OHG, Berlin, 1936.

Lange, J. *Verbrechen als Schicksal*, Georg Thieme Verlag, Leipzig, 1929.

Legras, A. M. *Psychose en Criminaliteit bij Tweelingen*, University of Utrecht, 1932, cited by Rosanoff et al., 1934.

Lombroso, C. *Crime, Its Causes and Remedies*, Little, Brown, Boston, 1918.

Robins, L. N. *Deviant Children Grown Up*, The Williams and Wilkins Co., Baltimore, 1966.

Rosanoff, A. J., Handy, L. M., and Plesset, I. R. Criminality and delinquency in twins, *J. Crim. Law Criminol.*, 1934, *24*:923–934.

Schulsinger, F. Psychopathy: heredity and environment, in L. Erlenmeyer-Kimling (ed.), *Int. J. Mental Health*, 1972, *1*:190–206.

Slater, E. Erbpathologie des manisch-depressiven Irreseins, Die Eltern und Kinder von Manisch-Depressiven, *Z. Ges. Neurol. Psychiat.*, 1938, *163*:1–47.

Stumpfl, F. *Die Ursprunge des Verbrechens am Lebenslauf von Zwillingen*, Georg Thieme Verlag, Leipzig, 1936.

Theilgaard, A., Nielsen, J., Sorensen, A., Froland, A., and Johnsen, S. G. A psychological-psychiatric study of patients with Klinefelter's syndrome, 47, XXY., *Acta Jutlandica* XLIII:1, 1971, Copenhagen: Munksgaard, 148 pp.

Wolfgang, M. E., Figlio, R. M., and Sellen, T. *Delinquency in a Birth Cohort*, University of Chicago Press, Chicago, 1972, 336 pp.

Yoshimasu, S. *Acta Crim. Med. Leg.*, Jap., 1961, 27:117–141, cited by Christiansen, 1968.

3

Will the XYY Syndrome
Abolish Guilt?

Nicholas N. Kittrie, S.J.D.

Reprinted from *Federal Probation* (June 1971), pp. 26–31, by permission of the publisher, the Administrative Office of the United States Courts.

Is guilt on its way out? The product of ecclesiastic thinking, guilt is inextricably tied to belief in free will. It consists of man's condemnation for failure to choose between the right and wrong paths of behavior. Guilt takes for granted man's capability and freedom to make such choices. But in this adherence to the concept of individual responsibility, guilt comes in direct conflict with diverse modern theories of behavioral determinism—the belief of some that man acts out of innate hereditary forces ("nature") and the conviction of others that criminal action is a result of environmental influences ("nurture")—a product of acquired traits and of situational forces.

There have been many assaults on the validity and viability of guilt during the last century. Yet it has survived all these attacks, defended by those who contend that the abolition of the concept of guilt would do away also with social restraints and order. Slowly, however, new breaches are being made in the dogma of man's free will, which underpins the whole citadel of criminal justice. One recent battering ram has been provided by evidence of the XYY syndrome.[1]

THE NEW DETERMINISM

The September 4, 1965, murder of a prostitute in a cheap Paris hotel set the dramatic scene. Marie-Louise Oliver, the prostitute, was found strangled in an apparently motiveless slaying, and the French police set out looking for 28-year-old Daniel Hugon, the central suspect. Hugon, who fled Paris and went to Normandy, was found working on the farm of actor Jean Gabin. Surrendering to the gendarmerie, Hugon confessed and expressed remorse.

The day before he was to stand trial, Hugon attempted to take his life in the State Prison. Concerned, the court ordered elaborate physical and mental examinations of the accused. One analysis, called a karyotyping, was made of his chromosomes, the strands of genetic material contained in every living cell. The chromosomes hold the biochemical code which determines a person's physical traits, such as skin, hair and eye color, and also hold the key to sexual characteristics. Hugon was found to have a chromosomal abnormality.

The cells of the human body have 46 chromosomes, each set of 23 derived from one of the parents. Two of those 46 chromosomes, designated either X or Y because of their form, determine the person's sex. The cells in a woman's body contain two X chromosomes. Each male cell has one X and one Y chromosome. But deviations from this norm appear from time to time when nature produces such unusual chromosomal combinations as XXY, XXYY, and XYY.

Daniel Hugon possessed an XYY variant. This deviation occurs in about one out of every 2000 men, but had previously been observed in much larger proportion among mental hospital and prison inmates. The examination of large numbers of inmates in maximum security wards in Scottish institutions prior to the Hugon case led to the conclusion by Edinburgh's Dr. Patricia Jacobs that 3 percent of these men had extra Y chromosomes. As a result, geneticists in other parts of the globe commenced a search for evidence linking criminality and chromosomal abnormalities.

In Melbourne, Australia, Robert Peter Tait was convicted of bludgeoning to death an 81-year-old woman from whom he had sought a handout. He was sentenced to death in 1962 but his sentence was commuted to life imprisonment. In the Pentridge Prison, Dr. Saul Weiner, a geneticist, found that Tait as well as three other inmates convicted of murder, attempted murder, and larceny were XYY. Writing in the leading British medical journal *Lancet*, Dr. Weiner claimed: "These results strongly support the concept that an extra Y chromosome is associated with antisocial or criminal behavior."

Support for the claim of a causal connection between crime and chromosomal irregularities kept growing. New evidence disclosed that XYY men tended also to be abnormally tall and to possess low intelligence. Dr. Mary A. Telfer, a biologist in Philadelphia, reported that a study of four Pennsylvania prisons and mental hospitals disclosed five XYY cases among 129 tall inmates. Similar results were reported from the Atascadero State Hospital in California.

An outburst of legal maneuvers and writings challenging the criminal responsibility of XYY offenders followed. In Sydney, Australia, a 21-year-old laborer charged with the murder of a 77-year-old widow, found stabbed to death in her apartment, was shown to have 47 chromosomes in each body cell instead of the normal 46. The jury bypassed this issue, however, and found him not guilty by reason of insanity. In the French Hugon case the XYY question was finally likewise abandoned. In the United States, the attorneys for Richard Speck, the convicted murderer of eight Chicago nurses, suggested in April 1968 that they may mount an appeal on the basis of Speck's genetic abnormality. Similarly, this never came to fruition.

Although the XYY defense has not obtained its full test in court, the proponents of determinism nevertheless have gained a new handle. Evidence of the XYY syndrome lent support to a long line of believers in genetic determinism—going back to Cesare Lombroso and his disciples. Nor are the claims with regard to genetic determinism a lonely development. Emphasis upon socioeconomic environment as the source of criminality goes back to Karl Marx and his followers. William Adrian Bonger, a Dutch professor of sociology and a Marxist, claimed that the capitalist society which emphasizes private property and individual gain was essentially inimical to the development of altruism and social responsibility. The conflicts of economic competition, he argued, made man more egoistic and more capable of crime. Economic, social, and educational deprivation, as well as the corrupting influence of criminalized peer groups, have thus been pointed to as causes of antisocial behavior.

More recently, social determinism has gained new support. Responding to the 1967 Baltimore civil disturbances, a Maryland NAACP leader asserted: "The laws and the system have turned our children into criminals and looters." Commenting on the killing of a white policeman by black militants in 1969, the Democratic National Committeeman for the District of Columbia simply laid the blame upon social conditioning. It is the white discrimination, he asserted, that compels blacks to respond through violence. Going a few steps further toward practical application, a Manhattan Criminal Court experiment was designed in 1967 to deal with offenders from deprived backgrounds, whom Mayor John V. Lindsay described as "persons forced into crime by economic or social pressures." Instead of the traditional criminal process and conviction, a selected group of underprivileged youth was offered special training and employment and at the end of a successful trial period would be relieved of prosecution.

How will traditional guilt fare in a society which is increasingly discovering the impact of hereditary and environmental forces upon human choice and behavior?

GUILT, FREE WILL, AND CRIMINAL JUSTICE

Guilt is a legal concept, not a scientific fact. In modern society it is the function of courts of law, rather than witch doctors, legislatures, or bureaucrats, to decree guilt and innocence and to assess punishment upon those found guilty. Today's method for finding guilt consists of an elaborate legal ritual, called trial, where witnesses come forward like actors in a play to give evidence. It is from this evidence that guilt or innocence is distilled. While the measure of punishment is typically left to the discretion of judges, the determination of guilt has been delegated to juries both by early English legislation[2] and the American Constitution. It is thus one's own peer's who must weigh the evidence and decide the probability of guilt—whether it has been proven beyond a reasonable doubt.

Evidence is whatever courts consider proper and relevant for the weighing and determination of criminal guilt. Trial by fire—where guilt was proved by the accused's inability to put out the flames set by him, or by bitter waters, where the wife's infidelity was established by the swelling of her belly after drinking the testing concoction—were not uncommon until the Middle Ages. Trial by combat was another popular means for weighing evidence and determining guilt. Those not guilty were expected to prove their innocence through an armed victory over their accusers.

Trials through witnesses go back to biblical times. Yet one might assert that it was Europe's Age of Reason, with its emphasis upon communications and the rationality of man, which accounts for the emergence of the modern trial—where words rather than acts of faith take pre-eminence. In the courts of America proof is usually made today through either verbal testimony or demonstrative evidence. Most frequently, an eye witness will describe what he saw or heard. Occasionally, the murder weapon, including fingerprints, the forged paper, or the clothing of the suspect, may be introduced at the trial as demonstrative proof. Any one of these types of evidence may also be classified as either direct or circumstantial. Direct evidence means that the witness in fact saw the very fact he describes; circumstantial evidence relates only indirectly to the facts that need be proved. A witness who did not observe a burglary, yet who testifies to the accused's spending an unusual amount of money shortly thereafter, is offering circumstantial evidence.

A determination of guilt is not merely a factual finding; it is also a moral judgment. The proof of guilt usually consists of two parts: proof that the accused did the prohibited act and proof of his criminal intent or purpose. Most serious crimes require not only proof of the criminal act, but also proof that the offender intended to do wrong, or in legal language, a showing that he has *mens rea* (an evil mind). This requirement of *mens rea* goes back to the religious and moral foundations of the criminal law, where criminality was viewed as a personal fault—one's failure to resist to temptations and to steer away from wrongdoing.

Those who in fact lacked the necessary intent (consider a man picking up a coat in a restaurant believing it to be his own) or others who were generally considered immature or otherwise incapable of harboring such evil purpose (animals, infants, persons acting under a threat to their lives, and imbeciles) were accordingly held exempt from criminal responsibility.

Modern criminal law similarly exempts from guilt juveniles under given ages, adults suffering from mental illness and defects, and at times also chronic alcoholics and drug addicts.

It is the concept of individual responsibility that is at the core of the criminal process. Without the axiomatic acceptance of man's special endowment with responsibility there can be no guilt finding. The laws of primitive societies which prescribed punishment for goring oxen and biting dogs were finally abolished because of the recognition that morality requires that we not punish those incapable of personal guilt.

Reduced to simple terms, the criminal law is based on an assumption of free will—that is, a belief in man's capability to differentiate between the lawful and the unlawful and his ability to choose between the two. Criminal law therefore exempts from its process those who, due to some formulated legal criteria, have been determined to lack that amount of free will which is required for a finding of criminal responsibility.

THE INSANITY EXCEPTION TO FREE WILL

The insanity defense has grown over the years to accommodate departures from this basic axiom of criminal law—that people are responsible for their deeds. Punishing the mentally ill appeared inhumane even in fourteenth century England. Not only was the spectacle of punishing a raving maniac distasteful to the viewing audience, but it also seemed an ineffective measure for deterring the conduct of an unreasoning being. Yet the question of what degree of insanity should suffice to exempt a person of criminal responsibility was never solved satisfactorily.

Commencing with a crude test which equated those exempt from punishment to "wild beasts" the criteria grew in complexity with time. The most famous and still most common test for differentiating between the responsible and those not so is the *M'Naghten* rule, which was formulated in the forties of the last century. M'Naghten gained fame by attempting to assassinate English Prime Minister Sir Robert Peel. (His case demonstrates that even before the current flourishing of mass media the assassin could derive his fame from the glory of his victim.) After public complaints and Queen Victoria's assertion that M'Naghten was unduly relieved of punishment, the House of Lords in 1943 formulated uniform criteria for relief from responsibility. They required that to be found not guilty the accused must have such a defect of reason, as a result of a disease of the mind, as not to know the nature and quality of his act or else not to know the difference between right and wrong.

The middle of the current century saw many efforts to expand and liberalize the insanity defense. Most psychiatrists have complained that M'Naghten reflected psychiatric knowledge of days gone by. Some asserted that the test employed legal criteria which are not meaningful in psychiatry, others urged a new test less grounded in the cognitive or reasoning ability of the offender. The reformers noted correctly that a man may well suffer from severe mental illness which could dominate his behavior yet leave his knowledge of right and wrong unimpaired.

The desire of psychiatrists, as well as reforming judges, to subject increasing numbers of offenders to mental therapy instead of criminal punishment resulted in the 1954 *Durham* rule in the District of Columbia ("is the crime a *product* of mental illness or defect"), the 1961 *Currens* rule in the United States Court of Appeals for the Third Circuit ("did the accused, because of mental illness or defect, lack *substantial capacity* to conform his conduct to the law"), and the 1962 American Law Institute's model penal code, which offers a combination of these reforms for voluntary adoption by the various states. Each of these modifications is intended to broaden the classification of those found insane rather than guilty.

Yet all tests which curtail criminal responsibility are arbitrary. Judge Thurman Arnold keenly noted in 1945 that the law recognizes either full responsibility or total irresponsibility, permitting no middle ground between these absolutes. The sciences of human behavior, on the other hand, provide no support for such dichotomy and furnish no scientific delineation for distinguishing the evil from the ill. The line that the law draws is therefore not a product of science but a result of a social policy determination. This means that society can at best establish not a scientific line on the insanity defense, but rather a pragmatic one, which constantly weighs penal versus psychiatric alternatives and is fundamentally grounded in the public need for stressing individual responsibility as a means for promoting conformity and self-restraint. In the face of deterministic sciences, the concept of guilt is thus preserved primarily as a tool of education, to reinforce ordained behavior, and as a means for social control.

In reality much of the heat generated in the recent debates on the insanity criteria remains primarily academic. In our courts it continues the task of the jury to find a sufficient degree of insanity to negate guilt. Psychiatrists have and continue being the most influential witnesses in charting the insanity defense before the jury: by elucidating psychiatric knowledge and relating it to the accused's condition. What psychiatrists label as insanity has a considerable bearing on the jury deliberations. Yet despite the dramatic recent departures from the M'Naghten formula, psychiatrists usually continue to limit their diagnoses of insanity to psychotic cases only, leaving neurotics and the so-called psychopath to the traditional criminal process. Moreover, we have little insight as to the effect of the new insanity criteria upon jury decisions. Some research projects have reached the conclusion that juries pay little attention to legal or psychiatric refinements and that the determination of insanity is most often a result of jury instinct and common sense. "Is the accused nuts?" may still better summarize the question before juries than the more complex criteria of M'Naghten, Durham, or A.L.I.

To this precarious and artificial balance between responsibility, free will, guilt, and insanity, the XYY syndrome brought much turmoil.

THE XYY DEFENSE

To exempt those afflicted by it from guilt, the XYY syndrome must come within one of the doctrines vitiating personal responsibility in criminal law. The formula that comes most readily to mind is the insanity defense. It is this route which has been previously attempted or suggested in France, Australia, and in Chicago's Speck case.

To comply with the insanity defense requirements one must first establish the existence of a mental illness or defect. Accordingly, the typology of the XYY abnormality becomes central. Is the XYY syndrome a mental illness, a mental defect, a physical illness, or one of these? Indeed, what precisely are the confines of mental illness or deficiency?

Only after this first prerequisite is positively answered, can one move on to the diverse secondary tests. In those states adhering to the M'Naghten test, a further showing must be made of the offender's lack of knowledge of the quality and nature of his act or his inability to tell right from wrong. Where Durham controls, a showing that the criminal behavior was a product of the abnormality would be required. Under the Currens or the A.L.I. test, the accused must prove that because of the mental illness or defect he lacked substantial capacity to stay within the law. And in a number of other states which subscribe to the irresistible impulse test, an insane person will be found not guilty if the offense was induced by such impulse.

As one views this complex obstacle course, the insanity defense route does not appear without difficulties. XYY's adoption and classification as a mental disability by the psychiatric fraternity would be the first requirement, and no such development yet appears in sight. The next step would depend on the insanity test in effect in given state. The Durham, the A.L.I., or the irresistible impulse criteria could supply the causality requirement needed to exempt an XYY sufferer from responsibility by a showing that the criminal behavior was a product of or was caused by the XYY abnormality or else that the latter deprived the offender of the capacity to conform. Less certain would be the M'Naghten test's applicability to the XYY sufferer, unless it could be shown that the abnormality affects the cognitive faculties.

In the face of these prerequisites, it is not surprising that little progress has been made to date in endowing the XYY abnormality with the equivalents of the insanity defense. But other routes remain. One to be looked at is the defense of compulsion or coercion. Criminal law has traditionally exempted from responsibility those who offended while acting under an imminent and serious threat to their lives or those in their immediate family. The defense of compulsion permits one to commit a lesser offense in order to save his life; it acknowledges also that a prohibited act is not punishable unless accompanied by the requisite evil intent. Yet coercion must usually be externally imposed and must involve a fear of life or bodily harm rather than an inner compulsion. Moreover, it will not excuse homicides—for no trade-off is permitted between one's own life and that of others.

Another approach is possible to the relationship between XYY and guilt. This is similar to the law's past treatment of drug addiction and alcoholism. In 1962, in the landmark *Robinson* case, the Supreme Court held addiction to be an illness and concluded that those afflicted by it may not be punished for addiction. The law has not been willing, however, to go farther and exempt from guilt addicts charged with other criminal behavior, such as robbery and murder, or even such narcotic-connected offenses as importation and sale of drugs. More recently, several federal courts, in a similar vein, ruled that those suffering from chronic alcoholism may not be prosecuted for public intoxication. Again, however, this exemption from responsibility does not extend to behavior other than mere intoxication. In refusing to relieve an alcoholic of punishment for such offenses as disorderly conduct, assault, or larceny, the courts have stressed the need for a showing of a direct causality between alcoholism and the prohibited conduct. Absent such connection, guilt will prevail.

The implications for the XYY defense are significant. If the syndrome indeed is classified as an illness, those possessing it could certainly not be punished for its presence. But those claiming it as a defense to other offenses would be required to prove that but for XYY's existence the proscribed conduct would not have occurred. Such proof might be difficult if not impossible, as would be the proof of any single causative reason for crime.

The most radical approach to the relief of XYY sufferers from responsibility would be that undertaken in the juvenile process. There, by comprehensive legislative fiat, all youth under a given age were decreed criminally unaccountable due to chronological immaturity. Beginning with the end of the nineteenth century, determinations of guilt have been accordingly dispensed with for juveniles and a new system of social controls, within which concepts of guilt and personal responsibility are nonexistent, was introduced. This absolute abolition of guilt met with some opposition. It is arguable that not all youth under a given age, say 16 years, are in fact so immature that they are presumed to be incapable of criminal intent. The argument is valid. Yet here as in other areas of law, the line of responsibility is arbitrarily drawn or, more precisely, drawn to accommodate certain social policies. In the juvenile area this policy called for the exemption of youths from the branding and harsher sanctions of criminal law. The policy did not result, however, in the total exemption of children from social sanctions, for the juvenile courts offered a new formula for control.

THE ABOLITION OF GUILT

Where does all this leave the XYY offender? Although with some modifications he could be fitted within one of the traditional exceptions to criminal responsibility, none of these cubbyholes fit him precisely now. Yet the XYY findings are probably only the first of many new scientific insights into human behavior. Much additional understanding of the causes of criminality will inevitably follow. Some evidence will point to physiological or genetic factors, other evidence will be environmental, educational, social, or economic. The time has clearly come for an eclectic framework for the causes of crime and delinquency. Yet in each individual case the balance of forces that finally tilt the scales from lawfulness to criminality may be different.

As the evidence of behavioral determinism grows, how are we to cope with it? Should we go the old road and presume all persons sound and capable of free will, yet keep withdrawing from this universe those who fall within such narrowly defined criteria as insanity, youth, drug addiction, alcoholism, or whatever it may be? Or should we honestly traverse a new road toward a new model of social control: one where we admit that free will and responsibility are at best relative and terms of convenience only; one where we acknowledge the inability and irrationality of drawing an absolute line between those capable of guilt and those free of it?

The XYY discovery is merely one more piece of evidence that man is not his own master. The XYY evidence should make the framers of the criminal law stop and think. If we are willing to give the XYY sufferers the benefit of the doubt, according them special therapeutic measures in lieu of punishment, we should be willing to recognize that every other offender has his XYY equivalent, his mortal weaknesses and shortcomings—hereditary or environmental. The rational choice in a scientific age offers only two alternatives: We are either to hold all guilty and subject to punishment or else recognize that we are all imperfect, yet accountable to society. I would rather choose the second approach and commence seeking and offering not punishment for guilt but individual cures for men's misconducts. I would prefer to see a new emphasis in society's management of crime, a shift from the assessment of abstract guilt to the offering of pragmatic remedies—to each according to his need.

What I suggest is not as revolutionary as it may sound: In the face of deterministic evidence we should presume all offenders as having involuntarily entered the life of crime. Yet society's defense requires that we undertake measures for its protection even against those without moral guilt. Accountability without guilt is not a new approach. Enrico Ferri, the noted nineteenth century Italian criminologist, pointed in this direction. He insisted that we need not rely on concepts of individual responsibility and guilt in order to design social programs for dealing with offenders. Every person who lives in a society is accountable to it for his antisocial conduct. Society, in return, may seek to curb his future misdeeds, not as a punishment for the improper exercise of free will but as a remedy for his human failings.

NOTES

1. M. Amir and Y. Berman, "Chromosomal Deviation and Crime," *Federal Probation*, June 1970.
2. The Magna Carta guaranteed in 1215 that no freeman was to be imprisoned, outlawed or exiled "unless by the lawful judgment of his peers, or by the law of the land." In 1275 the Statute of Westminster I imposed jury trials upon felons. T. E. Plucknett, *A Concise History of the Comon Law* 24, 126 (1956).
3. For a detailed study of legal programs imposing accountability without a finding of guilt (in such diverse fields as mental illness, juvenile delinquency, alcoholism, and drug addiction) see Kittrie, *The Right to be Different: Deviance and Enforced Therapy* (Baltimore: Johns Hopkins University Press, 1971).

4

Crime and Conditioning

H. J. Eysenck

Appeared originally in Chapter 6 of *Crime and Personality*, by H. J. Eysenck (Boston: Houghton Mifflin, 1964): pp. 120–39. Reprinted with permission of the author and present copyright holder, Routledge & Kegan Paul Ltd., Boston.

"What sort of things do you remember best?" Alice ventured to ask.

"Oh, things that happened the week after next," the Queen replied in a careless tone. "For instance, now," she went on, sticking a large piece of plaster on her finger as she spoke, "there's the King's Messenger. He's in prison now, being punished: and the trial doesn't even begin till next Wednesday: and of course the crime comes last of all."

"Suppose he never commits the crime?" said Alice.

"That would be all the better, wouldn't it?" the Queen said, as she bound the plaster round her finger with a bit of ribbon.

—Lewis Carroll

We have now propounded our theory, that it is conscience which is, in the main, instrumental in making us behave in a moral and socially acceptable manner; that this conscience is the combination and culmination of a long process of conditioning; and that failure on the part of the person to become conditioned is likely to be a prominent cause in his running afoul of the law and of the social mores generally. We must now turn to a consideration of the evidence which may be in favour of, or counter to, this hypothesis, and we must also discuss some of the consequences which follow from it. Let us first have a good look at the evidence.

Now there are several deductions which we can make from our theory. In the first place, we would expect conditioning experiments to show that psychopaths and extraverts generally manifest less conditioning in these experimental situations than do normal people or dysthymic neurotics. Similarly, if we studied groups of criminals, we would also expect to find that they would be more difficult to condition than non-criminals. We have already noted, in a previous chapter, that extraverted people, both neurotic and normal, are indeed more difficult to condition than are introverted neurotics and normals. It will be remembered that, on the eye-blink conditioning test for instance, it was found that extraverts condition only about fifty per cent as well as introverts, and roughly similar results have been found with other types of conditioning. When we turn to psychopaths specifically, we find that, here too, there is a distinct tendency for such people to show poor conditioning.[1] Lykken, in America, and Tong, in England, have carried out extensive studies of psychopaths and have come to the conclusion that their conditioning is much less effective than that of various control groups. The work of Tong is perhaps more relevant to our hypothesis, because, in his work at Rampton (a hospital for criminal psychopaths), he was in a position to deal with psychopaths who, in addition to having this particular psychiatric label, had also in their actual life histories run afoul of the law and had been referred to this particular prison hospital. The evidence on conditioning then, as far as it is available, tends to favour our hypothesis. It should be noted, however, that the amount of work that has been done is far from conclusive. Many more studies, involving thousands of criminals, both those diagnosed as psychopaths and others, will be required before we can assert that our theory does in fact accord with reality. In particular, it will be necessary to try out a great many different types of conditioning experiments. It will be necessary to vary the parameters we mentioned before, such as the strength of the unconditioned stimulus, the length of time elapsing between the conditioned and the unconditioned stimulus, the spacing of the trials, and so forth. Furthermore, it will be necessary to distinguish between different types of criminals. As we shall see later, our theory is not intended to apply indiscriminately to all criminals, and for some criminals indeed we would predict a greater conditionability than average. This exception to our rule will be discussed later on in this chapter; here let us simply note that while the evidence from conditioning experiments favours our theory, it is by no means sufficient to establish it firmly as a general law. It is left as a theory for which some slight support is available.

Another deduction from our theory is, of course, the more general one that people who commit crimes and other antisocial or asocial acts would, on the whole, be more extraverted than people who refrain from carrying out such acts. Here the evidence is fortunately more extensive, indeed, so extensive that we can look at only a few typical studies. Let us begin by looking at the problem of traffic accidents and violations of traffic rules. In an earlier chapter, we mentioned the fact that severe violation of the traffic laws tends to be the responsibility of people who have also run afoul of the law in many other ways. What about less severe violations of the traffic code? There is an interesting study carried out by Bernard J. Fine of the U.S. Army Research Institute of Environmental Medicine, which was planned specifically to test this hypothesis. As subjects, he used 993 male freshmen in the general college of the University of Minnesota, who had been administered a personality questionnaire. For each of these students information was available regarding the date, type, number, and place of occurrence of traffic accidents and traffic violations. On the basis of the questionnaire responses, Fine grouped his subjects into the most extraverted, the most introverted, and an intermediate group, each constituting roughly one-third of the total group. He found that the extraverts had significantly more accidents and were also guilty of more traffic violations than were the intermediates or the introverts.[2]

Another study was reported by S. Biesheuvel and M. E. White, from the National Institute for Personnel Research in South Africa. They studied an accident group of 200 pilots in training who had been involved in flying accidents at elementary and advanced flying schools. As a control, they used 400 men who had completed both elementary and advanced training with an accident-free record. Comparison between the two groups showed significant differences, both for emotionality and also for extraversion. Those in the accident group were more emotional, more distractable, they tended to act on impulse, and were generally less cautious. Their behavior was more variable and they were more apt to be influenced by the mood of the moment. These are all extraverted tendencies which, added to the strong emotionality of the accident-prone group, put them squarely into the psychopathic quadrant of our personality field.[3]

Consider now a rather different field altogether. Sexual promiscuity is not considered a crime, but rather a sin; nevertheless, it is obviously a case of contravening the social morality which has been preached to us from early childhood, and consequently we would expect the more extraverted to be more promiscuous. One attempt to study this question was made by Sybil B. G. Eysenck, who contrasted the personalities of married and unmarried mothers. Personality questionnaires were administered to 100 mothers in the maternity wards of a large London hospital. The same questionnaire was administered to unmarried mothers in various moral welfare homes, who were seen after their confinements. The unmarried mothers were found to be both more extraverted and also to have much higher degrees of emotionality or neuroticism than did the married mothers. When compared with the general population norms too, it was found again that the unmarried mothers tended to fall into the psychopathic quadrant, i.e., were high on neuroticism and high on extraversion. Here too, then, our general hypothesis is verified.[4]

Traffic violators, people who suffer accidents, and unmarried mothers—these may seem to be a little outside the more general field of this book because, while their conduct is certainly counter to certain rules and precepts of our society, they have not committed any actual crimes. What would happen if we gave our questionnaire to actual criminals? One such study has been done by Syed,[5] who tested a hundred women criminals in a large

London prison. He found that, very much as predicted, they fell predominantly and significantly into the psychopathic quadrant, having high scores on extraversion and high scores on emotionality. Many other studies are available, both in America and in England, showing that criminals tend to be high on emotionality or neuroticism. Unfortunately, most of these studies have not used a questionnaire, which would enable us to get an uncontaminated measure of extraversion. However, in a number of cases, there has been used a very extensive questionnaire called the Minnesota Multiphasic Personality Inventory, which contains one scale, the so-called "psychopathic deviant" scale, which may be relevant in this connection. It is found, in general, that among criminal prisoners it is this psychopathic deviant scale which, more than any other contained in this inventory, discriminates this group from the normal control groups or even from neurotic groups tested in hospitals. It is also usually found that other scales measuring emotionality or neuroticism give higher scores for criminals than for normals. Here again, therefore, we find some support, at least for our general hypothesis.

Of particular interest is an unpublished study carried out by Frank Warburton, of the University of Manchester. He worked with a group of prisoners in Joliet Penitentiary near Chicago. These men were the most recalcitrant in a prison of some 2000 inmates and had consistently had their privileges taken away from them. They can thus be described as "second order prisoners," in the sense that if all the prisoners in the jail had been placed on an island, they would have found it necessary to provide a prison for these men. Warburton administered the Cattell Personality Scales to these men, and found that on five traits, which are grouped under the extraversion heading, four showed a highly elevated score. The fifth, dealing with social behaviour (sociability), did not properly apply to these men, since social behaviour in prison is very different from that outside. Of five traits related to neuroticism, all five showed highly elevated scales. When a combined score was derived for extraversion, and another for neuroticism, taking all scales used into account, these men were found to be very much in the psychopathic quadrant; that is to say, they had high scores on extraversion and very high scores on neuroticism. In addition, objective tests were given by Warburton, yielding results supporting the conclusions derived from the questionnaires.[6]

Further support for this theory of the position of the criminal in the personality framework outlined above comes from a recent book by R. G. Andry, *The Short-Term Offender*. His study was mainly concerned with the personality correlates of recidivism in prisoners serving sentences not exceeding six months, and his main conclusions were that recidivists were characterized by emotional disturbances (neuroticism), and by tough-minded, extrapunitive (extraverted?) behaviour, as well as by immaturity. On the basis of psychological arguments not unlike those to be presented, Andry makes certain suggestions for differential treatment of criminals of these various personality types; they will be only briefly quoted here, as a more detailed discussion will be given later in this book. Andry's first suggestion is that "among neurotic offenders it is unlikely that recidivism will be reduced by conventional prison treatment but, in fact, may well be increased"; he considers it "likely that it [recidivism] will be reduced by treatment involving regular psychotherapy (and/or behaviour therapy and chemotherapy)." His third suggestion is that "rigid discipline and some degree of punitive treatment over a fairly long period has more chance of modifying the antisocial attitudes of extrapunitive offenders than has any known form of therapy alone (although a combination of both seems indicated)." We shall see in a later chapter that there exists some experimental evidence to lend at least limited support to these suggestions.[7]

As typical of many studies, we may perhaps discuss, in greater detail, a recent book by T. C. N. Gibbens, of the Maudsley Hospital in London, in which he studied 200 Borstal boys, that is, juvenile delinquents who had committed crimes of some seriousness, who were roughly sixteen to twenty-one years of age, and who had been sentenced to attend the special punitive, corrective institutions commonly referred to as "Borstals" in England. In addition to intensive psychiatric investigation, Gibbens also administered the Minnesota Multiphasic Personality Inventory and compared the responses of the Borstal boys with those of a control group. As had been expected, it was the psychopathic deviant scale which gave the best discrimination between the groups.

Gibbens also administered an objective test which had previously been shown to be correlated with extraversion, the Porteus Mazes Test. Originally this had been introduced as a test of intelligence; it consists of a printed maze pattern through which the subject has to find his way, tracing his path with a pencil from start to finish, the score being simply the length of time it takes him for his relative success or failure. Now in this test, the subject has to obey certain rules; he must not lift his pencil from the paper, he must not cross lines printed on the sheet, and he must not cut corners. In terms of our theory, it had been predicted that the extraverted person would be more likely to contravene these rules because of his failure of socialization, due to inadequate conditioning. And in one or two studies, it had indeed been found that extraverts tended to give higher deviant scores in this test, when it is scored simply for the number of contraventions of the instructions. A special score, the Q score, was introduced by Porteus as being independent of intelligence and as measuring this particular tendency which, incidentally, has also been found to be strong in people who had been subjected to lobotomy, the brain operation which, as we have pointed out earlier, has the effect of making people more extraverted.[8]

Apart from the study by Gibbens which have been discussed, there have been five different investigations studying the scores of delinquents and comparing them with those of non-delinquents. All these studies have been done by Americans, and the findings have been that, on the average, delinquents have a score of only about twenty. A similar comparison was made by Gibbens, who found, for delinquents, a score of thirty-five, and for non-delinquents, a score of fourteen. Both, in other words, were much lower than the corresponding American norms, which, itself, may be of interest, in view of the much greater rate of crime in America as compared to England. The important thing to note, however, is that in both the American and the English studies, the delinquents have a much higher score than do the non-delinquents. In other words, we find that in relation to this test, delinquents, as compared with non-delinquents, behave very much as do extraverts when compared with introverts.

Gibbens continued his studies with an assessment of body build. Before we are ready to understand the meaning and significance of this, we will have to digress briefly. When we take even the most casual look at people, one of the first things to impress us is the enormous variability in their bodily configuration or physique. It has been assumed ever since Hippocrates, the famous physician who lived in 430 B.C., that the different types of body build which people show have related both to their temperament and personality, and also to their tendency to develop different diseases. Hippocrates was particularly impressed by the differences between the long, lean type of body build and the short, stocky one; he called the former the *habitus phthisicus*, or tubercular type, and the other the *habitus apoplecticus*, or apoplectic type, suggesting that the long, lean person was more prone to tuberculosis and the stocky one to apoplexy and heart disease. Many writers since have followed his lead, and we have a large number of different types named in a variety of different ways. The thick-set habitus apoplecticus has been named, among other things, the abdominal type, the digestive type, the nutritive, the phlegmatic, the vital, the hyperplastic, the food type, the connective type, the lateral type; and the habitus phthisicus has been called the cephalic type, the mental type, the cerebral-asthenic type, the sensation type, the linear type, and the asthenic type. Perhaps the most widely accepted typology was that suggested by the German psychiatrist Kretschmer, shortly after the first World War, who labelled the thickset type the *pyknic* and the lean, linear type the *leptosome*. He also introduced the third type, roughly intermediate between the other two, which he called the *athletic* type. He proceeded to link up this bodily typology with psychiatry, by postulating that psychotics of pyknic body build tended to suffer from manic-depressive insanity, whereas psychotics of leptosomatic body build tended to suffer from schizophrenia. There is indeed some such relation but it is not strong enough to be of any very great use for diagnosis.[9]

More recently, Kretschmer's system was taken over by the American anthropologist and psychologist, W. H. Sheldon, who applied it more widely and particularly related body build to normal personality. He postulated, like Kretschmer, the existence of three main body types, which he called *endomorph*, for the thick-set pyknic type; *mesomorph*, for the athletic type; and *ectomorph*, for the equivalent of Kretschmer's leptosome. He further postulated that there were three relatively independent factors of bodily growth, and that each person could be rated according to the strength of each of these components on a seven-point scale. Each person is accordingly given a number consisting of three digits which indicates the strength of the three components. Thus, 117 would be a person characterised by an almost complete lack in endomorphy and mesomorphy and a complete dominance of the ectomorphy component. All other combinations are similarly derived in terms of three numbers and it will be seen that there are 343 theoretical possibilities of deriving different somatotypes from these three components. Sheldon reports, however, that only 76 have been encountered by him in actual practice. Sheldon tends to favour photography rather than direct measurement. He lines up his nude subjects, takes photographs of them in a standard position, and then these photographs are rated for the relative contribution of the three components.

Sheldon believes that these components have a different embryological origin. There are three germ layers in an embryo: the ectoderm, endoderm, and mesoderm. Sheldon believes that it is the exaggerated functioning of one of these layers which produces the three types. Taking Kretschmer's pyknic type, for instance, Sheldon maintains that in him the digestive tract, especially the gut, held a more or less predominant position in the organic economy.

> In these people, the most manifest external characteristic is a conspicuous laying-on of fat, which is an indication of predominance of the absorptive function—the function of the gut—over the energy-expending functions. The functional elements of the digestive system are derived embryologically almost entirely from the endoderm, the innermost of the three original embryonic layers. We can quite naturally, therefore, refer to the extremes of type one as exhibiting a condition of *endomorphy*.

In a similar way, bones, muscles, connective tissue, and the heart and blood vessels were seen by him to predominate overwhelmingly in the variants of type two, which corresponds to Kretschmer's athletics. This type is, therefore, called the mesomorph, as these functions are derived predominantly from the mesoderm, the second embryonic layer. As regards the third type, Kretschmer's leptosome,

> the principal derivatives from the embryonic ectodermal layer are the skin itself, hair and nails, sense organs, and the nervous system, including the brain.

Relative to total bodily mass, all these organs are conspicuous in the bodily economy of the extreme variants of type three. Hence we have named them ectomorphs, or persons exhibiting ectomorphy.

To correspond to these bodily types, Sheldon also posits the existence of three different types of temperament, which he calls viscerotonia, which is supposed to go with the body type of endomorphy; somatotonia, which is supposed to go with the body type of mesomorphy; and cerebrotonia, which is supposed to go with the body type of ectomorphy. A brief description of these three temperaments is as follows.

The viscerotonic is relaxed in posture and movement; he loves physical comfort and eating, has slow reactions, loves polite ceremony and is sociable. He is amiable, greedy for affection and approval, tolerant and complacent, sleeps deeply, is relaxed and extraverted. The somatotonic is assertive, loves physical adventure, is energetic and likes exercise, loves domination and power, likes to take risks and chances, is physically courageous and aggressive and psychologically callous. He is rather ruthless, unrestrained, indifferent to pain, generally noisy and also extraverted. The cerebrotonic loves privacy, is mentally over-intensive, rather restrained, tends to be apprehensive, is rather self-conscious, and dislikes social intercourse. He is hypersensitive to pain, sleeps rather poorly, is introverted, and needs solitude when troubled. We may sum up Sheldon's system by saying that the cerebrotonic is the typical introvert, as we have described him before, whereas both the viscerotonic and the somatotonic are extraverts. They differ in that the two types stress different aspects of extraversion. The viscerotonic stressed the *sociability* side, the somatotonic stresses rather the *impulsive* side of extraversion.[10]

Sheldon reports quite high correlations between personality ratings and somatotype ratings of body build, both made by him. Indeed these are so high as to be quite improbable, and it has been pointed out that a person holding a definite theory about the relationship between body build and temperament, rating the same persons with respect to both body build and temperament, is almost bound to find that his ratings are contaminated by his knowledge. Thus the figures reported by Sheldon may mean little more than that he was consistent in applying his theory. Other people have duplicated his work and the general consensus of opinion is that the correlations are in the expected direction, but they are relatively low: at most, about 0.3. This indeed is in very good agreement with previous studies by English workers, which have shown, by and large, similar correlations between introversion and the leptosomatic type of body build, and extraversion and the pyknic type of body build. What Sheldon has added essentially is a division of the pyknic or thick-set type of body build into two sub-types: the mesomorphs, whose body build incorporates a great deal of muscle, and the endomorphs, whose body build incorporates a great deal of fat. As regards personality correlates, his main contribution has been to suggest that the pyknic with the considerable degree of muscle will tend to be impulsive, the pyknic with a good deal of fat, rather sociable.

Body build is determined by hereditary factors to a considerable degree, and its correlation with temperament has sometimes been suggested as proof of the hereditary determination of personality as well. This is not necessarily true. We might simply be dealing with a reaction on the part of the individual concerned to the limitations imposed on him by his body build. As has sometimes been said, the fat boy cannot fight and he cannot run away, so he might just as well be friendly and sociable if he wants to get on in life. In other words, on this hypothesis, we would not say that temperament is inherited as body build is, but rather that the behaviour of the person is determined by the body build which he has inherited, in a rather indirect way. Similarly, we would expect the mesomorphic type of boy to be more adventurous, simply because his strong musculature enables him to do things, to be aggressive, and to indulge in various activities which the fat or the lean boy are unable to do because they lack the appropriate muscular equipment. Heredity would thus play some part in the determination of behaviour, but it would be, as it were, at second remove.

How does all this apply to our problem of criminality and personality? We have already noted that Lombroso studied morphological anomalies in criminals and proposed the doctrine that the criminal, as found in prison, was an atavistic anomaly presenting morbid physical stigmata. We have also noticed that this doctrine is now completely discredited. (It may be noted incidentally that it was less obviously absurd in Lombroso's time than it is now. When he was investigating the nature of criminality there were no mental defective institutions and many mental defectives were in fact in prison, guilty of minor offenses of various kinds. At least a certain proportion of mental defectives suffer from quite specific disorders, such as monogolism, which indeed alter their appearance and make them look rather startlingly unlike ordinary people. It is presumably due to the presence of people of this type that Lombroso proposed his doctrine.)

In modern times, the famous American anthropologist, Hooton, studied 17,000 prison and reformatory inmates and measured their body configurations. He found quite significant differences in various body measurements between persons convicted of different types of crime. He found, for instance, that the criminals with pyknic body build (extraverts?) headed the list of crimes for rape, sex offences and assault, but were lowest in murder, whereas the leptosomatic criminals (introverts?) had the highest incidence of murder and robbery but the lowest incidences of crimes such as burglary, assault, rape, and other sex offences. This is interesting, because rape, sex offences, and assault are precisely the impulsive type of crime which we would expect to find in extraverted people who, as we have seen, tend to be of the pyknic type of body build. However, not too much should be made of Hooton's figures, because many different racial strains, in almost pure culture, are found in America, and it is quite possible that different nationalities such as the Italians and the Swedes, for instance, differ both with respect to body build and with respect to the lawbreaking habits which they have acquired in the courses of their lives. We cannot, therefore, make any very confident deductions from Hooton's figures.[11]

However, a very well-known pair of American criminologists, Sheldon and Eleanor Glueck, of the Harvard Law School, conducted an enquiry which gave some very important and interesting results. They compared a group of 500 delinquent boys aged eleven to eighteen years with 500 non-delinquent controls who had been matched for age, intelligence, racial origin, and residence in under-privileged neighbourhoods. Comparing an-thropometric measurements and somatotype distribution along the lines that Sheldon has pioneered, they found that there was little difference in general body size, but that the delinquent group was considerably more mesomorphic and less ectomorphic than the non-delinquent group.[12]

Sheldon himself, with some of his colleagues, carried out a study in which 200 delinquent youths, somatotyped according to his system, were compared with 4000 college students. It was found that this sample of delinquents differed very much from the college somatotype distribution, having a dis-tinct massing in the endomorphic-mesomorphic sector, as compared with the ectomorphic. The students, on the other hand, tended to be ectomorphic rather than either endomorphic or mesomorphic. In terms of our system of temperaments, these findings show the criminals to have body types typical of extraverts, whereas the students had body types typical of introverts.

In England, Epps and Parnell studied a group of 177 young women be-tween the ages of sixteen and twenty-one, who were undergoing Borstal training. They compared the body configuration of these young women with 123 university women aged eighteen to twenty-one. They found that delin-quents were heavier in body build, were more muscular and fat; in tempera-ment they showed a predominance of somatotonia and viscerotonia. Here also we find a distinct tendency for the criminals to be extraverted compared with the students, who are introverted.[13] It may be added that the Gluecks, in addition to carrying out their studies of body build, also carried out surveys of the main personality traits of their delinquents, and found that their temperaments were "restlessly energetic, impulsive, extraverted, ag-gressive, destructive." They also found them to be highly emotional.

We may now continue our discussion of Gibbens' studies. He also somatotyped fifty-eight of his lads, and the resulting distribution of body

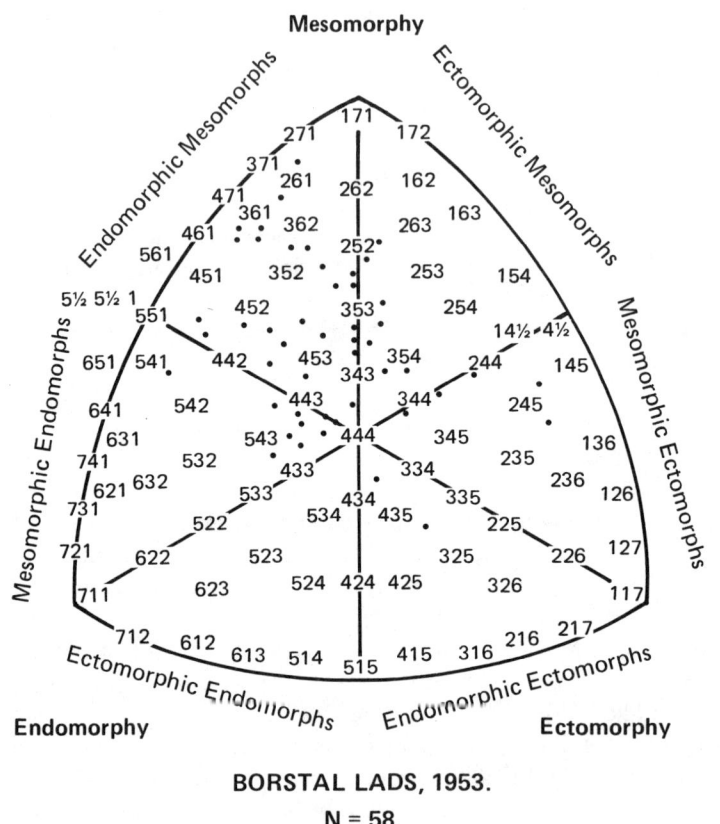

BORSTAL LADS, 1953.

N = 58.

FIGURE 4.1.

types is shown in Figure 4.1. This kind of semi-triangular scheme is customary for presenting data of Sheldon's body types. The numbers inside the diagram refer to various combinations of the three components, and help to identify the particular point in the diagram. It will be seen that nearly all the Borstal lads studied by Gibbens lie in the top, left-hand corner, with very few exceptions; in other words, they are very nearly all endomorphic mesomorphs. For comparison, we may look at 283 Oxford undergraduates, also presented in Gibbens' book. These are shown in Figure 4.2, and it will be seen that here the endomorphs are, if anything, under-represented and

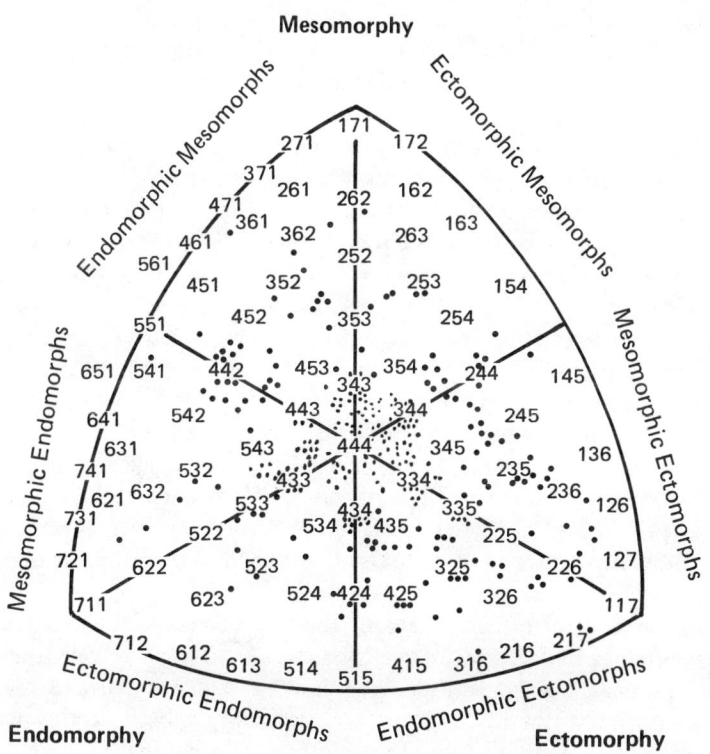

OXFORD UNDERGRADUATES. 1948-50
N = 283.

FIGURE 4.2.

that there is a great number of ectomorphs, a group of people almost entirely missing from the Borstal group. All these figures, both from America and from England, are in agreement then that criminals, on the whole, tend to be athletic in body build, that is, stocky and muscular rather than fat, and that they tend to show a temperamental tendency towards extraversion, particularly towards impulsiveness. These data, therefore, seem to support our general hypothesis.

Are there any contradictory data which might lead us to doubt the validity of our theory? We may perhaps begin by noting that questionnaire studies employing sociability items, that is, items which are usually diagnostic of extraversion, have not, on the whole, produced good differentiation between criminals and normals. Whether this is indeed an argument against our theory is difficult to say. As we pointed out before, it is the impulsive side of extraversion rather than the sociability side which we may consider to be associated with criminal behaviour. However, there is an even more power-ful reason for imagining that this unpredicted failure is little more than an artifact. Consider the position of a criminal, particularly a long-term criminal who has been in prison for perhaps ten or twenty years. Imagine his reaction when confronted with questions like the following. "Would you be very unhappy if you were prevented from making numerous social contacts?" "Is it difficult to 'lose yourself,' even at a lively party?" "Do you like to mix socially with people?" "Do you like to have many social engagements?" "Do you generally prefer to take the lead in group activities?" "Are you inclined to be shy in the presence of the opposite sex?" "Are you inclined to keep quiet when out in a social group?" "Can you usually let yourself go and have a hilariously gay time at a party?" If a prisoner, afer twenty years' incarcera-tion, comes out with a low score of sociability on questions such as these, this is not an altogether unforeseen result, and we need not consider it particu-larly inimical to our theory.

The same argument, of course, might apply in reverse to the observation which has often been referred to, that prisoners tend to score very high on tests of emotionality or neuroticism. It might be said, not without reason, that scores on questions of this type are high simply because the person answering the questionnaire is in prison; in other words, that it is his incar-ceration which produces the emotionality rather than the emotionality pro-ducing his criminal behaviour, in whole or part. This is not an unreasonable objection, but, on the whole, it may not be entirely correct. It has not been found, for instance, that the scores on emotionality tests rise as a function of the length of time a person has spent in prison. A person imprisoned for ten years does not score any higher than a person who has been in prison only a few days. Of course, it could be that the fact of imprisonment itself rather than the length of the sentence, or the length of time spent in prison, deter-mines the emotional reaction; but again it is doubtful whether this is a very good argument. We have found that even in cases where the violation of the rules of society has been less severe, and where the person has not gone to prison—as in the case of traffic violators or unmarried mothers—there is a considerable degree of emotionality which, quite obviously, could not have been due to their being incarcerated. Again, it might be said that possibly the emotionality in the unmarried mothers is produced by the precarious situa-tion in which they find themselves. This cannot be true of the traffic violators, because there the "crime" is too slight and the punishment too unimportant to influence responses on a questionnaire of the type used.

Nevertheless, it must be admitted that this is a point which requires much further study. In particular, it would be useful if predictive studies could be carried out with questionnaires; in other words, it would be desirable to study large numbers of subjects in a population where the rate of delinquency is known to be high. If these studies were carried out before individuals committed their crimes and were sent to prison, we could then follow them up and see whether a high score on emotionality on the original testing was correlated with a later tendency to commit crimes and be sent to prison. In the absence of any study of this kind, we can only conclude that this question had best be left open.

We must now turn to a rather different kind of objection which rests on a purely theoretical basis. We have argued that conscience is a conditioned response and we have also argued that extraverted people, because they condition poorly, will, on the whole, tend to have weaker consciences than introverts, who condition extremely well. This argument, however, makes an unwarranted assumption; it assumes that all people, extraverts and introverts alike, will be subjected to an identical system of conditioning or indoctrination. Now this is patently untrue, and we must next take up the question of determining what conclusions would follow from a more complicated and realistic state of affairs, where different degrees of conditioning are administered to different people. The argument we are now presenting may be put in experimental terms. If extraverts and introverts are conditioned on the eye-blink conditioning apparatus, and if both groups are given, say, twenty training trials, then we can demonstrate that introverts will condition about twice as well as extraverts; in other words, we will find that about 60 per cent of the introverted group will have formed strong conditioned responses but only 30 per cent of the extraverted group. But let us assume that instead of giving everybody the same number of conditioning trials, we give some people only two conditioning trials, others fifty, others a hundred, and others none at all. Under those conditions it would obviously be foolish to look for any very high correlation between introversion and conditioning; any such correlation would be over-shadowed by the incidental fact of whether the individual had had many or few conditioning trials. The final rate of conditioning would depend entirely on the number of trials he had in fact had. Now when we look at society as it is at present, we see that on the whole, it is this latter condition which obtains, rather than the hypothetical one of equal conditioning for all. We know, for instance, that in middle-class families there tends to be a much greater stress on moral and social behaviour, and firmer control over aggressive and sexual modes of conduct, whereas in some working-class families, far from frowning upon aggressive conduct and applying conditioning methods to suppress it, there is rather a tendency to encourage it and to take pride in the prowess of the growing boy. We also know that there are considerable differences in the childrearing practices of different nations. There is, for instance, considerably more stress on social conditioning in England than there is in the United States, where there has been a very marked tendency toward what might be called parental abdication of responsibility; that is, there has been a tendency for American parents to take some of the psychoanalytic and Freudian precepts of *laissez-faire* policy too literally. It is this, rather than any hypothetical differences in conditionability between Americans and English people, which may be responsible for the difference in crime rates in the two countries.

If we assume that there are indeed individual differences in the amount of conditioning which is given to the growing child, then we cannot expect a perfect correlation between extraversion and conditionability on the one hand, and criminality on the other. We would have to take into account the degree of conditioning which has in fact taken place; our general rule would only apply if we could, in some way, equate individuals with respect to their upbringing. We might also note, in this connection, another important feature which is implicit in much of what was said earlier. It will be remembered from our discussion of generality and specificity that emotional reactions, whether conditioned or unconditioned, tend to be relatively specific. Now it would also seem to follow from our hypothesis that conditioning itself will be relatively specific, depending on precisely what is included in the range of conditioned stimuli by the parents. Thus a boy may be brought up in an Irish family where there is a very severe process of conditioning in relation to sexual morality, but where there is a complete absence of conditioning with respect to aggressive, fighting behaviour. The child might then grow up to be a very "moral" member of society as far as sexual behaviour is concerned, but he might be involved in many fights and might even go to prison for his aggressive behaviour. There would be lacking, in his case, a congruence or concordance between one aspect of moral, law-abiding behaviour and another. This incongruity need not be interpreted as fatal to our general theory (rather it seems to follow from it), provided that we can demonstrate a deficiency in the conditioning schedule applied to this particular child with respect to aggression and a high amount of conditioning applied in the sexual sphere. In analysing individual cases and also in making predictions for group behaviour, it is extremely important to bear in mind this point. Specificity of responses is not universal but it does limit the generality of our theories and of our empirical findings, whether we are dealing with human or sub-human organisms.

We can extend the argument presented above a little further. We have so far postulated that human reactions will differ according to whether a particular type of reaction has been conditioned or not, and by conditioning in this sense we have always implied that the individual will be conditioned in what we call the "right" direction; that is, toward moral and social behaviour. This hypothesis unfortunately is not true of a small proportion of society. Consider the child whose mother is a prostitute and whose father is a thief. It is unlikely that the conditioning schedule which they will bring to bear on him will encourage him to behave in a socially acceptable manner. They probably will not label certain kinds of conduct as bad which society would prefer to have suppressed: on the contrary, they might even tend to encourage these. In other words, we may now be dealing with a situation quite different from that which we have envisaged so far. In our discussion hitherto we have assumed that a socialization process (conditioning in the "right" direction) was imposed on the child and we observed individual differences among children with respect to their ability to benefit from this socialization process. We must now consider those people who have had imposed on them an "antisocialization process," to coin a term, and consider the consequences in terms of their ability to "benefit" from this process. Clearly the exact opposite of what we have posited heretofore will take place. Now it will be the introverted child, the child who conditions well, who will condition to the precepts emerging from this "Fagin's kitchen." Instead of becoming conditioned to be a good and law-abiding citizen, we now have our introvert being conditioned to be a "good" law-breaking thief or prostitute. In line with our theory we should predict that now it would be the introvert who would become the less law-abiding citizen, whereas the extravert, by virtue of not conditioning so well, would have a better chance to escape from this fate.[14] The number of cases where this may have happened fortunately is probably quite small. It may be true that there is no honour among thieves; nevertheless, antisocial behaviour tends to be very disruptive, even in the smallest community such as the family, and a certain amount of training will be administered even under those conditions. Thus a mother or a father may have no objection to lying and stealing themselves; but they will tend to object to having their children lie to them or steal from them; they will, therefore, tend to administer punishment, if only intermittently, for antisocial activities, as long as these are directed against them. However, it must be borne in mind that the quality of the child's upbringing, the degree of conditioning, and the kind of conditioning which he receives, will be very important in his future development, and the degree to which we have concentrated on his own free activity, his own degree of conditionability, is too one-sided to make any prediction possible. It would follow from what has been said that factors militating against a consistent scheme of conditioning in the home and at school would work against the development of a socially responsible adult. There are many findings in the research literature to show that this is indeed so. The Gluecks, in their large-scale studies, showed, for instance, that there was a significant relationship between criminal behaviour and the incidence of unwholesome aspects of home life, notably in respect to such factors as family cohesiveness, affectional relations of parents and children, supervision, and discipline. There would be little point in cataloguing these findings or discussing them at any length; they are fairly obvious from a commonsense point of view and they are in good agreement with our general theory. What I would like to emphasize in this connection is rather that these factors of unsatisfactory upbringing, although undoubtedly important, are perhaps less so than one might have thought at first. Thus, for instance, D. J. West, who carried out a study of habitual prisoners on behalf of the Institute of Criminology at the University of Cambridge, found that:

> Most of the prisoners came of hard-working, respectable parents. Only four per cent had a parent with a record of criminal convictions, although seventeen per cent had either a parent or brother with a record. The total number of known brothers or half-brothers of the hundred prisoners amounted to 183, of whom twenty-three were known to have had convictions. The great majority of these brothers were not merely noncriminal but actually in satisfactory employment and behaving as responsible fathers of families and generally useful citizens. This contrast was frequently remarked upon by the prisoners, who time and time again described themselves as the only black sheep in the family.[15]

This study, which is typical of many, shows two things. In the first place, it shows that most habitual prisoners come from families where a reasonable system of conditioning is in force; and secondly, it shows that the great majority of the offspring of these families (almost ninety per cent) turn out to be good, decent, solid citizens who do not commit crimes of any kind. In these circumstances, we clearly cannot have recourse to differences in conditioning to account for the fact that a few are criminals and the majority are not; we must turn to individual differences in ability to condition to explain these otherwise inexplicable data.

However that may be, we must still explain one important fact which would seem to present some difficulty for our general theory. How is it possible that there are so many habitual prisoners: old lags, offenders who have been in and out of prison for many years, who have apparently never become conditioned, in spite of all these terrifying and painful experiences? Unless we postulate that we are dealing with persons who cannot be conditioned at all, it would seem that this accumulation of conditioning experiences should have been sufficient to finally inculcate in them an appreciation of the moral values. Is not the fact that this has not taken place a strong counter-argument to the general theory which we have put forward? There are two answers to this. The first is a very simple and straightforward one. Conditioning is a process which occurs only under certain highly specialised conditions. We have already noted, in connection with the eye-blink conditioning experiment, that conditions are optimal when the interval between the conditioned stimulus, the tone, and the unconditioned stimulus, the puff of air to the eye, is about 500 msec. (one-half second), and that when it is as long as two and one-half seconds, no conditioning takes place at all. In other words, for conditioning, the interval between conditioned and unconditioned stimuli is all-important. When we consider crime, however, and the punishment which society metes out to the criminal, we have seen that the interval may be very long indeed. It may be weeks, months, or even years, and under these conditions we do not expect conditioning to take place. This conclusion may have to be modified to some extent. Human beings, unlike rats, have what Pavlov called a second signalling system, that of speech, superimposed on the primary signalling system, namely that of conditioning. There is unfortunately very little work in this field, but it is conceivable that, at the time of sentencing the prisoner and while the prisoner is serving his sentence, the conditioned stimulus, which should have been the actual commission of the crime itself, may be substituted for by some kind of ideational representation, either verbally or sub-vocally. In other words, it is possible to assume that when the prisoner is being sentenced, he may, at that time, reiterate ideationally the circumstances of the crime, by thinking about it either in words or in images. It is possible that the connection between these images and the actual commission of the crime is sufficiently strong to potentiate a certain amount of conditioning. It is unfortunate that nothing, in practice, is known about the feasibility of this ideational mediation process in connection with social punishment of this kind, but it may be surmised that, at best, the conditioning that takes place would be much weaker than it would be if the proper conditioned stimulus had been applied.

Our second argument in accounting for the existence of the recidivist "old lag" is too complex to be presented here; its importance is such that it will be reserved for a separate chapter.

References

1. Recent work has been done by J. H. Johns and H. Quay, "The Effects of Social Reward on Verbal Conditioning in Psychopathic and Neurotic Military Offenders," *J. Consult. Psychol.*, 1962, *26*, 217–20; and H. Quay and W. A. Hunt, "Psychopathy, Neuroticism and Verbal Conditioning," *J. Consult. Psychol.*, 1965, *29*, 283.
2. B. J. Fine, "Introversion-Extraversion and Motor Vehicle Driver Behavior," *Percept. Mot. Skills*, 1963, *12*, 95–100.

3. S. Biesheuvel and M. E. White, "The Human Factor in Flying Accidents," *South African Air Force J.*, 1949, *1*, 25–31.
4. S. B. G. Eysenck, "Personality and Pain Assessment in Childbirth of Married and Unmarried Mothers," *J. Ment. Sci.*, 1961, *107*, 417–30.
5. I. Syed, unpublished study.
6. F. Warburton and R. B. Cattell, unpublished study.
7. R. G. Andry, *The Short-Term Offender*, Routledge, London, 1952.
8. T. C. N. Gibbens, *Psychiatric Studies of Borstal Lads*, Oxford University Press, New York, 1962.
9. A detailed discussion of the history and present status of work on body build is given in H. J. Eysenck, *The Structure of Human Personality*, Methuen, London; Macmillan, New York, 1970.
10. S. B. G. Eysenck and H. J. Eysenck, "On the Dual Nature of Extraversion," *Brit. J. Soc. Clin. Psychol.*, 1963, *2*, 46–55.
11. G. A. Hooton, *Crime and the Man*, Harvard University Press, Cambridge, Mass., 1939.
12. W. H. Sheldon, E. M. Hartt, and G. McDermont, *Varieties of Delinquent Youths*, Harper, New York, 1949.
13. P. Epps and R. W. Parnell, "Physique and Temperament of Women Delinquents Compared with Women Undergraduates," *Brit. J. Med. Psychol.*, 1952, *25*, 249–55.
14. This point has been particularly strongly made by C. M. Franks, "Recidivism, Psychopathy and Delinquency," *Brit. J. Delinq.*, 1956, *6*, 192–201. See also the excellent book by G. Trasler, *The Explanation of Criminality*, Routledge, London, 1962.
15. D. J. West, *The Habitual Prisoner*, Macmillan, London, 1963.

Part Two

Aggression and Violent Behavior

If we were to seek an act that is most universally defined as criminal behavior, there is no doubt that unprovoked violent aggression by one member of a social group against another member would elicit the widest consensus. The potentiality for unprovoked violent aggression is the class of criminal behavior, moreover, which is most certain to strike fear in the human heart. Thus, it need come as no surprise that, in the words of the psychologist Bandura, "Among the various human activities that are the subject of attention, none has aroused deeper concern than man's aggressiveness."[1] Or, that in a recent Gallup survey, nearly half (45 percent) of all respondents indicated fear of walking alone at night in their own neighborhoods. Observations on violence in the United States range from Abraham Lincoln's early characterization of "internal violence as the supreme threat to American political institutions" to H. Rap Brown's famous "Violence is American as cherry pie." Chief Constable Laurence Byford, of Lincolnshire, England, at a recent International Criminal Justice Seminar at the John Jay College of Criminal Justice, offered a comparative assessment of criminal violence, noting that in 1970 there were 16,000 murders in the United States and 167 in Britain. In 1974, more murders took place in the city of Detroit alone than in all of Great Britain. The May 31, 1976, issue of *The New Yorker* stated that there were almost as many robberies in Washington, D.C., as in England and Wales, and nearly fifty times as many rapes annually in the United States as in Great Britain.

Efforts to uncover the sources within individuals of violent behavior have generally reflected the theoretical assumptions of particular investigators. The contributions selected for inclusion here have one thing in common—an emphasis on intra-individual causation—as distinguished from broad socio-economic forces such as unemployment, political action, racial or ethnic strife, and climate. It is not our intent to minimize the significance of the latter, but rather to leave their consideration to authorities with competence in the disciplines relevant to them, while we here focus on the individuals who commit acts of violence commonly acknowledged as antisocial. In any event, it is obvious that even social, political, and economic causations gain expression through the acts of individuals, and that some selective psychological processes operate to determine which members of a given group will respond to "environmental" influences by means of violent acts.

As with most human behavior, efforts to explain (and, of course, ultimately to influence) overt aggressive behavior have tended to emphasize either environmental—i.e. learned—elements or biological causation. Jarvik et al. in introducing the initial paper in this section, put the question as follows: "Is human aggression an inborn biological urge which must become manifest in some form of violent or antisocial behavior, or is aggression learned as a response to particular environmental conditions or experiences which, under properly controlled circumstances, need not break through into overt acts of hostility?" They then proceed to consider one of the more

67

provocative—and potentially far-reaching—biological hypotheses of the present era, the "XYY Syndrome," and its corollary, "the association between maleness and violence." In what constitutes possibly the most extensive review of studies involving chromosomal analysis which has appeared to date, they conclude that "the data available so far, therefore, provide strong presumptive evidence for an association between criminal behavior and the extra Y chromosome." Having drawn this conclusion, they proceed with considerable caution in discussing its implications or applications. They note, for example, the existence of aggression in individuals lacking any Y chromosomes; and, on the other hand, those who were not particularly aggressive despite the presence of the additional Y chromosome. Moreover, the careful reader of this paper will undoubtedly have been impressed not merely with the disproportionate frequency of XYY's in the criminal population—"15 times that found in newborn males and normal adults"—but with the exceedingly small frequency in either population (1.9%; .13%). In other words, while biological predisposition to aggression is evidently a consideration not to be overlooked, by itself it does little to explain the totality of antisocial aggression.

The second and third papers in this section—Berkowitz and LePage and Eron et al.—serve to illustrate how aggression has been dealt with from the standpoint of environmental causation. Each is an attempt to gather data first-hand, each is related to a broader conceptualization of behavior as a product of external stimulus conditions, and each has significant implications for widely debated issues of public concern with respect to the control of violence.

In "Weapons as Aggression-Eliciting Stimuli," Berkowitz and LePage, in an ingeniously designed experiment, demonstrated the effects of visible weapons of aggression in the proximal environment on the aggressivity of previously frustrated subjects. Once a subject has been experimentally aroused (angered), the likelihood of his reacting violently toward the arouser is significantly facilitated by the (suggestive?) effects of weapons in his immediate environment. As Berkowitz and LePage recognize, "The findings contribute to the current debate as to the desirability of restricting sales of firearms," the so-called gun-control laws. (In this regard, it may be worthwhile to note that, in attempting to explain the greater incidence of violence in the United States, compared to that of Great Britain's, the British police official cited before is quoted further as saying, "I truly believe that the concept of violence in America is promoted by the fact that you are an armed society. In Great Britain, we have such strict control of firearms that the going rate for an illegally purchased handgun is now more than ten thousand dollars. But it is said that there are more firearms in American homes than in the combined armies of the United States, Russia, and NATO.")

These results, additionally, intersect with—and may help us to understand—another concept which has been adduced to explain eruptions of individual violence, "the subculture of violence."[2] Briefly, it points to the existence of geographical areas (neighborhoods) in which one finds a highly developed readiness among members of the resident population—particularly the males—to solve problems and to resolve interpersonal conflicts (including the most trivial) through violent means, where violence is seen as a relatively acceptable means of resolving conflicts, and where the implements of violence—knives, guns, tire-irons, chains—are frequently carried on their persons and brandished by members of the subculture. The latter feature of "the subculture of violence"—the visible presence of weapons—is, of course, the one that is of particular interest here. While the sequence of causality may be in doubt—which occurred first, the subculture of violence or the proliferation of instruments of violence—the findings of Berkowitz and LePage leave little room for doubt as to the potential for escalating aggressive behavior as a consequence of the presence of weapons in the environment.

The actual presence of weapons in the immediate environment may be seen as having direct stimulus impact. What impact can be attributed to stimuli of a less palpable—if more ubiquitous—sort, namely the depiction of violent aggression in the mass media? Much time, money, and research have been involved in the attempt to answer this question, particularly to the effect of television violence on the behavior of youth. The landmark report is "Television and Growing Up: The Impact of Televised Violence," a 1972 report to the Surgeon General of the United States from the Surgeon General's Scientific Advisory Committee on Television and Social Behavior. Based on some forty original studies and a review of earlier research, the Commission offered the following three "tentative and limited conclusions": "a preliminary and tentative indication of a causal relation between viewing violence on television and aggressive behavior; an indication that any such causal relation operates only on some children (who are predisposed to be aggressive); and an indication that it operates only in some environmental contexts."[3] The report is clearly intended to be extremely cautious in implicating television—certainly the most universal of the mass media in the United States—as a causative agent in aggressive acts by individuals. Yet, if one recalls the broader conceptual framework out of which such studies emerge, we might be inclined to question this hesitation. This refers to the body of theory and research known as "social learning," largely the work of Albert Bandura and others associated with him, and having at its center the process variously referred to as modeling, imitation, or observational learning. The essentials of this series of experiments can best be presented by citing Bandura directly: "Typically, these studies make use of a modeling paradigm . . . in which children observe models behaving in a physically and verbally aggressive manner. . . . Following exposure to the modeling influence, children are provided with opportunities to display what they have learned in a situation containing a variety of materials that can be used either for aggressive or nonaggressive purposes."[4] Of particular significance for the present discussion is Bandura's observation "that a person displaying aggression on film was as influential in teaching distinctive forms of aggression as those exhibiting it in real life."[5]

With this brief synopsis of the conceptual context, we may now turn to a consideration of the paper selected for inclusion here by Eron et al., "Does Television Violence Cause Aggression?" Whereas Bandura and his coworkers were able to observe relatively short-term effects on subjects observing aggressive models, Eron et al. attempt a determination of more enduring, longitudinal influences, a matter of considerably deeper societal concern. Studying a sizeable and relatively representative sample, they have been able to demonstrate an impressive relationship between exposure to television violence among third-graders and the tendency to aggressivity in the same subjects some ten years later, based on a variety of measures. Inevitably, when confronted with such a relationship, the question of causal sequence arises: Does watching television violence give rise to violent behavior? Or do violence-prone children prefer to watch violent television, and at the same time simply persist in their violent ways on into adulthood? By means of a sophisticated statistical analysis, Eron et al. have provided support for the hypothesis that watching violence on television does contribute significantly to subsequent behavior of an aggressive nature.

In attempting to bring the study of violence closer to the realities and concerns of the criminal justice system, Megargee has conducted a series of studies of subjects incarcerated for violent offenses, largely at the Federal Correctional Institution in Tallahassee, Florida. Where reports of Berkowitz and LePage and of Eron et al. emphasize the impact of external stimuli as producers of aggressive behavior, Megargee develops a framework whose focus is the personality structure of the individual, which disposes him to behave violently. In another context, these divergent approaches have been described as situational as against the dispositional hypotheses respectively. In Megargee's view, the crucial dimension is the ability of individuals to control their overt aggressivity. However, contrary to initial expectation, it is the individual with chronically *weak* control (Chronically Undercontrolled) who is *least likely* to erupt into extremely violent acts. Whenever those with strong controls (Chronically Overcontrolled) do express aggression, it is almost certain to be extreme and explosive. If this seems like a paradoxical hypothesis—the more controlled, the more extreme—the reader would do well, as he reads Megargee's paper, to keep in mind that both the overcontrolled and the undercontrolled groups studied by Megargee were composed of prisoners convicted of violent crimes. The difference between them lay in the "extremeness" of the violence. Readers familiar with psychodynamic formulations will not fail to discern Megargee's debt to Freudian energetics, in which the inborn aggressive drive, if not given normal opportunity for egress, accumulates quantitatively until its demand for expression becomes irresistible and it bursts through the control explosively. The undercontrolled individual, on the other hand, reduces the total force of the drive by frequent and more moderate acts of aggression, hence is less likely to carry out extreme acts of violence. (Megargee, it should be noted, does not propose total absence of more extreme types of violence among the undercontrolled, only a lesser likelihood.) A final point to be noted, with respect to Megargee's work, is the development of an instrument, the O-H scale, for differentiating between overcontrolled and undercontrolled assaultive individuals.

It is a truism that the ultimate purposes of psychological research are to predict and then to influence behavior. Almost as universal is the acknowledgment that efforts to predict—let alone influence—criminal behavior have thus far been of little success. This is no less true of the work by Wenk, Robison, and Smith, as reported in their paper, "Can Violence be Predicted?" Why then has it been selected for inclusion here? First, because it serves as an excellent exemplar of well-designed prediction research. More importantly, it brings into focus a major, but often overlooked, pitfall as one attempts to apply differences in between-group rates to predictions of the future behaviors of individuals—even when the observed differences are statistically significant. This is most clearly brought out with respect to Table 8.4, Violence History and Type of Recidivism. Table 8.4 reveals that violent recidivism occurs with significantly greater frequency among those with a history of actual violence (5.2%) than among either the group with no history of violence (1.8%) or the group with a history of aggressive crime, but no actual violence (1.3%). The *percentage* differences are of such a magnitude that one might be tempted to conclude that a history of actual violence might serve as a useful predictor of violent recidivism. What would happen if we were to implement this? It would, in fact, result in correctly identifying 50% of all those—in all three groups—who are prone to violent recidivism. However, in order to reach this level of predictive efficiency, some 95% (954 of the total of 1006 in the present group with history of actual violence) would have been incorrectly designated as prone to violent recidivism. It could result in creation of a program for the prevention of violence, in which 95% of the participants had been incorrectly labelled violence-prone ("false positing") in order to deal with the 5% who might realistically be expected to behave violently in the future.

A form of violence with which the criminal justice system is confronted

71

periodically is the prison riot. The attention of the entire world was, for a time, riveted on the bloody outbreak at Attica Prison, in western New York State, in 1971. As Straus and Sherman note in the introduction to their paper, included in this section, prison riots "have frequently occurred in the past and they are likely to recur in the future." Most post-mortem studies of prison riots have tended to emphasize causative factors arising out of the sociocultural conditions of the institution—repressive administration, racial antagonism, the parole process. Straus and Sherman have chosen instead to examine the personal characteristics of prisoners, which might correlate with participation or nonparticipation in riots. While containing the weakness inherent in *ex post facto* research, it represents an almost unique effort to seize the opportunity afforded by an unplanned series of events in order to focus attention on the antecedent characteristics of potential rioters, a research direction with obvious significance to administrators and personnel of correctional institutions. Of interest is their conclusion: "The group of inmates most likely to participate in the riot was predominantly composed of young, unmarried Blacks who had received disciplinary reports for institutional misbehavior and who had not participated in any of the available treatment programs." As the authors themselves recognize, these are conclusions that must be considered suggestive and tentative, rather than definitive, particularly in view of the reduced availability for study—due to transfer—of the heavily involved inmates. Before accepting the findings as a basis for administrative action, one would require several additional steps: (1) replication of the study in one or more alternative settings, to permit generalization of the conclusions; (2) cross-validation of the identified prisoner attributes, whereby the predictive power of the attributes are tested. Although prison riots are not the kind of variable readily susceptible to experimenter instigation or manipulation, these steps imply that institutions must assume a potential for riots and, in anticipation of them, make arrangements for antecedent records and data which could then be related to riot participation by individual inmates, as and when such an outbreak actually occurs.

The final selection in this unit serves to bring together, in summary fashion, information from a variety of sources, in "an attempt to present a panoramic examination of the violent offender." A number of points are highlighted by Sheppard: (1) violent crimes are a relatively small proportion of the total crime incidence; (2) the predominance of males as both perpetrators and victims of violent crime; (3) the high proportion of violence involving people previously known to each other; (4) uncertainty as to whether violent crime is increasing or declining; (5) the sometimes "provocative" behavior of the victim; (6) doubt about the popular assumption that a violent offense necessarily implies dangerousness of subsequent behavior, and, as a corollary, (7) the inappropriateness of extreme punishment for violent offenders; (8) the significance of "psychological, sociological, or cultural characteristics" in predisposing individuals to commit acts of violence. As Sheppard makes clear, there is little to justify lumping all violent behavior together etiologically, or to justify the tendency of the law to treat all violent offenders as if they were drawn from the same bolt of cloth.

NOTES

1. Bandura, A. *Aggression*. Englewood Cliffs, N.J.: Prentice Hall, 1973: p.1.
2. Wolfgang, M. E. and Ferracuti, F. *The Subculture of Violence*. London: Tavistock Publications, 1967.
3. Surgeon General's Scientific Advisory Committee on Television and Social Behavior. *Television and Growing Up: The Impact of Televised Violence*. Washington, D.C.: U.S. Government Printing Office, 1972: pp. 18–19.
4. Bandura, p. 72.
5. Bandura, p. 74.

5

Human Aggression and the Extra Y Chromosome: Fact or Fantasy?

Lissy S. Jarvik[1], Victor Klodin, Steven S. Matsuyama

Reprinted by permission from *American Psychologist* 28 (1973): 674–82. Copyright 1973 by the American Psychological Association. Author permission to reprint is gratefully acknowledged.

The goal of science has been to gain insight into the human condition, usually with the hope of improving it. No facet of human behavior has merited more serious attention than the problem of aggression: the predilection of man for violent and destructive acts, especially those directed toward his own kind. Recently, pioneering advances in the science of genetics have brought investigators to the verge of new insights into the problem of human aggression.

Man's capacity to commit violent and destructive acts has been recognized and well documented throughout history. By countless wars and other, more individual attacks, he has managed to kill literally millions of his fellow beings. The record of such destruction is a long one, dating back some two million years, to the time when *Australopithecus*, man's earliest known ancestor, roamed the Olduvai Gorge in what is now Tanzania in Africa. The remains of this ancestor, discovered by the archaeologist Louis Leakey, indicate that this early man killed others of his species. "Here the combination of heads severed from trunks and post mortem as well as ante-mortem damage is conclusive for some form of head hunting and at least suggestive of cannibalism (Howell, 1965, p. 139)."

What is perhaps more surprising and more dismaying than the knowledge that early man engaged in such acts is the realization that today, two million years later, the same behavior persists, virtually unchanged. "Neither natural, theological, moral, nor political barriers have appreciably inhibited the application of forms of violence . . . (Frazier, 1970, p. 14)." The only real change lies in the increase of our destructive capability. Our wars today seem no better motivated and certainly no less barbarous than any others in history, but more lives must be sacrificed. Over 300 years ago, Thomas Hobbes wrote that "the condition of man . . . is a condition of war of every one against every one (1960 printing, p. 85)." With our crises in Vietnam, the Middle East, and Pakistan, our snipers and assassins, our arsonists, bombers, and child beaters, and with the threat of nuclear annihilation for all, Hobbes' statement would seem to bear additional weight today.

Current, and well-founded, public concern over violence, exemplified by the recent staff report to the National Commission on the Causes and Prevention of Violence (Graham and Gurr, 1969), has stimulated the search for a means not only of understanding aggression, but of controlling it as well.

Unfortunately, the scientific community has been divided for many years by a major question: Is human aggression an inborn biological urge which must become manifest in some form of violent or antisocial behavior, or is aggression learned as a response to particular environmental conditions or experiences which, under properly controlled circumstances, need not break through into overt acts of hostility?

Despite a great deal of attention, this serious question has never been answered satisfactorily. Such a determination is critical, however, because applied research aimed at curbing unnecessary and excessive violence proceeds either from the assumption that as a biologically based urge, aggression can be treated biologically or else channeled into some socially acceptable areas, or from the hypothesis that as a learned response, aggressive modes of behavior are not acquired if neither the need nor the opportunity exists for such learning to occur.

Recently uncovered clues may herald the revival of a biological approach and may have a profound effect on all future studies of aggressiveness in man. These clues emanate from the discovery that a chromosomal aberration in some mentally retarded male criminals of exceptionally tall stature and unusually aggressive temperament may be responsible for their violent behavior characteristics.

Chromosomes are thin threads of genetic material (DNA) and contain hereditary instructions for the growth and reproduction of every living cell in an organism. Physical traits, such as eye color, hair color, and height, are controlled by these hereditary messages. New and improved methods for studying human cells have permitted an accurate description of the chromosome complement (karyotype) and have led to the discovery of many chromosomal aberrations. The cells of the human body normally contain 46 chromosomes, 2 of them ("X" and "Y") being sex chromosomes responsible for sex determination. Cells in a normal woman's body have 2 X chromosomes, whereas each cell in a normal man has 1 X and 1 Y chromosome.

Instead of the normal complement of 46 chromosomes, the cells of some mentally retarded, tall criminals were found to contain 47, the extra one being a Y chromosome. This abnormality is known as the XYY genotype. When the association of an extra Y chromosome with tall stature, mental retardation, and aggressive behavior was first made (Jacobs, Brunton, Melville, Brittain, and McClermont, 1965), it had a profound impact on the scientific community, the legal and medical professions, and the public at large. The reason for the excitement can be readily understood in the perspective of the knowledge available at the time, which consisted of only 11 cases in the entire world literature of what was then considered a rare syndrome. Suddenly, there was the study by Jacob et al. reporting 7 additional cases among 197 mentally retarded criminals. An outstanding feature of these 7 cases was that they had no physical stigmata that would differentiate them from other males, patients or not, except for their great height. Such had not been true of the earlier cases, many of whom had shown one or more physical abnormalities. Moreover, this was the first time that a specific behavioral abnormality, other than mental deficiency, had been linked to a chromosomal aberration. Soon, other investigators began to look for persons with the extra Y chromosome among tall retarded inmates of institutions for criminal offenders and discovered more than 100 of them in a scant four years.

Although there are exceptions, and they will be discussed later, the dominant features associated with the presence of an extra Y chromosome include unusual height, excessive episodic aggressiveness, and borderline intelligence. Not surprisingly, an extra Y chromosome has been detected in some of the most renowned murderers of our time. One of the first such cases was that of Robert Peter Tait, an Australian who was convicted in 1962 of bludgeoning to death an 81-year-old woman in a vicarage where he had gone seeking a handout. In 1965, Daniel Hugon, a 31-year-old French stablehand, brutally strangled a Paris prostitute, with no apparent motivation. During the course of his trial in 1968, he was found to have an extra Y chromosome. In April 1969, six-foot, eight-inch, 240-pound John Farley, nicknamed "Jolly Green Giant" because he was usually good-natured and "Big Bad John" because he was subject to fits of violent temper, confessed to having beaten, strangled, raped, and mutilated a Queens, New York woman. He was defended on the grounds that due to the presence in his cells of an extra Y chromosome, he had no control over his actions or his judgment, and should therefore be found not guilty "by reason of insanity resulting from a chromosome imbalance (Evansabury, 1969, p. 54)."

These and other similarly grisly cases were brought to public attention by attorneys who pleaded that their clients, charged with committing crimes of particular violence, could not be judged responsible for their actions. In some instances, the defense was successful; in others, it was not. A patient with the XYY genotype was located by us in an institution for the criminally insane when he was 26 years old (Abdullah, Jarvik, Kato, Johnston, and Lanzkron, 1969; Jarvik, 1969) and may serve as an example of the typical characteristics described in the literature. He had a history of antisocial behavior dating back to early childhood when, according to his mother's recollection, he was so uncontrollable that she finally tied him to a tree when doing her outdoor chores in order to prevent him from harming himself and others. Admitted to school at the age of 6, he created so much trouble that his parents were asked to remove him. Readmitted at the age of 7, he again beat up the other children and remained a disciplinary problem despite placement in a special ungraded class, until, at the age of 10, he was transferred to a boarding school for disturbed children. Ever since then he has been in institutions of one sort or another. He would escape whenever possible and invariably get into trouble on the outside. Among his favorite pastimes was that of killing chickens from neighboring farmhouses by cutting off their heads.

Though he is not known to have committed any sexual crimes, and specifically denies any homosexual or masturbatory practices, there is no dearth of other offenses with which he has been charged, ranging from pickpocketing to assault and robbery. At the age of 20, he was committed to a mental hospital because of increasingly abnormal behavior—quite aside from his aggressiveness—and was diagnosed as suffering from chronic schizophrenia. Some years later, after nearly killing an attendant and another patient, he was transferred to a hospital for the criminally insane, where he was regarded as *the* most difficult management problem.

He never belonged to a gang, or had any real friends, and in that respect resembled many other men with the XYY karyotype who have been characterized as "loners" (Money, 1970). The patient also described epileptiform attacks coinciding with his need to "strike out." The unpredictable, impulsive nature of his violence appears to be characteristic of persons with the extra Y chromosome, several of whom have shown a frank epilepsy and responded to anticonvulsant medication. Despite years of hospitalization and treatment with psychoactive drugs, as well as electroshock therapy, this patient has shown no signs of progress. Like so many XYY men, he is of borderline intelligence and has numerous old acne scars and a strong, muscular body, towering over all of those around him from his height of six feet, seven inches.

Is There an XYY Syndrome?

Even though the triad of tall physique, short temper, and limited intelligence, as exemplified by the patient described above, is characteristic of the XYY syndrome, not one of the attributes is either necessary or sufficient for its diagnosis. Thus, great height is typical, and yet, several cases of record did not even grow to be six feet tall. Of course, the possibility exists that without the second Y chromosome these particular persons might have been even shorter than they were. Similarly, with regard to intelligence, although there is a preponderance of cases on the borderline of the dull normal range, there is a fair representation of persons with average intelligence and even a few with superior intelligence. Finally, not even aggressive, antisocial, or criminal behavior is a *sine qua non* of the XYY karyotype, as first demonstrated by the accidental discovery in Australia of an extra Y chromosome in a solid citizen and family man whose only outstanding characteristic was that he volunteered as a blood donor and thus happened to have his chromosomes scrutinized.

Indeed, the mounting number of exceptions to the characteristic features of the extra Y syndrome led to a series of headlines at the time of the 1969 annual meeting of the American Psychiatric Association questioning the relationship between the extra Y chromosome and aggressive behavior. "It appears that the XYY males in general have been falsely stigmatized" proclaimed the headlines; and the consensus was that "most XYY men are solid citizens." This opinion was not restricted to newspaper reporters, but appeared in a learned journal under the title "XYY Chromosomes: Premature Conclusions." Kessler and Moos (1969) concluded from their survey of the literature: "That XYY males are uncontrollably aggressive psychopaths appears to be nothing more than a myth promoted by the mass media (p. 442)." Others have refused to accept this conclusion (Gardner and Neu, 1972).

Where are the data to resolve this controversy? Unfortunately, the tedious, time-consuming nature of human chromosome analysis and the requirement for highly skilled personnel make large-scale population surveys practically impossible.[2] Nonetheless, a thorough survey of the literature leads to the conclusion that a sufficient amount of information has been accumulated throughout the world to warrant an attempt at comparing the frequency of the XYY karyotype among various population groups.

Data from World Literature

In the largest single study so far reported (Jacobs et al., 1965), 1,709 noncriminal cases yielded only a single XYY karyotype. Three later studies (Casey, Blank, Street, Segall, McDougall, McGrath, and Skinner, 1966; Recherche Cooperative sur Programme No. 85, 1969; Wilton and Lever, 1967) added another 3 XYY individuals for a total of 4 out of 4,127 examined (.10%; see Table 5.1). However, these individuals were not truly a random sample; many of them had undergone chromosome analysis because they were related to an abnormal child or to a person with a chromosome anomaly.

In the absence of extensive general population screening, it would be highly desirable to have some other value with which to compare the fre-

TABLE 5.1.
CHROMOSOME SURVEYS OF NORMAL ADULT MALES

Reference	Year Published	Total Sample	XYY	XXY
Kjessler	1966	135	0	2
Goodman et al.	1968	36	0	0
Court-Brown & Smith	1969	924	0	2
Marinello et al.	1969	30	0	0
Noel et al.	1969	850	4	3
Stenchever et al.	1971	46	0	0
Total		2,021	4	7
Jacobs et al.	1965	1,709	1	—[a]
Casey et al.	1966	30	0	—[a]
Wilton & Lever	1967	750	1	—[a]
Recherche Cooperative sur Programme No. 85	1968	1,638	2	—[a]
Total		4,127	4	
Grand Total		6,148	8	(.13%)

[a]Not reported.

quency of extra Y chromosomes in different population groups. One such comparison group is provided by another sex chromosome. The XXY karyotype produces clinical symptomatology known by the eponym of Klinefelter's syndrome. Men thus afflicted are sterile, their testicular tissue never having developed properly. There is also a higher frequency of mental retardation among patients with Klinefelter's syndrome than there is in the general population, although superior intelligence is not excluded by Klinefelter's syndrome, just as it is not excluded by the XYY syndrome. An additional advantage to using persons with an extra X chromosome as a comparison group rests in the fact that for many years, techniques have been available to detect the presence of extra X chromosomes independent of karyotype analysis. Indeed it is not necessary to culture cells—a simple scraping of the mucous membrane lining the inside of the cheek will provide adequate material for the diagnosis of extra X chromosomes. These can then be verified by the usual culture techniques and chromosome analyses.

There are six series reporting chromosome surveys of normal adult males which provide data on both extra X and extra Y chromosomes (see Table

5.1). In the two large studies (Court-Brown and Smith, 1969, Noel, Quack, Durand, and Rethore, 1969) among 1,774 men, 4 were found to be XYY genotypes and 5 were found with an extra X chromosome. Four smaller series consisting of from 30 to 135 subjects did not provide any further cases with an extra Y chromosome and only 2 cases with an extra X chromosome. The frequency of XYY in the above studies is .20%, and the overall frequency of XYY in the normal adult population thus amounts to .13% (8/6,148), the latter percentage being based on an additional 4,127 cases for whom no information concerning extra X chromosomes was available.

For a disorder that occurs as infrequently as one or two times in a thousand cases, the samples are still too small for definitive conclusions. Nonetheless, it is of considerable interest that among presumably normal men, the frequencies of extra X and extra Y chromosomes were approximately equal.

Far larger than the samples of normal adult males are those of newborn males. Five major studies were conducted in Canada, in the United States (Boston, Massachusetts, and New Haven, Connecticut), and in Scotland, respectively, and together comprise nearly 10,000 cases (see Table 5.2). Among them there were 13 newborn boys with an extra Y chromosome and 14 with an extra X chromosome, giving frequencies of .13% and .14% respectively. The reliability of these results can be assessed indirectly by comparing the frequency of XXY among newborn males reported in these five studies with that found in Edinburgh as a result of a large-scale survey of newborn males (MacLean, Harnden, Court-Brown, Bond, and Mantle, 1964) by means of buccal mucosal smears (a technique revealing the presence of extra X but not extra Y chromosomes). Of 10,725 newborn males examined, there were .11% with the XXY karyotype. This incidence does not differ significantly from the .14% XXY reported in the 9,904 newborn males for whom data on extra Y chromosomes are also available.

We can feel reasonably confident, therefore, that the frequencies of extra X and extra Y chromosomes are about equal in newborn males and on the order of approximately one to two per thousand. Incidentally, this is also the frequency calculated by Penrose (1963) for mongolism among newborns. From the compilation of seven major studies on mongolism, with over one million newborns, the frequency of clinically diagnosed mongolism was computed as .15%. In the studies collected by Penrose, chromosomes had not been analyzed. The four major studies that do report chromosome analyses in newborns provide a frequency of .13% for trisomy G, the most common form of mongolism (see Table 5.2).

Again, the correspondence is remarkably close, even though in one group of studies diagnosis was based on clinical findings and in the other on chromosome examination. We may conclude, then, that all three

TABLE 5.2.
CHROMOSOME SURVEYS OF NEWBORN MALES

Reference	Year Published	Country	Total Sample	XYY	XXY	Trisomy-G
Court-Brown and Smith	1969	United Kingdom (Edinburgh)	1,788	1	2	4
Sergovich et al.	1969	Canada (Ontario)	1,066	4	1	0
Walzer et al.	1969	United States (Boston)	1,332	0	4	Normal, healthy infants
Lubs and Ruddle Personal communication (in Ratcliffe et al.)	1970	United States (New Haven)	2,222	3	4	2
Ratcliffe et al.	1970	United Kingdom (Edinburgh)	3,496	5	3	5
TOTAL			9,904	13	14	11/8,572

Note: For a comparison with the frequency of chromatin positive newborn males, see Maclean et al. (1964). Using a total sample of 10,725 newborn males, they found 21 chromatin positive infants (.20%) including 12 XXY (.11%).

For a comparison with the frequency of mongolism in all newborns, see Penrose (1963). From his total sample of seven studies, he found a mongolism frequency of 1,479/1,004,835. (.15%).

anomalies—mongolism, Klinefelter's syndrome (SSY), and XYY—occur with similar frequencies among newborns.

Among mental patients, some investigators have reported an elevated frequency of the XXY genotype, while others failed to detect such an increase. Many of the men with an extra Y chromosome have also been characterized as schizoid, and a number have been outright schizophrenics. The question arises, therefore, whether the frequency of an extra X and an extra Y chromosome is greater in persons admitted to mental hospitals than it is among males in general. There are four surveys of mental patients providing data on both extra X and extra Y chromosomes (see Table 5.3). Among the total of 597 men examined in Sweden, in France, and by two teams in New York (one upstate and one downstate), there were 6 men with an extra Y chromosome and 6 men with an extra X chromosome, giving a frequency of 1% for each category. This frequency is significantly higher than that found among newborn or adult males (ranging from .13% to .20%, P < .01).

It would seem, therefore, that patients in mental hospitals are more prone to have an extra sex chromosome than men in the general population, but that the tendency is nonspecific, the probability of an extra X chromosome being as great as that of an extra Y chromosome.

Since the XYY genotype has been associated with antisocial behavior, it would be reasonable to expect a higher frequency of this disorder among persons who have come in conflict with the law than among men in general. Twenty studies on criminal population providing information on both the XYY and XXY anomalies have been reported (see Table 5.4). Of 4,293 male

TABLE 5.3.
CHROMOSOME SURVEYS OF MENTAL PATIENTS

Reference	Year Published	Total Sample	XYY	XXY
Akesson et al.	1968	96	3	2
Abdullah et al.	1969	26	0	1
Marinello et al.	1969	76	1	0
Noel et al.	1969	399	2	3
Total		597	6	6
Casey et al.	1966	230	0	—[a]
Baker et al.	1970	30	0	—[a]
Total		260	0	
Grand Total		857	6	(.7%)

[a] Not reported.

TABLE 5.4.
CHROMOSOME SURVEYS OF CRIMINALS

Reference	Year Published	Total Sample	XYY	XXY
Goodman et al.	1967	100	2	2
Griffiths and Zaremba	1967	67	2	1
Welch et al.	1967	35	1	0
Armendares et al.[a]	1968	312	0	3
Bartlett et al.	1968	204	2	2
Close et al.	1968	68	2	3
Jacobs et al.	1968	315	9	1
Wiener et al.	1968	34	3	0
Abdullah et al.	1969	23	1	0
Court-Brown & Smith	1969	1,419	3	4
Marinello et al.	1969	86	2	0
McDanal	1969	100	2	0
MeInyk et al.	1969	200	9	2
Nielsen, Sturup, et al.	1969			
Nielsen, Tsuboi, et al.	1969	269	5	5
Noel et al.	1969	274	10	7
Baker et al.	1970	388	7	7
Davis et al.	1970	190	0	0
Fattig	1970	100	0	0
Falek et al.	1970	28	1	0
Masterson et al.	1970	81	0	0
Total		4,293	61	37
Casey et al.	1966	124	18	—[b]
Daly	1969	210	10	—[b]
Knox and Nevin	1969	67	0	—[b]
Griffiths et al.	1970	321	7	—[b]
Marcus and Richmond	1970	51	2	—[b]
Total		773	37	
Grand Total		5,066	98	(1.9%)

[a] S. Armendares, L. Buentello, G. Mora, C. Zavala, and R. Lisker, personal communication, 1968.
[b] Not reported.

criminals analyzed, 61 XYY individuals (1.4%) and 37 XXY individuals (.9%) were detected; the difference is statistically significant (P < .02). Another 773 males examined by investigators who reported only extra Y and not extra X chromosomes yielded 37 more XYY men (4.8%). Thus, the total frequency of XYYs in the criminal population amounts to 1.9% (98/5,066). This frequency is 15 times that found in newborn males and normal adults (.13% for each) and nearly three times that found in mental patients (.7%), the only other group to show an increased frequency of the XYY abnormality. In mental patients, however, an extra X chromosome is as common as an extra Y chromosome.

Thus, criminals are the *only* group in which an extra Y chromosome occurs significantly more often than an extra X chromosome. The data available so far, therefore, provide strong presumptive evidence for an association between criminal behavior and the extra Y chromosome. Within a short time, the question should be settled definitively, since a new technique (fluorescent staining), which has become available during the past two years (Capersson, Zech, Johansson, Lindsten, and Hulten, 1970; Pearson, Borrow, and Vosa, 1970; Zech, 1969), makes mass screening for extra Y chromosomes feasible.

XYY AND VIOLENCE

Whatever incidence may eventually be determined, it is safe to predict that persons with an extra Y chromosome will constitute but an insignificant proportion of the perpetrators of violent crimes. Yet, quite apart from questions of law and ethics, the XYY genotype may have importance exceeding by far its numerical impact in contributing to our understanding of aggressive behavior. As previously noted, the Y chromosome is the male-determining chromosome; therefore, it should come as no surprise that an extra Y chromosome can produce an individual with heightened masculinity, evidenced by characteristics such as unusual tallness, increased fertility (although most XYYs do not have children, some have produced as many as 10), and powerful aggressive tendencies.

The XYY genotype may be seen as highlighting the association between maleness and violence. Being genetic, such a relationship cannot depend exclusively on external factors, although undoubtedly home environment, early upbringing, and a host of sociocultural factors have either reinforcing or inhibiting effects. In this respect, the extraordinarily large size of many XYY males dating back to early infancy (Hook and Kim, 1971; Nielsen, Friedrich, and Zeuthen, 1971) may lead to their being taunted by their peers and encouraged to physically aggressive behavior as a means of retaliation. However, this explanation is not sufficient to account for the hostile behavior, since children afflicted with other forms of gigantism have not shown noticeably aggressive behavior (Stephenson, Mellinger, and Manson, 1968). Yet, further research on the relationship between physique and behavior may well help to elucidate the XYY genotype with its dominant features of tallness (physique) and aggressiveness (behavior). It is likely that both of these traits are linked to a third variable which is genetic in origin.

Although the majority of violent crimes are committed by chromosomally normal persons, the increased frequency of XYY individuals among perpetrators of such crimes suggests that an extra Y chromosome predisposes to aggressive behavior. If an extra Y chromosome can lead to excessive aggression or hostility, it is possible that the single Y chromosome with which each normal man is endowed may itself be the genetic root of "normal" aggressiveness and may be the reason that we have conclusive evidence that "males are the more aggressive sex (Maccoby and Jacklin, 1971)." Just as the amount and degree of aggressive behavior vary from one man to another, so we may assume that the presence of two Y chromosomes rather than one does not predispose all of the men so endowed to the same degree of aggressive behavior. If the genes on a single Y chromosome of a given individual are such as to produce a tendency toward marked aggression, then a double dose of such a Y chromosome would be expected to lead to extreme aggression. By contrast, if the genes on the Y chromosome of another man predispose him to minimal aggression, then a double dose of such a chromosome would not necessarily lead to unusually aggressive behavior. It is well known that aggressive behavior can be manifested even in the complete absence of any Y chromosome; although rare, there are aggressive women.

As discussed in the beginning of this article, many individuals have been recorded who, despite the presence of an extra Y chromosome, displayed no unusual aggressive behavior. How much the lack of aggression in certain persons with an extra Y chromosome can be ascribed to the particular genic content of their Y chromosome and how much can be attributed to a fortuitous combination of environmental circumstances remain to be established. Ideal subjects for this type of study would be a series of twins, but unfortunately, or fortunately, a disorder as rare as the XYY syndrome does not lend itself to twin studies. Indeed, to our knowledge, only one such pair has been described to date (Rainer, Abdullah, and Jarvik, 1972).

These twins were typical of persons with the XYY genotype in that they were unusually tall and of borderline intelligence. However, they displayed no aggressive behavior to the best recollection of their parents until the age of 5, when the transition from home to kindergarten was accompanied by uncontrolled outbursts of aggression. Following a stormy period of adjustment, there were no further episodes of aggression until puberty, the age of 15 to be exact. At that point, there were many repeated incidences of violence. One factor contributing to the lack of aggressive behavior between the ages of 5 and 15 may have been the unusually close family relationship and a good home environment. Were it possible to separate twins like the members of this pair, the effects of varying environmental conditions on a given genetic potential for aggressive behavior could be measured.

IMPLICATIONS FOR THE FUTURE

In order to understand, and perhaps control, inappropriate or extreme aggression, it is essential to determine the nature of the relationship that exists between the known internal state of the organism and the state of his environment. It may even be possible to define the circumstances under which a genetic tendency toward aggression will not become manifest, or will be channeled into socially accepted outlets. With the XYY syndrome as a research tool, it is conceivable that advances can be made in our understanding of the complexity of factors that together tend to either produce or curb aggressive responses.

The novelty of the XYY approach to aggression is most important, for this approach takes as its basis an inherent or internal predisposition, yet seeks its solution in an understanding of external or environmental variables. It is this synthesis of positions which gives such research its enormous potential.

The future of research into the nature and causes of aggression and hostility is of more than academic interest. The problem has been with us for countless generations, but as our population continues to spiral upward at an alarming rate and our planet becomes crowded to its very limits, the importance of working with, rather than against, each other also increases. Disaster will follow if we do not make a concerted effort to understand ourselves now. Hopefully, the XYY genotype can contribute to such an understanding. Hopefully, the condition of "war of every one against every one" will cease.

NOTES

1. This research was supported by General Research Support Grant No. 158 and HD No. 01615 from the National Institute of Child Health and Human Development.

   Lissy Jarvik, previously associated with Columbia University, is now at the University of California, Los Angeles, and the Veterans Administration Hospital (Brentwood), Los Angeles, California.

   Requests for reprints should be sent to Lissy F. Jarvik, 760 Westwood Plaza, Los Angeles, California 90024.

2. Recent technical advances are changing the situation.

REFERENCES

Abdullah, S., Jarvik, L. F., Kato, T., Johnston, W. C., and Lanzkron, J. The extra Y chromosome and its psychiatric implications. *Archives of General Psychiatry*, 1969, 21, 497–501.

Akesson, H. O., Forssman, H., and Wallin, L. Chromosomes of tall men in mental hospitals. *Lancet*, 1968, 2, 1040.

Baker, D., Telfer, M. A., Richardson, C. E., and Clark, G. R. Chromosome errors in men with antisocial behavior. *Journal of the American Medical Association*, 1970, 214, 869–78.

Bartlett, D. J., Hurley, W. P., Brand, C. R., and Poole, E. W. Chromosomes of male patients in a security prison. *Nature*, 1968, 219, 351–54.

Casey, M. D., Blank, C. E., Street, D. R. K., Segall, L. J., McDougall, J. H., McGrath, P. J., and Skinner, J. L. YY chromosomes and antisocial behavior. *Lancet*, 1966, 2, 859–60.

Capersson, T., Zech, L., Johansson, C., Lindsten, J., and Hulten, J. Fluorescent staining of heteropycnotic chromosome regions in human interphase nuclei. *Experimental Cell Research*, 1970, 61, 472–74.

Close, H. G., Goonetilleke, A. S. R., Jacobs, P. A., and Price, W. H. The incidence of sex chromosomal abnormalities in mentally subnormal males. *Cytogenetics*, 1968, 7, 277–85.

Court-Brown, W. M., and Smith, P. G. Human population cytogenetics. *British Medical Bulletin*, 1969, 25, 74–80.

Daly, R. F. Neurological abnormalities in XYY males. *Nature*, 1969, 221, 472–73.

Davis, R. J., McGee, B. J., Empson, J., and Engel, E. XYY and crime. *Lancet*, 1970, 2, 1086.

Evansabury, E. Chromosome slaying trial begins in Queens. *New York Times*, 1969, April 16, 69.

Falek, A., Craddick, R., and Collum, J. An attempt to identify prisoners with an XYY chromosome complement by psychiatric and psychological means. *Journal of Nervous and Mental Disease*, 1970, 150, 165–70.

Fattig, W. D. An XYY survey in a Negro prison population. *Journal of Heredity*, 1970, 61, 10.

Gardner, L. I., and Neu, R. L. Evidence linking an extra Y chromosome to sociopathic behavior. *Archives of General Psychiatry*, 1972, 26, 220–22.

Goodman, R. M., Miller, J. F., and North, C. Chromosomes of tall men. *Lancet*, 1968, 1, 1318.

Goodman, R. M., Smith, W. S., and Migeon, C. J. Sex chromosome abnormalities. *Nature*, 1967, 216, 942–43.

Graham, H. D. and Gurr, T. R. *Violence in America: Historical & comparative perspectives*. Washington, D.C.: U.S. Government Printing Office, 1969.

Griffiths, A. W., Richards, B. W., Zaremba, J., Abramowics, T., and Stewart, A. Psychological and sociological investigation of XYY prisoners. *Nature*, 1970, 227, 290–92.

Hobbes, T. *Leviathan*. Oxford: Basil Blackwell, 1960.

Hook, E. B., and Kim, D. S. Height and antisocial behavior in XY and XYY boys. *Science* 1971, 192, 284–86.

Howell, F. C. *Early Man*. New York: Time, Inc., 1965.

Jacobs, P. A., Brunton, M., Melville, M. M., Brittain, R. P., and McClemont, W. F. Aggressive behavior, mental subnormality and the XYY male. *Nature*, 1965, 208, 1351–52.

Jacobs, P. A., Price, W. H., Court-Brown, W. M., Brittain, R. P., and Whatmore, P. B. Chromosome studies on men in a maximum security hospital. *Annals of Human Genetics*, 1968, 31, 339–47.

Jarvik, L. F. Cytogenetic aspects of psychopathology. In J. Zubin & C. Shaggas (Eds.), *Neurobiological aspects of psychopathology*. New York: Grune & Stratton, 1969.

Kessler, S., and Moos, R. H. XYY chromosome: Premature conclusions. *Science*, 1969, 165, 442.

Kjessler, B. Karyotype, meiosis and spermatogenesis in a sample of men attending an infertility clinic. *Monographs in Human Genetics*, 1966, 2.

Knox, S. J. and Nevin, N. C. XYY chromosomal constitution in prison populations. *Nature*, 1969, 222, 596.

Maccoby, E. E., and Jacklin, C. N. Sex differences and their implications for sex roles. Paper presented at the annual meeting of the Am. Psych. Assoc., Washington, D.C., Sept. 1971.

MacLean, N., Harnden, D. G., Court-Brown, W. M., Bond, J. and Mantle, D. J. Sex chromosome abnormalities in newborn babies. *Lancet*, 1964, 1, 286.

Marcus, A. M., and Richmond, G. The XYY syndrome: A short review, a case study and investigatory model. *Journal of Forensic Sciences*, 1970, 15, 154–72.

Marinello, M. J., Berkson, R. A., Edwards, J. A., and Bannerman, R. M. A study of the XYY syndrome in tall men and juvenile delinquents. *J. of the Am. Medical Assoc.*, 1969, 208, 321–25.

Masterson, J., Power, M., and O'Brien, E. Cytogenetic studies in a maximum security hospital. *J. of the Irish Medical Assoc.*, 1970, 63, 362–64.

McDanal, C. E., Jr. A survey among tall male prisoners for the XYY karyotype. *Alabama J. of Medical Science*, 1969, 6, 295–96.

Melnvk, J., Derencsenvi, A., Vanacek, F., Rucci, A. J., & Thompson, J. XXY survey in an institution for sex offenders and the mentally ill. *Nature*, 1969, 224, 369–70.

Money, J. Behavior genetics: Principles, methods and examples from XO, XXY, and XYY syndromes. *Seminars in Psychiatry*, 1970, 2, 11–29.

Nielsen, J., Friedrich, U., and Zeuthen, E. Stature and weight in boys with the XYY syndrome. *Humangenetik*, 1971, 14, 66–68.

Nielsen, J., Sturup, G., Tsuboi, T., and Romano, D. Prevalence of the XYY syndrome in an institution for psychologically abnormal criminals. *Acta Psychiatrica Scandinavia*, 1969, 45, 383–401.

Nielsen, J., Tsuboi, T., Tuver, B., Jensen, J. T., and Sachs, J. Prevalence and incidence of the XYY syndrome and Klinefelter's syndrome in an institution for criminal psychopaths. *Acta Psychiatrica Scandinavia*, 1969, 45, 402–23.

Noel, B., Quack, B., Durand, Y., and Rethore, M. O. Les hommes, 47, XYY. *Annales de Genetique*, 1969, 12, 223–36.

Pearson, P. L., Borrow, M., and Vosa, C. G. Technique for identifying Y chromosomes in human interphase nuclei. *Nature*, 1970, 226, 78–80.

Penrose, L. S. *The biology of mental defect*. New York: Grune and Stratton, 1963.

Rainer, J., Abdullah, S., and Jarvik, L. F. XYY karyotype in a pair of monozygotic twins: A 17-year life history study. *British J. of Psychiatry*, 1972, 120, 543–48.

Ratcliffe, S. G., Stewart, A. L., Melville, M. M., Jacobs, P. A., and Keay, A. Chromosome studies on 3,500 newborn male infants. *Lancet*, 1970, *1*, 121.

Recherche Cooperative sur Programme No. 85. Frequence de la constitution XYY dans la population generale. *Annales de Genetique*. 1968, *11*, 245–46.

Sergovich, F., Valentine, G. H., Clien, A. J. C., Kinch, R. A. H., and Smout, M. S. Chromosome aberrations in 2159 consecutive newborn babies. *New England J. of Medicine*, 1969, 280, 851–55.

Stenchever, M. A., Chlebowski, R., and Jarvis, J. XYY syndrome. *J. of the American Medical Association*, 1971, 215, 798.

Stephenson, J. N., Mellinger, R. C., and Manson, G. Cerebral gigantism. *Pediatrics*, 1968, 41, 130–38.

Walzer, S., Breau, G., and Gerald, P. S. A chromosome survey of 2,500 normal newborn infants. *J. of Pediatrics*, 1969, 74, 438–48.

Welch, J. P., Borgaonkar, D. S., and Herr, H. M. Psychopathy, mental deficiency, aggressiveness and the XYY syndrome. *Nature*, 1967, 214, 500–501.

Wiener, S., Sutherland, G., Bartholomew, A. A., and Hudson, B. XYY males in a Melbourne prison. *Lancet*, 1968, 1, 150.

Wilton, E., and Lever, A. XYY male. *South African Medical Journal*, 1967, 41, 284–86.

Zech, L. Investigation of metaphase chromosomes with DNA binding fluorochromes. *Experimental Cell Research*, 1969, 58, 463.

6

Weapons as Aggression-Eliciting Stimuli

Leonard Berkowitz and Anthony LePage

Reprinted by permission from *Journal of Personality and Social Psychology* 7 (1967):
202–7. Copyright 1967 by the American Psychological Association. Author permission to reprint is gratefully acknowledged.

Human behavior is often goal directed, guided by strategies and influenced by ego defenses and strivings for cognitive consistency. There clearly are situations, however, in which these purposive considerations are relatively unimportant regulators of action. Habitual behavior patterns become dominant on these occasions, and the person responds relatively automatically to the stimuli impinging upon him. Any really complete psychological system must deal with these stimulus-elicited, impulsive reactions as well as with more complex behavior patterns. More than this, we should also be able to specify the conditions under which the various behavior determinants increase or decrease in importance.

The senior author has long contended that many aggressive actions are controlled by the stimulus properties of the available targets rather than by anticipations of ends that might be served (Berkowitz, 1962, 1964, 1965). Perhaps because strong emotion results in an increased utilization of only the central cues in the immediate situation (Easterbrook, 1959; Walters & Parke, 1964), anger arousal can lead to impulsive aggressive responses which, for a short time at least, may be relatively free of cognitively mediated inhibitions against aggression or, for that matter, purposes and strategic considerations.[1] This impulsive action is not necessarily pushed out by the anger, however. Berkowitz has suggested that appropriate cues must be present in the situation if aggressive responses are actually to occur. While there is still considerable uncertainty as to just what characteristics define aggressive cue properties, the association of a stimulus with aggression evidently can enhance the aggressive cue value of this stimulus. But whatever its exact genesis, the cue (which may be either in the external environment or represented internally) presumably elicits the aggressive response. Anger (or any other conjectured aggressive "drive") increases the person's reactivity to the cue, possibly energizes the response, and may lower the likelihood of competing reactions, but is not necessary for the production of aggressive behavior.[2]

A variety of observations can be cited in support of this reasoning (cf. Berkowitz, 1965). Thus, the senior author has proposed that some of the effects of observed violence can readily be understood in terms of stimulus-elicited aggression. According to several Wisconsin experiments, observed aggression is particularly likely to produce strong attacks against anger instigators who are associated with the victim of the witnessed violence (Berkowitz & Geen, 1966, 1967; Geen & Berkowitz, 1966). The frustrator's association with the observed victim presumably enhances his cue value for aggression, causing him to evoke stronger attacks from the person who is ready to act aggressively.

More direct evidence for the present formulation can be found in a study conducted by Loew (1965). His subjects, in being required to learn a concept, either aggressive or neutral words, spoke either 20 aggressive or 20 neutral words aloud. Following this "learning task," each subject was to give a peer in an adjacent room an electric shock whenever this person made a mistake in his learning problem. Allowed to vary the intensity of the shocks they administered over a 10-point continuum, the subjects who had uttered the aggressive words gave shocks of significantly greater intensity than did the subjects who had spoken the neutral words. The aggressive words had evidently evoked implicit aggressive responses from the subjects, even though they had not been angered beforehand, which then led to the stronger attacks upon the target person in the next room when he supposedly made errors.

Cultural learning shared by many members of a society can also associate external objects with aggression and thus affect the objects' aggressive cue value. Weapons are a prime example. For many men (and probably women as well) in our society, these objects are closely associated with aggression. Assuming that the weapons do not produce inhibitions that are stronger than the evoked aggressive reactions (as would be the case, e.g., if the weapons were labeled as morally "bad"), the presence of the aggressive objects should generally lead to more intense attacks upon an available target than would occur in the presence of a neutral object.

The present experiment was designed to test this latter hypothesis. At one level, of course, the findings contribute to the current debate as to the desirability of restricting sales of firearms. Many arguments have been raised for such a restriction. Thus, according to recent statistics, Texas communities having virtually no prohibitions against firearms have a much higher

homicide rate than other American cities possessing stringent firearm regulations, and J. Edgar Hoover had maintained in *Time* magazine that the availability of firearms is an important factor in murders (Anonymous, 1966). The
experiment reported here seeks to determine how this influence may come
about. The availability of weapons obviously makes it easier for a person who
wants to commit murder to do so. But, in addition, we ask whether weapons
can serve as aggression-eliciting stimuli, causing an angered individual to
display stronger violence than he would have shown in the absence of such
weapons. Social significance aside, and at a more general theoretical level,
this research also attempts to demonstrate that situational stimuli can exert
"automatic" control over socially relevant actions.

METHOD

SUBJECTS

The subjects were 100 male undergraduates enrolled in the introductory
psychology course of the University of Wisconsin who volunteered for the
experiment (without knowing its nature) in order to earn points counting
toward their final grade. Thirty-nine other subjects had also been run, but
were discarded, because they suspected the experimenter's confederate (21),
reported receiving fewer electric shocks than were actually given them (7),
had not attended to information given them about the procedure (9), or were
run while there was equipment malfunctioning (2).

PROCEDURE

GENERAL DESIGN

Seven experimental conditions were established, six organized in a 2×3
factorial design, with the seventh group serving essentially as a control. Of
the men in the factorial design, half were made to be angry with the confederate, while the other subjects received a friendlier treatment from him. All
of the subjects were then given an opportunity to administer electric shocks
to the confederate, but for two-thirds of the men there were weapons lying
on the table near the shock apparatus. Half of these people were informed the
weapons belonged to the confederate in order to test the hypothesis that
aggressive stimuli which also were associated with the anger instigator would
evoke the strongest aggressive reaction from the subjects. The other people
seeing the weapons were told the weapons had been left there by a previous
experimenter. There was nothing on the table except the shock key when the
last third of the subjects in both the angered and nonangered conditions gave
the shocks. Finally, the seventh group consisted of angered men who gave
shocks with two badminton racquets and shuttlecocks lying near the shock

key. This condition sought to determine whether the presence of any object near the shock apparatus would reduce inhibitions against aggression, even if the object were not connected with aggressive behavior.

EXPERIMENTAL MANIPULATIONS

When each subject arrived in the laboratory, he was informed that two men were required for the experiment and that they would have to wait for the second subject to appear. After a 5-minute wait, the experimenter, acting annoyed, indicated that they had to begin because of his other commitments. He said he would have to look around outside to see if he could find another person who might serve as a substitute for the missing subject. In a few minutes the experimenter returned with the confederate. Depending upon the condition, the person was introduced as either a psychology student who had been about to sign up for another experiment or as a student who had been running another study.

The subject and confederate were told the experiment was a study of physiological reactions to stress. The stress would be created by mild electric shocks, and the subjects could withdraw, the experimenter said, if they objected to these shocks. (No subject left.) Each person would have to solve a problem knowing that his performance would be evaluated by his partner. The "evaluations" would be in the form of electric shocks, with one shock signifying a very good rating and 10 shocks meaning the performance was judged as very bad. The men were then told what their problems were. The subject's task was to list ideas a publicity agent might employ in order to better a popular singer's record sales and public image. The other person (the confederate) had to think of things a used-car dealer might do in order to increase sales. The two were given 5 minutes to write their answers, and the papers were then collected by the experimenter who supposedly would exchange them.

Following this, the two were placed in separate rooms, supposedly so that they would not influence each other's galvanic skin response (GSR) reactions. The shock electrodes were placed on the subject's right forearm, and GSR electrodes were attached to fingers on his hand, with wires trailing from the electrodes to the next room. The subject was told he would be the first to receive electric shocks as the evaluation of his problem solution. The experimenter left the subject's room saying he was going to turn on the GSR apparatus, went to the room containing the shock machine and the waiting confederate, and only then looked at the schedule indicating whether the subject was to be angered or not. He informed the confederate how many shocks the subject was to receive, and 30 seconds later the subject was given seven shocks (angered condition) or one shock (nonangered group). The experimenter then went back to the subject, while the confederate quickly arranged the table holding the shock key in the manner appropriate for the subject's condition. Upon entering the subject's room, the experimenter asked him how many shocks he had received and provided the subject with a brief questionnaire on which he was to rate his mood. As soon as this was completed, the subject was taken to the room holding the shock machine. Here the experimenter told the subject it was his turn to evaluate his partner's work. For one group in both the angered and nonangered conditions the shock key was alone on the table (no-object groups). For two other groups in each of these angered and nonangered conditions, however, a 12-gauge shotgun and a .38-caliber revolver were lying on the table near the key (aggressive-weapon conditions). One group in both the angered and nonangered conditions was informed the weapons belonged to the subject's partner. The subjects given this treatment had been told earlier that their partner was a student who had been conducting an experiment.[3] They were reminded of this, and the experimenter said the weapons were being used in some way by this person in his research (associated-weapons group), and they too were asked to disregard the guns. For the last treatment, one group of angered men found two badminton racquets and shuttlecocks lying on the table near the shock key, and these people were also told the equipment belonged to someone else (badminton-racquets group).

Immediately after this information was provided, the experimenter showed the subject what was supposedly his partner's answer to his assigned problem. The subject was reminded that he was to give the partner shocks as his evaluation and was informed that this was the last time shocks would be administered in the study. A second copy of the mood questionnaire was then completed by the subject after he had delivered the shocks. Following this, the subject was asked a number of oral questions about the experiment, including what, if any, suspicions he had. (No doubts were voiced about the presence of the weapons.) At the conclusion of this interview the experiment was explained, and the subject was asked not to talk about the study.

DEPENDENT VARIABLES

As in nearly all the experiments conducted in the senior author's program, the number of shocks given by the subjects serves as the primary aggression measure. However, we also report here findings obtained with the total duration of each subject's shocks, recorded in thousandths of a minute. Attention is also given to each subject's rating of his mood, first immediately after receiving the partner's evaluation, and again immediately after administering shocks to the partner. These ratings were made on a series of 10 13-point bipolar scales with an adjective at each end, such as "calm-tense" and "angry-not-angry."

RESULTS

EFFECTIVENESS OF AROUSAL TREATMENT

Analyses of variance of the responses to each of the mood scales following the receipt of the partner's evaluation indicate the prior-shock treatment succeeded in creating differences in anger arousal. The subjects getting seven shocks rated themselves as being significantly angrier than the subjects receiving only one shock (F = 20.65, p <.01). There were no reliable differences among the groups within any one arousal level. Interestingly enough, the only other mood scale to yield a significant effect was the scale "sad-happy." The aroused-seven-shocks men reported a significantly stronger felt sadness than the men getting one shock (F = 4.63, p >.05).

AGGRESSION TOWARD PARTNER

A preliminary analysis of variance of the shock data for the six groups in the 3 × 2 factorial design yielded the findings shown in Table 6.1. As is indicated by the significant interaction, the presence of the weapons significantly affected the number of shocks given by the subject when the subject had received seven shocks. A Duncan multiple-range test was then made of the differences among the seven conditions means, using the error variance from a seven-group one-way analysis of variance in the error term. The mean number of shocks administered in each experimental condition and the Duncan test results are given in Table 6.2. The hypothesis guiding the present study receives good support. The strongly provoked men delivered more frequent electrical attacks upon their tormentor in the presence of a weapon than when nonaggressive objects (the badminton racquets and shuttlecocks) were present or when only the shock key was on the table. The angered subjects gave the greatest number of shocks in the presence of the

TABLE 6.1.
ANALYSIS OF VARIANCE RESULTS FOR NUMBER OF SHOCKS GIVEN BY SUBJECTS IN FACTORIAL DESIGN

Source	df	MS	F
Number of shocks received (A)	1	182.04	104.62*
Weapons association (B)	2	1.90	1.09
A X B	2	8.73	5.02*
Error	84	1.74	

*p < .01.

TABLE 6.2.
MEAN NUMBER OF SHOCKS GIVEN IN EACH CONDITION

Condition	Shocks received	
	1	7
Associated weapons	2.60_a	6.07_d
Unassociated weapons	2.20_a	5.67_{cd}
No object	3.07_a	4.67_{bc}
Badminton racquets	—	4.60_b

Note: Cells having a common subscript are not significantly different at the .05 level by Duncan multiple-range test. There were 10 subjects in the seven-shock-received-badminton-racquets group and 15 subjects in each of the other conditions.

weapons associated with the anger instigator, as predicted, but this group was not reliably different from the angered-unassociated-weapons conditions. Both of these groups expressing aggression in the presence of weapons were significantly more aggressive than the angered-neutral-object condition, but only the associated-weapons condition differed significantly from the angered-no-object group.

Some support for the present reasoning is also provided by the shock-duration data summarized in Table 6.3. (We might note here, before beginning, that the results with duration scores—and this has been a consistent finding in the present research program—are less clear-cut than the findings with a number of shocks given.) The results indicate that the presence of weapons resulted in a decreased number of attacks upon the partner, although not significantly so, when the subjects had received only one shock beforehand. The condition differences are in the opposite direction, how-

TABLE 6.3.
MEAN TOTAL DURATION OF SHOCKS GIVEN IN EACH CONDITION

Condition	Shocks received	
	1	7
Associated weapons	17.93_c	46.93_a
Unassociated weapons	17.33_c	39.47_{ab}
No object	24.47_{bc}	34.80_{ab}
Badminton racquets	—	34.90_{ab}

Note: The duration scores are in thousandths of a minute. Cells having a common subscript are not significantly different at the .05 level by Duncan multiple-range-test. There were 10 subjects in the seven-shocks-received-badminton-racquet group and 15 subjects in each of the other conditions.

ever, for the men given the stronger provocation. Consequently, even though there are no reliable differences among the groups in this angered condition, the angered men administering shocks in the presence of weapons gave significantly longer shocks than the nonangered men also giving shocks with guns lying on the table. The angered-neutral-object and angered-no-object groups, on the other hand, did not differ from the nonangered-no-object condition.

MOOD CHANGES

Analyses of covariance were conducted on each of the mood scales, with the mood ratings made immediately after the subjects received their partners' evaluation held constant in order to determine if there were condition differences in mood changes following the giving of shocks to the partner. Duncan range tests of the adjusted condition means yielded negative results, suggesting that the attacks on the partner did not produce any systematic condition differences. In the case of the felt anger ratings, there were very high correlations between the ratings given before and after the shock administration, with the Pearson *rs* ranging from .89 in the angered-unassociated-weapons group to .99 in each of the three unangered conditions. The subjects could have felt constrained to repeat their initial responses.

DISCUSSION

Common sense, as well as a good deal of personality theorizing, both influenced to some extent by an egocentric view of human behavior as being caused almost exclusively by motives within the individual, generally neglect the type of weapons effect demonstrated in the present study. If a person holding a gun fires it, we are told either that he wanted to do so (consciously or unconsciously) or that he pulled the trigger "accidentally." The findings summarized here suggest yet another possibility: The presence of the weapon might have elicited an intense aggressive reaction from the person with the gun, assuming his inhibitions against aggression were relatively weak at the moment. Indeed, it is altogether conceivable that many hostile acts which supposedly stem from unconscious motivation really arise because of the operation of aggressive cues. Not realizing how these situational stimuli might elicit aggressive behavior, and not detecting the presence of these cues, the observer tends to locate the source of the action in some conjectured underlying, perhaps repressed, motive. Similarly, if he is a Skinnerian rather than a dynamically oriented clinician, he might also neglect the operation of aggression-eliciting stimuli by invoking the concept of operant behavior, and thus sidestep the issue altogether. The sources of the hostile action, for him, too, rest within the individual, with the behavior only steered or permitted by discriminative stimuli.

Alternative explanations must be ruled out, however, before the present thesis can be regarded as confirmed. One obvious possibility is that subjects in the weapons condition reacted to the demand characteristics of the situation as they saw them and exhibited the kind of behavior they thought was required of them. ("These guns on the table mean I'm supposed to be aggressive, so I'll give many shocks.") Several considerations appear to negate this explanation. First, there are the subjects' own verbal reports. None of the subjects voiced any suspicions of the weapons and, furthermore, when they were queried generally denied that the weapons had any effect on them. But even those subjects who did express any doubts about the experiment typically acted like the other subjects. Thus, the eight non-angered-weapons subjects who had been rejected gave only 2.50 shocks on the average, while the 18 angered-no-object or neutral-object men who had been discarded had a mean of 4.50 shocks. The 12 angered-weapons subjects who had been rejected, by contrast, delivered an average of 5.83 shocks to their partner. These latter people were evidently also influenced by the presence of weapons.

Setting all this aside, moreover, it is not altogether certain from the notion of demand characteristics that only the angered subjects would be inclined to act in conformity with the experimenter's supposed demands. The nonangered men in the weapons group did not display a heightened number of attacks on their partner. Would this have been predicted beforehand by researchers interested in demand characteristics? The last finding raises one final observation. Recent unpublished research by Allen and Bragg indicated that awareness of the experimenter's purpose does not necessarily result in an increased display of the behavior the experimenter supposedly desires. Dealing with one kind of socially disapproved action (conformity), Allen and Bragg demonstrated that high levels of experimentally induced awareness of the experimenter's interests generally produced a decreased level of the relevant behavior. Thus, if the subjects in our study had known the experimenter was interested in observing their aggressive behavior, they might well have given less, rather than more, shocks, since giving shocks is also socially disapproved. This type of phenomenon was also not observed in the weapons conditions.

Nevertheless, any one experiment cannot possibly definitely exclude all the alternative explanations. Scientific hypotheses are only probability statements, and further research is needed to heighten the likelihood that the present reasoning is correct.

Notes

1. Cognitive processes can play a part even in impulsive behavior, most notably by influencing the stimulus qualities (or meaning) of the objects in the situation. As only one illustration, in several experiments by the senior author (cf. Berkowitz, 1965) the name applied to the available target person affected the magnitude of the attacks directed against this individual by angered subjects.

2. Buss (1961) has advanced a somewhat similar conception of the functioning of anger.
3. This information evidently was the major source of suspicion; some of the subjects doubted that a student running an experiment would be used as a subject in another study, even if he were only an undergraduate. This information was provided only in the associated-weapons conditions, in order to connect the guns with the partner, and consequently, this ground for suspicion was not present in the unassociated weapons groups.

REFERENCES

Anonymous. A gun-toting nation. *Time*, August 12, 1966.

Berkowitz, L. *Aggression: A social psychological analysis*. New York: McGraw-Hill, 1962.

Berkowitz, L. Aggressive cues in aggressive behavior and hostile catharsis. *Psychological Review*, 1964, *71*, 104–22.

Berkowitz, L. The concept of aggressive drive: Some additional considerations. In L. Berkowitz (Ed.), *Advances in experimental social psychology*. Vol. 2, New York: Academic Press, 1965. pp 301–29.

Berkowitz, L. & Geen, R. G. Film violence and the cue properties of available targets. *Journal of Personality and Social Psychology*, 1966, *3*, 525–30.

Berkowitz, L., & Geen, R. G. Stimulus qualities of the target of aggression: A further study, *Journal of Personality and Social Psychology*, 1967, *5*, 364–68.

Buss, A. *The psychology of aggression*. New York: Wiley, 1961.

Easterbrook, J. A. The effect of emotion on cue utilization and the organization of behavior. *Psychological Review*, 1959, *66*, 183–201.

Geen, R. G., & Berkowitz, L. Name-mediated aggressive cue properties. *Journal of Personality*, 1966, *34*, 456–65.

Loew, C. A. Acquisition of a hostile attitude and its relationship to aggressive behavior. Unpublished doctoral dissertation, State University of Iowa, 1965.

Walters, R. H. & Parke, R. D. Social motivation, dependency, susceptibility to social influence. In L. Berkowitz (Ed.), *Advances in experimental social psychology*, Vol. 1. New York: Academic Press, 1964, pp. 232–76.

7

Does Television Violence Cause Aggression?[1]

Leonard D. Eron,[2] L. Rowell Huesmann, Monroe M. Lefkowitz, and Leopold O. Walder

Reprinted by permission from *American Psychologist* 27 (1972): 253–63. Copyright 1972 by the American Psychological Association. Author permission to reprint is gratefully acknowledged.

With the increasing prominence of violence in our society, social scientists have been turning their attention to the antecedents of aggressive behavior in children and adults. Television programming, with its heavy emphasis on interpersonal violence and acquisitive lawlessness, has been assigned a role both in inciting aggression and teaching viewers specific techniques of aggressive behavior. The relation between overt aggression and television habits has been demonstrated in a few survey studies which, however, because of the nature of surveys have not been able to discriminate cause and effect (Bailyn, 1959; Eron, 1963; Schramm, Lyle, & Parker, 1961).

On the other hand, manipulative laboratory experiments have demonstrated an immediate effect on the extent of aggressive behavior of subjects who have witnessed aggressive displays on film (Bandura, Ross, & Ross, 1963a; Berkowitz, Corwin, & Heironimus, 1963). The latter studies, however, can be criticized for not duplicating real-life television viewing situations and possibly not accounting for anything more than a transient effect on the viewer. Hartup and Yonas (1971) stated in their review of development psychology in the latest *Annual Review of Psychology*,

> Current studies of the childhood determinants of aggression are not extensive. The report of a presidential commission, *Violence and the Media* (Baker & Ball, 1969), indicated that child psychologists possess much information concerning the determinants of aggression but very little stemming directly from naturalistic sources [p. 375].

One possible way of utilizing survey procedures to demonstrate cause and effect is to use a longitudial context. By contrasting the magnitude of contemporaneous and logitudinal correlations between two sets of variables, it is possible to account more clearly for which of the variables is antecedent and which consequent. The authors have now accumulated data on both aggressive behavior and television viewing habits over a 10-year period in a large group of subjects first seen when they were 8–9 years of age. Thus, we can implement such an analysis.

The hypotheses of this research are that a young adult's aggressiveness is positively related to his preference for violent television when he was 8–9 years old and, furthermore, that his preference for violent television during this critical period is one cause of his aggressiveness.

METHOD

Longitudinal data were collected on 427 teenagers of an original group of 875 children who had participated in a study of third-grade children in 1960 (Eron, 1963; Eron, Walder, & Lefkowitz, 1971). The original 875 constituted the entire third-grade population of a semirural county in New York's Hudson River Valley, while the 427 subjects were those who could be located and interviewed 10 years later.

The information collected about these subjects in both time periods falls into two classes: (a) measures of aggression and (b) potential predictors of aggression. During the third-grade interviews, four different data sources had been used: the subject, his peers, his mother, and his father. Ten years later, the data sources were the subject and his peers. For convenience, this later time period will be designated as the thirteenth grade.

The variables used in the study are listed in Table 7.1. Two variables are of particular importance: peer-rated aggression and preference for violent television programs. In the third grade, peer-rated aggression scores were obtained by asking each child to nominate any of his classmates on 10 "guess who" items describing aggressive behavior; for example, "Who pushes and shoves other children?" "Who takes other children's things without asking?" "Who starts a fight over nothing?" "Who says mean things?" These aggression items were interspersed among a series of other peer nomination questions. The validity and reliability of the aggression measure have been discussed elsewhere (Eron et al., 1971; Walder, Abelson, Eron, Banta, & Laulicht, 1961).

The peer rating instrument was revised slightly for the thirteenth-grade study. One item which was deemed inappropriate for 19-year-old subjects was dropped. Furthermore, since the subjects were no longer in school, the procedure was administered individually in a face-to-face interview. The

TABLE 7.1.
MEASURES OF AGGRESSION AND POTENTIALLY RELATED VARIABLES STUDIES AT TWO DIFFERENT TIMES

Variable	Third grade	Source
Measure of aggression		
Child's aggression (AGG3)		Peer ratings
Variables potentially related to aggression		
Father's occupational status		Father's report
Parents' aspirations for child		Parents' report
Parents' mobility orientation		Parents' report
Ethnicity of family		Parents' report
Mother's religiosity (frequency of church attendance)		Mother's report
Parental nurturance of child		Mother's report
Parental rejection of child		Mother's report
Parental punishment of child		Mother's report
Child's identification with father		Father's and child's report
Child's identification with mother		Mother's and child's report
Child's confessing to parents		Parents' report
Father's aggressiveness		Walters-Zak test
Mother's aggressiveness		Walters-Zak test
Parental disharmony		Parents' report
Child's IQ		Test
Child's hours of watching television		Mother's report
Child's preference for watching violent television (TVVL3)		Mother's report on favorite programs and violence scores by independent raters

Thirteenth grade

Measures of aggression

  Subject's aggression (AGG13)   Peer rating

  Subject's antisocial behavior (ASB13)   Subject's report

  Subject's psychological predisposition to delinquency (MMPI–49S)   Sum of Scales 4 + 9 on MMPI

Variables potentially related to aggression

  Father's occupational status   Subject's report

  Subject's occupational aspirations   Subject's report

  Subject's hours of watching television   Subject's report

  Subject's preference for watching violent television (TVVL13)   Subject's report on favorite programs and violence

number of possible peers any subject could nominate was widened beyond his own third-grade classroom to include his classmates through high school. Thus, each subject was rated by a larger set of raters in the thirteenth grade which included many of the raters from the third grade.

In the third grade, the children's preferences for violent television were obtained by asking each mother for her child's three favorite television programs. All programs mentioned were then categorized as violent or nonviolent by two independent raters with 94% agreement in their ratings. Differences in the remaining 6% of the programs were resolved by mutual discussion between the raters. Each subject received a score according to the number of violent television programs he was reported by his mother as favoring. Scores ranged from 1 (for no violent programs) to 4 (for three violent programs).

In the 10-year follow-up study, each subject *himself* was asked for his four current favorite television programs. All programs were then categorized for presence or absence of violence by two independent raters who were only a few years older than the subjects themselves. Scores were assigned to each program on the basis of agreement between the raters. If they both agreed a program was nonviolent, the program received a score of 0; if they both agreed it was violent, the score was 2; if they disagreed in categorization, the program was assigned a score of 1. Here again there was good agreement between the two raters. They agreed on 81% of 125 programs mentioned by the subjects. The score for each subject was the sum of the violence ratings of the four programs mentioned.

The designation by these raters of violent and nonviolent programs agreed very well with the assignment of programs by Feshback and Singer (1971) to aggressive and nonaggressive diets in their field experiment (see below). Furthermore, the judgments of our raters were in close agreement with the results obtained by Greenberg and Gordon (1970), who did an extensive rating study in which they used as raters both established television critics (approximately 45) and 300 subjects randomly selected from the Detroit, Michigan, telephone book. Of the 20 programs which Greenberg and Gordon indicated had the highest violence ratings, 19 were selected as violent by our raters. For the 427 cases in the 10-year follow-up study, there was a correlation of .94 between the Greenberg-Gordon average ratings and our ratings.

Results

The 427 subjects studied in both the third and thirteenth grades consisted of 211 males and 216 females whose modal age at the time of the thirteenth-grade interview was 19. The sample was at the higher end of the average range in intelligence with a mean IQ of 109 and was somewhat middle class in social status. The dropout rate from participation in the study between the third and thirteenth grade was considerably higher for subjects who displayed high aggression in the third grade than for those who displayed low aggression. For example, 57% of the low quartile in aggression were retained in the follow-up sample, while only 27% of the high quartile were retained. This can be explained by a number of factors including the finding that residential mobility was correlated significantly with aggression in the sample.

Preliminary analysis indicated that the measures of aggression distinguished the males from the females. There were statistically significant differences between males' and females' mean scores on every measure of aggression in both grades. The differences were more pronounced in the thirteenth grade. In addition, a principal component factor analysis of subjects' sex and the variables that were used in the study yielded a first principal factor whose largest loading was for the subjects' sex and whose next largest loadings were for the measures of aggression. Finally, a comparison of girls in the highest quartile on aggression with those in the lowest quartile revealed a difference in MMPI profiles; the high-aggressive girls were significantly more masculine in their interests and attitudes. Because of these findings, the data for males and females were analyzed separately.

CORRELATIONS BETWEEN PREFERENCE FOR TELEVISION VIOLENCE AND AGGRESSION

The correlations between preference for television violence and aggression at both grade levels are presented separately for boys and girls in Table 7.2.

These correlations must be interpreted in light of the total number of correlations being computed for the sample of 427 subjects and the distribution of the variables. Because of the large number of potential correlations, only those with a probability less than .01 on a two-tailed test were considered significant and only those with a probability less than .001 on a two-tailed test were called highly significant. On the other hand, it should be pointed out that the unusual skewness and kurtosis of many of the variables may impose a limit on the size of their intercorrelations.

From Table 7.2, one can see that there is a highly significant relation between boys' preferences for violent television programs in the third grade (TVVL3) and their peer-rated aggression in the thirteenth grade (AGG13). Similarly, there is a significant contemporaneous relation between the boys' television preferences in the third grade and peer-rated aggression in the third grade (AGG3). Neither of these effects was apparent for females. While the correlation between third-grade preferences and thirteenth-grade peer-rated aggression explains only 10% of the variance in aggression, 10% is impressive when one considers the probable limitations on the size of the

TABLE 7.2.
Correlations Among Violence Ratings of Preferred Television Programs and Measures of Aggression at Two Different Periods

	TVVL3	AGG3	TVVL13	AGG13	ASB13	MMPI-49S13
Boys						
TVVL3	1					
AGG3	.21*	1				
TVVL13	.05	.01	1			
AGG13	.31*	.38*	-.05	1		
ASB13	.10	.14	.01	.49*	1	
MMPI-49S13	.12	.21	.06	.39*	.46*	1
Girls						
TVVL3	1					
AGG3	.02	1				
TVVL13	.08	-.08	1			
AGG13	-.13	.47*	-.05	1		
ASB13	-.02	.01	-.10	.23*	1	
MMPI-49S13	-.05	.13	.11	.28*	.45*	1

Note: The number 3 or 13 following a variable indicates the period, third grade or thirteenth grade, when the data were obtained. TVVL is a measure of preference for television violence. AGG = peer-rated aggression; ASB = self-rating of frequency of antisocial behavior; MMPI-49S = sum of T scores on Scales 4 and 9 of MMPI.
*Indicates correlation is significantly different from zero beyond the .01 level of confidence.

correlation imposed by the skewed distributions of the variables, the large number of variables affecting aggression, the comparatively small explanatory power of these other variables (see below), and the 10-year lag between measurement times. The extremely low likelihood of achieving such a correlation by chance is a good indicator of the strength of the relation between preference for violent television at age 8 years and peer-rated aggression at age 19.

As has been pointed out previously (Eron et al., 1971), when distributions are unusual, an analysis of variance may, more clearly than a product-moment correlation, reveal the relation between the two variables. Hence, the male subjects were partitioned into low, medium, and high television violence groups, representing approximately the lowest 10%, the middle 80%, and the upper 10%, respectively. The results of one-way analyses of variance on this independent variable with aggression measures as the dependent variables are shown in Table 7.3. Now one can see that there is a highly significant relation between preference for violent television in the third grade and aggression in the thirteenth grade, whether the measure is one of peer-rated aggression or self-ratings of aggression (antisocial behavior and MMPI-49S).

CAUSAL ANALYSIS

Having established that there exists a highly significant relationship between a preference for violent television in the third grade and aggressive habits in the thirteenth grade, one can consider the alternative causal explanations for this phenomenon. Of course, one cannot demonstrate that a particular hypothesis is true. One can only reject untenable hypotheses and present evidence on the plausibility of the remaining hypotheses.

Cross-lagged correlations.

Consider the pattern of correlations diagramed in Figure 7.1. The correlations on the diagonals are called cross-lagged correlations. The cross-lagged correlation between a preference for violent television in the third grade and thirteenth-grade aggression was highly significant. When coupled with the lack of a relation between third-grade aggression and a preference for violent television in the thirteenth grade, this significant correlation supports the hypothesis that preferring to watch violent television is a cause of aggressive behavior. This causal hypothesis is diagramed in Figure 7.2a. The probability of a chance occurrence of the difference between the *cross-lagged correlations* is low (Fisher's $z = 3.07$, $p < .002$); however, a few rival hypotheses are seemingly consistent with the difference and deserve consideration.

One alternative hypothesis is that preference for violent television in the third grade stimulates concurrent aggression, and this aggression leads to

TABLE 7.3.
MEAN AGGRESSION SCORES AS A FUNCTION OF TELEVISION VIOLENCE RATINGS OF PROGRAMS PREFERRED BY BOYS IN THIRD GRADE

TVVL3	n	AGG3		AGG13		ASB		MMPI-49S	
		M	SD	M	SD	M	SD	M	SD
Low	31	9.06	9.91	5.14	5.05	25.58	12.12	121.97	20.50
Medium	139	11.19	11.54	8.14	9.88	22.06	12.69	122.50	19.33
High	14	21.00	13.79	16.46	13.01	30.86	14.23	135.86	18.14
Total	184	11.58	11.75	8.27	9.86	23.33	12.90	123.42	19.67
F^a		5.43****		6.82******	$t = 4.04***$	3.63**		3.11*	

Note: Abbreviations: AGG = peer-rated aggression; ASB = self-rating of frequency of antisocial behavior; MMPI-49S = sum of T scores on Scales 4 and 9 of MMPI.

[a] Because of heterogenity of variance, a t test between the two most discrepant means for AGG13 was performed. The t was conservatively evaluated by using degrees of freedom equal to the n for the smallest group, that is, 14.

*$p < .05$.
**$p < .03$.
***$p < .01$.
****$p < .005$.
*****$p < .001$.

108

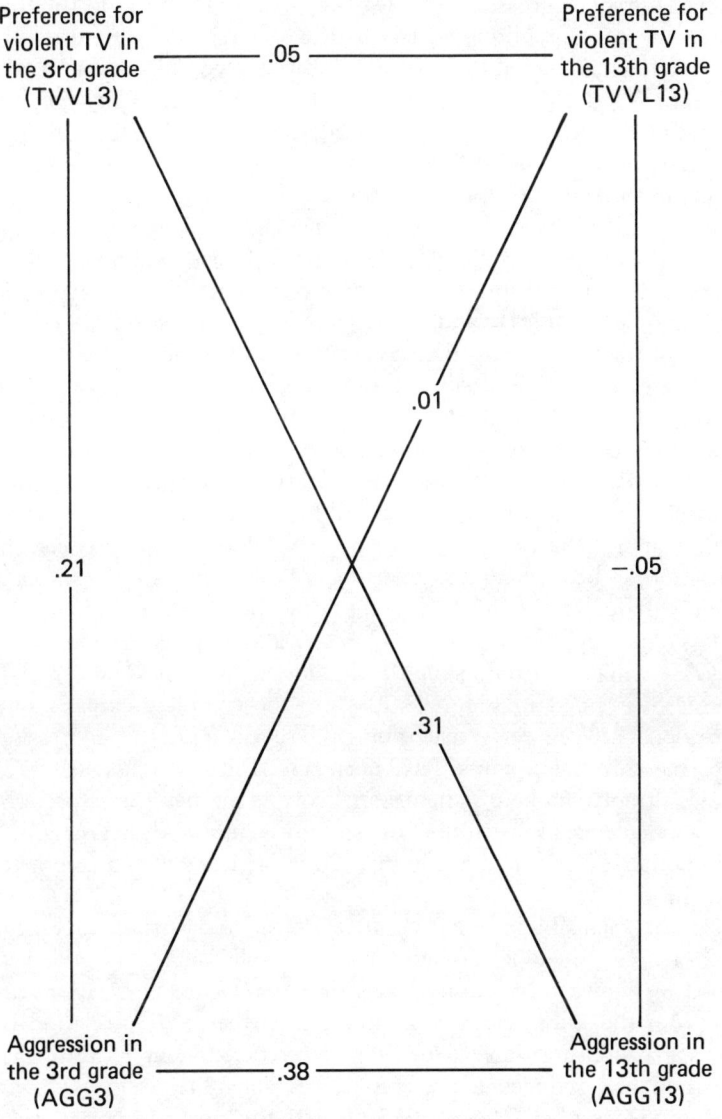

Preference for violent TV in the 3rd grade (TVVL3)

Preference for violent TV in the 13th grade (TVVL13)

.05

.01

.21

−.05

.31

Aggression in the 3rd grade (AGG3)

Aggression in the 13th grade (AGG13)

.38

FIGURE 7.1.
THE CORRELATIONS BETWEEN A PREFERENCE FOR
VIOLENT TELEVISION AND PEER-RATED AGGRESSION
FOR 211 BOYS OVER A 10-YEAR LAG

thirteenth-grade aggression or at least is being remeasured in the thirteenth grade. The corresponding causal chain is diagramed in Figure 7.2b. This interpretation can be rejected because if it were true, the relation between the end points of the causal sequence would have been no stronger than the product of the relations between all adjacent intermediate points. But the correlation between the end points was .31, which was much higher than the product of the intermediate correlations.

For a similar reason, the causal chain diagramed in Figure 7.2c can be eliminated as an alternative hypothesis. If early aggression caused a preference for violent television which in turn contributed to later aggression, the correlation between early and later aggression would have been less than the product of the two intermediate correlations. It was not.

One cannot reject so easily the more realistic alternative hypothesis diagramed in Figure 7.2d. This causal hypothesis asserts that early aggression causes both contemporaneous preferences for violent television and later aggression. Part of this hypothesis, that early aggression contributes to later aggression, is quite probably true. What is of interest here, though, is whether or not the relation between early television preferences and later aggression can be explained as an artifact of early aggression. One can obtain evidence to refute this idea by computing the partial correlation between third-grade television violence (TVVL3) and thirteenth-grade aggression (AGG13) while controlling for third-grade aggression (AGG3). If the hypothesis diagramed in Figure 7.2d were the complete explanation of the correlation between early television preferences and later aggression, then the partial correlation would have been zero. But it was not. It was .25 or a distance of only .06 below the original correlation between a preference for television violence in the third grade and thirteenth-grade aggression. Hence, the hypothesis diagramed in Figure 7.2d is implausible as a complete causal explanation.

The final plausible alternative to be considered is that early aggression causes a diminished preference for violent television. This theory is diagramed in Figure 7.2e. If one views the cross-lagged correlations as deviations from the initial cross-correlation, then the zero correlation between early aggression and later television preferences might indicate that early aggression had reduced a preference for violent television. However, as Rozelle and Campbell (1969) have indicated, the most appropriate base line is not the early contemporaneous correlation, but the average of the two contemporaneous correlations attenuated for the reliability of the variables. The higher the reliabilities, the less is the attenuation. With a conservative assumption of a very high temporal reliability of .70, the base line for Figure 7.1 would be $[.21 + (-.05) \times .70 \times .70]/2 = .06$. With this correction, the hypothesis that aggression diminishes a preference for violent television be-

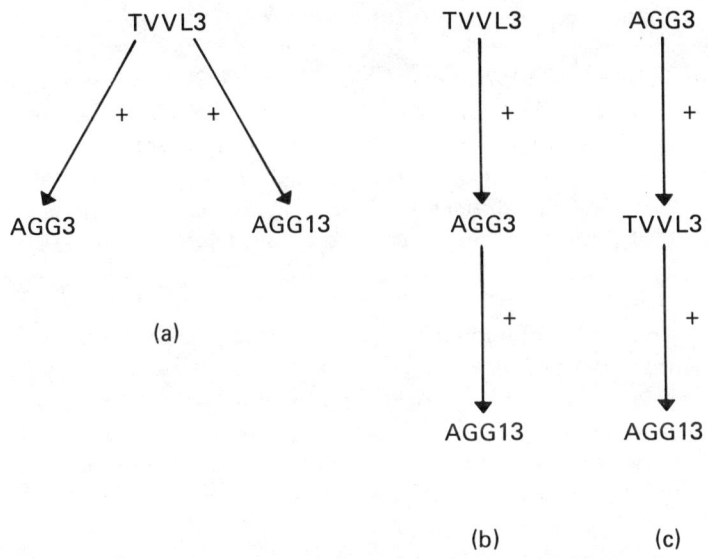

(a)

(b)   (c)

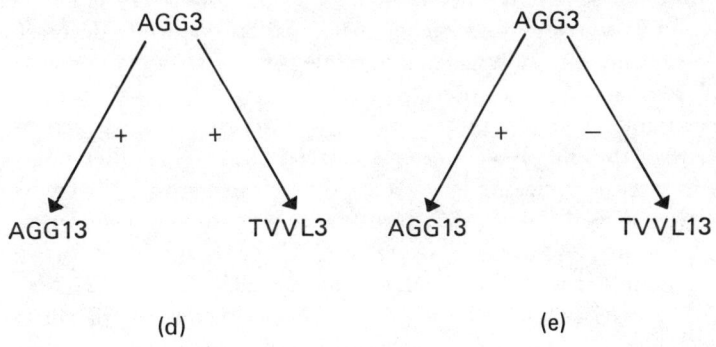

(d)   (e)

FIGURE 7.2.
FIVE FEASIBLE CAUSAL HYPOTHESES FOR THE
CORRELATIONS PRESENTED IN FIGURE 7.1

comes untenable, since the cross-lagged correlation from early aggression to later television preferences is very close to the base line.

As Rozelle and Campbell (1969), Kenny (in press), and others have pointed out, the validity of cross-lagged panel correlation inferences depends on the assumption that the underlying factor structure is stationary over time. If it is not, one must be very careful about the inferences drawn. The large difference between the third- and thirteenth-grade synchronous correlations is indicative of lack of stationarity and necessitates consideration of some artifactual effects.

One alternative is that the aggression measure increased in reliability between the third and thirteenth grades. Such an increase would have caused the measured correlation between third-grade television violence and thirteenth-grade aggression to increase even though the true correlation did not change. However, the reliability of the peer-rated aggression variable in the third grade was measured by a variety of methods and consistently found to be between .85 and .95 (Walder et al., 1961). Hence, an increase in reliability is not a plausible explanation of the pattern.

Similarly, a decrease in the reliability of the television violence ratings in the thirteenth grade could have caused the decrease in the correlation between third-grade aggression and thirteenth-grade television violence over the synchronous correlation. Low reliability for thirteenth-grade television violence is in fact plausible since thirteenth-grade television violence correlates poorly with most other variables. However, there is little evidence that third-grade television violence had much higher reliability. Furthermore, the reliability of thirteenth grade television violence could not affect the cross lagged correlation from television violence to aggression. Hence, a decrease in the reliability of the television violence variable is not sufficient to explain the pattern of cross-lagged correlations.

Basing the causality argument on the finding that the cross-lagged correlation is greater than the initial synchronous correlation raises another question. Was the increase significant? It is not appropriate to compare the cross-lagged correlation directly with the third-grade synchronous correlation since that correlation should erode over time. Using Kenny's (in press) method for estimating erosion rates yields a rate of .605 (.21) = .127. For $N = 184$, this comparison yields a Fisher's z of 2.33 which is significant at the .02 level.

On the basis of the cross-lagged correlations and the significant partial correlation between early preferences for violent television and later aggression with early aggression controlled, one concludes that the single most plausible causal hypothesis is that a preference for watching violent television in the third grade contributes to the development of aggressive habits. This does not mean that other variables are not of equal or greater importance in stimulating aggression, but only that a preference for television violence and the viewing behavior that the preference indicates probably are independent and important causes of aggressive habits.

Partial Correlations.

None of the data presented up to this point sheds evidence on the possibility that another variable such as IQ, social class, parental punishment, or parental aggression might have stimulated both the child's preference for violent television and his aggressiveness. However, one can test some of these hypotheses by computing the partial correlations between television violence and aggression with such variables controlled. Table 7.4 contains these partial correlations. Neither the child's aggression in the third grade, social class, mobility orientation of parent, IQ, parental punishment, parental aspiration

TABLE 7.4.
PARTIAL CORRELATIONS BETWEEN TVVL3 AND AGG13
WITH OTHER VARIABLES CONTROLLED

Controlled variable	*n*	Partial correlation between TVVL3 and AGG13
None	184	.31
Third-grade variables		
Peer-rated aggression	184	.25
Father's occupational status	140	.31
Child's IQ	179	.28
Father's aggressiveness	140	.30
Mother's aggressiveness	184	.31
Punishment administered	184	.31
Parents' aspirations for child	140	.30
Parents' mobility orientation	140	.31
Hours of television watched	184	.30
Thirteenth-grade variables		
Father's occupational status	182	.28
Subject's aspirations	149	.28
Subject's hours of television watching	183	.30

Note: Abbreviations: TVVL3 = a measure of preference for television violence in the third grade; AGG13 = peer-rated aggression in the thirteenth grade.

for child, nor parental aggression accounts for the relationship. Nor can the relation be explained by the total number of hours of television watched by the subject in either the third or thirteenth grade.

Multiple Regression.

As Darlington (1968) pointed out, one can treat the standardized coefficients in a multiple regression equation as measures of the causal contributions of the predictor variables to the criterion variable. This approach assumes that all causal variables not in the regression equation are uncorrelated with those that are and that the criterion variable is not "causing" any predictor variable. While it is quite possible that these assumptions are violated, it is still worthwhile to examine the coefficients as approximate measures of causal contributions. Hence, a multiple regression equation was computed by a step-wise method that entered the third-grade variables into the equation in order of their utility in predicting the criterion variable, thirteenth-grade aggression. The regression equation shown in Table 7.5 predicts thirteenth-grade aggression solely from third-grade variables.

The order in which the variables were entered reveals that a preference for watching television violence was the most "useful" third-grade variable in the prediction. It explained more of the variance than any other predictor. More important, however, for a causal analysis are the standardized regression coefficients in the final regression equation. Such a coefficient can be interpreted as the contribution of the predictor variable to "causing" the criterion variable independent of the other predictor variables. The coefficients in Table 7.5 show that a preference for violent television in third grade is the major contributor to thirteenth-grade aggression among the third-grade variables. This finding supports the hypothesis that a preference for watching violent television in the third-grade time period is a cause of aggressive habits later in life independent of the other causal contributors studied.

Path Analysis.

A more specialized technique for using multiple regression coefficients to estimate causal effects is path analysis (Heise, 1970). The path coefficients for television and aggression are shown in Figure 7.3. These coefficients are standardized partial regression coefficients. In other words, the path coefficients from third-grade television violence to thirteenth-grade aggression is the coefficient of third-grade television violence in a regression equation predicting thirteenth-grade aggression with third-grade aggression controlled. The obtained pattern of path coefficients adds further credence to the argument that watching violent television contributes to the development of aggressive habits.[3]

TABLE 7.5.

MULTIPLE REGRESSION PREDICTION OF THIRTEENTH-GRADE
AGGRESSION (AGG13) FROM THIRD-GRADE PREDICTORS

Step entered	Predictor	Multiple correlation	Final standardized coefficients for predictors
1	Television violence (TVVL3)	.31	.29
2	Parents' mobility orientation	.41	.28
3	Child's identification with mother	.44	−.03
4	Parental nurturance of child	.46	−.20
5	Parental disharmony	.47	.11
6	Parents' aspirations for child	.48	−.13
7	Child's IQ	.49	−.11
8	Mother's religiosity (frequency of church attendance)	.50	.09
9	Child's identification with father	.51	.12
10	Ethnicity of family	.51	−.09
11	Parental rejection of child	.52	.08
12	Parental punishment of child	.52	−.09
13	Child's confessing to parents	.52	−.07
14	Father's aggressiveness	.53	.06
15	Child's hours of watching television	.53	−.03
16	Mother's aggressiveness	.53	−.03
17	Father's occupational status	.53	.02

DISCUSSION

The above results indicate that television habits established by age 8–9 years influence boys' aggressive behavior at that time and at least through late adolescence. The more violent are the programs preferred by boys in the third grade, the more aggressive is their behavior both at that time and 10 years later. This relation between early television habits and later aggression prevails both for peer-rated aggression and for self-ratings of aggression.

Actually, these early television habits seem to be more influential than current viewing patterns since a preference for violent television in the thirteenth grade is not at all related to concurrent aggressive behavior, nor are early television habits related to later television habits.

It would be very difficult to explain these results as methodological artifacts. While the peer-rated aggression measure possesses demonstrated reliability (Walder et al., 1961), the thirteenth-grade scores represent more than the temporal reliability of the third-grade measure. Not only had 10 years of behavior intervened between the measurement periods, but the set of raters of each subject was substantially different as well. It is also unlikely that the findings were produced by a common method rather than content. Method refers to the form of the measuring device and the procedure for

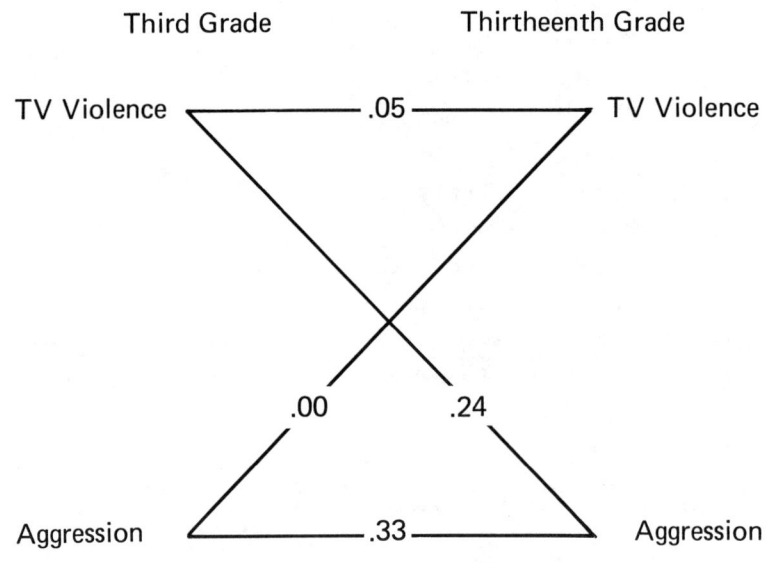

FIGURE 7.3.
THE PATH COEFFICIENTS FOR A PREFERENCE FOR
WATCHING VIOLENT TELEVISION AND PEER-RATED AGGRESSION

obtaining and calculating the score; content refers to what one intends to measure. Feshbach (1970), for example, warned that the

> predictive utility of sociometric, projective, and inventory measures is limited by the substantial method variance yielded by each procedure, and it is to the aggression criterion, the weaker are the relationships obtained [p. 181].

The peer-rated aggression measure employed in this study should not be susceptible to such criticism as it has been extensively validated over a 10-year period using a variety of techniques ranging from Campbell and Fiske's (1959) multitrait, multi-method technique to factor analysis. Peer-rated aggression scores agree closely with teacher ratings, clinical referrals, and overt behavior measured by such devices as the Iowa Aggression Machine (Williams, Meyerson, Eron, & Semler, 1967).

The ratings of the television programs for violence content also possess demonstrated reliability, as noted above, and were in close agreement with ratings made by at least two other groups (Feshbach & Singer, 1971; Greenberg & Gordon, 1970).

While only preferences for violent television were measured in both third and thirteenth grades, it is reasonable to assume that a child's preference for a television program is very highly correlated with the length of time that he attends to that program. The report of television preference in the third grade was made by the mother who probably was strongly influenced by her child's actual viewing habits, especially since the question regarding television was asked immediately following the question concerning the length of time the child watched television. Hence, it seems fair to conclude that a preference for violent television is indicative of viewing violent television by the child, particularly in the third grade. Furthermore, since the programs mentioned were the preferred ones, not only is it likely that they watched these programs regularly but that they also attended to the programs when they watched them. This would be a necessary condition for most theoretical explanations of a violence effect. While minor variations between preferences and watching certainly must have occurred, it is difficult to see how such variations could have enhanced our results.

These findings of a direct positive relation between the viewing of television violence and aggressive behavior on the part of the viewer corroborate in a long-term field study what has already been demonstrated as a short-term effect in the laboratory (Bandura et al., 1961, 1963b; Berkowitz, 1964; Berkowitz & Rawlings, 1963). Because the latter are manipulative studies in which systematically varied treatments were administered to randomly selected subjects under controlled conditions, statements about cause and effect relations based on their findings can be made with more confidence perhaps than those based on findings of field studies. In such studies, many uncontrolled variables are unaccounted for, and observation and measurement cannot be as precise. We feel that our findings relating television violence and aggressive behavior over a 10-year period strengthen the conviction that this is indeed a real relation. The causal direction indicated for the relation is that viewing violence regularly on television at age 8 leads to more aggressive behavior on the part of the viewer at that time and also in subsequent years than does viewing nonviolent programs. Thus, the significance of the laboratory studies is extended to indicate that the influence of television violence is not confined to short-term effects.

The laboratory studies of Bandura (Bandura, 1965; Bandura et al., 1961, 1963a, 1963b) furnish a theoretical model to account for these results. Bandura and his associates have demonstrated that aggressive behaviors new to the subject's repertoire of responses, as well as those already well established in his repertoire, can be evoked by observation of models performing such aggressive behaviors. The fact that the model does not get punished for the aggressive behaviors he develops serves to lower whatever inhibitions subjects have against the expression of similar behaviors. The likelihood of performance of the observed aggressive behaviors is stronger when the model is rewarded for his aggressive behavior (Bandura, 1965). It is not unusual on the more violent television programs for central characters to obtain desirable goals by violent tactics. Continued exposure to such models probably strengthens the conviction that these behaviors are permissible, and observation of acquisition of desired goals by aggressive behaviors increases the probability of performance of these behaviors by the observer. It is interesting in this regard that the more the subjects watch television at age 19 and the more violent the programs they prefer, the more likely are they to believe that situations depicted on television crime stories and westerns are realistic representations of life ($r = .28$ between judged realism of television programs and number of hours television is watched; and .36 between judged realism and television violence). Thus, subjects who watch television for many hours and prefer violent programs do not consider these aggressive behaviors as deviant but as appropriate ways of solving real-life problems.

The lack of an effect of television violence on girls also corroborates the Bandura laboratory studies which have consistently found that boys perform significantly more imitative aggression than girls (Bandura et al., 1961, 1963b). Why this is so probably has to do with the differential socialization of boys and girls in regard to aggression. Very early in life, girls learn that physical aggression is an undesirable behavior for girls, and so they acquire other behaviors more suitable to expectations for girls. Since they do not learn physical aggression as a response to instigation, they are rarely either rewarded or punished for such behavior and thus are not responsive to aggressive cues in the environment. Bandura (1965) has shown that when girls are positively reinforced for imitating aggressive behavior, they significantly increase such behavior and respond in a manner more similar to boys who are reinforced for the same behaviors. The results of Hokanson and Edelman (1966) would support this contention that lowered aggression levels in females are a function of lack of reinforcement for aggressive behavior. They found that females did not demonstrate the quickened reduction of physiological arousal after the opportunity to counteraggress against a confederate of the experimenter who had aggressed against them. However, such quickened reduction of heart rate and blood pressure to basal levels was routinely seen in male subjects. Finally, the frequency of occurrence of violently aggressive females shown on television is somewhat low. Hence, the female viewer is less likely to encounter an aggressive model to imitate.

It is interesting that the girls in the present sample had significantly higher masculinity scores on the MMPI. This suggests that in the past they had been reinforced for emitting aggressive (masculine) behaviors and were thus sensitive to aggression-arousing cues in the environment in the same way that boys are.

Regardless of the theoretical explanation of the results, however, the data support the concept of a critical developmental period in which the child is susceptible to the influence of violent television. His preference for violent television at ages 8 and 9 influenced his current aggressiveness and his aggressiveness 10 years later, but by age 19 his current preferences were unrelated to his aggressiveness. From this one might surmise that the role of imitation in the formation of the child's personality decreases drastically between ages 9 and 19.

One must compare the results of the current study with the somewhat different recent findings of Feshbach and Singer (1971). In a bold attempt to compromise between laboratory manipulation and a field setting, they provided findings which would indicate that the viewing of aggressive programs on television leads to a diminution of aggressive behavior on the part of some boys. Feshbach and Singer regulated the amount of television aggression viewed by their subjects over a six-week period by prescribing an aggressive or nonaggressive diet of television programs to two groups of subjects. The subjects were boys enrolled in residential private schools and homes for the underprivileged. The subjects watched television in groups of 10–18 boys at set times in specified locations. In two of the schools, participation by the subjects was compulsory. There was, of course, no voluntary choice of television programs. There are indications that at least initially this lack of preference was resented by boys assigned to the nonviolent diet since it meant they could not watch their favorite programs. In a few cases, the experimenters, in order to retain the cooperation of the subjects, permitted the boys in the nonaggressive group to watch one of the aggressive programs. Although all subjects were given the same cover story, some guessed the real purpose. Feshbach and Singer found that, of the boys around 13 years old, those who were exposed to the aggressive television diet decreased in manifestations of aggression, while the control subjects increased in aggression. Feshbach and Singer's limited and special sample, their subjects' ages, and their methodology all introduce factors sufficient to explain the discrepancy between their results and ours.

Actually the research of Feshbach and Singer addressed itself to a different question than did the present research which is more concerned with the long-range effects of viewing television violence and with the consideration of more pervasive dispositions. In this regard, it is of interest that Feshbach and Singer used the peer rating measure which we have developed for our studies (Walder et al., 1961) in order to assess pre-experimental aggression levels of their subjects and thereby separate them into high-aggressive and low-aggressive subsamples. They found:

> Regardless of experimental group, boys who score high on the peer aggression nomination measure display about twice as much aggressive behavior towards peers as boys who score low on the peer nomination measure [Feshbach & Singer, 1971, p. 91].

Thus, any manipulation that changes the peer nomination score would indeed have powerful effects, and we have demonstrated that it is this measure which is affected by television preference. While six weeks of violent television might be expected to stimulate more aggressive behaviors, it could not be expected to have the effect on the development of aggressive habits that 5–10 years of viewing violence might have.

The weight of evidence from this study, when coupled with previous laboratory studies, supports the theory that during a critical period in a boy's development regular viewing and liking of violent television lead to the formation of a more aggressive life style.

SUMMARY AND CONCLUSIONS

Among the results of a large-scale survey study of aggressive behavior in third-grade school children had been the finding that children at that age who preferred violent television programs were more aggressive in school as rated by peers than children who preferred less violent programs. In a 10-year follow-up study, 427 of the original 875 subjects, including 211 males and 216 females, were interviewed as to their television habits. They again rated their peers on aggressive behavior as well as responding to questions concerned with variables not treated extensively in the current report. It was found that the violence of programs preferred by the male subjects in Grade 3 were even more strongly related to aggression 10 years later. By the use of cross-lagged correlations, partial correlations, and multiple regression, it was demonstrated that there is a probable causative influence of watching violent television programs in early formative years on later aggression. Of course, it is not claimed that television violence is the only cause of aggressive behavior since a number of other variables are also related to aggression, including one in addition to the more than 20 variables we have reported on here, which could conceivably have had an influence over the 10 years covered by this logitudinal design. However, the effect of television violence on aggression is relatively independent of these other factors which we studied, including IQ, social status, mobility aspirations, religious practice, ethnicity, and parental disharmony.

Notes

1. This research was supported by Grant M1726 from the National Institute of Mental Health and Contract No. HSM 42-70-60 from the Surgeon General's Scientific Advisory Committee on Television and Social Behavior. Thanks are also due to the New York State Department of Mental Hygiene for their support and to Anne Karabin, Marjorie Kline, Ann McAleer, Victor Pompa, and Ann Yeager, who served as research assistants.
2. Requests for reprints should be sent to Leonard D. Eron, Department of Psychology, University of Illinois, Box 4348, Chicago, Illinois 60680.
3. The authors are indebted to John M. Neale, State University of New York at Stony Brook, for this path analysis of our data and to David Kenny, Northwestern University, for suggestions regarding interpretation of the cross-lagged correlations.

References

Bailyn, L. Mass media and children: A study of exposure habits and cognitive effects. *Psychological Monographs*, 1959, 73 (1, Whole No. 471).

Baker, R. K., & Ball, S. J. *Violence and the media.* Washington, D.C.: United States Government Printing Office, 1969.

Bandura, A. Influence of models' reinforcement contingencies on the acquisition of imitative responses. *Journal of Personality and Social Psychology*, 1965, 1, 589–95.

Bandura, A., Ross D., & Ross, S. A. Transmission of aggression through imitation of aggressive models. *Journal of Abnormal and Social Psychology*, 1961, 63, 575–82.

Bandura, A., Ross, D., & Ross, S. A. Imitation of film mediated aggressive models. *Journal of Abnormal and Social Psychology*, 1963, 66, 3–11. (a)

Bandura, A., Ross, D., & Ross, S. A. Vicarious reinforcement and imitative learning. *Journal of Abnormal and Social Psychology*, 1963, 67, 601–607. (b)

Berkowitz, L. Aggressive cues in aggressive behavior and hostility catharsis. *Psychological Review*, 1964, 71, 104–22.

Berkowitz, L., Corwin, R., & Heironimus, M. Film violence and subsequent aggressive tendencies. *Public Opinion Quarterly*, 1963, 27, 217–29.

Berkowitz, L., & Rawlings, E. Effects of film violence on inhibition against subsequent aggression. *Journal of Abnormal and Social Psychology*, 1963, 66, 405–12.

Campbell, D. T., & Fiske, D. W. Convergent and discriminant validation by the multitrait-multimethod matrix. *Psychological Bulletin*, 1959, 56, 81–105.

Darlington, R. D. Multiple regression in psychological research and practice. *Psychological Bulletin*, 1968, 69, 161–82.

Eron, L. D. Relationship of television viewing habits and aggressive behavior in children. *Journal of Abnormal and Social Psychology*, 1963, 67, 193–96.

Eron, L. D., Walder, L. O., & Lefkowitz, M. M. *Learning of aggression in children.* Boston: Little, Brown, 1971.

Feshbach, S. Aggression. In P. H. Mussen (Ed.) *Carmichael's manual of child psychology.* 3rd ed. Vol. 2. New York: Wiley, 1970.

Feshbach, S., & Singer, R. D. *Television and aggression.* San Francisco: Jossey-Bass, 1971.

Greenberg, B. S., & Gordon., T. F. *Critics and public perceptions of violence in TV programs.* East Lansing: Michigan State University, 1970.

Hartup, W. W., & Yonas, A. Developmental psychology, In P. H. Mussen & M. R. Rosenzweig (Eds.), *Annual review of psychology*, 1971, 22, 337–92.

Heise, D. R. Causal inference from panel data. In E. Borgatta & G. W. Bohrnstedt (Eds.), *Sociological methodology.* San Francisco: Jossey-Bass, 1970.

Hokanson, J. E., & Edelman, R. Effects of three social responses on vascular processes. *Journal of Personality and Social Psychology*, 1966, 3, 442–47.

Kenny, D. A. Cross-lagged and synchronous common factors in panel data. In A. Goldberger & O. D. Duncan (Eds.), *Structural equation models.* New York: Seminar Press, in press.

Rozelle, R. M., & Campbell, D. T. More plausible rival hypotheses in the cross-lagged panel correlation technique. *Psychological Bulletin*, 1969, 71, 74–80.

Schramm, W., Lyle, J., & Parker, E. B. *Television in the lives of our children.* Stanford: Stanford University Press, 1961.

Walder, L. O., Abelson, R. P., Eron, L. D., Banta, T. J., & Laulicht, J. H. Development of a peer-rating measure of aggression. *Psychological Reports*, 1961, 9, 497–556 (*Monograph Supplement*, 4-49).

Williams, J. F., Meyerson, L. J., Eron, L. D., & Semler, I. J. Peer rated aggression and aggressive responses elicited in an experimental situation. *Child Development*, 1967, 38, 181–90.

8

Can Violence Be Predicted?

Ernst A. Wenk, James O. Robison, and Gerald W. Smith

Reprinted from *Crime and Delinquency* (October 1972) pp. 393–402 by permission of the author and publisher, National Council on Crime and Delinquency.

This study was supported by ACORN grant NI-095 from the National Institute of Law Enforcement and Criminal Justice, LEAA, to the NCCD Research Center. Part of this work was supported by General Research Support Grant 1 SOL RR-05693-01 from the National Institute of Health to the NCCD Research Center. A more detailed presentation of the study will be issued through LEAA as a monograph entitled "Assaultive Youth: An Exploratory Study of the Assaultive Experience and Assaultive Potential."

The prediction of violence in offender populations has long been a dream of correctional decision-makers. The possibility of identifying those individuals who will engage in violent behavior in the future offers the prospect of treatment interventions to reduce such violence. Using elaborate case histories, current measures of mental and emotional functioning, and professional prognoses for a sample of 4,146 California Youth Authority wards, the present study sought to develop a classification device for estimating assaultive potential with sufficient accuracy to be useful in correctional program decisions. Simple classification procedures and multivariate approaches failed to yield an operationally practical prediction instrument that would warrent implementation in actual preventive or correctional practice. Much of the violent behavior we would wish to predict will probably never come to our attention and the part that does will be far from a representative sample. The prediction equations themselves contain the seed of self-fulfilling prophecy.

A large proportion of the public is alarmed about criminal violence. This alarm is commonly expressed as fear for one's own physical safety. Many are particularly apprehensive about danger in the streets and see the stranger as a menace.[1] They usually stay out of "dangerous areas" and sometimes purchase weapons with which to defend their homes and families. What many do not realize is that both of these responses are likely to elevate the overall level of public danger: as public traffic in an area diminishes, opportunities for victimizing those who remain may increase; and the chance of accidental injury, posed by the presence of a weapon in the home, may surpass the likelihood of deliberate injury by an intruder.

But citizens do not seem as concerned about the probability of personal injury as they are about the possibility of injury from a specific source: the stranger. General statistics showing the low probability of becoming a victim of homicide or physical assault do not appear to alleviate their concern, and comparative statistics showing that violence is most likely to be unleashed by a relative or personal acquaintance of the victim appear unlikely to alter their defense tactics. While some of the threat is perceived as coming from minority group members—political (e.g., "militant") and cultural (e.g., "hippie") as well as ethnic minorities—a great deal of suspicion is aimed toward those already adjudicated as criminal. Consequently, in recent years correctional agencies have been exposed to increasing pressure to "do something" about violent offenders.

In order to "do something" through treatment and intervention measures, it is first necessary to know to whom these measures are to be applied. Assuming that an effective and appropriate measure were available (a most unwarranted assumption[2]), the first move would be to identify a population of violent individuals—that is, individuals who will engage in violent behavior in the future.

PREDICTION: THE VIOLENT OFFENDER

There is little doubt that the known offender in general and the known violent offender in particular are more likely than members of the public at large to commit an assaultive act. Still, there has been no successful attempt to identify, within either of the offender groups, a subclass whose members have a greater-than-even chance of engaging again in an assaultive act. The best prediction available today, for even the most refined set of offenders, is that any particular member of that set *will not* become violent. Even so, since crimes of personal violence have such grave consequences for their victims, justification is often made for identifying—and extending special attention or treatment to—all members of a class with higher-than-average violence potential (for example, a class 10 per cent of whose members are likely to engage in serious violent acts during the period of official commitment or opportunity for intervention). Let us illustrate with two existing examples:

In 1965 the California Department of Corrections' Research Division developed a violence prediction scale for its population which employed, as predictor items, commitment offense, number of prior commitments, opiate use, age, length of imprisonment, and institution of release.[3] The result was the identification of a class of offenders (the most violent class isolated), 14 per cent of whom could be expected to violate parole by a violent or potentially violent discovered act. This likelihood was nearly three times as great as that for parolees in general, whose violence probability, by the same criterion, was only 5 per cent.

If a perfect correction intervention method were developed and applied to the members of the violence-prone class, all acts of violence by this class could be prevented. However, since the violence potential for the class is already low (14 per cent), 86 per cent of its members could be expected to refrain from violence without the special treatment, although the entire group must be exposed to it at a considerable treatment cost. Further, since this class is such a small part of the parole population (less than 3 per cent in this example), only 8 percent of total violence on parole would be prevented by its isolation and special treatment—leaving 92 per cent of violent parolee acts occurring as usual. If the treatment were less than entirely successful the violence reduction would be even less.

Our second example deals with the application of violence history classification to screening decisions by the California Department of Corrections' Parole and Community Services Division. All parolees released to supervision are classified into one of six categories according to past aggressive behavior. The categories range from the most serious, Aggressive Category No. 1, whose members have committed one or more acts of major violence (murder, assault with a deadly weapon, etc.), to the lowest level, Aggressive Category No. 6, consisting of parolees with no recorded history of aggression. The classification procedure involved both actual offender histories and psychiatric reports assessing violence potential.

The usefulness of this classification procedure can be examined by analyzing the effectiveness of decisions based on it in a correctional setting. Since the inception in 1965 of the parole division's Work Unit Program (a reduced-caseload, intensive-supervision operation), parolees in the two most aggressive categories were placed in Work Unit supervision instead of large-caseload or "conventional" supervision. For some period after their release from prison to parole, the men were required to receive "special" supervision—the highest of three intensity levels (or contact frequencies) in Work Unit parole. A modification was made late in 1967 which permitted the assignment of some of these cases to the conventional program. It then became possible to compare the two methods (see Table 8.1) and to assess the efficiency of the costly Work Unit intervention with violent offenders.

The findings presented in Table 8.1 indicate that the special precautions taken for identifying and handling the violent offender are unwarranted, given the actual level of danger. They can be justified only as token steps to alleviate fears about the possible occurrence of violence. One in every five parolees (1,630 out of 7,712) was assigned to the Potentially Aggressive categories (AC 1–2), and yet the rate of crimes involving actual violence for

Table 8.1.
One-Year Follow-Up of Returns to Prison for Violent Offenses Committed by Parolees Released Between January 1968 and June 1969

| Outcome | Type of Parole Supervision | | | |
| | Work Unit | | Conventional | |
Convicted and returned to prison for:	Aggressive (AC 1-2)	Less aggressive (AC 3-6)	Aggressive (AC 1-2)	Less aggressive (AC 3-6)
New crime involving actual violence*	0.3%	0.4%	0.4%	0.2%
New crime involving possible violence**	0.8%	0.4%	1.8%	1.6%
Number released	1,174	2,682	456	3,400

*Actual violence includes murder, manslaughter, assaults, rape, and kidnapping.
**Possible violence includes robbery, lewd and lascivious conduct, and escape.

this group was 3.1 per thousand cases (5/1,630), compared to 2.8 per thousand (17/6,082) among the Less Aggressive categories.

Our familiarity with the findings on past efforts at violence prediction left us little enthusiasm for developing a device that could have practical utility for correctional decision-makers. Nevertheless, many things convinced us of the importance of a contemporary study that could link its findings to their immediate social—and even political—implications. Public concern about the issue, the evident interest of officials and administrators in problems of offender classification (e.g., preventive detention), and the apparent belief of many that such practices are helpful or necessary and that instruments for effective prediction can eventually be perfected were all indications of the need for the study. A further incentive was the availability of a data pool[4] particularly suited to such an exercise by size of sample, character of population, and comprehensiveness of stored case information.

THE PRESENT STUDY—YOUTH AND VIOLENCE

In California, the most serious juvenile offenders are committed to the Department of the Youth Authority. The majority of this department's wards are maintained in the community under parole supervision (about 15,000 wards are on parole during any given year) and are therefore exposed to opportunities for violent crime. Youth Authority wards have both a proportionately higher recidivism rate and more violence recidivism than the Department of Corrections' adult parolees. The contribution of Youth Authority wards to total new crimes of violence in California is relatively small; however, with only a slightly larger population than adult parolees, Youth Authority wards account for twice as many new violent crimes on which Superior Court convictions are obtained in the state. Felony defendants who already had criminal status and were convicted and sentenced in Superior Court for willful homicide in 1967 numbered sixteen Department of Corrections parolees and thirty-three Youth Authority parolees; for robbery, 143 CDC parolees and 234 CYA parolees. Thus, while the vast majority of Youth Authority wards will not be convicted for a new crime of actual or threatened personal violence, the likelihood of such acts is still sufficiently high to make this population a prime target for the development and application of assault-proneness scales.

The study sample consisted of 4,146 California Youth Authority wards admitted to the Reception Guidance Center at Deuel Vocational Institution during 1964–65. The focus of the study was actual violence—primarily assault. Attention was given to the record of violence in each subject's career, including the offense for which he was incarcerated, past violent behavior not necessarily connected with the immediate offense, and violence during a fifteen-month exposure period on parole following his release from the in-

stitution. Extensive background information available on each subject included the following: (1) elaborate case histories containing possible predictor
items of violence proneness, such as past behavior (alcohol, drugs, suicide
attempts, homosexuality, escape, weapons-carrying) and past or present
diagnosed clinical conditions (psychosis, neurosis, brain damage, personality
trait disturbance, personality pattern disturbance); (2) current measures of
mental and emotional functioning (intelligence, maturity level, grade
achievement, MMPI, CPI); and (3) prognostic judgments (counselor's ratings
of academic and vocational potential, plus their recommendations for type of
training.

Using this information we hoped to determine whether it was possible to
construct a device for assessing potential assaultiveness with sufficient accuracy for program decisions.

In the sample of 4,146 wards, 250 or 6 per cent had a violent commitment
offense and 104 or 2.5 per cent were involved in a violent violation during the
fifteen-month period after their release. Our task was to identify as many of
the 104 violators as possible while misclassifying as "violent" a minimum of
the remaining cases. We began by developing subgroup classifications of
offenders. To control for sampling variability and to insure that findings
would have some utility for correctional decisions, subgroups were disregarded unless they contained at least one hundred subjects (about 2.5 per cent
of the population) or unless they could reasonably be merged with an adjacent category to exceed one hundred in total. A search was then conducted to
determine which groups had a favorable outcome rate notably different from
the entire study sample rate of 61.1 per cent. The thresholds applied were "at
or below 50 per cent favorable outcome" and "at or above 70 per cent favorable outcome." Only three sizable subgroups out of sixty (see Table 8.2) feel
outside these boundaries.

Thus, the recidivism rate for offenders who have already been admitted to
CYA institutions on several occasions and for those with more than a mild

TABLE 8.2.
SIZABLE AND DEVIATING OUTCOME SUBGROUPS*

Subgroup	No. of Cases	Favorable Outcome
Violent commitment offense	250	70.4%
Fourth or higher admission to CYA	351	46.5%
Moderate to serious opiate involvement	132	42.4%

*Subgroups numbering greater than one hundred, with favorable outcome 50 per cent or less, 70
per cent or more.

history of opiate usage was substantially higher than for the offender population in general. Neither of these groups contained a higher-than-average
proportion of members with violent commitment offenses—4.8 per cent for
the multiple admission group and 3.8 per cent for the opiate group, compared to 6.0 per cent overall. Violent recidivism was low for these groups—
4.8 per cent and 2.3 per cent, respectively; however, the rate of violent
recidivism for the multiple offender group was still twice as high as that for
the overall population (2.4 per cent).

We found that while recidivism among cases with a violent admission
offense was lower than average, this recidivism was more likely to be violent
when it occurred, and it accounted for 17.4 per cent of the violations for this
group, compared to 7.4 per cent overall. The rate of violent recidivism,
however, was 4.8 per cent—the same as the rate for the multiple recidivist
group. Further, since the total sample of offenders with violent commitment
offense numbered only 250, this group contributed a relatively small share to
the total violence on parole (twelve incidents out of 104). Thus, the odds
were about eight to one against a violent recidivist having had a violent
admission offense and about nineteen to one against a parolee with a violent
admission offense breaking parole by committing another violent offense.

Violent Recidivism

A second search was conducted within the sixty sub-groups to determine
which groups displayed a high proportion of violent offenses in their recidivism. For the full population, 7.4 percent of recidivism was violent, and all
sizable sub-groups in which the corresponding figure exceeded 10 per cent
were selected (see Table 8.3). Again, the convention of groups exceeding one
hundred was applied.

The multiple-recidivist and violent commitment subgroups have been discussed earlier. The four remaining groups all have general recidivism rates
quite close to the average but, for each, a greater than usual proportion of
recidivism is through violence. More than 10 per cent of the recidivism of
Chicano offenders and offenders diagnosed as having severe alcohol problems
is violent, but for each of these groups the rate of violence on parole remains
below 5 per cent.

The class of offenders with the highest level of violent recidivism is composed of subjects who have been referred to psychiatrists for evaluation of
their violence potential upon or during their CYA incarceration. This group
does not have a higher-than-usual rate of general recidivism, but nearly one
in five (17.6 per cent) of the violations that do occur are violent. Nevertheless,
the rate of violent recidivism remains relatively low (6.2 per cent) and the
group contains only 257 subjects—just over 5 per cent of the study population.

TABLE 8.3.
SIZABLE SUBGROUPS FOR WHICH VIOLENCE EXCEEDED 10 PER CENT OF SUBGROUP RECIDIVISM

Subgroup	Favorable Outcome	% of Cases in Group	% of Total Violations	Violent Recidivism Violent Commitment Offense	Total in Group
Psychiatric referral for evaluation of violence potential	62.3%	6.2%	17.6%	31.1%	257
History of actual violence	61.2%	5.2%	14.9%	20.3%	1,006
Fourth or higher admission to CYA	46.5%	4.8%	10.2%	4.8%	351
Violent commitment offense	70.4%	4.8%	17.4%	100.0%	250
Mexican-American	61.1%	4.3%	12.1%	9.5%	772
Severe alcohol problem	58.5%	4.0%	11.2%	11.7%	624
Entire sample	61.1%	2.4%	7.4%	6.0%	4,146

130

The "history of actual violence" category is of particular interest for several reasons. First, it is at least as capable of discriminating violence on parole as "violent admission offense" and is applicable to a relatively high proportion of the total admission population.[5] Second, relatively few (20.3 per cent) of the subjects in this category were admitted on an offense of labeled violence. Since this classification is based on actual behavior rather than on legal definitions, it should not be surprising that discrimination is improved with regard to future violence. But is a history of actual violence a useful indicator of potential violence on parole? Examine Table 8.4.

Since the first two categories have similar and low levels of violent recidivism, it appears reasonable to combine them into a single category containing 3,140 cases with fifty-two violent recidivists—a rate of 1.6 per cent. The category of offenders with a history of actual violence contains one-fourth of the total population and half the subjects who later became violent. This one category has a violent recidivism rate three times greater than that of the remainder. However, if the interest is in using this information for programming decisions to reduce the danger of violence, the practical consequences of this information are trivial. If a decision-maker were to consider all of the cases in the "history of actual violence" category as potentially violent and submit them to special programming, he would be sounding a false alarm nineteen times in twenty and wasting 95 per cent of the resources expanded in that endeavor. Further, there is no other form of simple classification available thus far that would enable him to improve on this level of efficiency.

The decision-maker might, nevertheless, apply the information in another fashion and determine that he will expend no energy on violence-preventive measures with regard to members of the two categories with no violent history, in which case he could ignore three-quarters of the population and miss only sixteen cases per thousand. He will notice, however, that this

TABLE 8.4.
VIOLENCE HISTORY AND TYPE OF RECIDIVISM

	Simple Recidivism	Violent Recidivism	Violent Recidivism	Total Cases
No history of violence	40.2%	1.8%	42	2,386
Aggressive crime, but no actual violence	34.7%	1.3%	10	754
History of actual violence	38.8%	5.2%	52	1,006
Total	38.9%	2.4%	104	4,146

informed decision is hardly more effective than an uninformed decision, owing to the general rarity of violence on parole. He would deal with the entire population in this way and miss 50 per cent more but still make only twenty-four errors per thousand cases. The quest for an operationally practical predictor of violence from simple classification appears to be futile.

MULTIVARIATE APPROACHES TO VIOLENCE PREDICTION

Several procedures were employed on the present study sample in the attempt to develop regression equations for application to violence prediction. William Meredith, Department of Psychology, University of California at Berkeley, and Peter Griffin, Department of Mathematics, Sacramento State College, conducted the statistical analyses.[6] The results of these analyses were similar to our previous efforts, although their interpretations were quite different. Griffin concluded:

Considering the rarity of the phenomenon (only one in forty exhibited subsequent violence), it is difficult to imagine that, even with the most refined techniques, one could do much better than, say, to double the best rates obtained here. The utility of such an optimal rate would seem highly limited for selection for remedial programs, etc. Of a group of 2,073 with fifty-two expected to be violent, if those with the fifty-two highest violence potentials, according to our predictive instrument, were separated for special treatment, we could expect to have correctly identified only eight of them while wasting treatment on forty-four false positives. In addition, more than 80 per cent of the actually violent would escape the sieve. This weakness is inherent in the limitations of the quantifiable variables we have available.

Using analytic procedures that were basically similar to those used by Griffin although varying in many details, Meredith arrived at markedly different conclusions:

It is apparent that this set of data offers numerous encouraging leads on the make-up and identification of potentially violent parolees. These results strongly suggest that a useful violence index could be constructed—although a great deal more research is obviously necessary.

He suggested that more accurate results might be yielded if different predictive equations were developed for each ethnic group and if multiple analyses of variance were applied, using the following four classes: violent history—violent parole offense; violent history—no violent parole offense; nonviolent history—violent parole offense; and nonviolent history—no violent parole offense. By such means, Meredith said, "it appears to be feasible to develop, in this sample at least, an index of violence-proneness that would correctly identify over 50 per cent of those individuals violating parole by violent offenses at the cost of misclassifying no more than 10 per cent of those not returned for violent offense.

But let us examine, for a moment, what the situation would be if this promise could be fulfilled:

50% of 104 violent offenders = 52

10% of 4,042 nonviolent offenders = 404

The ratio of false positives to true positives, although lower than any actually attained, remains a discouraging eight to one, and meanwhile, half of the true positives would continue to be ignored.

Griffin's rejection and Meredith's endorsement contain no reference to program applications other than "useful" (Meredith) and "special treatment" (Griffin). The policy question, if we may oversimplify it, is this: What represents an acceptable trade-off between the values of public safety and individual liberty? Answers to this question presuppose the existence of a concrete proposal that can be examined to determine whether and to what extent, if the plan is accepted, the realization of one value will entail the sacrifice of the other.

DISCUSSION

The present state of the art holds little promise for the development of a prediction instrument that would warrant implementation in actual preventive or correctional programs. The problem is fundamentally related to the nature of the phenomenon we studied: *reported violence*. A detailed examination of the 104 incidents of violence indicated that violence typically erupts out of a crisis. In these circumstances the labeled assailant may have been blamed for not avoiding the situation altogether, for contributing to the provocation within it, or for either losing control or asserting the control that became the violent act. Some of these incidents resulted in no injury or minimal injury to the labeled victim, and are recorded only because something transpired to bring official notice to the event, requiring its classification and acknowledgement.

Behavioral events of this type are not rare; they are probably quite common. Instead, it is the *certification* of the events that is rare, and this perhaps provides us with a major clue to the problems of prediction, as well as an alternate explanation of why we are capable at all of predicting better than "chance." The reason may lie in what the police choose to do about the event and how they choose to characterize it when it is brought to their attention. If the event is not clearly classifiable as violent, some part of their determination (as well as that of other relevant parties) is likely to be based on the prior record and reputation of the offender. Such processes will affect decisions about whether the subject is released, whether charges brought are subsequently dismissed, whether the violation will be noted and processed by the Youth Authority, whether parole revocation will result, and consequently whether the event will become available as a datum for research on violence prediction.

The problem, then, is this: Most of the violent behavior we would wish to predict probably never comes to our attention, and the part that does is far from a representative sample. The prediction equations contain the seed of self-fulfilling prophecy: those who have been noticed before will be noticed again. If this is so, the question of why "prediction" hasn't succeeded remains unanswered. It is relevant to raise questions about the reliability as well as the validity of the criteria, since the decisions involved vary by characteristics of persons other than the offender. The same kinds of influences also reduce the reliability of many of the predictor variables we employed, compounding the general problem.

As we approach incidents of greater gravity, such as those resulting in major injury or death, the reliability of the criteria changes. There is likely to be less variance in the handling of such events, and we can be more confident that they will be *reliably* brought to our attention.[7] These are the events to which everyone feels obligated to respond, and it is these events that we are most concerned with being able to predict and prevent. Twenty-six of our 104 cases involved in violence on parole inflicted major injury or death.

However, these twenty-six "violents" represent *only six-tenths of one per cent of the 4,146-member study sample.* The classification of events on the basis of the magnitude of their consequences may not be a true indicator of an individual's violence-proneness. The severity of injury resulting from a given interaction is only partly determined by the assailant's intent or factors within his control, and innumerable factors may make the difference between no injury and death, or between minor and major injury.

A still deeper question must also be asked: Once the potentially violent cases have been identified successfully, what then? Currently, violence prevention and treatment of known violent persons remain rather primitive, consisting largely of more secure confinement and the administration of calming drugs or counseling. Do such means accomplish anything besides a temporary reduction in the offender's social nuisance level? The adjustment centers within the California adult prisons were instituted, among other reasons, to control and reduce violence among prisoners, but today it is not certain whether they alleviate or exacerbate the problem. What are the available cures for "violence-proneness"?

Finally, we need to examine the important ethical problems that are a direct result of the present level of knowledge in identification of violence-prone individuals. Concern about violence will inevitably lead to the development of special treatment programs, but the majority of persons placed in such programs must be false positives—persons who would not commit the act which the program is designed to prevent. It must be acknowledged that involvement in a corrective program is a constraint on an individual as well as a possible help and that unnecessary constraint on human freedom should be avoided. Those who argue that treatment cannot harm the person who does not need it and those who would warp the definition of "need" are obviously ignorant of the effects of social stigma and of the difficulty of administering corrective interventions without social stigma as a result.

Confidence in the ability to predict violence serves to legitimatize intrusive types of social control. Our demonstration of the futility of such prediction should have consequences as great for the protection of individual liberty as a demonstration of the utility of violence prediction would have for the protection of society.

NOTES

1. "Public Attitudes toward Crime and Law Enforcement," in President's Commission on Law Enforcement and Administration of Justice, *Task Force Report: Crime and Its Impact—An Assessment* (Washington, D.C.: U. S. Government Printing Office, 1967: ch. 6.

2. James O. Robison and Gerald Smith, "The Effectiveness of Correctional Programs," *Crime and Delinquency*, January 1971, pp. 67–80.

3. "Predicting Violence Proneness on Parole," Crime Studies Section, California Department of Corrections Research Division, November 1965 (unpublished paper).

4. The authors are grateful to the Division of Research, California Youth Authority, for assistance in assembling the data base.

5. Because the temporal dimension is sacrificed in this classification, it is not possible to tell whether recency or distance in history is a relevant variable. However, considering the age of our subjects (mean age for total study population is 19.45 years, with a range of 16 to 25 years), this factor does not appear to be critical.

6. The statistical data and technical descriptions of the multivariate approaches have been omitted from the text of this article. This information is available in the LEAA Monograph, "Assaultive Youth."

7. The same probably holds true for one type of event that is ordinarily less violent—resisting arrest or battery on a police officer.

9

Recent Research on Overcontrolled and Undercontrolled Personality Patterns Among Violent Offenders[1]

Edwin I. Megargee

Reprinted from *Sociological Symposium* (Spring 1973), pp. 37–50 by permission of the author and publisher, Virginia Polytechnic Institute Sociological Symposium.

A dozen years ago, when the line of investigation to be discussed in this article was begun, violence was not a particularly respectable area for psychological research. Psychologists instead investigated the milder forms of aggressive behavior that could be studied rigorously in the laboratory without danger to subject or experimenter. Summarizing the results of such studies Megargee (1966: 1) wrote:

> The general formulation that has emerged from empirical studies of relatively mild aggression is that the overtly aggressive person has fewer controls and more need or instigation for aggression than does the overly nonaggressive person.
>
> The practical implications of this are clear: the way to discourage a person from acting aggressively is to build up his controls. Our prisons and reformatories typically base their programs upon this principle by instituting rewards for control and punishments for aggression. When an individual has demonstrated his controls by behaving in a nonaggressive fashion for a sufficiently long period, he is considered to be rehabilitated and is considered for release.

Clinical evidence, however, indicated that the principles derived from studies of mild aggression could not be safely extrapolated to explain all instances of individual violence. These observations suggested that more than one personality pattern might lead to violent behavior. After analyzing the psychological test results of several groups differing in assaultiveness, Megargee and Mendelsohn (1962: 437) speculated:

. . . that the extremely assaultive person is often a fairly mild-mannered, long suffering individual who buries his resentment under rigid but brittle controls. Under certain circumstances he may lash out and release all his aggression in one, often disastrous, act. Afterwards he reverts to his usual over-controlled defenses. Thus he may be more of a menace than the verbally aggressive, "Chip-on-the-shoulder" type who releases his aggression in small doses.

Two years later, Megargee (1964: i) expanded on this notion:

Extreme physical aggression, such as homicide, has frequently been regarded as a result of inadequate controls on the part of the offender. In this study, however, the writer proposes that physically aggressive people can be divided into two distinctly different types. The first type is termed Habitually Aggressive and consists of people who, because of particular family or social milieus, have failed to develop controls against the expression of aggression which are expected in our society. When they are frustrated or provoked they respond with aggression of an intensity proportional to the degree of provocation.

The other type is termed Chronically Overcontrolled because of their excessively rigid inhibitions against any form of expression of aggression. It is posited that in these people instigation to aggression accumulates over time through some form of temporal summation. If the chronically overcontrolled person ever does aggress, it is likely that he does so in an extreme fashion since (1) his instigation to aggression has had to reach a very high level to overcome his excessive inhibitions and (2) he has not learned socially acceptable or more moderate techniques of expressing aggression.

This paper will review studies designed to test these hypotheses and the development and validation of a psychological assessment instrument that appears to identify the overcontrolled type.

STUDIES INVESTIGATING THE OVERCONTROLLED–UNDERCONTROLLED TYPOLOGICAL DISTINCTION

Verification of the notion that overcontrolled as well as undercontrolled individuals might engage in violent behavior would have important implications for clinical practice as well as theory. As noted above, the treatment programs of most penal institutions were predicated on the assumption that the violent offender needs to develop more controls or inhibitions against aggressive behavior. Demonstration of the existence of an overcontrolled type would require some radical rethinking and provision for alternative treatment plans.

However, in the early 1960s this notion was supported only by clinical observations, case studies, and news reports, so it was first necessary to test the hypothesis empirically. From a purely scientific standpoint, the most cogent test would have been to take overcontrolled and undercontrolled individuals, expose them to extreme provocation, and then measure the violence that resulted. However, such an approach was impractical and unethical (as well as unsafe). Another straight forward approach would have been to select murderers with no previous histories of violence and demonstrate that on psychological tests they were assessed as more controlled than murderers with long records of antisocial behavior. However, that approach would have been circular, simply demonstrating the reliability of the original observations.

Therefore, as a first test of the hypothesis, it was decided to test a major prediction derived from the typology, one that on the face of it appeared so unlikely that its confirmation would provide strong evidence for the typology and against the prevailing notion that all violent offenders were undercontrolled sociopaths.

Megargee (1966) reasoned that if there is an overcontrolled type, characterized by massive defenses against the overt expression of aggression, then an extremely high level of instigation to aggression (anger, hostility, aggressive drive) would be required to overcome those defenses. If so, this high level of instigation would make it likely that the resulting act would be one of extreme violence, perhaps reaching homicidal proportions. However, for the undercontrolled type, no great instigation would be needed to overcome his minimal inhibitions against aggressive acting out. If he is mildly annoyed, he should respond with mild aggression, if moderately angered he should respond with moderate aggression, and if he is extremely provoked he should lash out with extreme aggression.

If Megargee's reasoning was correct, then a sample of extremely violent individuals should be composed of *both* undercontrolled and overcontrolled people. But moderately assaultive or mildly aggressive samples should contain only undercontrolled individuals, because the strong instigation needed to overcome the excessive inhibitions of the overcontrolled type should preclude a mild or moderate aggressive response.[2] If so, then a sample of extremely assaultive offenders should be assessed as *more* controlled and *less* hostile, *as a group*, than would samples of moderately or mildly aggressive offenders. This was the clearcut but rather paradoxical prediction tested in the first study.[3]

This hypothesis was tested by assessing the hostility and control of four groups of male juvenile delinquents. The first group consisted of nine delinquents detained in the Alameda County (California) Juvenile Hall for extremely assaultive offenses such as homicide, attempted murder and assault with a deadly weapon. The second group consisted of 21 moderately assaultive Ss detained for battery and gang fights. These two groups together constituted a population of all the seriously assaultive delinquents detained over a ten-month period. The third contrast group consisted of 20 boys detained for "incorrigibility," a group likely to be very verbally aggressive; the fourth consisted of 26 property offenders. Neither of the latter two groups were known to have committed any crimes of violence.

During the first ten days of detention, Juvenile Hall counselors rated the behavior of these boys, and staff psychologists administered a structured interview and an extensive battery of psychological tests. It was predicted that the extremely assaultive group would be lower, as a group, on measures of aggressiveness and higher on measures of control than the other groups in general and the moderately assaultive group in particular. In general, this proved to be the case; of the 28 observations made, 22 were in the predicted direction, with 14 receiving some measure of statistical support with p values ranging from .003 to .08. As predicted, the extremely assaultive group was found to have the highest proportion of first offenders, the best school attendance and conduct records, and to be assessed as the least aggressive and most cooperative and controlled by the unit counselors. Those interview and test measures that did differentiate the samples generally showed the extremely assaultive group to be the best socialized and least aggressive of the four. Given the rather gross nature of the independent and dependent variables, the involved chain of reasoning that led to this rather paradoxical prediction, the fact that the total pattern of the data was in the predicted direction, and the fact that there was no evidence for the contrary notion that assaultive delinquents are invariable undercontrolled, the results were interpreted as supporting the proposed typology (Megargee, 1966).

Further research was clearly needed, however, and this was soon forthcoming from other laboratories. Molof (1967) divided 4,344 California Youth Authority wards into three groups that were roughly comparable to Megargee's (1966) extremely assaultive, moderately assaultive, and nonviolent samples. The first consisted of boys convicted of homicide, assault or forcible rape; the second of boys convicted of battery or simple assault, and the third of boys convicted of nonviolent crimes. Comparing the three groups on 55 dependent variables, Molof found that the extremely assaultive group had more favorable family backgrounds and case histories indicative of better socialization. These findings were replicated on a new sample of 2,000 boys. Molof noted the similarity between his study and Megargee's (1966) and suggested that the overcontrolled-undercontrolled typology might account for his results.

Next, Blackburn (1968a, 1968b, 1969) performed a series of three studies testing the typology using assaultive individuals remanded for study to the Broadmoore Hospital at Crowthrone, Berkshire, England. In the first, he compared 38 extreme and 25 moderately assaultive patients on a number of MMPI scales and selected case history items. He concluded from his results:

The Extremely Assaultive (patients) were significantly more overcontrolled, introverted and conforming and less hostile than the Moderately Assaultives. The Extremely Assaultive group contained significantly fewer with a criminal record or a diagnosis of psychopathic disorder than the Moderately Assaultives, and in the majority of cases the offenses of the Extremely Assaultives involved individuals with whom they were acquainted in contrast to the Moderately Assaultives. The results support Megargee's hypothesis (Blackburn, 1968b:827).

In his next study, Blackburn (1968a) compared the incidence of homicidal aggression in paranoid and nonparanoid schizophrenic patients, reasoning, "Since extreme (i.e. homicidal) aggression appears to occur in individuals who are not characteristically aggressive (Megargee, 1966), it was predicted that such offenses would be more frequent among the non-paranoid schizophrenics." The reasoning that led to this prediction involved some assumptions that Megargee (1971) was reluctant to make, but Blackburn nevertheless obtained data in the predicted direction that approached statistical significance ($.05p < .10$). More direct support was obtained from Blackburn's (1968a: .302) finding of, ". . . a significant inverse relationship between extreme assaultiveness and persistent aggression (tetrachoric $= .56; p < .05$) indicating a tendency for those patients who have committed offenses of a homicidal nature to have no previous history of aggression."

In his most recent investigation, Blackburn (1969) performed a cluster analysis of the MMPI scores of all 56 male murderers admitted to the hospital over a 28 month period, a sample that comprised about one fourth of all the murderers in England and Wales who had not committed suicide as well. The cluster analysis showed four types, of which two appeared to be over-controlled and two undercontrolled.

> How far does this support Megargee's dual typology? As we have seen, Types 1 and 4 appear to correspond quite well to the overcontrolled and undercon-trolled types, and these account for more than two-fifths of the total. However, Types 3 and 2 could also be described in these terms. The most economic conclusion would appear to be that Megargee's typology is supported in that Types 1 and 3 combined, and Types 2 and 4 together represent the broad categories of overcontrolled and undercontrolled offenders, respectively (Black-burn, 1969:8).

The most recent and definitive study of the overcontrolled-undercontrolled typology is a doctoral dissertation recently completed by Dr. Howard Haven (1972). Since all of the studies completed thus far had supported the typology, Haven felt it was time to investigate the characteris-tics of the overcontrolled and undercontrolled types. Using the typology as an independent variable for the first time, Haven and the present investigator selected 20 overcontrolled and 20 undercontrolled youthful offenders at the

Federal Correction Institution, Tallahassee, Florida, (FCI) using a combination of offense descriptions and scores on the MMPI Overcontrolled Hostility *(O-H)* scale as criteria. (The derivation and validation of this scale will be described in the next section.)

For his study, Haven had access to data being collected by Megargee, Hokanson and Speilberger (1971) as part of a broad, logitudinal investigation of a cohort of over 1,400 consecutive admissions to the FCI.

In the first part of his dissertation, Haven used data from structured interviews to test the hypothesis that the overcontrolled *S*s would exhibit greater socialization and conformity throughout their overall life style. These interviews, which are administered to each entering inmate, were tape recorded and rated by two independent raters on over 250 five-point scales devised by the present investigator. Haven combined these discrete ratings into rationally constructed scales to assess five behavioral and attitudinal dimensions: (1) conservative attitudes, (2) achievement orientation, (3) aggressiveness, (4) authority conflict, and (5) poor socialization. He predicted the overcontrolled group would be significantly higher than the undercontrolled on scales 1 and 2 and significantly lower on scales 3, 4, and 5. These predictions were all confirmed with p values ranging from $< .0005$ to $< .00025$.

The second part of Haven's study investigated the developmental background of the two types. Turning again to the structured interview ratings, Haven constructed five more scales: (6) family cohesiveness, (7) nurturance, (8) adequacy of discipline, (9) mother's adequacy as a role model and (10) father's adequacy as a role model. He predicted that the overcontrolled group would be significantly higher on all five of these dimensions. This prediction was confirmed for scales 6, 7, 8, and 10 with p values ranging from $< .0005$ to $< .05$. For scale 9, mother's adequacy as a role model, the differences were in the predicted direction but failed to attain significance. In discussing this, Haven noted a strong tendency on the part of all the *S*s to describe their mothers in predominately favorable terms.

The accumulated quantitative evidence from these investigations all supported the hypothesis that overcontrolled as well as undercontrolled individuals may engage in extreme acts of violence.[4] We shall now turn to a series of studies deriving and validating a scale that appears to identify the overcontrolled individual.

DEVELOPMENT AND VALIDATION OF THE OVERCONTROLLED HOSTILITY SCALE *(O-H)*

The typological research reported above stemmed from Megargee's earlier efforts to predict individual violence from psychological tests. Over the years, a series of studies with the major personality tests, including the

California Psychological Inventory (CPI), the Minnesota Multiphasic Personality Inventory (MMPI), the Rorschach Inkblot Test, the Rosenzweig Picture-Frustration Study, and the Thematic Apperception Test (TAT), indicated that no available scale could be relied upon to distinguish assaultive from nonassaultive offenders, although a number could discriminate offenders from non-offenders (Megargee, 1964b, 1965b, 1966, 1967, 1970; Megargee & Cook, 1967; Megargee & Mendelsohn, 1962; Megargee & Menzies, 1971).

Therefore, an effort was made to derive a scale of assaultiveness by contrasting the MMPI protocols of violent criminals with those of nonviolent criminals and noncriminals. Cross-validation showed that this empirically derived scale was not a satisfactory measure of generalized assaultive tendencies. However, additional research indicated that it might well assess the dimension of overcontrolled hostility that, in its extreme form, could lead to crimes of violence (Megargee, 1971).

The original report of the derivation and validation of this scale (Megargee, Cook & Mendelsohn, 1967) included a number of converging bits of evidence that seemed to support this conclusion. First, the mean score of extremely assaultive offenders was significantly higher than those of moderately assaultive or nonviolent offenders; moreover, the extremely violent group had a bimodally distributed pattern of scores as one would expect if the two types were responding differently. Second, the item content of this empirically derived measure was surprisingly passive for a scale relating to assaultive tendencies.[5] Third, correlational data showed significant positive correlations with MMPI, CPI and Adjective Check List measures of control, and negative correlations with scales related to overt hostility and acting out. Fourth, a sample of 21 extremely assaultive Texas state prison inmates diagnosed as "overcontrolled" on the basis of rather sketchy case history data were found to have significantly higher scores than a sample of 24 extremely assaultive prisoners diagnosed as "undercontrolled" on the basis of extensive histories of antisocial behavior and violence ($p < .02$). Fifth, since women are more inhibited than men in their expression of physical aggression, it was predicted that a sample of 126 college women would obtain significantly higher scores than a sample of 100 college men. This hypothesis was confirmed ($p < .001$). On the basis of these data, the scale was christened the "Overcontrolled Hostility" scale *(O-H)* and published (Megargee, Cook & Mendelsohn, 1967).

Since then, several experiments have been performed testing the construct validity of the *O-H* scale. As noted above, Haven (1972) used the *O-H* scale to help select overcontrolled and undercontrolled offenders who were then found to differ predictably in their life style and developmental history.

White (1970) selected 30 youthful offenders with high *O-H* and 30 with low *O-H* scores and exposed them to an experimental procedure based on an adaptation of the Rosenzweig Picture-Frustration technique. As predicted, he found that the high *O-H* offenders emitted significantly more impunitive ($p < .001$) and significantly few extrapunitive ($p < .001$) responses.

White's findings were confirmed by Vanderbeck (1973) who placed 20 high, 20 medium and 20 low *O-H* youthful offenders into a complex experimental situation in which they were harassed while working on a simple matching task. Throughout the procedure, records were maintained of their autonomic response patterns and they periodically had an opportunity to indicate their feelings (angry, tense, or upset with themselves) and to deliver critical (extrapunitive), self-blaming (intropunitive), or impunitive messages to the experimenter. Vanderbeck predicted that the high *O-H* Ss would report feeling angry less often than would the medium or low *O-H* Ss. This prediction was confirmed ($p < .05$). He also predicted that the high *O-H* Ss would be least likely to deliver a critical message to the experimenter. The high *O-H* group did indeed deliver the fewest critical messages; it delivered significantly more impunitive messages than did either of the other two groups ($p < .05$). Vanderbeck concluded, "The results support the construct validity of high scores on the scale identifying the chronically overcontrolled personality who has very strong inhibitions against expressing angry feelings or aggressive behaviors.

White, McAdoo, & Megargee (in press) administered the 16 Personality Factor Questionnaire, Form C, to high and low *O-H* youthful offenders. This instrument was chosen since it is a factorially derived inventory that differs considerably from the MMPI. Significant differences in the predicted direction were found for each of the seven scales on which differences had been predicted with *p* values ranging from .002 to .01.

Efforts to relate the *O-H* scale to physiological or perceptual measures of behavior have not been successful. Vanderbeck (1973) failed to find any differences among his three groups on GSR, heart rate, or systolic or diastolic blood pressure. Wheeler (1971) presented violent and nonviolent pictorial stimuli to youthful offenders using a tachistoscope with exposure times ranging from the subliminal to suprathreshold. On the basis of perceptual defense theory, he had predicted that the mean difference in the recognition threshold between the violent and nonviolent stimuli would be greatest for his high *O-H* group. This proved to be the case, but although the means fell into the predicted pattern, the differences among them were not statistically reliable. Other studies have tested the concurrent validity of the *O-H* scale by comparing the mean scores of groups that should differ on this dimension. Megargee (1969) tested 20 members of a fundamentalist sect so adamantly opposed to violence that its members are not permitted to perform the civilian public service, such as hospital work, required of conscientious objectors but instead must go to prison. Their mean *O-H* score was significantly higher than that of a matched sample of 20 other Federal prisoners (p <.001) or the means of several samples of college students (p <.001). This provided convincing evidence that the *O-H* scale assessed extraordinary inhibition of aggressive tendencies. Dr. Carol Spencer of the California Youth Authority determined that the *O-H* scale reflected hostility as well when she found that a sample of 161 violent offenders had a mean *O-H* score significantly higher than a sample of 285 nonviolent offenders (p <.001).[6]

Table 9.1 shows the mean *O-H* scores of 12 male samples tested by Megargee and his colleagues. In general, these data suggest that extreme scores on the scale reflect a strong conflict between hostility and the inhibition of aggression. The resolution of this conflict may be an assaultive crime, a life style bordering on reaction formation, or, as other data suggest, a psychosis (Megargee, Cook & Mendelsohn, 1967). In any event, they are clinically significant.

Midrange *O-H* scores usually indicate either control or hostility. However, a midrange score does not rule out the possibility of overcontrolled hostility. Fisher (1970) compared the mean *O-H* scores of three groups of offenders diagnosed as overcontrolled violent, undercontrolled violent and nonviolent on the basis of extensive case history data. Although the mean score of the overcontrolled sample exceeded that of the other two, the difference was not statistically significant and the mean score itself was not particularly high (k = 14.52). Fisher (1970) attributed his results to a serious confounding of race and offense category, a problem that is especially acute since blacks' *O-H* scores are significantly higher than whites' (Haven, 1969). Nevertheless, Fisher's study points up the need for caution in interpreting midrange scores.

Low scores on *O-H* suggest that an individual is neither overly hostile nor overly controlled. This point should be emphasized since some investigators have erroneously treated the scale as if it were bimodal, with high scores reflecting overcontrol and low scores undercontrol. However, it can be seen that undercontrolled violent individuals typically score in the midrange.

How useful is the *O-H* scale? Its primary value to the clinician or researcher is that it appears to assess a construct, overcontrolled hostility, that is not yet assessed by other personality assessment devices. The diagnostician has little difficulty identifying the undercontrolled assaultive type because by definition they have accumulated an extensive record of aggressive behavior and antisocial acting out. But what about the person with no history of violence? Is he just a normal everyday individual, as the base rates would suggest? Or is he one of these excessively controlled people who might someday lash out? This is the differentiation that is most difficult to make and it is fortunate that all the data thus far indicate that the *O-H* scale is at its best in discriminating between overcontrolled individuals and normals.

TABLE 9.1.
MEAN O-H SCALE SCORES OF 12 MALE SAMPLES DIFFERING IN
HOSTILITY AND CONTROL MEAN O-H SCORES

Sample	Source	N	Raw Scores	T Scores
Extremely Assaultive Probation Applicants	Alameda County (Calif.) Probation Dept. (ACPD)	14	18.43	71
Fundamentalist Conscientious Objectors	Federal Correctional Institution, Tallahassee, Florida (FCI)	10	18.40	71
Overcontrolled Assaultive Prison Inmates	Texas State Prison (TSP)	21	16.24	64
Moderately Assaultive Probation Applicants	ACPD	28	15.07	59
Violent Inmates	California Youth Authority (CYA) (Spencer, 1966)	161	14.94	59
Federal Prisoners (Consecutive admissions)	FCI	678	14.56	58
Undercontrolled Assaultive Prison Inmates	TSP	24	14.00	56
Nonviolent Inmates	CYA (Spencer, 1966)	285	13.78	54
Nonviolent Probation Applicants	ACPD	44	13.39	53
Peace Corps Volunteers	University of Texas (UT)	22	12.77	52
Undergraduates	UT	50	12.36	51
Undergraduates	UT	100	12.21	50

NOTES

1. Preparation of this paper and some of the research reported therein were supported by USPHS Grant No. 18468: NIMH (Center for Studies of Crime and Delinquency).
2. For a more detailed discussion of the psychodynamics of aggression see Megargee (1972).

3. It should be pointed out that Megargee did not propose that *all* extremely violent people are overcontrolled as Robins (1965) inferred from an early report of this research (Megargee, 1965a). Instead, he simply suggested that *some* are overcontrolled so their inclusion in the groups would alter its mean relative to the other groups' (Megargee, 1965c).

4. The fact that we have focused on these two types does not mean that these are the only assaultive syndromes that can be identified. These dynamics are not meant to apply to instrumental acts of violence (Buss, 1961) in which aggression is a means to some other end, as in the case of an executioner (private or public), a soldier, or a robber. On an *a priori* basis, a typology of individual violence should probably provide for normal people acting under extreme provocation and psychotics suffering from grossly disorganized ego.

5. The *O-H* scale is scored from the standard group MMPI according to the following key:
   True: 78, 91, 229, 319, 338, 373, 394, 425, 488, 559.
   False: 1, 30, 81, 90, 102, 109, 129, 130, 141, 165, 181, 183, 290, 329, 382, 396, 439, 446, 475, 501, 534.

6. Personal communication, 1966.

REFERENCES

Blackburn, R.
  1968a   "Emotionality, extraversion and aggression in paranoid and nonparanoid schizophrenic offenders." *British J. of Psychiatry 115:* 1301–1302.
  1968b   "Personality in relation to extreme aggression in psychiatric offenders." *British J. of Psychiatry 114:* 821–28.
  1969   "Personality patterns in homicide: A typological analysis of abnormal offenders." Paper presented at the Fifth International Meeting of Forensic Sciences, Toronto, Canada. (June).
Buss, A. H.
  1961   *The Psychology of Aggression.* New York: Wiley.
Fisher, G.
  1970   "Discriminating violence emanating from overcontrolled versus undercontrolled aggressivity." *British J. of Social and Clinical Psychology 9:* 45–49.
Haven, H.
  1969   "Racial differences on the MMPI *O-H* scale." *FCI Research Reports 1* (6): 1–18. Federal Correctional Institution, Tallahassee, Florida, 32304.
  1972   Descriptive and developmental characteristics of chronically overcontrolled hostile prisoners. Unpublished doctoral dissertation: Florida State University.
Megargee, E. I.
  1964a   Undercontrol and overcontrol in assaultive and homicidal adolescents. Doctoral dissertation: University of California, Berkeley.
  1964b   "The utility of the Rosenzweig Picture-Frustration study in detecting assaultiveness among juvenile delinquents." Paper presented at the meeting of the Southwestern Psychological Assoc., San Antonio. (April).

1965a   "Assaultive with intent to kill." *Trans-Action 2* (6): 27–31.
1965b   "The relation between Barrier scores and aggressive behavior." *J. of Abnormal Psychology 70:* 307–11.
1965c   "A reply to Robins," *Trans-Action 3*(1): 45.
1966   "Undercontrolled and overcontrolled personality types in extreme anti-social aggression." *Psychological Monographs 80* (3, Whole No. 611).
1967   "Hostility on the TAT as function of defensive inhibition and stimulus situation." *J. of Projective Techniques and Personality Assessment 31*(4): 73–79.
1969   "Conscientious objectors' scores on the MMPI *O-H* (Overcontrolled Hostility) scale." Proceedings of the 77th Annual Convention of the American Psychological Association. Washington: APA.
1970   "The prediction of violence from psychological tests." In C. D. Spielberger (ed.), *Current Topics in Clinical and Community Psychology*, Vol. 2 New York: Academic Press.
1971   "Role of inhibition in the assessment and understanding of violence." In J. E. Singer (ed.), *Cognitive and Physiological Factors in Aggression*. New York: Academic Press.
1972   *The Psychology of Violence and Aggression*. New York: General Learn. P.

Megargee, E. I., and P. E. Cook.
1967   "The relation of TAT and inkblot aggressive content scales with each other and with criteria of overt aggressiveness in delinquents." *J. of Projective Techniques and Personality Assessment 31*(1): 48–60.

Megargee, E. I., P. E. Cook, and G. A. Mendelsohn.
1967   "Development and validation of an MMPI scale of assaultiveness in over-controlled individuals." *J. of Abnormal Psychology 72*: 519–28.

Megargee, E. I., J. R. Hokanson, and C. D. Spielberger.
1971   "The behavior research program at the Federal Correctional Institution, Tallahassee. I: Goals and initial data collection procedures." *FCI Research Reports 3* (5). Federal Correctional Institution, Tallahassee, Florida.

Megargee, E. I., and G. A. Mendelsohn.
1962   "A cross validation of 12 MMPI indices of hostility and control: *J. of Abnormal and Social Psychology 65:* 431–38.

Megargee, E. I., J. S. McGuire, V. H. Elion, H. Steuber, R. E. Nuehring, and D. Gilbert.
1972   "The behavior research program at the Federal Correctional Institution, Tallahassee. II: Later data collection procedures." *FCI Research Reports 4* (3). Federal Correctional Institution, Tallahassee, Fla. 32304.

Megargee, E. I., and E. S. Menzies.
1971   "The assessment and dynamics of aggression." In P. McReynolds (ed.), *Advances in Psychological Assessment*, Vol. 2, Palo Alto: Science and Behavior Books.

Molof, M. J.
1967   "Differences between assaultive and nonassaultive juvenile offenders in the California Youth Authority." Research report No. 51, Div. of Research, State of California, Dept. of the Youth Authority.

Robins, L. H.
    1965   "Psychology of the killer." *Trans-Action 3* (1): 55–56.
Vanderbeck, D. J.
    1973   A construct validity study of the *O-H* (Overcontrolled Hostility) scale of
                the MMPI, using a social learning approach to the catharsis effect. Un-
                published doctoral dissertation: Florida State University.
Wheeler, C. A., Jr.
    1971   "Overcontrolled hostility in the perception of violence." *FCI Research
                Reports 3* (3). Federal Correctional Institution, Tallahassee, Fla. 32304.
White, W. C., Jr.
    1970   "Selective modeling in youthful offenders with high and low *O-H* (Over-
                controlled Hostility) personality types." *FCI Research Reports 2* (3) Federal
                Correctional Institution, Tallahassee, Fla. 32304.
White, W. C., W. G. McAdoo, and E. I. Megargee.
    In press   "Personality factors associated with over- and undercontrolled of-
                fenders."

10

The Violent Offender: Let's Examine the Taboo

Colin Sheppard

Reprinted from *Federal Probation* (December 1971), pp. 12–19 by permission of the publisher, the Administrative Office of the United States Courts.

No criminal acts cause more concern to society than crimes which kill or seriously injure some of its members. Consequently, the perpetrators of such acts—violent offenders—are under constant scrutiny. Many people regard them with continuing fear, believing their extermination is the only safeguard to future public safety. Others, however, are more optimistic and perceive the violent offender as a salvageable human being.

What follows is an attempt to present a panoramic examination of the violent offender, utilizing findings from psychology, sociology, psychiatry, criminology, and penology. Up-to-date research reports and statistical studies will be examined. Such data will be cautiously interpreted for the benefit of legislators, correctional administrators, and practitioners who are prepared to direct their efforts toward the reconstruction of the violent offender rather than his destruction. Although violent behavior can encompass a multitude of destructive acts via a wide range of expression—against both property and the person—it was found necessary to impose some limits on the extent of violence to be considered. For the purposes of this article, therefore, the violent offender will refer to those persons who have committed a criminal act which resulted in either death or injury to a fellow human being. Thus, research information and statistical data will be presented on murder, manslaughter, and aggravated assault, with the focus of attention on the most serious of offenders—the murderer.

Those who advocate both the retention and utilization of capital punishment usually do so because of a deeply felt personal sentiment and a commitment to the sanctity of human life. Those who favour abolition are as adamant in their position which they often support by attempting to discredit the arguments of their adversaries. It is contended that the cogency of both arguments could benefit from a more rational understanding of the violent offender and a less emotional perception of the crime he commits.

149

UNIFORMITIES AND DEFORMITIES IN VIOLENT CRIME

How pervasive is violent crime? Is it a phenomenon which cuts across all strata of society or can it be identified with particular groups or subcultures? Is there a distribution factor by race and sex? How vulnerable are we as victims—is it "safer" to live in one particular area as opposed to another? Are there any characteristics that distinguish the assailant–victim relationship? Despite the fact that the vast majority of people never experience violence, either as participant or observer, and violent crime is but a small proportion of all criminal acts, its seriousness has prompted many researchers to try to provide answers to these questions.

Within the context of all types of crime, the numbers of violent crime are quite small. Of all crimes of violence (homicide, robbery, rape, and assault), murder in the United States occurs once in 50 offenses and represents less than 0.5 percent of all types of crime. Aggravated assault is more frequent, representing nearly half of all crimes of violence and 6 percent of crimes committed. The Federal Bureau of Investigation's *Uniform Crime Reports*[1] indicate further that the chances of being a victim of violent crime are higher by about 2 to 1 in a metropolitan area than a rural area. This, however, is a recent trend. In 1962, murder rates per 100,000 population were approximately equal for rural and metropolitan areas—4.9 and 4.7 respectively. By 1969 this ratio appeared to have changed dramatically—the murder rate for the whole United States was reported at 7.2 per 100,000 population, but the rates for rural and urban areas had now changed to 5.6 and 15.7 respectively. In other words, over a 7-year period the rural picture has not changed appreciably whereas the urban rate has more than tripled. Aggravated assault has weighed in favour of the cities. In 1969, the rates per 100,000 inhabitants were 318.6 and 85.2 for urban and rural areas respectively.

Further studies of violence reveal that a high concentration of homicides and assaults occurs in the poorer and dilapidated areas of a city. Most killings are centered in the downtown skid row areas frequented by vagrants, alcoholics, prostitutes, and drug addicts. Aggravated assaults were found to be more frequent in the inner-city area. Significantly, violent crime was found to be predominately contained in specific areas, whereas robberies and burglaries tended to be far more widely dispersed throughout the city.

It would appear that violent crime has come to the cities concomitant with the urbanization trend of the 1960's. Not surprisingly, therefore, criminologists have focused their attention on patterns of crime in such densely populated areas. A study of criminal homicide in Philadelphia between 1948 and 1952[2] and a later Chicago study in 1965[3] gave some insights which have proven invaluable to the better understanding of violent crime. In comparison to the general distribution of males and females, males are disproportionately involved both as assailants and victims and 83.1 percent of the assailants were males. In both areas the majority of males were nonwhite. A similar disproportion to the general population was found in a study of aggravated assault in St. Louis in 1961[4] where it was shown that nonwhites were more involved, both as assailants and victims. These findings indicated many similar patterns in crimes of homicide and aggravated assault.

A comparison of male to female involvement in murder in the U.S., Canada, and England indicates some disparities. In the U.S. in 1968 and 1969, males outnumbered females as victims by more than 3 to 1; the male/female ratio of arrests for murder was 5 to 1.[5] In Canada in 1968 and 1969, males outnumbered females as victims but by less than 2 to 1;[6] male murder suspects outnumbered female by 8 to 1 in 1968 and 6 to 1 in 1969.[7] In England, male offenders outnumbered female by nearly 5 to 1.[8] However, females consistently outnumbered males as victims in the proportion of 6 to 4.[9]

The relationship between the victim and his assailant has been another aspect of violent crime that has been carefully studied. An analysis of violent behaviour in the U. S. in a single year revealed "about 70 percent of all wilful killings, nearly two-thirds of aggravated assaults and a high percentage of forcible rapes are committed by family members, friends, and other persons previously known to their friends."[10] A further study which examined 2,700 murders in the U. S. found that only 37 were planned for economic, political, or other considered ends such as vengeance or relief from suffering. Most were the spontaneous product of quarrels.[11] Such data do not give us any insight into the causes of violent crime, but they do suggest a primary group aspect to the largest proportion of cases. In Canada, murders within the extended family approximate to 40 percent of the total number annually. The latest figures for the year 1969 indicate that 38 percent of murders were of a domestic nature.[12] The analysis of criminal homicides in Philadelphia revealed that only 12.2 percent of the murders were committed by strangers. In over 65 percent of the cases, a relationship existed between the murderer and his victim.[13]

These studies indicate that, contrary to popular belief, the majority of murders are committed within the home and not at the hands of strangers marauding through city streets.

Is Violent Crime Increasing?

Although the evidence in the United States and other countries is not precise, it appears that all types of crime have continued to rise in recent decades. This is hardly surprising and can be understood as a concomitant development to an increasing population. A specific examination of homicide and aggravated assault indicates a decline up until the middle 1960's followed by an increase. The most recent figures point to a tapering off.

Over a 30-year period, from 1933 to 1963, the homicide rate in the United States has approximately halved from 9.6 deaths per 100,000 population in 1933 to 4.9 in 1963.[14] Between 1963 and 1969, however, the murder rate increased from 4.9 to 7.2 per 100,000 population.[15] In Canada similar fluctuation has been observed, although the murder rate in that country is much lower. In 1954 the rate was 1 per 100,000 and by 1969, it had increased to 1.9.[16] England, which attests to an even lower murder rate by computing its figures on the basis of a million population, experienced no murder increase over a 30-year period. The average yearly murder rate in the 1930's was 3.2 per 1,000,000 population and by 1960 had decreased slightly to 3.0.[17]

Although the United States and Canadian figures for 1970 are not yet available, there is the suggestion that the rate may be leveling off. The police of Canada's most violent-prone city, Montreal, have reported a 6 percent decline in numbers of murders in 1970 over 1969.[18] In the United States, the murder rate declined in 1969 from 1968 which may reflect the veering away from the outburst of violence experienced in that country in the second half of the 1960's.[19]

THE VICTIM OF VIOLENT CRIME

As pointed out earlier, in more than two-thirds of murders and assaults, a relationship existed between the two participants prior to the altercation taking place. This is sometimes described as domestic violence, the most frequent relationship being that of husband and wife. The notion, therefore, that the majority of violent crimes are calculated attacks by vicious criminals on helpless victims is hopefully dispelled. In fact, it is the minority of cases where the victim plays a passive role.

The studies cited previously revealed that the victim very often plays a key role in violent interaction, sometimes "provoking" the other person, and often "precipitating" the violent interchange leading to injury or death. In the Philadelphia study, 26 percent of the 588 cases investigated were homicides initiated by the victim.[20] The Chicago study reported that 118 of 311 cases were precipitated by the victim, i.e., 40 percent of the victims initiated the violence which led to their own death. From these 311 cases, 140 or 45 percent were cases of domestic nature, and of these 140 cases, 59 or 42 percent were victim-precipitated.[21] In other words, nearly half of all domestic murders were initiated through the aggressive behaviour of the eventual victim.

Provocation by the victim is another mode of behaviour which can help to escalate the intensity of a violent interaction. Common examples are the constant crying of a child leading to a parental beating; the unfaithful wife; the harlot who repels sexual advances when they arise. Provocation by a victim has undoubtedly led to violence from the hand of a frustrated assailant and in fact has been successfully used in court as a plea to reduce the charge laid against an offender.[22]

Society's fears of crimes of violence are often expressed by an attitude which exonerates the victim (particularly if he is dead) for the crime, placing complete responsibility with accompanying demand for retribution upon the accused. As Morris and Blom-Copper point out, the idea of innocence is a quality often attributed to the victim of murder, whereas, in fact, the victim's behaviour may have a great deal to do with the initiation of violence and his eventual death.[23] Just as the difference between murder and assault can depend solely on factors of chance, so also can chance determine who ends up as the victim and who as the offender. The polarization of society's attitudes, therefore, from great sympathy for the victim to repugnance for the offender, needs to be moderated. The crime of murder is, of course, an irreversible act and no amount of financial recompense can compensate for death or serious injury to the victim. Yet in those crimes where the victim has provoked or initiated the violence, the onus of responsibility should not be placed entirely upon the offender.

THE VIOLENT OFFENDER AND THE LAW

Violent crime induces an emotional response which significantly shapes the views of most people toward the individual who committed such a crime. Unfortunately, the criminal law in relation to the violent offender has been molded largely out of this emotional reaction and is often unable to put forth a rationale for the penalties it prescribes. The foundation of the legislation in many jurisdictions has been formulated in an arbitrary manner, stemming from an attitude of punitiveness, moral condemnation, and usually an utter disregard for any empirical information which suggests that change is needed.

Legal rhetoric, by and large, continues to equate the violent offender, so defined in this paper, with the dangerous offender. It is presumed, *a priori*, that if a person kills or injures a fellow being, then he is dangerous and a menace and must be sentenced as such. Whereas it is acknowledged that this presumption is congruent with the propensities of some violent offenders, many, and in fact the majority, may well not be of continuing danger. Although the act of murder is the most serious of crimes, the murderer is not necessarily the most dangerous of offenders. Yet he is the offender who most often received the severest of punishments that our society can bestow upon its members—death by legal execution.

How does the violent offender stand in relation to two tenets which are currently in fashion in correctional circles, namely, individual sentencing and rehabilitation through community treatment? As far as the first is concerned, the act of murder or assault, rather than the offender committing them, tends to become the focus of the court's attention. In many jurisdictions, Canada for example, the finding that the defendant is guilty of capital murder leaves no sentencing option available to the presiding judge. If the victim was a policeman or prison guard, the death penalty is mandatory. The legal procedures at this point in the trial disregard any notions pertaining to the sentence necessary for the offender's rehabilitation.

With the focus of attention upon the offense rather than the offender, community treatment is rarely, if ever, an option. Yet it is paradoxical that this is so. If individual sentencing is being practised and if some violent offenders can be diagnosed as not being dangerous, then, one wonders, why is not probation considered as a viable alternative to imprisonment?

THE VIOLENT OFFENDER IN PRISON

The violent offender is scarcely ever accorded any leniency by the court in the form of a suspended sentence or release under conditions of probation. If the extreme penalty of death is not invoked, the violent offender is imprisoned, usually for life if the offense was capital murder but otherwise for long periods of time. One of the arguments put forth by the retentionists is the increased danger to the lives of prison guards when violent offenders are not executed but "warehoused" in penal institutions. Legislative measures sometimes attempt to protect the prison official from this alleged danger by placing violent acts against him under the umbrella of offenses which are punishable by death. Such is the situation existing in Canada at the present time where the death penalty has been abolished, but where exceptions have been made for the killers of policemen and prison officers.*

Is the violent offender a menace during his captivity? Does the danger of injury or death to officials and other inmates increase because of his presence in prison and the inevitability of contact with other persons?

A recent Canadian study examined incidents of assault on penitentiary officials and inmates over a 2-year period. Of the 37 acts of assault against penitentiary officers, seven were instigated by violent offenders. The vast majority of the assailants were serving sentences for theft and robbery. Of the 37 officers, 12 were severely beaten, one of whom died as a result. The assailant in this case was a robber. Between 1945 and 1964, three officers were killed while on duty in Canadian penitentiaries—one by a robber, one by fellow guards in a moment of panic, and in one case the offender was

---

*This situation existed in 1973 when this study was completed and is still current today. (Ed.)

never discovered. Inmates serving sentences for murder inflicted only three minor injuries to three officers.[24]

Data on prison homicides in the United States was gathered by Thorsten Sellin, for the year 1965, from 45 States, the District of Columbia, and the Federal Bureau of Prisons: a total of 61 victims (8 of whom were officials) and 59 assailants were identified. Of the latter, 16 were murderers, one had committed manslaughter, two assault to murder, one rape, and three assault.[25] Although this United States study indicates that the violent offender continues to be dangerous under conditions of incarceration, Jayewardene found from a study of seven state penal institutions that between 1949 and 1958 only 110 incidences of homicide and aggravated assault had occurred. Of these, 90 were committed by inmates not serving sentences for homicide. Jayewardene concluded that in the prison setting, "homicide does not appear to be the prerogative of homicide convicts."[26] When a group of 621 incarcerated murderers was compared with a similar number of nonmurderers, the findings revealed that the murderer appeared to have a lower "criminality level" than his nonviolent counterpart. That is, fewer murderers were recidivists and the murderers had a better behaviour record during previous incarcerations and fewer escapes.[27]

Thus there is no conclusive evidence as to the overall adjustment of the murderer to prison life and whether the violent offender poses a danger to custody staff. Sellin noted that prison administrators, broadly speaking, regard lifers as among the best behaved in an institution.

THE VIOLENT OFFENDER IN THE COMMUNITY

What happens to the violent offender when he is eventually allowed to return to the outside community after he has served a period of imprisonment? Does he continue to kill and injure other people once his freedom has been restored?

Although such questions are very difficult to answer, followup data on the offender's adjustment are available through information supplied by various parole jurisdictions. It is the exception rather than the rule for the violent offender, particularly the murderer, to be released unconditionally. Many violent offenders do apply for parole, either because they are attempting to shorten a lengthy sentence or because it is the only avenue available for their release. Such a release does not give the offender absolute freedom. He is under restraints which demand of him good behaviour at the risk of being returned to prison. This control of his outside behaviour provides the means of obtaining information on him.

The crucial question with regard to the violent offender on parole is not so much his parole violation rate, but rather his further resorting to the use of violence. There is substantial evidence from Canada and various jurisdictions in the United States which indicates that the murderer, particularly, is a better parole risk when compared with other offender groups. In California, 10.8 percent of 342 first-degree murderers violated parole between 1945 and 1954. Only one violation caused further death. In Michigan, 175 death-commuted murderers were paroled between 1937 and 1961. Of these, four ended up as parole violators none of whom killed again.[28] In New York, over a 31-year period from July 1930, 63 first-degree murderers were paroled. By 1961, none had committed further murder and of the three violations, two were technical infractions of parole conditions.

Similar findings were found in Ohio. Between 1945 and 1965, 273 first-degree murderers were paroled and only 15 (5.5 percent) violated. Of these, none caused further loss of life.[29] In Canada, 119 first-degree murderers were paroled between 1920 and 1947. By April 1968, 89 were still on parole, 19 had either died or left the country, and 22 had been returned to prison because of other offenses or parole violations. Only one offender killed a second time, and he was executed.[30]

As pointed out previously, incarcerated murderers have a lower criminality profile than non-murderers.[31] Thus it would be expected that murderers are better parole risks than groups of other types of offenders. The New York State Division of Parole made a comparison of 576 murderers and large groups of non-murderers. It was found that the rate of violations and new convictions of paroled murderers was lower at a very significant statistical level than those of paroled nonmurderers.[32]

Despite their rate of success and minimal risk to the community, parole boards have seemed reluctant to release the violent offender and, in turn, governments have displayed hesitancy to entrust the release of such individuals to the wisdom of parole boards. The reason why this is so is suggested as follows:

> The clusters of offenses associated with the lowest violation rates on parole are crimes which least often serve as vocations. These include homicide and rape. However, the strong public demand for punishment as an expression of revenge against such offenders, plus the extreme importance of preventing reoccurrence of these crimes, makes parole boards exceptionally cautious in paroling those who commit these offenses.[33]

Although the figures cited above may help to assuage the fears of those who advocate the ultimate of punishments for the murderer, the problem of isolated incidents of violence by paroled murderers remains. In the California figures cited earlier, 1 of 342 first-degree murderers released over a 9-year period killed a second time. Had the death penalty been invoked, this second murder would not have occurred; on the other hand, over 300 persons would have been executed, all of whom had eventually proven themselves to be of no further danger to society. This is the dilemma facing parole boards in considering the release of the violent offender. Despite the high rate of success of this group of offenders, it is unlikely that parole boards can improve their predictive techniques to the point of being able to identify the isolated offender who would commit further violence.[34] While errors in predictions are anticipated by parole boards, they will have to be prepared to face open criticism from police and citizens should a violent offender murder again.

Etiological Factors in Violent Crime

Violent offenders form a group of lawbreakers who have in common the fact that they have killed or injured other members of human society. They are in one legal category extracted from the heterogeneous population of men and women who have become variously defined as "criminal." Such a typology can tell us little about behavioral patterns since it is clear that violent offenders are as diverse a group as any selected at random from the general population. Thus, in discussing causation, no attempt is being made to present a simplistic explanation of why violent crime occurs. What follows is merely an overview of some of the variables that have been causally linked to some incidents of violent crime.

The variables to be presented will be categorized, utilizing the format of "predisposing" and "precipitating" causes. The former are either psychological, sociological, or cultural characteristics which are instrumental in explaining why violent behaviour occurred. Precipitating factors are always present even if it is merely the presence of the victim. However, as Toch has pointed out in reference to violence-prone persons, "although incidents that finally trigger violence may be provocative, their role is often minor."[35] In fact, the precipitating factor may be irrelevant and the victim incidental. Incidents of murder characterized by the ferocity and brutality of the offender can often only be explained by examining predisposing factors.

Many clinical studies of murderers and assaulters have referred to the violence and brutality they have experienced during their developing years. Bach-Y-Rita and colleagues psychiatrically examined 130 violent patients over a 2-year period. None was obviously suffering from a psychosis during the study. Of the 130 cases, 30 percent experienced violence within their parental family structure.[36] In another study of five adolescents who killed or threatened to kill a parent, the victim's brutal behaviour toward the child in question was seen as a significant variable.[37] Duncan and associates investigated the background of six first-degree murderers looking for reasons for their violent behaviour. None had suffered from previous psychosis, addiction to drugs, alcohol, epilepsy, or brain damage. According to the authors, the six individuals had all suffered "remorseless physical brutality at the hands of the parents."[38]

Further credibility to the thesis that parental enmity produces violent-prone offspring was indicated in a study of more than 100 subjects, all of whom had made threats of homicide. It was the author's clinical impression that parental brutality played a significant part in the development of these homicide threats.[39] In a comparative study of groups of assaultive and nonassaultive offenders, Peterson, Pittman, and O'Neal detected a pattern of erratic parental care and a disrupting environment in the early years of life in the violent group. This study tentatively concluded that early life experiences were a determinant as to whether an offender veered towards a violent or nonviolent criminal career.[40] In a study of 51 male murderers, Palmer revealed the extreme frustration—both physical and psychological—that his subjects had suffered as children. Accidents, disease, physical beatings, traumatic incidents were far more evident among the murderers than a similar group of average citizens and led Palmer to focus his attention on these factors in order to better understand the origins of murder.[41]

A variety of other psychological and psychiatric variables have been cited as offering an understanding of the genesis of the violent offender's personality. Among these are paranoia, incipient schizophrenia, brain damage, defective ethical standards, depression, psychopathy, and parental alcoholism. It is clear, however, that they are present as predisposing factors in only a relatively small number of cases. To gain an understanding of the origins of violent behaviour for perhaps the largest proportion of offenders, it is helpful to consider the concept of the "subculture of violence." It is hypothesized that this subculture provides an environment in which violent behaviour is learned. According to Wolfgang and Ferracuti, the subculture of violence suggests ". . . a potent theme of violence current in the cluster of values that make up the life style, the socialization process, the interpersonal relationships of individuals living in similar conditions."[42] This subculture thesis proposes a socio-psychological genesis for violence. Within the subculture, a slum area of a large city for example, the use of aggression is an accepted and reinforced mode of behaviour. Those children who grow up in such an area are likely to learn militant values and attitudes and thus become predisposed to react violently in later life.

So far, we have considered predisposing factors which undoubtedly play a major role in understanding the reasons for violent behaviour. Precipitation can be understood as an adjunct to more entrenched factors. Rarely can an explanation for violence rest wholly with precipitating reasons. Equally well, not all children subjected to parental brutality or reared in the depths of a violent-prone subculture end up as violent offenders. Precipitating factors can, however, provide some further momentum towards violence.

Kinzel, for example, reports a clinical finding that some violent persons become highly sensitized to the physical closeness of other human beings. Most people become "alert" when a stranger touches them or moves "uncomfortably" close; for violent persons, discomfort occurs at distance up to four times further away.[43] The anxiety induced when others move within this sensitized area can trigger a violent reaction. Both alcohol and drugs have been related to violent outbursts. Lanzkron,[44] Guttmacher,[45] and others have reported from clinical observations the relationship between alcohol consumption and homicides. Guttmacher found that half of 105 sane murderers had drunk heavily immediately prior to the commission of the offense. Only 10 percent of a group of psychotic murderers had imbibed. The contribution of alcohol to violence has long been known. Precipitating violence by overindulgence of narcotics is not new, but it is perhaps an escalating problem. A recent clinical study described the histories of 13 persons who committed homicide while under the influence of amphetamines. Like alcohol, which is thought to lower an offender's control over his impulses, amphetamines appear to create a state of intoxication in the individual which largely contributes to his committing the violent act.[46]

Mental disorders have also long been known as variables in murders and assaults. Palmer reported that most of the murderers in his study were "severely upset emotionally" at the time of the offense.[47] In Guttmacher's study, 53 of 175 cases were diagnosed as psychotic at the time of the murder and of these, two-thirds had no previous psychiatric history.[48] As already pointed out, mental illness is not a large factor in violence, accounting for less than one in 20 murders in the United States.

Conclusion

This article has tried to present a broad, dispassionate perspective of the violent offender, the crime he commits, and to suggest the reasons why. It was contended that a taboo surrounds this particular offender—that societal reaction to his behaviour stems from the emotions and not from the intellect; that the sizeable accumulation of empirical data about him is not being put into practice; that reluctance to act is continually strengthened by those who advocate the need for more research. Everyday recommendations and judgments about violent offenders are being made by policemen, magistrates, lawyers, probation officers, parole officers, and institutional correctional workers. However, the making of these various decisions is undoubtedly affected by bias, fear, and ignorance such that the violent offender is not being dealt with in accordance with knowledge available about him and the understanding to go with it.

There has been no intention of proposing a policy of leniency toward the violent offender. Many such individuals are dangerous and pose a potential and continuing threat to society. Their future should be decided with caution and perhaps imprisonment for an indeterminate period is the only recourse. However, many violent offenders are not dangerous and yet their return to society is marred by the mythology surrounding their act of violence.

Although the use of capital punishment is declining, it is still an issue in many parts of the world. In the United States, nobody has been executed since 1967 when two violent offenders were put to death.* Yet many languish on death row, their fate in the hands of indecisive legislators. As previously pointed out, there is no evidence to link the homicide rate with the availability of the death penalty. Individual sentencing is rarely an option for the violent offender. If the conviction is for homicide, the judge is often left with no discretion in disposing of the case. The prescription of a life sentence does not include the needs of the offender. When released on parole, the violent offender has a high rate of success and has been of minimal risk to the community. Yet parole boards continue to be overly cautious in their decisions despite this very optimistic feedback.

Violent offenders vary from persons who commit a single aggressive act in their lifetime to others where violence was learned early in life and is an everyday behavioural characteristic. There is no one simple explanation for violent crime nor will any one typology satisfactorily characterize all such offenders. Rehabilitation of such offenders is, therefore, a complex matter. In striving to act on the basis of our current knowledge, and to be continually aware of the need to reappraise our values and attitudes, society must continue its efforts to rehabilitate all its offenders, including the violent offender.

NOTES

1. *Uniform Crime Reports—1969*, Washington, D. C.: Federal Bureau of Investigation, 1970: 5–9.
2. Melvin E. Wolfgang, *Patterns in Criminal Homicide*. Philadelphia: University of Philadelphia Press, 1958.
3. Harwin L. Voss and John R. Hepburn, "Patterns in Criminal Homicide in Chicago," *J. of Criminal Law, Criminology and Police Science*, Vol. 59 (December 1968): 499–508.
4. David J. Pittman and William Handy, "Patterns in Criminal Aggravated Assault," *J. of Criminal Law, Criminology and Police Science*, Vol. 55 (December 1964): 462–470.
5. *Uniform Crime Reports*, op. cit. (1), p. 7.

*This was true until 1978 when the death penalty was reinstituted in the United States (Ed.)

6. Dominion Bureau of Statistics, *Murder Statistics 1969*. Ottawa: Queen's Printer, September 1970, p. 20.

7. *Ibid*, p. 15.

8. Home Office, *Murder—A Home Office Research Unit Report*. London: Her Majesty's Stationery Office, 1961, p. 27.

9. *Ibid*, p. 17.

10. President's Commission on Law Enforcement and Administration of Justice, *The Challenge of Crime in a Free Society*, Washington, D. C.: Government Printing Office, 1967, p. 18.

11. N.C.C.D. Board of Trustees, "Policy Statement on Capital Punishment," *Crime and Delinquency*, Vol. 10 (April 1964), p. 106.

12. *Murder Statistics 1969*, op. cit. (6), p. 13.

13. President's Commission on Law Enforcement and Administration of Justice, *op. cit.* (10) p. 39.

14. U. S. Department of Health, Education and Welfare, *The Violent Offender*, by Daniel Glaser, Donald Kenefick, and Vincent O'Leary, Washington, D. C.: Government Printing Office, 1968, p. 8.

15. *Uniform Crime Reports, op. cit.* (1), 1963–1969.

16. *Murder Statistics—1969, op. cit.* (6), p. 8.

17. Minister of Justice, *Capital Punishment: Material Relating to Its Purpose and Value*. Ottawa: Queen's Printer, 1965, p. 7.

18. *Globe and Mail* (Toronto), December 28, 1970: 48.

19. *Uniform Crime Reports, op. cit.* (1), p. 6.

20. Marvin E. Wolfgang, "Victim Precipitated Criminal Homicide," in Marvin E. Wolfgang, ed., *Studies in Homicide*. New York: Harper & Row, 1967, p. 75.

21. Harwin L. Voss, *op. cit.* (3).

22. Terrence Morris and Louis Blom-Cooper, *A Calendar of Murder*. London: Michael Joseph, 1964, p. 72.

23. *Ibid*, p. 321.

24. Dogan D. Akman, "Homicides and Assaults in Canadian Penitentiaries," *Canadian J. of Corrections*, 8 (1966): 284–299.

25. Thorsten Sellin, "Prison Homicides," in Thorsten Sellin, ed., *Capital Punishment*. New York: Harper and Row, 1967.

26. C. H. S. Jayewardene, "Are Murderers Dangerous?" *Probation and Child Care J.*, (Colombo, Ceylon), 2 (1962): 33–35.

27. Gordon P. Waldo, "The Criminality Level of Incarcerated Murderers and Non-Murderers," *J. of Criminal Law, Criminology and Police Science*, 61 (1970): 60–70.

28. N.C.C.D., *op. cit.*, (11), p. 107.

29. G. I. Giardini and R. G. Farrow, "The Paroling of Capital Offenders," in Thorsten, Sellin, ed., *Capital Punishment*. New York: Harper and Row, 1967, p. 185.

30. Colin Sheppard, "Towards a Better Understanding of the Violent Offender," *Canadian J. of Criminology and Corrections*, 13, (1971): 60–67.

31. Gordon, P. Waldo, *op. cit.* (27).

32. John M. Stanton, "Murderers on Parole," *Crime & Delinquency* 15 (1969): 149–155.

33. U. S. Dept. of Health, Education & Welfare, *Personal Characteristics & Parole Outcome*, by Daniel Glaser and Vincent O'Leary. Washington, D. C.: Government Printing Office, 1965, p. 16.

34. *The Violent Offender, op. cit.* (14), p. 34–37.

35. Hans Toch, *Violent Men: An Inquiry Into the Psychology of Violence*, Chicago: Aldine, 1969.

36. George Bach-Y-Rita, et al., "Episodic Dyscontrol: A Study of 130 Violent Patients," *American J. of Psychiatry*, 127 (1971): 1473–1478.

37. Jane Watson Duncan and Glen M. Duncan, "Murder in the Family: A Study of Some Homicidal Adolescents," *American J. of Psychiatry*, 127 (1971): 1498–1502.

38. Glen M. Duncan, et al., "Etiological Factors in First-Degree Murder," in Marvin E. Wolfgang, ed., *Studies in Homicide*. New York: Harper & Row, 1967.

39. John J. MacDonald, "The Threat to Kill," *American J. of Psychiatry*, 120 (1963): 125–130.

40. Richard A. Peterson, David J. Pittman, and Patrician O'Neal, "Stabilities in Deviance: a Study of Assaultive and Non-Assaultive Offenders," *J. of Criminal Law, Criminology and Police Science* 53 (1962): 462–470.

41. Stuart Palmer, *The Psychology of Murder*, New York: Thomas Y. Crowell, 1960.

42. Marvin E. Wolfgang and Franco Ferracuti, *The Subculture of Violence: Towards an Integrated Theory in Criminology*. London: Tavistock, 1967.

43. Augustus F. Kinzel, "Body—Buffer Zone in Violent Prisoners," *Am. J. of Psychiatry*, 127, (1970): 99–140.

44. John Lanzkron, "Murder and Insanity: A Survey," *American J. of Psychiatry*, 119 (1963): 754–758.

45. Manfred S. Guttmacher, *The Mind of the Murderer*. New York: Farrar, Straus and Cudahy, 1960.

46. Everett H. Ellinwood, "Assault and Homicide Associated With Amphetamine Abuse," *American J. of Psychiatry*, 127, (1971): 1170–1175.

47. Stuart Palmer, *op. cit.* (41), p. 180.

48. Manfred S. Guttmacher, *op. cit.* (45), p. 4.

11

Inmate Rioters and Non-Rioters: A Comparative Analysis

Alan C. Straus and Robert Sherwin

Reprinted from *American Journal of Corrections* (May–June 1975), pp. 34–35 and (July–Aug. 1975) pp. 54–58 by permission of the author and publisher, American Correctional Association.

Abstract

Following a prison riot, the research reported here examined similarities and differences between inmate riot participants and non-participants. Findings support a "birds of a feather" hypothesis whereby inmates with certain characteristics reflect differential susceptibility to riot participation. These characteristics are identified and suggestions made to Prison Administrators for minimizing the Human and material damage which may occur as a result of a prison riot.

Introduction

Prison riots are not new in the history of American Penology. They have frequently occurred in the past and they are likely to recur in the future. They can range from serious episodes involving immense property damage and loss of human life to fairly short-lived, abortive efforts which are quickly contained. Regardless of the outcome, it is quite possible that the spectre of a riot is a constant concern that lurks in the minds of prison administrators, officials, and custodians. Social scientists have also exhibited a fair amount of research interest in prison riots (Fox, 1971). Most of this research has been directed at understanding the precipitating events and underlying causes of riots. Yet, when a prison riot occurs, some inmates participate while other do not. Furthermore, the participants are likely to vary in their degree of involvement. Some inmates become "ringleaders"—totally and exclusively involved, others become moderately involved, while still others are but marginal or non-participants. Since research on prison riots has been predominantly directed at understanding "why" such riots occur rather than "who" becomes involved, little is known about the characteristic features of

163

the inmate rioter and non-rioter. Yet, such knowledge may be valuable not only to students of penology but to correctional officials and administrators as well who daily confront the ever present possibility that the seemingly tranquil nature of the prison will be shattered by a riot. It was in an effort to provide information in this area that the research reported here was undertaken.

METHODOLOGY

The research reported here was conducted following an August, 1968, inmate riot at the Lebanon Correctional Institution, Lebanon, Ohio. The institution is classified as medium security and predominantly houses young, first-felon offenders. The riot itself lasted about six hours and was ultimately controlled by the combined efforts of the correctional staff and the Ohio Highway Patrol. While no loss of life occurred, a number of inmates were injured during the control efforts, and property damage inflicted upon the institution during the riot was substantial. Post-riot investigations conducted by institution officials concluded that approximately one-fourth of the twelve hundred incarcerated men had participated to some extent in the riot.

Following the riot, our major research interest focused on the examination of whether or not and to what degree those inmates who participated in the riot differed from those who had not. On the one hand, it seemed that if participants and non-participants were indistinguishable from each other on a variety of measurements, then this would imply that an inmate's degree of involvement was influenced not so much by the kind of person he was but rather by his proximity to the point of the riot eruption; that all inmates were equally susceptible to participation and that the best or only defense against involvement was distance from the point of eruption. On the other hand it seemed that if participants did differ from non-participants, then this would imply that factors other than, or in addition to, proximity influenced the likelihood of participation and that if these factors could be identified, a profile of a likely candidate for riot involvement could be developed. Our purpose, then, was to examine as best we could, with the resources at our disposal, these two alternative interpretations of inmate riot involvement.

Conducting research in the aftermath of a prison riot is not an easy task. People are tense, nerves are taut, and an anomic pall of uncertainty hangs heavy in the air. Because of this, we decided not to directly interview any of the inmates but to instead focus our analysis exclusively upon the material contained in the inmates' institutional records. Indeed, this was the only research technique acceptable to the prison administration. Once this was decided, our next task was to separate the inmate population into riot participants and non-participants. To accomplish this, we depended upon the post-riot investigation conducted by the prison administration. This investigation relied heavily upon three major sources of information: (a) the Ohio State Patrolmen, who were able to identify some of the rioters they had observed; (b) the institution's correctional staff, who either knew the inmates involved or were able to identify them at a later time; and (c) from questioning hundreds of inmates who were promised anonymity and reminded that perjured testimony would jeopardize future parole consideration. While it is certainly possible that the use of these techniques resulted in some inmates being erroneously charged with riot participation by overzealous guards, patrolmen, or by inmates who "had a score to settle," as far as we were able to determine, the administration's ultimate judgment of an inmate's involvement was made with a high degree of accuracy.

The results of the investigation revealed that 343 inmates had participated to some degree in the riot. Of this number, 107 were defined as instigators, agitators, and leaders of the riot by the prison administration. We placed these men in the "heavily involved" category. Unfortunately, an unannounced transfer of these men and their files from Lebanon to other institutions created data collection problems. Only as the last group of twenty-four inmates was being processed for the transfer was it possible to collect data from their files. Our attempts to secure the needed information from the institutions to which the other "heavily involved" inmates had already been transferred were unsuccessful. Thus, this particular category of riot participants contains approximately twenty-five percent of the universe we had hoped to examine.

The remaining 236 men who were found guilty of riot participation were defined by the prison administration as being followers rather than leaders, and of having played a less active part in the riot. These inmates remained at Lebanon, their files were therefore accessible, and we placed these men in the "moderately involved" category.

Finally, as a control group, we randomly selected 267 men from the remaining inmate population. These men had not been charged by the prison administration with any involvement in the riot, and we placed these men in the "non-involved" category. Collectively, the three categories total 527 men.

The data extracted from institutional records used to compare the characteristics of the heavily involved, moderately involved, and non-involved rioters consisted of information concerning each man's (1) age, (2) marital status, (3) educational achievements level, (4) number of disciplinary actions received during present confinement, (5) amount of time before scheduled parole hearing, (6) religion, (7) race, (8) offense convicted of, (9) minimum and maximum sentence being served, and (10) degree of involvement in institutional programs. These ten items were selected for examination because from a logical perspective, it was our judgment that they might be statistically associated with riot involvement or non-involvement.

RESULTS: RACE

One of the most perplexing issues found in American society is that of race. Some blacks believe that the United States is a racist society and by its discriminatory practices has nullified any allegiance to the "system" and its rules by blacks. Indeed, some black inmates refer to themselves as political prisoners rather than criminals. In recent years, attempts by blacks to redress grievances have included both violent and non-violent techniques. Because of this phenomenon, it seemed logical to predict that the degree of black inmate riot involvement would be high. This information is presented in Table 11.1.

At the time of the riot, black inmates comprised approximately one-third of the total inmate population at Lebanon. When this figure is compared with the data presented in Table 11.1, it indicates that black inmates participated in the riot out of proportion to their total representation in the inmate population. Moreover, as the degree of riot involvement increases, so too does the percentage of black inmate participants. For white inmates, this tendency is reversed. Thus, our prediction concerning a statistical relationship between race and riot involvement is supported. Yet, care must be exercised in interpreting these results to avoid concluding that what happened at Lebanon was a race riot of black inmates against the prison administration. On the contrary, over fifty percent of the riot participants were white inmates. Thus, a more balanced conclusion to be drawn from the data in Table 11.1 would suggest that while the racial factor is significant, it is more influential than deterministic and that if our contention is accurate that blacks are alienated from "the system," this feeling is by no means absent from segments of the white inmate population.

RESULTS: AGE

Typically, increasing age is associated with increasing cautiousness and insight into the consequences of one's actions. Since Lebanon is a medium

TABLE 11.1.

DEGREE OF RIOT INVOLVEMENT AMONG BLACK AND WHITE INMATES

	Non-Involved (N = 267)		Moderately Involved (N = 236)		Heavily Involved (N = 24)		Chi Square	Gamma
	No.	%	No.	%	No.	%		
Black	90	34	103	44	13	54	$X^2 = 7.61^*$	$G = +.22$
White	177	66	133	56	11	46		

*Statistically significant at .05 level using a one-tailed test.

TABLE 11.2.
DEGREE OF RIOT INVOLVEMENT—BY AGE

Ages	Non-Involved (N = 267)		Moderately Involved (N = 236)		Heavily Involved (N = 24)		Chi Square	Gamma
	No.	%	No.	%	No.	%		
16–20	78	30	103	44	7	29		
21–24	108	40	98	42	13	54	$X^2 = 23.61^*$	$G = +.26$
25+	81	30	35	35	4	17		

*Statistically significant at the .05 level using a one-tailed test.

security institution designed for younger offenders, it seemed logical to conclude that the older inmates would be more cognizant of the possible consequences of riot participation and more leery about becoming involved. One of the outcomes could be a transfer to a maximum security institution for older, more hardened criminals, where life is even less enjoyable than at Lebanon. Indeed, as we have seen, this is precisely what happened to a number of riot participants. We therefore predicted that the older inmates would be more likely to refrain from participation in the riot than the younger inmates. The data which examines this issue is presented in Table 11.2.

The data presented in Table 11.2 indicates that, as predicted, the younger inmates were more likely to be riot participants than the older inmates. While the differences in age and riot involvement may seem modest, it must be kept in mind that the age of inmates at Lebanon is tightly compressed. With the fairly rare exception of parole violators, no one is committed to Lebanon who is more than 32 years of age. Viewed from this perspective, the difference between age and riot involvement is striking. In addition, further suggestive insights into the relationship between age and riot involvement are generated when the ages of the twenty-four men defined as "ringleaders" are examined. The majority of these men were found neither among the youngest nor the oldest age category. Instead, they predominantly fell in the 21–24 age category. Combined, these findings support the following conclusion. By and large, the youngest inmates are likely to participate in a riot but particularly as followers. The oldest inmates are most likely to stay out of it. The inmates between these two age groups are likely to participate, particularly as leaders. If this finding is accurate, the wisdom of the fairly widespread penological practice of age segregation of inmates may be questioned. The presence of larger numbers of older people in an inmate population may serve as a stabilizing or deflecting force in an institutional environment where tensions seem persistently high and a riot is an ever-present possibility.

RESULTS: PARTICIPATION IN TREATMENT PROGRAMS

In contemporary society, the prison is not only expected to act as a custodian for the convicted offender, but also to attempt to change or "rehabilitate" the inmate so that he may become a law-abiding member of society upon release. Thus, in most institutions, in addition to cells, walls, and fences, a variety of treatment programs are made available to the inmate population. In this regard, Lebanon is no exception. At the time of the riot, the treatment program available to inmates included: (1) a high school, (2) elementary school, (3) four separate vocational schools, (4) accredited college courses from a nearby college, (5) psychological classes, (6) an effective communications class, (7) speech therapy, (8) Alcoholics Anonymous, and (9) vocational guidance. Because inmate participation in any or all of these programs is voluntary and because we defined such participation as indicative of an effort at self-improvement, we hypothesized that inmates who participated in the treatment programs would be less likely to become involved in the riot than the non-participants. The data to test this hypothesis is presented in Table 11.3.

The data presented in Table 11.3 reveals a substantial relationship between participation in the institution's treatment programs and riot involvement. Those inmates who had for perhaps very diverse reasons voluntarily involved themselves in programs designed to "rehabilitate" were not nearly as frequently involved in the riot as were those inmates who had remained aloof from participation in such programs. Note that we are not suggesting here that inmate participation in treatment programs did produce a "rehabilitative" change effecting the likelihood of recidivism. This may or may not have occurred. What we can say is that inmate participation in treatment programs may produce a deterrent to riot involvement. Precisely why this should occur is uncertain. Perhaps, those inmates who involve themselves in treatment programs have a greater interest in self-improvement or a greater fear of jeopardizing parole possibilities than those inmates who do not. It is also possible that participation in such programs may produce at least one link between the inmate and legitimate, non-deviant society and may thus militate against the complete absorption of the inmate into an inmate subculture where riot instigation and participation may be overtly or covertly approved. At any rate, if this finding holds up in future research, this would suggest that institutional treatment programs, irrespective of their impact upon rate of recidivism, do produce a deterrent to riot involvement. Thus, for this reason alone penal administrators may wish to improve the quality and quantity of such programs.

TABLE 11.3.
DEGREE OF RIOT INVOLVEMENT—BY PARTICIPATION IN
TREATMENT PROGRAMS*

	Non-Involved (N = 267)		Involved (N = 260)		Chi Square	Yule's Q
	No.	%	No.	%		
No participation in treatment programs	89	33	173	67		
					$X^2 = 57.98^{**}$	$Q = +.59$
Participation in one or more treatment programs	178	67	87	33		

*Shortly after data analysis had begun, an accidental clerical error combined the information culled from the institutional files of the moderately and heavily involved inmates. Since the initial data collection sheets had been discarded, we were unable to re-identify the moderately and heavily involved rioters. Thus, in this and subsequent tables, the two categories will be blended into one.
**Statistically significant at the .05 level using a one-tailed test.

RESULTS: INSTITUTIONAL BEHAVIOR

Prisons are full of rules and it is quite easy for an inmate to run afoul of any of them. Yet, inmates do vary in the degree to which they violate institutional norms. Some maintain relatively unblemished records while others accumulate numerous citations for institutional infractions. Since riot involvement appears to represent a rather severe rule violation, we hypothesized that those inmates with heavy records of violation of institutional rules would be more likely to participate in the riot than those inmates whose records reflected infrequent rule violations. The information which bears upon this issue is presented in Table 11.4.

As Table 11.4 reveals, all inmates who had no record of institutional rule violations are exclusively found in the non-involved riot category. On the other hand, all of the riot participants had accumulated one or more citations for institutional misconduct. On the basis of this evidence, it seems clear that an inmates' history of institutional rule violations is associated with the likelihood of riot participation. This particular finding may not come as much of a surprise to prison officials. They appear to have learned long ago that the bellicose or troublesome inmate is much more of a threat to the security and tranquility of the prison than the inmate who is pursuing a "keep my nose clean" routine.

In addition, it also appears that the relationship between institutional rule

TABLE 11.4.
DEGREE OF RIOT INVOLVEMENT—ACCORDING TO PRIOR
INSTITUTIONAL MISCONDUCT*

	Non-Involved (N = 236)†		Involved (N = 186)†		Chi Square	Gamma
	No.	%	No.	%		
No citations	76	32	0	0		
1–6 Citations	122	52	139	75	X² = 73.17‡	G = +.51
7 or more Citations	38	16	47	25		

*Institutional misconduct is measured here by the number of court citations the individual inmates received prior to the riot.
†The number of individuals compared in this table is smaller than in previous tables because of the lack of precise information regarding court appearances in a number of inmates' files.
‡Statistically significant at the .05 level using a one-tailed test.

violation and riot involvement is not explained by the length of time incarcerated. While the length of institutional time served was not systematically examined for each and every inmate, a cursory sampling of inmate files did not reveal noticeable discrepancies in time served by rioters and nonrioters. "Short-term" and "long-term" inmates seemed to be found with the same regularity in both the involved and non-involved categories. Yet, despite this important recognition, the information revealed in Table 11.4 did produce some surprises. We had anticipated that as the degree of institutional rule violations increased, so too would the likelihood of riot participation. However, this did not occur to any substantial degree. Among those inmates who had accumulated from one to six citations, 53 percent participated in the riot while 47 percent did not. Among those inmates who had accumulated seven or more rule violation citations, 55 percent participated in the riot while 45 percent did not. Thus, it would appear that the chances of an inmate's participation in a riot are indeed influenced by the presence or absence of a record of institutional rule violation. Those who have such records are likely candidates while those who do not have such records are very unlikely candidates for riot participation. However, the size or quantity of that institutional record does not appear to be a particularly important influencing condition.

RESULTS: MARITAL STATUS

In the United States, there appears to be a long-standing cultural belief that married men are somewhat more responsible creatures than single men.

If we can assume that remaining aloof from riot involvement represents a more responsible judgment than the futility of riot participation—an activity that seldom improves life conditions and often makes them worse—then it seems logical to hypothesize that marital status might be related to riot involvement. We thus predicted that married men would be less frequently found as riot participants than single men. The data which bears on this issue is presented in Table 11.5.

As the information in Table 11.5 indicates, single men were somewhat more likely to be involved in the riot. Slightly more than 60 percent of the married inmates examined did not participate. While this information supports our prediction, the statistical discrepancies are not striking and the measure of association reveals a fairly weak relationship between marital status and riot involvement. Thus, while marital status may make a difference in susceptibility to riot participation, the degree of influence is not large. Yet, it should be noted that the marital status information concerning the twenty-four heavily involved inmate rioters is not included in Table 11.5. This particular item of information was the last item scheduled for extraction from inmate records. The day before this process was to begin, the twenty-four heavily involved inmates and their files underwent the previously mentioned transfer to another institution. Our efforts to secure marital status information for these men from the new institution were unsuccessful. As a result, the question of whether or not the conclusions drawn from Table 11.5 would have been modified had this information for these men been included must remain open.

Summary and Conclusions

In the research reported here, a number of characteristics of inmate rioters and non-rioters were contrasted. Some of the characteristics examined did

TABLE 11.5.
DEGREE OF RIOT INVOLVEMENT—BY MARITAL STATUS*

	Non-Involved (N = 267)		Involved (N = 236)		Chi Square	Yule's Q
	No.	%	No.	%		
Single	198	74	193	82	$X^2 = 3.67**$	$Q = +.22$
Married	69	26	43	18		

*Because divorced inmates were quite rare, the few cases which did appear were combined into the single category.
**Statistically significant at the .10 level using a one-tailed test.

not reveal statistically significant differences. These non-significant characteristics consisted of: (1) the length of sentence being served, (2) length of
time before scheduled parole hearing, (3) whether the examined inmates had
been convicted of person or property offenses, (4) religious affiliation, and
(5) amount of completed education. Inmate variation on each of these items
was not statistically associated with riot involvement or non-involvement.
The failure of some of these examined items to achieve statistical significance
was surprising. In particular, the length of imposed sentence and the amount
of time before scheduled parole hearing seemed to be logically associated
with variable inmate feelings of frustration and futility which might be expressed in riot participation. Yet, at the time of the research, a fairly unique
parole policy was in operation at Lebanon and this policy may have
minimized variable inmate sentence and parole frustration. Under this policy, no inmate, regardless of the length of minimum sentence, had to wait
longer than 38 months before meeting the parole board. Thus, inmates serving 5–10, 10–20, and 20–40 year sentences all met the board after 38 months
of incarceration. While the likelihood of receiving parole certainly may have
varied among men serving sentences of different lengths, the hope that parole
would be granted at initial parole hearing may have been uniform. Hope, in
turn, may have minimized the "I've got nothing to lose" feeling thereby
inhibiting an inordinate amount of riot participation by those serving lengthy
sentences. At the present time, this unique parole policy is being recon-
sidered by State of Ohio officials and it is quite possible that it will be
changed to the more standard policy of three-fourths minimum time served
before parole eligibility is achieved. Should this occur, variations in hope
and despair among inmates serving sentences of different lengths may appear
and inadvertently influence differential susceptibility to riot participation.

Other characteristics examined did reveal a number of statistically
significant relationships. Generally speaking, it seems that the group of inmates most likely to participate in the riot was predominantly composed of
young, unmarried blacks who had received disciplinary reports for institutional misbehavior and who had not participated in any of the available
treatment programs. To the extent that the percentage of the inmate population reflecting these characteristics is increasing, to that extent may the number of riot participants increase when and if a prison riot erupts. Based upon
these findings, it would appear that the amount of physical distance between
a given inmate and the point of riot eruption—what we have earlier called the
proximity hypothesis—is not a wholly sufficient technique for predicting
who may and who may not participate in a riot. Instead, our data would
support a "birds of a feather" hypothesis, whereby inmates with certain
characteristics have differential susceptibility to riot participation. If this
conclusion is accurate, this may mean that prison officials are in a position to

minimize, to some extent, the amount of inmate participation in a riot should one occur.

On the one hand, some of the statistically significant characteristics of inmate rioters are beyond the control of prison officials. A man's race, age, and marital status are beyond the regulatory capacity of prison officials. Fortunately, however, these non-modifiable characteristics seemed to be less influential than the characteristics of institutional misbehavior and participation in treatment programs. These latter characteristics, in turn, may be subject to administrative influence. With reference to prison rules, for example, it is evident that inmates have long claimed that the plethora of rules found in prisons tend to accumulate over time to such a degreee as to virtually guarantee by their sheer weight that most inmates will run afoul of them at one time or another. Perhaps periodic reviews of institutional rules for the purpose of modifying or eliminating those which are no longer necessary for maintaining institutional security or for facilitating a smoothly operating organization would be valuable.

With reference to involvement in institutional treatment programs, perhaps administrative efforts to increase inmate participation would produce beneficial dividends. While the data collected here will not permit inferences to be drawn concerning a possible relationship between participation in treatment programs and subsequent recidivism, the relationship between participation in such programs and non-involvement in the riot was striking.

Should successful steps in these suggested directions be taken, this will not necessarily produce an immunity against the possibility of a prison riot occurring. The nature of American prisons may be such that the possibility of riots erupting will be ever present. However, if steps can be taken which will minimize the number of riot participants, then the resultant human and material damage may be reduced.

REFERENCES

Fox, Vernon. 1971, "Why Prisoners Riot." *Federal Probation*, XXXV (March): 9–14.

Part Three

Abnormal Patterns: Broad Perspectives

Possibly no other topic is better calculated to provoke angry debate among "correctionists" than is that of the role of abnormality in the etiology of crime and the treatment of criminals. Everyone is familiar with the frequently repeated courtroom drama involving opposing testimony by psychiatric and psychological experts as to the mental status of the defendant. In the preface to this volume, we noted that there is currently underway a widespread reaction against behavioral science contributions to the solving of crime problems. As a corollary to this movement, there has arisen much scepticism regarding the concept of abnormality as explaining or—in more radical form—defining criminality. In a limited sense, this has shaped up as an effort to discard the so-called medical or disease model, which places the primary accent on the inner condition of the individual offender—as distinct from the social, economic, and political conditions of society as breeding-grounds of crime. We have encountered several variants of the medical model in earlier sections, including the genetic, the constitutional (XYY syndrome), and the psychodynamic. The psychodynamic position, rooted in Freudian theory and interpreting criminal behavior as the outward expression of internal and largely unconscious forces, has been particularly influential. This is easy to understand since it carried the *cachet* of the burgeoning post-World War II mental health movement, with its optimistic assumption that, by uncovering the interior roots of criminal behavior (insight), one could hope to change such behavior. The name most closely identified with this medical model is Karl Menninger, and we can hardly hope to improve on his words:

> Can doctors cure willful aberrant behavior? Are we to believe that crime is a *disease* that can be reached by scientific measures? Isn't it merely "natural meanness" that makes all of us do wrong things at times even when we "know better"? And are not self-control, moral stamina, and will power the things needed? Surely there is no medical treatment for the lack of those!
>
> Let me answer this carefully, for much misunderstanding accumulates here. I would say that according to the prevalent understanding of the words, crime is *not* a disease. Neither is it an illness, although I think it *should* be! It *should* be treated, and it would be; but it mostly isn't (Menninger, 1969, p. 254).

While Menninger was decrying the failure of society to adopt wholeheartedly the treatment philosophy implied in the medical model, a whole chorus of voices have recently been heard in deprecation of it, pointing to its presumed ineffectiveness in the reformation of criminals or the reduction of crime. Some of this criticism was touched on in the preface to this anthology. David Fogel, Executive Director of the Illinois Law Enforcement Commission, has called for an abandonment of the treatment model in favor of an alternative which he has dubbed a "justice model": "All clinical programs can be dismantled. . . . The spectacle of organizing inmates into therapy groups or caseloads is embarrassingly tragic. It is best described as a psychic lock-step. When the indomitability of the human spirit could not be crushed by our 'break the spirit' forefathers, we relinquished the task to the technology of psychiatry." (Fogel, 1975, p. 262)

The raging debate over the "disease model" in criminality is a subsidiary of a larger ferment regarding the definition and etiology of all forms of abnormal or deviant behavior. Thomas Szasz, himself a medically trained psychiatrist, has given' the issue a slogan: "the myth of mental illness." Szasz has contended: "Strictly speaking, then, disease or illness can affect only the body. Hence, there can be no such thing as mental illness. . . . [Since] the vocabulary of psychiatry serves to redefine systematically moral and political problems as diseases, we must repudiate and stop this abuse of our language." (Szasz, 1973, pp. 305–307) Consequently, efforts to treat criminal behavior as a form of illness must be rejected, unless such behavior is palpably and directly expressive of bodily defect. In Szasz's view, behavior which is threatening to society—and only if there is a threat—ought to be dealt with by controlling or removing the poser of the threat and, if possible, affording him the opportunity to acquire less dangerous forms of behavior.

By removing both mental illness and criminality from the domain of medicine, i.e. psychiatry, Szasz is, by implication, obliterating the distinction between normal and abnormal, insofar as the distinction reflects divergence at the level of behavior. On the one hand, such a point of view harks back to the Freudian hypothesis that normal and abnormal are merely arbitrary positions on a continuum, both being expressive of instinctual strivings held in common by all individuals. On the other hand, it places a premium on evidence for the biological causation of criminality; presumably, to the degree that such causation is demonstrated, to that degree might there, in Szasz's view, be support for an illness interpretation of criminalty (although not necessarily for a psychiatric role, as traditionally conceived). It highlights, for example, the potential significance of work concerned with inheritance of traits (i.e. co-twin studies), chromosomal anomalies (e.g. the XYY syndrome), and toxic conditions produced by ingesting various substances, such as alcohol and other drugs. (In fairness to Szasz's position, it should be noted that, even in these examples, he would most likely reject an illness interpretation, insisting that even here a destinction should be drawn between *organic condition*, which *should* be treated by physicians, and *behavior* which, if antisocial, should be dealt with through traditional legal processes. In contrast to the position in the paper by Kittrie, presented earlier in this book, Szasz would reject the notion that an XYY chromosmal structure [or alcoholism, or drug addiction] be taken as extenuations of responsibility for criminal behavior.)

As we have seen, the psychoanalytic conception posits a commonality between normal and abnormal behavior. However, it is generally recognized

178

as an exemplar of the illness approach, inasmuch as it tends to view deviant—including criminal—behavior as symptomatic of disturbance; elimination of the symptoms requires eradication of the underlying cause, that is, by analogy with physical medicine, the disease process. Eliminating the surface symptom, while neglecting to restructure the basic substratum of personality, will result in the replacement of the eradicated symptom by a new one serving the same basic purpose in the psychic economy of the individual. By treating the drinking behavior of offenders, for example, without helping them to deal with the passive-dependency which the drinking stems from, new behaviors, reflecting this basic personality dynamic, such as a turn to heroin, may be substituted.

With this brief background, we may now turn to a consideration of a major contemporary approach, representing a radical departure from the various illness models of abnormality or social deviance. Referred to by Ullman and Krasner as sociopsychological, it represents an attempt to combine the learning theories of the American behaviorist, B. F. Skinner, with principles of personality development rooted in sociology. Behavior, in this perspective, is acquired, maintained, eliminated, or modified on the basis of the environmental consequences of that behavior. To the extent that the environment—especially the social or interpersonal environment—reacts to behavior emitted by the individual in ways that he experiences as positive (rewarding, pleasurable, approving, etc.), to that extent does the probability increase of such behavior being repeated. The behavior, in psychological terms, has received positive reinforcement from the environment. Behavior which fails to elicit gratifying consequences tends to decline in frequency of emission until it ultimately drops out of the individual's behavioral repertoire; that is, it undergoes extinction. Finally, behaviors can give rise to aversive or punishing environmental consequences, the outcome of which is a tendency to suppress such behaviors as long as the risk of punishment exists, e.g. in the presence of the punishing agent.

Several mutually interrelated elements stand out in the reinforcement model of behavior. First is the crucial significance of the environment's reaction to behavior performed by the individual in determining the destiny of the behavior. Second, of particular influence on human behavior, is the role of the social, i.e. the interpersonal, environment. Except in the most primitive conditions of physical deprivation, it is the consequential behavior of fellow humans that determines each individual's subsequent behavior. Third, and as a corollary to the second element, is the total denial of internal causes of behavior; rather than a mere symptom of more fundamental underlying causation, observed behavior is construed as subject to the control of the external environment. This constitutes a radical break with the medical model—including its psychodynamic version. Fourth—and here we note a point of commonality with the psychodynamicists—is that the socio-psychological approach affirms the continuity of normal and deviant behaviors. *All* behavior is controlled by environmental consequences, and whether it comes to be viewed as normal or deviant is entirely a matter of social definition (labelling, stigmatization) and social reaction (differential reinforcement).

In presenting the sociopsychological model of abnormality, Ullman and Krasner employ the concept of labelling to demonstrate, for one thing, the haziness of the line between the broad classifications of normal and abnormal and, for another, between those forms of abnormality labelled psychiatric and those labelled criminal. The latter, particularly, is seen in their interweaving of illustrations from both realms throughout their discussion. Such labels are seen by them as means whereby any social group gains the adherence of its members to the values of the group. Where a member's behavior is deemed by the group to be "upsetting . . . psychiatric intervention permits a form of social control where no control has been legally legislated."

The deviant label in itself is of limited significance. Despite the loose references in contemporary conversation to self-fulfilling prophecies, it is not the label as such which results in an individual behaving in consonance with the label. It is still largely true that "Sticks and stones may break my bones, but names will never harm me." Sticks and stones may, however, follow from names, as in the form of penal sanctions; labels may imply social consequences of significance to the labelled, thereby influencing his or her subsequent behavior. It is a process whose steps can be visualized approximately as outlined on page 181.

In examining our schematic representation, the reader will recognize that the assumption of a criminal self-definition is dependent on the behavior of the social environment toward the individual, with its withdrawal of attention from his prosocial behavior, noticing (and punishing him for) his antisocial behavior, depriving him of opportunities to enact (and gain positive reinforcement for) socially approved behavior, as when a teacher ignores a stutdent's efforts to master academic subjects, but notices immediately when the student misbehaves in school. As this process proceeds—or unless the environment is somehow influenced to reverse the process by having its attentional emphasis refocussed on prosocial behaviors—the individual finds himself forced increasingly to seek positive reinforcement from alternative sources. Among the latter, one possibility would be sub-groups already actively criminal or delinquent. Among these, there is a tendency to applaud behaviors of a socially disapproved character. Each time such applause is experienced, in the absence of reward for competing prosocial behavior, the probability of repeating the positively reinforced antisocial behavior is increased. As it takes over a larger and larger proportion of the individual's

1	2	3	4	5
Deviant act (or deviant appearance)	Public label	Public expectancy	Environmental consequences	Self definition
		Social definition steps		
Steal; get caught	"Thief"	Will steal again	a. Environment ignores prosocial behavior ("all bad") b. Environment attends to antisocial behaviors c. Isolated, rejected by prosocial community deprived of opportunity to observe, and gain reinforcement for prosocial behavior d. Forced into association with antisocial peer community; observes, and is reinforced for, antisocial activity.	a. "I *behave* like a criminal; I must *be* a criminal." b. "This is what I know" (criminality as occupational role) c. "These antisocial peers are my people; I am one of them."

total behavior, he may at some point acknowledge its predominance in his life, taking on the character of a long-term "vocational" commitment, much as might occur following apprenticeship in one of the more traditional occupations.

We see, from the above brief description, that the distinction between criminal and lawful behavior is far from dichotomous, insofar as the process of acquisition is concerned. At the same time, it is well for the student to recognize that there are several broad patterns of abnormal behavior—syndromes, in the language of traditional psychopathology—which have been implicated in criminal behavior with particular frequency. Two such patterns are sociopathic (psychopathic) personality and paranoid personality, and we have selected to present in this unit the sociopsychological description of their development through excerpts from the book by Ullman and Krasner, *A Psychological Approach to Abnormal Behavior*. As might be anticipated from what we have said thus far, the emphasis is not on any *intrinsic* abnormality in behavior but rather on the way in which the environment responds to the individual enacting the behavior. Describing the behavior of the paranoid as involving "the expression of beliefs that are *considered so improbable* as to be false . . . a paranoid person is extinguished for attending and collecting evidence for the true (i.e. the majority's) belief and acts *rationally* on the information and choices available to him" (emphasis added). Again, in other words, by being deprived of opportunity to acquire (and express) socially accepted beliefs, he is left to fall back upon beliefs of presumably lesser probability (or social acceptability) which when expressed cause him to be seen as delusional and to be still further distanced from the community. Simultaneously, the opportunity for the delusional beliefs to be extinguished are reduced by reduced exposure to the nonreinforcing behavior of others. Instead, there may be a tendency on the part of those hearing the false beliefs to laugh at, or even to persecute, the one expressing them. This might cause the latter to suppress their utterance, while continuing to harbor them privately, and fatefully, to gain support for his delusions of persecution, for his belief that he is surrounded by enemies. The reader may have noted that the emphasis here is not on the intrinsic truth or falsity of the belief expressed, but rather on its perceived probability (or, put in other terms, its consensual validity).

We can illustrate the process of becoming paranoid in the following example which, while hypothetical as to details, is by no means remote from true-to-life observation. Consider the instance of "George Williams," who had been employed for some years as a correctional officer at a maximum security prison. From the day of his arrival on the job, Mr. Williams was imbued by his fellow guards with the need to be cautious in the presence of inmates—"Never turn your back on one;" "they're constantly scheming;" "It's us against them," and so on. Conversations among the guard force were filled with accounts of incidents reflecting this belief, and it was perfectly evident that the ones expressing it most fervently were the ones who were held in highest esteem by their colleagues, while any inclination to question it was soon snuffed out by derision as well as other forms of subtle pressure. Mr. Williams soon discovered that by demonstrating both verbally and nonverbally his agreement with this outlook, his acceptance increased among the more experienced guards (i.e., he was reinforced). Thus, in a relatively short period of time, he had been indoctrinated with the prevailing ideology of the prison guard force. And the more accurately he enacted the ideology, the more (positive) reinforcement he received—social acceptance, admiration, even promotions and merit raises. By now, he was thoroughly convinced that danger pervades the relationship between prisoner and guard, that the prisoners eye the officers with a hatred ever alert for an opportunity for violent— behind the back—attack, and that most people on the outside (especially those naive "reformers" expressing sympathy for prisoners) just have no idea how vicious prisoners really are. But then, after some years have passed, Mr. Williams received the report of his required annual physical check-up, which stated that a cardiac defect had been discovered and informed him that he was eligible for either extended sick leave benefit or for early retirement with full pension based on disability. Selecting the latter option, he and his family moved to a new place, somewhat closer to his native hometown. In an effort to get to know some of his fellow-townsmen, he started to drop in of an evening at a tavern downtown. On one of these occasions, when he had been drinking to the point of "feeling no pain," he overheard a conversation in which one of the participants expressed a belief that people were much to "up-tight" on the question of crime, that most criminals are "not all that different from you and me." The former guard immediately recognized the subject as an opening for him to join in. Not surprisingly, his comments reflected the years just recently ended, the belief in the inherent evil of those who commit crimes. The discussion became increasingly heated, fueled by the participants' intake of alcohol. The ex-guard experienced a growing sense of frustrated rage at the naivete of his opponents and their unwillingness to acknowledge his expertise regarding the topic. Soon he was shouting how dumb they were, what did they know, the streets were filled with danger, and one of these days one of them would get it, and it would serve him right. The others in the group found themselves not knowing what to make of his intensity and when one finally told him to cool it, Mr. Williams proceeded to throw a punch, which rapidly escalated into a melée, bringing in the police to break it up. Everyone questioned reported that it was started by Mr. Williams, who had been talking and acting like a nut. Mr. Williams was arrested and brought before an arraigning magistrate who, upon hearing of the event in the tavern as well as Mr. Williams' agitated assertion that he was "just telling the real truth, but those idiots wouldn't listen," ordered Mr. Williams remanded to the close security section of a nearby mental hospital for psychiatric evaluation prior to trial. At the hospital, Mr. Williams' agitation increased, and at one point he wrote a letter to the hospital administration repeating his story, insisting on both his innocence and his sanity. He ended it with a threat to sue for false arrest the man he had struck at the tavern, the arresting policeman, the magistrate, and the hospital administrator—all of whom he accused of acting in coordination to deprive him of his freedom. Moreover, he proceeded to talk in a like vein to other patients and to attendants at the hospital, at times pleading, other times threatening. Approximately one week after his admission to the hospital, he attempted to "walk away" from a recreational lounge, was discovered hiding in a storeroom, and when one of the attendants approached him, Mr. Williams struck the attendant. The psychiatric report to the magistrate contained the words "belligerant," "assaultive," "delusions of persecution," and ended with a tentative diagnosis of "paranoid personality (delusional)." It recommended that he be committed to the state hospital for the criminally insane until certified no longer dangerous by the staff of the institution.

Several elements in the experience of the fictitious George Williams illustrate the sociopsychological processes of abnormality.

By utilizing a correctional officer, as an example, we hope to show that the process is not restricted to segments of the population traditionally identified as dangerous; given the right combination of environmental consequences, the concept asserts, any individual could come to be perceived as dangerously abnormal. Note, for example, that his trouble begins when responses acquired *and positively reinforced* in a previous setting were transferred to an environment in which the very same responses proved dysfunctional. Several circumstances in his background might have to be assumed as contributory: (a) violence as an approved—or at least understood—response in the previous environment; (b) a rather limited experience of the larger world, resulting in Mr. Williams' failure to recognize the inappropriateness of his previous responses—acquired in the special circumstance of a prison, itself part of a "prison town"—to a significantly different community. We saw, moreover, that the response-pattern of paranoid personality, namely delusions of persecution, has a way of snowballing in that each individual behavioral response served to elicit further environmental punishment. This, of course, strengthened Mr. Williams' sense of being put down, rejected, misunderstood. Ultimately, feeling increasingly helpless to reverse the process—Mr. Williams strikes out violently. The first link between paranoid and criminal violence has been forged in the crucible of interaction between individual and environment.

Even more regularly associated with criminality is the class of abnormality known as sociopathic or psychopathic personality. While both terms are in currency, the former is of more recent vintage. It reflects the interesting observation that abnormality is inferred from the social (antisocial?) behavior of the individual, rather than from any significant evidence of bizarre thinking or felt discomfort on the part of the individual. Case reports of people diagnosed as sociopathic personality contain few references to delusional thinking, hallucination, inner conflict and anxiety; instead we read such phrases as "egocentric;" "a long history of theft;" "lives off the proceeds of crime;" "appears unable to learn from experience, from punishment;" "is parasitic, exploitative, and manipulative of others;" "no remorse or guilt;" "impulsive;" "lacks conscience." Often, the "sociopath" is described as a person of charm and intelligence, and as verbally smooth. In some descriptions, he comes through as, *par excellence*, the confidence man.

The chronicity of antisocial—or perhaps more to the point, dissocial—behavior and its resistance to efforts at reform has led numbers of theorists to the conclusion that sociopathy is a constitutionally determined defect, hence relatively intractable in the face of environmental manipulation. The socio-psychological position, on the other hand, proposes an explanation consistent with its emphasis on environmental consequences. Ullman and Krasner do attempt to integrate a number of essentially constitutional formulations with hypothesized reinforcement history in the causation of sociopathy.

In attempting to summarize their position, it might be well to start with some commonplace observations. Many workers have commented on the fact that habitual criminals become quickly bored with normal, day-to-day activities and constantly seem to be seeking new excitement, new sensations, and new thrills. Another set of observations focuses on the failure of the sociopath to avoid repeating behaviors which have previously resulted in aversive consequences, that is, failure to learn from experience, and more specifically, from punishment. Such observations have led some to the conclusion that the sociopath is constitutionally less capable of processing external stimuli at a level necessary to maintain normal levels of arousal. To reach such levels, he requires greater than normal amounts of stimulation, hence the constant pursuit of new and exciting experience. To borrow a phrase from an earlier era, he appears to receive less bang for a buck. This has suggested the notion that the sociopath suffers from stimulus-hunger (Quay) and is a stimulus-seeker. Since the acquisition of moral judgments and moral behaviors is a function of learning, based on environmental inputs (punishment, reward), a reduced capability for experiencing such inputs would ensue in reduced learning.

Ullman and Krasner introduce an additional concept—inconsequentiality. If moral behavior—like all behavior—is acquired on the basis of reinforcing consequences from the environment, then the seemingly amoral and egocentric behavior of the sociopath must be the outcome of a reinforcement history from which *consistent* patterns of reinforcement for "right and wrong" behaviors were absent. Thus, early in his development, the sociopath may have learned that it did not much matter whether he behaved acceptably or unacceptably, insofar as rewarding or punishing consequences were concerned. Hence, his morally relevant behavior could be described as inconsequential. He may have discovered, in addition, that he could avoid punishment for misbehavior by staying out of his parents' way till they cooled down. Or that rewards were more readily earned by being charming (conning; psyching out) than by behaving in socially approved ways. In such early learning encounters, presumably, behavioral responses having little relation to morality are acquired. Instead, we find the seeds of responsibility-avoidance and the early signs of interpersonal manipulativeness.

Our present knowledge does not permit, or even require, that we choose from among the concepts which we have reviewed, in our efforts to understand the significance of abnormality for criminal behavior. Each of them has sufficient plausibility to warrant consideration by the correctional practitioner in his or her efforts to develop approaches to individual offenders. To the extent that stimulus-hunger may be significant, it suggests that responses to the behavior of sociopathic clientele ought to be emphatic, clear-cut, impressive. Inconsequentiality implies an obligation to draw clear and unmistakable lines between acceptable and unacceptable behavior, and to provide consistently differentiated environmental consequences for such behaviors. Given the fact, finally, that stimulus-hunger and inconsequentiality are completely compatible, may, in fact, be additive in their effect; the practitioner would be well advised to take them both into account in the planning of programs for changing sociopathic behavior patterns.

We conclude our consideration of psychopathology with the study by Chesno and Kilman, which focuses on the stimulus-seeking behavior attributed to sociopathic offenders. Their grouping of subjects is of interest, highlighting the generally observed absence of anxiety—guilt feelings—among sociopaths. The authors used this characteristic to divide their population into primary sociopaths, those with little or no prior evidence of anxiety; neurotics, characterized by high levels of anxiety; and an in-between group of "normals." Varying the level of auditory stimulation accompanying a shock-avoidance response to be acquired, they were able to demonstrate that the sociopathic group had greater difficulty in learning such a response under conditions of reduced stimulation. This is a finding consistent with the hypothesis that sociopaths require greater environmental stimulus. By extension, it may help to explain the limited capacity of sociopaths to learn from normal levels of punishment for transgression of social rules.

REFERENCES

Fogel, D. *We Are the Living Proof*. Cincinnati: W. H. Anderson, 1975.
Menninger, K. *The Crime of Punishment*. New York: Viking Press, 1969.
Szasz, T. S. "Mental Illness as a Metaphor." *Nature*. 242 (1973): pp. 305–307.

12

A Sociopsychological Model[1]

Leonard P. Ullmann and Leonard Krasner

From Leonard P. Ullmann and Leonard Krasner, *A Psychological Approach to Abnormal Behavior*, © 1969, pp. 186–218. Reprinted by permission of the authors and of Prentice-Hall, Inc., Englewood Cliffs, New Jersey.

In order for a human activity to be designated as abnormal, a social situation must be involved. . . . This position has a number of implications. The first is in terms of definitions: *deviance* has been defined as failure to act in accordance with the expectations of others,[2] and *abnormality* as the type of deviance that sanctioned the professional attention of people such as psychologists and psychiatrists. This leads to the observation that what was expected and what was deviant depended on variables of time, place, and person.[3] An understanding of abnormality must therefore take into account the sociological context of the act and its evaluation.

LABELING AS BEHAVIOR

Given the considerations of time, place, and person as crucial variables in the formulation of abnormality, it is impossible to designate either a particular act or a particular actor as abnormal *per se*. . . . No fully satisfactory operational definition of abnormality has been devised. . . . Different professional groups or situations call forth special definitions of abnormality. Labeling behavior is a social act and, like any other social act, is one that is developed and maintained by reinforcing contingencies.

This point has been aptly expressed by Pronko (1963, p. 34): "Classification is, first of all, a human activity. It always involves a person observing phenomena in which he can perceive similarities and differences. There is always another essential but easily overlooked point: the observer has a *purpose* or *aim* in ordering those same data. . . ."

THE LABELER'S PROBLEM

An important analysis of the diagnostic act has been made by Scheff (1966a, pp. 105–127). Consider the physician's situation of having to decide whether to hospitalize a person or not. There are essentially two natural verifications of his decision: the person was indeed sick, or the person was not sick. It is possible to make a fourfold table in the manner of Table 12.1.

Following the letter designation of cells in Table 12.1, it is possible to evaluate the various outcomes for physical ills. If, as in A, the patient is indeed sick and the physician has hospitalized him, the physician has done the proper thing and his judgment has been verified. If, as in C, the physician hospitalizes the person and it is found that the person was not ill, the physician has not lost a great deal: he has practiced sound, conservative medicine, and, if anything, the patient will be grateful to him for his concern and care. If, as in D, the physician does not hospitalize and the person is indeed not ill, the physician has not made any visible professional gain and has had to reject the patient's complaints. If, finally, as in B, the physician does not hospitalize the patient and it is found that there was indeed an illness justifying hospitalization, the physician is a bad diagnostician and has poorly served both the patient and his profession. Because there is no stigma attached to being physically ill, because a careful physical checkup takes only a few days, and because there is relatively little expense, the medical patient has little to lose by being hospitalized. When in doubt, the physician does the rational thing: he hospitalizes the patient.

The situation is different for the patient in the case of psychiatric hospitalization. While there is a strong carryover of the concept "When in doubt, hospitalize," psychiatric hospitalization may lead to increased rather than decreased behavioral problems. These problems may occur through the training received in the hospital milieu (Sommer and Osmond, 1961; Barton, 1959; Wing, 1962) and the stigma attached to having been a patient in a psychiatric hospital (Lamy, 1966). Additional problems are raised by the greater length of psychiatric hospitalization. For these reasons, contemporary community mental health programs aim at keeping the person out of the hospital and continuing to strive in the environment which provides the ultimate criterion of adjustment. In short, the individual has much more to lose by psychiatric hospitalization than by hospitalization for a physical ailment.

TABLE 12.1.
PATIENT HOSPITALIZATION DECISIONS

| | | Physician's Decision | |
		Hospitalize	Do Not Hospitalize
Case Outcome	Sick	A	B
	Not Sick	C	D

Two additional pieces of information offered by Scheff on diagnostic practices are worth noting. That the trend for physicians dealing with physical illness is to err in a "conservative" (sick) direction may be noted in Garland's (1959) study of 14,867 X-ray films for signs of tuberculosis. There were 1,216 positive (sick) readings that turned out to be clinically negative (i.e. false alarms) and only 24 negative (not sick) readings that later turned out to be clinically active. The bias to call a film "sick" or pathological was 50 times greater than the bias in the direction of health. Because the cost to the patient of extra clinical tests is slight compared to the cost of untreated tuberculosis, this type of bias is socially acceptable. A similar result was reported by Bakwin (1956) in a study of the advisability of tonsillectomy for 1,000 school children. Of these children, 611 had their tonsils removed. The remaining 389 children were then examined by other physicians and 174 were selected for tonsillectomy. This left a group of 215 children, and when another group of physicians examined them, 99 were adjudged in need of tonsillectomy. Still another group of physicians examined the remaining children, and nearly half were again judged to be in need of the operation.

Shifting to the psychiatric situation, Scheff (1966a, pp. 130–132) reports on ratings of patients by 25 psychiatrists admitting patients to a state psychiatric hospital. The two main reasons for admitting patients to such a hospital are to protect the patient and to protect other members of society. Of 164 involuntarily confined patients, 102 or 63 per cent were rated as neither dangerous to others nor severely mentally impaired (i.e., needing protection for themselves). Mechanic (1962) writes: "In the two mental hospitals studied over a period of three months, the investigator never observed a case where the psychiatrist advised the patient that he did not need the treatment. Rather, all persons who appeared at the hospital were absorbed into the patient population regardless of their ability to function adequately outside the hospital." Kutner (1962) and Miller and Schwartz (1966) made similar observations. Scheff reports on observations of court proceedings as follows:

> Our observations of 116 judicial hearings raised the question of the adequacy of the psychiatric examination. Eighty-six of the hearings failed to establish that the patients were "mentally ill" (according to the criteria stated by the judges in interviews). Indeed, the behavior and responses of 48 of the patients at the hearings seemed completely unexceptionable. Yet the psychiatric examiners had not recommended the release of a single one of these patients. Examining the court records of 80 additional cases, we found still not a single recommendation for release. (1966a, p. 139.)

THE SOCIAL FUNCTION OF LABELING

It has been pointed out that psychiatric diagnosis is a social act made in the light of prior training that is manifested by biases toward the conservative or "sick" decision. The next question is why such behavior is maintained, or to put the issue bluntly, what are the conditions that lead social agencies to pay psychiatrists for such behavior? What function is served by such diagnoses?

This chapter started with a recapitulation of the basic definition of abnormality used in this book: abnormal behavior is behavior that is deviant in such a manner that a mental health professional's intervention is sanctioned. Szasz (1966b, p. 153) makes this point when he writes, "When people perform their social roles properly—in other words, the social expectations are adequately met—their behavior is considered normal." Accurate prediction of the response of another person, and especially being able to predict what is a response adequate to evoke a favorable response from another, is an act for which the individual has been frequently reinforced. . . . [It has been] noted how bringing a coat to a volunteer was sufficient to have her take a patient for a walk. There is a chain . . . in which one person's behavior becomes a stimulus for another person's response, which in turn is a discriminative stimulus or acquired reinforcer. . . . A person who acts in a manner that is unexpected *in an area in which someone else has a stake* poses a problem for the other person. This problem can be solved in a number of ways, *one* of which is to call the person mentally ill.

Szasz (1966b, pp. 150, 153) points out that terms like "waiter," "stenographer," and "judge" not only classify occupations but also define role expectations. He then offers an example: "The waiter refuses to wait on tables. He sits in the back of the café and scribbles endlessly on scraps of paper. When asked what he is doing, he either scowls condescendingly and refuses to answer, or confides to friends that he is writing a treatise on philosophy that will save the world. He is taken to a mental hospital by the police." First of all, the man raised a problem, but it might have been solved by coercing him to wait on tables or by firing him. He might have been begged by his wife and children who depended on his wages. Calling the police and having the man taken to the psychiatric hospital was but one possible solution.

The second aspect of this example is that the act of calling the police and the steps in the sequence of hospitalization represent human behaviors. . . . The acts must be in the individual's repertoire and must, whether learned through direct or vicarious reinforcement, be matched to a particular situation. In short, the situation must be labeled by the café owner as one fitting the category "Call the cops to take the guy to the loony bin." As with any other act, if prior experiences in similar situations have not worked out well—for example, led to endless red tape and court appearances—the café owner would not emit the acts. If however, through his reading of the mass media or prior personal experience, the café owner has learned that this is the effective and correct act, he will perform it.

A third issue touched on by the example of the waiter is that he broke no specific written, legislated rule. He committed no criminal act. On the other hand, his behavior was upsetting. In this instance, psychiatric intervention permits a form of social control where no control has been legally legislated. The psychiatric intervention is a solution. The situation is similar to that of the *Shaw* case in England. Shaw published a *Ladies Directory* in which were paid advertisements by women whose monetary approach to sex was at variance with official moral expectations. There was involved an alleged conspiracy to corrupt public morals: an offense that broke no statute. The judges in the House of Lords permitted the charge to stand, and one of the judges advanced the view that:

> ". . . the Court of King's Bench was *custos morum* of the people and had superintendency of offences *contra bonos mores* . . . there is in that Court a residual power, where no statute has yet intervened to supersede the common law, to superintend those offences which are prejudicial to the common welfare. Such occasions will be rare, for Parliament has not been slow to legislate when attention has been sufficiently aroused. But gaps remain and will always remain, since no one can foresee every way in which the wickedness of man may disrupt the order of society." (Hart, 1966, p. 9.)

The use of psychiatric intervention may permit controls to be extended in much the same way as illustrated by the Court of King's Bench: where no written rules exist, social control may be effected through psychiatric intervention. The particular value that is sacrificed or circumvented, depending on one's viewpoint, is that offenses should be carefully defined so that an individual may know beforehand what acts are criminal and what are not. The use of the concept of mental illness in this manner fits in with empirical observation. For example, Karl Menninger (1963, p. 77) writes: ". . . we can define illness as being a certain state of existence which is uncomfortable to someone and for which medical science offers or is believed by the public to offer relief. The suffering may be in the afflicted person or in those around him or both, but a disturbance has occurred in the total economics of a personality which becomes the focus of our clinical attention."

Up to the point of the last clause, starting with "but a disturbance has occurred," the quotation is not contradictory to the viewpoint taken in this volume. The agreement is that there is a difficult social situation for which the mental health profession is believed to offer an answer. A second aspect of this quotation is that the term "illness" is given a very broad meaning, "an uncomfortable state of existence." Szasz (1966a, p. 40) has correctly pointed out that this permits intervention in literally any area of human activity. Such intervention might be justified if mental illness actually existed in nature as entities in the manner that atoms and bacteria exist factually and distinct from social evaluations. The difference may be expressed in another way: if one calls a rock granite, it does not change; but if one calls a person schizophrenic, both his behavior and the behavior of those who come in contact with him may be changed. The third aspect of the quotation, then, is the clause that indicates the presence of a deviation in "personality." . . . A diagnosis of deviation from an accepted standard of functioning would conceivably permit the intervention of the specialist. Such intervention has social advantages: it becomes possible to say that the person was sick and that the actions which followed were not matters of control and infringement on personal freedom, but rather actions, scientifically grounded, taken for the person's own good. As a result, a medical model offers a chance to have one's cake and eat it: one can control others while feeling virtuous rather than guilty over not being democratic. A corollary is that treatment rather than punishment will be given; the reality at the majority of large psychiatric hospitals and prisons belies this hope.

PUBLIC INFORMATION AND LABELING

The second point derived from the example of the waiter who wrote rather than served at table was that calling the police was a learned response to the situation. This point in turn leads to two considerations. The first is that such an act is the right, the proper, the humane thing to do. In general (Nunnally, 1961), the opinion of the public about mental illness is not very different from that of experts in the field, such as psychiatrists and psychologists. However, the attitudes of the public (as measured by semantic differential scales) are in general far more negative toward the mental patient than those of professionals. Giovannoni and Ullmann (1963) found that hospitalized psychiatric patients gave responses very similar to those obtained by Nunnally. Manis, Houts, and Blake (1963) also found that psychiatric and nonpsychiatric patients held similar views about mental illness. In short, there is widespread and shared conception of the characteristics of the mental patient and his role.

It is generally viewed as good and desirable that the public share the views of mental health experts, notably that mental illness is like any other illness and should be treated by a physician. Woodward (1951) reports on data gathered by the procedures of a Roper survey. Woodward writes: "The first major conclusion that emerges from an analysis of the study results in that people (at least in Louisville) are definitely moving toward a humanitarian and scientific point of view toward mental illness . . . that mental illness is a sickness that should evoke sympathetic understanding and . . . requires some form of professional treatment." Two brief case histories were presented, and respondents were given a list from which they could select what would be the best thing to do. The assumptions of the investigators are clear from Woodward's statement about the subject of one of the case histories: "The lady described in the question . . . is a paranoid type clearly in need of professional treatment." The question was as follows: "Mrs. B had always been a little suspicious and inclined to take the worst view of things, but she had led a fairly happy married life until she began to accuse her husband of not loving her any more. When she saw him speak politely to an attractive widow next door, Mrs. B waited until he had left, got hold of his gun, and then went over and threatened to kill the widow. Mrs. B's husband hadn't done anything wrong and doesn't know what to do about her." Of the total sample, 26 per cent thought it would be best for her minister to talk with her, 21 per cent thought her husband should give her a good talking-to and see if she came to her senses, 21 per cent said the family doctor should be called and give a sedative to calm her down, 13 per cent thought the husband should stay home and prove to Mrs. B he loved her, 7 per cent said Mrs. B should be taken to a mental hospital where she could be treated and not do anyone any harm, 1 per cent said the police should be called to lock her up immediately, and 11 per cent of the respondents "did not know" or "did not like any of these alternatives."

A second matter derived from the waiter incident needs further comment; it is exemplified by the café owner's calling the police. This involves the designation of abnormal behavior by nonprofessionals. . . . It is a crucial problem in epidemiological studies. Zubin puts the matter as follows:

> The detection, rather than diagnosis, of mental disorders is made largely by laymen—the patient himself, his family, friends, neighbors, the community and its public officials, such as policemen, sheriffs, etc. . . . Thus, at least the initial detection of mental illness is based largely on those aspects of the patient's behavior which deviate from expected social and cultural norms. As a result, sociocultural forces tend to bias the apparent prevalence of mental illness.[4] (1966, p. 47.)

The two important points, that mass media disseminate information about the roles of both the abnormal person and his significant others, and that the vast majority of actions leading to people's being called to the attention of professional workers are initiated by laymen, are brought together in a statement by Jerome Frank:

> An interesting, if somewhat unfortunate, consequence of the fact that social attitudes play such a big role in the definition of mental illness is that mental health education may be a two-edged sword. By teaching people to regard certain types of distress or behavioral oddities as illnesses rather than as normal reactions to life's stresses, harmless eccentricities, or moral weaknesses, it may cause alarm and increase the demand for psychotherapy. This may explain the curious fact that the use of psychotherapy tends to keep pace with its availability. The greater the number of treatment facilities and the more widely they are known, the larger the number of persons seeking their services. Psychotherapy

is the only form of treatment which, at least to some extent, appears to create the illness it treats. It can never suffer the unfortunate fate of Victor Borge's physician uncle, who became despondent on realizing that he had discovered a cure for which there was no disease. (Frank, 1961, pp. 6–7.)

SOCIAL EVENTS LEADING TO THE LABEL "ABNORMAL"

Up to this point the discussion of the implications of the definition of mental illness has centered on the referral situation and its social function. This section will examine the specific cultural and class variables likely to lead to the person's being labeled abnormal.

CROSS-CULTURAL CONSIDERATIONS

Benedict (1934) noted that "localized social norms" among "simpler" people offered an opportunity to test cultural concepts which might have been considered as universal and inevitable if only standardized Western European people were available for study. One of her most striking findings was that many people who would be considered abnormal in our culture would fit into other cultures with ease and honor. Benedict points out the valued place of cataleptic and trancelike states in the role of the shaman in diverse cultures. She cites work by Fortune (1932) describing a Melanesian culture in which the major theme was a belief that other people were trying to harm the individual. Belief in the malevolence of others was omnipresent. A flavor of this belief may be gathered by the fact that the polite phrase at the acceptance of a gift was, "And if you now poison me, how shall I repay you this present?" Benedict writes, "Now in this society where no one may work with another and no one may share with another, Fortune describes the individual who was regarded by all his fellows as crazy. He was not one of those who periodically ran amok and, beside himself and frothing at the mouth, fell with a knife upon anyone he could reach. Such behavior they did not regard as putting anyone outside the pale. They did not even put the individuals who were known to be liable to these attacks under any kind of control. They merely fled when they saw the attack coming and kept out of the way. 'He would be alright tomorrow.' But there was one man of sunny, kindly disposition who liked work and liked to be helpful. The compulsion was too strong for him to repress it in favor of the opposite tendencies of his culture. Men and women never spoke of him without laughing: he was silly and simple and definitely crazy. Nevertheless, to the ethnologist used to a culture that has, in Christianity, made his type the model of all virtue, he seemed a pleasant fellow."

Reports such as this one, particularly as they involve aggression against one's fellows, from cultures such as the Kwakiutl (Benedict, 1934) and the Mundugumor (Mead, 1935) have a major and continuing place in theoretical formulations of abnormal behavior. Compared to normal people in these cultures, Mrs. B, the lady who in Woodward's (1951) study threatened the attractive widow next door, is a living doll. Yet, Mrs. B "is a paranoid type clearly in need of professional treatment." Such comparisons question the very nature of the concept of abnormality. Benedict (1934) wrote: "Most of those organizations of personality that seem to us most incontrovertibly abnormal have been used by different civilizations in the very foundations of their institutional life. . . . We recognize that morality differs in every society, and is a convenient term for socially approved habits. . . . The concept of the normal is properly a variant of the concept of the good. It is that which society has approved. A normal action is one that falls well within the limits of expected behavior for a particular society."

The use of ethnological material for purposes of cross-cultural psychiatric purposes must start with a clear conception of what is abnormal. Benedict, in the material cited above, represents a view called *cultural relativism*. In this view, what is abnormal is a function of cultural training and labeling, and the very behavior that is abnormal in one group is valued and considered not only normal but admirable in another. Two alternative views exist. The first is one which presumes that there is a normal distribution or *continuum* of behaviors ranging from normal to abnormal. The quotation from Rosen and Gregory (1965, p. 11) . . . represents a sample of this viewpoint: statistical frequency, degree of conformity, and extent of feelings of being unhappy and uncomfortable are all relative to a supposedly healthy group and represent quantitative rather than qualitative differences. The second alternative view is that health and illness are *discontinuous* and that there are qualitative differences between them. The quotation from Wegrocki (1939) . . . is an illustration of this type of thinking. All three views currently have their adherents, as indicated in recent volumes such as those by Eron (1966) and DeReuck and Porter (1965). Not infrequently the latter two views may be implied by the same author: certain answers to questionnaire items may be considered symptoms and the person with more symptoms is then considered sicker and hence suitable for diagnostic labeling. Generally the worker in the field of cross-cultural psychiatry is attracted to a discontinuous format as definitive of abnormality. . . . Thus, frequently, the very questions posed are already answered by the way in which they were asked.

Among the more interesting items of anthropological work is the description of "ethnic" psychoses: *amok*, a homicidal rampage; *piblokto*, an endemic convulsive disorder among the polar Eskimos; *windigo* psychosis among the Algonquin Indian hunters, in which the starved man becomes convinced he is in the power of a supernatural monster with an insatiable craving for human flesh; *ufufunyane*, noted among South African tribes such as the Zulus and Zhosa, which consists of attacks of shouting and sobbing, sometimes accompanied by abdominal pains and loss of consciousness and sight, attributed to the operation of magical love potions administered by rejected lovers. Among Siberian groups, especially women, there at times appears a copying mania called *amurakh; menerik* is similar but there is wilder screaming and dancing, often ending in an epileptiform seizure. *Kere*, observed among the people of the Malayan archipelago and South China, is an acute anxiety reaction in which the person (usually but not always male) fears that his sex organ will shrink and disappear into his abdomen; one type of *latah* observed among Malaysian people is similar to *amurakh*, but another type begins with a startle reaction under which all normal activity is suspended. It requires quite a bit of compromise with the definitions used in the United States to place these behaviors in the diagnostic system presented.

CROSS-CULTURAL INCIDENCE OF MENTAL DISORDERS

The availability of professional resources is a major determinant of the incidence of mental disorder. This makes it difficult to determine whether one society or one period of history is especially conducive to mental disorders. Goldhamer and Marshall (1949) reviewed hospital records in Massachusetts from 1840 onwards to determine the effect of cultural changes on the frequency of mental disorders. Their conclusion was that other than an increase in people over age 50, made possible by increases in life expectancy, admission rates remained stable throughout the various changing periods of history surveyed.

There formerly was a popular notion that there were no instances of mental illness among the relatively isolated, closely knit Hutterites. Eaton and Weil (1955), on close investigation, found that roughly one in 43 of the Hutterites displayed symptoms of mental disorder or had recovered from such symptoms. While the rate is far lower than the estimates made by studies of prevalence in other groups (which will be noted below), it is not, as had been rumored, zero. What was perhaps most useful to the Hutterite who was "mentally ill" was to be encouraged to participate in the normal life of the family and community, and most were able to do some useful work. The person was neither rejected nor cast away into a state hospital. It would seem that the favorable "mental health" record of the Hutterites was as much dependent upon what the group did when a person took the role of the mentally ill as it was that the society did not recognize or permit such a role or was so "healthy" that no one ever emitted such behaviors.

Moloney (1952, pp. 36–37), though his conclusions are not based on the careful checking of impressions that characterized the work of Eaton and Weil, argued that the Okinawans, Dyaks, Lepchas, and natives of Truk were relatively immune to psychoses. Aside from the problems noted previously, what may be a crucial variable in cross-cultural comparisons is whether the mentally ill role itself is in the repertoire of the society as a manner of handling interpersonal difficulties and what alternative are possible. This is most notably indicated in Lambo's observation: "Our clinical work in Nigeria shows that the diagnostic criteria and assessment of prognostic possibilities which hold in Western culture are equally applicable to the Nigerian patients who have been in contact with this culture. However, this does not seem to hold for patients whose social and cultural background is as different from a Western background as that of the non-literate African. In this group schizophrenic symptomatology in the main shows a considerable degree of diversity, polymorphism and affective swings." (1965, p. 70.)

Complexity of culture may be considered as a situation in which alternative behaviors are likely to be available, and when the traditional or normal acts are extinguished, new available role enactments are emitted. This is considerably different from a notion that cultural complexity in and of itself leads to stress.

Beyond the problems of diagnostic reliability . . . the role of the physician himself must be brought into consideration in evaluating the social implication of the diagnostic situation. Lin (1965, p. 22) noted: "It seems to me that the education and training background of the psychiatrist is more decisive than cultural variations in the identification of symptom-complexes." Loudon (1965), reviewing his work in South Wales, notes the important role of the general practitioner in the referral-labeling process. The general practitioner's attitudes toward the psychiatric specialist influenced public concepts about psychiatrists in general and types of symptoms about which psychiatrists should be consulted. Further, Loudon suggests that variations between socioeconomic segments of the population affect the general practitioner's concepts of both prevalence of psychiatric problems and appropriate referrals. Awareness of the individual's social characteristics may have as much influence on the physician as the purely clinical picture.

The physician is not alone in the diagnostic interchange, and Rubin (1965, p. 355) comments that in order to interact with the psychiatrist-anthropologist, the native must assign a role to him. The anthropologist may, therefore, first be categorized as, for instance, a Voodoo priest; after this has been done, the people have a role available for interaction with him, but it is as they would interact with a Voodoo priest rather than as they would interact with a "scientist" or *our* type of psychiatrist, neither of which they have conceptualized.

When discussing the waiter who would not serve, it was noted that the café owner had to have had various experiences prior to the act of calling the police. On a broader level, there must be some overlap of labeling procedures so that whatever behavior the professional calls mental illness fulfills the social function of such labels. While this overlap is far from perfect, both in specific cases (rater reliability) and in long-term social values (Szasz, 1961, 1963), it still must exist. There are in the final situation two immediate participants. The first is the non-professional public which does the majority of case finding, and which may evaluate symptoms very differently from the medical specialist whether physical or behavioral. Murphy and Leighton (1965) point out that the non-Western groups may describe a wide range of behaviors that would fall in the province of psychiatrists, but they do not necessarily use the same concepts employed in our culture. Similarly, Leighton points out that (1) behaviors may be agreed upon, but (2) conceptualizations (and hence, eventual evaluations) may differ: "An intriguing fact here is that there is no word for depression in Yoruba. When we described individual symptoms—crying spells, feeling blue, loss of appetite, waking early in the morning and so on—these were immediately recognized by the Yoruba, although the whole constellation of symptoms still did not form a syndrome in their minds; to us the various features all fitted together, but it had not occurred to our informants that they made a pattern. On the other hand, there was one disorder, puzzling to us, that was frequently reported, both by the native healers who were our key source of information and also by certain members of our sample who were questioned about their previous illnesses. They would quite often say that they suffered from *inorun*, which was translated to us as heavenly fire. *Inorun* quite clearly is a syndrome in their minds, although I still cannot make it form a pattern in mine."[5] (1965, p. 83.)

Epidemiological Studies

These conceptual difficulties are crucial in epidemiological studies: studies "of the health condition of a population in relation to any conceivable factors existing in or affecting that population which may influence the health state or affect its distribution in that population." (Lemkau and Crocetti, 1967, p. 225.) Epidemiological studies are correlational in nature: they endeavor to find what factors are associated with high or low rates of mental illness. These procedures have served mankind well—for example, in public health measures against cholera—but they are dependent upon a clear diagnosis.

While diagnostic and sampling procedures vary from one study to another, the rates of mental illness found on such surveys of the general population have been alarmingly high. A quotation from Alexander Leighton, who has been as responsible as any other person for serious work in this field, provides a summary:

In this connexion, some figures may be quoted. In a rural district in North America, one of our studies has shown that at least 29 per cent of the adult population have psychiatric symptoms and are impaired by these to a significant degree (D. C. Leighton et al., 1963a, b). A similar study in Manhattan (Srole et al., 1962) yields a figure of 23 per cent. Another sampling study (not yet published) of a small commune in France shows 26 per cent affected. The investigation of the entire population of two rural parishes in Sweden (Essen-Moller, 1956; Hagnell, 1964) indicates that 25 per cent have psychiatric difficulties. Studies in other areas are comparable. Research work conducted by professor Lambo and myself (A. H. Leighton et al., 1963a, b) in the Western region of Nigeria points to 16 per cent of the adults in rural villages and 17 per cent of the adults in a segment of a city having psychiatric symptoms to a significant degree. . . . As soon as one begins to look at subdivisions of these populations, marked differences on a considerable range appear. Thus, in some communities in the North American rural area, 62 per cent of the population were estimated to have a significant degree of disorder. In Nigeria, the range was from 6 to 50 per cent. (1965, pp. 219–220.)

The work by Srole et al. (1962) is the most widely cited one in this area and deserves some description. A part of Manhattan's East Side including 174,000 people was selected as the area to be studied. Blocks, homes in the blocks, and people in the homes were randomly sampled. People over 60 and transients were systematically excluded, and of 1,911 people drawn, 1,660 answered a rather long structured questionnaire about their past and present physical and mental symptoms. *Symptoms* were categorized as absent, mild, moderate, and serious, and *interference with life adjustment* as none, some, great, and incapacitating. The basic data were collected by trained nonmedical professionals and then evaluated by psychiatric clinicians. Sources of unreliability . . . may arise from data gathering or interviewer methods, from variability of the interviewee, and the method of evaluation by the psychiatric clinician. The bias toward diagnosing illness noted earlier in this chapter could operate, and, in fact, rater reliability was far and away greatest in the area of incapacity of functioning. Socioeconomic status was estimated from father's education and occupation, and it was found that the percentage of people rated "healthy" declined and the percentage of people rated "impaired" rose as socioeconomic status declined. In addition, as age increased, rated incapacity increased. But the most generally interesting finding was that fewer than one in four people was "well" and close to one in five was "incapacitated."[6]

The repeated finding of a large percentage of the general population as acting in a manner suitable for labeling as "mentally ill" emphasizes the importance of the evaluative process noted above. This finding and the additional datum that relatively few people of any kind are symptom-free also relates to the problem encountered by those who attempt to define mental illness operationally in terms of positive mental health. Intensive studies of samples whose adjustment should have been superior to that of the general population have found discouragingly few people manifesting "positive mental health." Heath (1945) found that only 60 per cent of Harvard sophomores had well-integrated personalities. Bond (1952) found that only 39 of 64 student council members of three Philadelphia colleges were well-balanced or had strengths outweighing their liabilities. Bond noted that 57 per cent of his sample could benefit from psychiatric help, while 14 per cent were in urgent need of help. Golden et al. (1962) found that of 1,953 adolescent males who took the Minnesota Multiphasic Personality Inventory, only 73 gave no significant indication of pathology. When 50 of these 73 men were extensively interviewed and tested 12 years later, only 23 were found to be without significant symptomatology, and perhaps more disturbing, these men were found to have little imagination, generally limited social interests, and were most notable for their contentment with their spouses. It seems clear that if an investigator seeks symptomatology, he will almost certainly find it.[7]

ECOLOGICAL AND SOCIAL CLASS STUDIES OF MENTAL DISORDERS

Two areas of investigation that have yielded interesting results are those of geographical location and social class. The former has been called ecological study. The seminal work in this area was by Robert Faris, and the single most important publication is that of Faris and Dunham (1939). The technique uses admission to psychiatric institutions as an index of mental health, a definition which, while open to question . . . , is both reliable and culturally relevant. It was found by these authors, and frequently substantiated thereafter, that a disproportionate number of schizophrenics entered hospitals from "disorganized" ecological areas. Faris argued that where social contacts are "adequate" and the person is neither sheltered nor ostracized from the mainstream of his culture, schizophrenia is rare, and where it does arise, the response to it by the individual's social milieu is generally therapeutic. The basic datum, of increased rates of schizophrenics admitted to hospitals from deteriorating sections of a city and a decrease of rate of admissions as distance of residence increases from this center, has been replicated; these studies have been reviewed by Faris (1944) and by Dunham (1955, 1966).

Associated with ecological research are studies of the association of social class with mental illness. As noted in the discussion of the work by Srole et al. (1962) on the prevalence of mental illness to the point of impairment in Manhattan, lower social class was associated with higher percentages of impairment and lower percentages of people evaluated as "well." While there have been exceptions to this rule (Kleiner and Parker, 1963), in broad outline it has been substantiated by a number of independent investigators.

The study that is deservedly the most widely cited in this area is by Hollingshead and Redlich (1953). The first step taken in this project was to delineate the social class structure of the population (New Haven, Connecticut, and surrounding towns). Five classes were defined: Class I were essentially wealthy, high-social-prestige business and professional men; Class II, managers and lesser ranking professionals; Class III, small proprietors, white collar workers, and skilled laborers; Class IV, semiskilled workers; and Class

V, factory laborers and unskilled laborers. While the occupation of those being studied was highlighted, factors such as education and place of residence were also taken into consideration. Next, a psychiatric census was taken to ascertain which residents were receiving psychiatric care on a given day, December 1, 1950. A control group was established by taking a 5 per cent sample of community households from the *City Directory*. The psychiatric and normal samples were categorized on the basis of the social class system described above. A highly significant association was found between social class and being under psychiatric care. A smaller percentage of the higher classes (I–IV) were under psychiatric care than would have been expected by the frequency of such people in the population, and a far greater number of the people under psychiatric care came from the lowest social class (V) than would have been expected by chance. Class V comprised 17.8 per cent of the general population but accounted for 36.8 per cent of the people under psychiatric care. The diagnosis of the person under psychiatric care was also significantly associated with his social class. The upper classes (I and II) were likely to be diagnosed as neurotic, while people from the lower classes (IV and V) were likely to be diagnosed psychotic. The respective percentages of each class diagnosed neurotic and psychotic were as follows: I: 53 per cent neurotic and 47 per cent psychotic; II: 67 per cent neurotic and 33 per cent psychotic; III: 44 per cent neurotic and 56 per cent psychotic; IV: 23 per cent neurotic and 77 per cent psychotic; V: 8 per cent neurotic and 92 per cent psychotic. Finally, the type of therapy given members of the social classes differed, the upper classes being more likely to receive psychotherapy, the lower classes being more likely to receive physical treatments such as shock or no specific treatment other than custody.

Two obvious social variables which deserve mention, albeit in passing, are sex and race. Different rates of sexual incidence for varying diagnoses have been frequently noted (Rose and Stub, 1955). While these differences are striking, at present little practical or theoretical use has been made of them other than in psychoanalytic theories. Perhaps an illustration of how such differences may best be used is indicated by Frumkin (1955), who presented correlations among income, occupational prestige, and rates of first admission to psychiatric hospitals separately for men and women. The correlation between income and prestige was .90 and .74 respectively for men and women; that between rate of admission and prestige was .81 and .53; and that between rate of admission and income was .71 and .15. The association of occupational prestige and income with admission to psychiatric hospitals is greater for males than females. These data indicate that it would probably be wiser to look for the correlates of variables such as occupational status than to stop with the sociological variable itself. Tuckman and Kleiner (1962) illustrate this point, using an index of discrepancy between education as an indicator of aspiration and occupation as an indicator of achievement. Rates of admission to hospitals for schizophrenia were more accurately predicted by such an index than by measures of social status alone. This finding seems to have particular relevance to Negroes, who as a group probably face this kind of problem more frequently than whites.

Kleiner, Tuckman, and Lavell (1960) replicated the broad findings of the New Haven study (Hollingshead and Redlich, 1953) in Philadelphia, but also reported differences between males and females, whites and nonwhites. The schizophrenic diagnosis was applied to one in three white persons, while it was given to one in two nonwhites. This finding was true for both males and females. It was also of interest that across nine diagnostic categories, for males and females separately (i.e., 18 comparisons), in every case nonwhites were younger at the time of first admission than whites of the same sex and diagnosis.

Before leaving this topic, it is worth noting that the belief that a *drift* toward lower socioeconomic status is positively associated with mental illness, either as a cause or as an effect, is not borne out by the data (Kleiner and Parker, 1963; Turner and Wagenfeld, 1967). Nor is there an increase in mental illnesses, such as psychosis, found among those individuals who have risen in socioeconomic status.[8]

Learning to Be Normally Abnormal

Both in the definition of abnormal behavior used in this book and in frequent quotations from other authors, the point has been made that being normal is acting in a manner expected or valued by other people. It was noted that mental health professionals fulfill a social function by providing a means of social control over behavior that violates expectations and causes discomfort to the individual, his significant others, or both. The act of diagnosing someone is a social act, involving the material on which this decision is based, the pressures on the professional person making the diagnosis, and a special set of concepts. Sociologists and anthropologists have sought to determine whether there are specific types of social situations likely to lead to a greater number of people acting in an abnormal manner. In essence the question is whether there are conditions under which the professional group will apply the label more frequently. It is clear from the reports of cross-cultural studies that the emission of deviant acts and their labeling are learned. General practitioners, mass media, and other social influences work to delineate *when* a person is to be labeled abnormal and *how* he is to be handled. Beyond this, all the problems of formulating concepts of abnormality are also involved in epidemiology. If one were to take the view of the upper-middle-class professional with his current concepts of mental illness, it would be easy to accept the conclusions of the many studies that find that a quarter of the population is mentally ill and that only a minority, perhaps one in six, is well adjusted. As has been described above, people from disorganized slum areas and people in the lower socioeconomic groups are more likely to receive diagnoses indicating social impairment in general, and in particular to be designated schizophrenic. Yet these findings are themselves manifestations of the current social concepts of mental illness and do not reflect an accurate picture of behavior in American society, since they do not take into consideration the rules of the game by which they were derived.

This section will approach the question of the conditions of the individual, relatable to broader groups such as class, residence area, sex, race, that are likely to lead to behavior called abnormal. If abnormal behavior is defined as deviance (rule and/or expectation breaking) that sanctions psychiatric intervention, then the obvious place to start a discussion of abnormality is not with the people who break the rules, but with the rules themselves and the ways in which they are learned.[9]

RULES

The first thing about rules is that they are constantly changing. Opportunities for behavior that previously did not exist now do, and some behaviors that only a short time ago were frowned upon are today considered normal. In our society the area of sexual expression is the most notable example. There are many ways of focusing on social change, but the following law passed by the British Parliament in 1770 dramatically points up the difference in social rules then and now. "All women, of whatever age, rank, profession or degree, whether virgins, maids or widows, that shall impose upon, seduce or betray into matrimony any of his Majesty's subjects, by scents, paints, cosmetics, washes, artificial teeth, false hair, iron stave hoops, high-heeled shoes, bolstered hips or padded bosoms shall incur the penalty of the law enforced against witchcraft and like misdemeanors, and upon conviction, that marriage shall stand null and void."

Another example of changes in rules, this one in the area of religion, deals with how a small New England private school gained the reputation of "godless Harvard." ". . . the very limits of religious irresponsibility were not reached until 1760, when the Harvard faculty granted permission to Anglican students to attend Christ Church, Cambridge, instead of the Congregational meetinghouse." (Rudolph, 1965, p. 17.) During the same era Yale demonstrated a proper attitude by expelling two students for attending a revival with their parents during vacation time.

The second thing about rules is that there are many of them. At a formal, legal level, the complexity of written rules is basic to the existence of professions such as law and accounting. Because there are so many of them, it is obvious that rules may conflict. . . . It was noted that a person might act in a manner that was unexpected and upsetting to those around him if he guided his behavior by discriminative stimuli that were temporally or geographically distant and not shared by those immediately present. Proper behavior for a fraternity brother may lead to role enactments that are not expected from a good churchgoing son who is also a gentleman and a serious student.[10]

At times academic advisers help cut red tape and break rules so that the very purpose of the institution responsible for the rules may be served. Such nonconformity in the service of the organization is perhaps characteristic of much of bureaucratic society, and is certainly a necessary feature of large psychiatric hospitals (see Ullmann, 1967a). Conflicts among rules are made more likely by the varied nature of our society. The cultural richness and pluralism of America as a "melting pot" and its relative degree of openness or opportunity for upward mobility increase the opportunity for the individual to be faced with choices in terms of religion, occupation, and personal conduct. There is even the choice to reject the dominant value structure of the society, as manifested by the "hippies." Conversely, the symbols of having made a choice may in and of themselves lead to aversive consequences. There are periodic reports of court battles over whether high school students should cut their hair. The ultimate of such pressures is exemplified by an Iowa court's decision (reported in *Time*, February 25, 1966, pp. 45–48) to refuse permission for a son to return to a father who was a political liberal, a reader of works on Zen Buddhism, and a writer-photographer without concern for formal religious training, so that his son could be raised by more conventional grandparents.

It is practically impossible to obey all the rules. Again, the area of sex is one that most readily offers illustrations. There is the repeated observation, based on work such as the Kinsey report, that in their sexual behavior at least 95 per cent of the American population has broken some written rule at some time or other. Wallerstein and Wyle (1947) report 99 per cent of respondents from the general population admitted to having committed one or more offenses serious enough to draw a maximum sentence of not less than a year. For example, among men, 84 per cent had committed malicious mischief, 85 per cent disorderly conduct, and 89 per cent larceny. Of the men, 57 per cent admitted to tax evasion, while only 40 per cent of women admitted to this offense. Among the women 81 per cent admitted to malicious mischief, 76 per cent to disorderly conduct, and 83 per cent to larceny. Approximately three-fourths of both men and women admitted to indecency.

Rules stand functionally in the same light as the concept of positive mental health: perfect adherence to the criteria is rarely found. If a policeman enforced all the minor violations he noticed in his rounds, he would spend so much time testifying in court that he would not be able to fulfill his function of protection against and detection of major crimes. Further, rigorous and complete enforcement of the laws would fill beyond capacity the community's mental hospitals and jails. Finally, complete enforcement of rules would probably bring a reaction that would lead to the termination of many rules and aversive consequences to the promulgators.

If all rules cannot be enforced, there are two important considerations. The first is that breaking the rule is not sufficient for the label of deviant or abnormal. It can well be argued that being caught and publicly labeled is an integral and possibly even necessary step in a career of deviance.

The second consideration is that justice in the form of apprehension and public labeling is unevenly administered. Many breaches of rules are overlooked or minimally punished because they are not "worth the trouble" of enforcing. Specifically in the realm of abnormal behavior, the same actions may meet with tolerance or with professional treatment depending on the degree to which significant others are annoyed.

Associated with the unenforceability of all rules is the concept that rules may be so breached that their violation is itself institutionalized. Rule following, like any other behavior, must be worthwhile. If the cost of breaking a rule is less than the cost of following it, the rule is likely to be broken. Lemert (1967, p. 11) makes this point in terms of compliance with weight regulations by trucks on northern California highways. If the cost of two trips is greater than the cost of a single trip plus fine, the law is likely to be broken, and fines for violations will be accepted as a normal cost of business. This is accepted by state officials to the extent that trucking companies are sent monthly statements of fines due.

The fact that change in the expectations of individuals is controlled by subsequent reinforcement is illustrated on a community-wide scale by two parallel studies. Leighton (1965, pp. 231–232) tells how a power company built a dam and provided employment over three years for a poverty-stricken community. The people discovered credit and appliances, particularly television, which introduced them to general American values. "The breadwinners also discovered something else about television sets; if they did not retain their jobs and pay premiums on the sets, somebody came along and took them away. They were thus trapped into working steadily. One result of this was that the men from this community, who had previously had a reputation for being poor employees, gradually developed the opposite kind of reputation." The parallel instance is where employment ceases. Cottrell (1951) relates how a shift to the use of diesel engines disrupted the economy of a town. The lower classes, lacking a major investment, could move to other places, but the more settled, propertied classes shifted toward radicalism and ideological rebellion.

Rules, informal expectations, and written laws are discriminative stimuli. That is, they indicate the conditions under which certain behaviors will have reinforcing consequences. With association, either simultaneous or chained, they become acquired reinforcers. But as such, they may be extinguished. An overwhelming inflation such as that in Germany during the 1920's is an example of one of Western civilization's most widely used secondary reinforcers becoming invalid for an entire population.

Rules will be adhered to only if adherence is worthwhile. Lemert (1967, p. 15), for example, notes that the Naval supply section in San Francisco observed weight distribution guidelines on axles of trucks in a manner not done by private concerns. The private firms could write off trucks as depreciated equipment, while the Navy could not do this and had a low budget for maintenance. Thus the latter were involved in a situation in which there was reinforcement for rule adherence which was not true for the former.

A key point on the development of rules was made by Leighton's example of the men who were trapped into work. Not only must the role enactment by physically possible, but its continuance must be worthwhile. A good example of this is King's (1956, p. 116) quotation of a manifesto by an American Indian tribe that was backsliding in terms of the rules laid down by missionary workers: "No more blanket, no more hallelujah!" There is in rules an implied reciprocal obligation that when a person enacts a role, he will be reinforced for it by other people. When this contract is broken, alternative behaviors are emitted. The Indians had been shaped into religious practices deviant for them, namely, Christianity, but they were not adequately maintained by subsequent reinforcement.

Riots in the Negro ghettos display similar principles. If a person has studied and followed the rules properly and then cannot find a job, he may question the entire procedure. As one young man said, "I put my faith in the Man and he didn't come through." A riot is an alternative behavior to playing by the rules. In addition, some riots have obtained short-run benefits that should have been forthcoming without the riots but were not.

A third point about rules is that frequently virtue is its own reward, there being no other. The likelihood of reinforcement for rule-following behavior is not as great as might be desirable. While the mass media glorify the self-made man, and while the religious ethos of the country is one of self-responsibility and opportunity limited only by personal effort (Fromm, 1941, 1947; Tawney, 1926), the facts of life are that room at the top is restricted rather than unlimited. The majority of the large organizations in which Americans increasingly live, work, worship, and play are pyramidal, so that the further one rises, the fewer are the positions available above him. Aside from limitations in opportunity, there are limitations in ability which have little if anything to do with effort. There is frequently a gap between aspiration (what one labels as the good life) and accomplishment. The culture influences what the good life will be. In the United States today mass media such as television provide models of the good life (e.g., appliances) which are frequently unattainable by the general public.

A fourth feature of rules is that they are made by people in power, that is, by people who are in positions to dispense reinforcers. To make a formal rule, especially a written one such as a law, is a major enterprise on the part of many people. By implication there are conditions that those in power wish to perpetuate and other conditions, acts by people (usually specific individuals), that they wish to minimize. The English law against the use of deceit by women in the attraction of men was made by men.

In terms of unwritten rules, there must be a standard of what is expected and normal behavior. As noted in the review of prevalence studies earlier in the chapter, there are many individuals in the population who might be termed mentally ill but who manage to make some sort of socially appropriate adjustment. The societal agent who imposes rules is likely to be a member of the class currently holding power. If a person has not been taught the rules of a particular group, he will be considered strange and abnormal by members of it. On the one hand, he may have had, at best, minimal exposure to such rules, or having had such exposure, little opportunity or reinforcement for following such rules. It is in this regard that it is reasonable that lower socioeconomic classes should have higher rates of both prevalence and incidence of severe "abnormalities." In similar fashion, it is reasonable that the better organized the person's social group and the more reinforcing contact he has with other people, the lower will be the rates of incidence and prevalence of mental illness. Finally, the closer the person is in socioeconomic, educational, and common value system to the societally sanctioned labeler, the more likely it is that his behavior will be understandable to the labeler and hence not as readily diagnosed as mentally ill.[11]

Rule Learning and Social Movements

Considering the wide range of behaviors that are appropriate across different cultures, the specific acceptable pattern of behavior in any given time and place is severely restricted. The conformity of college students and professors is an example: college education is an elaborate preparation covering many years and many courses. Some of the courses have little immediate value, either in terms of the students' current interests or future jobs. Healthy, intelligent young people delay the acquisition of various material goods and of certain interpersonal relations in order to master this material. In similar fashion the typical college professor leads a life of unparalleled poverty, chastity, and obedience in which scholarly activity is highly valued, although his more esoteric publications are rarely read and his more popular productions such as textbooks are infrequently understood. To an objective observer, student and professorial behavior may seem peculiar. The point is that if one can formulate the development of a "normal" person, be he student or professor, one will have a description and set of principles for dealing with any learned bizarre behavior. Timothy Leary made this point cogently when he said there is nothing so far out as a square.

At this point it needs only to be recapitulated that the cues must be present, the messages attended to, acted upon, and reinforced. A person may emit "abnormal" behavior because he has failed to learn the accepted normal pattern of behavior or because, having learned it, he was extinguished for its emission and reinforced for emission of alternative behaviors.

Ullmann (1968) has pointed out that just as there is no clear definition of abnormal behavior, so there is no clear definition of a social movement. Working with definitions of various social movements, Ullmann noted a marked similarity between definitions of members of a social movement and definitions of abnormality such as that of Rosen and Gregory (1965, p. 11, cited in the first chapter of this book): members of social movements are statistically different from the majority or dominant group of the culture; are upset or unhappy with current affairs as indicated by their working toward social change; and do not conform to all aspects of the dominant culture. A person joining or defecting from a social movement may be used as a model for a person starting or ceasing to follow the accepted norm. In this regard, some quotations from Toch are enlightening:

> Usually, the hold of the movement is thus weakened gradually. First a few outposts are sacrificed; doubts about minor matters come to the fore; other "weaknesses" are perceived; and eventually, the bonds linking member to movement become sufficiently tenuous to snap under stress. [Toch, 1965, p. 165.] The convert is a disillusioned person, and disillusionment is a slow, surreptitious type of change. It begins with undercover reservations to the effort of remaining loyal. It represents a cumulative record of the costs of adaptation. Whether it dies in its suppressed state or becomes publicized in awareness depends on the number and the import of disillusioning experiences that are encountered. . . . A person will tend to become disillusioned if he becomes actively involved in life situations for which he has been ill-prepared by socialization. (1965, p. 128.)

A good illustration of these concepts was presented by Rosenthal (1954), who described the abandonment of the traditional Jewish pattern by young lower-class people in a small Polish town between the two world wars. The main determinant of status for the total group lay in learning, charity, and good deeds. Being able to play this role depended in turn on wealth and leisure, and young people in the lower class were at a severe disadvantage. Since they could not compete in a way of life in which the central values were difficult if not impossible to attain, they were more likely to forsake the way of life altogether.

The development of behaviors that are labeled abnormal may teach a great deal about the development of behaviors labeled normal. This is the import of many of the case examples. . . . The areas in which shaping to a recognized abnormal pattern have been most extensively presented . . . are in terms of marijuana smoking (Becker, 1963) and schizophrenia (Ullmann, 1967a).

To become a marijuana smoker, first of all a person must physically be in a geographical, temporal, and social environment where marijuana is available. A student who had lived in a protected environment in which marijuana was not available and who had therefore followed other patterns may, upon entering college, find that his previous patterns of social behavior, such as dependence on parents and teachers, serious and dedicated memorization of textbooks, and the like, are no longer rewarded as they were in high school. He may be extinguished for square behaviors and go to pot. After having the role available, he must smoke (enact the role). And even that is not enough; he must learn to smoke marijuana properly in order to get the kick. Next he must identify the effect of the drug, and finally he must label the changes . . . as being good and pleasurable. These considerations represent successive stages, and failure to enact or be reinforced for any stage is likely to lead to a decrease of the behavior.

This model is directly applicable to the use of alcohol or indulgence in sexual intercourse and involves reduction of ties to a prior evaluative system and of aversive consequences for deviation from it. Such a step-wise progression is called shaping . . . but it may also be called a career. To become a physician a person must get into college, take pre-med courses, then move through medical school and internship. Failure (cessation of reinforcement) at any point will terminate the career.

At the point of being extinguished or, in Toch's terms, disillusioned, the person may emit many different behaviors. The ones that are reinforced are likely to increase in emission, while those not reinforced are likely to decrease. Once again the important element making for the stability of a pattern of behavior, whether labeled normal or abnormal, is reinforcement. The fact that prevalence rates (the number of people who might be labeled) are so much higher than incidence rates (the number of people who are actually labeled, hospitalized, and treated) is taken by Scheff (1966a) to be indicative of the fugacious nature of much "mental illness." From this datum, the great amount of "residual deviance," the difference between prevalence and incidence, and, more generally, the near universal presence of some deviant (rule-breaking) behavior, Scheff, like a number of other sociologists, points out that it is the act of being labeled that stabilizes the mentally ill role. In the material that follows, this important step in the role of being mentally ill will be discussed.

LABELING: A FURTHER STEP IN BEING NORMALLY ABNORMAL

Nearly four decades ago, in *As I Lay Dying*, William Faulkner spoke of the effects of labeling a person sane or crazy:

> Sometimes I ain't so sho who's got ere a right to say when a man is crazy and when he ain't. Sometimes I think it ain't none of us pure crazy and ain't none of us pure sane until the balance of us folks talks him that-a-way. It's like it ain't so much what a fellow does, but it's the way the majority of folks is looking at him when he does it. (p. 510.)

It has been stressed that failure to learn socially approved habits or the extinction of such behavior is one condition leading to the emission of acts that will be labeled abnormal. Benedict (1934) talks of those individuals who are liable to serious disturbances because "their habits are culturally unsupported." One form of disturbance, the behavior pattern of the disillusioned man who becomes a convert, is also a learned behavior mediated by social labeling. Benedict made this point:

> The particular forms of behavior to which unstable individuals of any group are liable are many of them matters of cultural patterning like any other behavior. . . . Even in trance the individual holds strictly to the rules and expectations of his culture, and his experience is as locally patterned as a marriage rite or an economic exchange. . . . The particular behavior of an unstable individual in these instances is not the single and inevitable mode in which his abnormality could express itself. He has taken up a traditionally conditioned pattern of behavior in this as in any other field. Conversely, in every society, our own included, there are forms of instability that are out of fashion.

Being labeled in itself has an enormous effect. The crux of the matter conceptually is that while some specific aspect of the person's behavior leads to labeling, in practice it is the total person who is labeled and who is then reacted to in terms of his label. This difference in behavior of other people toward him makes it possible for him to take some roles and emit some acts that will be reinforced, but it also makes it more difficult for him to emit and be reinforced for other behaviors.

The student mentioned in the previous section who went to college, experienced a change of reinforcing contingencies, and fell into "bad" or "swinging" company eventually acted in a manner that deviated from the expectations of the larger, dominant group. His deviant behavior may have an adverse effect on him even if he was not caught and publicly labeled. In behavioral terms his behavior did not match the model. In social-psychological terms, his overt behavior was at variance with his beliefs, a situation called cognitive dissonance (Festinger, 1957), inconsistency (Lecky, 1945), or incongruity leading to an increase of unassimilated percepts (McReynolds, 1960).

Whatever the term used, marked differences between overt behavior and attitude are likely to have been previously associated with aversive consequences. The person is vulnerable to being found out. Being labeled as inconsistent, whether by oneself or others, is an acquired reinforcer. It places the person in the position of an increased likelihood of being in situations in which he may be called upon to play roles which are inconsistent with each other, that is, situations which have been called conflictual. Given this background, the person may emit behavior in order to make his behavior more consistent. The most likely action is to alter one's previous attitudes. That is, if one's labeling of proper behavior and one's own behavior do not match, the procedure requiring the least effort is to alter one's concepts of proper behavior. In addition, many behaviors labeled improper may be considered so on irrational grounds so that having acted in an improper way, the person may relabel the act as "not so bad." An example which comes to mind is cutting classes, a matter that in grade school is the grave sin called truancy but in college is normal, mature, independent behavior.

Probably the majority of people who commit deviant acts and are not publicly labeled show the effect in greater tolerance of others. Some people, however, do not make use of this alternative: they may refer themselves for treatment, make restitution anonymously, or avoid assiduously the conditions that led to their deviance. To therapists, the most tragic response to deviance is the one in which a person labels himself an outcast and acts in accordance with the most negative stereotypes and false information present in our culture. A prime example of this with college students occurs when a boy labels himself a homosexual and by no longer dating girls confirms his diagnosis (this is an example of the self-validating hypothesis) . . . or when a girl labels herself a nymphomaniac and stops being discriminating. In this latter case feelings of disgust and frustration may lead to a further high turnover of lovers and added confirmation of the label.

The examples just cited lead to the concept of secondary deviance. Lemert (1951, 1967) summarizes this concept as follows:

> Primary deviation is assumed to arise in a wide variety of social, cultural, and psychological contexts, and at best has only marginal implications for the psychic structure of the individual; it does not lead to symbolic reorganization at the level of self-regarding attitudes and social roles. Secondary deviation is deviant behavior, or social roles based upon it, which becomes means of defense, attack, or adaptation to the overt and covert problems created by the societal reaction to primary deviation. (1967, p. 17.)

Leaving aside Lemert's concepts of psychic structure and bearing in mind that societal reaction may be applied by the person himself, the key concept is that the act itself probably does not have as long-term consequences as do reactions to the act. Rather than taking the view that deviant acts precede their social control, it is possible to take the position that in a society where there are many value systems and where reinforcing stimuli are neither equitably nor rationally distributed, the breaking of some rules occurs through chance, ignorance, or extinction of rule-following behavior. The acts will not particularly affect the individual until his life is changed as a consequence of the enforcement of the rules. From this point on, the person's behavior is altered either through new sources of positive reinforcement or through exclusion from previous sources of positive reinforcement. Further behavior may then be the result of reactions to the deviance rather than the deviant behavior itself.

While such a process can occur without public condemnation, it most frequently happens and is easiest to demonstrate in instances where there has been public labeling of the act rather than the act itself that is crucial in the shaping of succeeding behavior. The most obvious aspect of public labeling is punishment. Incarceration, whether in a prison or a psychiatric hospital, limits the person's range of social contacts and occupational activities. Entrance into an institution may involve depersonalization and other degrading circumstances—for example, being assigned a number in place of a name (see Goffman, 1961). The public labeling may stigmatize the person, that is, mark him as defective, degenerate, or otherwise infamous. He is then treated in terms of the label. All the negative concepts, many of them demonstrably erroneous, held about members of the class are ascribed to the labeled individual. The result, on the one hand, is that he may not be able to obtain a job commensurate with his abilities, may not be trusted, and may be put under special observation on the job, while, on the other hand, he is placed in a position where major interpersonal satisfactions such as friendship and acceptance are found only with social outcasts like himself.

A prime example of such a situation is that of the drug addict, who is believed to be untrustworthy, impulsive, and criminal. Drug addicts have a special language and culture. In major part this is due to the illegal act typically involved in obtaining drugs: friendship is knowing where to make a connection. In part this is also due to the aversive reaction of society to the addict. In the United States, physicians who are addicts and obtain drugs without criminal connections do not develop the secondary characteristics of the addict culture. The same finding is true of the general population in the United Kingdom, where addicts may obtain their supplies through legitimate (and far less expensive) channels. In the United States, supplies for a heroin habit are expensive and call for frequent, large expenditures. The addict, especially if deprived of legitimate employment, is forced to crime to raise money. An addict's characteristic behavior ("personality") seems more likely to be the effect of the addiction rather than a predisposing or causative element.

The point illustrated by reference to the addict is that characteristics associated with perpetrators of deviant behavior may be secondary to the act. How the person labeled as abnormal is treated after he has been labeled may lead to uniformities of behavior based on uniformities of reinforcing contingencies. "The ultimate example of these [additional rules placed on labeled deviants] is found in prisons. In a list of forty punishable rule violations held to in one state prison only six corresponded to what would be misdemeanors or felonies outside of the prison" (Lemert, 1967, p. 61). In similar fashion, men released from prison may have their parole revoked if they drink, get married without permission, leave the vicinity without permission, or have intercourse with someone other than their wives. In this case, the very onerousness of the rules makes compliance less likely.

Implicit in the definition of abnormality and the deduction from it discussed in this chapter is the concept that normality is a social evaluation. This evaluation depends on the standpoint of the observer, and this standpoint, in turn, has been learned and continues to be maintained by reinforcement. The view, then, is that there is not a single, universal standard of normality, but rather normality within groups. There are different sorts of normal, conventional insiders and different sorts of deviants or outsiders. For all groups there are insiders and outsiders. The member of a small religious sect may see the majority of other people as sinners; the marijuana user may see himself as swinging and cool, and nonusers as squares; the sexually liberated may see the conventional person as a prude if not downright sad. An article on Weight Watchers, Inc. (*Time*, April 7, 1967, p. 54) makes the point: ". . . people who are not fat are known as 'civilians' to the members with weight problems."

Once a person has been "converted" and has joined a group or received a new label, the same variables that led him to defect from the larger, modal social group are involved if he is to be reconverted. The reasons for maintaining group membership within the square society are the same as those involved in maintaining membership in swinging cultures. Continuing personal support and understanding as well as biological pleasure are involved in the difficulties of the confirmed homosexual going straight. Movement from one group to another not only means different positive reinforcement, it also frequently means new responsibilities. For example, being mentally ill may sanction severing of family ties and responsibilities. The person who is "normal" is expected to work, to support his wife, and adhere to many social restrictions. The person who is mentally ill need not face these challenges and is permitted, within limits, to be irascible and dependent.

The crucial difference between the square and the swinger is that they do not share the same values. Operationally, the behavior of people in the two groups is not altered by the same reinforcing stimuli. Much of the unpredictability of the deviant or outsider is that he does not act the way he should, that is, the way the labeler himself acts or would want others to act. There are few things more difficult to accept and more upsetting for a person than for another not to respond to the stimuli he emits, especially when they are intended as kindnesses. The first person's well-practiced operant behavior is literally being extinguished when a second person does not respond "correctly." Its social functions aside, the act of labeling some people as abnormal confirms the correctness of the labeler's values and the adequacy of his repertoire of social reinforcement. This may be particularly vital to young psychologists and psychiatrists: a person who is not responsive to them must be mad.

A prime example of the furor over people who will not respond to the dominant culture's values is the current hippie movement. Against the typical ethic of work, acquisitiveness, delay of gratification, and personal self-discipline, this group poses the values of sensory experience and an emphasis on inner rather than outer experience. Very explicitly, the hippie "drops out," that is, will not follow the accepted pattern of normality. The hippie minority poses the question of whether it is necessarily good to accumulate worldly possessions and status, especially if these are acquired at the expense of other people or of one's own inner peace.

Another prime example, one directly in the nosological system of the American Psychiatric Association, is the category of dyssocial reaction. . . . This term refers to "individuals who manifest disregard for the usual social codes, and often come into conflict with them, as a result of having lived all their lives in an abnormal moral environment." (DSM-I, p. 38.) As good a picture of what is meant in this regard as has ever been drawn is Shaw's monograph "The Jack-Roller" (1930). Jack-rolling is taking a drunk's money after luring him to some deserted spot by some inducement such as the offer of homosexual practices. Shaw's jack-roller learned as proper behavior what the dominant culture would consider deviant:

> One day my stepmother told William to take me to the railroad yard to break into box-cars. [The subject was six at the time.] William always led the way and made the plans. He would open the cars, and I would crawl in and hand out the merchandise. In the cars were foodstuffs, exactly the things my mother wanted. We filled our cart, which we had made for this purpose, and proceeded toward home. After we arrived home with our ill-gotten goods, my stepmother

would meet us and pat me on the back and say I was a good boy and that I would be rewarded. (p. 53.)

Whenever the boys got together they talked about robbing and made more plans for stealing. I hardly knew any boys who did not go robbing. . . . Fellows who had "done time" were big shots and looked up to and gave the little fellows tips on how to get by and pull off big jobs. (p. 54.)

[At age 15] I was looked up to as the hero of the quartet because I had done 56 months in St. Charles, more than all the others put together. They naturally thought I was one who had a vast experience and was regarded as one might regard the big social hit of society. (p. 96.)

A final quotation from Shaw serves two purposes: first, to indicate that an ousider may have a clear set of values about which he feels as strongly and righteously as the insiders do about theirs; and second, to show that this set of values may be in direct opposition to the dominant culture's set of values and may make difficult the altering of the outsider's behavior.

I believe that any game should be played according to the rules of the game. Violators of rules should be punished. Crime is a game, and therefore as a rat violates the rules or code by informing the "dicks" and the "screws," he should be punished when caught, just like other criminals are punished. I think everyone will agree with me in my feelings about these low rats. All prisoners who are worthy of the name will agree with me. (p. 112.)

Having been labeled abnormal may lead to reinforcement for the emission of behaviors consistent with the label but not necessarily part of the behavior that originally led to the labeling. The jack-roller's pride in his prison record and attitude toward informers are examples. Often having been labeled a deviant may make normal behavior illegitimate and lead to further rule-breaking as a safeguard against being caught. The abnormal label then places the person under a new set of rules: the convict must lead a more restricted life than the nonconvict; the hospitalized patient may be ignored because he is mentally unbalanced.

Once a person assumes a role, whether it be that of swinger or square, there are additional elements of behavior that are typically considered part of the role. People respond to him in a particular manner, and if he does not react as expected, that is, does not respond to the cues given to him, others are upset with him and do not reinforce him. Being a real boy may mean doing daring or foolish things (the evaluation depends on the age of the evaluator). A girl who has become pregnant may obtain a criminal abortion, a far graver crime to cover for a lesser one. A man who has engaged in homosexual acts may open himself to blackmail and far worse consequences than the original act. A very interesting example is provided by Kai Erikson (1957). Erikson noted that a group of hospitalized psychiatric patients organized and produced dramatic plays before outside audiences with a skill that surprised professional drama critics: "At a prizewinning performance in a neighboring city, some of the audience were and remained under the impression that the players were members of the medical staff rather than patients in the institution." Yet one of the patients, after doing a very fine job in the play, returned to the patients' dormitory and tried to set fire to it. There may have been any number of reasons or reinforcing contingencies involved, but Erikson uses this as an example of role-expressive behavior, and the present authors concur.

To obtain the benefits of being a patient within the social usage of the medical model, the patient must present himself (and his "illness") in the manner recognized by the culture. The public idea of the mentally ill includes a breakdown in intellect, irrational behavior, and an inability to control one's impulses. The person who does well in an activity such as a public performance may thus raise questions about his sanity. Falsely enacting the sick role is called malingering. Cohen (1966, p. 15) notes that such behavior is considered very bad: "Indeed, he is now guilty of a type of deviance that is everywhere regarded with a special odium. He has claimed an identity that he does not really have. . . . To make such a false claim is to force other people to take up and play the correlative roles, to subject themselves to a certain discipline, to go through elaborate and sometimes stressful motions that turn out to be meaningless and 'don't count.' It is a flagrant violation of trust." The patient who performed in the play was in the difficult position of having to look incompetent to justify his release from normal social responsibilities.

In summary, being labeled as deviant or abnormal has consequences in terms of further behavior. These consequences change reinforcing contingencies, and the general pattern is toward shaping action in the direction of the pattern of behavior appropriate to the label. These concepts will be illustrated with two extended examples selected in accordance with the general view that normal and abnormal behavior are similar in their development and maintenance. In the next section of this chapter the psychiatric hospital therapist will be the focus.

LEARNING TO BE A BUGHOUSER

Earlier, Jerome Frank was quoted to the effect that "Psychotherapy is the only form of treatment which, at least to some extent, appears to create the illness it treats." Throughout previous sections of this chapter it has been noted that a pattern of abnormality is learned social acts dependent upon the responses of other people to the signals emitted by the "abnormal" individual. Consistent with these considerations is the notion that people who do not break the rules support the deviant. Tannenbaum (1938) made this point in regard to lawbreaking deviants, that is, criminals. He noted that monetary "backers," lawyers, bondsmen, dishonest police, and crooked politicians have supported the criminal element. It is possible to go further and note that law enforcement and rehabilitation agencies literally depend on apprehended criminals as much as schoolteachers depend upon students. To quote Tannenbaum (1938, p. 63): "It is not too much to say that the development of the criminal career as here described is possible only because there are more or less well-organized recognized agencies that live off, and depend upon, the profit-making opportunities which the criminal supplies." The gatekeeper to the role of abnormality, the person who legitimizes the role and over time teaches the public its changing characteristics, is the mental health professional. Aside from the formal educational requirements . . . it is proper to ask what are the conditions which shape him, for an understanding of the mental health worker will aid in understanding the psychiatric patient.

There are few data on the conditions that lead to the selection of a career in mental health. The most pertinent material lies in research on the performance of residents in psychiatry (Holt and Luborsky, 1958) and medical specialists (Strong and Tucker, 1952). Because the people tested in these studies were well along in their careers, it is impossible to give the reasons they chose the profession they did.

While it does not solve the problem of self-selection, the following material is of use because of the relative youth of the individuals concerned and the author's insightfulness:

> I spent one summer as a member of the senior clinical staff of a treatment camp for emotionally disturbed children. The junior staff consisted of college students training for work with children as teachers, social workers, psychologists, and sociologists. For these students the situation was initially largely "unstructured"; they did not know how they were to respond to the provocative behavior of the youngsters in their roles as "clinicians." These expectations were defined for them by the senior staff. They included the ways in which a clinician is supposed to define the behavior of his charges, how he is supposed to feel about it, and what he is supposed to do about it. They were expected to see the children as victims of uncontrollable impulses somehow related to their harsh and depriving backgrounds, and in need of enormous doses of kindliness and indulgence in order to break down their images of the adult world as hateful and hostile. The clinician must never respond in anger or with intent to punish, although he might sometimes have to restrain or even isolate children in order to prevent them from hurting themselves or one another. Above all, the staff were expected to be warm and loving and always to be governed by a "clinical attitude"—that is, to respond in terms of what was therapeutically appropriate rather than in terms of their own notions of morality or emotional needs. This demanded of the junior staff what would ordinarily be regarded as superhuman patience in the face of intolerable provocation.

To an extraordinary degree, they fulfilled these expectations, including, I am convinced, the expectation that they feel sympathy and tenderness and love toward their charges despite their animal-like behavior. The speed with which these college students learned to behave in this way cannot be easily explained in terms of gradual learning through a slow process of "internalization." They did, however, have a tremendous investment in their clinical roles. The investment was partly a product of their isolation, for a period of eight weeks, from the outside world, so that there were no seriously competing roles. Because of this isolation and the inexperience of the junior staff, the authority of the senior staff as reference group was unchallenged. These and other features of the social organization created a powerful need to demonstrate, to themselves and others, that they were authentic clinicians as defined by the senior staff. They had made certain claims about themselves, they had learned what constituted evidence of these claims, and they produced that evidence by behaving in a "clinical" manner.

In all probability, however, their conformity to the expectations of the clinical role was more than merely role-expressive behavior. Their assumption of the clinical role and their effort to live up to it were also instrumental to their other roles. They were, after all, students looking forward to graduation, to jobs, and to graduate school. They were being evaluated by the senior staff, and the impressions they made would become part of their "record," which could be used for or against them at later stages in their careers. (Cohen, 1966, pp. 104–105.)

There are three aspects of the shaping of a recruit to the mental health profession. The first is that the situation is ambiguous; this volume has indicated at least that there is controversy in the field, and has taken the stance that in dealing with people labeled as abnormal there is a large measure of social evaluation and self-fulfilling prophecy. Social psychologists have made detailed investigations of situations in which people may be influenced to alter their responses. Crutchfield (1955), among others, indicated that people are more easily influenced on matters of opinion whose validity derives from a social frame of reference than on matters of fact. Next, conformity is more likely if the task is difficult for the person, that is, if the person does not know what to do or how to do it. If external cues or alternative information is withheld, the person cannot match his behavior to any but the available models, and this also leads to conformity. Finally, the greater the prestige of the models or leaders, the more likely the person will be to conform. To these generalizations from social psychology should be added the fact that continuing reinforcement plays a vital role, both as avoidance of unpleasant situations such as censure and as maximization of praise and advances in status and salary.

The second aspect of the training situation is the bureaucratic nature of the institutions in which professional training takes place. The vast majority of public psychiatric hospitals number their patients in the thousands. The decline of the more personal approach of the era of moral treatment and the development of large psychiatric hospitals [has been] described. . . . The task of dealing with large numbers of people makes a bureaucratic model increasingly probable if not necessary. Blau (1956) has noted that the four basic characteristics of bureaucratic organization are specialization of function, hierarchical status, rules, and impersonality. Specialization in a psychiatric hospital is an analogue to the medical model, a consideration that will be discussed below. Hierarchical status means that there is a pyramidal ordering of authority such that theoretically no order goes unchecked.

Ideally, each person reports only to his immediate superior. In a large psychiatric hospital this has the effect that the people most intimately involved with patients, trainees and attendants, being on the lowest level of the hierarchy, report to people whose job is to supervise them rather than interact with patients. The effects are to denigrate interacting with patients; advancement and authority are negatively associated with interaction with patients. The supervisor makes his decisions on the basis of acts that he can see, acts that are visible, and these are rarely interactions with patients. On the one hand this leads to a bias of activities that the supervisee will engage in with patients. Henry (1964) made this point when he quoted a psychiatric nurse: "When you go off duty, they don't know whether you have spent time with the patients, but they do know whether you have written in the chart." The visible and reinforced activity is not interaction with patients, but records that the supervisor can check. Interaction with the supervisor rather than with patients is the major supervisee activity about which the supervisor knows. To the extent that the supervisor is separated from the patients, his knowledge about them is general. The interaction with the supervisor then becomes theoretical rather than practical, and consistency with the supervisor's views rather than the reality of service is what is likely to be reinforced. A social worker once muttered as she was on her way to a supervisory conference, "Well, I'm going in and vague it up."[12]

Because every new situation cannot be taken up, rules to cover situations must be developed. The rules may proliferate so that few people know them all, but they exist and can be applied when it serves someone's ends. The safest thing is to abide by rules that are generalizations. Etzioni makes this point:

> For example, a welfare worker may fear the risks of making a decision on his own; he plays it safe by observing minutely the organization's rules and policies with the result that more important treatment considerations are underplayed. This is illustrated, for example, when a social worker in violation of his own judgment as to what would be most beneficial for the clients, recommends that a mentally disturbed child remain with his family, because the agency has a

policy of not breaking up family units, even though the child's presence at home may disrupt the adjustment of other children in the family. Instead of making procedures means to the organization's goal, he makes them ends in themselves. The policy becomes the prevailing criterion for decision, and the worker bends the clients' needs to fit the policy. (1964, p. 12.)

Cases are matched to rules, and when the fit is clear enough, the rules provide the decision. The individual merits of the case are a source of confusion. The bureaucrat may be curt, not because he is basically an anal-sadistic person à la Freud, but because the more he hears, the more he is put in a situation where his role as an effective employee is put in opposition to his role as a pleasant human being. If he makes an exception, he is faced with the problem of explaining to his supervisor how he, the employee, came to do something different from what the supervisor would have done. The supervisor, in turn, is under constraints, and at the policymaking level of the hierarchy the very funding of the hospital may be based on appeals to legislatures made in terms of patients "in bed" or residing at the hospital rather than people once again living in the community. For example, Ullmann (1967a) found that the percentage of patients attaining a rapid release and the percentage of patients with more than two years of continuous hospitalization were significantly associated (the former positively, the latter negatively) with the number of new applications per bed, even when size, staffing, and nonpsychiatric medical activities were held constant. In short, as Ullmann pointed out (1967a, especially pages 117–143), the hospital personnel are under strong control of reinforcing contingencies.[13]

A third and final general comment about the training situation in the hospital is the widespread adoption of the medical model by the staff. This is reflected in the very use of the word "hospital," the historical development of hospitals after the era of moral treatment, and the training of treatment staff as medical and "paramedical" specialists. In physical medicine the body is conceptually a complicated biochemical apparatus, and the person is the rather boring address of an interesting malfunction. Specialization is appropriate to physical medicine as is large hospital size which makes possible enough cases to support such specialization. While not an ideal situation for the individual who is also a patient, specialized techniques of physical medicine may be successfully separated from each other: X-ray, dentistry, surgery, and the like. This fragmentation fits neatly with bureaucracy, where the line of authority is easiest when drawn by profession and specialty rather than by the total functional task, the person.

A psychoanalytic variant of the medical model also has impact on the staff and particularly the trainee. As noted . . . all behavior may be related within psychoanalytic theory to deprivations and defenses. If a person does something that is not "right" as defined by the professional supervisor, it is appropriate to ask why he did so. Since the supervisor is rational and right, the answer is some flaw in the supervisee's personality. In addition to the other pressures on the recruit discussed earlier in this section, he is faced with a situation in which his supervisor may evaluate his behavior as a manifestation of personality difficulty rather than as mature ideation which deserves answers based on evidence. Once labeled as a person "having authority problems," whatever the trainee says may be evaluated in terms of his motivations rather than the truth or falsity of the specific verbalization. Stanton and Schwartz (1954, p. 205) make this point when they write that ". . . modern psychiatrists and psychologists make up one of the few groups in history where ad hominem argument may be treated with greater respect than an argument confined to the subject matter under discussion."

Under these conditions, the trainee learns to fit in and act as his mentors think he should. Advancement is usually given to those who are liked by (Holt and Luborsky, 1958) and like (Ullmann, 1967a, pp. 136–141) the supervisor. In this manner there is a reduction of information contrary to the supervisor's views. An extreme example of this may be seen in Frank's review of the training of the psychoanalyst (1961, pp. 116–134).

Among the aspects of the therapist role the student learns are the jargon and the approach to patients.[14] He may believe that the problem is insufficient "giving" on the part of others and therefore "give" in an endlessly loving manner (as in the example of the college students at the beginning of this section), or he may ask what the patients are getting out of the interchange and make his own responses differentially favorable depending on the sort of behavior the patient emits. The trainee comes to the hospital relatively naïve, but he is trained in the manner described so that he is quite different from either the way he previously was or the way normal people, including himself, act with other normal people. A person who put up with taunting, testing behavior in the manner of the ideal "clinician" in Cohen's material, if he were not doing so in the context of mid-twentieth century psychotherapy, would be considered either a saint or a masochist. Yet this behavior is what is reinforced professionally, even if there is a paucity of empirical evidence to support its value to the patient and hence to the society that supplies the institution with money.

This section has dealt with the pressures that bear on the mental health trainee and lead him to have views of patients and responses to them that are different from the views and responses he had before he was trained and also different from his current responses to people he labels as normal. In short, the trainee learns to conform, where "conforming behavior is regarded as behavior reflecting the successful influence of other persons" and deviant behavior is regarded as "behavior reflecting the rejected influence of other persons" (Bass, 1961, pp. 38, 40). The setting of the psychiatric hospital and clinician's role are aspects of environment that must be considered in any account of the behavior of psychiatric patients. . . . The point remains that both patient and staff learn special roles, and, having learned them, interact in terms of these roles and thereby influence each other.

Summary

Starting from the definition of abnormal behavior as that type of deviance or rule- and expectation-breaking which sanctions the intervention of the mental health professional, the pressures on the labeler were investigated. The social function of labeling was described: calling a person mentally ill is a way of solving a social problem. The concept of abnormality is particularly useful in instances where people are distressed by behavior that is upsetting but not specifically criminal. Successful use of the solution of labeling someone as needing a mental health professional is a learned behavior, and presumes that the laymen who are case finders and initiators of the labeling cycle have some concepts of the mentally ill role.

The behaviors that will lead people to designate someone as mentally ill vary with time, place, and person. This insight is one of the major contributions of cross-cultural psychiatry. Within a given culture, such as ours, there is evidence from epidemiological studies that the rate of people emitting behavior that might properly be labeled abnormal (prevalence) is far higher than the rate of people hospitalized or treated for such behavior (incidence). This raises the possibility that the label itself is applied with discretion within the culture, again probably in terms of solving a social problem rather than in terms of the classic abnormal pattern per se.

Race, sex, location of home, and social class are among the variables associated with differential rates of hospitalization for various abnormal behaviors. One possible unifying theme is that among racial minorities, lower classes, and people living in slum areas there is less social reinforcement, less opportunity to follow and be reinforced for the behaviors considered normal by white, middle-class standards. Rather than being reinforced, a person who finds his vocational opportunities not commensurate with his educational abilities will be extinguished for trying. Such a person may be thought of as acting in a manner analogous to a person who becomes disillusioned and joins or becomes converted to a new social movement. The pattern of behavior in the former role has not been reinforced, and the aversive consequences of deviation from such standards are therefore reduced. At the same time, the new identity may be entered into gradually in the step-by-step sequence of a career or of shaping. Such a process is more likely when there are changing rules, numerous rules, rules that may well conflict and cannot all be either obeyed or equally enforced, and rules that are made by and for the benefit of special groups.

Having either labeled himself or been publicly stigmatized, a person is affected by the fact of his designation. This process follows the concept of self-fulfilling prophecy. People act toward the person labeled as abnormal not only in terms of the person and his behavior as they are, but also in terms of concepts about the category of persons into which he has been placed. The person may therefore be subjected to extremely stringent rules that militate further against normal patterns for acquiring reinforcement; or he may be more likely to engage in acts consistent with the new role he has adopted or to which he has been assigned. Examples of how this may occur were presented in terms of smoking marijuana, becoming a jack-roller, and becoming a clinician or staff member of a large psychiatric hospital.

NOTES

1. The present chapter draws on but also is a modification and extension of previous work (Ullmann and Krasner, 1965a; Ullmann, 1967a, 1967b, 1968). The work is deeply indebted to sociologists such as Becker (1963), Cohen (1966), Homans (1961), Lemert (1967), and Scheff (1966a). This chapter, however, will move among schools of sociological thought in a manner that may well horrify sociologists. The explication and full discussion of distinctions drawn by different sociological viewpoints is beyond the scope of this book, and not infrequently beyond the scope of laymen, such as the present authors, no matter how well-intentioned they may be. Different professions at times use the same words to denote different things. For example, some sociologists call psychoanalysis the psychological model. To avoid semantic confusions, sociological insights have been recast within the framework adopted for this book. One major difference exists between the present authors and the majority of sociologists and social psychologists who write about social movements and related phenomena. The present authors eschew concepts such as needs and cognitions and endeavor to define the specific reinforcing stimuli contingent upon behavior. The same data may be described in more than one way and may be placed in more than one theoretical system. What cannot be changed is the actual observation, the empirical data. A variety of observations will be presented in this chapter from the intellectual domain of sociologists, and to a lesser extent social psychologists, anthropologists, and psychiatrists. Hopefully, the behavioral viewpoint will provide a worthwhile integration of this material.
2. What appears at first to be an obvious exception is the behavior of a person already designated as abnormal. . . . This is not necessarily an exception because the "sick role" is one that is learned. A person who does not play it properly may be punished and one who plays it correctly may be reinforced.
3. Or more accurately, the person's status, a concept Linton describes: "The place

in a particular system which a certain individual occupies at a particular time will be referred to as his status with respect to that system. . . . The second term, role, will be used to designate the sum total of the culture patterns associated with a particular status. It thus includes the attitudes, values and behavior ascribed by the society to any and all persons occupying this status. It can even be extended to include the legitimate expectations of such persons with respect to the behavior toward them of persons in other statuses within the same system." (1945, pp. 76–77.)

4. It is interesting to note, in passing, that this definition of disease is at variance with that of Menninger previously mentioned in this chapter. By this latter definition, mental illness is based on deviance from cultural norms as judged by an observer and may not at all involve a person's being so uncomfortable that he must turn to medical science in order to alleviate his discomfort. Zubin's definition is closer to those involved in physical medicine (e.g., early stages of tuberculosis may go undetected, but still a disease is present) in that it indicates that there are disease entities separate from the reactions of the person and his environment. This is true, of course, of organic disorders such as toxic psychoses, paresis, and vitamin deficiencies such as Korsakoff's syndrome. Whether it is true of the functional psychoses is debatable.

5. Even when there is agreement on a particular behavior itself, it is still questionable whether or not it will be considered a disease. There are a number of reports of "hysterical epidemics" usually involving at most a dozen cases. To males in general, and fathers of teenage daughters in particular, these manifestations seem slight compared to the shrieking, fainting, and generally unusual behavior of thousands of girls on the occasion of the Beatles' giving a recital at New York's Shea Stadium or San Francisco's Cow Palace.

6. Similar results are reported by Plunkett and Gordon (1960), Pasamanick (1961), and Phillips (1966).

7. An excellent critical review of epidemiology is that of Mishler and Scotch (1963). A related topic is the degree to which general medical patients may manifest symptoms justifying psychiatric referral. Stoeckle, Zola, and Davidson (1964), who provide an excellent review and new data, might set the figure as high as between 50 and 80 per cent. Similar additional reports are by Silbert (1964) and Denney et al. (1966), who, like Zusman (1967), make the point that the practitioner in physical medicine requires training in identifying psychiatric disorders.

8. Kleiner and Parker (1963) provide an excellent review of the area, as does Scott (1958b). Additional examples of work in this area relate to the reciprocal relationship of the patient's social class and the psychiatrist's response (Myers and Roberts, 1959; Moore, Benedek, and Wallace, 1963; Aronson and Overall, 1966; and Michael, 1967). Vail, Lucero, and Boen (1966), surveying 123 variables across 87 counties, "demonstrated that half the variance in state hospital load was associated with socio-economic variables. Poor counties showed a higher incidence and prevalence of major mental illness than did wealthier counties." Examples of two other variables are work on dwelling-unit density (Kahn and Perlin, 1967) and ethnic discrimination (Wignall and Koppin, 1967).

9. Rules develop in much the same way as the concept of abnormality advocated in this volume: "Law . . . begins when someone takes to doing something someone else does not like." (K. Llewellyn, cited in Mayer, 1967, p. ix.)

10. This example touches on two points which are integrated into the following material: first there may be "role conflict." The second is that a person will not break rules unless there is opportunity to attain goals through "illegitimate means" (Cloward, 1959).

11. Education, religion, and race are examples of variables that may affect relative frequency of self-referral (Scheff, 1966b) or utilization of a clinic (Rabkin and Lytle, 1966). Educational differences within professions may also affect frequency of referral (Bentz, 1967).

12. Gerber (1967) found that those practitioners who were closer to the ward setting were better able to differentiate psychotic variables than those practitioners who were further away from the ward setting.

13. Three other lines of investigation add support to this point. Ekman (1961) relates how when psychiatric screening was ordered for all first courts-martial in these regiments. This drop was not matched in two control regiments in which this procedure had not been instituted. When the new procedure was terminated, the rate of courts-martial increased in the experimental regiments and became similar to that of the control regiments. In short, to the extent that psychiatric intervention in military procedures was aversive, when courts-martial became a discriminative stimulus for such intervention, the calling of courts-martial decreased. A second source of data is by Butterfield, Barnett, and Bensberg (1966), who found that turnover rate of attendants at institutions for the mentally retarded was in large measure accounted for by the economic climate of the counties in which the institutions were located. A third area deals with prescription of medication. Klerman et al. (1960) reported a significant positive correlation between ethnocentrism of resident psychiatrists and their prescription of drugs. Mendel (1967) noted that experienced therapists used fewer tranquilizing drugs to manage hospitalized psychotic patients. Because of lower staffing, patients admitted on weekends had a greater chance of receiving medication. A rule was made that no patient admitted to the ward was to receive a tranquilizer during the first 12 hours of hospitalization. Prior to this rule, 82 per cent of all schizophrenics admitted to the ward were placed on tranquilizers at some time during a seven-day stay. After the change, only 27 per cent received such medication during their stay. The number of patients discharged with a prescription for medication decreased from 85 per cent to 6 per cent. To recapitulate, responses of the professional personnel are influenced by administrative and economic variables and not solely by the behavior of the patient.

14. It has long been noted that differences between professions, such as teachers compared to mental health practitioners, will lead to different evaluations of the seriousness of problem behaviors (Wickman, 1929; Stouffer, 1952, 1956). Needless to say, differences exist between children of different ages and teachers (Mutimer and Rosemier, 1967). Similar findings have been reported in the psychiatric setting (Dietze, 1966; Goldschmid and Domino, 1967) with differences between professional groups reflecting their different responsibilities.

REFERENCES

American Psychiatric Association. *Diagnostic and statistical manual: mental disorders (DSM-1).* Washington: American Psychiatric Association, 1952; special printing, 1965.

Aronson, H., and Overall, B. Treatment expectations of patients in two social classes. *Social work,* 1966, *11,* 35–41.

Bakwin, H. *Pseudocia peditricia.* New England journal of medicine, 1956, 232, 691–697.

Barton, R. *Institutional neurosis.* Bristol, Eng.: Wright, 1959.

Bass, B. M. Conformity, deviation, and a general theory of interpersonal behavior. In I. A. Berg and B. M. Bass (eds.), *Conformity and deviation.* New York: Harper, 1961, 38–100.

Becker, H. S. *Outsiders: Studies in the sociology of deviance.* New York: Free Press, 1963.

Benedict, R. Anthropology and the abnormal. *Journal of mental deficiency,* 1934, *69,* 674–679.

Bentz, W. K. The relationship between educational background and the referral role of ministers. *Sociology and social research,* 1967, *3,* 185–189.

Blau, P. M. *Bureaucracy in modern society.* New York: Random House, 1956.

Bond, E. D. The student council study; an approach to the normal. *American journal of psychiatry,* 1952, *109,* 11–16.

Brackbill, Y. Extinction of the smiling response in infants as a function of reinforcement schedule. *Child development,* 1958, *29,* 115–124.

Butterfield, E. C., Barnett, C. D., and Bensberg, G. J. Some objective characteristics of institutions for the mentally retarded: implications for attendant turnover rate. *American journal of mental deficiency,* 1966, *70,* 786–794.

Cloward, R. A. Illegitimate means, anomic, and deviant behavior. *American sociological review,* 1959, *24,* 164–176.

Cohen, H. L., Filipczak, J. A., Bis, J. S., and Cohen, J. E. *Contingencies applicable to special education of delinquents.* Silver Spring, Md.: Institute for Behavioral Research, 1966.

Cottrell, W. F. Death by dieselization. *American sociological review,* 1951, *16,* 358–365.

Crutchfield, R. S. Conformity and character. *American psychologist,* 1955, *10,* 191–198.

Denney, D., Quass, R. M., Rich, D. C., and Thompson, J. K. Psychiatric patients on medical wards: I. prevalence of illness and recognition of disorders by staff personnel. *Archives of general psychiatry,* 1966, *7,* 265–271.

DeReuck, A. V. S., and Porter, R. (eds.). *Transcultural psychiatry.* Boston: Little, Brown, 1965.

Dietze, D. Staff and patient criteria for judgments of improvement in mental health. *Psychological reports,* 1966, *19,* 379–387.

Dunham, H. W. Current status of ecological research in mental disorder. In A. M. Rose (ed.), *Mental health and mental disorder.* New York: Norton, 1955, 168–179.

Dunham, H. W. Epidemiology of psychiatric disorders as a contribution to medical ecology. *Archives of general psychiatry,* 1966, *14,* 1–19.

Eaton, J. W., and Weil, R. J. *Culture and mental disorders.* Glencoe, Ill.: Free Press, 1955.

Ekman, P. Research as therapy? *Journal of nervous and mental disease,* 1961, *133,* 229–232.

Erikson, K. T. Patient role and social uncertainty: a dilemma of the mentally ill. *Psychiatry,* 1957, *20,* 263–274.

Eron, L. D. (ed.). *The classification of behavior disorders.* Chicago: Aldine, 1966.

Etzoni, A. *Modern organizations,* Englewood Cliffs, N. J.: Prentice-Hall, 1964.

Faris, R. E. L. Ecological factors in human behavior. In J. McV. Hunt (ed.), *Personality and the behavior disorders* (Vol. 2). New York: Ronald, 1944, 736–757.

Faris, R. E. L., and Dunham, H. W. *Mental disorders in urban areas.* Chicago: University of Chicago Press, 1939.

Faulkner, W. *As I lay dying.* New York: Modern Library, 1946.

Festinger, L. *A theory of cognitive dissonance.* Evanston: Row, Peterson, 1957.

Fortune, R. F. *Sorcerers of Dobu.* New York: Dutton, 1932.

Frank, J. D. *Persuasion and healing.* Baltimore: Johns Hopkins Press, 1961.

Fromm, E. *Escape from freedom.* New York: Rinehart, 1941.

Fromm, E. *Man for himself.* New York: Rinehart, 1947.

Frumkin, R. M. Occupation and major mental disorders. In A. M. Rose (ed.), *Mental health and mental disorder.* New York: Norton, 1955, 136–160.

Garland, Z. H. Studies on the accuracy of diagnostic procedures. *American journal of roentgenology, radium therapy and nuclear medicine,* 1959, *82,* 25–38.

Gerber, I. Practitioners' perceptual consistency of mental patients' behavioral characteristics. *Journal of social psychology,* 1967, *72,* 129–134.

Giovannoni, J. M., and Ullmann, L. P. Conceptions of mental health held by psychiatric patients. *Journal of clinical psychology,* 1963, *19,* 398–400.

Goffman, E. *Asylums,* Garden City, N. Y.: Doubleday Anchor, 1961.

Golden, J., Mandel, N., Glueck, B. C., Jr., and Feder, Z. A summary description of fifty "normal" white males. *American journal of psychiatry,* 1962, *119,* 48–56.

Goldhamer, H., and Marshall, A. W. *Psychosis and civilization,* New York: Free Press, 1949.

Goldschmid, M. L., and Domino, G. Differential patient perception among various professional disciplines. *Journal of consulting psychology,* 1967, *31,* 548–550.

Hart, H. L. *Law, liberty and morality.* New York: Vintage, 1966.

Heath, C. W. *What people are: a study of normal young men.* Cambridge, Mass.: Harvard University Press, 1945.

Henry, J. Space and power in a psychiatric unit. In A. F. Wessen (ed.), *The psychiatric hospital as a social system.* Springfield, Ill.: C. C Thomas, 1964, 20–34.

Hollingshead, A. B., and Redlich, F. C. Social stratification and psychiatric disorders. *American sociological review,* 1953, *18,* 163–169.

Holt, R. R., and Luborsky, L. *Personality patterns of psychiatrists: a study of methods of selecting psychiatrists.* New York: Basic Books, 1958.

Homans, G. C. *Social behavior: its elementary forms.* New York: Harcourt, 1961.

Kahn, R. L., and Perlin, S. Dwelling-unit density and use of mental health services.

Proceedings of the 75th annual convention of the American Psychological Association, 1967, 175–176.

King, C. W. *Social movements in the United States.* New York: Random House, 1956.

Kleiner, R. J., and Parker, S. Goal-striving, social status, and mental disorder: a research review. *American sociological review*, 1963, *28*, 189–203.

Kleiner, R. J., Tuckman, J., and Lavell, M. Mental disorder and status based on race. *Psychiatry*, 1960, *23*, 271–274.

Klerman, G. L., Scharaf, M. R., Holzman, M., and Levinson, D. J. Sociopsychological characteristics of resident psychiatrists and their use of drug therapy. *American journal of psychiatry*, 1960, *117*, 111–117.

Kutner, L. The illusion of due process in commitment proceedings. *Northwestern University law review*, 1962, *57*, 383–399.

Lambo, T. A. Schizophrenic and borderline states. In A. V. S. DeReuck and R. Porter (eds.), *Transcultural psychiatry.* Boston: Little, Brown, 1965, 62–75.

Lamy, R. E. Social consequences of mental illness. *Journal of consulting psychology*, 1966, *30*, 450–455.

Lecky, P. *Self-consistency.* New York: Island Press, 1945.

Leighton, A. H. Discussion. In A. V. S. DeReuck and R. Porter (eds.), *Transcultural psychiatry.* Boston: Little, Brown, 1965, 83.

Lemert, E. M. *Social pathology,* New York: McGraw-Hill, 1951.

Lemert, E. M. *Human deviance, social problems, and social control.* Englewood Cliffs, N. J.: Prentice-Hall, 1967.

Lemkau, P. V., and Crocetti, G. M. Epidemiology. In A. M. Freedman and H. J. Kaplan (eds.), *Comprehensive textbook of psychiatry.* Baltimore: Williams and Wilkins, 1967.

Lin, T. Discussion. In A. V. S. DeReuck and R. Porter (eds.), *Transcultural psychiatry.* Boston: Little, Brown, 1965, 22.

Linton, R. *The cultural background of personality.* New York: Appleton, 1945.

Loudon, J. B. Social aspects of ideas about treatment. In A. V. S. DeReuck and R. Porter (eds.), *Transcultural psychiatry.* Boston: Little, Brown, 1965, 137–161.

Manis, M., Houts, P. S., and Blake, J. B. Beliefs about mental illness as a function of psychiatric status and psychiatric hospitalization. *Journal of abnormal and social psychology*, 1963, *67*, 226–233.

Mayer, M. P. *The lawyers.* New York: Harper, 1967.

McReynolds, P. Anxiety, perception and schizophrenia. In D. D. Jackson (ed.), *The etiology of schizophrenia.* New York: Basic Books, 1960.

Mead, M. *Sex and temperament in three primitive societies.* New York: Morrow, 1935.

Mechanic, D. Some factors in identifying and defining mental illness. *Mental hygiene*, 1962, *46*, 66–74.

Mendel, W. M. Tranquilizer prescribing as a function of the experience and availability of the therapist. *American journal of psychiatry*, 1967, *124*, 54–60.

Menninger, K., with M. Mayman and P. Pruyser. *The vital balance.* New York: Viking, 1963.

Michael, S. T. The family with problems, social class and the psychiatrist. *International journal of social psychiatry*, 1967, *13*, 93–100.

Miller, D., and Schwartz, M. County lunacy commission hearings: some observations of commitments to a state mental hospital. *Social problems*, 1966, *14*, 26–35.

Mishler, E. G., and Scotch, N. A. Sociocultural factors in the epidemiology of schizophrenia. *Psychiatry*, 1963, *26*, 315–351.

Moloney, J. C. *The battle for mental health.* New York: Philosophical Library, 1952.

Moore, R. A., Benedek, E. P., and Wallace, J. G. Social class, schizophrenia and the psychiatrist. *American journal of psychiatry*, 1963, *120*, 149–154.

Murphy, J. M., and Leighton, A. H. Native conceptions of psychiatric disorder. In J. M. Murphy and A. H. Leighton (eds.), *Approaches to cross-cultural psychiatry.* Ithaca, N. Y.: Cornell University Press, 1965, 64–107.

Mutimer, D. D., and Rosemier, R. A. Behavior problems of children as viewed by teachers and the children themselves. *Journal of consulting psychology*, 1967, *31*, 583–587.

Myers, J. K., and Roberts, D. H. *Family and class dynamics in mental illness.* New York: Wiley, 1959.

Nunnally, J. C., Jr. *Popular conceptions of mental health.* New York: Holt, 1961.

Pasamanick, B. A survey of mental disease in an urban population. IV: An approach to total prevalence rates. *Archives of general psychiatry*, 1961, *5*, 151–155.

Phillips, D. L. The "true prevalence" of mental illness in a New England state. *Community mental health journal*, 1966, *2*, 35–40.

Plunkett, R. J., and Gordon, J. E. *Epidemiology and mental illness.* New York: Basic Books, 1960.

Pronko, N. H. *Textbook of abnormal psychology.* Baltimore: Williams and Wilkins, 1963.

Rabkin, L. Y., and Lytle, C. Further information on the ecology of service. *Journal of consulting psychology*, 1966, *30*, 146–150.

Rose, A. M., and Stub, H. G. Summary of studies on the incidence of mental disorders. In A. M. Rose (ed.), *Mental health and mental disorder.* New York: Norton, 1955, 87–116.

Rosen, E., and Gregory, I. *Abnormal psychology.* Philadelphia: Saunders, 1965.

Rosenthal, C. S. Deviation and social change in the Jewish community of a small Polish town. *American journal of sociology*, 1954, *60*, 177–181.

Rubin, V. Discussion. In A. V. S. DeReuck and R. Porter (eds.), *Transcultural psychiatry.* Boston: Little, Brown, 1965, 355.

Rudolph, F. *The American college and university: a history.* New York: Vintage, 1965.

Schachter, S., and Singer, J. E. Cognitive, social and physiological determinants of emotional state. *Psychological review*, 1962, *69*, 379–399.

Scheff, T. J. *Being mentally ill.* Chicago: Aldine, 1966a.

Scheff, T. J. Users and non-users of a student psychiatric clinic. *Journal of health and human behavior*, 1966b, *7*, 114–121.

Scott, W. A. Social psychological correlates of mental illness and mental health. *Psychological bulletin*, 1958b, *55*, 65–87.

Shaw, C. R. *The jack-roller.* Chicago: University of Chicago Press, 1930.

Silbert, R. Psychiatric patients in the admitting emergency room. *Archives of general psychiatry*, 1964, *11*, 14–30.

Sommer, R., and Osmond, H. Symptoms of institutional care. *Social problems*, 1961, *8*, 254–263.

Srole, L., Langner, T. S., Michael, S. T., Opler, M. K., and Rennie, T. A.C. *Mental health in the metropolis. Midtown Manhattan study*. Vol. I. New York: McGraw-Hill, 1962.

Stanton, A. H., and Schwartz, M. S. *The mental hospital*. New York: Basic Books, 1954.

Stoeckle, J. G., Zola, I. K., and Davidson, G. E. The quality and significance of psychological distress in medical patients: some preliminary observations about the decision to seek medical aid. *Journal of chronic diseases*, 1964, *17*, 959–970.

Stouffer, G. A. W., Jr. Behavior problems of children as viewed by teachers and mental hygienists. *Mental hygiene*, 1952, *36*, 271–285.

Stouffer, G. A. W., Jr. The attitudes of secondary school teachers toward certain behavior problems of children. *School Review*, 1956, *64*, 358–362.

Strong, E. K., Jr., and Tucker, A. C. The use of vocational interest scales in planning a medical career. *Psychological monographs*, 1952, 66, 9 (whole no. 341).

Szasz, T. S. *The myth of mental illness: foundations of a theory of personal conduct*. New York: Hoeber-Harper, 1961.

Szasz, T. S. *Law, liberty, and psychiatry: an inquiry into the social uses of mental health practices*. New York: Macmillan, 1963.

Szasz, T. S. The psychiatric classification of behavior: a strategy of personal constraint. In L. D. Eron (ed.), *The classification of behavior disorders*. Chicago: Aldine, 1966b, 125–170.

Tannenbaum, F. *Crime and the community*. Boston: Ginn, 1938.

Tawney, R. H. *Religion and the rise of capitalism*. New York: Harcourt, 1926.

Toch, H. *The social psychology of social movements*. Indianapolis: Bobbs-Merrill, 1965.

Tuckman, J., and Kleiner, R. J. Discrepancy between aspiration and achievement as a predictor of schizophrenia. *Behavioral science*, 1962, *7*, 443–447.

Turner, R. J., and Wagenfeld, M. O. Occupational mobility and schizophrenia: an assessment of the social causation and social selection hypotheses. *American sociological review*, 1967, *32*, 104–113.

Ullmann, L. P. An empirically derived MMPI scale which measures facilitation-inhibition of recognition of threatening stimuli. *Journal of clinical psychology*, 1962, *18*, 127–32.

Ullmann, L. P. *Institution and outcome: a comparative study of psychiatric hospitals*. New York: Pergamon, 1967a.

Ullmann, L. P. Abnormal psychology without anxiety. Paper read at Western Psychological Association convention, 1967b.

Ullmann, L. P. Behavior therapy as social movement. In C. M. Franks (ed.), *Assessment and status of the behavior therapies*. New York: McGraw-Hill, 1968.

Ullmann, L. P., and Krasner, L. Introduction: what is behavior modification? In L. P. Ullmann and L. Krasner (eds.), *Case studies in behavior modification*. New York: Holt, 1965b.

Vail, D. J., Lucero, R. J., and Boen, J. R. The relationship between socioeconomic variables and major mental illness in the counties of a midwestern state. *Community mental health journal*, 1966, *2*, 211–212.

Wallerstein, J. S., and Wyle, C. J. Our law-abiding law-breakers. *Probation*, 1947, *25*, 107–112.

Wegrocki, H. J. A critique of cultural and statistical concepts of abnormality. *Journal of abnormal and social psychology*, 1939, *34*, 166–178.

Wickman, E. K. *Children's behavior and teachers' attitudes*. New York: Commonwealth Fund, 1929.

Wignall, C. M., and Koppin, L. L. Mexican-American usage of state mental hospital facilities. *Community mental health journal*, 1967, *72*, 50–52.

Wing, J. K. Institutionalism in mental hospitals. *British journal of social and clinical psychology*, 1962, *1*, 38–51.

Woodward, J. L. Changing ideas on mental illness and its treatment. *American sociological review*, 1951, *16*, 443–454.

Zubin, J. A cross-cultural approach to psychopathology and its implications for diagnostic classification. In L. D. Eron (ed.), *The classification of behavior disorders*. Chicago: Aldine, 1966.

Zusman, J. The psychiatrist as a member of the emergency room team. *American journal of psychiatry*, 1967, *123*, 1394–1401.

13

Paranoid Behaviors and Personality Disorders

Leonard P. Ullmann and Leonard Krasner

From Leonard P. Ullmann and Leonard Krasner, *A Psychological Approach to Abnormal Behavior,* © 1969, pp. 429–43. Reprinted by permission of the authors and of Prentice-Hall, Inc., Englewood Cliffs, New Jersey.

This chapter will be devoted to a number of borderline and less reliably, although not necessarily less frequently, used diagnostic categories. The major topic will be paranoid behavior, but the concepts of personality pattern disturbance and personality trait disturbance will also be discussed.

The term "paranoia" comes from Greek, meaning beside or beyond reason. This accurately touches the major behavior involved: a false belief not susceptible to logical argument. The word has been used at least since the second century A.D. Currently paranoid behavior is a major element in a number of diagnostic categories: the paranoid type of schizophrenic reaction, the categories of psychosis called paranoid reactions (i.e., paranoia and paranoid state), and the personality disorder of personality pattern disturbance, paranoid personality. Clinical observation indicates that paranoid behavior may occur in cases with brain damage such as paresis and senility, and may, as all other patterns of abnormal behavior, be observed in transient situational maladjustments.

The behaviors likely to be designated paranoid range from sensitiveness to slights, cautiousness, rigid adherence to rules, social isolation, overcriticism of others, and self-righteousness all the way to full-blown overt delusions of persecution, influence, grandiosity, and reference. The delusion of persecution is usually considered the prototypical behavior. The person believes that other people are trying to destroy him; they may endeavor to control him, either through bizarre means such as radio waves and nighttime attacks or by keeping information from him and spreading malicious gossip about him. A reason for such influence on the part of others is their jealousy of him; hence, by implication, he is particularly important. This is the delusion of grandiosity. To the extent that the person called paranoid has "insight" into the workings of other people that the remainder of the population does not have, he is superior: like the college professor, he knows something other people do not and are not intelligent enough to grasp. The person may be on the alert for attacks and thus misinterpret aspects of his environment. He may manifest delusions of reference and give a personal meaning to events that are fortuitous or do not particularly apply to him.

Other behaviors which have been noted in connection with the label "paranoid" but which have not been assigned as central a position as the four delusions just mentioned are unusual beliefs dealing with religion, politics, legal processes, and sex. Eventually, any aspect of social life may be the focus of beliefs considered exaggerated if not downright false: there are health nuts, academic freedom nuts, and even some people who think psychology is interesting.

PARANOID REACTIONS

The paranoid reactions are placed in DSM-I (p. 28) as psychotic reactions: "In this group are to be classified those cases showing persistent delusions, generally persecutory or grandiose, ordinarily without hallucinations. The emotional responses and behavior are consistent with the ideas held. Intelligence is well preserved. This category does not include those reactions properly classifiable under schizophrenic reaction, paranoid type."

The only symptom in this category is that of paranoia, specifically a delusion or false belief. Although the individual is psychotic, the behaviors which would lead to a schizophrenic diagnosis are not manifest.

As the reader will remember, psychoses are "characterized by a varying degree of personality disintegration and failure to test and evaluate correctly external reality in various spheres. In addition, individuals with such disorders fail in their ability to relate themselves effectively to other people or to their own work." (DSM-I, p. 24.) The psychotic elements of the paranoid reaction would involve incorrect interpretation of external reality manifested in delusions, and ineffective (that is, inappropriate) relations to other people. Theoretically, when applying the label of paranoid reaction there should be little if any evidence of the schizophrenic manifestations: "fundamental disturbances in reality relationships and concept formations, with affective, behavioral, and intellectual disturbances in varying degrees and mixtures," strong tendency to retreat from reality, emotional disharmony, unpredictable disturbances in stream of thought, or "regressive" behavior. It is difficult to conceive of a psychotic, especially one with delusions, who would not manifest some aspect of schizophrenia. Empirically, such cases are extremely difficult to find. Sullivan (1956) puts it this way: "Yet the fact is that every person who gets lost in the schizophrenic morasses has paranoid feelings and can be led to express paranoid content at times; and, on the other hand, every paranoid person that I have encountered has in his history a period of schizophrenic content. . . . But how few people ever approach the absolute pole of pure paranoia may be suggested by the fact that out of, I suppose, fully three thousand veteran cases with which I had some contact in one of the hospitals where I have worked, only one even raised the diagnostic problem of whether he might be a pure paranoid."

Within the paranoid reactions there are two subcategories. The first is paranoia. "This type of psychotic disorder is extremely rare. It is characterized by an intricate, complex, and slowly developing paranoid system, often logically elaborated after a false interpretation of an actual occurrence. Frequently, the patient considers himself endowed with superior or unique ability. The paranoid system is particularly isolated from much of the normal stream of consciousness, without hallucinations and with relative intactness and preservation of the remainder of the personality, in spite of a chronic and prolonged course." (DSM-I, p. 28.)

The other subcategory is paranoid state. "This type of paranoid disorder is characterized by paranoid delusions. It lacks the logical nature of systematization seen in paranoia; yet it does not manifest the bizarre fragmentation and deterioration of the schizophrenic reactions. It is likely to be of a relatively short duration, though it may be persistent and chronic." (DSM-I, p. 28.)

In both the categories there are no symptoms other than the delusional beliefs. In the first of these, paranoia, the belief is conceived of as possible, following an actual occurrence which is logically elaborated. The concept of the system being isolated from much of the normal stream of consciousness may be interpreted as either that the illness is "latent" or that it is "defended against" by mechanisms such as denial and dissociation. The individual is socially appropriate save in one area of life or in terms of one topic on which he holds beliefs differing from the remainder of the population.

When the paranoid state is of relatively short duration it may well overlap with a transient situational maladjustment. . . . However, the definition continues, it may be persistent and chronic. Throughout the definition of paranoid reaction there is a notion that all that is wrong are the delusions. Intelligence and personality are well-preserved. No mention is made of the individual being capable or incapable of maintaining his economic freedom and working. The defining consideration is the presence of beliefs not shared by other people.

Formulations of Paranoia

There have been three pivotal formulations of paranoia: those of Freud (1915, 1922), Cameron (1959, 1967), and Lemert (1962). Each has had important consequences for the conceptualization and treatment of paranoia.

FREUD'S FORMULATION

Freud made two contributions. The first was a formulation of paranoid behaviors in terms of a defense mechanism that is ascribed to normal people and, in exaggerated form, to neurotics and psychotics. This mechanism is projection, the attribution of one's own unacceptable traits to another person. The second aspect of Freud's work on paranoia was the hypothesis, since questioned by psychoanalysts as well as other workers, that paranoid projection necessarily involves unacceptable and unsublimated homosexual impulses. Freud's major formulation of paranoia occurred in his analysis of an autobiography written by Daniel Paul Schreber, *Memoirs of My Nervous Illness.* "Although Freud had no contact with Schreber's autobiography, he made a masterful analysis of its paranoid contents. Freud's conclusions from this study and from his own and his colleagues' experiences was that paranoid reactions and homosexuality were inseparable." (Cameron, 1967, p. 667.) Aside from failure of clinical evidence to support Freud's hypothesis, Freud has been criticized because Schreber was quite overtly schizophrenic and thus far from a "pure" paranoid.

Freud did report on paranoid patients with whom he had direct contact. In a 1922 essay on "certain neurotic mechanisms in jealousy, paranoia and homosexuality," Freud illustrates some of the ideation. . . . "When I saw him he was still subject only to clearly defined attacks, which lasted for several days and, curiously enough, regularly appeared on the day following an act of intercourse [with his wife] which was, incidentally, satisfying to both of them. The inference is justified that after every satiation of the heterosexual libido the homosexual component, likewise stimulated by the act, forced for itself an outlet in the attack of jealousy." (p. 235.)

The use of the term "homosexual" to describe a man who obtains heterosexual gratification with his wife and with other women and who has emitted no overt adult homosexual act differs from contemporary usage such as that of Kinsey. . . . It might be possible to hypothesize, both generally and from the few details Freud presents, that the man was attracted to his wife and was upset when she emitted in the presence of other men those cues which successfully aroused him. Freud continues (p. 235): "His abnormality really reduced itself to this, that he watched his wife's unconscious mind much more closely and then regarded it as far more important than anyone else would have thought of doing." The same observation might be applied to the behavior of Freud vis-à-vis his patient. In similar fashion, in his 1915 paper "A case of paranoia running counter to the psychoanalytical theory of the disease" (pp. 150–161), one may observe a normal man (Freud) searching for information which will maintain a specialized view of the world. The two points to be made by these references are that the data on which Freud based his theory are skimpy and that much of the behavior of the paranoid lies well within the realm of normal, appropriate, and socially acceptable activity.

CAMERON'S FORMULATION

Cameron's concept of the paranoid pseudo-community represents a major step forward in the formulation of paranoid behavior. Cameron hypothesizes the existence of a threat or stress and a great likelihood that the person involved has had a lifelong pattern of finding fault with everyone but himself. It is difficult to reason with such a person, who finds himself isolated and estranged at the very moment when he most needs someone to confide in and to give him a more balanced view of a situation. Having no one whom he can trust, he may withdraw both socially and emotionally. Rather than change his false beliefs and his mode of approach to situations, he reconstructs the realities around him to fit his views. He is therefore not subjected to contradictory information which a close friend might provide. Because his own behavior may increase the threat, the person is indeed in a difficult situation; and as people in difficult, threatening situations often do, he becomes watchful, uneasy, puzzled, and, by searching for it, finds further confirmatory evidence of threat. Delusions of reference, the belief that others are paying special attention to him, laughing at him, or disturbing his work and home situation, which develop as minor everyday frustrations are reinterpreted. The individual may become actively suspicious and seek causes for his difficult interpersonal situation. If he tells someone else about his ideas, he is likely to find that the other person disagrees with him. He may interpret such behavior as meaning that other people do not understand him or even that they are part of the general conspiracy of people and events against him.

The person may question why this should occur. Many puzzles are solved when a false belief makes sense of the prior confused situation. The false belief helps assimilate many experiences which were previously contradictory. It does so, however, at the expense of accuracy and long-term interpersonal adjustment. Given the power and effectiveness of the organizing belief, there develops a further belief in a group of "them" who plot against the person. Because "they" do not really exist in the manner the paranoid believes, he is living in a "pseudo-community." The belief is considered false because it is based on evidence that seems inadequate, contradictory, and invalid to the normal person or the assessing mental health professional.

The paranoid's activities are ones which would be considered rational for any person who actually was threatened or persecuted. Running throughout Cameron's formulation is the thread of the person's increasing isolation from others, both as an effect and as a further cause for an inability to see things from other people's point of view. Cameron's formulation places the paranoid individual within the realm of normal people. There is a reasonable and inexorable progression in the development of his behavior, a progression which when sublime is called Greek drama and when mundane is called shaping.

LEMERT'S FORMULATION

Another major step forward in the formulation of paranoid behavior was made by Lemert (1962), who argued that the individual's suspiciousness might be a realistic response to the situation. Rather than saying that the paranoid construes the world as if the "others" were against him, Lemert introduces evidence that the world may indeed be against the individual. The feelings that he is being watched, that he is being specially treated, that other people are against him may be true. Whether it is because the individual is difficult to get along with, differs from others in some manner, or is placed by chance in a situation where reinforcement contingencies are sparse or suddenly altered, he may emit behaviors which are aversive to others. He may seem abrupt, lacking in sensitivity, and overly aggressive. These behaviors may be realistic responses made in order to obtain clear overt responses from others and hence establish what the situation really is. For example, many paranoids are litigious and seek public trials or written documentation so that they can hold other people to their words at later times. If a person needs to find solid evidence that others are trying subtly to exclude him or to deprive him of his job, this sort of behavior is eminently realistic.

Lemert thus shifts the spotlight away from the individual in isolation to an investigation of both the paranoid and the other people around him. Lemert studied a series of people committed to the Los Angeles County Department of Health and eight other cases, all of which were characterized by paranoid behavior. The requirement for inclusion in his sample was that there be no history of evidence of hallucinations and that the people studied were intellectually unimpaired. Lemert's intensive and acute observation of these individuals is the basis of his formulation of paranoia.

Lemert indicates that calling a person paranoid (or mentally ill) permits others to disregard their social obligations to him and, as an excuse, especially in contemporary organizations, to kick the person upstairs, to isolate him from the mainstream of information and responsibility, or to remove him from the scene by psychiatric hospitalization. The question remains, however, why people should pick on one particular individual. Lemert hypothesizes that there are frequently genuine issues centering around differences of opinion. In such situations, or in situations involving a sudden change in the environment caused by the death of relatives, loss of position, loss of professional certification, failure to be promoted, age, or physiological life-cycle changes, there may indeed occur threats to the person's status which he endeavors to ameliorate in the only ways he knows. Unfortunately, he may do so in a manner disruptive to others.

Lemert has a phrase which excellently describes the pressures on the individual. He says that the paranoid often may have the feeling of having the status of a stranger on trial in each new group he enters. That is, he seems to have been deprived of his prior sources of reinforcement and modes of adaptation and thus feels he must prove himself in each new situation. Such an individual may be very difficult for others to adjust to. He may act in a manner contrary to the way they accept as appropriate. The observers then may employ different methods to avoid taking him or their obligations to him seriously. They may develop what is, in fact, a pseudo-community as they are falsely polite or cooperative.

In a formal organization the individual may indeed be watched by others, who develop a network around him, making sure that they gather together when he is not present, shift the conversation when he approaches, start collecting evidence against him, or withhold information from him. In some instances, as Lemert points out, the individual may be placed under actual surveillance, and people, on police initiative or on their own, may watch his home, seeking new signs of deviation. There is a crystallization of the rationale for official action as the people in power positions observe the watched individual and seek further data to maintain or to document their viewpoint.[1]

Lemert portrays the individual called paranoid as one who indeed is excluded by others. If he has difficulty taking the viewpoint of the others, it is because others are indeed against him and have isolated him.

The concepts and formulations presented by Lemert are beautifully illustrated in a volume by Mrs. E. P. W. Packard (1875) called *Modern Persecution*. From 1861 through 1863, Mrs. Packard was a patient at an Illinois state psychiatric hospital. She was at first treated with great consideration and personal closeness by the superintendent of the asylum, Dr. McFarland. Her treatment, as she describes it, would be considered today as within the best traditions of the then declining moral treatment. After she had been in the hospital a number of months and been treated in a very humane way, she wrote Dr. McFarland a "reproof" for his abuse of patients. This reproof was 17 printed pages long. The quotations are presented here to ask the reader whether a woman who is a patient in a mental hospital and writes the superintendent (whom she reports as having treated her very well) in the following manner is paranoid or not.

> The office of a Reprover is put upon me; and this to me, the hardest of all crosses, I bear for Christ's sake. Christ is now my only Master, and His will,

not my own, is now my only choice. Oh! my Master, help me to do this duty under Thy special guidance and dictation. In Christ's own expressive language, I say, "Come let us reason together!" . . . Yes, in our insane asylums may be found the only real sane beings in the world, who, like the righteous of Sodom, are to become the world's saviors. . . . I have proof from a personal observation of your own actions . . . that you, sir, have exhibited more evidence of insanity of your part, than I have seen on any person since I entered this institution! and I think your insanity deserves and merits, imprisonment for life, in a state of extreme torture. . . . You have merited the reputation of Nero, and that reputation you will have, unless you repent. . . . I feel called of God, and I shall obey this call, to expose your character by exposing your actions, to the light of 1861, unless you repent. I have ability—I have influence—I have friends—I have money—I have God's promised aid . . . to aid me in doing this. . . . And what is worse for you, sir, is the fact this is known—and known by those who are determined . . . to have your character exposed and your insanity punished. . . . I am also a monument for the age—a standing miracle, almost—of the power of faith to shield one from insanity. . . . Besides, Dr. McFarland, there are others in this institution, that have now become invulnerable. . . . They are protected by a spiritual power that is invincible, and all your skillfully worked machinery for making maniacs, cannot make maniacs of them. As your friend, I advise you to beware! There are more for us, than there are against us. You are the weaker party. . . . Remember, Dr. McFarland, this is your last chance. The fatal dyke is but a few moments ahead of you. Repentance or exposure! (Packard, 1875, pp. 120–137.)

Dr. McFarland had Mrs. Packard transferred to a more disturbed ward, and Mrs. Packard wondered if her reproof had offended him (an illustration of the lack of sensitivity or ability to take the other person's point of view).

Knowing only the foregoing segment, most readers would agree that Mrs. Packard displayed poor judgment and false beliefs, including touches of delusions of persecution and grandeur. (Throughout the volume Dr. McFarland, despite what Mrs. Packard says, comes through as an outstandingly kind and patient man.)

Mrs. Packard's book was written a dozen years after her release from the hospital. One cannot say at that point whether she was abnormal as a result of her hospitalization or had been abnormal before being hospitalized. The title itself, *Modern Persecution*, is perhaps indicative. The entire tenor of the book is that Mrs. Packard is perfect and utterly loving. She is always right; she is always on a higher plane. She has excellent ability to reason logically, to take another person's statements out of context, and to make them appear illogical. She makes very acute and accurate observations on the treatment of mental patients at a period when moral treatment was changing to large institutional treatment. Even in 1875, when she was writing, there are elements of what might be called disordered communication or examples of assertion of the predicate and grandiosity. In her dedication she lists her children and then writes, "Yes, it is for you, my jewels, I have lived—it is for you I have suffered the agonies of Gethsemane's garden—it is for you I have hung on this cross of crucifixion; and have been entombed three years in a living cemetery; and Oh! it is for your sakes that I hope to rise again, to find my maternal joys immortalized." (p. v.) In addition: "Yes, the mother had died. But she has risen again—the mother of her country—and her sons and daughters are—The American Republic." (p. vi.)

Mrs. Packard was a minister's daughter who married a minister who had been her father's assistant. Both men were dominant and patriarchal. After some twenty years of marriage and six children, she developed theological views at variance with those of her husband. "In short, from my present standpoint, I cannot but believe that the doctrine of total depravity conflicts with the dictates of reason, common sense and the Bible. And the only offense my persecutors claim I have committed, is, that I have dared to be true to these my honest convictions, and to give utterance to these views in a Bible-class in Manteno, Kankakee County, Illinois." (pp. 33–34.)

Mrs. Packard's theological views would be accepted today as quite reasonable and not even particularly liberal. However, they did conflict with those of her husband and, given the milieu of an Illinois rural town in 1860, they were a source of great interest in the community. Attendance at the Bible class she taught increased, and there was some danger of the congregation splitting or, at least, of her husband losing his job. "These questions troubled both our teacher, Deacon Smith, and their pastor. They could not answer them satisfactorily to themselves or to the class; and it was to extricate themselves from this unpleasant dilemma that they at once agreed that this question was the result of a diseased brain, from whence it had emanated, and therefore it was unworthy of their consideration! Thus their reputation for intelligence and ability was placed beyond question, and the infallibility of their creed remained inviolate! And their 'poor afflicted Christian sister' must be kindly cared for within the massive walls of a prison lest the diseased brain communicate its contagion to other brains, and then what will become of our creed! for we cannot afford to follow the example of this 'Man of God,' and sacrifice our wives and mothers to save our creed!" (p. xvii.) (This quotation is exact and in sequence—it is an illustration of flight of ideas.)

In short, for whatever reason—change of life, difficulties with her husband, a more humane and liberal interpretation of the Bible, a desire for notoriety, or even a desire to embarrass her husband, who might have been flirting with a younger member of the congregation—Mrs. Packard proceeded to discuss and give vent to ideas that were disturbing to her husband and disruptive of the congregation.

During the ensuing period, Mrs. Packard noticed meetings being held which she thought were concerned with her. These ideas might have been delusions of reference. However, it is safe to presume that pressure was put on her husband and that he discussed with others what to do ". . . in most earnest conversation, which was always carried on in a whisper whenever I was in hearing distance, and my presence seemed always to evoke manifestations of guilt on their part. I think the theme of conversation at these clandestine interviews was, my abduction and how it should be secured." (p. 44.)

It would seem reasonable that Mrs. Packard's behavior had led to what Lemert would call exclusion. In trying to deal with Mrs. Packard's disruptive behavior, it is reasonable to assume there were discussions about her, observations of her, and the devising of plans to which she was not privy. Mrs. Packard was taken to the state hospital at Jacksonville, Illinois. Her removal from her home, placement on the train, and the ensuing trip were, to say the least, dramatic. She refused to walk, since that might be interpreted as compliance with her husband's ideas. She had to be carried. A maximum of embarrassment to her husband was a not unforeseen result. The reader may imagine the discussion provoked by the minister's wife's being forcibly picked up and placed on the train to the state psychiatric hospital.

Mrs. Packard prayed in front of the sheriff for divine forgiveness for Mr. Packard; she writes, "In fact, if I know anything of my own heart, I do know that it did not cherish a single feeling of resentment towards him." Despite this disclaimer, rarely in all literature is there a more thorough blackening of a man's reputation than Mrs. Packard's job on her husband.

It should be noted that the Illinois legal system at that time did not recognize a married woman as a separate entity. Once a woman was married, she was a dependent of her husband. As a result, a husband could place his wife in the state hospital. All that was required was the acceptance of the patient by the superintendent of the hospital. There was not the recourse to a legal body that would have been required for a male or for an unmarried woman. This law was eventually changed, a step for which Mrs. Packard was in part responsible.[2]

With this additional background, the reader may again want to consider whether Mrs. Packard should be categorized as paranoid or as normal. Her history illustrates various aspects of the situation described by Lemert. She was excluded by others who planned her final disposition. Her cause, both theological and legal, was just if one accepts the standards current a century later. Whether the cause or the effect of her experiences, however, the book written a dozen years later provides ample indications of unusual thinking. If the reader is not sure whether Mrs. Packard was paranoid or normal, the basic point of the chapter has been made.

A SOCIOPSYCHOLOGICAL FORMULATION

The question that follows from formulations of paranoid reactions such as those of Cameron and Lemert is how an individual comes to hold a false belief or, in fact, any belief at all. The viewpoint manifested throughout this book is that there is no such thing as abnormal behavior per se, but rather that all behavior is normal, understandable, and appropriate given the person's history of reinforcement.

All that is known of a person's beliefs are his actions, i.e., what he says and what he does, both of which are operant behaviors. Therefore, the problem becomes to determine how a person develops behaviors which later disturb observers who are in positions of power to reinforce positively or aversively.

The individual is always responding to his environment. His responses alter the behavior of other people; and because he has behaved and been reinforced in a particular manner, his own behavior is also altered. When a person's behavior is reinforced, his selection of stimuli from the environment is altered. He pays attention to what has been useful to him in the past. As a result of his experience he becomes sensitive to particular stimuli within the environment. An instance is the sensitivity of a mother to the crying of a child. Frequently she will respond to auditory cues which nonparents in the same room do not "hear."

One empirical example is found in studies noting a relatively greater likelihood of people diagnosed as paranoid reporting threatening material than reporting neutral material (Ullmann, 1958, 1962; Shannon, 1962). The problem, then, is a delineation of conditions under which a person is particularly sensitive to stimuli that others label as threatening.

Paranoia may be approached in terms of information and its evaluation. Isolation, difficulty in taking another person's viewpoint, and Cameron's pseudo-community may all be considered disruptions in information-gathering: the paranoid person is one who thinks straight about a biased sample of information. This leads to the core behavior of paranoia, the expression of beliefs that are considered so improbable as to be false. In day-to-day living, people do not check every story; rather, they make decisions that something is so unlikely that it is reasonable to presume that it is false. In other words, they act like scientists rejecting the null hypothesis.

The material . . . would lead to a formulation that a paranoid person is extinguished for attending and collecting evidence for the true (i.e., the majority's) belief and acts rationally on the information and choices available to him. . . . The analogy was made between such attitude development and careers in marijuana smoking, social movements, and religious conversion. The alteration of beliefs in brainwashing [has been illustrated]. Once the person has converted or has been given a special label, the effects of his changed identity lead to further changes in how people act toward him. Mrs.

Packard's style of writing in 1875 may have been, in part at least, the result rather than the cause of her hospitalization. An example of these considerations is provided by material excerpted and commented on by Szasz (1963, pp. 166–168) from *The New York Times* of September 28, 1962:

"After four years at the Matteawan State Hospital for the Criminal Insane, 39-year-old Victor Rosario became a free man yesterday, largely because he finally got someone to look into a fantastic story that he had tenaciously insisted was true.

"The core of the story was that his wife's love had been stolen by another man who drew blood from his arms and drank it in beer to prove his vigor. Mr. Rosario told this story to everyone, including at least eleven psychiatrists, but not until a woman lawyer verified it did anyone believe him. Yesterday charges of assault that had been brought against him in 1958 were dismissed in Bronx Criminal Court.

"In 1957 Mr. Rosario had been placidly married for almost eight years. He and his wife, Caen, had two children, Martha and Victor, now 9 and 7 years old respectively. Then Mr. Rosario introduced a male boarder into their home at 725 Fox Street, the Bronx. It was this man who won Mrs. Rosario's affection. The wife, from whom Mr. Rosario is separated, signed a sworn affidavit in June stating that this was true.

"Mr. Rosario, a waiter and longshoreman, ordered the boarder to leave. He refused and the two men lived in the apartment in considerable tension until Mr. Rosario left.

"He returned later, however, in a jealous rage and allegedly struck and kicked his wife and threatened her with a bailing hook. She called the police, who said they arrested him on June 22, 1958.

"Mr. Rosario was charged with simple assault, resisting arrest, and illegally using a weapon. *He was sent to Bellevue Hospital for observation and was committed to Matteawan on October 14, 1958, on the testimony of two psychiatrists.* They said that he appeared to be a paranoiac and was incapable of understanding the charges against him.

"Matteawan is a large and formidable-looking institution in the Hudson Valley hills at Beacon, about 60 miles north of the city. There Mr. Rosario worked in the kitchen cleaning silverware and paring vegetables, and he began his long campaign to free himself.

"He had come to New York in 1946 from Puerto Rico and his English was very limited, but he labored painstakingly with a dictionary and wrote to a great many Government figures, to friends and lawyers. *He also drew up six writs of habeas corpus, all of which were dismissed by State Supreme Court in Dutchess County or were ignored.*

"Mr. Rosario told everyone who interviewed him the story of the drawn blood. 'The doctors told me that if I forgot that story, they might let me go, but the truth is the truth no matter what anyone says,' he said yesterday. So he never changed his story.

"Last November he wrote the first of several appeals to Mrs. Sara Halbert of Zapata and Halbert, a New York City law firm. He was told that a relative would have to confer with Mrs. Halbert. At length two cousins flew up from Puerto Rico and prevailed upon the lawyer to visit Mr. Rosario.

"After a second visit, Mrs. Halbert went to Mr. Rosario's wife. She confirmed his story and signed the affidavit, asserting that the boarder had taken the blood in beer and had written on a wall in letters of blood.

"Mrs. Halbert said she presented the affidavit to Dr. Cecil Johnston, director of the hospital on Aug. 27. She asked that Mr. Rosario be released immediately. *The following day, four psychiatrists interviewed him, and he was shortly declared fit to return to the Bronx to face trial.*

"Dr. Johnston said by telephone yesterday that more than the affidavit had entered into the decision, but he acknowledged that the new information had caused the staff to look on the patient in a little different manner. He said Mr. Rosario had been interviewed on seventeen occasions by nine psychiatrists in four years.

"Mrs. Halbert moved in court yesterday that the case be dismissed. The motion was granted by Judge Ambrose J. Haddock, after Assistant District Attorney Joseph Tiger had agreed." [Italics added by Szasz.]

It seems that poor Mr. Rosario's "delusions" were true, after all. And yet, according to the account in the *Times*, the psychiatric authorities did not feel that a mistake had been made. On the contrary. They implied that whatever the circumstances surrounding Victor Rosario's incarceration might have been, the "fact" of his "mental illness," proved by nine psychiatrists over a period of four years, justified his involuntary "hospitalization." [p. 168.]

A crucial point here is that the "delusion" did not instigate hospitalization but rather justified it. Mrs. Rosario asked for help when physically threatened, but Mr. Rosario's beliefs justified the diagnosis of paranoia, which in turn permitted psychiatric hospitalization.

The authors' clinical experience does not include a case as dramatic as that of Mr. Rosario. However, it does include an instance of a patient who claimed that another patient had stolen his teeth. The fact of the matter was that the second patient had been a corpsman a decade before when the first patient was wounded, had indeed removed his dentures, and in the normal confusion of events they had been lost.

TREATMENT OF PARANOID BEHAVIOR

Following the sociopsychological formulation, behavior labeled paranoid is learned as a response to situations which extinguish appropriate responses and shape the person toward the target (paranoid) behavior. Treatment is directed, as with other behaviors, toward the emission of an alternative and more socially appropriate act. An example of a behavioral program which altered a paranoid delusion was presented in . . . the case of a positive reinforcing stimulus generated by avoidance of an aversive situation. The woman who would not feed herself did so when such activity avoided food-spilling on her clothes. The delusion that her food was poisoned "spontaneously" dropped out. Cowden and Ford (1962) reported systematic desensitization with paranoid schizophrenics, while Rickard, Dignam, and Horner (1960) and Rickard and Dinoff (1962) illustrate the use of verbal conditioning of delusional material in a framework similar to that of Ayllon and Haughton (1964) . . . and Ullmann, Krasner, and Collins (1961) and Ullmann et al. (1965).

A further illustration of how paranoia may be treated in the present conceptual framework is provided by Davison (1966). Upon admission to the hospital, Mr. B was diagnosed paranoid schizophrenic by one psychiatrist and paranoid state by another. His history was as follows: After a medical discharge from the military for an eye imbalance, he had frequently encountered difficulties arising from actions and schemes that had "a paranoid flavor." His current admission to the hospital was at his wife's insistence, and Mr. B structured his concern as finding out about twitches over his right eye, heart, and solar plexus. His problems seemed to have started four years earlier after the suicide of his only brother. At that time he became preoccupied with "pressure points" over his right eye, which he interpreted as being caused by a spirit that helped him make decisions. Tranquilizers and surgery had been of little help. The behavior therapist interviewed Mr. B and asked him to describe tension-producing situations likely to lead to "pressure points." Mr. B was taught relaxation procedures and how to apply them in his daily life. During therapy, which comprised eight sessions in a nine-week period, the therapist introduced games that would increase tension and hence provide additional, on-the-spot training in relaxing under pressure. After the first month, Mr. B's speech changed: he talked of "sensations" rather than "pressure points." The therapist taught him better ways to label his own behavior. He began to assert himself at home, and his marriage improved.

Discussing treatment of paranoids, Henderson and Batchelor (1962, p. 317) write: "The cases, however, which are completely established are not susceptible of therapeutic success, and can only be regarded as extremely disappointing." Noyes and Kolb (1963, p. 376) write: "It is doubtful if a case of traditional paranoia ever recovers." Cameron (1967, p. 673) writes: "Classical full blown paranoia is by definition incurable."

In contrast to this pessimistic view, the behavioral formulation leads to treating paranoid ideation in a manner similar to other behaviors: to withdraw reinforcement for the socially disturbing operants and to shape alternative reactions to social situations. Frequently, after changed behavior has provided new experiences contrary to prior beliefs, the beliefs themselves "spontaneously" change.

Personality Disorders

Personality disorders, one of the major divisions of the functional disorders, "are characterized by developmental defects or pathological trends in the personality structure, with minimal subjective anxiety, and little or no sense of distress. In most instances, the disorder is manifested by a life-long pattern of action or behavior, rather than by mental or emotional symptoms." (DSM-I, p. 34.)

That the theoretical foundation of this category bears the full weight of psychoanalytic theory and the reification of personality . . . is made explicit in the following: "The personality disorders are divided into three main groups with one additional grouping for flexibility in diagnosis (Special symptom reactions). Although the groupings are largely descriptive, the division has been made partially on the basis of the dynamics of personality development. The Personality pattern disturbances are considered deep-seated disturbances, with little room for regression. Personality trait disturbances and Sociopathic personality disturbances under stress may at times regress to a lower level of personality organization and function without development of psychosis." (DSM-I, pp. 34–35.)

As was noted [earlier] the diagnostic revision represented here introduced these terms in order to be able to categorize every instance of morbidity observed in the military situation. Data provided [earlier] indicate that the reliability with which these particular diagnoses are applied is low and in some studies approaches the level of chance.

Within the three major groupings of personality disorder, the personality pattern disturbances are the most severe. "The depth of the psychopathology here allows these individuals little room to maneuver under conditions of stress, except into actual psychosis." (DSM-I, p. 35.) In short, these people are operationally ones who either are in remission after psychosis or currently not psychotic only because of favorable environments. The very definition has in it the concept that chances are poor for improvement even after prolonged therapy and that "basic change is seldom accomplished."

The four subtypes of personality pattern disturbance parallel psychoses. Inadequate personality is similar to the simple type of schizophrenic reaction. "Such individuals are characterized by inadequate response to intellectual, emotional, social, and physical demands. . . . they do show inadaptability, ineptness, poor judgment, lack of physical and emotional stamina, and social incompatibility." (DSM-I, p. 35.)

Cyclothymic personality is analogous to manic–depressive psychosis.

"Characteristic are frequently alternating moods of elation and sadness, stimulated apparently by internal factors. . . ." (DSM-I, p. 35.) The schizoid personality is analogous to the more general category of schizophrenia, particularly the hebephrenic and undifferentiated types manifested by avoidance of close relations with others, inability to express negative feelings directly, and autistic thinking. Finally, paranoid personality is analogous to paranoid schizophrenia and paranoid reactions being characterized by many traits of the schizoid personality "coupled with an exquisite sensitivity in interpersonal relations, and with a conspicuous tendency to utilize a projection mechanism, expressed by suspiciousness, envy, extreme jealousy, and stubbornness." (DSM-I, p. 36.)

The second major group of the personality disorders is called personality trait disturbance. "This category applies to individuals who are unable to maintain their emotional equilibrium and independence under minor or major stress because of disturbances in emotional development. Some individuals fall into this group because their personality pattern disturbance is related to fixation and exaggeration of certain character and behavior patterns; others, because their behavior is a regressive reaction due to environmental or endopsychic stress." (DSM-I, p. 36.) The comments made previously about the theoretical concepts incorporated in the definition of personality pattern disturbance apply here. Further material along this line is the stipulation that neurotic features are relatively insignificant and "the basic personality maldevelopment is the crucial distinguishing factor."

There are four subcategories within personality trait disturbance. The first is emotionally unstable personality, in which the person reacts with excitability and ineffectiveness when faced with minor stresses. He is presumed undependable under stress and to have poor relationships with others because his emotional responses fluctuate and because he has "strong and poorly controlled hostility, guilt, and anxiety." (DSM-I, p. 36.)

The passive–aggressive personality is described by three subtypes. The passive–dependent type is characterized by helplessness, indecisiveness, and a tendency to cling to others "as a dependent child to a supporting parent." (DSM-I, p. 37.) The passive–aggressive type pouts, procrastinates, and is inefficient, stubborn, and passively obstructive. The aggressive type is irritable, resentful, and may have temper tantrums.

The compulsive personality displays excessive concern with adherence to standards of conscience and conformity. The person may be overinhibited, overconscientious, and have a great capacity for work. These people are characterized as rigid, and lack relaxing and enjoyable pursuits.

The final category is called personality trait disturbance, other, and, by definition, "This category is included to permit greater latitude in diagnosis. Instances in which a personality trait is exaggerated as a means to life adjustment (as in the above diagnoses), not classifiable elsewhere, may be listed here." (DSM-I, p. 37.)

A function similar to "personality trait disturbance, other" is served by a division of personality disorders called special symptom reactions. "This category is useful in occasional situations where a specific symptom is the single outstanding expression of the psychopathology. . . . Thus, for example, the diagnosis special symptom reaction, speech disturbances, would be used for certain disturbances in speech in which there are insufficient other symptoms to justify any other definite diagnosis." (DSM-I, p. 39.)

A SOCIOPSYCHOLOGICAL COMMENT ON PERSONALITY DISORDERS

The category of personality disorders arose as a solution to administrative pressures. It is in its very definition a deduction from psychoanalytic theory in terms of psychosexual development, fixation, and regression. If psychoanalytic theory is incorrect, the categories are without foundation. The empirical evidence for the exact and reliable use of these labels is sparse and, when carefully measured, disappointing. A sociopsychological formulation of a person's behaviors likely to lead to such designations is therefore unwarranted. What is necessary is a formulation of the conditions leading professional people to make this diagnosis.

An application of the sociopsychological model would ask, first and foremost, what the person is doing. What acts is he making that are disturbing to others? The overt activity should be the focus of clinical endeavors. Given categories such as personality trait disturbance and special symptom reaction, this procedure becomes a crucial matter not only of appropriate scientific procedure but of fundamental respect for the individual. The standard of what is an exaggeration of personality is so poorly defined that a person may be deprived of his place in society and his self-respect as a result of uncritical application of labels. While this is true with respect to other labels as well, the personality disorders are the clearest examples of the need for specification of behavior as a method for ethical as well as effective clinical practice.

SUMMARY

This chapter dealt primarily with paranoid reactions. Descriptions, theories, and clinical practice were touched on. It was suggested that false beliefs must be studied in the same way as true beliefs, and, given the person's history of reinforcement, cannot be differentiated from them. Because paranoid reactions are essentially disturbing behaviors with few if any other indications of abnormality, the opportunity was taken to review briefly and comment on the label "personality disorder," and two of its three major subcategories.

NOTES

1. In formal outline, this procedure is no different from the method by which a scientist develops his theories. He collects data, thinks about them and develops various explanations to fit the facts. Eventually he develops hypotheses that integrate his information. He may then proceed to search the literature for further information consistent with his hypothesis, and look for reasons why information that does not fit with his theory is incorrect, inappropriate, or spurious. Finally, he may devise experiments to create additional information.

2. Deutsch (1937, p. 307), writes of Mrs. Packard: "Her allegations created a national sensation and resulted in a wave of sentiment in favor of legislation providing better safeguards for persons 'accused' of insanity." A bill to this effect passed the Illinois legislature in 1867. Mrs. Packard lectured throughout the country, and her books sold well. It is possible that such vindication might have provided a realistic basis for some allegations that, in her 1875 volume, touch on grandiosity. The professional reader may also wish to contrast the following quotation with concepts such as those espoused by Szasz (1963, 1965) and by the present authors: ". . . in 1865, she presented two bills for the consideration of a legislative committee. The first read: 'No person shall be regarded or treated as an insane person or a monomaniac simply for the expression of opinions, no matter how absurd these opinions may appear.' This bill, she explained with much reason, was intended to protect reformers and progressive thinkers from being adjudged insane merely because their ideals might seem too 'queer' to their more backward contemporaries. Her second bill read as follows: 'No person shall be imprisoned and treated as an insane person except for irregularities of conduct, such as indicate that the individual is so lost to reason as to render him an unaccountable moral agent.' By these bills she hoped to establish general behavior rather than particular opinions as a criterion for determining insanity." (Deutsch, 1937, p. 424.) It [has been] . . . noted that each era reinterprets the past: Deutsch, writing in 1937, has glowing things to say about Dorothea Dix and generally unfavorable things about the impact of Mrs. Packard, while the present authors reverse the procedure.

REFERENCES

American Psychiatric Association. *Diagnostic and statistical manual: mental disorders (DSM-1)*. Washington: American Psychiatric Association, 1952; special printing, 1965.

Ayllon, T., and Haughton, E. Modification of symptomatic verbal behaviour of mental patients. *Behaviour research and therapy*, 1964, *2*, 87–97.

Cameron, N. A. Paranoid conditions and paranoia. In S. Arieti (ed.), *American handbook of psychiatry*. New York: Basic Books, 1959, 508–539.

Cameron, N. A. Paranoid reactions. In A. M. Freedman and H. I. Kaplin (eds.), *Comprehensive textbook of psychiatry*. Baltimore: Williams and Wilkins, 1967, 665–675.

Cowden, R. C., and Ford, L. I. Systematic desensitization with phobic schizophrenics. *American journal of psychiatry*, 1962, *119*, 241–245.

Davison, G. C. Differential relaxation and cognitive restructuring in therapy with "paranoid schizophrenic" or "paranoid state." *Proceedings of the 74th annual convention of the American Psychological Association*, 1966, 177.

Deutsch, A. *The mentally ill in America.* Garden City, N.Y.: Doubleday, 1937.

Freud, S. A case of paranoia running counter to the psychoanalytical theory of the disease (1915). In *Collected papers* (Vol. 2). London: Hogarth Press, 1950, 150–161.

Freud, S. Certain neurotic mechanisms in jealousy, paranoia and homosexuality (1922). In *Collected Papers* (Vol. 2). London: Hogarth Press, 1950, 232–243.

Henderson, D., and Batchelor, I. R. C. *Henderson and Gillespie's textbook of psychiatry* (9th ed.). London: Oxford University Press, 1962.

Kinsey, A. C., Pomeroy, W. B., and Martin, C. E. *Sexual behavior in the human male.* Philadelphia: Saunders, 1948.

Lemert, E. M. Paranoia and the dynamics of exclusion. *Sociometry*, 1962, *25*, 2–25.

Noyes, A. P., and Kolb, L. C. *Modern clinical psychiatry* (6th Ed.). Philadelphia: Saunders 1963.

Packard, E. P. W. *Modern persecution.* Hartford: Case, Lockwood and Brainard, 1875.

Rickard, H. C., Dignam, P. J., and Horner, R. F. Verbal manipulation in a psychotherapeutic relationship. *Journal of clinical psychology*, 1960, *16*, 364–367.

Rickard, H. C., and Dinoff, M. A follow-up note on "verbal manipulation" in a psychotherapeutic relationship. *Psychological reports*, 1962, *11*, 506.

Shannon, D. T. Clinical patterns of defense as revealed in visual recognition thresholds. *Journal of abnormal and social psychology*, 1962, *64*, 370–377.

Sullivan, H. S. *Clinical studies in psychiatry.* New York: Norton, 1956.

Szasz, T. S. *Law, liberty, and psychiatry: an inquiry into the social uses of mental health practices.* New York: Macmillan, 1963.

Szasz, T. S. *Psychiatric justice.* New York: Macmillan, 1965.

Ullmann, L. P. Clinical correlates of facilitation and inhibition of response to emotional stimuli. *Journal of projective techniques*, 1958, *22*, 341–347.

Ullmann, L. P. An empirically derived MMPI scale which measures facilitation-inhibition of recognition of threatening stimuli. *Journal of clinical psychology*, 1962, *18*, 127–132.

Ullmann, L. P., Forsman, R. G., Kenny, J. W., McInnis, T. L. Jr., Unikel, I. P., and Zeisset, R. M. Selective reinforcement of schizophrenics' interview responses. *Behaviour research and therapy*, 1965, *2*, 205–212.

Ullmann, L. P., Krasner, L., and Collins, B. J. Modification of behavior through verbal conditioning: effects in group therapy. *Journal of abnormal and social psychology*, 1961, *62*, 128–132.

14

Sociopathic Personality Disturbance: Antisocial and Dyssocial Reactions

Leonard P. Ullmann and Leonard Krasner

From Leonard P. Ullmann and Leonard Krasner, *A Psychological Approach to Abnormal Behavior*, © 1969, pp. 444–65. Reprinted by permission of the authors and of Prentice-Hall, Inc., Englewood Cliffs, New Jersey.

Three of the major subcategories of personality disorder have been discussed. The fourth is that of sociopathic personality disturbance: "Individuals to be placed in this category are ill primarily in terms of society and of conformity with the prevailing cultural milieu, and not only in terms of personal discomfort and relations with other individuals." (DSM-I, p. 38.) There are four groups within the sociopathic personality disturbance label: antisocial reaction, dyssocial reaction, sexual deviation, and addiction. This chapter will be devoted to the first two.

Antisocial reaction is defined as referring to "chronically antisocial individuals who are always in trouble, profiting neither from experience nor punishment, and maintaining no real loyalties to any person, group, or code. They are frequently callous and hedonistic, showing marked emotional immaturity, with lack of sense of responsibility, lack of judgment, and an ability to rationalize their behavior so that it appears warranted, reasonable, and justified." (DSM-I, p. 38.)

The DSM-I designation of dyssocial reaction applies to "individuals who manifest disregard for the usual social codes, and often come in conflict with them, as the result of having lived all their lives in an abnormal moral environment. They may be capable of strong loyalties. These individuals typically do not show significant personality deviations other than those implied by adherence to the values or codes of their own predatory, criminal, or other social group." (DSM-I, p. 38.)

A DISCUSSION OF TERMS

These two types of sociopathic personality were previously included within the older term "psychopathic personality." Although now officially discarded for diagnostic purposes, the term "psychopath" has become part of the clinician's everyday vocabulary. The newer terms implicitly recognize the "social" forces which shape and maintain the kinds of behaviors described in this chapter, but the continued use of the word "ill" in the definition undoes the special meaning of the new label.

A review by Preu, over two decades ago, of the confusions and ambiguities involved in the concept of psychopathic personality (the current "sociopath") remains a fair representation of the current situation. Preu reformulated the then current definitions concerning psychopathic personalities as follows: "The diagnostic labels psychopathic personality and constitutional psychopathic inferiority designate those individuals who have manifested considerable difficulty in social adjustment over a period of many years or throughout life, but who are not of defective intelligence nor suffering from structural disease of the brain or epilepsy, and whose difficulties in adjustment have not been manifested by the behavioral syndromes which are conventionally referred to as neuroses and psychoses." (1944, p. 923.)

Preu emphasized that whatever the particular current version of this category of "psychopath," it is used to indicate the presence of human behaviors that do not fit conveniently in any of the established clinical categories. "The diagnosis has never been made dependent on the recognition of particular symptoms or kinds of behavior in the direct descriptive sense, nor on the demonstration of the existence of any definite etiologic factor. The emphasis has been predominantly but not exclusively on the occurrence of persistent social maladjustment in the absence of the symptoms of the traditional clinical entities of psychiatry." (p. 924.) Preu's conclusion that the concept of psychopathic personality "illustrates the futility of orienting psychiatric research about the traditional clinical entities as 'diseases' of 19th century psychiatry" (p. 936) summarizes a viewpoint that is still applicable.

The reader may have noted that Preu's definitions would fit the other personality disorders described at the end of the previous chapter, as well as antisocial and dyssocial reactions. In fact, DSM-I notes that the term "emotionally unstable personality" is synonymous with the no-longer-used term "psychopathic personality with emotional instability." If not a waste basket, the category represents a set of conflicting compromises. The definition of the general category "personality disorder" states that "these disorders are characterized by developmental defects or pathological trends in the personality structure. . . ." (DSM-I, p. 34.) The definition of sociopathic personality disturbance notes that the person is "ill primarily in terms of society," while the dyssocial reaction applies to individuals who come in conflict with social codes "as a result of having lived all their lives in an abnormal moral environment."

This is an uncomfortably muddled situation just where clarity is called for: clear diagnostic meaning is a necessary condition for progress in research and eventually in treatment. One solution is to take the view expressed by Robins (1967, p. 951): "In the author's opinion, dyssocial reaction either does not refer to a psychiatric illness or has not been studied in a manner to differentiate it clearly from antisocial reaction. . . . The term 'dyssocial reaction,' although a logically and psychologically impeccable concept, appears to be so rare that it may safely be assumed that the overwhelming majority of criminals would fit into the diagnostic category of sociopathic antisocial personality, and not dyssocial reaction."

The problem to be dealt with is that there are people who act in a manner that is socially disturbing. Their behaviors do not fall into recognizable patterns of psychosis, neurosis, or psychophysiological disorders, there are no immediately apparent overwhelming environmental stresses (which would "justify" a person, such as the psychiatrist, in acting the way these individuals do), and there is no evidence of either mental retardation or brain injury. Yet the people act in an incomprehensible manner: if they break laws it is in such a repetitive, almost self-defeating, foolish manner that it seems unlikely that they act as a result of having compared the risk of being caught with the gain that could result if they were not caught. Having given up concepts of demonology, how is one to understand such people? In a simple phrase, the behavior these people manifest is considered poor social judgment but is not psychotic. The diagnostic concept, the group of people denoted, and the social puzzle will become clearer through the following historical survey.

The History of a Label

Although the behaviors described within the current category of sociopathic disturbances, particularly antisocial reaction, have been a part of the human scene since ancient times, the concept of "psychopath" as a psychiatric classification began with Pinel's diagnosis of a patient as suffering from manie sans délire (McCord and McCord, 1964). Despite coming from a wealthy, noble family and having been given everything he wanted, this patient could never satisfy his desires. He was aroused to fury at any obstacle in his way and kicked a dog to death, whipped a horse, and threw a peasant woman into a well. Pinel's label of manie sans délire appears to have included more behaviors than are currently attributed to the "sociopath," but the existence of a label focused interest on this "disorder" and led to additional reports and descriptions.

Other labels important to the understanding of modern viewpoints on psychopathy were those of "moral insanity" and "moral derangement." The former term was introduced in 1835 by Pritchard and referred to an individual who was without "insane illusion or hallucination" and whose condition did not affect the "intellect or knowing and reasoning facilities." Such a person was one in whom "the moral and active principles of the mind are strongly perverted or depraved." Rush (1812) defined "moral derangement" as a state "when the will becomes the involuntary vehicle of vicious actions through the instrumentality of the passions." He included among "the morbid operations of the will" the behaviors of murder, theft, lying, and drinking. Rush refers to such individuals as having "derangement of the moral faculties," which he thought of as innate; he considered the condition to be due to "an original defective organization in those parts of the body which are occupied by the moral faculties of the mind." (Lowrey, 1944.) Ray (1838), who had a major influence on concepts of sanity and legality classified moral insanity in the category of affective mania. Ray felt that these people would commit crimes for reasons inexplicable to themselves and others. He attributes such events to the working of a blind, instinctive, and irresistible impulse.

The views of Pinel, Rush, Pritchard, and Ray evoked considerable controversy because the implication of their argument was that socially disturbing behaviors of an extreme nature, including crime, were actually a form of insanity and, as such, came within the province of medicine. The counter arguments described these behaviors as "sinful" or "evil," but not as "sick." It was argued that the act of describing such undesirable action as "illness" destroyed the grounds for human responsibility. This dispute reached a peak in the trial of Guiteau, the assassin of President Garfield. Defense psychiatrists argued that Guiteau was morally insane and thus not responsible for his behavior. The prosecution produced psychiatrists who argued that Guiteau was sane since he knew the difference between right and wrong. The jury upheld the latter group, and Guiteau was executed. Much the same debate might have occurred if Lee Harvey Oswald had stood trial for the assassination of President Kennedy.

The professional concept of psychopathy began to slowly move in the direction of the belief that these behaviors were due to innate, inherited causes. In 1888, Koch contributed the term "psychopathic inferiority," implying a constitutional predisposition to such behavior. Tredgold (1915, p. 321) argued that the "moral defective" was really feebleminded: ". . . my experience is that most persistent criminals are the offspring of a decidedly neurotic or mentally abnormal stock, and that they possess many characteristics identical with those occurring in ordinary aments."

Fernald (1908) presented the other side of the coin with the belief that every imbecile is a potential criminal needing only a particular environment and opportunity to express his criminal tendency. Thus, in contrast to the earlier ideas, the tendency became that of equating immoral behavior with stupid behavior. This view culminated in the British Mental Deficiencies Act of 1913 in which moral imbeciles were defined as "persons who from an early age display some permanent mental defect coupled with strong vicious criminal propensities on which punishment has had little or no deterrent effect."

The approach linking psychopathy with innate characteristics culminated in the Italian school of criminology led by Lombroso (1911). It was claimed that the criminal was a born "type" who had clear "stigmatizing" facial features which were signs of degeneracy and discernibly different from those of normal people. Among the signs of the degenerate criminal were a cleft palate, a low forehead, unusual shaped head or nose, protruding ears, high cheekbones, and a scanty beard. These features were a direct throwback to the savage caveman. Lest the reader's mirror cause him too much anxiety, it must be clearly stated that, Hollywood type-casting notwithstanding, this theory has been almost universally abandoned.

The next important development was the introduction of more careful gathering of empirical data about these people. The first person generally credited with empirical study in this field was Bernard Glueck, a psychiatrist at Sing Sing prison in the early 1920's. He labeled approximately 20 per cent of the inmates as constitutional psychopaths and found that these were the individuals who also had the greatest recidivism, drunkenness, and addiction.

In 1924 Bolsi reported the observation that encephalitis (a brain inflammation) can result in psychopathic symptoms in individuals who had previously been "normal." The consequences of Bolsi's findings in the behavior of the professional investigators were equivalent to those that followed the demonstration that syphilis caused paresis. The organically minded investigators hailed this as evidence that malfunction of the brain accounted for psychopathic behavior, which, if true, would have eventually solved the puzzling problem.

In the 1930's and 1940's the influence of psychoanalysis began to be manifested in the field of psychopathy. For example, Alexander and Staub (1929) hypothesized that the criminal was unconsciously motivated by a desire for punishment and argued that the psychopath was fixated at the phallic stage of development.

DESCRIPTION AND THEORIES OF PSYCHOPATHY[1]

The behaviors which may result in a person's being designated as an antisocial personality are listed below. As is true in other "reactions," not all these behaviors are characteristic of any one "sociopath"; rather, they are representative of general types of behaviors. Further, many people who act in this manner may not come to the attention of authorities; that is, there is a great amount of residual deviance. First of all the individual must perform an act or series of acts that bring him to the attention of the authorities. Often this is a behavior designated as criminal by the legal code or as morally wrong in terms of custom. As the representative of authority learns more about the behavior of the offending individual, various of the following characteristics frequently emerge:

1. The individual does not play by the usual rules of society. He generally does not seem responsive to the kinds of reinforcements that are effective with most people. He does not "play the game" the way everyone else does. It seems as if he wants special rules (or none) to apply to him alone.

2. He talks a good game. There is a façade of competency or maturity. He is often charming and verbalizes the right things, the things others want to hear. His behavior, however, is at marked variance with his verbalization. There is an inconsistency between words and actions, and between words at various times.

3. He may perform illegal or unusual behaviors characterized by "impulsiveness."[2] He is likely to react to stimuli in the immediate situation without regard for the consequences of his behavior for himself or for others, consequences which may seem apparent to an observer, but not to him.

4. He may repeatedly commit crimes involving pettiness and deceit, such as fraud, forgery, and "con-man" behavior.

5. He may be a chronic liar, but his lies are often difficult to spot because of the sincerity with which he emits them. It is only after considerable contact that the untruthfulness of many of his statements becomes obvious. He will often express regret or sorrow, but the question is whether he really means it. The evidence is that this is an example of saying the thing most calculated to placate others. But there seems to be no "real self-blame" or "insight."

6. He usually does not display anxiety or guilt about his behavior.

7. He does not seem to learn from experience. He will repeatedly emit a behavior that seems self-defeating or simply stupid. Even if he is caught and punished for his behavior, he may repeat the same stupidity.

8. He is likely to be uninfluenced by any form of authority and discipline. Although he may be intelligent, he usually will not go very far in formal schooling since he is likely to get into difficulty with school authorities.

9. He seems unable to sustain any close interpersonal relationship. He uses other persons as objects rather than as individuals. He dehumanizes others; he cannot empathize with, identify with, or "role-play" other human beings. He is likely to disappoint anyone who has prolonged contact with him, such as family or friends. He usually will change jobs frequently, desert

his family, borrow money and fail to pay it back, and yet continually ask for another chance and usually get it because of his verbal assurances of repentance.

10. He seems unable to wait, to forego present pleasures for future gratifications. Consequently there is little successful long-term planning or achievement of long-range goals.

Not everyone who is labeled an antisocial personality manifests all these behaviors, and all the behaviors may be emitted to some degree by people not labeled as psychopathic.

The problem of categorization in this area is complicated by the conflicting views of the relation of antisocial personality to the concept of anxiety. There has been previous discussion of the limited usefulness of the concept of anxiety, but assuming for the moment that the concept is measurable, are antisocial personalities deviant in regard to anxiety? The lack of anxiety is taken to be one of the characteristics clearly distinguishing the personality disorders in general from the psychoneuroses. However, observers (from Alexander and Staub, 1929) have noted individuals called antisocial or psychopathic who are "anxious." To resolve this dilemma with any kind of consistency, the notion developed of two types of psychopath, the true or primary psychopath and the secondary, neurotic psychopath. In some regard this is implicitly recognized in DSM-I when it is noted that "sociopathic reactions are very often symptomatic" of various other disorders. Cleckley (1964) has been the major proponent of the lack of anxiety of the "real" or "primary" sociopath. Cleckley (1964), Karpman (1941), and Lykken (1957) all argue for a designation of the category "primary sociopathy or primary psychopath" characterized as being: "(a) clearly defective as compared to normals in their ability to develop (i.e., condition) anxiety, in the sense of an anticipatory emotional response to warning signals previously associated with nocioceptive stimulation. Persons with such a defect would also be expected to show (b) abnormally little manifest anxiety in life situations normally conducive to this response, and to be (c) relatively incapable of avoidance learning under circumstances where such learning can only be effected through the mediation of the anxiety response" (Lykken, 1957).

Lykken (1957) reports a study in which he compared these two types of psychopaths with normal subjects on galvanic skin response (GSR) conditioning and avoidance learning. The task involved the measurement of GSR in anticipation of electroshock. Lykken found that anxiety was highest in the normals and lowest in the primary sociopaths, and the order of conditioning and avoidance learning differed in the same magnitude. Other similar studies using GSR as the measure of anxiety (Hare, 1965) have tended to support this difference in conditionability between psychopaths and normals. Since many theorists argue that some anxiety is necessary for an individual to learn a new task, the absence of anxiety is taken as an explanation of the sociopath's failure to learn by experience and his repeated behaviors leading to social punishment.

As to the conditions or causes which have led to the socially deviant behavior of the psychopath, theories have run the gamut from heredity through physiology to the family, social, and cultural environment.

Heredity and the Sociopath

The historical material presented earlier in this chapter indicated how closely the term "psychopath" has been tied to the notion of an inborn lack of moral sense. The investigation for hereditary factors in psychopathy runs into the same kinds of methodological problems as do all studies involving the effects of heredity and environment. McCord and McCord, after reviewing relevant studies, conclude "that the research on the constitutional or genetic basis of psychopathy is inconclusive and contradictory. . . . Heredity cannot yet be excluded as a causal factor. With more adequate delineation, with more rigidly controlled experiments, and with more sensitive measurement, an hereditary link may possibly be established. Given our current knowledge, however, the extravagant claims of the geneticists must be questioned." (1960, pp. 60–61.)

Brain Function and Sociopathy

The only current evidence that might support a belief in the constitutional nature of psychopathy is the finding that some psychopaths have abnormal EEG's. This finding, however, has been equivocal. Many sociopaths have normal EEG's, and it is not clear that the percentage of abnormal EEG's among sociopaths is any greater than among other groups such as psychotics or neurotics.

Two key concepts are exemplified in this argument. The first is that of the baserate of the sign, in this case the abnormal EEG. Ostrow and Ostrow (1946) collected the EEG's of 440 convicts. From these, they designated as their psychopathic group 69 men who were very impulsive, unable to accept social limitations, and had severe difficulties in empathy. Of this group, 50 per cent had abnormal EEG's. Among comparison groups, Ostrow and Ostrow report that 56 per cent of homosexuals, 98 per cent of epileptics, 80 per cent of schizophrenics, and 65 per cent of conscientious objectors had abnormal EEG's. The second problem is the effect of baserate when a finding is applied to the entire population. This has been discussed as the problem of false positives and false negatives. It may be stated that not all psychopaths have abnormal EEG's nor do all law-abiding citizens have normal EEG's. Since there are far more people in the latter group than the former, the number of misdiagnoses indicates that abnormal EEG's are certainly not a sufficient cause for antisocial behavior and probably not even a necessary one.

Robins's summary statement reflects the opinion of the present authors: "Despite numerous electroencephalographic (EEG) studies indicating varying but high rates of abnormality in adult criminals, there is no proof that brain damage or abnormality as reflected in the EEG is a necessary precondition for the development of antisocial reaction." (1967, pp. 955–956.)

FAMILY RELATIONS OF THE SOCIOPATH

Early investigators such as Partridge (1928), Knight (1933), and Haller (1942) all considered rejection, usually by mothers, as a causative factor in the development of psychopathy. Another group of investigators (Szurek, 1942; Lindner, 1944; Greenacre, 1945; Bowlby, 1952) also emphasized rejection, but by the father. In one of the more comprehensive studies of criminal behavior, McCord, McCord, and Zola (1959) found a strong link between the emergence of psychopathic behavior and emotional deprivation as indicated by parental conflict, cruelty, erratic punishment, and neglect.

Bender (1947) concluded that all psychopathic children have experienced emotional deprivation and neglect, particularly in the first three years of life. Bender's formulation is that the child who has little opportunity to learn socially desirable behavior from adult models and who does not experience the adult as a socially reinforcing object is likely to display subsequently nonsocial or antisocial behavior. Bowlby et al. (1956) investigated cases of early deprivation and concluded that children who are isolated at a very young age are unable to relate to others in adult situations. Most reports of "feral children" raised in isolation (Davis, 1940) or in deprived institutional atmospheres (Freud and Burlingham, 1944) propose a definite relationship between isolation and lack of response to human beings.

McCord and McCord (1964) come to the conclusion that there are three causal patterns in the development of psychopathy. The first is severe rejection itself. The second is mild rejection combined with damage to the brain (possibly the hypothalamus). The third is mild rejection, even in the absence of neural disorder, if the environment fails to provide behaviors alternative to psychopathic ones. While this type of work is persuasive, one must note that, as with the EEG, there is a baserate of deprivation among normals and that research from studies meeting minimal standards of comparison have been uniformly disappointing (Frank, 1965).

ROLE-TAKING AND SOCIOPATHY

Gough (1948) presented a theory of psychopathy based upon role-taking theory. He defined a deficiency in role-playing as the incapacity to look upon oneself as an object or to identify with another's point of view. The psychopath presumably cannot foretell the consequences of his behavior because he is unable to look at his own behavior from another's point of view. The social emotions of embarrassment, loyalty, or gregariousness are not experienced by the psychopath. Being deficient in the ability to take the role of others, he is surprised and resentful when others disapprove of his behavior. The psychopath is unable to form deep attachments because he cannot identify with other people.

An example of this inability to experience the usual social emotions is given by Hathaway (1939). A female psychopath was unable to reply to a question about "humiliating experiences" because she did not understand what such experiences were. She knew what the words meant, but she was unable to tell whether she had ever had such an experience herself. If the psychopath were indeed deficient in role-taking skills, the therapy of choice would involve role-playing. And there are in fact reports of role-playing being a therapeutic procedure having a beneficial effect on psychopaths (Baker, 1952).

The Sociopath and Conditionability

Eysenck (1957) presents a theory of the origin of sociopathic behavior which is based upon learning theory. He postulates two inherent and basic variables: introversion–extraversion and neuroticism. The individual who is high on extraversion and low on neuroticism (anxiety) would condition slowly, and would build up reactive inhibition quickly and dissipate it slowly. Eysenck relates socialization to the ability to be conditioned, from which it would follow that the sociopath, unable to be conditioned properly, would be less likely to become socialized. Eysenck also has a category of secondary psychopath which represents a combination of high neuroticism (anxiety) and high extraversion.

Another source of experimental evidence on the responsivity of sociopaths comes from verbal conditioning studies. It should follow from the various views that if sociopaths have a learning deficit, then it is reasonable to assume that they should react less strongly to the kinds of stimuli that evoke emotional reactions in others. As illustrated by the Hathaway anecdote above, the sociopath lacks appreciation of emotionally laden statements. Johns and Quay (1962, p. 217) succinctly express this point: "The psychopath can thus be said to be one who knows the words but not the music." Yet the experimental evidence in the verbal conditioning studies is contradictory as to the responsiveness of sociopaths to such social reinforcement as "good" (Johns and Quay, 1962; Quay and Hunt, 1965; Persons and Persons, 1965; Bernard and Eisenman, 1967). It is clear from these studies that it cannot be conditioned. Rather, conditionability of the sociopath, as with any other group of individuals, is a function of the many variables present in conditioning studies. (See Weiss, Krasner, and Ullmann, 1960, for a study illustrating how situational variables in a conditioning study may be manipulated.)

STIMULATION-SEEKING AND THE SOCIOPATH

An important conceptualization of the nature of psychopathic personality is the stimulation-seeking theory advanced by Quay (1965), which in many ways complements both Eysenck's theory and the social learning viewpoint to be presented below. Quay observes that the impulsivity of the sociopath can be interpreted as the "lack of even minimal tolerance for sameness. . . . The basic hypothesis is that psychopathic behavior represents an extreme of stimulation-seeking behavior and that the psychopath's primary abnormality lies in the realm of basal reactivity and/or adaptation to sensory inputs of all types." (1965, p. 180).

Quay argues that if the psychopath has a lessened basal reactivity or an increased rate of adaptation, then he must frequently find himself in a condition of stimulus deprivation. This state of affairs is highly unpleasant, and the psychopath seeks new stimulation. In a highly organized and restrictive society this stimulation often involves breaking some kind of legal or moral code.

Strong support for Quay's theory was provided by Skrzypek (1967). Skrzypek selected 33 "psychopathic" and 33 "neurotic" delinquents by use of ratings of overt behaviors made on a checklist (Quay, 1964; Peterson, 1961). The groups did not differ as to age, I.Q., length of stay in the institution at which the study was made, or number of school grades completed. The flavor of the concept of primary ("true") and secondary ("neurotic") psychopathy may be gained by contrasting the following two sets of behaviors. The unsocialized or psychopathic delinquents were high on the following characteristics: restless, attention-seeking, disruptive, boisterous, short attention span, inattentive to what others say, fighting, temper tantrums, lazy on assigned tasks, irresponsible, undependable, disobedient, uncooperative, distractible, negativistic, impertinent, profane, and irritable. The disturbed, neurotic, or anxious delinquents were characterized, on the other hand, by higher ratings on the following characteristics: doesn't know how to have fun, self-conscious, feelings of inferiority, preoccupied, shy, socially withdrawn, lacks self-confidence, easily flustered, generally fearful, daydreaming, tense, depressed, lethargic, and easily startled. After a period of perceptual isolation, "psychopathic" delinquents increased their preference for novel stimuli, while "anxious" delinquents increased in self-rated anxiety and decreased in preference of complex figures. In Skrzypek's work, on pretest measures of (self-rated) anxiety, the "psychopathic" delinquents were very significantly lower than the "neurotic" delinquents; high self-rated anxiety was very highly related to low novelty preference ($-.84$), low

"psychopathic" behavior rating ($-.86$), and high "neurotic" behavior rating
(.83).

A SOCIOPSYCHOLOGICAL FORMULATION OF ANTISOCIAL
(PSYCHOPATHIC) PERSONALITY

The behavior to be conceptualized in the sociopsychological formulation is
that of a person who shows poor social judgment, who is continually breaking rules and promises, who seems unaffected by stimuli that control the
behavior of most other people in his society. Specifically, other people do not
seem to act as acquired reinforcers for him.[3] In this sense, there is no real
distinction between the psychopath and the schizophrenic; both are not
under the control of typical social stimuli. Both emit behavior that disturbs
other people, in part, because it is so unexpected. The similarity between the
psychopath and schizophrenic has been pointed out by a number of authors,
most notably Cleckley (1964), who emphasized the semantic dementia of the
psychopath; that is, his words or promises are meaningless. Cleckley terms
the apparent nonpsychotic behavior of the psychopath as merely "the mask
of sanity" which hides the true psychotic nature of the disorder.

The poor judgment of the psychopath, however, takes the form of antisocial, impulsive behavior. Such behavior seems shortsighted, childish, and
self-defeating. An important point, as relevant to the psychopath as to the
schizophrenic, is that in the vast majority of his behaviors the person appears
normal, i.e., acts in an expected, undisturbing manner. Perhaps the easiest
way to illustrate this is to let the reader note that a person cannot "break a
promise" unless someone trusts him, and cannot be a forger, embezzler, or
cash checks without sufficient funds without having been trusted.

A typical pattern of behavior for the psychopath is to hold a job, to do
well, and, after the novelty and challenge have gone, to emit a disturbing
behavior such as telling off the boss, not reporting for work, or embezzling,
and then to suffer the consequences by losing the job. The act is perceived as
impulsive; to cite a common quip, the lid is off the id. The person acts in a
manner that many other people have at times wished to but refrained from
for fear of the easily foreseen consequences. It is this behavior of failing to
evaluate consequences that leads to formulations of psychopathy as involving
a deficit of "anxiety."[4]

Gough's (1948) concept, described above, of the psychopath as one who is
deficient in role-playing ability further extends this notion.[5] It is a fair description of the psychopath's behavior to say he is poor at playing social roles,
but the problem of specifying the conditions leading to and maintaining such
behavior remains.

From the general sociopsychological formulation it follows that the
psychopath has either been insufficiently trained in the crucial steps in the

procedure of emitting a social response or else has been trained in a manner different from that typical in the core culture. Several kinds of observations on psychopathy seem to offer leads in this direction. One group of observations would point to the view that the "wrong" things were reinforced.

Buss (1966) argues that two kinds of parental models foster the development of psychopathy. First is the parent who is cold and distant to the child. Buss argues that the child imitates the parent and becomes cold and distant in his own relationships. He learns the formal attributes of social situations without ever becoming involved with them. The second parental model comprises inconsistencies of rewards and punishments which make it difficult for the child to learn a definite role model, with the result that a consistent self-concept does not develop. The parents reward both "superficial conformity" and "underhanded nonconformity." Because the parent behaves arbitrarily and inconsistently, punishment is the result, but it is unpredictable. Therefore, the child learns how to avoid blame and punishment rather than how to differentiate right from wrong. A frequently observed behavior is that of a child either lying to avoid punishment or making superficial responses such as, "I'm sorry and I won't do it again." The child has then been rewarded for escaping punishment without feeling guilt.

Maher (1966) offers a variation of this theory. He points out that the sociopath is not behaving as a result of any defect at all but rather as the end result of "a particular set of learning experiences which happen to equip him poorly for adult responsibility." In effect one may hypothesize that the child must learn to emit the responses called "being lovable." If he emits these "lovable" or "ingratiating" responses, he is likely to avoid unpleasant consequences and later increase positive responses. The psychopath may (Maher, 1966) be a person who has been reinforced for emitting such acts at the wrong time; that is, when they help him avoid the consequences of his acts. Therefore, he has learned to apologize but not to avoid that for which he must apologize. Observations such as those of Buss and Naher are particularly helpful in conceptualizing the psychopathic behavior of middle-class children.

The present authors would go a step further in arguing that the psychopath frequently finds himself in a situation in which his behavior is treated as if it were inconsequential. The effects of his behavior are unpredictable for him, and hence he has difficulty learning about himself. Where such training in eliciting feedback is provided—in making amends, in being charming—the person later to be called psychopathic learns very well indeed.

A related point is that if what he does is considered inconsequential, then there may be no reason for him to attend to certain social stimuli. In this sense the psychopath may have found himself frequently in a situation similar to that of the schizophrenic, for whom there also may have been no "payoff" for attention.

Given this formulation, there is a different schedule of reinforcement for the psychopath. The unexpected behavior that wrecks success may be related to the lack of adequate feedback of behavior to the individual. The psychopath appears stimulus-deprived (Quay, 1965) because he has been (and is) deprived of major sources of stimuli. What would be adequate to shape most people in the society is not sufficient to maintain conforming behavior. The result is extinction rather than reinforcement. As noted, "impulsiveness" is behavior that an observer (usually middle-class) does not consider situation-appropriate. The person acts impulsively because the amount of effective reinforcing stimuli is insufficient to maintain his current behavior. That is, the job others consider "good" is "not good enough," and the consequences of losing it then are trivial.

A different set of circumstances may also lead to similar behavior. Case histories of people later called psychopaths who came from broken and/or extreme lower-class homes frequently indicate that they had been recipients of very severe physical punishment. The child had learned, quite rationally, that people are anything but positive reinforcers. Staying away from others and avoiding trouble would thus be very reasonable behavior. It is also likely that inconsistency, that is, punishment based on the adults' shifting moods rather than on the child's objective behavior, is involved. The result is twofold. First, the child's behavior is inconsequential; it seems that no matter what he does, if he interacts with people he will be punished. In this regard extreme punishment and extreme indulgence have similar eventual consequences. Second, whereas the inconsistent overindulged pattern leads to reinforcement of escape through apology and ingratiation, the inconsistent brutally punished pattern leads to avoidance by physical distance. Again the behavioral results are identical; when one's own behavior fails to serve as a meaningful stimulus for others, the consequences for the person are much the same whether the others have been seemingly too kind or too mean.

Other people do not become effective secondary reinforcing stimuli for this individual. This is important because the vast majority of actions by others that are typically reinforcing are acquired or secondary reinforcing stimuli. The person called a psychopath is, if anything, more skilled than average in emitting behavior that will influence others to act in a manner that is explicitly reinforcing. He is able to sell himself to others, and the payment they make by not punishing him or by giving him a good job is indeed reinforcing. Other people, then, seem to serve as secondary reinforcing stimuli. The distinction here is between the seducer and the genuine lover. The psychopath may indeed sell himself well and apparently be influenced (i.e., reinforced in the sense that his behavior is altered) by the extrinsic reinforcement of the other person's compliance. In fact, he may be even more effective as salesman or seducer than the average person because he is not paying attention to the other person's welfare: he is less likely to avoid lying to the other person and to worry about the ultimate aversive consequences for the other person.

In a heterosexual interpersonal relationship the psychopath can display a great deal of energy and enthusiasm at the beginning of a relationship just as he does at the start of a job or when "turning over a new leaf." However, curiosity ("Can I do it?" "What will it be like?") is soon satisfied. Where other people mature in their relationships in terms of the development of the other person's happiness as a reinforcing stimulus, the psychopath soon is satiated: there is a surplus of the reinforcing stimulus, there is nothing new. Not unlike the Madison Avenue stereotype, the psychopath asks, "What have you done for me recently?" He (or she, for women have been known to act in this manner) then breaks the relationship, usually by transferring his attention and favors to another. The psychopath is surprised when the other person is disturbed or hurt. He frequently expresses puzzlement that the other person is so immature, weak, or dependent as to be depressed: it was fun, it's over now, why is she bugging me and trying to make me feel bad?

It is in this regard that Quay's formulation of the psychopath as a stimulus-seeker fits with the sociopsychological formulation: the psychopath does indeed act as if rapidly satiated or as if new stimuli are continually required to maintain desired levels of behavior. This is not necessarily physiological in etiology, and it may be hypothesized that a host of stimuli based on his own and others' behavior are simply not effective for the psychopath. To the psychopath relationships are only skin-deep, love is a frenzy, and the object of work is to attain a status, not any intrinsic accomplishment and satisfaction. There is indeed deprivation of experience and an emphasis on sensory newness, turmoil, and large muscle activity. The psychopath experiences these; he does not experience the subtler, less direct, but more humanizing long-term aspects of the interpersonal environment. The pattern of behavior may in the long run lead not only to overt stimulus seeking, but to differences in perceptual and somatic input and processing.

If this formulation is correct, then treatment should involve making the person's behavior meaningful. This indeed seems the common thread in the reports of effective treatment of the psychopath. Case reports by people with philosophies as divergent as Aichorn (1935), Makarenko (1936), and Maxwell Jones (1953) illustrate this.

The present formulation (and the majority of writing in this field) has so far overlooked the "neurotic" delinquent (the second group described in Skrzypek's 1967 work). The people in this group commit violations of the social and legal code which are similar to those of the "primary" or "true" psychopathic person just described. It is possible to hypothesize that they may be reacting to situations in a manner similar to that of some people variously labeled hysteric, schizophrenic, and, particularly, obsessive. That is, the core difficulty may well have been failure in training in the emission of the socially expected and desirable act. The socially disruptive behavior may be a response which is immediately reinforced either by short-term gain or as an escape or avoidance of a situation. The formulation of compulsive behavior may be appropriate here and treatment should focus more on the development of appropriate operant behavior than on the sources of appropriate reinforcing stimuli (as with the "true psychopathic" group).

In summary, consistent with the views expressed throughout the book on other categories of abnormal behavior, it is not conceived that there is an entity called psychopath or sociopath into which an individual can be fitted. It is only possible to describe the behaviors that are disturbing to a society and that therefore receive labels. Whereas most individuals have experienced in their early environment a set of circumstances which have led to the development of their own and other people's behavior as secondary reinforcers, there are some individuals whose early environment militated against the full development of this source of meaningful stimuli. From this concept the observations of authors such as Gough, Quay, Buss, and Maher have been used to present a sociopsychological formulation of sociopathy.

DYSSOCIAL REACTION

Including the dyssocial reactions among the current mental illnesses highlights the question of whether criminal behavior is necessarily sick behavior.[6] The dyssocial category, as previously defined, is a label used for individuals with no obvious pathology other than criminal behavior. These people may be excellent fathers and husbands with deep loyalty to their families, friends, and "organizations." Their behavior is not sick, it is illegal. The reader may wish to consider how his behavior would be viewed by his peers if he found himself suddenly living in a ghetto area to which he brought his "ivory tower" academic interests and respect for authority. He might well be viewed as a stoolie, a fink, and worse as a result of having lived all his life in an abnormal moral environment.

The distinction between dyssocial and antisocial should be explicit. While both categories refer to people who may emit criminal acts, the dyssocial person is considered "normal" by the APA because there is no major intrapsychic defect. The antisocial person is conceived of as defective in an intrapsychic way as well as in interpersonal behavior.

The legal definition of criminal behavior may change from age to age: Buying alcohol in 1923 was a crime; in 1933 it was not. There are rules of the game or social norms at any given time in history. Sociologists classify norms into four major types—folkways, mores, customary law, and enacted law. Folkways are social rules enhanced by informal social controls such as gossip, ridicule, or ostracism. Mores are rules whose violation calls for strong moral indignation. Customary law involves those norms enforced by the community as a whole or by the community's formally chosen representatives. Enacted law designates the rules or norms that are formally instituted by a king or a legislative body. In the United States the enacted law comprises the state and federal constitutional provisions. Customary law consists of maxims, principles, and customs of long usage developed in England over the course of centuries and then transplanted to America. These legal rules, known as the common law in the Anglo-Saxon legal system, are enforced by the courts in spite of the fact that they have not been decreed by a governmental body. Despite the growth of enacted law, the common law continues to provide norms backed by the power of the state for the control of social behavior (Sykes, 1956).

The sociopsychological formulation of behavior labeled as dyssocial reaction is the same as applied to any normal behavior. This is implied in the very definition in DSM-I. Membership in Students for a Democratic Society or the Ku Klux Klan, patterns of earning money, or ways of relating to authority are all learned. The model of joining and defecting from a religious or social movement applies directly to the behavior called dyssocial. Such behavior is proper or improper depending on the view of the observer, and is maintained and altered by reinforcing contingencies. If the person is not extinguished for the "deviant" social mode and given opportunity to emit and be reinforced for socially appropriate behavior, he will continue in his mode of adjustment. It is not a matter of "knowing" what is "good" but of how "good" is defined. There are supports for antiauthoritarian behavior in the deviant group: the wrongness (the label leading to avoidance) is nullified and social support is given for the anti-middle-class act. Dyssocial behavior, then, is a prime example of the present sociopsychological formulation. It illustrates the manner in which normal behavior may be viewed as "sick." If dyssocial behavior is sick, then any learned behavior may be called sick.

JUVENILE DELINQUENCY

The incidence of delinquency is difficult to estimate because the definition depends on legal procedures, and most states differ as to what constitutes a juvenile offender. Also, not all offenders are treated in a similar manner. There are social class differences in the detection of and disposition of the juvenile. Clearly it is the behavior of "being caught" that counts in identifying delinquency. A series of investigators (Porterfield, 1946; Murphy, Shirley, and Witmer, 1946; Miller, 1962) have found strong evidence of hidden delinquency; for example, college students may admit to having committed acts during their high school years that, if discovered at the time, would have resulted in their having been classified as delinquent. They were not so classified because they were not caught.

Wirt and Briggs (1965) cite FBI figures as one source of information on the incidence of juvenile offenses. For the years from 1953 to 1961 there was a tripling of juvenile crime nationally from about 300,000 to almost a million arrests annually. These increases have been reflected not only in absolute numbers, but also in the rate of delinquency in the adolescent population.

As in every other category dealt with in this book, a precise definition of the behavior involved is difficult. Wirt and Briggs emphasize that the term "delinquency" is a legal term and offer a definition focusing on behavior that is labeled by society, at a given time, as a "relatively serious legal offense . . . not committed as a result of extremely low intellect, intracranial organic pathology, or severe mental or metabolic dysfunction," which "is alien to the culture in which [the person] has been reared." (1965, p. 23.)

Ellingston (1948) has offered a definition of delinquency and crime which is similar to a social learning position. He views crime as whatever the dominant elements of a particular society believe to be dangerous to the security and solidarity of the society at any particular time. Thus the individual would learn from his culture what is delinquent and what is not. All societies have codes of conduct, but there are wide differences in time and place among groups as to what behaviors are acceptable and what immoral. Thus when one discusses delinquency, one speaks about a series of behaviors in a given time and culture.

There are many illustrations of the argument that delinquent behavior is reinforced and maintained within family and peer groups. Shaw and McKay (1942) report that 84 per cent of the delinquents in Massachusetts reformatories came from homes in which there were criminals.

However, the complexities of the home environment for the delinquent go beyond the mere presence and encouragement of criminal behavior. It has frequently been reported that a majority of institutionalized delinquents come from broken homes. It is not the broken home per se that causes difficulty for the youth, but the fact that broken homes result in many more adult figures coming into his life. It may be argued that the presence of many parental figures in the home increases the likelihood of noninterest or rejection by some, if not all, of them, which leads, in turn, to inconsistency of reinforcement and a lack of the necessary consistent model of socialized behavior.

A good illustration of the relation between the availability of role models and subsequent delinquent behavior is given by McCord and McCord (1958). A five-year observation of 253 boys and their families from a lower-class urban area in the Cambridge-Somerville vicinity of Massachusetts was followed up by a study 20 years later of those who became delinquent. The environmental combination that was most likely to lead to delinquent behavior was the presence of a criminal role model in the father and the absence of maternal warmth. On the other hand, consistent discipline and love from at least one parent to a large extent counteracted the father's criminal role model. It may be argued that rejection is likely to reduce reinforcement of prosocial behaviors, and the presence of the criminal role model gives the information as to one alternative form of behavior, namely crime.

Further evidence along this line comes from studies by Bandura and Walters (1959) of 26 aggressive delinquent boys. These authors found a pattern of father rejection plus inconsistent handling by both parents. The fathers frequently used physically punitive methods of discipline. Thus there was a combination of rejection, hostility, and a lack of clear socially approved guidelines as to what kind of behavior would receive parental reinforcement. Further, the boy may be described as being inadequately socialized, or having failed to make the discrimination necessary for the development of people as sources of secondary reinforcement.

This pattern of father rejection of the delinquent was also found by Andry (1960). Various kinds of sociopathic behavior in the fathers of delinquent boys, such as alcoholism, brutality, nonsupport, and frequent absence from home have been reported repeatedly (Glueck and Glueck, 1962).

Of major importance in the development of delinquent behavior are opportunity, peer models, and immediate reinforcement for delinquent behavior. This is exemplified by the role of gangs in fostering delinquent behavior. Vedder (1963) describes three different types of gang activities. One he calls "criminal," where the activities of the gang are directed toward illegal ways of obtaining money. A second represents "conflict," in which violence is used to gain status. A third is "retreatist," in which drugs and promiscuous sex are stressed. An additional category with high delinquency potential is the large, amorphous group of youths, frequently school dropouts, who spend their time in a loose-knit streetcorner, drive-in, or bowling alley society. The evidence seems to indicate that most gangs are not delinquent. However, the small percentage that are cause problems for society. It is clear that the gangs supply the kinds of social approval, peer reinforcement, status, meaning, and value system that are not obtained from the home, school, or other typical socially approved organizations. The gang becomes the principal agent of socialization for many teenagers. Unfortunately, the acts reinforced are not the ones considered desirable by the dominant adult middle-class culture.

If the development of delinquent and/or criminal behavior is viewed in social reinforcement and modeling terms, then what is the data concerning the role of the parents or other adults in the delinquent's early life in the family? Peterson and Becker summarize the many studies on family interac-

tion and delinquency by stressing the differences in social-class value emphasis. It is the middle class that defines laws and designates behaviors to be
classified as delinquent. "Emphasis on toughness, worldly smartness, and
independence from authority is sometimes coupled with a de-emphasis of
achievement, consideration for others, and self-control among members of
the lower class. In terms of behavior theory, this means that models for
behavior of the kind that are 'tough,' 'smart' and so on are plentifully available, and social reinforcement for such behavior is frequent, immediate and
strong." (1965, p. 92.) Further, peer groups as well as parents may reinforce
the kind of behavior likely to eventuate in a label of delinquency.

Despite the many significant social-class variables, the fact remains that
most lower-class children do not behave in a manner leading to the label
"delinquent" and many middle-class children do. The primary source of
learning of delinquent behavior seems to be the home. The figures in the
home represent the source of reinforcement for delinquent behavior and the
source of failure to develop socially desirable behavior. Among the home
variables are the presence or absence of both parents (broken homes, divorce,
illness, death, mother's employment) and the specific parental behavioral
attributes. As has been described, some investigations place etiological
significance on the father's behavior (Bandura and Walters, 1959); others
place more on that of the mother (McCord, McCord, and Zola, 1959). Peterson and Becker conclude, "The development of stable behavior tendencies
depends on the intensity and consistency with which emotionally effective
rewards and punishments are administered. Excessively harsh treatment,
especially if unaccompanied by generally affectionate acceptance, ordinarily
arouses resentment, and this reduces the effectiveness of discipline. Excessive leniency is tantamount to neglect. The regulatory emotional expectancies are never established." (1965, p. 94.) Thus the general picture in
delinquent families is of parents whose discipline is either severe or lax or,
most likely, an inconsistent alternation between the two.

The argument is often presented that delinquent behavior is an expression
of a youth's frustration with his poor living conditions, poor economic situation, or poor family relationships. In effect, it has become a socially accepted
myth that such frustration tends to lead to aggression. However, recent
studies indicate that aggressive behavior is likely to occur as a function of
reinforcement of such aggression. Bandura and Walters (1959) found that
parents of aggressive boys were more likely to condone aggression than
parents of nonaggressive boys. Lovaas (1961) demonstrated that when children's aggressive behavior is positively reinforced, it is likely to increase and
generalize. Children who were reinforced for aggressive verbalization and for
hitting a toy doll increased both behaviors significantly. Further, in a free
play situation, after the experimental procedures, children who had been

reinforced for verbal aggression increased their motor aggression (doll hitting) when given an opportunity.

TREATMENT OF DELINQUENCY

Throughout the years, there has been considerable controversy as to the goals and methods of treatment to be used in institutions dealing with individuals who have been labeled antisocial or delinquent. The problem is usually expressed in terms of whether the use of punishment or some other procedure is the best method of bringing about rehabilitation. It may be initially concluded that a strictly punitive atmosphere in a correctional institution will result in the ignoring of desirable behavior, generate hostility, and defeat the goals of rehabilitation. In fact, as in treatment of any problem behaviors, the indiscriminate use of punishment and/or positive reward for all behaviors does not teach the individual to make the kind of discriminations that are necessary in his social environment.

An illustration of treatment of delinquent behavior is the program in effect at Camp Butner, North Carolina, as described by Burchard (1967). Burchard conceptualized antisocial behavior as behavior which is "acquired, maintained and modified by the same principles as other learned behavior." Therefore, he argued that an individual "can learn constructive, socially acceptable behavior by being placed in an environment where the behavioral consequences are programmed according to the principles of operant conditioning. Instead of administering an excess of reinforcement or punishment on an indiscriminate, non-contingent basis, behavior should be punished or reinforced systematically on a response-contingent basis. This has been the objective of the Intensive Training Program." The result was an experimental residential program in behavior modification for mildly retarded delinquent adolescents. Burchard utilized techniques based on the principles of "reinforcement, punishment, and programmed instruction." It was a standardized program, involving mostly nonprofessional people, and developed to teach the delinquent individuals the practical skills essential for adjusting adequately to the community and for eliminating or markedly reducing forms of antisocial behavior. As in other operant programs, the procedures involved the definition of the behaviors to be reinforced, selection of an effective reinforcer, and programming the reinforcement contingencies. The two criteria for the selection of the behaviors to be reinforced were, first, behaviors that produce a physical and identifiable change in the environment that can be reliably observed and reinforced, and, second, behaviors which provide the individual with a behavioral repertoire that will lead to reinforcement in a community environment. Behaviors selected were those involved in maintaining a job, staying in school, budgeting money, buying and caring for clothes, buying food and meals, and cooperating with peers and adults.

Because previous studies (Johns and Quay, 1962; Quay and Hunt, 1965) had implied that verbal reinforcement is not effective for individuals emitting antisocial behavior, Burchard used aluminum tokens as reinforcers. The tokens were stamped with the individual's residence number. Thus, he could utilize only those tokens stamped with his own number.

Burchard also made use of punishment procedures deduced from operant conditioning work (Azrin and Holz, 1966). In applying these principles Burchard's aim was to develop a procedure that (1) would have the characteristics of immediate administration following the response, and, (2) while of short duration, would be sufficiently intense to decrease the frequency of response. In developing these procedures he followed the same pattern as in developing positive reinforcement procedures, that is, defining the behaviors to be punished, selecting effective stimuli, and programming the punishment contingencies. The behaviors selected for punishment were those that typically evoke some negative response from the community, such as fighting, lying, stealing, cheating, physical or verbal assault, temper tantrums, and property damage. One form of punishment was the withdrawal of positive reinforcement, that is, tokens. Other aversive stimuli consisted of two verbal responses, "time out" and "seclusion." These responses involved the loss of opportunity to obtain tokens. When a staff member said "Time out," the resident was charged four tokens and had to sit in a row of chairs at one side of the day room for three to five minutes until his behavior became appropriate. Seclusion was used contingent upon more serious disturbing behavior such as fights, serious property damage, or refusal to go to the time-out area. Upon verbalization of "Seclusion," the resident was charged 15 tokens and taken to a nearby seclusion area, an empty room with one outside window covered with a metal screen and a drawn shade. He had to stay in this room until he had been quiet for 30 minutes. If the boy went to the room and behaved in an orderly manner, staying the minimum of time, he was rewarded with five tokens on his return to the living quarters. Burchard also made use of the concept of response cost developed by Weiner (1963). If a resident did not pay up his daily debts by the end of the day, he lost what was called one behavior credit. This was the response cost. If he could not maintain his minimum number of behavior credits, then all reinforcers cost additional tokens. If he did maintain his minimum number, he also had free access to the yard area outside his unit and could purchase a trip to town (for 90 tokens) or an hour of recreation time with female residents, each hour costing 15 tokens.

Within this context Burchard completed a series of specific illustrative experiments. He selected a specific behavior such as sitting at a desk during workshop and school time. The design of the experiment was based on "an A-B-A type of analysis": reinforcement was contingent on the response during the first phase, noncontingent during the second phase, and then contingent again during the third phase. Each phase lasted five consecutive days. The resident received five tokens for accumulating time while sitting at his desk and also for doing specific school tasks. In the second five days he received an equivalent number of tokens, but noncontingently. In the third five-day period the contingent reinforcement was resumed. Figure 14.1 illustrates that there was an immediate decline in performance during the non-contingent phase and a reinstatement of performance under reinforcement during the third phase.

Another illustration of recent applications of behavioral principles to modifying the behavior of juvenile delinquents is Project CASE (Contingencies Applicable for Special Education) at the National Training School for Boys (Cohen et al., 1966). The target behavior shaped was academic work in the form of programmed instruction. If the student completed a unit of the program with a score of at least 90 per cent, he was eligible to take an examination on which he could earn reinforcement in the form of points each worth one cent. These points could be used to buy Cokes, potato chips, Sears Roebuck items, or entrance into a lounge where his friends were; to register for a new program; to rent books; or to get time in the library or a private "office" with a telephone. The points, unlike the tokens described in the studies of Ayllon and Azrin (1965), Atthowe and Krasner (1968), and Burchard (1967), were not transferable. The only way the student could obtain points was by emitting the desired behavior, namely studying.

The study by Cohen et al. also illustrated that the systematic contingent application of reinforcement was most effective when it took place within an environment programmed so that the likelihood of desirable behavior was enhanced and undesirable behavior decreased. Thus the investigators built a special environment, including classrooms, study booths, control rooms, library, store, and lounge. Cohen et al. also used the principle of gradually incorporating newer and more relevant payoffs. The students gradually switched from working for Cokes to working for the more educationally relevant behavior of library time or new programs.

The results on the 16 students in the project indicated that the program was enormously successful in generating desirable educational activities. There were also other favorable changes in behavior. In four and one half months there were no discipline problems, and the boys did not in any way destroy or deface the facilities. The social behavior of the delinquent boys matched that of nondelinquents.

One of the most unique approaches toward the modification of delinquent behavior is that developed by the Schwitzgebel brothers and their co-workers (Schwitzgebel, 1960, 1961, 1963, 1964, 1967; Schwitzgebel and Kolb, 1964; Schwitzgebel, Schwitzgebel, Pahnke, and Hurd, 1964) based on the earlier work of Slack (1960). This group of investigators developed a pioneering approach to the delinquent involving a functional analysis of behavior. The

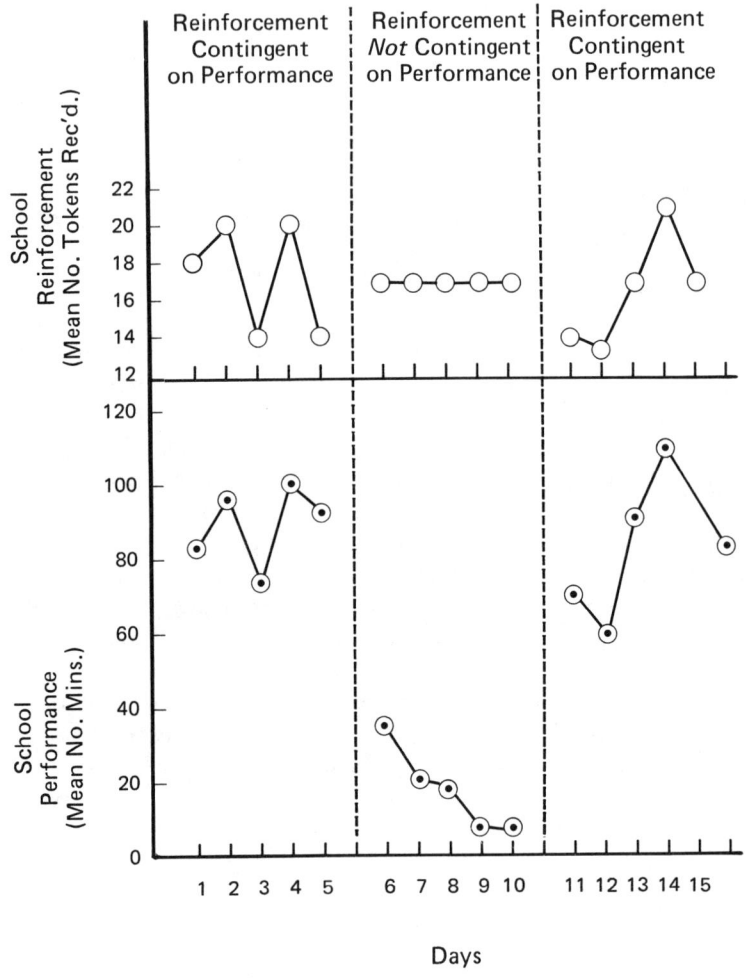

FIGURE 14.1.
MEAN NUMBER OF MINUTES OF SCHOOL PERFORMANCE BY NINE
RESIDENTS. REDRAWN FROM BURCHARD, 1966, P. 470

adolescents working within the project had been labeled delinquents by a court. The laboratory for the project was set up in a large storefront on a streetcorner in a respectable business district, and the project received the name of "Street Corner Research." The experimental group comprised 30 white males employed by the project for six months or longer. Of these 30 boys, 25 had appeared in courts and 20 had spent six months or more in correctional institutions. At the time of the project they averaged 18 years of age and had an average of 9½ years of education. A control group was formed by matching each member of the experimental group with a male offender chosen from police records.

The techniques used with the experimental group of delinquents involved a four-step sequence:

1. Defining in measurable units the final, desired behavior as specifically as possible.

2. Determining the available reinforcers that were most likely to be effective.

3. Determining the subject's repertoire of present and previous behavior.

4. Applying the reinforcers according to an explicit theoretical model and modifying application according to results (feedback).

The initial goal of the project was to get the adolescent into the laboratory. The experimenters accomplished this by going into the community and offering to hire people with delinquent records as subjects in a study of delinquency. Subjects were paid for their participation, which initially involved talking into a tape recorder about their experiences as a delinquent. For those who initially did not report to the laboratory, gradual shaping procedures were used in which the subjects were given cigarettes or food as over a period of time they came closer to the laboratory. They received different sums of money depending on how close they approximated the agreed-upon time of arrival at the laboratory. A number of interviewers gradually built up a close relationship with the subjects. The interviews included philosophic discussions, moral guidance, or "psychoanalysis." The boys were paid for specific jobs in the laboratory, such as soldering. Then gradually jobs were obtained outside the laboratory in the community.

A follow-up study of the first 20 subjects in this program (Schwitzgebel, 1964) three years after termination of employment in the program showed that the number of arrests and months of incarceration of the employees was about half that of a matched control group. Within the overall program Schwitzgebel (1967) reports the results of seven controlled studies which demonstrate the points previously made about the effects of response-reinforcement contingent on the behavior of delinquents. Schwitzgebel matched two groups of his delinquent employees and treated them differentially during the course of 20 tape-recorded interviews on four classes of operants: hostile statements, positive statements, prompt arrival at work, and general employability. Hostile statements were followed by mild aversive consequences (inattention and mild verbal disagreement) while the other target operants were followed by a positive consequence (verbal praise or a small gift such as cigarettes, candy, or cash). The results in both a laboratory and natural setting (restaurant) indicated that there was a significant increase in the frequency of the three target behaviors that were followed by positive consequences. The hostile statements, however, which were followed by "punishment," did not significantly decrease. Schwitzgebel's (1967, p. 141) conclusion is very relevant to the general approach to sociopathy described in this chapter. "The fact that a series of interviews with an operant-conditioning orientation could develop dependable and prompt attendance and certain other social behaviors in juvenile delinquents may not surprise therapists familiar with experimental analysis of human learning. What is more difficult to explain, however, is why this knowledge has not been put to systematic use in the large majority of treatment programs. This may be related to a still broader problem; namely, the extent to which usual clinical assumptions about the 'character structure' of delinquency is an artifact of the traditional clinical procedure itself."

SUMMARY

This chapter discussed antisocial and dyssocial reactions, considered subgroups of the category sociopathic personality disturbance. The term "sociopath" has replaced the older term "psychopath" and thus implicitly recognizes the social forces involved in the development of antisocial behavior. Historically the psychopathic label has been applied to people who act in a socially disturbing way. Further, these behaviors are usually not characteristic patterns of other psychiatric categories, nor is there evidence of brain injury or retardation. The puzzling behaviors of the antisocial person were described, and various explanatory theories were presented. The socio-psychological formulation of antisocial personality argues that there is no entity called sociopath into which an individual can be fitted. Rather there are individuals whose history of reinforcement decreased the effectiveness of other people's behavior as secondary reinforcers. In addition, culturally approved behavior must be maintained by ongoing reinforcement. A formulation of juvenile delinquency and illustrations of its behavioral treatment were presented.

NOTES

1. Given the confusion of terminology, the words "sociopath," "psychopath," and "antisocial" as used in this section reflect their interchangeable nature in the literature under discussion.

2. McCord and McCord (1964) point out the "warped capacity for love" on the part of the psychopath. "Either because he is incapable of forming them, or because his experience has not shown him how to form them, the psychopath wards off close attachments." (p. 16.) "The psychopath feels little, if any, guilt. He can commit the most appalling acts, yet view them without remorse. . . . [G]uiltlessness and lovelessness conspicuously mark the psychopath as different from other men." (McCord and McCord, 1956.)

3. Anxiety may be defined here in terms of the various physiological measures used by Lykken (1957), or the self–rating used by Skrzypek (1967) or, more generally, as Wolpe (1958) did, as anticipation of unpleasant or aversive consequences.

4. Following from Gough and the immediately preceding material, it might also be hypothesized that the psychopath is deficient in vicarious reinforcement, a hypothesis which, as far as the present authors know, has not been tested.

5. By definition criminal behavior is rule breaking, i.e., deviance. The question is whether all rule breaking is in the province of the professional mental health worker, i.e., abnormal as used in this volume. The problem becomes vital in the area of sexual behavior.

References

Aichorn, A. *Wayward youth.* New York: Viking, 1935.

Alexander, F., and Staub, H. *The criminal, the judge, and the public: a psychological analysis* (1929). Rev. ed.: Glencoe, Ill.: Free Press, 1956.

American Psychiatric Association. *Diagnostic and statistical manual: mental disorders (DSM-1).* Washington: American Psychiatric Association, 1952; special printing, 1965.

Andry, R. G. *Delinquency and parental pathology.* London: Methuen, 1960.

Atthowe, J. M., Jr., and Krasner, L. A preliminary report on the application of contingent reinforcement procedures (token economy on a "chronic" psychiatric ward). *Journal of abnormal psychology,* 1968, *73,* 37–43.

Ayllon, T., and Azrin, N. H. The measurement and reinforcement of behavior of psychotics. *Journal of the experimental analysis of behavior,* 1965, *8,* 357–383.

Azrin, N. H., and Holz, W. C. Punishment. In W. K. Honig (ed.), *Operant behavior: areas of research and application.* New York: Appleton, 1966, 380–447.

Baker, A. A. The misfit family: a psychodrama technique used in a therapeutic community. *British journal of medical psychology,* 1952, *25,* 235–243.

Bandura, A. and Walters, R. H. *Adolescent aggression.* New York: Ronald, 1959.

Bender, L. Psychopathic behavior disorders in children. In R. Lindner and R. Seliger (eds.), *Handbook of correctional psychology.* New York: Philosophical Library, 1947, 360–377.

Bernard, J. L., and Eisenman, R. Verbal conditioning in sociopaths with social and monetary reinforcement. *Journal of personality and social psychology,* 1967, *6,* 203–206.

Bowlby, J. *Maternal care and mental health.* Geneva: World Health Organization, 1952.

Bowlby, J., Ainsworth, M., Boston, M., and Rosenbluth, D. The effects of mother-child separation, a follow-up study. *British journal of medical psychology,* 1956, *29,* 211–247.

Burchard, J. D. Systematic socialization: a programmed environment for the habilitation of antisocial retardates. *Psychological record*, 1967, *17*, 461–476.

Buss, A. H. *Psychopathology*. New York: Wiley, 1966.

Cleckley, H. *The mask of sanity* (4th ed.). St. Louis: Mosby, 1964.

Cohen, H. L., Filipczak, J. A., Bis, J. S., and Cohen, J. E. *Contingencies applicable to special education of delinquents*. Silver Spring, Md.: Institute for Behavioral Research, 1966.

Davis, K. Extreme social isolation of a child. *American journal of sociology*, 1940, *45*, 554–564.

Ellingston, J. R. *Protecting our children from criminal careers*. New York: Prentice-Hall, 1948.

Emprey, L. T., and Erickson, M. L. Hidden delinquency and social status. *Social forces*, 1966, *44*, 546–554.

Eysenck, H. J. *The dynamics of anxiety and hysteria*. New York: Praeger, 1957.

Fernald, W. E. The imbecile with criminal instincts. *American journal of insanity*, 1908, *65*, 731–749.

Frank, G. H. The role of the family in the development of psychopathology. *Psychological bulletin*, 1965, *64*, 191–205.

Freud, A., and Burlingham, D. *Infants without families*. New York: International Universities Press, 1944.

Glueck, S., and Glueck, E. T. *Unraveling juvenile delinquency*. Cambridge, Mass.: Commonwealth Fund, 1950.

Glueck, S., and Glueck, E. T. *Family Environment Delinquency*. Boston: Houghton, 1962.

Gough, H. G. A sociological theory of psychopathy. *American journal of sociology*, 1948, *53*, 359–366.

Greenacre, P. Conscience in the psychopath. *American journal of orthopsychiatry*, 1945, *15*, 495–509.

Haller, B. L. Some factors related to the adjustment of psychopaths on parole from a state hospital. *Smith College studies of social work*, 1942, *13*, 193–194.

Hare, R. D. Psychopathy, fear arousal and anticipated pain. *Psychological reports*, 1965, *16*, 499–502.

Hathaway, S. R. The personality inventory as an aid in the diagnosis of psychopathic inferiors. *Journal of consulting psychology*, 1939, *3*, 112–117.

Johns, J. H., and Quay, H. C. The effect of social reward on verbal conditioning in psychopathic and neurotic military offenders. *Journal of consulting psychology*, 1962, *26*, 217–220.

Jones, M. *The therapeutic community*. New York: Basic Books, 1953.

Karpman, B. On the need of separating psychopathy into two distinct clinical types: the symptomatic and the idiopathic. *Journal of criminal psychopathology*, 1941, *3*, 112–137.

Knight, E. M. A descriptive comparison of markedly aggressive and submissive children. *Smith College studies in social work* (Vol. 4), 1933.

Lindner, R. *Rebel without a cause—the hypoanalysis of a criminal psychopath*. New York: Grune & Stratton, 1944.

Lombroso, C. *Crime, its causes and remedies.* Translated by H. P. Horton. Boston: Little, Brown, 1911.

Lovaas, O. I. Effect of exposure to symbolic aggression on aggressive behavior. *Child development,* 1961, *32,* 37–44.

Lowrey, L. G. Delinquent and criminal personalities. In J. McV. Hunt (ed.), *Personality and the behavior disorders* (Vol. 2). New York: Ronald, 1944.

Lykken, D. F. A study of anxiety in the sociopathic personality. *Journal of abnormal and social psychology,* 1957, *55,* 6–10.

Maher, B. A. *Principles of psychopathology,* New York: McGraw-Hill, 1966.

McCord, J., and McCord, W. The effects of parental role model on criminality. *Journal of social issues,* 1958, *14,* 66–75.

McCord, W., and McCord, J. *Psychopathy and delinquency.* New York: Gruen & Stratton, 1956.

McCord, W., and McCord, J. *The psychopath: an essay on the criminal mind.* Princeton: Van Nostrand, 1964.

McCord, W., McCord, J., and Gudeman, J. *Origins of alcoholism.* Stanford, Calif.: Stanford University Press, 1960.

McCord, W., McCord, J., and Zola, I. *Origins of crime.* New York: Columbia University Press, 1959.

Makarenko, A. S. *Road to life.* London: Stanley Nott, 1936.

Miller, W. B. The impact of a "total community" delinquency control project. *Social problems,* 1962, *10,* 168–191.

Murphy, F. J., Shirley, M. M., and Witmer, H. L. The incidence of hidden delinquency. *American journal of orthopsychiatry,* 1946, *16,* 686–696.

Ostrow, M., and Ostrow, M. Bilaterally synchronous paroxysmal slow activity in the encephalograms of non-epileptics. *Journal of nervous and mental disease,* 1946, *103,* 346–358.

Partridge, G. E. A study of 50 cases of psychopathic personality. *American journal of psychiatry,* 1928, *7,* 953–973.

Persons, R. W., and Persons, C. E. Some experimental support of psychopathic theory: a critique. *Psychological reports,* 1965, *16,* 745–749.

Peterson, D. R. Behavior problems of middle childhood. *Journal of consulting psychology,* 1961, *25,* 205–209.

Peterson, D. R., and Becker, W. C. Family interaction and delinquency. In H. C. Quay (ed.), *Juvenile delinquency: research and theory.* Princeton: Van Nostrand, 1965, 63–99.

Porterfield, A. L. *Youth in trouble.* Fort Worth, Texas: Leo Polishman Foundation, 1946.

Preu, P. W. The concept of psychopathic personality. In J. McV. Hunt (ed.), *Personality and the behavior disorders* (Vol. 2). New York: Ronald, 1944.

Quay, H. C. Personality dimensions in delinquent males as inferred from the factor analysis of behavior ratings. *Journal of research in crime and delinquency,* 1964, *1,* 33–37.

Quay, H. C. Psychopathic personality as pathological stimulation-seeking. *American journal of psychiatry,* 1965, *122,* 180–183.

Quay, H. C., and Hunt, W. A. Psychopathy, neuroticism and verbal conditioning: a replication and extension. *Journal of consulting psychology*, 1965, *29*, 283.

Ray, I. *Medical jurisprudence of insanity*. Boston: Little, Brown, 1838.

Robins, E. Antisocial and dyssocial personality disorder. In A. M. Freedman and H. I. Kaplan (eds.), *Comprehensive textbook of psychiatry*. Baltimore: Williams and Wilkins, 1967, 951–958.

Rush, B. *Medical inquiries and observations upon the diseases of the mind*. Philadelphia: Kimber & Richardson, 1812.

Schwitzgebel, R. A new approach to reducing adolescent crime. *Federal probation*, March 1960, pp. 20–24.

Schwitzgebel, R. Reduction of adolescent crime by a research method. *Journal of correctional psychiatry and social therapy*, 1961, *7*, 212–215.

Schwitzgebel, R. Delinquents with tape records. *New Society*, January 1963, pp. 14–16.

Schwitzgebel, R. *Street-corner research: an experimental approach to the juvenile delinquent*. Cambridge, Mass.: Harvard University Press, 1964.

Schwitzgebel, R. Short-term operant conditioning of adolescent offenders on socially relevant variables. *Journal of abnormal psychology*, 1967, *72*, 134–142.

Schwitzgebel, R., and Kolb, D. A. Inducing behaviour change in adolescent delinquents. *Behaviour research and therapy*, 1964, *1*, 297–304.

Schwitzgebel, R., Schwitzgebel, R., Pahnke, W. N., and Hurd, W. S. A program of research in behavioral electronics. *Behavioral science*, 1964, *9*, 233–238.

Shaw, C. R. *The jack-roller*. Chicago: University of Chicago Press, 1930.

Shaw, C. R., and McKay, H. D. *Juvenile delinquency and urban areas*. Chicago: University of Chicago Press, 1942.

Skrzypek, G. J. The effect of perceptual isolation and arousal on anxiety, complexity preference and novelty preference in psychopathic and neurotic delinquents. Unpublished doctoral dissertation, University of Illinois, 1967.

Slack, C. W. Experimenter-subject psychotherapy: a new method of introducing intensive office treatment for unreachable cases. *Mental hygiene*, 1960, *44*, 238–256.

Sykes, G. M. *Crime and society*. New York: Random House, 1956.

Szurek, S. A. Notes on the genesis of psychopathic personality. *Psychiatry*, 1942, *5*, 1–6.

Tredgold, A. F. *Mental deficiency*. Baltimore: William Wood, 1915.

Vedder, C. B. *Juvenile offenders*. Springfield, Ill.: C. C. Thomas, 1963.

Wallerstein, J. S., and Wyle, C. J. Our law-abiding law-breakers. *Probation*, 1947, *25*, 107–112.

Weiner, H. Response cost and the aversive control of human operant behavior. *Journal of the experimental analysis of behavior*, 1963, *6*, 415–421.

Weiss, R. L., Krasner, L., and Ullmann, L. P. Responsivity to verbal conditioning as a function of emotional atmosphere and pattern of reinforcement. *Psychological reports*, 1960, *6*, 415–426.

Wirt, R. D., and Briggs, P. F. The meaning of delinquency. In H. C. Quay (ed.), *Juvenile delinquency*. Princeton: Van Nostrand, 1965, 1–26.

Wolpe, J. *Psychotherapy by reciprocal inhibition*. Stanford, Calif.: Stanford University Press, 1958.

15

Effects of Stimulation Intensity on Sociopathic Avoidance Learning

Frank A. Chesno and Peter R. Kilmann

Reprinted by permission from *Journal of Abnormal Psychology* 84 (1975): 144–50. Copyright 1975 by the American Psychological Association. Author permission to reprint is gratefully acknowledged.

Ninety public offenders were selected to represent low, medium, and high levels of anxiety and low and high levels of sociopathy. Subjects were exposed to an avoidance situation under either low, medium, or high levels of background auditory stimulation. The avoidance task allowed shock to be averted through appropriate active and passive avoidance responses in the presence of visually presented cues. Anxiety, sociopathy, and auditory stimulus intensity interacted in their effects on avoidance behavior. Primary sociopaths learned to avoid shock more effectively under conditions of higher auditory stimulus intensity, while avoidance behavior of control subjects was not affected by changes in the level of auditory stimulation.

Recent investigators (e.g., Hare, 1970) hold that Cleckley (1964) has provided the most accurate description of sociopathy. His detailed account includes 16 criteria of sociopathy, emphasizing inconsistencies in interpersonal behavior, deficits in emotionality, and failure to profit from punishment. Cleckley makes a distinction between primary or true sociopathy and its secondary or neurotic counterpart; primary sociopathy is associated with defects in emotionality, while secondary sociopathy emphasizes the neurotic motivation behind acting out behavior. Thus, while the overt behavioral patterns of both categories may be remarkably similar, important etiological and motivational differences distinguish the two groups from each other.

Studies conducted in a variety of experimental conditions have consistently found that primary sociopaths are less responsive to sensory input from exteroceptive sources and lack normal levels of internally generated stimulation, such as anxiety and fear (e.g., Hare, 1965a, 1965b, 1970; Lindsley,

1952; Schoenherr, 1964; Sutker, 1969). Other studies (e.g., Lykken, 1955; Skrzypek, 1969; Wiesen, 1965), have found evidence that sociopaths share a strong urge toward seeking stimulation. Quay (1965) proposed that the primary sociopath may be best understood as an individual whose restricted sensitivity to stimulation forces him to seek intense and varied sensory input in order to increase arousal to a more comfortable level. This drive toward stimulation causes him to periodically transgress interpersonal, moral, and legal boundaries and may therefore account for his sociopathic behavior. Quay reasons that sanctions are so easily violated by sociopaths because their impact is subordinated to a more immediate need for stimulation, and whatever fear may be generated by the possibility of punishment is often inhibited by the rewarding consequences of gaining access to additional sensory input.

Viewing the sociopath as a chronically underaroused individual in constant search for added sources of stimulation may help to explain his inability to profit from punishment. Clinical descriptions (e.g., Cleckley, 1964) and experimental studies of sociopathy (e.g., Lykken, 1955; Schmauk, 1968) have documented the sociopath's seeming inability to inhibit punished responses. Hare (1970) accounts for this deficit on the basis of Mowrer's (1947) two-factor avoidance conditioning theory, which may be interpreted to suggest that the sociopath's low arousal level precludes strong fear conditionability and therefore limits drive reduction as a source of reinforcement for performing the avoidance response.

The purpose of this study was to propose an alternative explanation of defective sociopathic avoidance conditioning based on the model of sensory reinforcement (Duffy, 1962) and the principle of optimal stimulation (Leuba, 1955). The collective evidence suggested that the sociopath is a chronically underaroused individual who experiences this condition as aversive and who makes attempts to increase sensory input. The findings also indicated that sociopaths even seek stimulation in situations where added stimulus acquisition is punished. This study attempted to test the possibility that among sociopaths punishment may serve a relatively nonaversive function. Punishment often consists of some type of increased stimulation (e.g., attention, censure, shock) and, according to the principle of optimal stimulation, could be experienced as reinforcing to the extent that it brings stimulus input to an optimum level. To the extent that sociopaths are underaroused, they are more likely to accept punishment, which produces the stimuli needed for achievement of an optimal level of stimulation.

For the purposes of this study, three comparison groups were identified: Subjects who scored low in anxiety and rated high in sociopathy were designated *primary sociopaths;* subjects who scored in the median anxiety range and rated low in sociopathy were designated *normals;* and subjects who scored

high in anxiety and rated low in sociopathy were designated *neurotics*. The
following hypotheses were tested:

1. Primary sociopaths will perform poorly on a shock avoidance task
where stimulation other than shock is limited; however, as nonshock stimulation is increased, the need for further sensory input will be reduced and will
be reflected in improved shock avoidance rates.

2. Normals who, by definition, are optimally aroused will do well in the
shock avoidance situation and will not be affected by the manipulation of
sensory input to the extent that sociopaths and neurotics are.

3. Neurotics, who theoretically represent the opposite of sociopathy with
respect to the arousal continuum by showing high internal stimulation and
low need for additional stimuli (Skrzypek, 1969; Wiesen, 1965), will vigorously avoid the stimulation associated with shock; however, higher levels of
sensory input will raise their arousal level beyond an optimal range, lead to
response interference, and result in decreases in shock avoidance proficiency.

METHOD

SUBJECTS

The subjects were 90 male public offenders incarcerated in a large state-
administered maximum security penitentiary. The mean age of these subjects was 27.2 years; the mean educational level was 10.5 years; and the mean
IQ (Revised Beta) was 99.9. Due to selection procedures requiring a moderate level of reading skill, illiterate inmates and those of less than 80 IQ were
eliminated from consideration. Of those qualifying, 323 inmates voluntarily
participated in the completion of the following battery of tests: (a) the Taylor
Manifest Anxiety Scale (TMAS), (b) the Institute for Personality and Ability
Testing (IPAT) Anxiety Scale, and (c) the Wolpe-Lang Fear Survey (FS).

On the basis of the results of these tests, the following groups were established:

1. The low-anxious group consisted of 30 subjects who scored in the
lowest 20% on the TMAS and IPAT measures and below the median on the
FS. Mean age, Revised Beta IQ, and years of education were, respectively,
27.4, 103.1, and 10.7. Mean TMAS, IPAT, and FS scores were, respectively, 5.1, 12.8, and 16.8.

2. The medium-anxious group consisted of 30 subjects who scored in the
middle 30% range of the TMAS and IPAT measures and in the middle 50%
range on the FS. Mean age, Revised Beta IQ, and years of education were,
respectively, 28.2, 98.9, and 10.7. Mean TMAS, IPAT, and FS scores were,
respectively, 16.4, 28.0, and 34.3.

3. The high-anxious group consisted of 30 subjects who scored in the upper 20% on the TMAS and IPAT measures and above the median on the FS. Mean age, Revised Beta IQ, and years of education were, respectively, 26.0, 97.8, and 10.0. Mean TMAS, IPAT, and FS scores were, respectively, 30.9, 49.2, and 44.8.

Subjects qualifying for the above groups were rated on Cleckley's (1964) criteria of sociopathy. Two ratings were independently completed for each subject, and their mean was used to represent the subject's level of sociopathy. Reliability between the two sets of ratings was .77. The raters were the subject's vocational counselor and his job supervisor. To insure consistency of interpretation of the Cleckley items and to encourage serious consideration of subjects' behavior patterns, the experimenter interviewed all raters to discuss their decisions regarding the applicability of each item to each subject. All subjects were rated on a scale of 1–5 on Cleckley's criteria, with 1 representing maximum agreement and 5 representing maximum disagreement. The range of mean ratings for the two judges for all subjects participating in the study was 25–60. Subjects designated as primary sociopaths achieved a mean rating of 33.2, with a standard deviation of 3.51. Subjects rated low in sociopathy (i.e., neurotics and normals) achieved a mean rating of 51.2, with a standard deviation of 4.7. On the basis of these ratings, 15 subjects high in sociopathy and 15 low in sociopathy were selected for each anxiety group. A matching procedure was employed to insure that sociopathy scores did not differ over anxiety levels.

APPARATUS AND STIMULUS VARIABLES

Auditory stimuli consisted of white noise randomly and repeatedly interrupted at 1, 2, and 3 seconds by .5 seconds of silence. White noise was taped from a 1524 Lehigh Valley white noise generator on a Sony Solid State 260 tape recorder. Playback arrangements were calibrated to replay white noise at either 65 or 95 db. through standard stereo earphones. Decibel levels were calibrated with a Bruel and Kjaer sound level meter, Type 2203, with Artificial Ear, Type 4152. Attenuation factor of the earphones reduced ambient noise to approximately 35 db. in the low frequencies (= masking level). All decibels use as a reference $20\mu N/m^2$.

Visual stimuli consisted of 10 randomly selected two-digit numbers. Each was projected on a white screen for 2 seconds followed by a 2-second blank interval. The 10-number series was presented for a total of 17 blocks and was randomly reordered for each block. The intertrial interval was 2 seconds.

Electric shock was produced by a CJA Model 228 constant current stimulator. The dial was set on "continuous" and was adjusted to 2.5 mA. Shock administration was regulated by a spring-back button which, upon depression, completed a circuit and released a .5-second shock to the subject. Electrodes were fashioned of 1-inch (2.54-cm) diameter stainless steel disks and were attached to the dorsal and ventral surfaces of the subject's left wrist with 2-inch (5.08-cm) "electroplast" bandage. H-R electrode contact jelly (potassium bitartrate, sodium chloride, and pumice) was applied before electrode attachment to reduce individual differences in skin moisture.

PROCEDURE

Subjects were tested individually in a relatively quiet prison administration building. When the subject arrived at the testing room he was asked if he would be willing to participate in an experimental task involving the use of electric shock. He was offered $1 as an incentive. Only two subjects elected not to participate; both were replaced by individuals with similar scores on the measures described above.

After the experimenter had secured the subject's cooperation the nature of the experimental task was explained. Two-digit numbers were projected on a screen. On certain numbers preselected by the experimenter, the subject received a shock unless he touched a white disk on a table in front of him (active avoidance) within 2 seconds of the number's presentation. On the other numbers, the subject did not receive a shock unless he did touch the disk (passive avoidance). Five numbers were associated with the active avoidance response and five with the passive. The numbers were presented in randomly reordered fashion for a total of 17 blocks. On the initial presentation of each number, the subject has no way of knowing the appropriate response; he learned by experiencing shock for an incorrect response. Touching the disk on a passive number was scored as a passive avoidance error, and failing to touch the disk on an active number was scored as an active avoidance error. Shock was discontinued after Block 12 to allow measurement of extinction on Blocks 13–17.

Subdued lighting and quiet conditions were maintained in the testing room. However, auditory stimulation was varied to alter the degree of sensory input. One third of the subjects performed under a 35-db. masking level associated with wearing mute stereo headphones. Another third performed under a randomly interrupted white noise input of 65 db. through the earphones, and the last third was subjected to the same white noise arrangement at 95 db. Random interruption of white noise causes a higher level of stimulation due to the novelty and complexity associated with the patterning (Berlyne, 1960). The auditory stimulation was maintained for the duration of the avoidance task. The experimenter, seated alongside but slightly behind and out of sight of the subject, administered shock for incorrect responses and recorded the subject's active and passive acquisition and extinction errors.

RESULTS

The nature of the avoidance task used in this study was such that subjects were initially unaware of which cues demanded the active avoidance response and which demanded the passive avoidance response. This information could only be acquired through experience with the punishment contingencies, which were revealed as the task proceeded. As a result, initial trials were associated with random responding and chance performance. In order to diminish the influence of these effects and to gain a purer estimate of differential acquisition of avoidance behavior under the various experimental conditions, responses over the first 7 blocks were not included in the following data analysis, which examined performance on Blocks 8–12. Blocks 13–17 were not included in this analysis, since punishment contingencies were withdrawn during these blocks. During the blocks analyzed, each subject was exposed to 25 active avoidance cues and 25 passive avoidance cues, allowing for a total of 50 possible errors.

ANALYSIS OF TOTAL AVOIDANCE ERRORS

Avoidance errors were analyzed in a 3 × 2 × 3 analysis of variance design, which included three levels of stimulation, two levels of sociopathy, and three levels of anxiety. The three levels of anxiety and two levels of sociopathy provided six subject groupings at which to investigate the effects of stimulation: (a) low anxiety, low sociopathy-low-anxious nonsociopaths, (b) low anxiety, high sociopathy-primary sociopaths, (c) medium anxiety, low sociopathy-medium-anxious nonsociopaths, (d) medium anxiety, high sociopathy-medium-anxious sociopaths, (e) high anxiety, low sociopathy-neurotic nonsociopaths, and (f) high anxiety, high sociopathy-neurotic sociopaths.

No main effects were found to be significant. However, changes in stimulation resulted in differential avoidance acquisition among three of the groups (see Table [15.1]). Primary sociopaths were clearly affected by stimulation change, $F(2,72) = 12.51$, $p<.01$. The Newman-Keuls test showed that this group made significantly more avoidance errors at the 35-db. level than at either of the higher levels of stimulation ($p<.01$). Neurotic sociopaths were also influenced by changes in stimulation, $F(2,72) = 6.83$, $p<.01$. The Newman-Keuls test indicated that they made significantly more avoidance errors at the 65-db. level of stimulation than either the higher or lower levels ($p<.05$). A third group of subjects, neurotic nonsociopaths, was also affected by stimulation changes, $F(2,72) = 5.34$, $p<.01$. Like primary sociopaths, they made more avoidance errors at the 35-db. level of stimulation than at either of the higher levels (Newman-Keuls test, $p<.01$). Avoidance acquisition among the remaining groups (low-anxious nonsociopaths, medium-

TABLE 15.1.
MEAN ACTIVE AND PASSIVE AVOIDANCE ERRORS BY SUBJECT GROUP

Subject group	Stimulation level											
	35 db.				65 db.				95 db.			
	Active		Passive		Active		Passive		Active		Passive	
	M	SD	M	SD	M	SD	M	SD	M	SD	M	SD
Low-anxious nonsociopaths	1.4	1.7	.8	.8	3.4	1.7	4.4	1.1	6.8	5.8	4.8	4.4
Primary sociopaths	13.0	6.4	8.0	3.2	4.4	4.3	2.4	2.4	2.2	2.2	.8	1.3
Medium-anxious nonsociopaths	5.6	6.5	6.4	5.1	9.2	4.1	3.6	2.9	7.0	3.7	3.4	.9
Medium-anxious sociopaths	3.4	4.3	3.2	3.9	4.4	4.8	3.8	3.6	1.6	.9	3.0	4.5
Neurotic nonsociopaths	9.6	4.5	9.2	4.9	4.2	4.5	2.8	2.6	5.4	4.4	4.2	3.6
Neurotic sociopaths	2.2	3.3	1.0	1.4	10.4	4.0	5.0	3.4	3.4	4.8	.8	.4
M	5.9		4.8		6.0		3.8		4.4		2.8	

Note: Each subject group contains 15 subjects.

anxious nonsociopaths, and medium-anxious sociopaths) was not significantly affected by changes in stimulation.

Among low-anxious subjects, an interaction occurred between stimulation level and sociopathy, $F(2, 72) = 13.91$, p.<.01. Table [15.1] shows that subjects rated low in sociopathy tended to make relatively fewer avoidance errors as stimulation level was decreased, while subjects rated high in sociopathy learned to avoid more rapidly as stimulation level was increased. Primary sociopaths made more errors than low-anxious nonsociopaths when stimulation level was low, $F(1, 72) = 24.60$, p.<.01. However, at the 95-db. level of stimulation, primary sociopaths committed fewer errors than nonsociopaths $F(1, 72) = 5.14$, p.<.05.

Subjects in the middle range of anxiety did not differ in avoidance responding as a function of sociopathy. Among high-anxious subjects, an interaction was seen between stimulation level and sociopathy, $F(2, 72)-10.08$, p<.01. Table [15.1] indicates that neurotic subjects rated low in sociopathy performed relatively better at higher levels of stimulation than at low or intermediate, while neurotic subjects rated high in sociopathy did relatively better under low and high levels of stimulation than under an intermediate level. Neurotic sociopaths made fewer errors than neurotic nonsociopaths at the 35-db. level of stimulation, $F(1, 72) = 16.91$, p.<.01. At the 65-db. level, neurotic sociopaths made more errors than neurotic nonsociopaths, $F(1, 72) = 4.90$, p<.05. The groups did not differ at the 95-db. level.

At the 35-db. level of stimulation, an interaction occurred between anxiety and sociopathy levels, $F(2, 72) = 21.70$, p<.01. Table [15.1] shows that among subjects low in sociopathy, those at higher anxiety levels committed relatively more avoidance errors than low-anxious subjects; among subjects high in sociopathy, those at higher anxiety levels avoided shock relatively more effectively than low-anxious subjects. Both sociopathic and nonsociopathic subjects differed in avoidance behavior as a function of anxiety, $F(2, 72) = 12.41$, p<.01; $F(2, 72) = 9.68$, p<.01. Newman–Keuls analysis indicated that among subjects high in sociopathy primary sociopaths made more errors than medium-anxious sociopaths or neurotic sociopaths (p<.01). Low-anxious nonsociopathic subjects made significantly fewer errors than medium-anxious nonsociopaths and neurotic nonsociopaths (p<.01). Anxiety did not appear to differentially influence avoidance acquisition at the 65-db. and 95-db. levels of stimulation.

ANALYSIS OF ACTIVE VERSUS PASSIVE AVOIDANCE ERRORS

Further analysis of avoidance performance was concerned with the relationship between active versus passive types of avoidance (see Table [15.1]). There was a significant relationship between the two types of errors (r = .48, p<.01) and a tendency toward making more active than passive errors, t(89) = 3.42, p<.01. An active error reflected a failure to avert shock through reaching out and tapping a disk. The less prevalent passive error consisted of reaching out and tapping the disk when no response was called for.

Closer examination of the data revealed that the tendency toward making active errors was accounted for by subjects rated high in sociopathy, t(44) = 2.89, p<.01. Among low-sociopathy subjects, the difference between the number of active and passive errors did not reach significance, t(44) = 1.99, p<.05. Anxiety level also showed some relationship to error type. Low-anxious subjects made more active than passive errors, t(29) = 2.46, p.<.05. However, medium– and high-anxious subjects showed no reliable tendency toward either type of error, t(29) = 1.67, p<.05; t(29) = 1.98, p<.05. Active and passive errors were committed at relatively equal frequency at the 35-db. level of stimulation, t(29) = 1.21, p<.05. However, both higher levels of stimulation were associated with a significant tendency toward making active error t(29) = 2.81, p<.01; t(29) = 2.05, p = .05. In summary, the features favoring the commission of active versus passive errors were high sociopathy, low anxiety (= primary sociopathy), and relatively high levels of stimulation. Granted these conditions, the subject was more likely to err in the direction of passively accepting noxious stimulation than of actively attempting to avert it.

DISCUSSION

One of the most revealing findings in this study was that stimulation level exerted considerable influence on shock-avoidance behavior. Despite the fact that the independent manipulations of sensory input were restricted to the auditory modality, three of the six groups showed differential behavior as a function of this manipulation. Primary sociopaths, as predicted by the first hypothesis, were least effective at avoiding shock at the lowest level of stimulation. Viewing this finding in terms of optimal stimulation theory (Leuba, 1955) leads to the explanation that an underaroused subject under conditions of inadequate stimulation (35 db.) would respond so as to augment sensory input. Since avoidance errors led to shock stimulation in the experimental task employed here, primary sociopaths were most likely to commit and benefit by these errors when other stimulation was minimal (35 db.). Increases in auditory stimulation to 65 and 95 db. resulted in significant reduction in incorrect avoidance responses, suggesting that increased auditory input better approximated the primary sociopath's optimal level of stimulation and reduced his need for additional stimuli, namely, stimulation via shock.

It might be argued that Mowrer's (1947) explanation of avoidance conditioning accounts for the same results, in that increased auditory stimulation may have augmented fear conditionability among sociopaths and thereby allowed the reinforcing effects of drive reduction associated with successful shock avoidance to reinforce and increase avoidance responding. While both explanations of sociopathic avoidance behavior are compatible with the results of the present study, the optimal stimulation interpretation offers the dual advantages of easier quantification and less reliance on hypothetical constructs. Assessing stimulus intensity and measuring subjects' response on a dependent variable providing further stimulation (e.g., shock) seems to constitute a more precise and concrete operation than that associated with Mowrer's model, which theorizes about and relies upon the less definable concepts of fear conditionability and drive reduction.

The use of subjects derived from a population of convicted, institutionalized, public offenders left the present study devoid of the usual normal control group. The closest approximations to this were represented by the low- and medium–anxious nonsociopath groups. The other four groups were atypically high in either sociopathy, anxiety, or both. The two groups considered closest to normal controls were found to be relatively unaffected on the avoidance task by changes in the auditory stimulation. This finding supports the second hypothesis, which predicted that normals would be less affected by changes in sensory input than sociopaths or neurotics. Both of the latter groups were subsequently found to alter their avoidance performance as a result of changes in stimulation level.

Since anxiety interacted with the other independent variables employed in this study, the appropriate control group for primary sociopaths was the low-anxious nonsociopath group. Under conditions of low stimulation, primary sociopaths made significantly more avoidance errors than controls. As pointed out previously, deficient avoidance conditioning among sociopaths is a typical finding in the experimental literature (Lykken, 1957; Schachter and Latane, 1964; Schmauk, 1968). In the present study, however, it was found that increases in the level of auditory stimulation to which the subject was exposed removed the deficit in avoidance performance among primary sociopaths. This finding raises the possibility that sociopaths' defective avoidance acquisition in experimental situations may be an artifact of the long, monotonous, and unstimulating nature of the avoidance task employed (e.g., Lykken's Mental Maze used in the studies mentioned above). It also suggests the possibility that the primary sociopath's clinically noted failure to profit from punishment (Cleckley, 1964; Hare, 1970) may be restricted to situations providing little sensory input. Conversely, this deficit may disappear in environments which are highly stimulating. If this possibility proves valid, it suggests the plausibility of therapeutic intervention in the primary sociopathic process through the application of sensory inputs aimed at controlling a chronic need for additional stimulation. Providing adequate prosocial sensory input could conceivably eliminate the primary sociopath's indiscriminate drive toward attaining added stimulation regardless of its source.

Present findings corroborate the need for sociopaths to be classified along the dimension of anxiety. Hare (1970) argued that such a classification is essential, since persons who engage in sociopathic behavior may be differently motivated, that is, some may have a need for increased sensory input (e.g., primary sociopaths) while others may have a need to reduce neurotic conflict (e.g., neurotic or secondary sociopaths). In the present study, anxiety interacted with sociopathy in avoidance responding. Primary and neurotic sociopaths were both significantly affected by stimulation changes, but differently, while medium-anxious sociopaths were relatively unaffected. Primary sociopaths made more avoidance errors than the other groups of sociopaths under the low-stimulation condition (35 db.). Unlike primary sociopaths, whose level of internal stimulation, as reflected by anxiety measures, is very low, medium-anxious and neurotic sociopaths, with their higher levels of internal stimulation, may have experienced less stimulus deprivation under conditions of low sensory input and less corresponding need for the added stimulation available through commission of avoidance errors leading to shock.

One of the most puzzling performances was that of neurotic non-sociopaths, who made significantly fewer avoidance errors at the higher levels of stimulation than at the 35-db. level. The third hypothesis, based on Spence and Spence's (1966) response interference hypothesis, had predicted the opposite effect—that neurotics should do poorest under conditions of high stimulus input, since high stimulation would presumably raise their anxiety even higher and result in inefficient, disintegrating performance. A post hoc interpretation of the data found here might show that among neurotics, conditions of low external stimulation (35 db.) permit sensitization to disturbing internal stimuli, which are capable of producing response interference and, therefore, defective avoidance acquisition. Another puzzling result was produced by neurotic sociopaths, who also performed in a manner difficult to interpret. They committed more avoidance errors at the intermediate level of stimulation (65 db.) than at either the higher or lower levels. These results presently defy even a post hoc interpretation, suggesting a need for replication.

While no differences were predicted regarding the relative frequency of active versus passive types of avoidance errors, a significant tendency toward making active errors (failure to respond) was noted among subjects high in sociopathy and among those low in anxiety. Primary sociopaths, who represent both of these extremes, demonstrated an especially strong tendency toward committing active errors. In terms of the principle of optimal stimulation, these subjects were not motivated to avert the experience of shock stimuli that might help to provide a more appropriate level of sensory input. As a result, they were relatively unsuccessful in acquiring active avoidance responses. McCleary (1966) has emphasized that separate physiological mechanisms are involved in active and passive avoidance behavior. One of the productive areas for future research in sociopathy and psychopathology might be in the direction of investigating the nature and function of these mechanisms, including their role in avoidance behavior. Tentatively, it appears that among the variables affecting avoidance behavior, those of internal stimulation (anxiety), need for additional stimulation (sociopathy), and level of external stimulation are influential.

REFERENCES

Berlyne, D. E. *Conflict, arousal, and curiosity*. New York: McGraw-Hill, 1960.
Cleckley, H. *The mask of sanity*. St. Louis, Mo.: Mosby, 1964.
Duffy, E. *Activation and behavior*. New York: Wiley, 1962.
Hare, R. D. Psychopathy, fear arousal, and anticipated pain. *Psychological Reports*, 1965, *16*, 499–502. (a)
Hare, R. D. Temporal gradient of fear arousal in psychopaths. *J. of Abnormal Psychology*, 1965, *70*, 442–45. (b)
Leuba, C. Toward some integration of learning theories: The concept of optimal stimulation. *Psychological Reports*, 1955, *1*, 27–33.
Lindsley, D. B. Psychological phenomena and the electroencephalogram. *Electroencephalogram and Clinical Neurophysiology*, 1952, *4*, 443–56.
Lykken, D. T. *A study of anxiety in the sociopathic personality*. Unpublished doctoral dissertation, University of Minnesota, 1955.
Lykken, D. T. A study of anxiety in the sociopathic personality. *J. of Abnormal and Social Psychology*, 1957, *55*, 6–10.
McCleary, R. A. Response-modulating functions of the limbic system: Initiation and suppression. In E. Steller and J. M. Sprague (Eds.) *Progress in physiological psychology* (Vol. 1). New York: Academic Press, 1966.
Mowrer, O. H. On the dual nature of learning—a reinterpretation of "conditioning" and "problem solving." *Harvard Educational Review*, 1947, *17*, 102–48.
Quay, H. C. Psychopathic personality as pathological stimulation seeking, *American J. of Psychiatry*, 1965, *122*, 180–88.
Schachter, S., and Latane, B. Crime, cognition and the ANS. In M. R. Jones (Ed.), *Nebraska Symposium on Motivation* (Vol. 12). Lincoln: U of Nebraska Press, 1964.
Schmauk, F. *A study of the relationship between kinds of punishment, autonomic arousal, subjective anxiety and avoidance learning in the primary sociopath*. Unpublished doctoral dissertation, Temple University, 1968.
Schoenherr, J. C. *Avoidance of noxious stimulation in psychopathic personality*. Unpublished doctoral dissertation, U of California, Los Angeles, 1964.
Skrzypek, G. J. Effect of perceptual isolation and arousal on anxiety, complexity preference, and novelty preference in psychopathic and neurotic criminals. *J. of Abnormal Psychology*, 1969, *74*, 321–29.

Spence, J. T., and Spence, K. W. The motivational components of manifest anxiety: Drive and drive stimuli. In C. D. Spielberger (Ed.), *Anxiety and behavior*, New York: Academic 1966.

Sutker, P. S. *Vicarious conditioning, empathy and sociopathy.* Unpublished doctoral dissertation, U of Georgia, 1969.

Wiesen, A. E. *Differential reinforcing effects of onset and offset of stimulation on the operant behavior of normals, neurotics, and psychopaths.* Unpublished doctoral dissertation, U of Florida, 1965.

Part Four

Abnormal and Deviant Behavior: Special Considerations

In the preceding section, we attempted to provide two things: first, a foundation for the conceptualization of behavior—the sociopsychological model—and second, a consideration of the two broad categories of abnormality most frequently identified among offender populations—paranoia and psychopathy. In this unit, we undertake presentations of research approaches to several specialized forms of deviation which are often implicated in criminality. This section is, in a sense, a potpourri of "abnormality," with little or no pretense of commonality among the groups, other than the fact that they all involve behavior which, in varying degrees, illustrates the sociopsychological process of deviance-formation. Significantly, each occupies a rather ambiguous position between radical psychological and penological approaches to their treatment.

The ambiguity is well demonstrated in the rapidly changing definition of rape, from an aberrant *sexual* act to an act primarily of criminal *violence*. This has come about largely in response to the organized activity of the "women's movement," which has put forth such a redefinition as an essential element in acknowledging the full "personhood"—and hence bodily inviolability—of women. According to Susan Brownmiller, in her widely-discussed book, *Against Our Will*, rape—rather than being perpetrated by a few depraved or abnormal men—has been the act, par excellence, whereby males have perpetuated their dominance over females throughout human history. In this position, its more flagrant manifestations are more appropriately grouped with assault and armed robbery as crimes of violence than with behaviors thought of as psychopathological. The impact of this position on the criminal justice system is evident in the trend toward revision of laws defining rape. More and more, violence (or the threat of violence) becomes the paramount legal consideration—while de-emphasizing such recently and widely accepted concepts as "sexual psychopathy," with their implication of chronic abnormality. This is well illustrated in legislation approved in the Spring 1976 session of the Wisconsin State Assembly, "moving the crime of rape from the section of Crimes Against Sexual Morality to the section of Crimes Against Life and Bodily Security . . . [and placing] emphasis on the amount of force used by the rapist . . ." (Miller, 1976, 1–5). The novelty of this shift in emphasis is revealed in the fact that even in full-scale recent treatments of aggression, there are to be found no specific references to rape or sexual assault.

Goldner, in his paper summarizing the research to date, calls our attention to the limited information available in regard to rape. However, one does get the impression that, from the standpoint of normality, rapists are not notably different from the rest of the population—particularly control groups of non-sexual offenders—except perhaps with regard to aggressivity or control of aggressive behavior. This conforms with the contention by spokespersons for the women's movement, that rape is primarily an act of violence by men

297

against women, for the purpose of inducing fear or humiliation through sexual violation.

Rada, in *Alcoholism and Forcible Rape*, reports on an effort to comprehend the act of rape within the framework of alcohol ingestion. While far from conclusive in establishing a causal relationship, it does suggest an area of research warranting more definitive investigation. It would be of significance, for example, if it could be shown that the probability of rape increases at a rate different from other types of offenses—particularly nonaggressive ones—under the influence of alcohol. Again, does sexual violence grow out of drinking, or does the rapist drink in order to facilitate commission of the premeditated act (i.e. reduce his fear or inhibition)? Rada draws the properly cautious inference of "an important, but not necessarily direct or causal relationship between alcohol and rape."

If the psychopathological implications of rape are in question, there appears to be less doubt with respect to the other major category of sexual crime, pedophilia, or the sexual molestation of children. This is not to imply that there exists a clear conception of the etiological factors in pedophilia, or that persons committing pedophilic acts represent a unitary model of abnormality. In fact, the contrary is true; a review of the literature leaves an impression of a veritable smorgasbord of causal explanations including functional psychoses, organic disease (neurological and endocrinological), toxic conditions, mental deficiency, neuroses, personality disorders (including psychopathic states), as well as a number of transitory contingencies. A similar range of theoretical positions emerges in efforts to elucidate the causes—and treatment—of pedophilia: psychoanalytic (in all its varieties), general developmental, behavioral, situational, etc. Not surprisingly, given such a plethora, no single explanation proves completely persuasive or satisfying. As in so many efforts to explain deviant human behavior, conviction all too readily takes precedence over empirical findings, or findings are tortured into conformity with *a priori* conviction. The situation is well summarized in a volume based on the work carried out at the Forensic Clinic of the Toronto (Canada) Psychiatric Hospital:

> The precise identification of the etiological factors of behavioral symptoms depends greatly on the theory to which one subscribes. Immaturity, for example, which is the problem most consistently raised with pedophiles, can be seen as an organic malfunction, as a deficient learning process, as a lack of proper conditioning, or as psychodynamic fixation or regression. Many of these concepts overlap. Their relative importance in explaining the symptom is still unexplored. (Mohr, Turner, and Jerry, 1964, p. 87.)

In the report by Rada included in this section, the relationship between pedophilia and alcohol is explored. While his failure to utilize nonpedophilic control groups represents a serious shortcoming of this investigation, the report does call to our attention several frequently noted characteristics of the group, especially the high average age (35.2) and the high proportion of unmarried (41%). Most treatments of the topic cite advanced age—suggesting either reduced opportunity or neurological deterioration—as an earmark of the pedophilic offender group. Single status may be related to the common description of pedophilics, as a group, as tending to social timidity (passive-inadequate personality). With regard to the role of alcohol, perhaps the most interesting finding is the fact that exactly half of the group had been "drinking at the time of commission of offense" (DATCO). Additionally, it would be pertinent to know how this compares to the conditions surrounding non-sex crimes, as well as the causal (temporal) link between alcohol use, conceiving of the offense, and its actual perpetration. Even lacking such information, however, we can accept Rada's suggestion "that alcohol may play an important role in the commission of these offenses." Should Rada's findings be supported by further research, the potential for reducing the incidence of sex offenses (to say nothing of other crimes), through treatment of alcoholism, is clearly implied.

If alcohol is generally perceived as a facilitator of crimes, the role of narcotic substances such as heroin is far less self-evident. Much energy has been expended in debating whether antisocial or criminal behavior is a direct outcome of the pharmacological action of heroin on the organism, or is rather a secondary consequence of the criminalization of heroin usage and marketing, where addicted individuals are forced into criminality to support their habits. For example, the report of a Joint Committee of the American Bar Association and the American Medical Association on Narcotic Drugs was entitled, "Drug Addiction: Crime or Disease?" (Joint Committee of the American Bar Association and The American Medical Association on Narcotic Drugs, 1971.) This report acknowledges an apparent increase in drug addiction in the United States since World War II, particularly in urban slums and among minority groups, accompanied by increasingly severe penal sanctions imposed on both users and dealers. As to whether it is the illegality—and consequent scarcity—of drugs, or the direct effect of drugs on the organism, the report concludes that "the weight of evidence is so heavily in favor of the former point of view that the question can hardly be called a controversial one" (Joint Committee of the American Bar Association and the American Medical Association on Narcotic Drugs, 1971, p. 165). Readers of this anthology will be interested to note the report's observation that crimes of violence and sexual crimes are almost never committed by addicts (Joint Committee of the American Bar Association and The American Medical Association on Narcotic Drugs, 1971, p. 165).

While this is not the place to comment extensively on these conclusions, the fact remains that in most parts of the United States, narcotics possession, use, and dealing are still severely punished, so that the correctional system will, for some time to come, continue to be confronted with clients convicted of drug or drug-related offenses. Thus, it behooves the correctional worker to acquire some awareness of the typological variety constituting the population of drug users. The paper by Lewis and Glazer, "Lifestyles Among Heroin Users," maintains that five subgroups can be identified, characterized by distinctive "lifestyles" and involving little overlapping. All five groups have passed through the correctional system. They vary with respect to socioeconomic origin, ethnic affiliation, capacity for social integration, tolerance for incarceration, intellectuality, legal attitude, criminality, and potential for rehabilitation. It should come as no surprise that the subgroups from the most affluent circumstances and with the highest levels of intellectual capacity, the Expressive Students and the Social World Alternators—in other words, those closest to middle-class mainstream values—should prove to be most responsive to rehabilitative approaches; or that the least rehabilitatable would be those addicts with the poorest prospects of socioeconomic achievement, those from the *barrios*, the ghettos, and the neighborhoods of high delinquency.

The two final selections included in this section represent somewhat differing types of "special problems." Rather than deviant forms of criminal behavior, female criminals and suicidal inmates are frequently discussed from the standpoint of administrative management. Women, because of their disproportionately low incidence in the criminal justice system, constitute an anomalous subgroup within a world of mostly male clientele and staff. At the end of 1973, for example, there was a known total of 6,684 female inmates in U.S. Federal and State Institutions, compared to 197,665 incarcerated males (National Prisoner Statistics Bulletin, May 1975, pp. 14–16). Despite the small numbers involved, there has emerged in recent years a growing interest in female criminality and the position of women vis-à-vis the criminal justice—including the correctional—system. Several comprehensive treatments have appeared, including a review by Velimesis (Velimesis, 1975, pp. 94–112) and the entire Fall 1973 issue of *Issues in Criminology*. Velimesis refers to "the mediocrity and irrelevance of correctional programming for women." In *Prisons for Women*, Eyman—who has served as warden at women's prisons in South Carolina and Tennessee—lists a series of discrepancies between male and female prisons, to the disadvantage of the latter. In her view, a heavily masculine bias is responsible: "Male directors, male wardens, and male legislators seem incapable of providing acceptable conditions in many women's prisons. Indeed, they often refuse to believe that conditions are anything but acceptable." (Eyman, 1971, p. 166).

Findings with regard to "the nature of female criminality" are brought together and summarized by Hoffman-Bustamente (Hoffman-Bustamente, 1975), who purports to see "a close relationship to sex roles [such that women] tend not to be arrested for crimes that require stereotyped male behavior, i.e. robbery, burglary. Even in crimes where women are more frequently arrested, i.e., homicide, shoplifting, the close ties are still evident. Where the crime requires behavior that is consistent with expected female roles, women appear to make up a large number of the petty criminals (forgery, fraud, embezzlement, prostitution, vagrancy, curfew, and runaway)."

As with the male population, women in the correctional system are a small proportion of the total who commit offenses or undergo adjudication. Again, as with males, there is an oft-heard suspicion that the ones who do come into corrections tend to be unrepresentative of the totality of women offenders—more of them poor, black, and at the lower ranges of the educational-intellectual distribution. In fact, as Velimesis' review makes clear, there is little agreement among the reported studies as to the characteristics of incarcerated females.

One major source of data regarding the personal characteristics of female criminals is the series of reports by Guze and his colleagues at the Department of Psychiatry of Washington University School of Medicine in St. Louis. We have selected for inclusion here a paper by Cloninger and Guze that focuses on the prevalence of diagnosed sociopathy and hysteria, in relation to the personal, social, and familial backgrounds of the sixty-six women observed in lengthy (two- to six-hour) interviews. As one might expect in a population of convicted felons—of either sex—the most common diagnostic label was sociopathy, 65 percent. Hysteria was diagnosed in 41 percent of the cases, including 25 percent identified as both sociopathic and hysterical. One feels hard put to evaluate the significance of the diagnostic labels, particularly with respect to etiology of crime and responsiveness to treatment. In fact, if one takes into consideration the backgrounds of these women, in combination with the well-known contagiousness of behavioral reactions within confined settings, it becomes difficult to imagine how they could have avoided falling into sociopathic or hysterical behavior patterns.

The question that remains unanswered here—as in so many post–conviction psychiatric studies—has to do with the temporal relationship between psychiatric diagnosis and criminality. The selections from Ullman and Krasner in the preceding section would be worth rereading, particularly those dealing with the processes of labeling and institutional indoctrination (e.g., "Learning to be a Bughouser") which affects inmates as well as staff. The aspect of the paper by Cloninger and Guze that justifies its inclusion in this work is the description of the background histories of their women. While these will undoubtedly vary somewhat from place to place, it should provide the corrections worker who may be assigned to work with women clients, with a framework for relating to them.

After individual or group violence against other inmates or against institutions, the client behavior most prone to induce insomnia in correctional administrators is that of self-directed violence—suicide. As a form of deviant behavior, there probably has never been a time in the history of corrections when suicide has not been part of the catalog of prisoner behavior. Perhaps the prototypical occurrence is to be found in the biblical account of Samson, the Israelite hero who, taken into captivity by the Philistines, proceeded to bring the Philistine temple crashing down upon his captors and himself. Samson may be the earliest example in recorded history of what Wicks, the author of the final selection in this unit, refers to as "suicidal manipulation," where self-destruction (or its attempt) is incidental to the primary end, namely vengeance toward the hated captor.

Most suicides in correctional settings lack the heroic trappings of the Samson legend. Wicks offers a useful enumeration of the more common motivations or antecedents. None will surprise the experienced correctional worker. While Wicks' article is aimed, ostensibly, toward the corrections officer, it is just as applicable to others whose duties bring them into interaction with correctional clients, including counselors, teachers, physicians, chaplains, and recreational leaders. Of particular interest currently is his calling our attention to the significance of "confinement for a long period in an unsentenced status." The newspapers of the larger cities report numerous incidents in which inmates of so-called houses of detention—awaiting trial or sentencing for from months up to a year or more in overcrowded, verminous, violent conditions—are found in their cells hung or poisoned. As court calendars continue to lengthen and the criminal justice system becomes ever more glacial in its pace, the potential for suicide and suicide attempts can be expected to increase, making it all the more imperative that correctional workers be capable of recognizing the signs, and of acting to prevent the occurrence of suicide attempts.

REFERENCES

Eyman, J. S. *Prisons for women.* Springfield, Ill.: Charles C. Thomas, 1971.

Hoffman-Bustamente, D. The Nature of Female Criminality. *Issues in Criminology*, 8 (1975): 117–36.

Joint Committee of the American Bar Association and The American Medical Association on Narcotic Drugs. *Drug addiction: crime or disease?* Bloomington: Indiana University Press, 1971.

Miller, M. Wisconsin Adopts Rape Reform Legislation. *Criminal Justice Digest*, 4 (1976): 1–5.

Mohr, J. W., Turner, R. E., Jerry, M. B. *Pedophilia and exhibitionism*. Toronto: University of Toronto Press, 1964.

National Prisoner Statistics Bulletin, No. SD-NPS-PSF-1. U.S. Department of Justice, Law Enforcement Assistance Administration, National Criminal Justice Information and Statistics Service, May 1975, pp. 14–16.

Velimesis, E. The Female Offender. *Crime and Delinquency Literature*, 7 (March 1975): 94–112.

16

Rape as a Heinous but Understudied Offense

Norman S. Goldner

Reprinted by special permission of the *Journal of Criminal Law, Criminology and Police Science*, copyright © 1972 by Northwestern University School of Law, Vol. 63, No. 3. Author permission to reprint is gratefully acknowledged.

Law enforcement personnel generally form their opinions about sex offenders and their victims on the basis of their experiences in the field.[1] Realistically, neither police officers, their supervisors nor the court can be expected to search the social science literature and collate the available information about the many types of sex offenders. The purpose of this paper is to present, to those who most frequently deal with it, a cross-section of the available literature on forcible rape (hereafter also referred to as rape). This paper will summarize some of the available data concerning the frequency, time, place and methods of forcible rape as well as that concerning the personality characteristics of both the rapist and his victim. It will also indicate certain questions about rape which have been given scant attention in criminological publications.

LEGALISTIC DEFINITIONS OF RAPE

Perhaps the most inclusive legalistic definition of rape was given by the English jurist and legal historian, Sir William Blackstone: "Rape in the first degree . . . includes cases in which intercourse was had without conscious and voluntary consent, when the woman was unable to give consent, or when resistance was prevented by stupor, intoxication, narcotics, etc."[2] Refinements of this definition have been offered. One includes the stipulation of violence and states that "Rape means to seize against the wishes of the female and by means of physical force."[3] Another elaborates on the means by which the deed can be accomplished: "Rape is unlawful carnal knowledge . . . without her consent either by force, fear or fraud (fraud vitiates consent)."[4]

The specific language of present laws dealing with rape varies but two types of rape are generally recognized:(1) rape by force or various kinds of deceit; and (2) statutory rape, intercourse with someone below statutorily stipulated age.[5] For example, section 213.1 of the Model Penal Code provides in part:

(1) Rape. A male who has sexual intercourse with a female not his wife is guilty of rape if:
   (a) he compels her to submit by force or by threat of imminent death, serious bodily injury, extreme pain or kidnapping, to be inflicted on anyone; or
   (b) he has substantially impaired her power to appraise or control her conduct by administering or employing without her knowledge drugs, intoxicants or other means for the purpose of preventing resistance; or
   (c) the female is unconscious; or
   (d) the female is less than 10 years old.[6]

FREQUENCY

The paucity of studies on rape may be explained by the facts that " . . . the number of forcible attacks on women and children represents but a small fraction of all sex offenses"[7] and that statutory rapes far outnumber forcible rapes.[8] For example, in New York between 1930 and 1939 there were 2,366 convictions for rape; 82 percent were statutory.[9]

According to the Federal Bureau of Investigation Uniform Crime Reports (hereinafter referred to as UCR) "crime clocks," only murder occurs less frequently than forcible rape. However, over the nine-year period from 1960–1969, forcible rapes increased from 16,860 to 36,470, or 116 percent.[10] However, it is unclear whether forcible rape is increasing disproportionately to population increases. There is some evidence it is not. For instance, between 1960 and 1969 the number of rapists arrested under the age of eighteen increased 86 percent, those eighteen years and over, about 51 percent (UCR). This increase is consistent with an increasingly youthful population. However, numerous variables affect such measurements. Changes in arrest rates are influenced by changes in laws, in reporting procedures by the police to the federal authorities, and in police efficiency. Furthermore, the publicizing of a dramatic incident of rape often leads to an increase in reports of rape for a time thereafter.[11] And in any event, reporting a rape has such unpleasant ramifications for the victim—both because of her "reputation" and the necessary caution of the police in accepting these charges—that rapes frequently go unreported.

TIME, PLACE, METHOD

According to UCR, it has been true for decades that forcible rape is most prevalent from May through October, reaching its peak in August. Little data has been collected to indicate more precisely the times during which rapes most frequently occur, however. Amir, studying 646 cases of rape in

Philadelphia during 1958 and 1960, found that Saturday was the peak day for this offense and that the highest risk hours were between 8:00 P.M. and 2:00 A.M.[12]

The UCR reveal that forcible rape as a "known offense" is most frequent in the city, least frequent in rural areas. Low rates also characterize suburban areas. The rate tends to increase with the increasing size of the city, though between 1968 and 1969 the largest percent increase in forcible rape (20.7 percent) was in 451 cities with populations between 25,000 and 50,000. No locale showed a decreased rate between 1968 and 1969 as had been the case in some previous years. No explanation of these rates is readily available in criminological literature.

Only limited evidence exists correlating place and rape, and it was collected in two of our largest cities. A survey in 1940 by the Homicide Bureau in Chicago revealed that there was a substantial relationship between place of the offense and the residence of the sex offenders. Eighty-two percent of male sex offenders committed their crimes within their own neighborhoods.[13] The next most prevalent area of offense was in a district adjacent to their area of residence.[14] A similar pattern was discovered by Amir: "In the majority of cases (82 percent) offenders and victims lived in the same area, while in 68 percent a 'neighborhood triangle' was observed, i.e., offenders lived in the vicinity of victim and offense."[15] He found that rapist and victim most often met on the street and in the residence of either the victim or the offender.[16] The offense usually took place at the site of the initial meeting with a tendency for the crime scene to move from outdoors to inside.[17]

Only Amir seems to have published data relevant to the techniques or methods utilized for rape.[18] He noted that the most dangerous meeting place was the street, and found that most of the rapes were planned, and that most of those planned were intraracial when they took place in one of the participants' homes or when it was a group rape.[19] Non-physical methods to accomplish the rape included verbal threat, intimidating physical gestures and the menacing use of some type of weapon in 87 percent of the cases.[20] Violent practices accompanying the rape included roughness (29 percent), nonbrutal beatings (20 percent) and choking (12 percent). Extreme violence was significantly associated with intraracial Negro rapes or when the offender was Negro and the victim was white. Force and multiple rape, that is, rape by more than one offender, were also correlated, especially when the event took place out of doors.[21] Sexual humiliation through the use of practices usually referred to as sexually deviant occurred in a quarter of the cases (27 percent).[22]

Forty-three percent of the rapes studied by Amir were multiple. The initial interaction and the rape usually took place outside; both were usually planned as opposed to "explosive." Multiple rapes were accomplished more often by intimidation and nonbrutal beatings than by the extreme violence and brutality which characterized single offender rapes.[23]

Only 4 percent of the rapes coincided with other felonies such as burglary or robbery, and in these cases the offender was often at least ten years younger than the victim.[24] In 48 percent of the rapes, the offender and the victim already knew one another, and in these cases, the closer the prior relationship the greater the degree of force used. As is the pattern with murder, neighbors and acquaintances, though not relatives, most often committed brutal rapes.[25] Multiple rape more often took place between strangers. So-called victim-precipitated rapes occurred in only 19 percent of the rapes Amir studied.[26]

THE OFFENDER: VITAL STATISTICS

Arrest statistics for 1969 show that eighteen year olds commit the greatest number of rapes; nineteen year olds follow closely as principal offenders. Considering five-year age spans, the range from 15–19 years contains the largest number of offenders with high but steadily decreasing rates exhibited as the intervals proceed from 20–24, 25–29 and 30–34 years. These UCR figures are consistent with previous ones showing a gradual increase in rape with increasing age from ten to a peak at eighteen, whereafter the rates gradually decline past the 35–39 age bracket. They are supported by studies through time in specific locales. For example, a study in New York showed that rape was committed mainly by those under thirty-one;[27] later findings in Los Angeles gave the average age of rapists as 23.[28]

UCR figures for 1969, consistent with previous years, indicate that the rapist population is composed primarily of whites and Negroes, with the former in far greater proportion than the latter. However, Amir's Philadelphia study found that "Negroes exceed whites . . . among offenders in absolute numbers as well as in terms of their proportion in the general population. . . . The proportion of Negro offenders was four times greater than their proportion in the general population. . . ."[29] Substantially more Negroes than whites have been executed for rape (375 Negroes, 41 whites), the vast majority of these executions taking place in the South.[30]

Data concerning the religion of offenders is scanty. Karpman[31] has indicated that 53 percent of all sex offenders are Roman Catholic, but provided no specific figures for rapists. The same lack of information exists for educational, occupational and social class levels. We do know that sex offenders are usually single, unskilled workers from low education and income groups.[32]

Our knowledge about the general criminality of convicted rapists is inadequate and somewhat contradictory.[33] Karpman, though, has concluded that "rapists appear to have a greater tendency toward criminal records of nonsexual crimes than do other sex offenders."[34]

There is virtual unanimity among those who study rapists that they possess a below-average I.Q. Gillin found this to be the case for a Wisconsin State Prison population in which rapists had a lower I.Q. than sodomists.[35] Caldwell administered a revised Army Beta Intelligence Test to inmates of various Alabama prisons and correctional camps and found both whites and blacks convicted of rape to have below-average scores for that inmate population.[36]

THE OFFENDER: PSYCHOPATHOLOGY
AND OTHER CAUSAL FACTORS

Psychoanalysts, psychiatrists and other clinicians have written at length about the psychopathology of sex offenders. The following interpretations of sex offenders' behavior are a sample of available psychodynamic and psychostructural explanations. The sample demonstrates that no agreement has been reached on whether the motivation of rapists is different from that of other offenders in degree, kind or pattern.

A study by the University of Minnesota Medical School of prisoners in Sing Sing Prison led to the conclusion that none of the sex offenders had a normal personality while 70 percent had symptoms of schizophrenia.[37] Another study of convicted sex offenders at the State of New Jersey Diagnostic Center concluded that high rates of disturbed behavior were "found among those convicted of forcible rape and exhibitory acts. . . . Underlying or overt hostility was particularly evident in those convicted of sexual assault, forcible rape, and incestuous relationships."[38] Hammer and Glueck conducted a five-year study of the psychodynamic patterns of 200 sex offenders and found that other inmates were differentiated in the degree but not the kind of their mental processes.[39]

A number of behavior explanations and personality descriptions have been offered for rapists, as distinguished from sex offenders generally. Hammer and Glueck found rapists to have less intense feelings of castration than other sex offenders. They suggested ". . . that the rapists' castration feelings are not overwhelmingly incapacitating, which allows them to employ the mechanism of overcompensation and diminution under a cloak of overassertive and aggressive virility."[40] They also suggested that, "The rapist, feeling rejected by his mother, feels he cannot be wanted or desired by any woman; hence he attempts to command a woman physically."[41]

Karpman reports a study by Manfred Guttmacher in which he concluded on the basis of Rorschach tests that rapists show ". . . conflict, inner disharmony, and social isolation."[42] Also using the Rorschach, Padcal and Herzberg compared rapists with a control group but found that the two were indistinguishable from one another; "If we take heterosexual behavior between adults as our standard, then it is difficult to see how the rapists differ from the controls in sexual behavior."[43]

According to Karpman, the probable motivation for rape is that for some men, only the resistance of the woman makes them potent: "In many cases, rape may be related unconsciously to early incestuous desires and the fury aroused by the Oedipus complex. . . . The victim may be a substitute for the criminal's mother who would naturally resist the attack by her son."[44]

A few studies have been made of the wives and mothers of rapists. In the first study of its kind, Palm and Abrahmsen analyzed the wives of eight rapists by use of the Rorschach.[45] They found these women remarkably alike in that they had an image of the father figure as threatening and sexually aggressive and responded in a masochistic way; they had latent homosexual inclinations; their husbands—then in Sing Sing—complained about their wives' lack of sexual spontaneity.[46] Checking case histories, Palm and Abrahmsen found that these same rapists had been overstimulated sexually in their childhood by their mothers: "In most cases, seductive behavior by the mother alternated with cruelty and harshness. . . ."[47] Gillin also found difficulties in the rapists' family situations and suggested that the homes of sex offenders in general seem to have "an outstanding lack of emotional tone."[48]

THE VICTIM

An area of inquiry which has received even less attention than those already reviewed concerns the rapist's victim. Both men and women are the victims of rape, though judging from the UCR, males are very seldom raped. Karpman points out that

> Indecent assault by an adult woman on a small boy is more common than is thought. In 1842 The Court of Assizes of the Seine convicted a girl of rape on two children. A case has been reported where several women seized a young man. Such cases are rare. The mores of the community . . . define sexual deviation as acts committed by males. . . .[49]

Female victims of rape ordinarily do not wish to cooperate in studies of their own behavior. This may be due largely to the shame involved in being a victim. Furthermore, the issue of victim-precipitated rape is often raised. Did the victim appear to agree but then retract consent before intercourse was "forced," or did she place herself in a situation which implicitly invited a sexual encounter?[50]

Clinical literature contains numerous psychiatric studies of rape victims, but these tend to be both unsystematic and individualistic[51] and plagued by problems of police and victim non-cooperation. One study partly circumvented these problems by focusing upon seventy-three girls from the ages of four to sixteen who were the victims of adult sex offenders.[52] In those cases in which the girls were "participant," as opposed to "accidental," victims, three factors were discovered: (1) deprivation and rejection of the child by the mother along with inconsistent attitudes toward the child; (2) intense sexual stimulation of the child by the parent; (3) conflict within one parent or disagreement between them over the child's expression of her sexual impulses.[53] It should be noted that the above traits were also considered important etiological factors in the motivation of the rapist.[54]

CONCLUDING OBSERVATIONS

If rape is regarded as such a serious offense by the victim, society and its legal enforcement agencies, why is our knowledge of it so incomplete and why had so little formal study been devoted to it? At least a partial explanation is provided by the following observations:

1. Statistical representations of rape are subject to all of the well-known limitations of garnering valid and reliable data about crime in general.

2. Statistically, rape is a relatively infrequent offense. Of those acts regarded as major offenses, only "murder" and "non-negligent manslaughter" occur less often.

3. Rape is a highly personal and unorganized offense. There is little likelihood of gathering participant observation data[55] or acquiring information from active participants, informers or "plants" as has been the case with organized crime, the drug culture, and many kinds of property offenses.

4. The legalistic definitions of "forcible" and "statutory" often make it difficult to determine which kind of rape has occurred or whether rape has occurred at all.[56]

5. Rapists as well as their victims are reluctant to discuss the act, especially when it has not already been officially reported. Even known rapes may go unprosecuted because of the victim's reluctance to press charges and bear witness.

6. Rapists sometimes plead guilty to a lesser offense such as simple assault, or otherwise evade the charge. It is possible and perhaps likely that rape is less frequently reported to the police than some other types of crime. The effect is for known crimes, arrests, prosecutions, convictions and penalties to be lower for rape than for crimes comparable in occurrence but whose victims are more prone to see the case through.[57]

7. Rape, like homosexuality, falls into that category of lurid crime which is usually discussed in a circumspect manner and which may also arouse doubts as to the motives of the investigator.

Many benefits could accrue from further inquiry about rape. A better understanding of the motivation to commit rape would probably result in fewer victims. The task of the police, courts and penal system in their investigation, prosecution and rehabilitation of the offender would also be made easier. Furthermore, legislatures would be able to work on more enlightened and less emotional bases. Finally, the adjustment of the rape victim to the social and psychological stress caused by rape would be facilitated.

NOTES

1. The way in which the public, through its attitudes and actions, influences the treatment and punishment afforded sex offenders was discussed in Falk, "The Public Image of the Sex Offender," 48 *Mental Hygiene* 612 (1964). Falk concludes that the urban middle class is most influential in disseminating attitudes toward sex offenders; that mass communication surveys these attitudes; that fear and hysteria surround sexual issues in the United States; that sex criminality is exaggerated; that the laws which attempt to regulate sexual conduct fail to do so; that a gradual trend is evident from punishment to treatment.
2. B. Karpman, *The Sexual Offender and His Offenses* 12 (1954) [hereinafter cited as Karpman].
3. Id.
4. Id.
5. Bornstein, "Investigation of Rape: Medicolegal Problems," 9 *Med. Trial Tech. Q.* 61 (March 1963). In statutory rape, age is the salient criterion; force is not a primary issue even when it accompanies the act.
6. *American Law Institute, Model Penal Code* (Proposed Draft 1962).
7. *Sex Habits of American Men: A Symposium on the Kinsey Report* 25 (A. Deutsch ed. 1948).
8. Karpman at 12, 27.
9. Id. at 12.
10. All UCR "serious" crimes except murder and aggravated assault showed a greater relative increase during the same period.
11. This may be similar to the phenomenon that citizens reported more prowlers than usual when a mysterious "gasser" was believed to be at large. Johnson, "The 'Phantom Anesthetist' of Matoon: A Field Study of Mass Hysteria," 40 *Abnormal & Social Psychology* 175 (1945).
12. Amir, "Forcible Rape" in *Deviance* 67, 69 (S. Dinitz, R. Dynes, A. Clarke eds. 1969).
13. Erlanson, "Scene of a Sex Offense as Related to the Residence of the Offender," 31 *J. Crim. L. & C.* 339 (1940).
14. Id.
15. Amir, supra note 12, at 69.
16. Id. at 71.
17. Id.

18. Amir identifies five phases in the process and characteristics of the rape situation. Id. at 70.
19. Id. at 71.
20. Id.
21. Id.
22. Id. at 71–72.
23. Id. at 72–73.
24. Id. at 73.
25. Karpman at 39, maintains that sex offenses involving force are more prominent among youthful offenders, especially during rape.
26. Amir, supra note 12, at 73–74.
27. New York Mayor's Committee Reports on the Study of Sex Offenses (1943).
28. Guttmacher & Weihofer, "Sex Offenses," 43 *J. Crim. L.C. & P.S.* 78 (1953).
29. Amir, supra note 12, at 68.
30. *Federal Bureau of Prisons, National Prison Statistics* No. 20 (1959).
31. Karpman at 33.
32. Id. at 33–34.
33. See Rothenberg & Steffens, "Rape Victim," 73 *Am. Mercury* 78 (1951).
34. Karpman at 28.
35. Gillin, "Social Backgrounds of Sex Offenders and Murderers," 14 *Social Forces* 288 (1935).
36. Caldwell, "Personality Trends in the Youthful Male Offender," 49 *J. Crim. L.C. & P.S.* 413 (1959). Prision populations generally fall within the normal range on I.Q. tests, although federal prision populations are an exception because of the select nature of the inmates. Federal inmates tend to have higher than average I.Q.'s. However, since I.Q. tests in general are affected by superficial factors in the testing situation and suffer from other problems of meaning and interpretation, I.Q. scores may be of limited use in understanding the rapist.
37. The study is summarized at 42 *Science Digest* 22 (Sept. 1957).
38. Brancale, "Psychiatric and Psychological Investigations of Convicted Sex Offenders: A Summary Report," 109 *Am. J. Psychiatry* 18 (1952).
39. Hammer & Glueck, "Psychodynamic Patterns in Sex Offenders: A Four-Factor Theory," 31 *Psychiatric Q.* 327 (1957).
40. Id. at 329.
41. Id. at 337. A similar interpretation is set forth in Roth, "Factors in the Motivation of Sexual Offenders," 42 *J. Crim. L.C. & P.S.* (1952).
42. Karpman at 38.
43. Pascal & Harzberg, "The Detection of Deviant Sexual Practice from Performance on the Rorschach Test," 16 *J. Projective Techniques* 370 (1962).
44. Karpman at 347.
45. Palm & Abrahmsen, "A Rorschach Study of the Wives of Sex Offenders," 119 *J. Mental Disorder* 167 (1954).
46. Id. at 168–70.
47. Id. at 170–71.
48. Gillin, supra note 35.

49. Karpman at 37. Other accounts of female rape offenders are given in *Juvenile Offenders for a Thousand Years* (W. Sanders ed. 1970), and Gebhard & Gagnon, "Male Sex Offenders Against Very Young Children," 121 *Am J. Psychiatry* 576 (1964).
50. Amir, supra note 12, at 74, classified 19 per cent of the cases he studied as victim-precipitated. It should be noted that the literature on forensic medicine is much concerned with techniques whereby the truth of an alleged rape can be determined.
51. See, e.g., Factor, "A Woman's Psychological Reaction to Attempted Rape," 23 *Psychoanalytic Q*. 243 (1954).
52. Weiss, "A Study of Girl Sex Victims," 29 *Psychological Q*. 1 (1955).
53. Id. at 25–27.
54. It may well be that information derived from cross-cultural studies can assist our understanding of rape in America. Suggestive hypotheses have come from Robert LeVine's anthropological study of the Gusii in southwest Kenya. Rape rates in that culture were relatively high: 4,712 per 100,000 population between 1955 and 1956. (In the U.S. for this same period the ratio was 13.85 per 100,000 urban and 13.1 per 100,000 rural residents.) LeVine suggested that "four factors should be regarded as necessary but not sufficient for rapes:"
    1. Severe formal restrictions on the nonmarital sexual relations of females;
    2. Moderately strong sexual inhibitions on the part of females;
    3. Barriers to marriage prolonging the bachelorhood of some males into their late twenties;
    4. Absence of physical segregation of the sexes.

    Notably absent from these factors are the psychological concerns so prominent in the U.S. literature. LeVine, "Gusii Sex Offenses: A Study in Social Control," 61 *Am. Anthropologist* 965 (1959).
55. An exception is Connell, "Notes from the Diary of a Rapist," in *Mirror of Man* 58–64 (J. Dabaghian ed. 1970).
56. This is also true in other Western societies. In 1911 Thoinat estimated that in France, from 60 to 80 percent of the accusations of sex crimes were recognized as unfounded. For every real case of rape brought to trial in England there were at least twelve false accusations. Karpman at 211.
57. A paradox is evident here in that a Committee on Uniform Crime Reporting saw fit to include forcible rape as a Type 1 offense on the ground that these are the most likely to be reported to the police.

17

Alcoholism and the Child Molester

Richard T. Rada, M.D.

Reprinted from *Annals of the New York Academy of Sciences: Work in Progress on Alcoholism* 273 (1976):492–96, by permission of the author and the New York Academy of Sciences.

INTRODUCTION

Although considerable attention has been given to the problem of the sex offender in our society, little study has been given to the problem of a relationship between alcohol and the commission of sexual offenses. Several studies, [1,2] however, have indicated a high association between child molesting and drinking at the time of the commission of the offense, and one[2] reports an alcoholism rate of 28%. The relationship between drinking, alcoholism, and child molesting has important implications not only for etiology and diagnosis but for the subsequent long-term treatment of the pedophilic sex offender.

The purpose of this paper is to present data on 203 pedophilic sex offenders committed to Atascadero State Hospital for child molesting. The data will include demographic data, drinking at the time of the commission of the offense (and if so, whether heavily, moderately, or lightly) and an alcoholism rating based on the Michigan Alcoholism Screening Test (MAST) devised by Seltzer.[3] In addition to the total group, data will be presented on three subgroups of the child molester based on the sex of the victim; namely child molesters offending a female subject, those offending a male subject and those offending both sexes, called an ambisexual group.

PATIENT POPULATION AND DATA COLLECTION

The California state program for the treatment of mentally disordered sex offenders was initiated with the opening of Atascadero State Hospital in 1954. At any one time there are approximately 500 inmates with the diagnosis of mentally disordered sex offender of whom approximately 40 to 60 percent are classified as child molesters. The others include those committed for rape, statutory rape, incest, exhibitionism and other sex offenses. In general, the child molester in Atascadero State Hospital has committed a non-violent sexual offense other than sexual intercourse with a child under the age of 14 years.

After completing an informed consent form, 405 mentally disordered sex offenders of all types completed a questionnaire of basic demographic data including whether they were drinking at the time of the commission of the offense, and if so, whether heavily, moderately or lightly. Heavily is defined as 10 or more beers or the equivalent, moderately, 5–9 beers and lightly, under 5 beers. Subjects also completed the 25-question Michigan Alcoholism Screening Test devised by Seltzer. The 405 subjects comprised over 80% of the total sex offenders in the hospital population at that time. Two hundred and three were child molesters and comprise the study population for this report.

RESULTS

Of these 203 child molesters, 108 (53%) were female molesters, 82 (40%) male molesters and 13 (7%) ambisexual molesters. The age range for the total group was 18 to 69 years with a mean of 35.2 years. The racial breakdown was Caucasian 85%, Indian 7%, Black 5%, and Spanish-American 3%. Religious preference showed Protestant 62%, Catholic 18%, Jewish .5% and other 20%. The mean education level for the group was approximately the 11th grade. There were little differences in age, race, religious preference, and education between the three subgroups of child molesters. Marital status, however, showed a definite difference between the three groups. Table 17.1 shows the marital status statistics for the total group and for the three subgroups of child molesters. Forty-one percent of all child molesters were single; but 57% of the male child molesters were single whereas only 28% of the female child molesters were single. It is nevertheless interesting to note that 43% of the male child molesters had been married at some time in their lives. This statistic at least suggests that a homosexual object, whether

TABLE 17.1.
MARITAL STATUS OF CHILD MOLESTERS

Marital Status	Total Group	Male Molesters	Female Molesters	Ambisexual Molesters
Single	41%	57%	28%	38%
Married	27%	15%	36%	31%
Separated	9%	10%	9%	8%
Divorced	20%	13%	26%	23%
Widower	3%	5%	1%	0%

TABLE 17.2.
PERCENTAGE DATCO* AND AMOUNT

Degree of Drinking	Total Group	Female Molesters	Male Molesters	Ambisexual Molesters
DATCO	49%	57%†	38%	54%
Heavily	34%	43%	25%	23%
Moderately	10%	10%	7%	23%
Lightly	5%	4%	6%	8%

*DATCO—Drinking at the time of commission of offense.
†Difference between Female-Male molesters significant at 0.025 level.

child or adult, was not the exclusive sexual preference for all the child molesters of male victims.

Table 17.2 presents the percentage drinking at the time of the commission of the offense and if so, the percentage drinking heavily, moderately or lightly. Forty-nine percent of the total group were drinking at the time of the commission of the offense of whom 34% were drinking heavily. Fifty-seven percent of the female child molesters were drinking at the time of the commission of the offense as opposed to 54% of the ambisexual molesters and 38% of the male molesters. The difference between the female molesters and male molesters is significant at the .025 level. Another way of looking at this data is to note that if the subject were drinking at all at the time of the commission of the offense there was a 70% chance that he would be drinking heavily.

Table 17.3 gives the percentage alcoholism rate based on results from the Michigan Alcoholism Screening Test. In Seltzer's original scoring of his 25-question screening test he states that a score of 5 or above can be considered to be alcoholic. For purposes of this study only subjects who scored 7 or above on the MAST were rated as alcoholic. On that basis, 52% of the total group are classified as alcoholic. Percentage for the subgroups were: female molesters 58%, ambisexual molesters 54% and male molesters 44%. The difference in alcoholism rate between the female and male molesters shows a strong trend but does not reach statistical significance.

Pokorny et al.[4] have recently presented a report in which they took 10 questions from the Michigan Alcoholism Screening Test and developed a brief version of the MAST. In this report they showed that there was a very high correlation between the alcoholism rate found on the MAST and the alcoholism rate found on the 10 selected questions from the MAST. Table 17.3 shows the difference, however, between the alcoholism rate as measured by the total 25 question MAST and the Pokorny Shortened Version of the MAST for this population. The Brief MAST shows a 33% alcoholism rate with 38% for the female child molester, 25% for the male child molester and 46% for the ambisexual. I believe that the Brief MAST is a more stringent screening test for alcoholism than the MAST, which accounts for the different alcoholism rates between the two. Nevertheless, whether one accepts the Pokorny Shortened Version or the Michigan Alcoholism Screening Test, the alcoholism rate for the group is considerable.

To further illustrate the effect of alcohol on this population, the positive response by the total group to various questions on the MAST will be presented. Thirty-five percent have been previously arrested for drunk behavior; 26% have been arrested for drunk driving; 17% had sought professional help for an emotional problem in which drinking had played a part; 17% had experienced delirium tremens or severe withdrawal symptoms; and 8% had been told that they had liver trouble or cirrhosis. Question number 10 states, "Have you gotten into fights when drinking?" This is the only question on the MAST directly related to violence. Forty-one percent of the group (a group generally considered to be nonviolent) admitted to having gotten into fights when drinking.

DISCUSSION

The data in this study suggest a high association between drinking, alcoholism and child molestation. The finding of nearly 50% drinking at the time of the commission of the offense suggests that alcohol may play an important role in the commission of these offenses. Swanson[2,5] has pointed out the necessity for differentiating between pedophilia (the morbid sexual interest in children which implies a predictable personality structure) and the

TABLE 17.3.
ALCOHOLISM RATE BY SCREENING TEST

Screening Test	Total	Male Molesters	Female Molesters	Ambisexual
Michigan Alcoholism Screening Test (MAST)	52%	44%	58%	54%
Brief MAST (Pokorny Shortened Version)	33%	25%	38%	46%

child molester, the individual who has committed a sexual offense against children. He suggests that labeling all child molesters as pedophiliacs tends to underestimate the importance of the circumstances such as conflict with or loss of a suitable adult partner, availability of a passive if not willing victim, and the heavy use of alcohol. In a previous study[6] the author reported that rapists also showed a high association between drinking and the commission of violent sexual crimes. Nevertheless, it is my clinical view that the rapist does not drink to lower his inhibitions but rather to increase his sense of confidence and power prior to the commission of the offense.[7] In the case of the child molester, however, I believe the use of alcohol does lower his inhibitions and facilitates the commission of an offense much less likely in the sober state. An interesting and unexplained finding is the statistically significant difference between the male child molester and the female child molester. I have no clearcut understanding to account for this difference but offer the following speculation: female child molesters frequently view themselves as healthy in terms of their heterosexual orientation and use many rationalizations for their pedophilic interests or offenses. It may well be, however, that the male child molester with a more predominantly homosexual orientation already views himself as deviant. As a result, he may not have as great a need to use alcohol to facilitate engaging in a further sexual deviance. The female child molester, on the other hand, may be inclined to use alcohol to dull the inhibitions and moral judgment which even his rationalizations cannot completely quiet.

Whether one accepts the findings of the Michigan Alcoholism Screening Test or the Brief MAST, an alcoholism rate of either 33% or 52% is exceedingly high. For many of these alcoholics, child molestation is just one of a number of indices of the social maladjustment secondary to the chronic deteriorating effects of long-term alcoholism. As their alcoholism removes them further and further from acceptable and potential adult sexual objects, the willing or at least passive early pubescent victim becomes an attractive sexual outlet. In addition, the impotence[8] frequently associated with pedophilic offenders is exacerbated by the long-term effects of alcohol[9] and again undoubtedly prompts the type of regressed sexual contact such as fondling and oral genital contact to which the offender gravitates. The finding of eight percent cirrhosis of the liver in this population also suggests a possible biological factor contributing to a more regressed sexual behavior. Cirrhosis has been shown to be associated with a decrease in the plasma testosterone level, the male sex hormones.[10] It may very well be that in a certain number of these subjects a lowered plasma testosterone level may contribute to decreased libido and more primitive forms of sexual expression. In a recent study examining the plasma testosterone level in rapists and child molesters, the author found a lower mean plasma testosterone level in the child molester as compared with a normal population or the rapist group. Although this lowered level did not reach statistical significance, it does suggest further study of the potential biological mechanisms involved in the behavioral expression of certain deviances.

This study adds to the growing list of antisocial behaviors associated with drinking and a history of alcoholism. If long-term treatment programs are to be effective, the child molester will need ongoing treatment not only for his sexual deviance but also for his addiction-proneness. For example, in a study of patterns of drinking by offenders before their commitment and after discharge to the community, those labeled problem drinkers showed an actual increase in drinking following discharge despite specific legal prohibition against any drinking.[1] At present, most treatment programs tend to focus on one aspect of the problem or the other which suggests that even the best currently available follow-up care may be inadequate.

Summary

This study shows a high association between drinking, alcoholism and child molestation. Forty-nine percent of the child molesters were drinking at the time of the commission of the offense and 34% were drinking heavily, defined as 10 or more beers or the equivalent. The alcoholism rate for the group was 52% using the Michigan Alcoholism Screening Test or 33% using the more stringent Pokorny Shortened Version of the MAST. An interesting and unexpected finding was a statistically significant lower incidence of drinking at the time of the commission of the offense in male child molesters compared with female child molesters. In addition the male child molesters had a definitely lower alcoholism rate compared with female child molesters. The importance of these findings for treatment programs is emphasized.

Acknowledgements

The author thanks Drs. Richard Laws and Al Rucci, Atascadero State Hospital, Atascadero, Calif., for valuable assistance.

Notes

1. Frisbie, L. V.: *Another Look at Sex Offenders in California*. Research Monograph No. 12, Sacramento, California, Department of Mental Hygiene, 1969, p. 196.
2. Swanson, D. W.: Adult Sexual Abuse of Children. *Dis. Nerv. Syst. 29*:677, 1968.
3. Seltzer, M.: The Michigan Alcoholism Screening Test: The Quest For a New Diagnostic Instrument. *Am. J. Psychiat. 127*:1653, 1971.
4. Pokorny, A. K., Miller, B. A. and Kaplan, H. B.: The Brief MAST: A Shortened Version of The Michigan Alcoholism Screening Test. *Am. J. Psychiat. 129*:342, 1972.

5. Swanson, D. W.: Who Violates Children Sexually? *Med. Aspects Human Sexuality* 5:184, 1971.
6. Rada, R. T.: Alcoholism and Forcible Rape. *Am. J. Psychiat.* April, 1975 (In Press).
7. Rada, R. T.: Alcohol and Rape. *Med. Aspects of Human Sexuality.* (To be published).
8. Bowman, K. M.: The Problem of the Sex Offender. *Am. J. Psychiat. 108*:250, 1951.
9. Lemere, F. and Smith, J. W.: Alcohol-Induced Sexual Impotence. *Am. J. Psychiat. 130*:212, 1973.
10. Galvao-Teles, A., Anderson, D. C., Burke, C. W., Marshall, J. C., Corker, C. S., Bown, R. L. and Clark, M. L.: Biologically Active Androgens and Oestradiol in Men with Chronic Liver Disease. *Lancet 1*:173, 1973.

18

Lifestyles Among Heroin Users

Virginia Lewis and
Daniel Glaser, Ph.D.

Reprinted from *Federal Probation* (March 1974), pp. 21–28, by permission of the publisher, The Administrative Office of the United States Courts.

Social separation produces cultural differentiation. This basic law of sociology and anthropology accounts for the dramatic language, dress, and eating differences among peoples largely separated from each other, for example, France and Japan. It also explains subcultures, those variations of group custom and belief that occur within large societies. Among the Federal offenders committed under the National Addict Rehabilitation Act (NARA) to the Los Angeles area we found not one homogeneous drug culture but several, all apparently the consequences of social separation.

The first author has in the past 5 years interviewed nearly all the approximately 150 persons released from the Federal Correctional Institution at Terminal Island to NARA aftercare in and around Los Angeles. She has seen many of them repeatedly, at scattered locations, with close rapport indicated by their frequently revealing information to her that might have penalized them had she divulged it to others. The second author has been a part-time participant and consultant in those followup studies for about 2 years. Statistics presented here are rough estimates tabulated from subsamples.

From this endeavor there gradually emerged a recognition of five rather distinct lifestyles among the subjects, which we call: (1) Expressive Student; (2) Social World Alternator; (3) Low-Rider; (4) Barrio Addict; and (5) Ghetto Hustler. The first two categories come mainly from middle or upper class socioeconomic backgrounds, and the last three from working class or even extremely impoverished homes, although there are exceptions within each group. That is why those in the last three categories are often called "low-lifers" by themselves and others. The Barrio Addicts are mostly Mexican-American and the Ghetto Addicts mostly Black but there are a few white "Anglo" women in each of these groups. The Social World Alternators were very mixed ethnically, but the Expressive Students were exclusively white, and the Low-Riders were almost all white.

Questioning and observation revealed that with the exception of Social World Alternators, members of each of these groups usually do not mingle extensively or intimately with those in the other groups, either when in correctional institutions or when in the community. There is some shifting from one group to another, but only over an extended period of time, so that very few of the NARA cases in the Los Angeles area are difficult to classify into one of these five categories.

EXPRESSIVE STUDENTS

This group has variations of what used to be called the "hippie" lifestyle. They all share some form of intellectual or quasi-intellectual "counter-culture." They argue for alternative marital arrangements on moral grounds, for being "at one with nature" through "living off the land," for being "free of the 9 to 5 routine," and for gaining new types of aesthetic experience. We call them "students," regardless of their academic status, because of their orientation to learning, to searching for new forms of understanding or appreciation.

The Expressive Students were especially adept at rationalizing their previous drug use, even after they asserted no further interest in it. For example, a man with a degree in psychology before his NARA incarceration and currently a graduate student said that he told himself his use of heroin was experimental, to study dreams, because heroin produced a state of "waking sleep." Actually, most members of this group seemed to become involved in heavy drug use less deliberately than their rationalizations suggest.

Expressive Students usually started heroin use by "chipping"—using a small amount on a somewhat regular basis—instead of "getting strung out"—using heavily enough to become psychologically dependent on opiate use because its cessation gives them withdrawal sickness. Many developed a third pattern that we call "episodic use"—taking heroin heavily but only on widely scattered occasions, months or even years apart. When initial heavy use resulted in withdrawal discomforts, those who had these symptoms but got over them without more opiates nevertheless went back to heavy heroin use rather than chipping, to regain the feeling of extreme narcoticization. One observed that chipping produces a "good" but not a "great" feeling, and that heroin users "do not know the feeling they're after until they've been there" (experienced it).

Thus addiction among the Expressive Students seems to be a consequence of participation in a social milieu with heroin frequently available and any drug use acceptable. Some smuggled or traded in marihuana and other drugs, and thereby had opportunity periodically to get heroin at low cost. This contributed to their using it rather than drugs less accessible to them at the moment, as the following case indicates: "The first time I tried it was

1960. I was 18 years old. Only once. In the next few years I tried it several more times. At that time none of it affected me since I wasn't relating to seeing the consequences of being addicted. It never affected me until I started smuggling grass in my boat from Mexico around 1966. More into it for the excitement than the money, I used money from the grass to buy some heroin. I started dealing this to make money and shooting dope around the same time. My sister was living with me at that time and I think both of us just decided to do it—see, we'd been involved with it over the years but never addicted. Both of us felt, well, it might be a bad thing if we didn't have any money, but we had a lotta money. That is, for about 6 months. Then we ran out, and took to the streets, the downhill road. By the time I got busted, I didn't have a friend in the world. I had burned everyone out."

The Expressive Students were all in their late teens or early twenties at the time of their heaviest heroin use, and all were under 30 when seen on NARA aftercare. About three-fourths remained completely abstinent after their release from the NARA program in the Federal Correctional Institution at Terminal Island, and the remainder are known to have used drugs but did not become readdicted. Only one was a clear "failure" on aftercare, having been convicted for sale of heroin to a state narcotics agent. Several of the successful releasees are now self-employed: One owns a fishing boat, another works as a waterbed maker, a third is a musician. The last two also go to college part-time. Two work as paraprofessionals in drug programs.

Rehabilitation of Expressive Students seems to result in large part through a series of traumatic experiences alienating them from the heroin-using world. This is illustrated by the following account: "I would have stopped no matter what. Any prison you would have sent me, I would have stopped. See, I decided before I went to jail to stop, but I didn't know how. I tried to kick in Mexico for 9 days, but couldn't. In fact, I decided to get busted when I crossed the border. I had gone through some really traumatic stuff before this. Also, right before I went to Mexico I bought a sailboat with $7,500 I'd ripped off. I lost the sailboat. I went down to Mexico with a guy on the boat, thinking I'd kick on board. I couldn't and one night he just sailed off without me. I lost a lot of things behind dope. A wife and family, a girlfriend, a boat. I'll never forget when she died. I called an ambulance. The cops came and hassled me a lot. About 10 minutes after they left, I started crying like I couldn't stop. Probably this is why I'll never shoot it again."

Many of the Expressive Students were especially rejected by others in the institutional setting, and were ridiculed because of their ideological or philosophical interests. Frequently other inmates and some of the custodial staff were highly critical of their reading tastes, unconventional attitudes toward sexuality or business, or in some instances what was seen as their sloppiness and lack of cleanliness. Other inmates complained that "the dirty hippies smell." Expressive Students, on the other hand, complained that many prisoners "played foolish games," resorted to violence or threats of violence to get their way, and were indiscriminately loyal to their own ethnic groups. For the Expressive Students more than for other prisoners, incarceration was a highly unpleasant experience, often perceived as life-threatening.

The intellectuality of some psychotherapeutic programs was especially appealing to many Expressive Students. Both the antidrug-use obligations and the associations that participation in these programs fostered appeared to be rehabilitative for this group. One reports: "In the joint I was a loner at first. I was reading a lot; psychology, Eastern Philosophy, Buddhism, Jung, Freud, Adler. I met a counselor there who was interested in me. I told him my ideas on revolutionary life-styles. He listened but didn't agree. Most people who rebel are rebelling against themselves. He helped me a lot. The groups at that time were very undynamic. Several of us got together and developed a core group and then several months later a TA (Transactional Analysis) therapist came in. We were dedicated to learning about ourselves and pledged to pull each other's covers. It got very intense. Then I went on school release . . . I see a lot of these people that were in the groups with me, and I see the counselor who helped me and we support each other. I'm still very lonely. I didn't know anybody from Long Beach when I was first released. Since I've been out, I've experienced a lot of pain and depression. My job helps. At the clinic (where he works as a paraprofessional counselor) I have a few intimate friends and I've been teaching classes there, in TA. Been getting good feedback."

In this, as in other cases, it is significant that inmates sympathetic with rehabilitation objectives help each other when on aftercare. They give each other support in coping with personal problems and checking each other's occasional inclination towards resuming heroin use. While there is much evidence that many on NARA aftercare who became readdicted obtained heroin from other NARA clients, it is clearly the quality of the association which is symptomatic, rather than the mere fact of association among releasees. Indeed, lack of a sense of social support in the community outside of drug-using groups seems to have been a factor in prior failures of some Expressive Students in other treatment programs before their NARA experience. The secure rehabilitation of ex-addicts appears to require their developing a multiplicity of positive social resources, and their being kept from feeling completely rejected in the new relationships should they have some disagreements there.

SOCIAL WORLD ALTERNATORS

Subjects were included in this category if their life histories suggested movement back and forth among social worlds with sharply contrasting expectations and activities. They had learned several alternative roles in life, each acquired as a temporary expedient to meet the contingencies of their momentary situation. A prototype of this group is the 39-year-old Black man, the son of a Texas minister, who came to Los Angeles in 1959 where he has since been a ghetto street hustler, a pimp, the area campaign manager of a prominent white political candidate, a dealer-addict, and a paraprofessional in addiction therapy. Another, a 27-year-old white from Los Angeles, is bisexual, an accomplished writer and poet, was an award-winning university student film maker. He became involved with heroin while making a film on motorcycle gangs, then stole rare art books from museums and libraries to support his opiate habit.

Social World Alternators are about 40 percent white, 40 percent Black, and 20 percent Chicano. Their mean age on aftercare is 31, and about a quarter are women. Their drug use patterns are highly diverse, with only about half using heroin predominantly, and a few claiming never to have experienced severe withdrawal symptoms. About a quarter used cocaine. Their chipping and eventual addiction usually occurred during periods when they were with drug-using criminal groups—narcotics dealers, thieves, or prostitutes.

The pattern of drug involvement by Social World Alternators is illustrated by one whom we shall call "Mike." Though a "delinquent teenage tough," he was from a well-to-do family but had grown up and gone to school with several future members of a group well known to the police. He first tried heroin at 17, but after his return from military service at 21 he took a responsible well-paying job, married, had two children and even "attended church occasionally." He also led something of a double life, since he still sometimes associated with his former friends. When job pressures and marital difficulties developed, Mike quit his job, left his family, and rejoined the "police character" groups. He began chipping, burglarized some drug and grocery stores, and wrote bad checks. This was more for excitement than for financial need, he claims, but he continued for a year and a half before his forgeries brought a 3-year incarceration in a state penitentiary. In prison, he became a trusty and thereby controlled prisoner-visitor exchanges to a considerable degree, which allowed him to obtain heroin fairly readily through bargaining with other prisoners. It was there that he first became addicted. When released from the institution, Mike was "strung out," reentered the criminal world, and remained addicted until he was charged with a Federal offense and received the NARA commitment.

The Social World Alternators participated in crime–oriented groups before and during their period of heroin use. About two-thirds have remained relatively drug-free on aftercare and have not resumed criminal roles. About half, however, have engaged in episodic heroin use without starting a pattern of chipping and without becoming readdicted. They apparently "slipped into" chipping or episodic use in conjunction with seeing old friends or attending parties where heroin was available. This reflects their adaptability to the expectations of whatever social situation they happen to be in. About a quarter have not used heroin at all and about a quarter have become read-dicted.

None of the Social World Alternators has low-status employment on aftercare. One, a script-writer, received local publicity for a drama he wrote and produced for network television. Another received recognition as a paraprofessional addiction therapist and became an administrator of a narcot-ics prevention program. Several others in this group currently are para-professional therapists, a role for which they are particularly well-suited because of their communication skills with persons of diverse background. Several are enrolled in local universities.

Firm rehabilitation of the Social World Alternators appears frequently to be a consequence of their perception of severe risks in heroin use or in association with heroin users. One almost died of a kidney ailment and was impressed with his health risk in drug use. Another described a sojourn into his former social world, while on aftercare, as a turning point alienating him from drug-takers: "I went and got it (heroin). After not having it for such a long time, I wanted to know what it was like. I had always known I would fix one more time before I die. Everything was going good, my life, I had a job, money, and I just wanted to fix again. See if the feeling was really that good. It wasn't. The whole experience was traumatic. I cried. I could see myself getting right back into it again. I was really depressed afterward for a week and then I went and fixed again, and not since. (Why?) The first time, I couldn't relate to why I was feeling so bad the first time, so I went to fix again. The second time was really a funky scene with scuffy types and they started arguing about dope. I could stand back and look at the scene and see how funky it was. I even had a batch to take home with me and then I threw it out the window on the way home. I knew I had to try it again, and I did. Since then I've been clean."

"Scott," another Social World Alternator, received paraprofessional train-ing at Terminal Island, in which he had to conduct group therapy sessions for fellow inmates. During a heated argument a member of his group asked, while staff were present: "Do you believe I've been using (heroin) in here?" Scott angrily replied: "Yes," thereby violating an inmate code of silence, and after lights out he was beaten by several members of an inmate clique. This acquisition of a "snitch jacket," as the inmates call it, prevented his associat-ing with most inmates, and forced him to cultivate the friendship of staff and of those inmates least criminally oriented. While he had at first engaged in the therapy training primarily as a means of getting out early, he soon found that it provided his only social life in the institution and his most promising postrelease opportunity. He immediately obtained a paraprofessional job on release, but he says his therapy clients know that he now can influence decisions on whether or not to return them as parole or aftercare violators, so if he himself were returned to the institution his life would be threatened by inmates intent on revenge.

Our observations suggest that Social World Alternators are the type most successful in paraprofessional roles, because of their skills in communication. Their lack of close cohesion with other addicts, however, especially with "low-lifers," may impair their ability to recruit other addicts to therapy groups; yet those of the "low-lifer" groups who recruit successfully may not learn to perform well as paraprofessionals, at least as judged by the professionals. Regardless of type, the paraprofessional gradually becomes a marginal man, accepted and at ease neither in the addict world nor the "square" world. Frequently those acquiring this role in the institution "place all their eggs in one basket" and will accept no other employment, but often their expectations of a therapy job and of joy at it are highly unrealistic. It may be that explicit presentation of the paraprofessional job as a stepping-stone would maximize its rehabilitative value. Future role incumbents could be informed that in performing the role, they are acquiring skills useful in other less stressful types of legitimate careers, which they should be encouraged to explore while given security in the therapist employment.

LOW-RIDERS

The term "Low-Rider" is used by Terminal Island inmates to designate peers who assume a defiant stance with persons in authority, and who walk, talk, and dress in a rather aggressive and provocative manner. This behavior frequently is designed to intimidate either the unwise, other Low-Riders, or persons of other subcultures, particularly middle-class "Squares." Originally the term "Low-Rider" was applied mainly to older juveniles, but currently it is used also for persons ranging well into their middle thirties. It is synonymous in some respects to the label "greaser," a term originally applied by Anglos to Chicanos, but now losing ethnic connotations.

Motorcycle gang members fall into this category, as do Anglo neighborhood street gang members. They share with the Barrio and Ghetto "lowlifers" the prominent activity of "high rolling." This is the spending of a large amount of money for material goods, or for an evening "on the town," in one grand gesture, and in a manner suggesting that this is their usual behavior, when in fact it is a special occasion. The customary activity in these three lifestyles is "hanging out," that is, idling at a particular eating or drinking place, such as a hot dog stand or a bar which peers frequent. They wait in these places for "something to happen," for some excitement accessible for participation or observation, such as a fight, the appearance of a hostile gang, or "shooting dope" (usually "speed," cocaine or heroin).

Two salient differences between Low-Riders and the Barrio or Ghetto drug subcultures are a lesser cohesiveness among the Low-Riders and an earlier age of "pulling-up"—reducing or terminating their commitment to this lifestyle. Both features reflect the greater occupational opportunities for whites than for minorities in the square world.

About three fourths of the Low-Riders are male, all are Caucasian and their mean age on aftercare is about 30. An appreciable fraction are of Italian descent, mostly migrants from New York. They often claim ties with the "Mafia," probably more to exploit its reputation than because of actual association with Mafiosi. Although reared in working-class homes, about half the Low-Riders had extremely unstable family experiences. For example, one woman, repeatedly diagnosed as schizophrenic, ran away from her Brooklyn home at 13, hitch-hiked to California, and whenever not confined in the next 18 years lived with various "old man" protectors or procurers. Several grew up in orphanages, most were mainly in one-parent households, most have juvenile court records, and about 40 percent were in correctional or mental health institutions as juveniles. Most had not completed high school, but had a variety of short-term manual employment jobs, such as spray-painter, machinist's helper, waitress, truck driver, and carpenter.

Involvement of Low-Riders with drugs occurred on the basis of social expectation in the groups with which they "hung out." One reports: "I grew up in a traditional Italian neighborhood in Brooklyn. At 14, I left school and got into hanging out, smoking grass and stuff, meeting groovy people. I thought, 'Wow, these people are beautiful.' So, when the heroin came around I wasn't frightened—it was a part of the scene." A female Low-Rider relates: "I started using uppers around people at school (at 14). I've always been with the 'worst' crowd, according to straight people, I don't know why. I've always been opposite though. About 50 percent of the people I was with as a kid ended up having trouble with the law, not necessarily around drugs. When I first used heroin I only knew two guys who used. I was alone at the house a lot and they brought the stuff over."

While their initial drug use was diverse, about two-thirds of the Low-Riders later used heroin exclusively, and about a third became readdicted on aftercare. Most return to their pre-NARA types of intermittent employment, and long for the comaraderie and excitement of their drug-using groups. "Tony," a Low-Rider from New York but arrested in California for drug smuggling, eventually became an enthusiastic participant in the therapeutic program at Terminal Island. He was released daily to attend a local college, which he continued when placed on aftercare, but he explains his subsequent failure as follows: "I was living by myself. I'd learned how to recognize the signs I was going to start to use, so I kept myself super busy. School, work, no recreation. Sort of overcompensating, trying for terrific grades. Somehow I tied the two together—good grades, no heroin. I had 3.8 on school release and wanted to continue. I didn't know anyone except for those from the joint, so I stayed alone a lot. I was lonely. This is why I started using again. Stupid. I went to give a urinalysis and ran into an old partner of mine. He was stoned and I got some stuff, a spur of the moment thing. Hadn't planned to use. Nothing different about the day. It just fell before me and I couldn't resist. Almost immediately I got into it again. Started stealing to get the money for dope."

Tony's case suggests the need for intensive attention to the involvement of relocators in gratifying new social relationships. Those who transfer have the advantage of separation from their former drug-using associates. But if they are at their new locations without close ties to relatives or friends who do not use drugs, when extremely lonely they readily renew intimacy with drug users. The latter prospect is enhanced by the inevitable association of the abstinent with the readdicted at supervision offices, which is one of many factors in the superiority of field to office contacts of supervisors with clients, despite the greater costs of field contacts.

Some Low-Riders seem simply to have found steadier gratification from life as addicts than from any conventional alternatives they have experienced or can perceive as accessible. "Janet," a 37-year-old Low-Rider, says: "I was first strung out in 1961–62. See, my husband got out of the joint. Things were O.K. for a while. But he got busted for sales—grass—and was in jail 3 or 4 months. I was pregnant and depressed. Lost all our money fighting the case. I got strung out. Always before, he had gotten the dope. I left him after he got out because he wouldn't let me use. See, I use cause I like to use. I've said this to you before, you know. They could lock me up the rest of my life and as long as I got my dope every day, I'd be fine." Her various romantic liaisons have always been with addicts, and she remarked during an interview: "Well, you know I've been around dopers so long I can't communicate with lames." She was readdicted on aftercare. Clearly, her NARA programs have not fostered a change from the addict lifestyle, and fear of incarceration does not deter her from drug use.

"Sam," a Low-Rider, is a dramatic aftercare success despite maintaining close ties with former associates. He is a "biker" who designs, builds or modifies motorcycles for a living, and has a reputation as a superior craftsman. The bulk of both his work and leisure activities involve riding and "hanging out" with bikers, many of whom are heroin users. Thus he has retained much of the Low-Rider lifestyle, but has traded its addict and criminal components for a legitimate entrepreneurial role. Many others who have achieved aftercare success through stable employment and marriage still pursue some Low-Rider activities during their free time, but without jeopardizing this stability by felonious behavior.

BARRIO ADDICTS

Most in this category are of Mexican-American descent, some are other "Latins" and a few—all females—are Anglos, but all speak Spanish most of the time. A slight majority were reared mainly in California, the rest in other Southwestern states but relocated in the Los Angeles area just before or after NARA confinement. The latter group keep somewhat apart from the California Chicanos both in and out of the institution, and are more successful than other Barrio Addicts on aftercare.

The Barrio Addicts were almost all from very impoverished families, employed mainly at day labor, farm labor, railroad work and restaurant or domestic work. The mean age of those in this group on NARA aftercare was just under 30, and over a third reported that they had never held a single legitimate job for as long as one month. Many had much experience as hired smugglers, carrying drugs over the Mexican-American border in exchange for some for themselves. Most first became addicted in adolescent peer groups. A majority of the Barrio Addicts reported "runs" of uninterrupted heroin use for over a year in the 5 years preceding their NARA commitment, but the length of runs was not as predictive of addiction on aftercare as was the number of separate runs. Many had been repeatedly incarcerated in jails and in juvenile and adult state institutions, "kicking" their habits only when confined, and not always then, for they frequently were able to smuggle drugs into places of incarceration through visitors.

Many Barrio Addicts obtained low-status jobs on leaving school in late adolescence, married at that time, and had children. One recounts his first addiction, 3 years after his first heroin use, as follows: "It was in 1957, I was 18. My first wife and I were living in New Mexico—I had bought a car and the only job I could find paid $1.25 an hour. I couldn't make the payments. We were living in a dumpy apartment. Things started to go downhill. I started using heavy, and stealing construction stuff, copper and brass. I bought dope in large quantities and my personal friends bought off me." Most of their heroin use is in their neighborhood, often with members of their gangs as adolescents, and their joint activities also include joyriding, petty theft, rowdy drinking, and smoking marihuana. Once addicted, however, the activities associated with obtaining and using narcotics became a preoccupation. It is our impression that all Barrio Addicts who return to their former neighborhoods on aftercare resume heroin use, though perhaps a third merely chip or use episodically without becoming readdicted. They work at sporadic jobs, including truck driver, busboy and construction worker, although three are presently part-time paraprofessional drug therapists in Los Angeles and two of these are also college students.

Among the Barrio Addicts the social obligation to use drugs appears to be more prevalent than in any other group. A common observation among addicts themselves is "Blacks deal, Chicanos use, and whites feel guilty." Typical is the following account: "It was late, my birthday. We were drinking. Some dude came down with some stuff. He offered me a birthday fix, a present. I don't know why I didn't continue. The guy only lived two blocks away. Course, this was Saturday and I had to test Wednesday, and I didn't want to come up dirty, so I just forgot about it." Another relates: "Well, see—I came back to the old neighborhood. I went to trade school. All my old friends were at the school. They were all using. I started coming to school and getting loaded every day. When I was in another environment I was O.K., but when I get around old friends, it's all over. See, when I first started using I had no responsibilities. But now I have a family, kids, and no money for shoes, even, if I shoot stuff. I don't want to start stealing again." This man is now in a methadone program, and his present successful adjustment for over 2 years has been achieved despite a number of difficulties, including an occasional apparently irresistible sense of obligation to use heroin. It appears that methadone had provided a workable solution to his narcotics problem, on which his remarks are revealing: "I got tired of trying all these illusions. I went through all those programs, nalline, therapeutic community. See, I don't want to be found dead, or spend my life in jail and on the street; never have a penny in my pocket. So my PO and the director of the place where I work told me to try methadone. At first I thought it was just another trip. They didn't give me enough and I started drinking every day, thought I'd turn into an alcoholic. But finally they upped the dosage and it's O.K. I'd rather be off it, but it's better to be on it and walking around taking care of business than ripped up on heroin."

For Barrio Addicts, the Terminal Island education programs were sometimes a major employment resource, even if they still led only to manual jobs. With Chicanos at the bottom of America's occupational ladder, even low-skill jobs were often an improvement over prior opportunities. Several of those who relocated in Los Angeles from border towns in the Southwest appear to have achieved success as a consequence of their exposure to other ways of life through participation in NARA. They spoke little English when they entered the institution, and they previously had been employed mainly as "mules"—carriers of illicit drugs over the border. One told of the self-imposed regimen he adopted while incarcerated in order to "make himself over." He taught himself to walk, talk, and relate to other inmates as Anglos did, practicing these activities daily. Upon release he worked for a year as a clothes presser, a skill acquired on work release, and at the same time attended college with the goal of a BA in Spanish. He is now married, works as a paraprofessional, and plans to continue his education in graduate school.

The Barrio Addicts who were successful differ from the other types in the extent to which they credit the urine tests with being a factor in their success. This reflects the fact that they had more difficulty than most other released addicts in avoiding social contacts that generated a sense of obligation to join in the use of heroin. Several related that the urine tests helped because other addicts "did not take it personally" if their excuse for not taking a "fix" was that they had an imminent test. Indeed, some seemed to need the excuse of the test as a justification to themselves during moments of temptation when they could find no other reason for not joining a gathering where heroin would probably be used.

GHETTO HUSTLERS

Persons were placed in this category because of their participation in so-called "hustling" activities centered in Black ghetto areas, although several of the women in this group are not Black. "Hustling" refers to any illegal scheme to obtain money, mainly confidence or "bunco" games, theft, and prostitution.

Some prostitutes marry men who act as procurers for them and also supply them with heroin. A higher status female role is that of carrier or smuggler of drugs for male dealers. Occupationally, the men in this group have been extremely disadvantaged in legitimate employment, having only low status and poorly paid jobs, whereas several of the women had had office jobs. About two-thirds of the Ghetto Hustlers confined their drug use almost exclusively to heroin, while the remainder also used other drugs and several frequently drank to excess.

The average age of the Ghetto Hustlers is about 34. About 60 percent have had periods of readdiction since release from Terminal Island, and about half have been declared violators, mainly following new felony convictions. Most of the women in this group ultimately were successful in obtaining above-average employment at office jobs, while most of the men had only low status jobs with frequent unemployment. An exception was one man with an art background, continued in the institution, who has become a successful fashion designer. Another was a paraprofessional therapist for a while, but the strains of his marginal relationships with staff and clientele were too difficult for him to handle, and he reverted to drug use.

"Susan," a Black Ghetto Hustler, was reincarcerated within 3 months after first release. She resumed use on the day she got out, became readdicted, was arrested for theft, and then returned to Terminal Island. Released again, this time to a halfway house, she overdosed three times—twice on barbiturates and once on heroin. Some of the aftercare staff felt that these were suicide attempts, and she was then sent to a state mental institution instead of being returned to Terminal Island. She had been placed in a religious correctional institution at the age of 12 and released to live on her own in San Francisco when she was 17. She became involved with a dealer-pimp whom she later married, and after his arrest and imprisonment she eventually lived with another "old man" procurer. During her 2½-year first incarceration she is reported to have developed strong homosexual relationships, and it appears possible that her failures on aftercare were related to the fact that prison provided her with the most stable and satisfactory relationships she had experienced.

CONCLUSION

Realistic decisions in dealing with addicts require some comprehension of the culturally rooted expectations of the social worlds in which they live. Five distinct lifestyles associated with drug use have been described, each having unique features of emphases, although all foster dependence on opiates.

The Expressive Student lifestyle appears to be the most conducive to rehabilitation, and the most reachable by group therapy programs, because its members are accustomed to trying to guide their lives by intellectual processes, and because incarceration is an extremely aversive experience for them. The lifestyle of the Social World Alternators makes them highly adaptable to both legitimate and illegitimate social roles, including that of paraprofessional therapist, thus making it probable that they will be among both the spectacular successes and the dramatic failures of correctional efforts. The Low-Riders, Barrio Addicts, and Ghetto Hustlers are poorer rehabilitation risks than the other two types because they have poorer prospects of achieving a legitimate way of life as gratifying to them as their careers in crime and addiction. They require the most drastic efforts to alter their experiences, not only in employment, but also in social relationships where they can feel at ease, involved and well regarded among law-abiding persons.

19

Female Criminals:
Their Personal, Familial,
and Social Backgrounds: The
Relation of These
to the Diagnoses of
Sociopathy and Hysteria

C. Robert Cloninger and
Samuel B. Guze

Reprinted from the *Archives of General Psychiatry* 23 (March 1970), pp. 554–58, by permission of the authors and publisher. Copyright 1970, American Medical Association.

Among convicted male felons, the prevalence of sociopathy, alcoholism, and drug dependency is increased.[1,2] An increased prevalence of these same conditions and of hysteria is found among the felons' first-degree relatives: hysteria in the female relatives, and the others predominantly in the male relatives.[3] On the other hand, family studies of women with hysteria show an increased prevalence of hysteria in the female relatives, and of sociopathy and alcoholism in the male relatives.[4,5] In addition, Robins[6] reported that 20 of 76 girls referred to a child guidance clinic between the ages of 12 and 16 because of antisocial behavior received a diagnosis of hysteria as adults. Finally, Forrest[7] noted that some patients with hysteria, as defined in this study, would in Great Britain be diagnosed as hysterical psychopaths or psychopathic personalities. He presented data indicating significant antisocial behavior and alcohol or drug abuse in such patients.

Since these results all suggested a significant association between sociopathy and hysteria, a study of female criminals seemed appropriate to investigate the apparent association further and to determine what psychiatric disorders characterize such women. We recently reported some of the results of such a study of a consecutive series of 66 convicted female felons.[8] Each woman received at least one psychiatric diagnosis. Sociopathy, alcoholism, drug dependency, hysteria, and homosexuality were seen more frequently than would be expected in the general population. Sociopathy or hysteria was found in 80% (regardless of other diagnoses): sociopathy alone in 39%, hysteria alone in 15%, and both in 26%. The high prevalence of hysteria, over 20 times that seen in the general population,[5] was striking. We concluded that the results, confirming the other work, indicate a significant association between sociopathy and hysteria.

The first report primarily described the psychiatric disorders in these women. This report will describe other personal, familial, and social characteristics, relating these, where appropriate, to the psychiatric disorders. Since antisocial behavior and crime are much less common in women than in men, familial and social influences that are associated with female criminality are of particular interest. Further, because the psychiatric illnesses associated with criminality most often begin early in life, the early environmental experiences of these women deserve careful study. We were particularly interested in any significant differences between women with sociopathy and women with hysteria.

METHOD

Details of the subject selection, interview arrangements, interview content, and diagnostic criteria are described elsewhere.[8] The statistical analyses were done using X^2 with Yate's Correction.

RESULTS

Age and Race.—Ages ranged from 17 to 54 years with a median of 27. A total of 75% were between 20 and 35 years. There were 34 whites, 30 Negroes, one American Indian, and one woman of mixed (American Indian and white) descent.

Socioeconomic Background.—The head of the homes in which the women had been raised had been an unskilled laborer in 56%, semiskilled or a clerical worker in 32%, and a professional or managerial worker in 12% of the cases. A total of 21% had been reared in a rural environment until adulthood.

Parental Home Experience.—Sixty-five percent of the women reported at least one parent permanently absent from the household before the women reached age 18. Parental loss included only the father in 30%, only the mother in 8%, and both in 27% of the cases. Parental death was reported by 18%; parental divorce or separation by 50%. Nine percent were illegitimate. One woman had been removed from her home by a welfare agency because of parental neglect.

As a consequence of the high rate of parental loss, the women had been reared in a variety of settings when they were growing up. For various reasons, 55% of the women had lived away from their parents for more than three months. Twenty-six percent had lived with relatives or friends, 14% had lived in foster homes or orphanages, and 15% had lived "on their own" for several months at a time but then returned to the parental home.

Parental antisocial behavior was frequent. The father, or surrogate, was reported as a heavy drinker by 53% of the women, as neglecting the family by 29%, as having been in prison or jail by 20%, as an erratic worker by 14%, and as cruel or physically abusive by 12%. Similarly, the mother, or surrogate, was said to have been a heavy drinker by 21%, to have been cruel or abusive by 12%, to have been in prison or jail by 9%, and to have neglected the family by 9%. On the basis of the family history, the biological father of 55% of the women received a diagnosis of suspected sociopathy or suspected alcoholism; the corresponding figure for the biological mother was 27%. More mothers than fathers, however, were considered to warrant some psychiatric diagnosis (76% vs 59%).

School History.—Eleven of the women did not finish elementary school. Eight stopped after completing the eighth grade. Twenty-nine dropped out of high school. Seven stopped after graduating from high school. Ten spent some time in college but did not get a degree, and one was a college graduate. Thus, failure to complete the last level of education entered was reported by 76%. Fourteen women quit school because of pregnancy.

Expulsion or suspension from school was reported by 33%, repeated truancy was reported by 32%, repeated fights in school leading to trouble with teachers was reported by 36%, and having to see the principal by 52%. Parents had been required to come to school for academic or disciplinary reasons in 33%.

Mental deficiency was infrequent, but low academic achievement was common. Fifty-five percent of the women reported failing one or more subjects, and 26% had to repeat one year of school. The 66 women reported attending a total of 271 primary and secondary schools. In addition to their formal academic education, 41% of the women had attended one or more technical training programs, often while in prison.

Work History.—Fifty-five percent were unemployed and 33% were on welfare. There were only two whose income exceeded $5,000 a year. Over 70% had incomes less than $3,000 a year. Thirty percent were working in unskilled jobs. Seventy-three percent reported that they had worked at only unskilled jobs when they did work, despite the fact that 41% had attended technical training programs. Thirty-five percent reported paramedical employment as their current or usual job, and most of these worked as nurses' aids. Often the women worked at various types of unskilled labor, most often domestic or janitorial work, factory labor, or as a waitress.

Forty-seven percent reported having been fired from a job for poor performance at least once. Seventy percent had quit a job without having another one to go to at least once. The 66 women reported 395 jobs in the last ten years, or six jobs per woman. Forty-two percent had never held a job for as long as one year and 65% had never held a job for as long as two years.

Sexual History.—The median age for first sexual intercourse was 16. Sexual intercourse before the age of 18 was reported by 76%. Premarital sexual intercourse was reported by 80%. Eight women reported being raped, and two of these reported being raped twice. In four cases, the offender was the victim's father (one case) or stepfather (three cases). Three women reported other forms of incest.

Thirteen women were known to have had some homosexual activity. In five cases, the homosexuality was significant both in extent of experience and in psychological orientation. In the other eight cases, the experience was casual and occurred principally during prolonged prison confinement.

Seventeen women were known to have been prostitutes. Venereal disease was reported or documented by medical records in 21%.

Sexual inadequacy was reported by 79%, sexual indifference by 67%, frigidity by 52%, and dyspareunia by 36%.

Marital History.—Twenty percent of the women had never been married; all of these were under age 30. Twenty-two women had married before the age of 18. Twelve women had lived in common-law relationships for two years or more, and all of these had also been legally married to another man at some time. Among the 53 women who had been married, 23 had been divorced at least once. Nine had been divorced twice, and three women had been divorced three times. Twenty-one women had been separated, but not divorced. Thus, divorce or separation was reported by 83% of those who had been married. At the time of the interview, 33 women were divorced or separated, 6 were widows, and 14 were living with a husband. Seventy-two percent of those who had been married had married at least one sociopathic or alcoholic husband. Fighting with her husband or being beaten by him was reported by 64% of those ever married. Thirty-one women complained of their husbands' nonsupport. Twenty-three complained of their husbands' infidelity. On the other hand, 29 women reported being unfaithful to their husbands. In 30 of the 44 cases of separation or divorce, the woman claimed that she had left her husband.

Pregnancy and Motherhood.—Fifty-five of the women had been pregnant at least once, and 51 had given birth to at least one child. These women reported a total of 144 children. Nineteen of the children had died: six were stillborn, seven others died in the first year, and six more died before the age of 3. Ten women reported 17 abortions: 16 spontaneous and 1 illegal. Forty percent of the children were conceived out of wedlock. Thirty-one women reported at least one illegitimate pregnancy.

Nine women had been declared to be "unfit mothers" by the court; four of these had been convicted of child abuse. Three of the nine had been required by the court to give up their children for adoption. Two other women voluntarily placed their children for adoption. A total of ten children had been placed for adoption. The children of another 21 women lived with relatives (36 children). A total, then, of 46 children (37% of those alive) did not live with their mothers.

Religion.—Thirty-five women reported an interest in religion; in 22 of these women, this had begun after their index conviction. (The term "index" is used to designate the crimes that brought the subjects to our attention.) Twenty-eight women said they prayed often; in 18 this represented a recent change. Twenty-three women read the Bible often; in 15 cases this was a recent change. Ten women reported communication with God and expressed the belief that they had actually talked with Him or received a message from Him. Six women reported being currently active in church organizations. Fifteen others attended church regularly. Twenty-five were affiliated with a church but seldom attended. Nineteen were uninterested, and one was hostile. Various sects were represented, but none of the women were Jewish.

Other Features.—Forty-five women reported repeated fighting or using a weapon in a fight. Twenty-six women reported a history of running away from home overnight, and 15 women reported at least one period of wanderlust. Most of the women denied significant feelings of guilt, sinfulness, or worthlessness. Pathological lying characterized ten women. Lack of close friends or activity in any organization was reported by 19 women.

Problem drinking, defined as reporting any of the symptoms of alcoholism whether or not the full diagnostic criteria were fulfilled,[1,2] was reported by 34 women. Twenty-five women reported some experimentation with illicit drugs, again independent of whether or not the diagnostic criteria for drug dependency were met.

Histrionic personality traits (dramatic overstatement, seductive and manipulative behavior, ostentatious grooming and dress) were present in 22 women. Five women spontaneously described themselves as having a "split personality" or a "multiple personality." Circumscribed persecutory feelings of being specially watched, followed, or plotted against (as by the police) were reported by seven women.

Aggravating Influences and the Index Crime.—It has already been noted[8] that 44% of the women were acutely intoxicated (alcohol, drugs, or both) at the time of the index crime. Another important factor was the presence of accomplices. Thirty-seven women had an accomplice at the index crime; 16 had only male accomplices, 8 had only female accomplices, and 13 had both. Thus, male accomplices were present in 44% of all the crimes. Index property crimes (shoplifting, burglary, auto theft, check offenses, and embezzlement) more often involved an accomplice than did the other crimes (65% vs. 35%, P<0.05). Accomplices, intoxication, or both, were present in 82% of the crimes.

Jealousy or sex-related emotional stress, such as infidelity, was involved in 12 index offenses: 11 of the 14 homicides and 1 of the 2 cases of aggravated assault. There were 13 male victims and 3 female victims.

Variables Associated with Sociopathy.—Fifty-six percent of the sociopathic women were Negro compared to 26% of the other women (P<0.05).

Seventy percent of the sociopathic women had not lived with their parents the whole time they were growing up compared to 22% of the others P<0.001). The corresponding figures for white women were 67% versus 33% and for Negro women 42% versus 24%, but neither difference is significant.

The sociopathic women reported first sexual intercourse earlier (age 15) than did the others (age 18). Ninety-three percent of the former had experienced sexual intercourse by the age of 18 compared to 44% of the latter (P<0.001). All of the Negro women had begun sexual intercourse during adolescence. Among the white women, 89% of the sociopaths had done so as compared to 18% of the others (P<0.001).

Twenty-eight percent of the sociopathic women had a history of homosexual experiences compared to 4% of the others (P<0.05). The corresponding figures for the white women were 32% versus 0% (P<0.05), and for the Negro women 25% versus 17% (NS).

Drinking problems were more common among the sociopathic women than the others (67% versus 22%, P<0.01). For the white women, the corresponding figures were 79% versus 12% (P<0.001); for the Negro women, 58% versus 50% (NS).

The sociopathic women were more likely to have a history of various forms of school delinquency, repeated fighting, previous juvenile and other arrests, reform school, and prostitution. Since each of these variables was directly or indirectly part of the diagnostic criteria for sociopathy, these findings were expected, and only indicate that each form of delinquency or antisocial behavior is usually associated with other forms of such behavior.

Variables Associated with Hysteria.—Twenty-six percent of the hysterics had lived in a foster home or orphanage compared to 5% of the others (P<0.01).

Sixty-seven percent of the hysterics presented histrionic personality traits compared to 13% of the others (P<0.001). Twenty-six percent of the hysterics presented circumscribed persecutory feelings; none of the others did so (P<0.01).

The hysterics were much more likely to report sexual difficulties, suicide attempts, conversion symptoms, hospitalizations, and surgical procedures, but since these variables were directly or indirectly part of the diagnostic criteria for hysteria, these findings were expected.

Variables Associated with Sociopathy Plus Hysteria.—Women who received both diagnoses were more likely to report being raised in a foster home or orphanage, and to show histrionic personality traits. These findings, however, probably reflect only the association between these variables and the diagnosis of hysteria alone (above).

Only one variable was significantly associated with the presence of both diagnoses without being significantly associated with either one separately: the loss of both parents by the age of 18. This was reported by 53% of the women who received both diagnoses compared to 18% of the others (P<0.02).

Variables That Did Not Distinguish Sociopathy or Hysteria.—The following variables were not associated with either diagnosis: age, socioeconomic status, being illegitimate, parental divorce or separation, parental antisocial or criminal behavior, poor academic performance in school, poor work record, history of rape, marital discord and psychopathological disturbances in the husbands, pregnancy and motherhood experiences, religious attitudes and practices, feelings of guilt, pathological lying, social isolation, or type of index crime.

COMMENT

The severe social and familial pathological disturbances are striking! While similarly disturbed social and family settings characterize male felons, our impression is that the situation is worse for the women. From the home environment in which they were raised to the home environment they are providing for their own children, the findings indicate a dishearteningly grim picture.

The sociopaths and the hysterics apparently come from the same social and family backgrounds. While each diagnostic group was significantly associated with a different measure of parental deprivation (more of the sociopaths had not lived with their parents the whole time the children were growing up, more of the hysterics had lived in foster homes or orphanages, and more of those with both diagnoses had lost both parents by the age of 18), on balance, parental psychopathological disturbance and home disruption were very similar for each diagnosis.

In fact, aside from the more extensive antisocial and criminal history of the sociopaths and the typical history of recurrent symptoms in many organ systems of the hysterics, few differences were observed between the two diagnostic groups. An increased proportion of Negroes, an earlier onset of sexual intercourse, an increased prevalence of homosexual experiences, and a more frequent history of problem drinking characterized the sociopaths, while histrionic personality features and circumscribed persecutory feelings were more likely in the hysterics. Rather than differences between sociopaths and hysterics, the data emphasize the similarities, and thus strengthen the hypothesis derived from other work that these two conditions arise from similar etiologic and pathogenetic factors.

Summary

The personal, familial, and social backgrounds of convicted female felons are characterized by marked parental deprivation and psychopathological disturbance and by severe disturbances in all areas of life. Poor school performance, school delinquency, poor job records, running away from home, periods of wanderlust, frequent fights, sexual maladjustment, prostitution, repeated marital discord, and poor performances as mothers are very frequent.

Female criminals with sociopathy and with hysteria apparently come from similar backgrounds and have similar life styles, except for the features that are part of the diagnostic criteria for the two disorders.

This study was supported in part by Public Health Service grants MH-05938 and MH-09247 and in part by a Student Research Scholarship (Dr. Cloninger).

Mr. Vearl Harris and the staff of the Missouri State Board of Probation and Parole cooperated with this study.

Notes

1. Guze S. B., Tuason V. B., Gatfield, P. D., et al: Psychiatric illness and crime with particular reference to alcoholism: A study of 223 criminals. *J Nerv Ment Dis 134:*512–521, 1962.
2. Guze S. B., Goodwin D. W., Crane J. B.: Criminality and psychiatric disorders. *Arch Gen Psychiat 20:*583–591, 1969.
3. Guze, S. B., Wolfgram E. D., McKinney, J. K., et al: Psychiatric illness in the families of convicted criminals: A study of 519 first-degree relatives. *Dis Nerv Syst 28:*651–659, 1967.
4. Arkonac O., Guze S. B.: A family study of hysteria. *New Eng J Med 266:* 239–242, 1963.
5. Woerner P. I., Guze S. B.: A family and marital study of hysteria. *Brit J Psychiat 114:*161–168, 1968.
6. Robins L: *Deviant Children Grown Up.* Baltimore, Williams & Wilkins Co, 1966.
7. Forrest A. D.: The differentiation of hysterical personality from hysterical psychopathy. *Brit J Med Psychol 40:*65–78, 1967.
8. Cloninger C. R., Guze S. B.: Psychiatric illness and female criminality: The role of sociopathy and hysteria in the antisocial woman. *Amer J Psychiat*, to be published.

20

Suicide Prevention: A Brief for Corrections Officers

Robert J. Wicks

Reprinted from *Federal Probation* (September 1972) pp. 29–31 by permission of the publisher, the Administrative Office of the United States Courts.

Though prison mental health staffs are trained to handle abnormal behavioral episodes, they usually are not present in the blocks or near the cells when there is a sudden violent outburst. If a suicide attempt or disturbance occurs, the corrections officer, not the psychologist, is the one who must act promptly to prevent unnecessary loss of life and property damage.

In recognition of this situation a great deal of information on crowd control has been disseminated to officers to help them stunt the development of spontaneous riots. Yet, in the case of suicide prevention, in most civilian and military confinement facilities guidelines have been lacking or, at best, incomplete. The officer has often been left to himself in this area and expected to be capable of determining overt signs which indicate an inmate is potentially suicidal and ultimately prevent him from attempting to kill himself. This attitude is clearly unfair to the officer.

And so, to help alleviate this problem the author has developed a basic brief on suicide prevention that can be distributed to the individual officer. Though it is obviously not the ultimate fact sheet on the subject, it does contain pertinent information which should prove to be of practical value to the corrections personnel who come into direct contact with the prison population.

The areas which will be covered are: (1) Organic and functional causes of suicide; (2) signs of depression; (3) suicidal manipulator; and (4) acting to prevent a suicide.

ORGANIC AND FUNCTIONAL CAUSES OF SUICIDE

Three functional (psychological) causes of suicide are extreme fear, depression, and psychotic hallucinations. Fear and depression strong enough to precipitate a suicide attempt may be triggered by the following:

1. Bad news (sickness or death at home, rejection by family or infidelity of spouse);
2. homosexual rape;
3. no news;
4. sudden confinement (first offender);
5. unexpected sentence of unusually long duration handed down by the courts;
6. guilt arising from a crime committed by the individual which had particularly unpleasant overtones (child molesting, murder of a relative or close friend);
7. receiving a beating from an inmate or corrections officer;
8. confinement for a long period in an unsentenced status.

Psychotic hallucinations can be experienced by a person who has temporarily lost touch with reality. They may give the inmate the feeling that he hears or sees things. These apparent sensations may scare or even "instruct" him to kill himself or someone else.

Therefore, a psychotic, since he may be quite divorced from reality at times, must always be considered as being possibly dangerous. Too often a confinee who is severely disturbed is allowed to withdraw and not referred for treatment, causing him to strike out. This show of aggression (suicide or murder) is a last desperate effort to prove to himself that he can still find reality. Unfortunately, this last effort may well cost him his life.

As well as the above functional causes, death could also result due to organic (physical) problems such as drug overdose or withdrawal, high fever and delerium tremens (alcoholic). Though these conditions do not usually induce a person to take his own life they present the same danger as suicide because death might result if the individual were left alone and unaided.

Too often inmates suffering from some type of physical reaction are left to "sleep it off" without medical attention while in city or county jails. Even in penal institutions where prisoners are often detoxified before being received, the confinees may have a drug "flash back" or become suddenly ill, and not be sent for medical attention. Such inaction on the part of an officer in these circumstances could prove fatal for the prisoner and result in serious disciplinary action being taken against the officer on duty.

SIGNS OF DEPRESSION

A psychotic's bizarre actions and an organic disorder's physical symptoms of sweating, vomiting, disorientation, squirming, and trembling are easy-to-observe signs indicating that a person needs medical or psychological attention. On the other hand, signs of depression are often imperceptible unless one is particularly sensitive to them. And so, the corrections officer who is versed in suicide prevention principles should be alert to the following symptoms. If they are present in a combination or exaggerated form they are indicative of depression serious enough to lead to possible suicide: (1) Loss of appetite; (2) difficulty sleeping; (3) lethargic; (4) extremely tense, restless and agitated; (5) prone to upset easily; (6) shuns company of other inmates and doesn't attend normally popular recreational events.

SUICIDAL MANIPULATOR

Bona fide attempts to take one's own life are often made by the inmate when the officer on duty is least available, and thus able, to intervene. It could happen right after the officer has finished his check of the area during the night or when he is distracted by other duties.

When an attempt is made in the day or just before the officer is due to check the area, the inmate could quite possibly be a manipulator since it appears he is purposely trying to be seen and stopped by the officer when he makes his attempt. Accordingly, some officers might be tempted to take lightly attempts which they consider are not genuine. To have such an attitude however would be a serious mistake. There are numerous cases of would-be manipulators who made a dramatic attempt in order to get attention and tragically lost their lives by mistake.

ACTING TO PREVENT A SUICIDE

Referral is the first line of defense against potentially suicidal inmates. If the officer sees an individual who is manifesting organic and/or functional symptoms which may end in death for the confinee if he is left alone, a superior should naturally be notified and briefed.

After the report is made, the officer should then see that the officer coming on for the next shift is informed about the confinee in question. In addition, the officer should follow up his original report to ensure that medical and psychiatric assistance for the inmate is, in fact, imminent.

Once attention has been provided for the troubled inmate, care must be taken to prevent a future attempt from being successful. Often a subsequent attempt is made by a depressed person soon after he seems to be improving through the aid of psycho-narcotherapy.

In the instance where the officer observes a suicide attempt, obviously he should first take steps to eliminate the danger immediately (i.e., cut the person down, stop bleeding, etc.) and then notify his superior. However, the case of an inmate who is threatening to jump from one of the prison's tiers is an exception to this rule. If the officer moves too quickly he might precipitate more fear in the confinee, causing him to jump.

In a prison located in a major United States city, a youth threatened to jump and kill himself. Upon hearing the threat by the inmate situated on the edge of a walkway up on the third tier, the officer became excited. He yelled, "I'm coming up to get you, don't move!" When the inmate heard this and saw the officer dashing up the steps he became frightened and jumped.

In the above situation instead of moving quickly toward the inmate the officer should have: (1) Tried to quiet the block; (2) avoided making a sudden move or doing anything which the inmate might interpret as threatening; (3) attempted to assure the individual and motivate his native will to live; (4) moved slowly and calmly toward him; (5) referred him immediately for psychiatric attention once he was out of danger.

Conclusion

No effort is too great to save a life. And with a minimum amount of knowledge and willingness a corrections officer can save many lives by preventing needless suicides. This brief article should provide the basic knowledge; the responsibility for applying it now remains in the hands of the officer.

Part Five

The Experience of Institutionalization

A dominant theme of contemporary writing on corrections deals with the impact of the system on the client—particularly the impact of correctional institutions on inmates. This concern has reached the wider public in such phrases as "crime schools" and "factors of crime." While a full-scale presentation of all that has been written in this area would take us beyond the scope of this introduction, it would be well to summarize several of the more influential contributions that form the background to this section of the book.

In 1940, Donald Clemmer's classic work, *The Prison Community*, made its appearance. Based on extensive observation of a state penitentiary housing some 2,300 inmates, Clemmer introduced the term "prisonization" to describe a series of processes "which breed or deepen criminality and antisociality and make the inmate characteristic of the criminalistic ideology in the prison community" (Clemmer, 1971, p. 94). While not all inmates are fully assimilated to the "criminalistic ideology" of the prison, Clemmer makes it clear that the longer an individual remains incarcerated and the weaker his ties to the community outside, the greater his vulnerability to the influence of the prison community. While various details of Clemmer's description have been revised by researchers following upon Clemmer's work, there is by now almost universal recognition that incarceration in a correctional institution represents more than a temporary time-out from the course of normal life; rather, it encompasses socialization processes which are uniquely characteristic of self-contained involuntary settings—"total institutions," in the famous phrase introduced by the social psychologist Goffman (Goffman, 1961).

While Goffman refers repeatedly to correctional environments to illustrate his conceptions, he is quite explicit in recognizing that they constitute but an instance: "Prisons serve as a clear example, provided that we appreciate that what is prison-like about prisons is found in institutions whose members have broken no laws" (Goffman, 1961, p. xiii). What all such institutions share is the effort to force inmates into behavior patterns and self-definitions conforming to the needs or values of their staffs and administrators. The latter, according to Goffman, make use of a system (composed of three basic elements—formal prescriptions and proscriptions, rewards for obedience, and punishment for rule breaking) whose purpose is to ensure "that cooperativeness is obtained from persons who often have cause to be uncooperative" (Goffman, 1961, p. 52).

Along with inducing inmate behavior which can be termed "cooperative," the institutional process appears to have a second objective of potentially far more profound consequences both for the inmate and for the larger society. This involves an intense pressure to force the inmate to perceive himself as deviant (i.e., antisocial or insane), hence justifying his confinement in the institution; it is a process not dissimilar to the socio-psychological process of acquiring an "abnormal" identity, discussed in Part 3. In essence, what can be seen taking place—in varying degrees of subtlety—is the manipulation of the environment by the staff, so that the inmate comes in time to adopt (at least verbally) the institution's estimate of him as a deviant person, deserving of the institution's treatment of him.

Ken Kesey, in *One Flew Over the Cuckoo's Nest*, has provided us with an incomparable depiction of the process as it takes place at a group therapy session in a mental hospital:

> . . . When twenty minutes had passed, she [the head nurse] looked at her watch and said, "Am I to take it that there's not a man among you that has committed some act that he has never admitted?" She reached in the basket for the log book. "Must we go over past history?"
>
> That triggered something, some acoustic device in the walls, rigged to turn on at just the sound of these words coming from her mouth. The acutes stiffened. Their mouths opened in unison. Her sweeping eyes stopped on the first man along the wall.
>
> His mouth worked. "I robbed a cash register in a service station."
>
> She moved to the next man.
>
> "I tried to take my little sister to bed."
>
> Her eyes clicked to the next man; each one jumped like a shooting-gallery target.
>
> "I—one time—wanted to take my brother to bed."
>
> "I killed my cat when I was six. Oh, God forgive me, I stoned her to death and said my neighbor did it."
>
> "I lied about trying. I did take my sister."
>
> "So did I! So did I!"
>
> "And me! And me!"
>
> It was better than she'd dreamed. They were all shouting to outdo one another, going further and further, no way of stopping, telling things that wouldn't ever let them look one another in the eye again. The nurse nodding at each confession and saying yes, yes, yes." (Kesey, 1964, pp. 48–49)

In this brief excerpt, Kesey graphically portrays for us the pressures that institutions apply to inmates to adopt the deviant status that enables the institution to feel justified in exercising coercive control over the inmates—"for the benefit of the inmate." While most of Kesey's characters have been incarcerated for fairly long periods and have learned to do what is expected in order to please the staff, the first paper included in this section, "On Being Sane in Insane Places," experimentally documents the early steps in the process. Here we see the total blindness, on the part of institutional staff, to inmate behaviors which might in any way tend to negate the initial judgment of deviance. We see, moreover, how any and all inmate behaviors are used to underpin the same judgment of deviance. It takes no leap of the imagination to visualize inmates anxious to be released discovering that the best route is to "play the game," that is, to acknowledge their deviance and demonstrate

350

efforts to "improve themselves" for the benefit of parole or release boards. As John Irwin, himself a former prison inmate, put it in his book *The Felon:*

> Finally, time-doers try to get out as soon as possible. . . . And in recent years, with the increasing emphasis on treatment, they "program." To program is to follow, at least tokenly, a treatment plan which has been outlined by the treatment staff, recommended by the board, or devised by the convict himself. It is generally believed that to be released on parole as early as possible, one must "get a program." A program involves attending school, vocational training, group counseling, church, Alcoholics Anonymous, or any other special program that is introduced under the treatment plan of the prison. (Irwin, 1970, p. 70)

Rosenhan describes the twin processes of powerlessness and depersonalization, conditions forming the foundation for the institutionalization process, whether the institution be a mental hospital, a correctional institution, or even a large university.

If writers such as Rosenhan emphasize the role of institutional *staffs*, others have made us aware that the inmates as well participate in the prison socialization process through the creation of a so-called inmate culture. This culture is a system of values, attitudes, and behavioral modes that on the one hand offers some relief from the pains of imprisonment, and on the other hand encourages inmates to accept a criminalistic ideology and self-identity. For example, Schrag, who studied leadership among prison inmates, found that the most important factors were extensive criminal history, long sentence, and aggressive and violent habits. This led him to conclude that "the group identifications of the inmates are generally organized around the activities and interests of the least improvable offenders, and that the values of the prison culture encourage rebellion and non-conformity" (Schrag, 1971, p. 88). Thus, we see that the coercive pressures emanating from the staff combine with those of the inmate culture to produce and enforce a sense of asocial or antisocial deviance on the part of the inmates.

While the effects of prisonization upon adult inmates has by now begun to penetrate the consciousness of social and behavioral scientists and even informed citizens, less attention has been given to similar processes among confined youths. Much of our knowledge is still reflective of the Dickensian descriptions of orphanage–workhouses of early nineteenth century England—as experienced by the young Oliver Twist, for example. The emphasis in such works, of course, is on the cruelty to children by the adults employed in such institutions. Today, with growing awareness of the significant contribution of youth to the totality of crime—particularly violent crime—we find ourselves asking whether the climates of institutions to which youths are confined may not be characterized as criminogenic just as adult

351

prisons were found to be. In 1946, George Bernard Shaw wrote "The Crime of Imprisonment," in which he commented on the hypocrisy of a society that would "inflict on the child the prison demoralization and the prison stigma which condemn it for the rest of its life to crime as the only employment open to a prison child" (Shaw, 1975, p. 22).

The demoralization and stigmatization noted by Shaw are well illustrated in the study by Bartollas and Miller, the second selection in this section. It will come as no surprise to most readers that homosexuality is a pervasive characteristic of closed institutions populated entirely by same-sex inmates. Of particular interest here is the use of homosexual as well as other forms of exploitation as an expression of the status and power structure of the inmate society, dependent in turn on the willingness to assert physical strength coercively over other inmates. The degree to which a boy's reputation follows him from institution to institution or from street to institution, causing him to be indelibly stigmatized as a scapegoat ("punk"), is one of the more poignant aspects of the inmate socialization system.

Both Rosenhan and Bartollas and Miller emphasize that experiences they describe are typical and pervasive of the institutions studied. Thus, we may with some justification infer that such experiences are reflective of an overall psychosocial climate. At first blush, "psychosocial climate" may strike us as a rather nebulous concept, subjective and indefinable from an operational standpoint. Nonetheless, Moos, in the final item in this section, demonstrates that institutional climate is a concept amenable to quantitative measurement and definition. The Social Climate Scale (SCS) had been developed earlier as a measure of several aspects of institutional climate. Moos here shows significant relationships between several subscales of the SCS (spontaneity, affiliation, insight, variety, autonomy) and feelings of residents about themselves, attitudes toward institutional staffs, and types of initiatives they perceived themselves as taking. It would appear, then, that the climates characterizing institutions vary—they are not all alike; it may be possible to measure institutional climate reliably with instruments such as the SCS; such measured variations in climate may be related to the ways in which inmates perceive their own possibilities; and we may have a more reliable way of identifying and monitoring desirable changes in institutional climates, so as to bring about changes in variables—inmate attitudes and behaviors, e.g.—which are related to climate.

REFERENCES

Clemmer, D. The process of prisonization. In L. Radziniwicz & M. E. Wolfgang (Eds.) *The criminal in confinement*. New York: Basic Books, Inc., 1971.

Goffman, E. *Asylums*. Garden City, New York: Anchor Books, 1961.

Irwin, J. *The felon*. Englewood Cliffs, New Jersey: Prentice-Hall, Inc., 1970.

Kesey, K. *One flew over the cuckoo's nest*. New York: Viking Press, 1964.

Schrag, C. Leadership among prison inmates. In L. Radziniwicz & M. E. Wolfgang (Eds.) *The criminal in confinement*. New York: Basic Books, Inc., 1971.

Shaw, G. B. The crime of imprisonment. Excerpted in J. E. Trupin (Ed.) *In prison*. New York: New American Library, 1975.

21

On Being Sane in Insane Places

D. L. Rosenhan

Reprinted from *Science* 179 (19 January 1973): 250–58, Copyright © 1973 by the American Association for the Advancement of Science. Author permission to reprint is gratefully acknowledged.

If sanity and insanity exist, how shall we know them?

The question is neither capricious nor itself insane. However much we may be personally convinced that we can tell the normal from the abnormal, the evidence is simply not compelling. It is commonplace, for example, to read about murder trials wherein eminent psychiatrists for the defense are contradicted by equally eminent psychiatrists for the prosecution on the matter of the defendant's sanity. More generally, there are a great deal of conflicting data on the reliability, utility, and meaning of such terms as "sanity," "insanity," "mental illness," and "schizophrenia."[1] Finally, as early as 1934, Benedict suggested that normality and abnormality are not universal.[2] What is viewed as normal in one culture may be seen as quite aberrant in another. Thus, notions of normality and abnormality may not be quite as accurate as people believe they are.

To raise questions regarding normality and abnormality is in no way to question the fact that some behaviors are deviant or odd. Murder is deviant. So, too, are hallucinations. Nor does raising such questions deny the existence of the personal anguish that is often associated with "mental illness." Anxiety and depression exist. Psychological suffering exists. But normality and abnormality, sanity and insanity, and the diagnoses that flow from them may be less substantive than many believe them to be.

At its heart, the question of whether the sane can be distinguished from the insane (and whether degrees of insanity can be distinguished from each other) is a simple matter: do the salient characteristics that lead to diagnoses reside in the patients themselves or in the environments and contexts in which observers find them? From Bleuler, through Kretchmer, through the formulators of the recently revised *Diagnostic and Statistical Manual* of the American Psychiatric Association, the belief has been strong that patients present symptoms, that those symptoms can be categorized, and, implicitly, that the sane are distinguishable from the insane. More recently, however, this belief has been questioned. Based in part on theoretical and anthropological considerations, but also on philosophical, legal, and therapeutic ones, the view has grown that psychological categorization of mental illness is useless at best and downright harmful, misleading, and pejorative at worst. Psychiatric diagnoses, in this view, are in the minds of the observers and are not valid summaries of characteristics displayed by the observed.[35]

Gains can be made in deciding which of these is more nearly accurate by getting normal people (that is, people who do not have, and have never suffered, symptoms of serious psychiatric disorders) admitted to psychiatric hospitals and then determining whether they were discovered to be sane and, if so, how. If the sanity of such pseudopatients were always detected, there would be prima facie evidence that a sane individual can be distinguished from the insane context in which he is found. Normality (and presumably abnormality) is distinct enough that it can be recognized wherever it occurs, for it is carried within the person. If, on the other hand, the sanity of the pseudopatients were never discovered, serious difficulties would arise for those who support traditional modes of psychiatric diagnosis. Given that the hospital staff was not incompetent, that the pseudopatient had been behaving as sanely as he had been outside of the hospital, and that it had never been previously suggested that he belonged in a psychiatric hospital, such an unlikely outcome would support the view that psychiatric diagnosis betrays little about the patient but much about the environment in which an observer finds him.

This article describes such an experiment. Eight sane people gained secret admission to 12 different hospitals.[6] Their diagnostic experiences constitute the data of the first part of this article; the remainder is devoted to a description of their experiences in psychiatric institutions. Too few psychiatrists and psychologists, even those who have worked in such hospitals, know what the experience is like. They rarely talk about it with former patients, perhaps because they distrust information coming from the previously insane. Those who have worked in psychiatric hospitals are likely to have adapted so thoroughly to the settings that they are insensitive to the impact of that experience. And while there have been occasional reports of researchers who submitted themselves to psychiatric hospitalization,[7] these researchers have commonly remained in the hospitals for short periods of time, often with the knowledge of the hospital staff. It is difficult to know the extent to which they were treated like patients or like research colleagues. Nevertheless, their reports about the inside of the psychiatric hospital have been valuable. This article extends those efforts.

PSEUDOPATIENTS AND THEIR SETTINGS

The eight pseudopatients were a varied group. One was a psychology graduate student in his 20's. The remaining seven were older and "established." Among them were three psychologists, a pediatrician, a psychiatrist, a painter, and a housewife. Three pseudopatients were women, five were men. All of them employed pseudonyms, lest their alleged diagnoses embarrass them later. Those who were in mental health professions alleged another occupation in order to avoid the special attentions that might be accorded by staff, as a matter of courtesy or caution, to ailing colleagues.[8] With the exception of myself (I was the first pseudopatient and my presence was known to the hospital administrator and chief psychologist and, so far as I can tell, to them alone), the presence of pseudopatients and the nature of the research program was not known to the hospital staffs.[9]

The settings were similarly varied. In order to generalize the findings, admission into a variety of hospitals was sought. The 12 hospitals in the sample were located in five different states on the East and West coasts. Some were old and shabby, some were quite new. Some were research-oriented, others not. Some had good staff-patient ratios, others were quite understaffed. Only one was a strictly private hospital. All of the others were supported by state or federal funds or, in one instance, by university funds.

After calling the hospital for an appointment, the pseudopatient arrived at the admissions office complaining that he had been hearing voices. Asked what the voices said, he replied that they were often unclear, but as far as he could tell they said "empty," "hollow," and "thud." The voices were unfamiliar and were of the same sex as the pseudopatient. The choice of these symptoms was occasioned by their apparent similarity to existential symptoms. Such symptoms are alleged to arise from painful concerns about the perceived meaninglessness of one's life. It is as if the hallucinating person were saying, "My life is empty and hollow." The choice of these symptoms was also determined by the *absence* of a single report of existential psychoses in the literature.

Beyond alleging the symptoms and falsifying name, vocation, and employment, no further alterations of person, history, or circumstances were made. The significant events of the pseudopatient's life history were presented as they had actually occurred. Relationships with parents and siblings, with spouse and children, with people at work and in school, consistent with the aforementioned exceptions, were described as they were or had been. Frustrations and upsets were described along with joys and satisfactions. These facts are important to remember. If anything, they strongly biased the subsequent results in favor of detecting sanity, since none of their histories or current behaviors were seriously pathological in any way.

Immediately upon admission to the psychiatric ward, the pseudopatient ceased simulating *any* symptoms of abnormality. In some cases, there was a brief period of mild nervousness and anxiety, since none of the pseudopatients really believed that they would be admitted so easily. Indeed, their shared fear was that they would be immediately exposed as frauds and greatly embarrassed. Moreover, many of them had never visited a psychiatric ward; even those who had, nevertheless had some genuine fears about what might happen to them. Their nervousness, then, was quite appropriate to the novelty of the hospital setting, and it abated rapidly.

Apart from that short-lived nervousness, the pseudopatient behaved on the ward as he "normally" behaved. The pseudopatient spoke to patients and staff as he might ordinarily. Because there is uncommonly little to do on a psychiatric ward, he attempted to engage others in conversation. When asked by staff how he was feeling, he indicated that he was fine, that he no longer experienced symptoms. He responded to instructions from attendants, to calls for medication (which was not swallowed), and to dining-hall instructions. Beyond such activities as were available to him on the admissions ward, he spent his time writing down his observations about the ward, its patients, and the staff. Initially these notes were written "secretly," but as it soon became clear that no one much cared, they were subsequently written on standard tablets of paper in such public places as the dayroom. No secret was made of these activities.

The pseudopatient, very much as a true psychiatric patient, entered a hospital with no foreknowledge of when he would be discharged. Each was told that he would have to get out by his own devices, essentially by convincing the staff that he was sane. The psychological stresses associated with hospitalization were considerable, and all but one of the pseudopatients desired to be discharged almost immediately after being admitted. They were, therefore, motivated not only to behave sanely, but to be paragons of cooperation. That their behavior was in no way disruptive is confirmed by nursing reports, which have been obtained on most of the patients. These reports uniformly indicate that the patients were "friendly," "cooperative," and "exhibited no abnormal indications."

THE NORMAL ARE NOT DETECTABLY SANE

Despite their public "show" of sanity, the pseudopatients were never detected. Admitted, except in one case, with a diagnosis of schizophrenia,[10] each was discharged with a diagnosis of schizophrenia "in remission." The label "in remission" should in no way be dismissed as a formality, for at no time during any hospitalization had any question been raised about any pseudopatient's simulation. Nor are there any indications in the hospital records that the pseudopatient's status was suspect. Rather, the evidence is strong that, once labeled schizophrenic, the pseudopatient was stuck with that label. If the pseudopatient was to be discharged, he must naturally be "in remission"; but he was not sane, nor, in the institution's view, had he ever been sane.

The uniform failure to recognize sanity cannot be attributed to the quality of the hospitals, for, although there were considerable variations among them, several are considered excellent. Nor can it be alleged that there was simply not enough time to observe the pseudopatients. Length of hospitalization ranged from 7 to 52 days, with an average of 19 days. The pseudopatients were not, in fact, carefully observed, but this failure clearly speaks more to traditions within psychiatric hospitals than to lack of opportunity.

Finally, it cannot be said that the failure to recognize the pseudopatients' sanity was due to the fact that they were not behaving sanely. While there was clearly some tension present in all of them, their daily visitors could detect no serious behavioral consequences—nor, indeed, could other patients. It was quite common for the patients to "detect" the pseudopatients' sanity. During the first three hospitalizations, when accurate counts were kept, 35 of a total of 118 patients on the admissions ward voiced their suspicions, some vigorously. "You're not crazy. You're a journalist, or a professor [referring to the continual note-taking]. You're checking up on the hospital." While most of the patients were reassured by the pseudopatient's insistence that he had been sick before he came in but was fine now, some continued to believe that the pseudopatient was sane throughout his hospitalization.[11] The fact that the patients often recognized normality when staff did not raises important questions.

Failure to detect sanity during the course of hospitalization may be due to the fact that physicians operate with a strong bias toward what statisticians call the type 2 error.[5] This is to say that physicians are more inclined to call a healthy person sick (a false positive, type 2) than a sick person healthy (a false negative, type 1). The reasons for this are not hard to find: it is clearly more dangerous to misdiagnose illness than health. Better to err on the side of caution, to suspect illness even among the healthy.

But what holds for medicine does not hold equally well for psychiatry. Medical illnesses, while unfortunate, are not commonly pejorative. Psychiatric diagnoses, on the contrary, carry with them personal, legal, and social stigmas.[12] It was therefore important to see whether the tendency toward diagnosing the sane insane could be reversed. The following experiment was arranged at a research and teaching hospital whose staff had heard these findings but doubted that such an error could occur in their hospital. The staff was informed that at some time during the following 3 months, one or more pseudopatients would attempt to be admitted into the psychiatric hospital. Each staff member was asked to rate each patient who presented himself at admissions or on the ward according to the likelihood that the patient was a pseudopatient. A 10-point scale was used, with 1 and 2 reflecting high confidence that the patient was a pseudopatient.

Judgments were obtained on 193 patients who were admitted for psychiatric treatment. All staff who had had sustained contact with or primary responsibility for the patient—attendants, nurses, psychiatrists, physicians, and psychologists—were asked to make judgments. Forty-one patients were alleged, with high confidence, to be pseudopatients by at least one member of the staff. Twenty-three were considered suspect by at least one psychiatrist. Nineteen were suspected by one psychiatrist *and* one other staff member. Actually, no genuine pseudopatient (at least from my group) presented himself during this period.

The experiment is instructive. It indicates that the tendency to designate sane people as insane can be reversed when the stakes (in this case, prestige and diagnostic acumen) are high. But what can be said of the 19 people who were suspected of being "sane" by one psychiatrist and another staff member? Were these people truly "sane," or was it rather the case that in the course of avoiding the type 2 error the staff tended to make more errors of the first sort—calling the crazy "sane"? There is no way of knowing. But one thing is certain: any diagnostic process that lends itself so readily to massive errors of this sort cannot be a very reliable one.

The Stickiness of Psychodiagnostic Labels

Beyond the tendency to call the healthy sick—a tendency that accounts better for diagnostic behavior on admission than it does for such behavior after a lengthy period of exposure—the data speak to the massive role of labeling in psychiatric assessment. Having once been labeled schizophrenic, there is nothing the pseudopatient can do to overcome the tag. The tag profoundly colors others' perceptions of him and his behavior.

From one viewpoint, these data are hardly surprising, for it has long been known that elements are given meaning by the context in which they occur. Gestalt psychology made this point vigorously, and Asch[13] demonstrated that there are "central" personality traits (such as "warm" versus "cold") which are so powerful that they markedly color the meaning of other information in forming an impression of a given personality.[14] "Insane," "schizophrenic," "manic-depressive," and "crazy" are probably among the most powerful of such central traits. Once a person is designated abnormal, all of his behaviors and characteristics are colored by that label. Indeed, that label is so powerful that many of the pseudopatients' normal behaviors were overlooked entirely or profoundly misinterpreted. Some examples may clarify the issue.

Earlier I indicated that there were no changes in the pseudopatient's personal history and current status beyond those of name, employment, and, where necessary, vocation. Otherwise, a veridical description of personal history and circumstances was offered. Those circumstances were not psychotic. How were they made consonant with the diagnosis of psychosis? Or were those diagnoses modified in such a way as to bring them into accord with the circumstances of the pseudopatient's life, as described by him?

As far as I can determine, diagnoses were in no way affected by the relative health of the circumstances of a pseudopatient's life. Rather, the reverse occurred: the perception of his circumstances was shaped entirely by the diagnosis. A clear example of such translation is found in the case of a pseudopatient who had had a close relationship with his mother but was rather remote from his father during his early childhood. During adolescence and beyond, however, his father became a close friend, while his relationship with his mother cooled. His present relationship with his wife was characteristically close and warm. Apart from occasional angry exchanges, friction was minimal. The children had rarely been spanked. Surely there is nothing especially pathological about such a history. Indeed, many readers may see a similar pattern in their own experiences, with no markedly deleterious consequences. Observe, however, how such a history was translated in the psychopathological context, this from the case summary prepared after the patient was discharged.

> This white 39-year-old male . . . manifests a long history of considerable ambivalence in close relationships, which begins in early childhood. A warm relationship with his mother cools during his adolescence. A distant relationship to his father is described as becoming very intense. Affective stability is absent. His attempts to control emotionality with his wife and children are punctuated by angry outbursts and, in the case of the children, spankings. And while he says that he has several good friends, one senses considerable ambivalence embedded in those relationships also. . . .

The facts of the case were unintentionally distorted by the staff to achieve consistency with a popular theory of the dynamics of a schizophrenic reaction.[15] Nothing of an ambivalent nature had been described in relations with parents, spouse, or friends. To the extent that ambivalence could be inferred, it was probably not greater than is found in all human relationships. It is true the pseudopatient's relationships with his parents changed over time, but in the ordinary context that would hardly be remarkable—indeed, it might very well be expected. Clearly, the meaning ascribed to his verbalizations (that is, ambivalence, affective instability) was determined by the diagnosis: schizophrenia. An entirely different meaning would have been ascribed if it were known that the man was "normal."

All pseudopatients took extensive notes publicly. Under ordinary circumstances, such behavior would have raised questions in the minds of observers, as, in fact, it did among patients. Indeed, it seemed so certain that the notes would elicit suspicion that elaborate precautions were taken to remove them from the ward each day. But the precautions proved needless.

The closest any staff member came to questioning these notes occurred when one pseudopatient asked his physician what kind of medication he was receiving and began to write down the response. "You needn't write it," he was told gently. "If you have trouble remembering, just ask me again."

If no questions were asked of the pseudopatients, how was their writing interpreted? Nursing records for three patients indicate that the writing was seen as an aspect of their pathological behavior. "Patient engages in writing behavior" was the daily nursing comment on one of the pseudopatients who was never questioned about his writing. Given that the patient is in the hospital, he must be psychologically disturbed. And given that he is disturbed, continuous writing must be a behavioral manifestation of that disturbance, perhaps a subset of the compulsive behaviors that are sometimes correlated with schizophrenia.

One tacit characteristic of psychiatric diagnosis is that it locates the sources of aberration within the individual and only rarely within the complex of stimuli that surrounds him. Consequently, behaviors that are stimulated by the environment are commonly misattributed to the patient's disorder. For example, one kindly nurse found a pseudopatient pacing the long hospital corridors. "Nervous, Mr. X?" she asked. "No, bored," he said.

The notes kept by pseudopatients are full of patient behaviors that were misinterpreted by well-intentioned staff. Often enough, a patient would go "berserk" because he had, wittingly or unwittingly, been mistreated by, say, an attendant. A nurse coming upon the scene would rarely inquire even cursorily into the environmental stimuli of the patient's behavior. Rather, she assumed that his upset derived from his pathology, not from his present interactions with other staff members. Occasionally, the staff might assume that the patient's family (especially when they had recently visited) or other patients had stimulated the outburst. But never were the staff found to assume that one of themselves or the structure of the hospital had anything to do with a patient's behavior. One psychiatrist pointed to a group of patients who were sitting outside the cafeteria entrance half an hour before lunchtime. To a group of young residents he indicated that such behavior was characteristic of the oral-acquisitive nature of the syndrome. It seemed not to occur to him that there were very few things to anticipate in a psychiatric hospital besides eating.

A psychiatric label has a life and an influence of its own. Once the impression has been formed that the patient is schizophrenic, the expectation is that he will continue to be schizophrenic. When a sufficient amount of time has passed, during which the patient has done nothing bizarre, he is considered to be in remission and available for discharge. But the label endures beyond discharge, with the unconfirmed expectation that he will behave as a schizophrenic again. Such labels, conferred by mental health professionals, are as influential on the patient as they are on his relatives and friends, and it should not surprise anyone that the diagnosis acts on all of them as a self-fulfilling prophecy. Eventually, the patient himself accepts the diagnosis, with all of its surplus meanings and expectations, and behaves accordingly.[5]

The inferences to be made from these matters are quite simple. Much as Zigler and Phillips have demonstrated that there is enormous overlap in the symptoms presented by patients who have been variously diagnosed,[16] so there is enormous overlap in the behaviors of the sane and the insane. The sane are not "sane" all of the time. We lose our tempers "for no good reason." We are occasionally depressed or anxious, again for no good reason. And we may find it difficult to get along with one or another person—again for no reason that we can specify. Similarly, the insane are not always insane. Indeed, it was the impression of the pseudopatients while living with them that they were sane for long periods of time—that the bizarre behaviors upon which their diagnoses were allegedly predicated constituted only a small fraction of their total behavior. If it makes no sense to label ourselves permanently depressed on the basis of an occasional depression, then it takes better evidence than is presently available to label all patients insane or schizophrenic on the basis of bizarre behaviors or cognitions. It seems more useful, as Mischel[17] has pointed out, to limit our discussions to *behaviors*, the stimuli that provoke them, and their correlates.

It is not known why powerful impressions of personality traits, such as "crazy" or "insane," arise. Conceivably, when the origins of and stimuli that give rise to a behavior are remote or unknown, or when the behavior strikes us as immutable, trait labels regarding the *behavior* arise. When, on the other hand, the origins and stimuli are known and available, discourse is limited to the behavior itself. Thus, I may hallucinate because I am sleeping, or I may hallucinate because I have ingested a peculiar drug. These are termed sleep-induced hallucinations, or dreams, and drug-induced hallucinations, respectively. But when the stimuli to my hallucinations are unknown, that is called craziness, or schizophrenia—as if that inference were somehow as illuminating as the others.

The Experience of Psychiatric Hospitalization

The term "mental illness" is of recent origin. It was coined by people who were humane in their inclinations and who wanted very much to raise the station of (and the public's sympathies toward) the psychologically disturbed from that of witches and "crazies" to one that was akin to the physically ill. And they were at least partially successful, for the treatment of the mentally ill *has* improved considerably over the years. But while treatment has improved, it is doubtful that people really regard the mentally ill in the same way that they view the physically ill. A broken leg is something one recovers from, but mental illness allegedly endures forever.[18] A broken leg does not threaten the observer, but a crazy schizophrenic? There is by now a host of evidence that attitudes toward the mentally ill are characterized by fear, hostility, aloofness, suspicion, and dread.[19] The mentally ill are society's lepers.

That such attitudes infect the general population is perhaps not surprising, only upsetting. But that they affect the professionals—attendants, nurses, physicians, psychologists, and social workers—who treat and deal with the mentally ill is more disconcerting, both because such attitudes are self-evidently pernicious and because they are unwitting. Most mental health professionals would insist that they are sympathetic toward the mentally ill, that they are neither avoidant nor hostile. But it is more likely that an exquisite ambivalence characterizes their relations with psychiatric patients, such that their avowed impulses are only part of their entire attitude. Negative attitudes are there too and can easily be detected. Such attitudes should not surprise us. They are the natural offspring of the labels patients wear and the places in which they are found.

Consider the structure of the typical psychiatric hospital. Staff and patients are strictly segregated. Staff have their own living space, including their dining facilities, bathrooms, and assembly places. The glassed quarters that contain the professional staff, which the pseudopatients came to call "the cage," sit out on every dayroom. The staff emerge primarily for caretaking purposes—to give medication, to conduct a therapy or group meeting, to instruct or reprimand a patient. Otherwise, staff keep to themselves, almost as if the disorder that afflicts their charges is somehow catching.

So much is patient-staff segregation the rule that, for four public hospitals in which an attempt was made to measure the degree to which staff and patients mingled, it was necessary to use "time out of the staff cage" as the operational measure. While it was not the case that all time spent out of the cage was spent mingling with patients (attendants, for example, would occasionally emerge to watch television in the dayroom), it was the only way in which one could gather reliable data on time for measuring.

The average amount of time spent by attendants outside of the cage was 11.3 percent (range, 3 to 52 percent). This figure does not represent only time spent mingling with patients, but also includes time spent on such chores as folding laundry, supervising patients while they shave, directing ward clean-up, and sending patients to off-ward activities. It was the relatively rare attendant who spent time talking with patients or playing games with them. It proved impossible to obtain a "percent mingling time" for nurses, since the amount of time they spent out of the cage was too brief. Rather, we counted instances of emergence from the cage. On the average, daytime nurses emerged from the cage 11.5 times per shift, including instances when they left the ward entirely (range, 4 to 39 times). Late afternoon and night nurses were even less available, emerging on the average 9.4 times per shift (range, 4 to 41 times). Data on early morning nurses, who arrived usually after midnight and departed at 8 A.M., are not available because patients were asleep during most of this period.

Physicians, especially psychiatrists, were even less available. They were rarely seen on the wards. Quite commonly, they would be seen only when they arrived and departed, with the remaining time being spent in their offices or in the cage. On the average, physicians emerged on the ward 6.7 times per day (range, 1 to 17 times). It proved difficult to make an accurate estimate in this regard, since physicians often maintained hours that allowed them to come and go at different times.

The hierarchical organization of the psychiatric hospital has been commented on before,[20] but the latent meaning of that kind of organization is worth noting again. Those with the most power have least to do with patients, and those with the least power are most involved with them. Recall, however, that the acquisition of role-appropriate behaviors occurs mainly through the observation of others, with the most powerful having the most influence. Consequently, it is understandable that attendants not only spend more time with patients than do any other members of the staff—that is required by their station in the hierarchy—but also, insofar as they learn from their supervisors' behavior, spend as little time with patients as they can. Attendants are seen mainly in the cage, which is where the models, the action, and the power are.

I turn now to a different set of studies, these dealing with staff response to patient-initiated contact. It has long been known that the amount of time a person spends with you can be an index of your significance to him. If he initiates and maintains eye contact, there is reason to believe that he is considering your requests and needs. If he pauses to chat or actually stops and talks, there is added reason to infer that he is individuating you. In four hospitals, the pseudopatient approached the staff member with a request which took the following form: "Pardon me, Mr. (or Dr. or Mrs.) X, could you tell me when I will be eligible for grounds privileges?" (or " . . . when I will be presented at the staff meeting?" or ". . . when I am likely to be discharged?"). While the content of the question varied according to the appropriateness of the target and the pseudopatient's (apparent) current needs, the form was always a courteous and relevant request for information. Care was taken never to approach a particular member of the staff more than once a day, lest the staff member become suspicious or irritated. In examining these data, remember that the behavior of the pseudopatients was neither bizarre nor disruptive. One could indeed engage in good conversation with them.

The data for these experiments, are shown in Table 21.1, separately for physicians (column 1) and for nurses and attendants (column 2). Minor differences between these four institutions were overwhelmed by the degree to which staff avoided continuing contacts that patients had initiated. By far, their most common response consisted of either a brief response to the question, offered while they were "on the move" and with head averted, or no response at all.

The encounter frequently took the following bizarre form: (pseudopatient) "Pardon me, Dr. X. Could you tell me when I am eligible for grounds privileges?" (physician) "Good morning, Dave. How are you today?" (Moves off without waiting for a response.)

It is instructive to compare these data with data recently obtained at Stanford University. It has been alleged that large and eminent universities are characterized by faculty who are so busy that they have no time for students. For this comparison, a young lady approached individual faculty members who seemed to be walking purposefully to some meeting or teaching engagement and asked them the following six questions:

1: "Pardon me, could you direct me to Encina Hall?" (at the medical school: ". . . to the Clinical Research Center?").

2: "Do you know where Fish Annex is?" (there is no Fish Annex at Stanford).

3: "Do you teach here?"

4: "How does one apply for admission to the college?" (at the medical school: ". . . to the medical school?").

5: "Is it difficult to get in?"

6: "Is there financial aid?"

Without exception, as can be seen in Table 21.1 (column 3), all of the questions were answered. No matter how rushed they were, all respondents not only maintained eye contact, but stopped to talk. Indeed, many of the respondents went out of their way to direct or take the questioner to the office she was seeking, to try to locate "Fish Annex," or to discuss with her the possibilities of being admitted to the university.

Similar data, also shown in Table 21.1 (columns 4, 5, and 6), were obtained in the hospital. Here too, the young lady came prepared with six questions. After the first question, however, she remarked to 18 of her respondents (column 4), "I'm looking for a psychiatrist," and to 15 others (column 5), "I'm looking for an internist." Ten other respondents received no inserted comment (column 6). The general degree of cooperative responses is considerably higher for these university groups than it was for pseudopatients in psychiatric hospitals. Even so, differences are apparent within the

TABLE 21.1.
Self-initiated Contact by Pseudopatients with Psychiatrists and Nurses and Attendants, Compared to Contact with Other Groups.

Contact	Psychiatric hospitals		University campus (nonmedical)	University medical center Physicians		
	(1) Psychiatrists	(2) Nurses and Attendants	(3) Faculty	(4) "Looking for a psychiatrist"	(5) "Looking for an internist"	(6) No additional comment
Responses						
Moves on, head averted (%)	71	88	0	0	0	0
Makes eye contact (%)	23	10	0	11	0	0
Pauses and chats (%)	2	2	0	11	0	10
Stops and talks (%)	4	0.5	100	78	100	90
Mean number of questions answered (out of 6)	*	*	6	3.8	4.8	4.5
Respondents (No.)	13	47	14	18	15	10
Attempts (No.)	185	1283	14	18	15	10

*Not applicable.

medical school setting. Once having indicated that she was looking for a psychiatrist, the degree of cooperation elicited was less than when she sought an internist.

POWERLESSNESS AND DEPERSONALIZATION

Eye contact and verbal contact reflect concern and individuation; their absence, avoidance and depersonalization. The data I have presented do not do justice to the rich daily encounters that grew up around matters of depersonalization and avoidance. I have records of patients who were beaten by staff for the sin of having initiated verbal contact. During my own experience, for example, one patient was beaten in the presence of other patients for having approached an attendant and told him, "I like you." Occasionally, punishment meted out to patients for misdemeanors seemed so excessive that it could not be justified by the most radical interpretations of psychiatric canon. Nevertheless, they appeared to go unquestioned. Tempers were often short. A patient who had not heard a call for medication would be roundly excoriated, and the morning attendants would often wake patients with, "Come on, you m———f———s, out of bed!"

Neither anecdotal nor "hard" data can convey the overwhelming sense of powerlessness which invades the individual as he is continually exposed to the depersonalization of the psychiatric hospital. It hardly matters *which* psychiatric hospital—the excellent public ones and the very plush private hospital were better than the rural and shabby ones in this regard, but, again, the features that psychiatric hospitals had in common overwhelmed by far their apparent differences.

Powerlessness was evident everywhere. The patient is deprived of many of his legal rights by dint of his psychiatric commitment.[21] He is shorn of credibility by virtue of his psychiatric label. His freedom of movement is restricted. He cannot initiate contact with the staff, but may only respond to such overtures as they make. Personal privacy is minimal. Patients quarters and possessions can be entered and examined by any staff member, for whatever reason. His personal history and anguish is available to any staff member (often including the "grey lady" and "candy striper" volunteer) who chooses to read his folder, regardless of their therapeutic relationship to him. His personal hygiene and waste evacuation are often monitored. The water closets may have no doors.

At times, depersonalization reached such proportions that pseudopatients had the sense that they were invisible, or at least unworthy of account. Upon being admitted, I and other pseudopatients took the initial physical examinations in a semipublic room, where staff members went about their own business as if we were not there.

On the ward, attendants delivered verbal and occasionally serious physical abuse to patients in the presence of other observing patients, some of whom (the pseudopatients) were writing it all down. Abusive behavior, on the other hand, terminated quite abruptly when other staff members were known to be coming. Staff are credible witnesses. Patients are not.

A nurse unbuttoned her uniform to adjust her brassiere in the presence of an entire ward of viewing men. One did not have the sense that she was being seductive. Rather, she didn't notice us. A group of staff persons might point to a patient in the dayroom and discuss him animatedly, as if he were not there.

One illuminating instance of depersonalization and invisibility occurred with regard to medications. All told, the pseudopatients were administered nearly 2,100 pills, including Elavil, Stelazine, Compazine, and Thorazine, to name but a few. (That such a variety of medications should have been administered to patients presenting identical symptoms is itself worthy of note.) Only two were swallowed. The rest were either pocketed or deposited in the toilet. The pseudopatients were not alone in this. Although I have no precise records on how many patients rejected their medications, the pseudopatients frequently found the medications of other patients in the toilet before they deposited their own. As long as they were cooperative, their behavior and the pseudopatients' own in this matter, as in other important matters, went unnoticed throughout.

Reactions to such depersonalization among pseudopatients were intense. Although they had come to the hospital as participant observers and were fully aware that they did not "belong," they nevertheless found themselves caught up in and fighting the process of depersonalization. Some examples: a graduate student in psychology asked his wife to bring his textbooks to the hospital so he could "catch up on his homework"—this despite the elaborate precautions taken to conceal his professional association. The same student, who had trained for quite some time to get into the hospital, and who had looked forward to the experience, "remembered" some drag races that he had wanted to see on the weekend and insisted that he be discharged by that time. Another pseudopatient attempted a romance with a nurse. Subsequently, he informed the staff that he was applying for admission to graduate school in psychology and was very likely to be admitted, since a graduate professor was one of his regular hospital visitors. The same person began to engage in psychotherapy with other patients—all of this as a way of becoming a person in an impersonal environment.

THE SOURCES OF DEPERSONALIZATION

What are the origins of depersonalization? I have already mentioned two. First are attitudes held by all of us toward the mentally ill—including those who treat them—attitudes characterized by fear, distrust, and horrible expectations on the one hand, and benevolent intentions on the other. Our ambivalence leads, in this instance as in others, to avoidance.

Second, and not entirely separate, the hierarchical structure of the psychiatric hospital facilitates depersonalization. Those who are at the top have least to do with patients, and their behavior inspires the rest of the staff. Average daily contact with psychiatrists, psychologists, residents, and physicians combined ranged from 3.9 to 25.1 minutes, with an overall mean of 6.8 (six pseudopatients over a total of 129 days of hospitalization). Included in this average are time spent in the admissions interview, ward meetings in the presence of a senior staff member, group and individual psychotherapy contacts, case presentation conferences, and discharge meetings. Clearly, patients do not spend much time in interpersonal contact with doctoral staff. And doctoral staff serve as models for nurses and attendants.

There are probably other sources. Psychiatric installations are presently in serious financial straits. Staff shortages are pervasive, staff time at a premium. Something has to give, and that something is patient contact. Yet, while financial stresses are realities, too much can be made of them. I have the impression that the psychological forces that result in depersonalization are much stronger than the fiscal ones and that the addition of more staff would not correspondingly improve patient care in this regard. The incidence of staff meetings and the enormous amount of record-keeping on patients, for example, have not been as substantially reduced as has patient contact. Priorities exist, even during hard times. Patient contact is not a significant priority in the traditional psychiatric hospital, and fiscal pressures do not account for this. Avoidance and depersonalization may.

Heavy reliance upon psychotropic medication tacitly contributes to depersonalization by convincing staff that treatment is indeed being conducted and that further patient contact may not be necessary. Even here, however, caution needs to be exercised in understanding the role of psychotropic drugs. If patients were powerful rather than powerless, if they were viewed as interacting individuals rather than diagnostic entities, if they were socially significant rather than social lepers, if their anguish truly and wholly compelled our sympathies and concerns, would we not *seek* contact with them, despite the availability of medication? Perhaps for the pleasure of it all?

THE CONSEQUENCES OF LABELING AND DEPERSONALIZATION

Whenever the ratio of what is known to what needs to be known approaches zero, we tend to invent "knowledge" and assume that we understand more than we actually do. We seem unable to acknowledge that we simply don't know. The needs for diagnosis and remediation of behavioral and emotional problems are enormous. But rather than acknowledge that we are just embarking on understanding, we continue to label patients "schizophrenic," "manic-depressive," and "insane," as if in those words we had captured the essence of understanding. The facts of the matter are that we have known for a long time that diagnoses are often not useful or reliable, but we have nevertheless continued to use them. We now know that we cannot distinguish insanity from sanity. It is depressing to consider how that information will be used.

Not merely depressing, but frightening. How many people, one wonders, are sane but not recognized as such in our psychiatric institutions? How many have been needlessly stripped of their privileges of citizenship, from the right to vote and drive to that of handling their own accounts? How many have feigned insanity in order to avoid the criminal consequences of their behavior, and, conversely, how many would rather stand trial than live interminably in a psychiatric hospital—but are wrongly thought to be mentally ill? How many have been stigmatized by well-intentioned, but nevertheless erroneous, diagnoses? On the last point, recall again that a "type 2 error" in psychiatric diagnosis does not have the same consequences it does in medical diagnosis. A diagnosis of cancer that has been found to be in error is cause for celebration. But psychiatric diagnoses are rarely found to be in error. The label sticks, a mark of inadequacy forever.

Finally, how many patients might be "sane" outside the psychiatric hospital but seen insane in it—not because craziness resides in them, as it were, but because they are responding to a bizarre setting, one that may be unique to institutions which harbor nether people? Goffman[4] calls the process of socialization to such institutions "mortification"—an apt metaphor that includes the processes of depersonalization that have been described here. And while it is impossible to know whether the pseudopatients' responses to these processes are characteristic of all inmates—they were, after all, not real patients—it is difficult to believe that these processes of socialization to a psychiatric hospital provide useful attitudes or habits of response for living in the "real world."

SUMMARY AND CONCLUSIONS

It is clear that we cannot distinguish the sane from the insane in psychiatric hospitals. The hospital itself imposes a special environment in which the meanings of behavior can easily be misunderstood. The consequences to patients hospitalized in such an environment—the powerlessness, depersonalization, segregation, mortification, and self-labeling—seem undoubtedly counter-therapeutic.

I do not, even now, understand this problem well enough to perceive solutions. But two matters seem to have some promise. The first concerns the proliferation of community mental health facilities, of crisis intervention centers, of the human potential movement, and of behavior therapies that, for all of their own problems, tend to avoid psychiatric labels, to focus on specific problems and behaviors, and to retain the individual in a relatively nonpejorative environment. Clearly, to the extent that we refrain from sending the distressed to insane places, our impressions of them are less likely to be distorted. (The risk of distorted perceptions, it seems to me, is always present, since we are much more sensitive to an individual's behaviors and verbalizations than we are to the subtle contextual stimuli that often promote them. At issue here is a matter of magnitude. And, as I have shown, the magnitude of distortion is exceedingly high in the extreme context that is a psychiatric hospital).

The second matter that might prove promising speaks to the need to increase the sensitivity of mental health workers and researchers to the *Catch 22* position of psychiatric patients. Simply reading materials in this area will be of help to some such workers and researchers. For others, directly experiencing the impact of psychiatric hospitalization will be of enormous use. Clearly, further research into the social psychology of such total institutions will both facilitate treatment and deepen understanding.

I and the other pseudopatients in the psychiatric setting had distinctly negative reactions. We do not pretend to describe the subjective experiences of true patients. Theirs may be different from ours, particularly with the passage of time and the necessary process of adaptation to one's environment. But we can and do speak to the relatively more objective indices of treatment within the hospital. It could be a mistake, and a very unfortunate one, to consider that what happened to us derived from malice or stupidity on the part of the staff. Quite the contrary, our overwhelming impression of them was of people who really cared, who were committed and who were uncommonly intelligent. Where they failed, as they sometimes did painfully, it would be more accurate to attribute those failures to the environment in which they, too, found themselves than to personal callousness. Their perceptions and behavior were controlled by the situation, rather than being motivated by a malicious disposition. In a more benign environment, one that was less attached to global diagnosis, their behaviors and judgments might have been more benign and effective.

NOTES

1. P. Ash, *J. Abnorm. Soc. Psychol.* 44, 272 (1949); A. T. Beck, *Amer. J. Psychiat.* 119, 210 (1962); A. T. Boisen, *Psychiatry* 2, 233 (1938); N. Kreitman, *J. Ment. Sci.* 107, 876 (1961); N. Kreitman, P. Sainsbury, J. Morrisey, J. Towers, J. Scrivener, *ibid.*, p. 887; H O. Schmitt and C. P. Fonda, *J. Abnorm. Soc. Psychol.* 52, 262 (1956); W. Seeman, *J. Nerv. Ment. Dis.* 118, 541 (1953). For an analysis of these artifacts and summaries of the disputes, see J. Zubin, *Annu. Rev. Psychol.* 18, 373 (1967); L. Phillips and J. G. Draguns, *ibid*, 22, 447 (1971).

2. R. Benedict, *J. Gen. Psychol.* 10, 59 (1934).
3. See in this regard H. Becker, *Outsiders: Studies in the Sociology of Deviance* (Free Press, New York, 1963); P. M. Braginsky, D. D. Braginsky, K. Ring, *Methods of Madness: The Mental Hospital as a Last Resort* (Holt, Rinehart & Winston, New York, 1969); G. M. Crocetti and P. V. Lemkau, *Amer. Sociol. Rev.* 30, 577 (1965); E. Goffman, *Behavior in Public Places* (Free Press, New York, 1964); R. D. Laing, *The Divided Self: A Study of Sanity and Madness* (Quadrangle, Chicago, 1960); D. L. Phillips, *Amer. Sociol. Rev.* 28, 963 (1963); T. R. Sarbin, *Psychol. Today* 6, 18 (1972); E. Schur, *Amer. J. Sociol.* 75, 309 (1969); T. Szasz, *Law, Liberty and Psychiatry* (Macmillan, New York, 1963); *The Myth of Mental Illness: Foundations of a Theory of Mental Illness* (Hoeber-Harper, New York, 1963). For a critique of some of these views, see W. R. Gove, *Amer. Sociol. Rev.* 35, 873 (1970).
4. E. Goffman, *Asylums* (Doubleday, Garden City, N.Y., 1961).
5. T. J. Scheff, *Being Mentally Ill: A Sociological Theory* (Aldine, Chicago, 1966).
6. Data from a ninth pseudopatient are not incorporated in this report because, although his sanity went undetected, he falsified aspects of his personal history, including his marital status and parental relationships. His experimental behaviors therefore were not identical to those of the other pseudopatients.
7. A. Barry, *Bellevue Is a State of Mind* (Harcourt Brace Jovanovich, New York, 1971); I. Belknap, *Human Problems of a State Mental Hospital* (McGraw-Hill, New York, 1956); W. Caudill, F. C. Redlich, H. R. Gilmore, F. B. Brody, *Amer. J. Orthopsychiat.* 22, 314 (1952); A. R. Goldman, R. H. Bohr, T. A. Steinberg, *Prof. Psychol.* 1, 427 (1970); unauthored, *Roche Report 1* (No. 13), 8 (1971).
8. Beyond the personal difficulties that the pseudopatient is likely to experience in the hospital, there are legal and social ones that, combined, require considerable attention before entry. For example, once admitted to a psychiatric institution, it is difficult, if not impossible, to be discharged on short notice, state law to the contrary notwithstanding. I was not sensitive to these difficulties at the outset of the project, nor to the personal and situational emergencies that can arise, but later a writ of habeas corpus was prepared for each of the entering pseudopatients and an attorney was kept "on call" during every hospitalization. I am grateful to John Kaplan and Robert Bartels for legal advice and assistance in these matters.
9. However distasteful such concealment is, it was a necessary first step to examining these questions. Without concealment, there would have been no way to know how valid these experiences were; nor was there any way of knowing whether whatever detections occurred were a tribute to the diagnostic acumen of the staff or to the hospital's rumor network. Obviously, since my concerns are general ones that cut across individual hospitals and staffs, I have respected their anonymity and have eliminated clues that might lead to their identification.
10. Interestingly, of the 12 admissions, 11 were diagnosed as schizophrenic and one, with the identical symptomatology, as manic-depressive psychosis. This diagnosis has a more favorable prognosis, and it was given by the only private hospital in our sample. On the relations between social class and psychiatric diagnosis, see A. deB. Hollinshead and F. C. Redlich, *Social Class and Mental Illness: A Community Study* (Wiley, New York, 1958).

11. It is possible, of course, that patients have quite broad latitudes in diagnosis and therefore are inclined to call many people sane, even those whose behavior is patently aberrant. However, although we have no hard data on this matter, it was our distinct impression that this was not the case. In many instances, patients not only singled us out for attention, but came to imitate our behaviors and styles.

12. J. Cumming and E. Cumming, *Community Ment. Health* 1, 135 (1965); A. Farina and K. Ring, *J. Abnorm. Psychol.* 70, 47 (1965); H. E. Freeman and O. G. Simmons, *The Mental Patient Comes Home* (Wiley, New York, 1963); W. J. Johannsen, *Ment. Hygiene* 53, 218 (1969); A. S. Linsky, *Soc. Psychiat.* 5, 166 (1970).

13. S. E. Asch, *J. Abnorm. Soc. Psychol.* 41, 258 (1946); *Social Psychology* (Prentice-Hall, New York, 1952).

14. See also I. N. Mensh and J. Wishner, *J. Personality* 16, 188 (1947); J. Wishner, *Psychol Rev* 67, 96 (1960); J. S. Bruner and R. Tagiuri, in *Handbook of Social Psychology*, G. Lindzey, Ed. (Addison-Wesley, Cambridge, Mass, 1954) vol. 2, pp. 634-654; J. S. Bruner, D. Shapiro, R. Tagiuri, in *Person Perception & Interpersonal Behavior*, R. Tagirui and L. Petrullo, Eds. (Stanford Univ. Press, Stanford, Calif., 1958), pp. 277–288.

15. For an example of a similar self-fulfilling prophecy, in this instance dealing with the "central" trait of intelligence, see R. Rosenthal and L. Jacobson, *Pygmalion in the Classroom* (Holt, Rinehart & Winston, New York 1968).

16. E. Zigler and L. Phillips, *J. Abnorm. Soc. Psychol.* 63, 69 (1961). See also R. K. Freudenberg and J. P. Robertson, *A.M.A. Arch. Neurol. Psychiatr.* 76, 14 (1956).

17. W. Mischel, *Personality and Assessment* (Wiley, New York, 1968).

18. The most recent and unfortunate instance of this tenet is that of Senator Thomas Eagleton.

19. T. R. Sarbin and J. C. Mancuso, *J. Clin. Consult. Psychol.* 35, 159 (1970); T. R. Sarbin, *ibid.* 31, 447 (1967); J. C. Nunnally, Jr., *Popular Conceptions of Mental Health* (Holt, Rinehart & Winston, Inc., New York, 1961).

20. A. H. Stanton and M. S. Schwartz, *The Mental Hospital: A Study of Institutional Participation in Psychiatric Illness and Treatment* (Basic, New York, 1954).

21. D. B. Wexler and S. E. Scoville, *Ariz. Law Rev.* 13, 1 (1971).

22. I thank W. Mischel, E. Orne, and M. S. Rosenhan for comments on an earlier draft of this manuscript.

22

The White Victim in a Black Institution

Clemens Bartollas and Stuart J. Miller

This is a revision of an article which appeared in *Treating the Offender: Problems and Issues*, M. Rievel and P. Vales, Praeger Publishers, 1976. Reprinted by permission of the authors.

American society has seen the victimization of blacks by whites for many years. Sexual exploitation of black women, discrimination in housing, the granting of menial jobs only to blacks, and differential treatment by the criminal justice system have all contributed to feelings of resentment and frustration. These facts are especially salient for youths in black ghettos; jobless, unskilled, turned off by the schools, and yet trying to make it by any means possible, it is little wonder that some eventually find themselves in penal institutions where, in all probability, they should be able to expect further white domination. Paradoxically, this does not always happen, and blacks are occasionally able to experience the feelings of dominance and power ordinarily reserved for whites only. The result is black exploitation of whites, i.e., the creation of white victims.

THE PRESENT STUDY

To ascertain the nature of exploitation, we went to certain staff and asked them about the most serious types of exploitation in the institution.[1] They suggested that food, clothes and cigarettes were the primary items of non-sexual exploitation, while masturbation of others, oral and anal sodomy constituted the forms of sexual exploitation.[2] They also indicated that inmates fell into different categories—some youths were neither the exploiters nor the exploited, some were exploiters but weren't exploited, some were exploiters, but were also exploited, some did not exploit, but were exploited occasionally, and some did not exploit but were exploited often. Schedules were constructed enabling us to describe the sample and to test these ideas, and were given to all youth leaders and social workers in the institution.[3] In addition, in-depth interviews were conducted with certain staff and youth.

THE INSTITUTIONAL SETTING

The institution studied is considered end-of-the-line, and is reserved for overly hostile and aggressive males ranging in age from 15 to 18 years. These boys, 46% of whom are black and 54% white, are considered to be some of the hardest core delinquents in the state. The majority of these youths have committed serious personal and property offenses, with 2.4 being the average number of previous commitments to state institutions. In addition, one-half have been diagnosed as dangerous to others and one-fifth as emotionally disturbed. As one administrator put it, "There is no innocence here."

The boys are housed in eight cottages joined by corridors connecting school, vocational, and recreational areas. Each cottage has a living, dining and recreational area, offices for the youth leaders and a social worker, two four-bed dormitories, and sixteen single rooms. The institution can accommodate 192 boys although only 159 were in residence at the time of the study. The youth leaders, who have more contact with the boys than anyone else, are 97% black.[4]

FINDINGS

Our findings indicated clearly that whites were the most seriously exploited victims in this institution. Of the 16 boys who were being exploited sexually, for example, 13 were white; and in every cottage, even though whites usually outnumbered blacks slightly, whites were clearly at the bottom of the pecking order. To understand the dynamics of the exploitation, it was necessary to examine social class, institutional structure, boys' past institutional history and their physical and psychological characteristics. To understand why whites rather than blacks were victimized, it was necessary to understand the interplay of these factors.

Before coming to this institution, boys, both black and white, have heard rumors about it being underground, that staff whipped boys with hoses, that you have to stay a long time, and that all of the boys were big and tough.[5] Thus, boys coming to this institution are fearful for their own survival. Although this fearfulness usually subsides after several weeks, it is during this initial period that the greatest efforts will be made to victimize them, beginning, in fact, when the students first enter the institution.

When the student walks into the cottage that first day, all eyes are on him. His peers are attempting to answer four basic questions: "Is he a punk?," "How is he holding himself?," "Will he defend himself?" and "How much does he have?" These questions revolve around whether he has been sexually exploited, how fearful he is at the present time, whether he will fight back, and what can be exploited (food, cigarettes and/or sex) from him.

The answers to these questions begin to emerge when, if he is white, another white walks up to him and asks him what his name is, where he is from, where he has been, and what he is in for. After feeling him out with these questions, he will probably ask the new boy whether he has a cigarette. If so, his "new friend" will probably ask him for a pack, promising to pay him back in the near future. But more than exploiting a few cigarettes from him, the purpose of this initial contact is to set him up for later victimization and to determine where he is going "to fit" in the cottage social structure.

Other whites are watching this encounter and will get together later to talk with the student who made the first approach. Their attempts at exploitation over the next several weeks will be contingent upon what has been learned about him. But regardless how successful his "interview" was, it is very unlikely that the new student will receive any support from the other whites as he struggles to adjust to the institution.

With the black students, the situation is quite different. In the first place, there are usually three or four blacks in every cottage who are interested in sexually exploiting him, especially if he has feminine features. In addition, more blacks than whites are interested in exploiting cigarettes and food and may approach him even before the whites.

The degree of victimization of this new white boy depends upon this initial impression, as well as his size, number of friends in the cottage, criminal offenses, social class, and the ability of the boys trying to victimize him. Further, most successful sexual exploiters are subtle; they constantly remind the white boy that he is "punk" and that it would be easier on him if he would "give in." Experienced exploiters wait for a moment of weakness, and then pounce on their prey before he can change his mind. If they are not successful, they will eventually leave him alone. Nevertheless, he will still have to go through the same battles in the school and recreational areas.

It is at this point of beginning participation in other institutional activities that the new white may attempt to approach the "heavy" of the cottage and give him cigarettes or food in exchange for protection.[6] The heavy will usually accept his cigarettes, but he will not smoke after him, since smoking after a white boy, even one who is "together" and "all right" will result in loss of status to the black leader.[7] In addition, he may not protect the new student in other parts of the institution since, as a heavy, he can take favors from students without necessarily involving himself in reciprocal relationships.

After the other blacks see these initial "bribes" given to the heavy, they become very serious about taking his possessions from him. Initially, the youth generally overreacts, gives too much away and, following a period of harassment from the youth leaders in the cottage, tapers off in what he is willing to give away.

It is during these early weeks in the institution, in other words, that a youth earns his position in the pecking order. He will not be placed at the bottom of the social structure until he can be exploited sexually, but if he does "give away his manhood" then he becomes a scapegoat to the boys and "a vegetable" to the youth leaders. Sexual victims, moreover, differ to the extent they are ostracized from the group. Anal sodomy appears to receive the least social rejection, followed by masturbation and oral sodomy.[8]

Boys who commit oral sodomy or masturbate others are regarded as the worst type of outcasts, and their ability to get along with others is seriously weakened. In one cottage, for example, the black students went on a hunger strike for several days until a white social outcast was taken out of the kitchen. In this same cottage, another white outcast was stabbed for touching the cake of a black student. The reason for both of these incidents is that the black student feels that social outcasts are unclean and they do not want them handling their food.

VARIETIES OF HOMOSEXUAL BEHAVIOR

The boys in this institution regard anyone who engages in sex play with the same sex as homosexual, regardless of why it took place. Little if any distinction is made between the youth who is oriented toward homosexuality as a life-style, the youth who is forced to participate against his will, or the youth who has ulterior motives for his participation.[9] In this study, there appeared to be four types of homosexual behavior among the whites.

The first type consists of those who willingly have had homosexual experiences in other institutions. They generally come to this institution hoping to leave their past behind, but once their peers become aware they had been "punks" in other places, great pressure is placed on them to continue this life-style. It is rare for any youth with a homosexual history to be able to resist the type of persistent pressure he receives.[10]

A second type of homosexual is one who gives up sex in exchange for something else. There is the youth, for instance, who does not have any cigarettes and who will masturbate another for a pack of cigarettes. Another example is the fearful white boy who buys protection from a strong black peer because he does not want to be slapped around by others. Thus, he exchanges sexual privileges for protection. Although this appears to create consistent disruptive problems in the adult correctional system, the buying of protection is rather rare at this institution. When it does take place, it creates serious conflicts within the peer culture in this type of institution as well.

The third type of homosexual is the passive and dependent youth who submits strictly out of fear. He is afraid of being physically attacked, and is mentally fatigued from the abuse and harassment he has received from his black peers. While this boy is usually a middle-class white who is simply overwhelmed by his present environment, lower-class whites who come into the institution with a reputation of being a "tough guy" can sometimes be made into fearful homosexuals if they are gang raped. After one of these incidents several years ago, there was a drastic change in the personality of a particular boy, for instead of pushing others around as he had done in the past, he became quite passive and tried to withdraw from everyone in the cottage.

Finally, there is the youth who has anal intercourse with another white because they are friends and they feel close to each other. Most of these sexual relationships are characterized by the exchange of friendship, rather than the coercion of exploitation. Since their behavior is voluntary, they appear to come closest to what is considered to be true homosexuality. But even here, the relationship would appear to be temporary and is a function of the institutional life. It is not characterized by a life-style which theoretically, at least, should also include blacks.

OTHER RESULTS OF BLACK DOMINATION

In this institution, black students not only exploit cigarettes, food and clothing and sex from whites, but also socialize whites into black subculture. Blacks, by their position of power, are able to control what music will be played and what television programs will be seen; they, in addition, dictate the style of food, clothing and language to be used in the cottages.

Whenever a white puts an unacceptable record on the stereo in the program area, for example, a black student merely walks over to the stereo and changes the record.[11] In the dormitory at night, unless all four boys are white, white boys refrain from playing anything but "soul music." When watching television, blacks choose the programs, and whites are forced either to watch these programs or do something else. Whites must decide each night whether to go to bed early or to watch a television show preferred by the blacks.[12] Food is an even better indicator of the influence and pervasiveness of the black culture. Certain foods are considered "soul food," others are considered acceptable to be eaten but not to be liked, and there are other unacceptable foods which must not be eaten. Only a few strong whites are not co-opted in their taste in food by blacks. The major exception to this is the cottage scapegoat who seems to have an affinity for eating undesirable foods—probably in order to get attention.[13] Another indicator of black domination is clothing. Since students wear state clothing, black influence is difficult to perceive in daily dress, but it becomes much more obvious at dances and other special occasions where students dress up. The whites attempt to imitate the modish dress of blacks at these occasions. Finally, the language also is a sign of the black subculture's domination. Even though there is some resemblance between the language used by a ghetto black and a white boy who lives near the ghetto, there is a distinctive style of language used by the ghetto black which the white attempts to emulate after he has been exposed to it for a short period of time.

FACTORS RELATED TO VICTIMIZATION

There are several factors which contribute to the white being victimized more than the black in this institution and others like it. Social class background as it relates to race is of primary importance, with institutional structure and characteristics, past institutional history of the boys, and their personality and physical characteristics appearing to be secondary variables.

SOCIAL CLASS AND BLACK AGGRESSIVENESS

Jim Roberts, a youth leader in this training school, stated that there were three types of youths in this institution—the ghetto black, the white who lives near a ghetto, and the middle-class white. Roberts felt that these youths could be further divided into the haves and the have nots with the have-not blacks in control of whites who similarly were made up of haves and have nots.

Roberts attributed the domination of blacks to their becoming more aggressive, more cohesive as a group, and the fact that they had been victimized by whites in the community. He noted that "blacks are just naturally more aggressive because most of the black kids we get here are from the ghetto." In addition, he felt that the willingness of blacks to stick together made whites fearful of retaliation from other blacks if they were to fight back. Finally, the injustices suffered on the streets by blacks make them want to even the score with whites, and they utilize this opportunity to turn the tables on the whites. '

The social class of the white boy is an important variable in explaining the varying degrees of success in their victimization. The lower-class white, for example, is not as easy to victimize as the middle-class white. Part of the reason for this, according to Roberts, is that the lower-class white is not easily intimidated. Not only does he perceive of himself as someone who can take care of himself, he may, in fact, be looking for a good fight so that he can move up the status hierarchy in his cottage. What also makes it difficult to exploit a lower-class white is that he has never had much to begin with and therefore is extremely reluctant to give up such things as the food and cigarettes which his parents and friends bring from home.

In contrast, the middle-class white youth tends to have little savvy on how to survive in this hostile environment. Even though he probably was a troublemaker in his own community, he may not know how to defend himself physically. Furthermore, he frequently is afraid of bodily harm which makes him an easy mark for an aggressive peer. His parents also bring enormous amounts of food when they visit—far more than one person needs—and he tries to buy protection by giving away much of what he receives from home. When he discovers that he is becoming a victim, he usually withdraws from the cottage program, attempting to keep away from the other boys. He begins to stay close to staff, hoping that they will protect him.

INSTITUTIONAL STRUCTURE

Institutional structure, in which we include the physical location of institutional programs, the nature of staff supervision and attendance, climate of the cottage and racial characteristics of the staff, is quite influential in any victimization.

The cottage area, interestingly enough, is not the most popular area for exploitation. Sexual rape, for instance, most frequently takes place in the academic and vocational area since the educational staff are unable to supervise students as well as youth leaders in the cottages.[14] Also, exploiters from all the cottages are together in the school, and they seem willing to do things which three or four exploiters in a cottage usually are unwilling to do.

Staff alertness may make the difference in whether or not victimization occurs. Don Jennifer, a former youth leader, stated it explicitly when he said, "Supervision is a key word when it comes to exploitation." There is no question but that supervision is closer in some cottages than in others. When permanent staff are irregular in attendance or on-call leaders are inexperienced and fearful, the time is ripe for a new boy to be exploited quite easily, especially if there are several peers present who sexually exploit others. For example, there was no sexual exploitation whatever in three cottages. In one cottage, however, eight boys were exploited sexually, exactly one half of the number exploited in the institution as a whole. In the remaining four cottages, there were one, two, and three boys exploited respectively.

Another interesting structural characteristic is that nearly all of the cottage youth leaders are black. In fact, at the time of this study, only two of the 48 youth leaders working directly with boys were white. Generally, black staff made a real attempt to be fair with white students, and the evidence of their success is that black students constantly complain that whites have it easier than they do.[15] As a result of their experiences in white society, black leaders also tend to be more sensitive than white leaders to exploitation, and this helps them to be more aware of the exploitation matrices in their cottages.

But in spite of the positive attributes of their leadership, the fact remains that the institutional authorities with whom the white boy relates are black. This is especially difficult for whites from rural areas as well as many middle-class whites who have had little contact with blacks before coming to this training school. The fact that blacks are in authority positions would appear to identify power with blackness, and thus give a social-psychological edge to black students in confrontations, in spite of the fairness exhibited by the black staff.

PAST INSTITUTIONAL HISTORY AND PERSONAL FACTORS

When a new boy arrives, boys interested in sexual exploitation will attempt to find out who knows him and whether he was ever a "punk" in another institution. If he has a history of homosexuality, he—in the words of a youth leader—"is right smack on the floor, he's dirt." The boy's past can spread so fast around the institution that it is not uncommon for a boy to arrive one day and to be called derogatory sexual names the next.

Previous offenses are also important since there is a tendency to leave youths alone who have committed serious offenses or who were incarcerated for a violent offense. One of the few white boys to become a heavy in his cottage claimed that his committing offense of bank robbery protected him from being exploited. The converse to this would be the white boy committed to the Youth Commission for incorrigibility at home and who was then transferred to the present institution because he had tried to run away from other institutions. To some youths this type of history indicates that he does not belong here and encourages his peers to victimize him.

Also important is the number of friends a newcomer has in a cottage. If he has a friend or two, especially ones who are respected, he will have support should hostile peers wish to victimize him. It is a big advantage to have support when the pressure is on, particularly when you are new. Having a friend to talk with may make the difference as to whether exploitation will take place.

The importance of size cannot be underestimated and, generally, the greater the size of a youth, the less his chances of being victimized. The only exception would appear to be a very passive youth afraid of physical confrontation who, regardless of size, would rapidly be victimized.

Finally, one of the most important variables of all is the personality characteristics of the white. If he walks in the cottage looking fearful, does not answer questions directly, hesitates in answering why he has been sent up, and gives verbal and physical evidence of being passive, he will be recognized very quickly as someone who can be exploited sexually and will be placed under considerable pressure by black peers interested in sexual exploitation.

GETTING OFF THE BOTTOM

The white scapegoat ordinarily remains at the bottom of the peer hierarchy for the duration of his stay in the institution. This is almost always lengthy unless he chooses to end it by running away. Some scapegoats, however, suddenly come to life and escape their lowly plight. As one leader said, "They become tired of being walked over."

Experience has indicated that there is usually a strong and influential youth leader behind the emergence of any student off the bottom. Other peers and sometimes even other staff are reluctant to accept his "new identity" and there is often a concerted effort to keep him in his place. Consequently, it takes more than desire to get off the bottom and it involves at least one or two fights with white as well as black peers. While some of the blacks do not want to lose him as a sexual object, some whites are afraid that his upward movement may result in their downward movement, so it is likely that the scapegoat will confront physical conflict from both groups. The need to fight his way out tests the determination of the scapegoat because it was largely his refusal to fight which resulted in his becoming a scapegoat in the first place.

One of the more serious fires at this institution in recent years was started because a scapegoat became tired of being "messed over" and one day physically defended himself against another white peer. He surprised himself and the rest of the cottage by beating up the other student. This meant, of course, that the boy who really looked bad in the fight was a ripe candidate to become the scapegoat and to be placed at the bottom of the cottage's social hierarchy. He was despondent at this possibility and chose to handle it by setting his room on fire. He and several of his peers nearly lost their lives in this fire.

CONCLUSIONS

This study of a maximum security institution for hostile and aggressive youths showed that whites were exploited more often and more seriously than blacks. Although each and every boy coming into the institution potentially could be exploited, certain youths are at greater risk of becoming the victim of attacks. Social class background appears to be a major factor in that ghetto blacks carry their prejudice against whites into the institution. Other factors, including structural features of the institution, institutional history of the boy, personality and physical characteristics of the student are also influential.

With many different types of exploitation taking place in our institutions, our criminal justice system remains in quite a dilemma. It is given the charge by many officials to be rehabilitative, yet society continues to be discriminative by sending disproportionate numbers of blacks into the institution. Understaffing then results in all inmates being put under extreme pressure by other inmates so that their only desire is to survive in a jungle-like atmosphere so they may then get out. It may well be that as long as juvenile institutions are allowed to survive, their clients will not.

NOTES

1. We are very indebted to the Ohio Youth Commission, its research staff and institutional officers for their permission to conduct this particular study. Mr. Don Jennifer, Edward Redd, and James Roberts were of special assistance. These staff members gave extensively of their time and were willing to share with us the results of their many years of experience in working with the institutionalized youth and wherever possible, we will identify the special contributions of these men to the study.
2. When exploitation is discussed, it takes place in adult penal institutions and is usually limited to sexual exploitation. In this study we wanted to explore the types of exploitation taking place in a juvenile institution.
3. Although it is not possible to present the results here, data were collected on the criminal history, demographic and physical characteristics of the youths as well as their responses to the Gough Adjective Checklist, Jesness Personality Inventory, and Machover Draw-A-Figure Test. These data will be reported at a later date.
4. Even though whites outnumber blacks slightly, it is the fact that the staff are 97% black that leads us to classify this institution as black-dominated—and in spite of the fact that the black staff appear to be more than fair in dealing with whites.
5. Boys reported these rumors in interviews held with them, and it appears that staff of other institutions of the Ohio Youth Commission communicated this information to intimidate troublesome boys in their own institutions.
6. In the social organization of this training school, the inmate leader is called the "heavy."
7. Smoking after another youth means finishing a cigarette he has started.
8. There is some debate among staff whether masturbation or anal sodomy receives the greater social rejection.
9. The only exception to this labelling process is the black student who is the aggressor in the homosexual encounter.
10. It is interesting that at the time of the study there were no real "queens," i.e., males who dress as women, among white students at this institution. In fact, there have only been a few "queens" the past four years, and interestingly enough, all were black.
11. Each cottage has a large front area called a program area. It is in this area that boys spend the majority of their leisure time in the cottage. Cottage staff only permit one record player in this area.
12. Each cottage has a television set in the program area, and boys are permitted to stay up until 9:30 or so provided they will watch television.
13. This scapegoat is almost always white.

14. When a rape takes place in a cottage, it is almost always in the sleeping area. Rapes are actually quite rare and do not take place in the institution more than once or twice a year. The last two or three mass rape attempts began in play, and occurred at a time when racial tensions were high.
15. In his Ph.D. dissertation, "Runaways at the Training Institution, Central Ohio," Bartollas discovered that white boys do tend to receive privileges earlier than black boys in this institution.

REFERENCES

Clemmer, Donald (1958), *The Prison Community*. New York: Holt, Rinehart & Winston.

Davis, Alan J. (1968), "Sexual assaults in the Philadelphia prison system and sheriff's vans." *Transaction*, 12:9.

Ellenberger, Henri (1954), "Relations psychologiques entre le criminel et la victime." *Revue Internationale de Criminologie et de Police Technique II*, April–June.

Fry, Margery (1951), *Arms of the Law*. London: Gollancz.

Gough, Harrison and Heilbrun, Alfred B. (1965), *The adjective checklist manual*, Palo Alto, California: Consulting Psychologists Press, Inc.

Jesness, Carl F. (1962), *Manual for the Jesness Inventory*. Palo Alto, California: Consulting Psychologists Press, Inc.

Machover, K. (1949), *Personality Projection in the Drawing of the Human Figure*. Springfield, Ill.: C. C. Thomas.

Mendelsohn, B., "The origin of victimology." *Excerpta Criminologica* 3, May–June: 239–41.

Schafer, Steven (1968), *The Victim and His Criminal*. New York: Random House.

Schrag, Clarence (1944), "Social types in a prison community." University of Washington: M. A. Thesis.

Schultz, Leroy G., "The victim-offender relationship." *Crime and Delinquency*, Vol. 14, No. 2 (April, 1968) 135–41.

Von Hentig, Hans (1948), *The Criminal and His Victim*. New Haven: Yale University Press.

23

Differential Effects of the Social Climates of Correctional Institutions[1]

Rudolf H. Moos

Reprinted from *Journal of Research in Crime & Delinquency* 7 (1970): 71–82, by permission of the author and publisher, National Council on Crime and Delinquency.

The purpose of the study was to assess the differential effects of the social climates of 16 correctional units. The study hypothesized and showed that units which were different in social climate were also different on variables related to general resident reaction to the unit and on the initiatives which residents perceived themselves as taking on the unit. For example, the results indicated that units with greater emphases on spontaneity, affiliation, insight, variety, and autonomy had residents who were more likely to like the staff and to feel that they were able to test their abilities and to increase their self-confidence; . . . who perceived themselves as more likely to take both submissive and autonomous initiatives toward the staff, i.e., who generally interacted more with the staff. The results substantiate the idea that different unit social climates have different predictable effects on the residents who live within them. Practical implications and directions for future research are discussed.

There is currently growing interest in the physical and social aspects of planning for a variety of environmental systems, and in the variability in individual behavior which is induced by ecological, social, and situational factors.[2] In this connection, several investigators have found that both setting and person/setting interactions contribute importantly and significantly to the variance in types of behavior,[3] and others have demonstrated the important differences which may occur in the behavior of the same person in different settings or milieus.[4]

These results indicate that the systematic assessment of environments might substantially increase the accuracy of behavior predictions. Pace[5] and

385

Stern[6] have measured the social atmospheres of college environments. Findi-kyan and Sells[7] have quantified and measured the dimensions of 60 campus organizations; Bellows[8] has studied the dimension of cooperation-authority in over 100 different situations; Moos and Houts[9] have developed a Ward At-mosphere Scale to assess the social atmospheres of psychiatric wards; and Moos[10] has developed a Social Climate Scale which assesses the social cli-mates of units in correctional institutions.

There is substantial research evidence that different social climates have different consequences for the behavior of their inhabitants.[11] For example, Moos and Houts[12] found that the degree of emphasis on spontaneity and autonomy on psychiatric wards was positively related to the initiatives pa-tients perceived themselves as taking in the area of submission to the staff, and that the degree of emphasis on aggression (the open expression of aggres-sive feelings) was related positively to perceived aggression and negatively to perceived affiliation and variety initiatives.

At least two investigators have touched specifically on this issue with respect to correctional institutions. Street, Vinter, and Perrow[13] studied the organizational climates of six different juvenile correctional institutions whose goals were oriented toward obedience-conformity, reeducation-development or treatment. They hypothesized and showed that difference in institutional goals had consequences for staff perceptions about inmates, staff-inmate authority relations, and the patterns of social relations and lead-ership that emerged among inmates.

Jesness compared living units to which boys had been assigned according to their I-level subtype classification[15] with control living units. Quantitative estimates of unit climate were obtained from subjects' perceptions of their institutional experience and from ratings made by experts who had read and evaluated typed program descriptions gained through interviews with the senior group supervisors on each living unit. These measures of unit climate differentiated among the units and were generally similar for subjects and experts. The correlations between the scores of five subject-perceived treat-ment dimensions of unit climate were related to pre- to post-test differences on the Jesness Inventory and Behavior Checklist, indicating that certain psychological and behavioral changes may be predicted to follow from the introduction of defined treatment strategies.

The purpose of the present study was to assess the differential effects of the social climates of units in correctional institutions. An earlier paper[16] described the development of the Social Climate Scale (SCS) which measures twelve dimensions of environmental press and which significantly differ-entiates unit social climates. The press of the environment, as the resident perceives it, establishes the directions his behavior should take if he is to find satisfaction and reward within the unit culture. The particular twelve dimensions were chosen by a literature search through previously identified press, and the choice of items on each press subscale was guided by the general conceptualization of environmental press.

This logic closely follows that of Murray[17] and of Stern.[18] For example, the following question was asked: what would be characteristic of an environment which exerts a press toward affiliation, or toward autonomy, or spontaneity? Conversely, what in an environment would tend to satisfy an individual patient who had a high need for affiliation, or for autonomy, or spontaneity? Needs may be inferred from an individual's characteristic modes of response. Press may be inferred from the characteristic pressures, rewards, and conformity-demanding influences of the unit culture. Press includes the characteristic demands or features of the environment as perceived by those who live in the particular environment. To each statement in the SCS, the resident who takes the test answers "true" if he believes it is generally characteristic of the unit and "false" if he believes it is not generally characteristic. The logic of the development of the SCS is more fully described by Moos.[19]

The particular pattern of environmental press creates a group atmosphere or social climate which, as Lewin has pointed out, needs to be considered as something real, having demonstrable effects, just as a physical field of gravity. For example, Lewin showed that the aggressive behavior of two girls tended to change with the social atmosphere of the group. After transferring from one group to the other, each girl rapidly displayed the level of conduct shown by the other girl before the change.[20] Lewin theorizes that individual members of a group will tend to fall in line with the norms of that group. For example, an individual in a low aggression group will tend to express little aggression whereas an individual in a high aggression group will tend to express high aggression.

Lewin, Lippitt, and White[21] and Lippitt and White[22] have reported that different group climates affect group behavior on variables such as the spontaneity of the group, the number of friendly remarks made by group members to each other in meetings, the amount of aggressive behavior, the degree to which normal free sociability is inhibited, and the general amount of satisfaction or dissatisfaction within the group. Most of these results were replicated by Curfman[23] in a study in which the same person led both democratic and autocratic groups. Social climates have effects on individual behavior by creating "induced forces," and possibly new needs, which impel behavior in particular directions shaped by these social climates.[24]

The present study, following this logic, was concerned with investigating whether units which were different in social climate, as measured by the SCS, were also demonstrably different on two sets of dependent variables: (1) general resident satisfaction and reaction to the unit; and (2) initiatives which residents perceived themselves as taking in order to cope with, and possibly change, the unit environment. It was hypothesized that different social systems and climates would result in different reactions to the unit and would have different reward qualities for different types of coping mechanisms.

More specifically, it was hypothesized that unit climates emphasizing individual resident responsibility (autonomy), general freedom of emotional expression (spontaneity, insight, aggression), and/or high staff-resident and resident-resident interaction (affiliation) would tend to have residents who were generally more satisfied, who liked each other and the staff more, and who felt that the unit was having a greater impact on the development of their abilities and their self-confidence.

In addition, it was hypothesized that high emphasis in a particular environmental press dimension would tend to "induce" greater resident initiatives either in that area or in one closely related. Different social climates were thought to produce pressures which direct coping behavior and channel initiatives in particular directions.

This study was designed to parallel an earlier study of the relationship between the psychological atmospheres of psychiatric wards and a similar set of dependent variables.[25]

METHODS AND SUBJECTS

Each of three questionnaires was given to residents on each of sixteen correctional units. The first test was the SCS, the development of which has been previously described.[26] In brief, the questionnaires contain subscales which purport to measure the emphasis of social climate in correctional units on twelve different dimensions. These dimensions are spontaneity, support, practicality, affiliation, order, insight, involvement, aggression, variety, clarity, submission, and autonomy. An emphasis on affiliation, for example, would be inferred from items such as: "The staff help new residents get acquainted on the unit" and "Staff encourage group activities among residents." An emphasis on insight would be inferred from items such as: "Residents are expected to share their personal problems with each other" and "Personal problems are openly talked about." An emphasis on autonomy would be inferred from still other items, for example: "Residents are expected to take leadership of the unit" and "Staff encourage residents to start their own activities."

These twelve subscales significantly differentiate between correctional units. In addition, the subscale scores show only low correlations between resident background characteristics such as age or length of stay on the unit. Form B of the SCS consists of twelve ten-item subscales, each measuring one dimension of unit social climate (five items scored true and five scored false in each subscale), and two ten-item subscales measuring positive and negative halo, respectively.

The second test which was administered was the Resident Initiative Scale (RIS). Items were indicative of initiatives which residents could take in units. For each item residents were asked how often (i.e., always, often, sometimes, never) they acted in a given way while on the unit. Items which were in the scale had been shown to be sensitive to differences among units and relatively free of social desirability response set.

The RIS consisted of seven subscales: affiliation with residents, revealing self to others, involvement with the unit, aggression, seeking variety, submission to staff, and autonomy toward staff. For example, initiatives in the area of autonomy toward staff would be inferred from the following items: "I ask my counselor if he thinks I am improving" and "I make suggestions to the staff." Initiatives in the area of revealing self to others would be inferred from these items: "I try to share my personal problems with residents" and "I tell the staff about my feelings." Initiatives in the area of affiliation with residents would be inferred from items such as: "I try to have close personal relationships with people on the unit" and "I try to become friends with the other residents on the unit." An eighth scale measuring social desirability response set was also constructed.

The third test was designed to measure residents' general reactions to the unit. This test included six questions asking residents to rate their general satisfaction with the unit (six-point scale), how much they liked the residents and the staff on the unit, how nervous or tense they generally felt while on the unit, whether they felt that the unit gave them a chance to test their abilities, and whether what they did on the unit helped them to gain self-confidence (five-point scales).

The 16 units had been picked in order to obtain a sample of a variety of units in different types of correctional institutions. The 16 units included: 7 units from a training school for boys ranging in age from 16 to 20 years; four units from a training school for boys and young men ranging in age from 18 to 30 years and organized into program units with an extensive program of academic and vocational education; two units from a juvenile hall, one for males and one for females with average ages of approximately 15 years; three boys' camps with extensive vocational programs for boys with an average age of approximately 16 years. Some characteristics of the 16 units are shown in Table 23.1.

Two testing sessions were needed to complete the questionnaires. The SCS and the items measuring general reaction to the unit were given at the first session, and the RIS was given at the second session.[27] Each resident was also asked to fill out the Marlowe-Crowne Social Desirability Scale.[28]

Table 23.1.
Background Characteristics of the Sixteen Units

Unit No.	No. of Residents Tested	Sex	Avgr. Age Residents	Median Length Res. Stay (wks.)
101	20	M	17.8	18
102	22	M	16.6	18
103	27	M	17.3	18
104	25	M	17.6	39
105	21	M	17.6	30
106	20	M	17.4	31
108	19	M	17.4	22
109	26	M	16.0	12
110	23	M	15.7	18
111	22	F	15.0	04
112	17	M	14.9	01
114	32	M	15.5	13
115	24	M	22.5	26
116	32	M	21.6	27
117	30	M	26.3	44
118	24	M	23.2	54

Results

The total number of residents tested on the 16 units was 384. Almost all the residents approached were both willing and able to take the questionnaires. The three tests were scored for each patient and the following scores were obtained for further analyses: (1) twelve subscale scores for the twelve dimensions of the SCS; (2) six scores on the items measuring satisfaction and general reactions to the unit; and (3) seven subscale scores on the RIS. Unit means also were obtained for each of these 25 scores.

A one-way analysis of variance (between-unit variations versus within-unit variations) was calculated for each of the 12 SCS scores in order to see which scales differentiated significantly between the units. All 12 of the subscales did differentiate between the units. Next the intercorrelations among the twelve subscale unit averages were calculated. Several of the subscale scores were so highly intercorrelated (e.g., .88 between practicality and affiliation, and -.81 between submission and autonomy) that five subscales (support, practicality, involvement, clarity, submission) were dropped from further analyses to eliminate redundancy.

Since the results indicated that the 16 units had significantly different social climates as measured by the SCS, the next question was whether the social climates were related significantly to the dependent variables. Thus, Pearson correlations across units were calculated between each of the remaining seven SCS subscale scores and the six general reaction and seven resident initiative scores.

Table 23.2 presents the correlations between the SCS scores and general reactions to the unit. These results indicate that there were no significant relationships between the SCS scores and general satisfaction with the unit, liking of residents, and degree of nervousness or tenseness felt by residents. However, five of the seven SCS dimensions were related significantly to the other three dependent variables, indicating that the greater the emphases on spontaneity, affiliation, insight, variety, and autonomy on a unit, the more likely that residents liked the staff, felt that they were able to test their abilities on the unit, and felt that what they were doing on the unit helped them to have more confidence in themselves.

Table 23.3 presents the correlations between the SCS and the RIS scores. These results indicate that: (1) units with higher emphases on spontaneity, affiliation, insight, variety, and autonomy had residents who perceived themselves as taking more initiatives in the areas of affiliation, self-revealing, and involvement with the unit; (2) units with a higher emphasis on variety had residents who perceived themselves as taking more initiatives in the area of seeking variety; (3) units with higher emphases on affiliation, order, insight, and autonomy had residents who perceived themselves as taking more initiatives in the area of submission to staff; and (4) units with higher emphases on spontaneity, affiliation, insight, and autonomy had residents who perceived themselves as taking more initiatives in the area of autonomy toward the staff. The last two findings indicate that there may be much more interaction (both submissive and autonomous) between residents and staff on some units than on others.

In order to test for the possibility that an underlying tendency of individual residents to answer items in socially desirable directions might have mediated the across-unit relationships among the three tests, correlations were calculated across all residents between the Marlowe-Crowne Social Desirability Scale and all the other variables. These correlations, which are shown in Table 23.4, indicate that the relationships between social desirability and the seven SCS subscales, the six variables measuring general reactions to the unit and the RIS subscales, are all generally low, with the exception of the RIS aggression subscale. Importantly, the aggression sub-

TABLE 23.2.

CORRELATIONS OVER UNITS (N = 16) BETWEEN
SELECTED SCS SUBSCALES AND GENERAL REACTIONS TO THE UNIT

SCS Subscale	General Satisfaction	Like Residents	Like Staff	Nervous or Tense	Abilities	Self-Confidence
Spontaneity	.20	.09	.83**	.23	.67**	.74**
Affiliation	.09	.23	.70**	−.24	.88**	.89**
Order	.17	.11	.04	.22	.16	.17
Insight	.19	.10	.67**	−.12	.73**	.82**
Aggression	.22	.08	.04	.32	−.25	−.18
Variety	.29	.31	.48*	.07	.62*	.64*
Autonomy	.17	.01	.80**	−.28	.83**	.87**

*P.05 = .48.
**P.01 = .61.

392

Table 23.3.
Correlations over Units (N = 16) Between Selected SCS Subscales and Resident Initiative Subscales

SCS Subscale	Affiliation	Self-Revealing	Involvement	Aggression	Variety	Submission	Autonomy
Spontaneity	.87**	.65**	.63**	.11	.09	.26	.56*
Affiliation	.81**	.80**	.80**	-.03	.28	.60*	.54*
Order	-.15	-.04	.09	-.34	.14	.51*	-.14
Insight	.77**	.85**	.92**	-.14	.36	.52*	.62**
Aggression	.20	-.19	-.10	.00	-.09	-.31	.07
Variety	.50*	.49*	.60*	-.31	.50*	.30	-.01
Autonomy	.82**	.83**	.89**	-.07	.41	.64**	.58*

*P.05 = .48.
**P.01 = .61.

393

SCS Subscales	R	General Reactions to the Unit	R	RIS Subscales	R
Spontaneity	.13	General Satisfaction	+ .10	Affiliation	.05
Affiliation	.09	Like Patients	+ .07	Self-Revealing	.02
Order	.26	Like Staff	+ .21	Involvement	.20
Insight	.07	Nervous or Tense	− .09	Aggression	− .36
Aggression	− .28	Abilities	.08	Variety	.16
Variety	.03	Self-Confidence	+ .17	Submission	.27
Autonomy	.08			Autonomy	− .08

scale showed no significant across-unit correlations with the seven SCS subscales. These results indicate that the across-unit correlations between the SCS subscales and the two sets of dependent variables were not mediated mainly by social desirability.

A more detailed comparison was made of two of the units for illustrative purposes. Figure 23.1 compares the SCS profiles of units 101 and 105, which are two physically similar units from a training school for boys ranging in age from 16 to 20 years.

Unit 101 is higher than unit 105 on the dimensions of order and aggression, whereas unit 105 is higher on the dimensions of spontaneity, practicality, affiliation, insight, autonomy, and variety. The two units show little difference on the dimensions of support, involvement, clarity, and submission.

Some of the items which differentiate most strongly between these two units are: "There are lots of things going on around here (variety); Everyone on this unit has pretty much the same opinions about treatment (variety); Residents are expected to share their personal problems with each other (insight); Personal problems are openly talked about (insight); Residents here are encouraged to be independent (autonomy); The day room is often messy (order); Many residents look messy (order); There is very little emphasis on what the residents will be doing after they leave the unit (practicality); The staff spends very little time talking with the residents (affiliation); This is the friendly unit (affiliation)."

These two different social atmospheres have significantly different consequences for the behavior of their inhabitants. For example, the residents on unit 105, when compared to those on unit 101, stated more that they generally liked each other, less that they felt nervous and tense, and more that they felt that the unit gave them a chance to test their abilities and to increase their self-confidence. In addition, residents on unit 105 more than those on unit 101, stated that they took initiatives in the following four areas: (1) seeking variety; (2) revealing self to others; (3) affiliation with residents; (4) involvement with the unit.

This illustrates that unit social climates may have specific and predictable effects on the types of initiatives which the residents on these units perceive themselves as taking, on their liking for each other, and on the degree to which they feel they are being helped by their activities on the unit.

DISCUSSION

The results indicate that there are direct relationships between the social climate on a correctional unit and the general reactions of residents to that unit and the types of initiatives which residents perceive themselves as likely

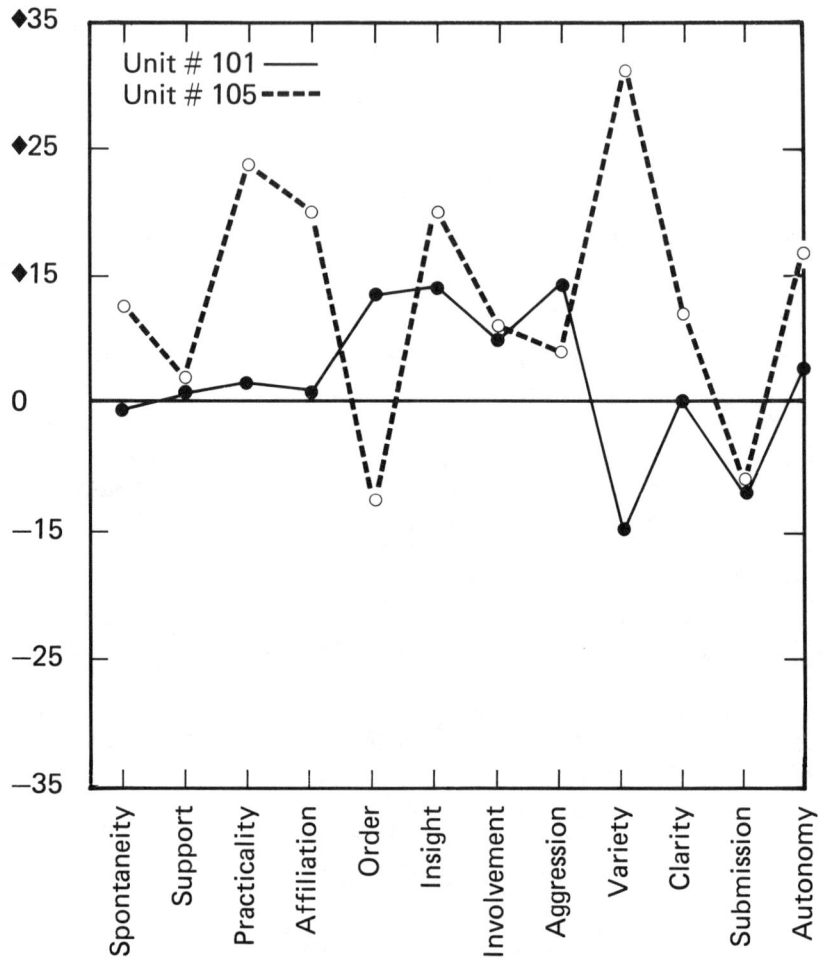

FIGURE 23.1.
COMPARISON OF SOCIAL CLIMATE SCALE PROFILES FOR
RESIDENTS ON UNITS 101 AND 105

to take on the unit. Different social climates have different predictable effects on the inhabitants who live within them.

Residents on units with high emphases on spontaneity, affiliation, insight, variety, and autonomy were more likely to like the staff, to feel that they were able to test their abilities and to feel that they were gaining self-confidence. The SCS dimensions were not related to general satisfaction, degree of liking for other residents, or extent of felt nervousness or tenseness. If replicated, this finding would suggest that different social climates on units may not have as many differential effects in these latter three areas as has sometimes been believed to be the case.

These same SCS dimensions were highly related to a number of different types of perceived initiatives, most importantly affiliation, revealing self to others, involvement with the unit, submission to the staff, and autonomy toward the staff. On the other hand, perceived initiatives in the area of aggression were uncorrelated with any of the SCS dimensions, indicating that unit climate may have less effect in this area than has previously been thought.

These results suggest that the social climates of units may have quite specific effects; i.e., that not all dependent variables are related to them. This would indicate that manipulations of unit climate might be expected to have effects on only certain variables. Further research needs to investigate which resident satisfaction, initiative, or other behavior variables are related to the dimensions of unit climate and which are not.

A comparison between the results of this study on correctional units and an earlier study on psychiatric wards[29] is particularly instructive. The results of the ward study indicated that various dimensions of ward atmosphere (support, affiliation, order, insight, autonomy) were significantly related to general satisfaction with the ward and liking of other patients, but not to how much patients felt able to test their abilities or whether they felt they were increasing their self-confidence. Furthermore, the ward atmosphere dimension most highly related to patient perceived initiatives was aggression; higher emphasis on aggression was related to more aggression but to less affiliation and variety initiatives. In the present study, emphasis on aggression on units was not related to any of the dependent variables. These sets of results, taken together, indicate that the social climates on both psychiatric wards and on correctional units have important effects on patient and resident behavior, but that these effects may derive from different aspects of the climate and may relate to different dependent variables. Thus, even though the conclusion that different social climates have differential effects may generalize from one type of institution (hospitals) to another (correctional units), the exact relationships between specific dimensions of social climate and specific dependent variables may differ.

There are a number of possible practical implications. First, the work has implications for social planning; i.e., for designing the type of social climate which staff want. The SCS can provide recurrent feedback to unit staff on whether or not they are creating the type of social climate which they wish to create. Since different social climates appear to have different predictable effects, this information might also enable staff to find out more about the kinds of effects they were creating.

Second, there are specific implications for planning and evaluation studies comparing different types of unit programs.[30] Some of the mediating variables which differentiate between different programs, i.e., the social climate and its effects, may be measured and thus may help to clarify why programs do or do not have differential effects. Unit programs which are different on paper and which appear to have different goals and utilize different correctional philosophies and methods may or may not create different social climates and have differential effects.

Third, the relationships between deviant perceptions of the environment and satisfaction and initiatives may be important. Wood et al.[31] have shown that inmates who perceive a correctional institution deviantly are more likely to be labeled "troublemakers" by institutional staff. Thus investigation of the relationship between accuracy of perception of the environment and satisfaction and initiative and/or other dependent variables may be particularly fruitful.

Fourth, it may be that both the measures of the psychological environment in which the resident is living in the correctional unit, and the measures of the similarity between in-unit and out-of-unit environments could substantially increase the range of predictability of the effects of different correctional treatment programs.

NOTES

1. This research was supported in part by NIMH Grant MH16461. The author wishes to express his appreciation to Ernst Wenk, who assisted in the development of the Resident Initiative Scale; to Karl Schonborn and Gordon Adams, who participated in various phases of the research; to Bill Lake, who coordinated the computer data analyses; and to the residents and staff whose cooperation made this research possible.

2. G. W. Allport, "Traits Revisited," *American Psychologist, 21* (1966), 1–10; W. Mischel, *Personality and Assessment* (New York: Wiley, 1968); S. B. Sells (Ed.), *Stimulus Determinants of Behavior* (New York: Ronald Press, 1963); J. Yinger, "Research Implications of a Field View of Personality," *American Journal of Sociology, 68* (1963), 580–92.

3. See: N. Endler, J. McV. Hunt, and A. J. Rosenstein, "An S-R Inventory of Anxiousness," *Psychological Monographs, 76* (Whole No. 536), (1962): H. Raush, A. Dittman, and T. Taylor, "Person, Setting, and Change in Social Interaction,"

Human Relations, *12* (1959), 361–78; R. Moos, "Situational Analysis of a Therapeutic Community Milieu," *Journal of Abnormal Psychology*, *73* (1968a), 49–61.

4. See: P. Gump, P. Schoggen, and F. Redl, "The Camp Milieu and Its Immediate Effects," *Journal of Social Issues*, *13* (1957), 40–46; W. Soskin and V. John, "The Study of Spontaneous Talk," in R. Barker (Ed.), *The Stream of Behavior* (New York: Appleton-Century-Crofts, 1963), pp. 228–87; L. Zinner, "The Consistency of Human Behavior in Various Situations: A Methodological Application of Functional Ecological Psychology," Unpublished Ph.D. Dissertation, University of Houston, 1963.

5. C. R. Pace, CUES: *College and University Environment Scales Preliminary Technical Manual* (Princeton, New Jersey: Educational Testing Service, 1963).

6. G. G. Stern, *People in Context* (New York: Wiley, 1968).

7. N. Findikyan and S. B. Sells, "Organizational Structure and Similarity of Campus Student Organizations," *Organizational Behavior and Human Performance*, *1* (1966), 169–90.

8. R. Bellows, "Toward a Taxonomy of Social Situations," in Saul B. Sells (Ed.), *Stimulus Determinants of Behavior* (New York: Ronald Press, 1963), pp. 197–212.

9. R. Moos and P. Houts, "The Assessment of the Social Atmospheres of Psychiatric Wards," *Journal of Abnormal Psychology*, (in press), (1968a).

10. R. Moos, "The Assessment of the Social Climates of Correctional Institutions," *Journal of Research in Crime and Delinquency*, (in press), (1968b).

11. See: R. G. Barker and P. Gump, *Big School, Small School* (Stanford, California: Stanford University Press, 1964); J. Kelly, "Naturalistic Observations and Theory Confirmation: An Example," *Human Development*, *10* (1967), 212–22; L. Porter and E. Lawlor, "Properties of Organization Structure in Relation to Job Attitudes and Job Behavior," *Psychological Bulletin*, *64* (1965), 23–51; H. J. Walberg, "Structural and Affective Aspects of Classroom Climate," *Psychology in the Schools*, *5* (1966), 247–53; J. Withall, "Assessment of the Social-Emotional Climates Experienced by a Group of Seventh-Graders as They Moved from Class to Class," *Educational and Psychological Measurement*, *12* (1952), 440–51.

12. R. H. Moos and P. Houts, "Differential Effects of the Social Atmospheres of Psychiatric Wards," in preparation.

13. D. Street, R. D. Vinter, and C. Perrow, *Organization for Treatment: A Comparative Study of Institutions for Delinquents* (New York: Free Press, 1966).

14. C. Jesness, The Preston Typology Study (Sacramento, California: Institute for the Study of Crime and Delinquency, unpublished manuscript, 1968).

15. M. G. Warren, *Interpersonal Maturity Level Classification: Juvenile Diagnosis and Treatment of Low, Middle, and High Maturity Delinquents* (Sacramento, California: California Youth Authority, 1966).

16. Moos, op. cit., 1968b.

17. H. A. Murray, *Explorations in Personality* (New York: Oxford University Press, 1938).

18. Stern, op. cit.

19. Moos, op. cit., 1968b.

20. K. Lewin, "Frontiers in Group Dynamics" in D. Cartwright (Ed.), *Field Theory*

and Social Science (New York: Harper and Row, 1951b), pp. 188–237, esp. p. 212; K. Lewin, "Behavior and Development as a Function of the Total Situation," in D. Cartwight (Ed.), *Field Theory and Social Science* (New York: Harper and Row, 1951b), pp. 238–303.

21. K. Lewin, R. Lippitt, and R. White, "Patterns of Aggressive Behavior in Experimentally Created 'Social Climates'," *Journal of Social Psychology, 10* (1939), 271–99.

22. R. Lippitt and R. White, "The 'Social Climate' of Children's Groups" in R. Barker (Ed.), *Child Behavior and Development* (New York: McGraw-Hill, 1943), Chapter 28.

23. M. M. Curfman, "An Experimental Investigation of Some of the Influences of Authoritarian and Democratic Atmospheres on the Behavior of Small Groups," unpublished M. A. Thesis, Stanford University, 1939.

24. Moos and Houts, "Differential Effects of the Social Atmospheres of Psychiatry Wards," unpublished manuscript (1968b).

25. Lewin, op. cit., 1951b.

26. Moos, op. cit., 1968b.

27. Copies of the scales are available on request to the author.

28. D. Crowne and D. Marlowe, *The Approval Motive* (New York: Wiley, 1964).

29. Moos and Houts, op. cit., 1968b.

30. Jesness, op. cit., 1968.

31. B. Wood, G. Wilson, R. Jessor, and J. Bogan, "Troublemaking Behavior in a Correctional Institution: Relationship to Inmates Definition of their Situation," *American Journal of Orthopsychiatry, 36* (1966), 795–802.

Part Six

Rehabilitation and Modification: Broad Perspectives

The correctional pendulum has lethargically swung from the "punishment only" model of public offender treatment to intervention strategies which include rehabilitative processes. However, the pendulum is now showing signs of a quickened pace in its regressive movement as it retraces its travels from offender rehabilitation to its historical foundations of retribution and retention. This trend is quite evident when one recalls that only a few years ago offender rehabilitation was the dominant theme of professional and popular literature and the cornerstone of speeches by public officials and statements issued by citizens' groups. Today these same sources are decrying rehabilitation and are lamenting its failure to stop crime and correct criminals. State legislatures are beginning to support this public outcry by passing legislation which emphasizes determinate sentencing procedures and de-emphasizes—and in some cases, abolishes—indeterminate sentencing. They, along with the federal government, are appropriating larger amounts for funding the creation of a greater profusion of correctional facilities to house the ever-increasing number of individuals who are sentenced to terms in prison.

Thus, rehabilitation has had only a brief moment in the limelight when one places it in the perspective of the entire historical context of offender treatment. Yet, it would appear to be an exercise in naivete to believe that offender rehabilitation and modification programs will be abandoned in favor of a complete return to the retribution/retention model. Even though rehabilitation programs gained the spotlight for only a relatively short period, it seems inconceivable, in this age of human and civil rights, to believe in a return to the inhumane treatment of merely warehousing and categorizing offenders in prisons or supplying only supervision for probationers, parolees and others. What, for example, beyond work, sleep and boredom, is planned for the greater number of individuals who will be placed in our growing number of correctional facilities? Making the individual more "accountable" for his or her crime by serving longer, non-parolable sentences will increase the time available for the rehabilitative programs that can be of benefit to an incarcerated individual. It is naive to believe that the public will not continue to expect the offender to be "cured" of his or her criminal behavior once he or she leaves the prison or is released from probation or parole status. Therefore, it is still incumbent upon the professional corrections worker to be knowledgeable in and have the ability to plan and carry out programs which can result in socially beneficial behavior change on the part of the offender.

It has taken a long time to weld the joint between corrections and rehabilitation and, although this coupling appears to be strained at present, it is not likely to break under the present duress. Underlying today's stress is the stronger desire to have offenders become productive members of society and the belief on the part of many that rehabilitative processes hold the only hope. We know historically that locking up prisoners and using silent intro-spective meditation have not worked. We also know, as Bindman points out, that most of our prison rehabilitative programs have been inadequately funded and funding has not been supplied to carry out longitudinal follow-up studies which could more adequately ascertain the effectiveness of the pro-gram (Bindman & Aaron, 1973). We need, further, to discover whether or not in the course of developing correctional rehabilitation it has become entangled in the web of outdated correctional practices currently in use. There now exists a confusing state of affairs due to the lack of consistency and continuity evident among various programs in both interstate and intrastate rehabilitation program development. In this light, it would appear that at this juncture one could legitimately ask two questions directly to correctional rehabilitation and modification programs: What has been done? and What must we do?

The response to the first question is easily summarized from the material which has been presented thus far. We have progressed from retribution and retention to humane rehabilitative programs for offenders. From this point there has developed an emphasis on rehabilitation as the *only* method of combatting criminal behavior, which has resulted in the eruption of a hodge-podge of rehabilitative programs in combination with outmoded correctional practices. Finally, rehabilitation as a means of eliciting offender behavior has begun to fall in disrepute and greater emphasis is now being given to punish-ment. Thus, we have almost completed the full circle. However, the impact that rehabilitation has had in the past and that it presently has on corrections has prevented this circle from being completed. It is this exact situation which calls for an answer to question number two, What must we do? To this end, we defer to the selections included in this section of the book. The authors of this collection of articles are knowledgeable about what effects rehabilitation can have on offender behavior change and how rehabilitation can be assimilated with corrections in accordance with the goal of supplying offenders with the opportunity to make behavior changes which are beneficial to them and to society as a whole.

Quay's paper initiates this section by undertaking the thorny task of dis-cussing what corrections can effectively correct and how this process can take place. It is obvious that there is little agreement among the lay public and professionals in corrections concerning the exact identification of and solu-tions for the problems which beset corrections and the criminal justice sys-tem. Quay indicates that a multitude of reforms for corrections have been proposed, developed and utilized without being effective. He specifies two areas which must be analyzed: why the offender offends, and how we can lessen the likelihood he will offend again. In dealing with the first issue, Quay indicates we must keep in mind that people become offenders because of their present behavior. This concept sets the stage for having offenders deal with the present and de-emphasize the past by spending less time searching for historical behavioral causes and more time learning skills which will help them function productively in society. Indeed, Quay alludes to these ideas when he states that corrections should deal directly with ineffective personal and social offender behavior related to criminality but should not deal with the origins of these behaviors. This, of course, seems to be the direction that would be most beneficial for corrections to pursue. It would appear to be more reasonable to help offenders replace their personally and socially dysfunctional behaviors with skills which have a greater likelihood of enhancing their ability to live within the boundaries set by society. It would also be more realistic to expect the majority of those individuals assigned to rehabilitation responsibilities to be better able to grasp and use the concept of skill training and modification techniques than to utilize in-depth therapeutic analysis. The skill training modification program would also appear to be more suitable for the majority of offenders since, as has been pointed out many times, only a minority of these individuals are actually in need of intensive psychotherapy.

Quay begins the examination of his second area of analysis—lessening the likelihood that the offender will offend again—by indicating that the first step one must take is to recognize that behavior change is the basic goal for establishing effective corrections. Before direct intervention into this realm can become a reality, agreement on this goal must be garnered in the sectors of professional correctional workers and policy makers for corrections. Quay firmly believes that corrections can correct within the limits of the mission he describes. When individuals make a total commitment to a readily understood philosophical goal that can be implemented through the rehabilitation model, and then analyze how this goal can be met, the layers of confusion can be stripped away. Until now, the voluminous amount of material attempting to define rehabilitation's niche in the context of correctional goals has aided only in creating a mire of confusion. General acceptance of a philosophical goal that is linked to the concept of working toward positive offender behavior change could be effectively carried out through the rehabilitation model.

Once this primary commitment has been made, a second commitment on which there must be concurrence is that of supplying the necessary training for all staff so programs can be instituted which will help accomplish offender behavior change. Quay adds a third prerequisite to effective corrections, that of providing adequate physical facilities. It is incumbent on those committed to the primary mission of effective corrections to lobby for facilities which are designed to promote positive behavior change.

Brodsky's writings, in turn, deal in specific terms with how to start positive diagnostic procedures with offenders. He first explores the professional literature relevant to psychological illness and strength in offenders. Although the review of literature presented in this article is representative of only a small group of studies done in this area, a major point which becomes evident is that of the importance of considering positive diagnostic procedures for offenders. Brodsky indicates that there appears to be a "split" which is dependent on disciplinary affiliation when the discussion centers on the psychological illness and strength in offenders. Those individuals occupied in sociological areas tend to find little information which supports the premise that offenders can be distinguished from non-offenders on the basis of a high incidence of mental illness in the offender group. Those persons engaged in work as psychiatrists, psychologists, and social workers seem to adopt the concept that offenders, as a specific population, show a high degree of psychological illness. Brodsky points out that professional affiliation, attitude, and expectations of those persons doing the diagnostic work "have a potential for leading to implicit self-fulfilling prophesies." He believes that agreement between all factions concerning the extent of the existence or non-existence of mental illness in offenders is inconsequential when the broader question of positive diagnostic procedures for offenders is considered. He believes that a strong effort should be made to develop positive expectations in diagnosticians and correctional workers at all levels. This suggestion is most important if a total commitment dedicated to the proposition of making positive offender behavior change is to occur.

Brodsky presents an "action" program which will accomplish the task of direct intervention for identification of the "most promising, psychologically healthy, or highest potential prisoners" entering a correctional system. By instituting this type of program, information could be supplied which could have effects on sentencing, probation, parole, and rehabilitation program development. Those inmates with the highest potential for functioning productively in society are likely to be the ones who could most benefit and would be most willing to participate in behavior change programs. By accentuating the positive, the negative may not be eliminated, but it certainly could be inhibited. This inhibition could be one of the greatest boons to corrections. The positive emphasis in the areas of diagnosis and behavior change program development could be the impetus needed to give offender rehabilitation a share of the limelight once again.

It is fitting that we close this section with the selection by Jacks, in which he presents an approach to counseling correctional clients that distills many of the most appropriate concepts and techniques from various psychological theoretical foundations into a practical, day-to-day usable intervention strategy which he calls "Positive Therapeutic Intervention" (PTI). In presenting these concepts and techniques in this manner, the author supplies to correctional practitioners a basic handbook for dealing with correctional clients in a counseling situation by showing them how to develop skills in listening and communicating. In addition, the author details several "facilitator techniques for positive therapeutic intervention," among which are role-modeling, role-rehearsal, desensitization, the "helper" principle, and analysis of client logic. The author's intention is to acquaint correctional practitioners with several counseling tools which have been, to this point, scattered throughout several different correctional treatment modalities and to bring them into practical focus within a single, useable approach. He has accomplished his task very well and has given to his readers a rehabilitative counseling approach which can be learned and used by many correctional counseling practitioners.

In developing his approach, Jacks builds his conceptional basis for Positive Therapeutic Intervention on eight basic principles: (1) Most social behavior amenable to modification is learned behavior; (2) Most learned social behavior is maintained by means of environmental consequences; (3) Rewarding consequences tend to be most effective in the production of new or modified social behavior; (4) Punitive consequences tend to be less effective; (5) Learning of new behaviors is a gradual process and requires practice; (6) Immediate consequences for social behavior are more effective than delayed consequences; (7) Our goal should be to change people's external behavior rather than to change their interior attitudes; (8) Nothing succeeds like success. From these principles, one sees that the practical orientation is positively based with little emphasis given to negatives, but still is not a Pollyanna approach because it emphasizes the client's responsibility for developing behavior skills which will allow him to function in society in a productive rather than destructive manner.

The material presented by Jacks makes sense when one views the disjointed hodge-podge of theories coming and going in various correctional settings. By pulling together under one umbrella those techniques which can be easily learned and used by correctional workers, Jacks has developed a workable set of criteria for immediate use as well as a firm foundation on which the practitioner can build increasing proficiency as a counselor to correctional clients.

References

Bindman, Aaron, Why Does Rehabilitation Fail? *International Journal of Offender Therapy and Comparative Criminology 17* (1973): 309–24.

24

What Corrections Can Correct and How

Herbert C. Quay, Ph.D.

Reprinted from *Federal Probation* (June 1973) by permission of the author and publisher, the Administrative Office of the United States Courts.

It has become obvious to both criminal justice professionals and the lay public that there are some fundamental problems with corrections and the criminal justice system in America. However, as to exactly what the problems are and what to do about them, there is less unanimity of opinion.

From the public sector and from some inspired but not necessarily enlightened elected representatives come cries for more and better law enforcement, for quicker justice and for more tranquil prisons. From the better informed segments of the public there are also concerns that these measures should be coupled with more humane and effective confinement.

From the professional side the recommendations are somewhat different: screening fewer people into the system in the first place, providing more legal safeguards for both the accused and convicted, and greater involvement of the community in the correctional process. But professionals are also concerned with more humane and effective confinement.

The need for all these things is clear. Better law enforcement can reduce serious crime; the decriminalization of petty offenses will enable the system to apprehend with more certainty and adjudicate more rapidly. Greater legal safeguards at all stages of the process will permit "justice" to have an operational meaning closer to its dictionary definition. Certainly more humane confinement in terms of more and better physical space, better nutrition, more recreation, is justifiable on the grounds that prisoners are, after all, human. Furthermore, to deny the offender these things is not in the best long-run interest of the general public.

However, for those thousands of persons remanded to the care of the correctional system for greater or lesser periods of their lives, all of these proposed reforms will not add up to an effective corrections.

An effective corrections can only be brought into being by detailed and systematic analysis of (1) what has this particular offender offended and

(2) what can be done to lessen the likelihood, other things being equal, that he will offend again. I wish to examine carefully each one of these questions in a somewhat different light than that under which they have usually been scrutinized.

WHY DOES THE OFFENDER OFFEND?

Even the casual student of crime and delinquency recognizes that we have a multitude of theories relative to this question. The criminal offends because he is poor, because he lacks opportunity, because he has a poor family background, because he has criminal associates, and on and on. Unfortunately, none of these conceptions is of very much help in corrections' effort to correct. What the correctional administrator is faced with is a person who, for probably a multitude of reasons, was unable to function effectively in a society in which the vast majority of people do function. In fact, most poor, opportunity-denied products of a discordant family do not become criminal offenders. Why then, did this individual offend? It seems to me that corrections is forced to accept a very simple working hypothesis: Offenders are offenders because of their present behavior. Then the task becomes that of asking what facet or facets of this person's behavior is critical for his having become an offender. Is it because he responds to frustration by uncontrolled aggression? Is it because he has no available work skill? Is it because he cannot read? Is it because he believes that theft is an appropriate form of acquisitive behavior? Is it because he meets adversity by flight? These are but a few examples of behaviors which offenders display which are likely to be associated with crime. For any given offender one or all could be involved.

Clearly, corrections has no control over the matrix of social forces in which behaviors related to offending have already been acquired. What corrections can deal with are those personally and socially ineffective behaviors related to criminality; *not* the origins of the behaviors but the behaviors themselves. An effective correctional institution *can* teach a man to respond to frustration with something other than unbridled aggression, it *can* teach him a saleable skill, it *can* teach him to read, it *can* show him that in the long run there are more effective ways to gain property than by theft. At the most basic level, then, what corrections can correct, given the appropriate circumstances, are those behaviors related to offending.

The next question is more difficult. How can corrections correct?

HOW CAN CORRECTIONS CORRECT?

The first step towards a conceptualization of how requires a recognition that behavior change is the basic mission for an effective corrections. Agreement as to this mission has to occur both within corrections itself and among policy makers for corrections. There must also be a recognition that behavior change demands, according to the needs of the individual, specific and definitive efforts; social, emotional, educational, and vocational. These efforts are the essence of an effective corrections; everything else is subsidiary.

There are, as even the casual scholar of behavioral science knows, a host of approaches to bringing about behavior change which have some degree of theoretical and/or empirical respectability. The best judgment that can currently be made about their effectiveness is that the majority of these approaches are effective for some people at some point in time under some conditions. None of them, however, are universally effective. At present we should neither accept any one approach as a panacea nor arbitrarily dismiss any technique that does not frankly go counter to known facts about behavior.[1]

However, it should be obvious that to effectively carry out any of these approaches requires staff with technical expertise well above that required for warehousing or for humane confinement. The assessment of the individual in terms of his social, academic, and vocational needs and the implementation of the behavior change strategy most appropriate to meet his needs are not at all simple tasks. Furthermore, the major part of the task of changing those ineffective personal and social behaviors becomes the responsibility of line correctional staff. Under current conditions the vast majority of these officers are undereducated and undertrained for the task facing them. Thus, it follows that corrections and its policy makers must commit themselves to both extensive and intensive training programs at all staff levels from correctional officer to institution director. Without this training, programs will fail and so will our chance for an effective corrections. With this training, the field moves toward becoming a true profession: a profession whose members function at various levels of responsibility and expertise but who share a common orientation toward systematic behavior change.

In addition to trained staff, adequate physical facilities must be provided. It is doubtful that those who are calling for a moratorium on construction have visited some of the large, overcrowded, totally antiquated institutions in which thousands of offenders are currently confined. The physical nature of these institutions makes the implementation of an effective corrections next to impossible. It is not that we simply need more institutions but we are in desperate need of adequate ones. These new institutions must be designed to facilitate positive behavior change. They should be small and near population centers where volunteers and part-time professionals are available; a facility need not be a halfway house on Main Street to involve the larger community in its correctional efforts.

Clearly, an effective correctional system, like an effective educational system or effective health care system, will require talented and trained people, material resources, a philosophical commitment among its professionals and public support. These talented people, their training and the resources needed for them to do their job will cost money. But the job they have to do is one of the most difficult imaginable. It cannot be done both successfully and cheaply. But the ultimate cost of not doing it is far greater.

How Much Can Corrections Correct?

Up to this point I have tried to indicate what corrections can correct and some of the requisites for implementation. The next issue is the question of how *much* can corrections correct. Can corrections, by the application of systematic methods to change social, emotional, academic, and vocational behaviors, forever insulate an individual against environmental forces acting to change his behavior in directions contrary to his success in society? The answer is, of course, corrections cannot. The new behaviors and skills which the offender takes with him when he returns to society must somehow be maintained in that society. Currently, we assume that such maintenance will be facilitated by some form of aftercare. This aftercare is only rarely under the control of those responsible for institutional correction. Equally rarely is aftercare anything more than a casual contact between agent and parolee with the content of the interaction generally about the wrong things. Until aftercare can become an integral part of the correctional process, oriented toward the same ends, the institution's responsibility essentially stops at the door of the correctional facility. Consequently, an evaluation of its efforts cannot be entirely based on success or failure in environmental circumstances over which institutional corrections has no control.

However, we can evaluate corrections on the basis of the extent to which it succeeds, in the correctional setting, in changing those behaviors which it has set out to change. Corrections must be prepared to offer evidence in terms of what it has done for a given individual and what the results have been. If reasonable and rational goals have not been met, it is the fault of the correctional program, not that of the individual or the community.

Should we not also be prepared to evaluate aftercare in the same way? What was done to maintain the effective behaviors demonstrated to have been acquired in the correctional program? Currently we talk about failures on parole but we actually assign the blame for these failures to the correctional institution. In point of fact, no one ever fails in prison. He fails in the community. Clearly, we need a reconceptualization of institutional corrections.

Community Corrections

Finally, I would like to make some comments on community corrections. It is now being suggested by some that rehabilitation cannot take place within a correctional institution. Evidence for this position consists mainly of impressionistic studies of the adverse effects of the inmate culture and reviews of those multitudes of studies which have applied some poorly defined treatment modality in blanket fashion to a totally undescribed inmate population and have obtained the almost inevitable indeterminate results.[2]

Following on the heels of the rejection of the institution as a setting for meaningful behavior change is a too ready acceptance of the notion that all one needs to do is to move corrections out of the institution and into the community and all will be well. Under current conditions, what this consists of is old wine in new bottles. The simple tactic of changing the locus of the delivery of services from hospital to community has not proved to be the expected panacea for mental health. Neither will it prove to be a panacea for corrections. What is needed in corrections are some fundamental and basic changes in the nature of the service delivered. Inadequately trained personnel charged with carrying out poorly thought out and minimally supported programs cannot be expected to do any better in the community than in the institution. In fact, there is a good possibility that they will do worse particularly from the standpoint of the community itself. The community is, after all, entitled to some protection during the process of correction.

We will be totally irresponsible if we continue to neglect the crying need for effective correctional programs in institutions using as the latest excuse the illusion that a loosely conceptualized and inadequately implemented "community corrections" will solve all of our problems.

It is my firm belief that corrections can, within the limited and reasonable definition of its mission proposed here, truly correct. While the institutional setting, with its unwilling clientele, may not be the *ideal* treatment setting, for a great many offenders we have no choice. In my view, it is totally unrealistic to consider the mission of corrections as that of "holding" the offender for some period of time, perhaps years, until society is willing to tolerate him in the community—where he can then be treated. We must begin to bring about positive changes in the offender from the day he enters the correctional system by the specification of behaviors which need to be changed and the application of an effective technology for changing them. It is erroneous to say that corrections has failed. Corrections has not yet been tried.

NOTES

1. This question of the match between offender characteristics and treatment modalities, i.e., differential classification and treatment, remains perhaps the most important problem for research in applied corrections.
2. An excellent example of the latter is the study by Kassebaum, Ward, and Wilner, *Prison Treatment and Parole Survival: An Empirical Assessment.* New York: Wiley, 1971. While there is little to criticize about the research design, the treatment which failed (to improve parole success rates) was group counseling, applied to inmates regardless of their amenability to this approach by minimally prepared non-professional counselors.

25

Prisoners with Promise: Psychological Illness and Psychological Strengths in Offenders

Stanley L. Brodsky

Reprinted by permission of the author.

This is the second report of a project entitled "Prisoners With Promise," funded as a planning grant by the Illinois Law Enforcement Commission in June, 1969. The first report contained developments in identifying psychological promise in prisoners. The current report presents a synthesis of (A) the evaluation of research and concepts for identifying promise in offenders and, (B) the needs and diagnostic functions of the correction system. This report addresses itself to the practical question of how actually to start positive diagnostic procedures with offenders.

A prominent characteristic of the psychological study of man has been the emphasis on abnormal functioning. Terms such as psychotic, neurotic, and psychopathic are commonly used, while expressions of creativity, positive functioning and mental growth occur with far less frequency. The imbalance is apparent in examination of texts for the study of adjustment and personality. Human adjustment books are described more accurately as maladjustment texts and the number of abnormal psychology books published very much outnumbers the number on normal personality. Although this imbalance has been criticized in some quarters, the viewing of personality functioning in American psychology and psychiatry generally does tend to be from the frame of reference of mental illness rather than mental health.

The mental illness model of behavior has accompanied the movement of psychological professionals into the prison and has led to an interest and sometimes emphasis on individual diagnosis, intensive psychological treatment and therapeutic change in prisoners. Thus to a degree the prison shares the same goals and the same problems as the mental hospital, including the implicit pessimism about the changeability of a variety of human behaviors

413

arising out of experience with patients with long-standing behavioral disorders. As psychiatrists and other mental health professionals become agents for deciding the appropriateness of release or confinement for prisoners, there develops an increasing need to re-examine the underlying psychological justifications of long incarceration of law breakers both by lay people and professionals.

A frequent operational assumption is made that a fundamental characteristic of offenders is psychological disturbance. The reasoning underlying this assumption follows this syllogism:

1. Most people don't commit crimes
2. Most people are normal
3. Therefore people who commit crimes are not normal

It is suggested not only that the syllogism itself is false, but that the final statement itself needs to be carefully examined. The origins of such conclusions tend to be varied, but it is rare that these observations are derived from reliable data.

The present report seeks to explore the professional literature on psychological well-being and strengths and psychological illness in offenders. Offenders will be defined as individuals who have been convicted in a court, and most studies draw samples from incarcerated populations. Initially the results of research and expert opinion will be tabulated. Then special attention will be directed toward the nature and identification of psychological strengths in offenders.

PSYCHOPATHOLOGY IN OFFENDERS

When basic criminology textbooks, review sources, and general professional statements about offender psychopathology are studied, the views seem to split according to disciplinary affiliation.[1] The sociologists find that insufficient information is available to conclude reasonably that offenders are different psychologically from non-offenders. (Barnes & Teeters, 1959; Waldo & Dinitz, 1967). Barnes & Teeters suggested that when all criminals are considered, those not apprehended as well as those arrested and convicted, that ". . . the criminal class as a whole is certainly as intelligent and stable, mentally and emotionally, as the general population."

The diagnostic systems are equally open to critical evaluation. Thus Tappan (1960) stated "figures on psychoneurosis and psychopathic personality are too variable, as are the concepts themselves, to offer much insight into the prevalence of these disorders among criminals." While disagreement exists among the sociological ranks (e.g. Roebuck, 1966), a general perspective is present of uncertainty or skepticism about offenders as a group with unusually high rates of psychological illness.

On the other hand psychiatrists, and often their colleagues in the professions of social work and psychology, report high rates of psychological illness. Abrahamsen (1952) stated "in all my experience I have not been able to find one single offender who did not show some mental pathology . . . the 'normal' offender is a myth." Similarly Karpman (1949) attributed all criminality to be symptomatic of abnormal mental states.

Research reports of psychiatric assessment of offenders have yielded highly variable results. Table 25.1 summarizes several such studies. Comparisons between studies are difficult because different populations were sampled, because diagnostic categories were not alike, and because a time period of over fifty years is represented. Nevertheless, it may be observed that the range of psychotic illnesses reported is quite narrow. The studies usually found between one and two percent of the populations psychotic.

The range of findings on psychological normality is much wider. Four studies found over eighty percent of the offenders sampled to be normal. (Overholser, 1935; Bromberg and Thompson, 1937; Schilder, 1940; Poindexter, 1955).

In a number of recent studies a very small percentage of offenders examined were found to be essentially normal. The reporting of normality, however, is subject to many administrative and non-psychological influences. For example in the diagnostic system of Illinois, none of the five official categories indicate general well-being or normal adjustment. The most positive of the categories is "no gross personality defects," and even that cautious indication of possible normality was made in less than two percent of the 4,453 prisoners seen in an Illinois diagnostic center (Twomey, personal communication, 1967).

These investigations fail to support the unequivocal theoretical statements of Abrahamsen and Karpman on psychological illness and criminality. However, there are a number of implications and limitations of these investigations that are important to note here.

1. The data suggested that the individual diagnostician, the setting, the population and the diagnostic formulae need to be considered. As more thorough psychiatric examinations are conducted, it is likely that more psychopathology will be reported. Conversely, the coarser the screening, the more likely that normality will be found. Psychiatric diagnoses thus are perceived here as relative bits of information which need to be viewed within a number of larger contexts.

2. Typically, psychiatric evaluations are illness-oriented and recent research findings tend to be reported in terms of presence or absence of behav-

TABLE 25.1.
STUDIES OF PSYCHIATRIC EVALUATIONS OF OFFENDERS

Source	Population		Percent
Glueck (1918)	608 Sing Sing Prisoners	Psychotic or mentally deteriorated	12.0
		Normal	41.0
		Mentally retarded	28.1
Overholser (1935)	5,000 Felons under Briggs Law in Massachusetts	Abnormal	15.0
		Normal	85.0
Bromberg and Thompson (1937)	9,958 Offenders before Court of General Sessions, New York City	Psychotic	1.5
		Psychoneurotic	6.9
		Psychopathic personalities	6.9
		Feebleminded	2.4
		Normal or mild personality defects	82.3
Schilder (1940)	Convicted Felons Court of General Sessions of New York City	Psychotic	1.6
		Neurotic	4.2
		Psychopathic personalities	7.3
		Feebleminded	3.1
		Normal	83.8
Banay (1941)	Sing Sing Prisoners	Psychotic	1.0
		Emotionally immature	20.0
		Psychopathic	17.0
		Normal	62.0
Ropa (1951)	Wakefield Prisoners	Neurotic	12.0
		Psychopathic	8.0
		Dullards	23.0
		Schizoid, hysteroid, or aggressive	20.0

(continued from preceding page)

Poindexter (1955)	100 Problem Inmates	Mentally ill Normal	20.0 80.0
Schlessinger and Blau (1957)	500 Typical Prisoners	Character and behavior disorders Normal	85.0 15.0
Shands (1958)	86 North Carolina Prisoners	No psychiatric disorder Transient personality disorder	4.7 19.8
Twomey (1967)	4,453 Prison- ers at Illinois Diagnostic Depot, Menard, Ill.	No gross personality defects	1.4
Brodsky	32,511 Military Prisoners	Character and behavior disorders No psychiatric disease	77.1 21.3

ioral and personality deficits rather than presence or absence of strengths and positive features.

3. The research does not reveal direct information about crime causation. The pathology could be a partial result of the events of arrest, trial, incarceration and the acquisition of stigma.

4. The research indicates offender psychiatric status, but does not give comparative non-offender information. Since, in the studies cited, there was no use of control groups, no base exists for concluding that offenders are more or less psychologically disturbed than non-confined persons.

The reviewed studies represent a small proportion of the research and practices reported in diagnosis and classification of offenders. There are psychometric methods derived from neutral- (as opposed to illness-) oriented theories of personality, and other methods evolved from empirical data organizing procedures, such as Quay's factor analytic research. However, such non-traditional approaches are rarely part of offender diagnostic procedures. The purpose of the next section of this paper will be to examine within the present framework the potential for moving toward positive and strength-oriented perspectives in offender behavior.

TOWARD PSYCHOLOGICAL STRENGTHS IN OFFENDERS

"Seek and ye will find." This quote may be used to summarize part of the diagnostic set in looking at offenders. From textbooks, social class differences, popular depictions of the offender, and informal professional conceptions of criminality, emerge a series of expectations about offender personalities. These expectations prompt diagnosticians to search for content in tests and interviews related to the expectations. We suggest that the searching process leads to a much greater likelihood of discovering personality characteristics to confirm the expectations and overlooking those that disagree. With the bias thus confirmed, the diagnostician then further uses the same stereotypes and expectations in looking at other offenders.

This view does not deny that some offenders have psychological maladjustments, which may or may not occur in differing types and degrees from the general population. Rather it is suggested that attitude and expectations of diagnosticians have the potential for leading to implicit self-fulfilling prophecies. The clinician whose professional antennae are raised and turned to psychopathic tendencies will indeed be prone to finding psychopathic tendencies. The clinician who is tuned to illness and problem behavior similarly is poised to discover it.

If this conception of diagnostic selectivity and discovery is accepted, the issue then arises of what should be the desirable characteristics, ideally and practically, to seek and to discover? We suggest that there is a need to develop a wide range of positive expectations in diagnosticians, correctional officers, job supervisors, parole agents and others in the criminal justice system. Behavior that may be labeled in several ways should acquire positive connotations. Shifty eyes might be described as perceptiveness and awareness. The term "independent thinker" could be used in place of "nonconformist and resistive." In offenders there rarely is unequivocal weakness and illness. As the examiner searches for the difficulties, let him search for the strengths that are just as surely there in every person. Similarly, as the correctional officer stands ready with his armamentarium of disciplinary rules and procedures, let him be equally equipped with formalized ways of rewarding and encouraging.

Within the Illinois correctional system diagnostic evaluations are made through central evaluation centers. This organization of administration into a very few diagnostic depots permits introduction of new evaluation procedures in ways that promote positive expectations. Appendix I presents concrete methods for introducing such procedures. [Appendix I immediately follows this selection.]

Empirical tests of such procedures might be developed. The words indicating illness or negative aspects and those indicating strengths or positive aspects can be counted in diagnostic reports on offenders. Currently we would hazard that the ratio of negative to positive terms is at least ten to one. We suggest that experimentally one might turn back to the diagnostician all reports with more negative than positive terms, and instruct him to look again. The professional persons would howl and protest, but radical approaches are needed to break the fixed stereotypes held by our professional sooth-sayers of pathology. The same quantitative device could be used to count positive versus negative "action reports" of on-the-spot reports of correctional officers.

For the entire penal rehabilitation system, there is a need to build a new vocabulary and a new vision. The old darkly shaded myths must be replaced by reasonable, positive and bright lenses through which the offender is viewed.

NOTES

1. The author is indebted to Richard Vandiver of the Department of Sociology.

APPENDIX I

THE DEVELOPMENT OF ACTION PROGRAMS

When an individual enters a correctional system, the question typically posed is, What problems will this prisoner give us? The present appendix poses an alternative question. That question is: What strengths and positive features does this prisoner have that we may capitalize on in our correctional system? One method to look for such promise or potential is to identify individuals who have the most personal promise from a large number of individuals entering the Illinois Correctional System, and to follow through in a rigorous, experimental design studying prisoners so identified. Subjects who have been found to be promising but who have not been identified within the system and another control group should also be studied.

PRISONERS WITH PROMISE AND THE ILLINOIS CORRECTIONAL SYSTEM

The integration of positive concepts into the Illinois system would best be accomplished through a procedure of gradual re-education of personnel, redevelopment of diagnostic report writing, and promoting of positive self-fulfilling prophesies at all levels. The first step could be to implement a pilot phase to introduce such a philosophy. A minimal number of pilot subjects would be 300 prisoners entering the Illinois Adult Correctional System. These prisoners would be newly committed from courts and entering at any of the Illinois State Diagnostic centers.

The Minnesota Multiphasic Personality Inventory is currently administered to all new entering prisoners at the Diagnostic Depots. In addition, several tests could be added to identify positive features and positive mental health. These include the California Psychological Inventory, the Kuder Vocational Preference Record, several attitude scales, including *The Law Scale*, and the Bills Index of Adjustment and Values, a measure for the assessment of self-concepts.

The tests can be administered through the normal depot procedures and a total of 1,000 prisoners are suggested for a pilot subject pool. Since it is our belief that diagnosticians often are bound by habitual and administrative constrictions, it is suggested to bring in at least two graduate assistants working half time at each depot. These graduate students from the behavioral sciences would be trained to look for and identify features of positive mental health in the prisoners.

Each graduate student would be under the professional supervision of the outside psychologists and maintain direct consultation with the staff members of the Diagnostic Depot. The students would evaluate those individuals who seem to have the most potential for benefiting from correctional experiences and who have the most inner strengths and psychological health. The top twenty percent of the individuals so identified, in terms of their potential, would be the total prisoners with promise group and would have special positive diagnostic reports written on them. A negative versus positive adjective count would be made and it would be required that more positive terms be present. Of these prisoners, half would have special diagnostic reports released and made public to their permanent correctional facility.

The reports would be written by the students with the supervision and agreement of the diagnostic depot staff. These reports would need to make very clear the subject's strength, potential, and indicate ways within the system of mobilizing the strength and potential of the "prisoners with promise" so identified.

As the one hundred identified prisoners are assigned to their institutions, they should be followed through. The graduate students would meet with cell supervisors, job supervisors, mental health workers, correctional officers, and others within the correctional system to appraise them of the prisoner's potential and identify these individuals as promising prisoners. Diaries would be kept by the students of the reactions. The "positively viewed" prisoners would be observed in terms of disciplinary incidents, level of custody, ratings by correctional officers and job supervisors, release dates, and recidivism rates.

A control group should consist of the anonymous (unreleased positive reports) groups of prisoners found to be "prisoners with promise." The identity of this second group of one hundred individuals would be maintained within confidential records. They would be followed through the system but not identified in any way different than other prisoners. Their released reports would be written by the normal diagnostic depot staff and have the customary foci. The effect of labeling versus the existence of the "promising condition" would be compared by noting the relative dispositions of these two groups. As prisoners are actually divided from the 200 total "prisoners with promise" into publicly identified and privately identified subjects, they would be matched by age and offense.

A third group, also of control subjects, should be maintained of prisoners from the remaining 80 percent of the entering population. These subjects also need to be matched for age and offense with the other groups of prisoners with promise. Their reports would be written in the customary fashion by the regular diagnostic depot staff.

The pilot method just outlined is likely to encounter problems in introducing change into the closed social systems. The students, the new diagnostic approaches and particularly the on-site consultation have high probability of meeting subtle and overt resistance. The current organization of records in the Illinois Department of Corrections suggests an alternative starting point in the search for prisoners with promise. This second alternative is a records-oriented approach in which minimal conflict with the system would occur, but which would have less immediate impact. In this alternative, the psychological test results, the psychiatric diagnoses, and the classification reports of perhaps 1,000 consecutive prisoners to enter the diagnostic depots would be examined. These individuals can then be rated on a 10-point scale in terms of general psychological health, potential for maintaining crime-free lives, and specific potential for benefiting from prison. The individuals who represent the top 10 percent, that is 100 subjects, in this category would then be identified from this rating system.

The subjects identified as having this kind of promise on the basis of records can then be followed. Data would be collected on what has happened and is happening in adjustment to prison and recidivism with these 100 subjects as well as a control group of 100 subjects selected from the remaining population. The questions such a project could seek to answer are:

a. What is the range and nature of psychological promise and health and potential for rehabilitation within a prison population?

b. Do these individuals indeed receive differential treatment currently within the system?

c. What is the disposition of these individuals with regard to parole, recidivism, vocational achievement in prison, academic achievement in prisons, and attitude changes indicated in periodic re-evaluation while confined?

IMPLICATIONS

We suggest there is a need to institute direct action for identifying the most promising, psychologically healthy, or highest potential prisoners entering the Illinois Correctional System. If indeed methods are developed and utilized for readily identifying such individuals and the characteristics of such prisoners are objectively known, then a number of possibilities occur for implementing these results further. These will include:

a. Supplying this information to other members of the criminal justice system, such as judges and probation officers, which may well affect decisions on sentencing and probation supervision. It is possible that, with an effective means of identifying early the most healthy and potentially useful offenders, officials may not wish to confine such individuals.

b. Mobilizing special programs and legislation to expedite the confinement process and focus the resources of the system on these individuals more selectively and efficiently.

c. To call to the attention of parole and prison authorities this kind of information that must be gathered and used.

d. To provide ways of avoiding the frequent prisonization and anti-social attitudes imposed by correctional systems on individuals who enter with positive and psychologically healthy attitudes.

REFERENCES

Abrahamsen, D. *Who Are the Guilty?* New York: Rinehart, 1952.

Banay, R. Mental Health in Corrective Institutions. *Proceedings, The American Prison Association.* New York: 1941.

Barnes, H. E. & Teeters, N. *New Horizons in Criminology*, 3rd ed. Englewood Cliffs, N.J.: Prentice Hall, 1959.

Brodsky, S. L. Mental disease and mental ability. In Brodsky, S. L. & Enggleston, N.E. (Eds.), *The Military Prison: Theory, Practice and Research.* Carbondale, Ill.: Southern Illinois University Press, 1970.

Bromberg, W. & Thompson, C. B. The relation of psychoses, mental defect, and personality to crime. *Journal of Criminal Law*, 1937, *28*, 70–89.

Glueck, B. Concerning prisoners. *Mental Hygiene*, 1918, *2*, 178.

Karpman, B. Criminality, insanity and the law. *Journal of Criminal Law and Criminology*, 1949, *39*, 584–605.

Overholser, W. The Briggs Law in Massachusetts. *Journal of Criminal Law*, 1935, *25*, 859.

Poindexter, W. R. Mental illness in a state penitentiary. *Journal of Criminal Law, Criminology and Police Science*, 1955, *45*, 559–64.

Roebuck, J. *Criminal Typology*, Springfield, Ill.: Thomas, 1967.

Schilder, P. The cure of criminals and prevention of crime. *Journal of Criminal Psychopathology*, 1940, *2*, 152.

Schlessinger, N. & Blau, D. A psychiatric study of a retraining command. *U.S. Armed Forces Medical Journal*, 1957, *8*, 397–405.

Shands, H. C. A report on an investigation of psychiatric problems in felons in the North Carolina Prison System. Chapel Hill, N. C.: Department of Psychiatry, University of North Carolina, 1958.

Tappan, P. *Crime, Justice & Correction*. New York: McGraw-Hill, 1960.

Twomey, J. L. Unpublished report. Illinois Diagnostic Depot, Menard, Ill., 1967.

Waldo, G. & Dinitz, S. Personality characteristics of criminals. *Journal of Research in Crime and Delinquency*, 1967, *3*, 1–20.

26

Positive Interaction: Everyday Principles of Correctional Rehabilitation

Irving Jacks

Modern approaches to the treatment of offenders have generally reflected the major fashions prevailing in the foundational fields of psychiatry and clinical psychology. These currents have included psychoanalysis, nondirective counseling, group psychotherapy, encounter and attack strategies, reality therapy, hypnosis, sensitivity training, transactional analysis, transcendental meditation, rational-emotive therapy, and behavior modification, to mention only the best-known. Each has tended—again imitating events in the foundational disciplines—to excite the hopes of practitioners that the ultimate rehabilitative panacea had at last made its appearance. Each has taken on a cult cast, attracting worshipful adherents and equally vociferous opponents. And each, alas, has in its turn proven to be chimerical, so far as the vast majority of offenders was concerned. The hopes, based on early reports of clinical successes, as each pressed for acceptance as the ultimate answer to crime and delinquency, soon enough turned to disillusionment, as it became apparent that the latest technique was not working its trumpeted magic in transforming the clientele.

For some, often the most enthusiastic supporters of a particular technique, lack of universal success meant that it was time to turn to new magic. Others have concluded that all treatment of offenders is hopeless and, as we have seen, have demanded a return to a more ancient retributive philosophy. Finally, there are correctional workers—such as the present writer—who have attempted to maintain a middle-range position between the extremes of cultism and nihilism. This group has recognized that each approach has had both successes and failures, and has taken elements from each, to form a new distillation of practical day-to-day concepts and techniques which, for lack of a better term, the present writer has dubbed positive therapeutic intervention (PTI). While making no claim to having originated any of the individual elements in this approach, the writer has undertaken to assemble them here, in the hope that they may provide both practitioners and students of corrections with some anchorage for resisting the current attacks on the viability of correctional treatment. They grow out of some fifteen years of almost daily personal contact with correctional clients, and have been further delineated in discussions with correctional staffs and correctional students taught by the writer.

CONCEPTUAL BASIS OF POSITIVE THERAPEUTIC INTERVENTION

Before describing the procedures which constitute PTI, it is worth devoting a bit of time to outlining the rather simple and straightforward concepts underlying the procedures. They may perhaps be better viewed as forming a kind of experience-based guide, rather than as a fully-developed dogmatic structure.

1. *Most social behavior amenable to modification is learned behavior*. In essence, this represents an acknowledgment that an important source of social (and antisocial) behavior is the biological-genetic endowment with which we are all born. To the extent that the behavior which we hope to change is either directly or closely reflective of biological-genetic causes, the likelihood of our being able to bring about significant change with the procedures presently available is probably quite limited. The individual, for example, who goes on aggressive rampages as a result of inherited brain dysfunction, or because of some central nervous system injury or disease, is probably best left to the care of the appropriate medical specialist. On the other hand, the offender who has *learned* to respond with aggression to life's frustrations in a social environment in which interpersonal aggression is an everyday experience (the so-called subculture of violence), may well be amenable to learning new, more socially appropriate ways of handling frustrating or anxiety-producing experiences.

2. *Most learned social behavior is maintained by means of environmental consequences*. As has been demonstrated repeatedly by experimental psychologists, we tend to go on doing those things that work for us, that give us some valued payoff, whereas behavior that fails to yield such payoff is likely to diminish or to be discarded entirely. In other words, if a teenager has discovered that the most effective means presently available to him for gaining the admiration of his friends is the performance of daring feats of theft or aggression, he is likely to go on stealing or beating up on others in order to retain this approval. The practitioner whose aim is to eliminate (or prevent) antisocial behavior should then be on the look-out for means of converting peer approval to disapproval and/or of providing new ways for his client to obtain rewarding payoffs.

3. *Rewarding consequences tend to be most effective in the production of new or modified social behavior*. In general, most of us tend to acquire and to retain

behavioral responses which have resulted in positive (pleasurable, rewarding) payoffs. This places the emphasis on behavior which is socially appropriate, rather than on antisocial behavior to be punished. The task of the practitioner, then, becomes one of eliciting or instilling prosocial behavior having a high probability of gaining rewarding consequences.

4. *Punitive consequences tend to be less effective.* This is the obverse of the concept just presented. There is a considerable body of research suggesting that the main effect of punishment is to suppress undesirable behavior only temporarily, primarily in the presence of the punishing agent. Moreover, it often produces avoidance of and hostility toward the punisher, as well as resistance to the learning of more appropriate social behavior.

5. *Learning of new behaviors is a gradual process, and requires practice.* The acquisition of any new skill, be it driving a car, speaking a foreign language, or playing the piano, will require that the learner go through a series of phases (sometimes referred to as "the learning curve"). Initially the learning will be slow, with numerous errors and relapses; this is succeeded by an acceleration during which the various elements blend together in a smoothly coordinated performance of the behavior being learned, with fewer and fewer errors. A similar process can be observed in the acquisition of new social behaviors. The latter are infinitely more complex than the learning of academic or motor skills, and it behooves the correctional practitioner to be constantly aware of the gradual nature of the learning process, and the need for clients to practice newly acquired skills, lest practitioner or client become discouraged too soon or too easily persuaded of the futility of it all.

6. *Immediate consequences for social behavior are more effective than delayed consequences.* This is a concept which is receiving wide current recognition in criticism of the creeping pace of the criminal justice system in dealing with offenders, who reap the rewards of their crimes almost immediately, while the rewards for prosocial behavior often remain far in the distant future. Consider, for example, the correctional practitioner whose goal may be to assist a client to become occupationally self-supporting. If the client has hardly ever in his/her life put in a full week on a job, the prospect of a successful outcome is enhanced if the initial stages result in payment for brief stretches of work, say at the end of each day, rather than postponing the payoff to the end of the week or month. Some readers may recognize, in the concept presented here, one of the origins of token economies, in which symbolic rewards are dispensed almost immediately following the production of prosocial behaviors. Of course, immediacy is a relative term, in that the concept involves rewarding of gradually expanding units of prosocial behaviors (e.g., slowly working up to pay for a full week's work), or the instilling of an increasing capacity to postpone immediate gratification with the expectation of greater rewards later.

7. *Our immediate goal should be to change people's external behavior rather than their interior attitudes.* Most current approaches to correctional rehabilitation reflect the idea that our goals ought to involve changing clients' attitudes as the basis for inducing socially appropriate behavior. This has overlooked what one might have thought was self-evident, namely that the only means we have for knowing the attitudes of another is through the other's behavior. From a practical standpoint, that which we refer to as a person's "attitudes" may well be viewed as simply a summarizing label for his/her observed behaviors. Thus, when we speak of an offender "lacking respect for the property rights of others," what else do we mean other than that he has been observed trespassing upon, or illegally appropriating to his own use, some-one else's property? And of what use is it socially if he verbally professes respect of others' property, but continues to steal? Obviously, the task of the correctional practitioner is to assist the client to change the larcenous (or assaultive) behavior, irrespective of his verbalized moral principles. And, if we succeed in accomplishing this task, we may find, willy-nilly, that the individual's expressed attitudes may then change to conform to his new pattern of behavior. An excellent illustration of this last point is to be found in one approach of Synanon in treating drug addicts. A cardinal rule of that program, which includes clients of various racial backgrounds living together in a therapeutic community, is that, no matter how a member feels about another's race, no comments of a racist nature will be permitted, and that each member will treat other members as individuals, rather than as social stereotypes. The underlying assumption would appear to be that if one *behaves* respectfully toward another, his *attitude* toward the other will shift toward one of respect.

8. *Nothing succeeds like success.* PTI is a success-oriented approach which makes the assumption that each time an individual succeeds in reaching a goal, he/she feels encouraged to work toward a higher or more difficult goal. The writer recalls a former correctional client who announced one day that he had decided to try for a college degree. He enrolled in a course in fresh-man math being offered at the institution by a nearby junior college. After about four weeks, he informed the writer that he had quit the course, that it was worthless, and that the man from the junior college was a "lousy teacher." In reviewing what had taken place, it quickly became obvious that the course assumed some proficiency in high-school algebra, which the in-mate—a high-school "push-out"—had never really grasped. Fortunately, the institution school offered high-school algebra which the inmate, after some initial resistance, was persuaded to pick up. Here he made rapid progress, earned an "A," and the following year enrolled again in the college math course. Flushed with his success, and having now the necessary background, he proceeded through the junior college curriculum, went on for a B.S. in

Psychology, got a Master's degree in Counseling, and presently heads a community-based program working with juveniles. While not all correctional treatment will yield such dramatic outcomes, the point is that it behooves the correctionist to know the client's strengths, and to use this knowledge to enable the client to have successful experiences. In the terminology of the poker player, whenever possible, one should deal to the power.

THE FUNDAMENTAL SKILLS OF PRACTICAL THERAPEUTIC INTERVENTION

While there exists a considerable range of intervention procedures available to the practitioner in working with a variety of client problems, there are two skills which are fundamental to all, and without which no intervention procedure can be expected to succeed. The two complement each other and are employed reciprocally. The reference is to the twin skills of *listening* and *communicating*. The reader may be reacting to this with a shrug, thinking that the skills of listening and communicating are so universally possessed that they hardly warrant such emphasis. After all, don't we, from infancy on, spend a large portion of our waking hours listening to and communicating with the people around us? Without belaboring the point in this limited space, the writer would simply respond that the verbal exchanges that pass for listening and communicating in ordinary social intercourse are a far cry from those needed for successful therapeutic intervention. It may suffice to note simply that their employment by therapists should, as much as possible, be unmotivated by exhibitionism, one-upsmanship, putting-down, or scoring points off the client.

Listening therapeutically is composed of three primary components: empathy; attention; selectivity.

1. Empathy may be seen as an effort to see things as the client sees them or, in contemporary jargon, where the client is "coming from." It implies, for example, understanding (not necessarily condoning; empathy is not synonymous with *sympathy*) the inner conflict experienced by a teenager who is taunted as a "chicken" if he resists the suggestion of his friends that he join them in breaking into a store for the purpose of stealing merchandise; or that of the parolee who learns that he is being paid less than the prevailing scale received by others with equal skill, doing the same work in the same plant, and who then explodes with anger when the foreman criticizes him. PTI takes the position that correctionists capable of placing themselves in clients' shoes while the latter describe their daily experiences are the only ones who can truly be said to understand—and therefore, be situated to deal with—the reality of their clients' experiences. Listening with empathy implies a willing-

ness to put aside temporarily the counselor's own values, attitudes, and biases, in the effort to perceive life as the client perceives it. While almost anyone can learn to be an empathic listener, its achievement is most likely to be attained by counselors who recognize and relish diversity of outlooks, and who are prepared to expose themselves to life experiences other than their accustomed ones. Take, for example, the counselor who has spent most of his life in rural or small-town environments, and who expects to be employed in a correctional system whose clients are drawn heavily from urban inner-city neighborhoods; this prospective correctionist might do well to spend some time, perhaps as a volunteer, working in an inner-city program and learning the life-style which may characterize his future clientele.

2. Listening with *attention* is a precondition for listening empathetically, as well as for the third component (described below)—listening selectively. On the one hand, it implies an effort initially to identify the client's perceptions and interpretations of what is going on, and ultimately, an effort to understand the relationship between actual events in the client's environment and the client's actual behavior. In general, attentive listening is listening that zeroes in as sharply as possible on the experiences and activities of a specific human being.

3. When we listen *selectively*, we are being guided by the frequently replicated finding that a listener—especially a listener who is valued by the speaker—can, by varying the mode of listening, significantly influence the nature of what is being said. It has been demonstrated, for example, that through the selective application of nonverbal behaviors, e.g., leaning forward, nodding vigorously, and looking at the speaker, the content of verbal discourse can be influenced both quantitatively and qualitatively. In addition, verbal responses such as repeating and/or rephrasing what the speaker has said, requesting further clarification, or even adding "uh-huh," "Oh?" or "I see" to the nod of the head can effect the flow of speech. An assumption underlying listening attentively is that not all of the verbal content produced by clients is of equal value in advancing the therapeutic process. Another assumption is that the correctionist functioning as counseling practitioner can and should utilize the techniques of attentive listening *selectively* for the purpose of eliciting interview content of greater value to therapy.

While the latter may vary somewhat among practitioners, depending on their therapeutic values, there are certain criteria which the present writer considers applicable to most current approaches. For example, since most counseling approaches assume that the client ought to produce material verbally during the interview, the attentive counselor will, *during the initial phases*, respond in relatively undifferentiated fashion to almost any verbalization produced by the client. This is of particular import in work with clients whose life experience has tended to make them somewhat shy of verbal interaction and who feel inadequate in situations which place a heavy emphasis on verbal description of experiences and attitudes. With such clients, it may be desirable to show attention at first to just about any type of verbal comment, no matter how irrelevant or trivial-sounding.

At some point, when the client has acquired some ease in speaking to the counselor, the latter will begin to vary his attention responses in order to help the client to focus on therapeutically useful content. To be in a position to provide such variable responses means that the counselor will have been listening attentively at all times. In other words, *it is the counselor's response, not his/her attention, that varies!*

Which client verbalizations constitute "therapeutically useful content"? (Here again, counselors of differing theoretical persuasions are likely to have differing ideas of what is important, and the present writer candidly acknowledges a major debt to the behavioral position [a leaning which will undoubtedly be apparent to the discerning reader]. The writer is of the opinion that the behavioral principles and procedures included in this chapter are those which are widely recognized as playing a role in many of the modern approaches referred to earlier.)

1. *References to self* vs. references to others or to atmospheres. While ostensibly in counseling for the purpose of understanding and changing their own behavior, many clients will find it easier to discuss the experiences and actions of others, sometimes focusing on abstractions, such as "society," rather than on themselves—their own experiences and actions. Correctional clients are particularly prone to use the counseling session to describe what others have done—the misfeasances committed by others or how they were victimized—as a means of making themselves feel less responsible for their own actions. The attentive counselor will be listening closely for any content references to self (e.g. "*I* went . . ."; "*I* said . . ."; "*I* thought . . .") and will respond vigorously to such remarks with any of the techniques noted above. On the other hand, the counselor will want to discourage messages emphasizing the experiences or actions of third parties by the withholding of responses implying interest or attention. Included in the "withholding" category would be such behaviors as remaining silent, closing one's eyes, yawning, shuffling papers, staring at the ceiling, and looking at one's wristwatch. When such low-key responses fail to bring about the desired shift in emphasis, direct prompting in the form of a question—"And so, what did *you* do?"—is by no means precluded.

2. *References to actions* vs. references to attitudes (or feelings). The reader may recall the concept noted above, that our targets for change ought to be behaviors rather than interior attitudes. From this, it follows that the counselor ought to be listening attentively for evidence of client behaviors, and

responding selectively to these, while giving less attention to references to thoughts, attitudes, or feelings. Needless to say, included among client behaviors are things the client said ("So I told him . . ."), as well as failure to act (the zero end of the scale of activity).

3. *References to our actions* vs. the actions of others. This, in a sense, represents an integration of the two categories immediately preceding—self-reference and reference to action. Not infrequently, counseling sessions deteriorate into a recounting of the behavior of others in the clients' lives—parents, spouses, friends, police, and lawyers. At times, listening to transcripts of such sessions, one almost forgets that the speaker is the client, not his nagging wife, or his critical employer, or the "corrupt" criminal justice system. Here, again, judicious interjection of prompts occasionally ("And so, what did you do when the foreman chewed you out for coming in late?") can be useful in moving the discussion in more profitable directions.

Thus far, we have focused on the elements involved in therapeutic *listening* skills. But as the reader surely has already observed for himself, the separation of listening from *communicating* is an artificial one, convenient perhaps for instructional purposes, but hardly tenable in practice. The practices of selective listening, nonverbal though they may be, are inevitably means of communicating to the client which behaviors are deemed most appropriate to the achievement of therapeutic progress. Thus, we discover that the skills of therapeutic communication are much the same as the skills of attentive listening, which was foreshadowed in the references above to prompts that might be utilized by the counselor. The purposes of the counselor's communications, stated briefly, are to convey to the client:

1. that you *are* paying attention;
2. that you *do value* him/her;
3. that it is the client's *actions* rather than his thoughts or feelings that interest you;
4. that you are interested primarily in *his/her actions* or experiences—not in what someone else experienced or did;
5. that it is the *present circumstances* of the client's life, as they elicit and perpetuate his/her present behavior, that is of therapeutic interest.

In this, we are, of course, diverging radically from the "psychodynamic" tradition, which assumes a necessity to explore the influence of early—especially childhood—experience on current behavior. On the other hand, the writer is pleased to acknowledge his debt to several more recent contributions, particularly rational-emotive therapy, reality therapy, and behavior therapy, all of them emphasizing the here and now of client experience.

In order to illustrate more concretely the quality of the counselor's responding, consider the following statement, made to a counselor by a client who was on probation at the time:

"I almost didn't come in to see you today. My boss started bugging me about some shipment being sent out late. I could hardly get anything done after that, even though it wasn't my fault . . . I figured, 'Why bother . . . Nothing is going to change'."

A counselor's response to this, incorporating several of the principles outlined above, might have gone something like this:

"It was after your boss started chewing you out that you found it hard to get your work done, even though it wasn't your fault. This discouraged you to the point where it didn't seem like you were going to be able to change anything, so you might as well not keep your appointment with me."

(Here the counselor demonstrates that he has been paying attention by reflecting back significant portions of the client's statement. In doing so, he emphasizes both the antecedent event—"It was after your boss . . ."—giving rise to the behavior in question, as well as the feelings—"This discouraged you . . ."—resulting from the experience.)

"There are a couple of things I'm wondering about. Did you do or say anything to your boss after he bawled you out—like trying to explain why it wasn't your fault the shipments were late? [If not,] how come? What do you suppose would have happened if you had tried to explain?"

(Here the counselor is focusing on possible client *behavior*—"Did you do or say anything . . ."—as well as on client antecedent expectancies, which might have inhibited client behavior—"What do you suppose would have happened if. . . ." At the same time, the counselor introduces the possibility that there may have been some alternative constructive response available to the client other than passive discouragement, namely ". . . trying to explain. . . .")

"Another thing I'm curious about . . . If you hadn't come in here today, what else do you suppose you might have done? . . . Where else would you have gone?"

(Here the counselor is attempting to elicit information regarding the behavior-pattern of the client when faced with antecedent circumstances of a discouraging or frustrating nature—possibly an extended drinking spree in violation of the rules of his probation, opening the door to loss of his job and to further illegal behavior.)

"Still, despite feeling discouraged, wondering if it was worth continuing, you did keep your appointment with me. It took a lot of guts and will-power to make it in today; and it proves that you actually are making progress."

(Finally, and perhaps most significantly, the counselor takes the opportunity to give explicit recognition of the client's effort, thereby reinforcing the client's constructive response to a frustrating experience, as well as to his continued participation in counseling.)

Let us take a moment to summarize the points illustrated in our "hypothetical" client-counselor interaction:

1. The client tells how the action of a third party gives rise to feelings and actions by the client.

2. The counselor rephrases what the client has said, placing the emphasis on:

    a. *the client's behavior* in response to the antecedent event;
    b. inhibition of client behavior due to client expectancies of (painful) consequences of his behavior;
    c. the possibility of more *constructive alternative behaviors* being available to the client;
    d. the potentially damaging client behavior-pattern in the face of frustrating circumstances.

3. The counselor seeks to strengthen constructive behavior through explicit recognition and appraisal.

Facilitator Techniques for Positive Therapeutic Intervention

We turn our attention now to a consideration of several procedures which, in the writer's experience, are particularly compatible with the concepts and goals of PTI. Once again, no claim of originality is implied; each of these techniques has been described individually elsewhere. It is the belief in the value of bringing them together in one place that emboldens the author to present them here albeit in relatively skeletal fashion. In fact, one might hope that the reader's appetite will be sufficiently whetted by this overview to look into the more detailed descriptions available elsewhere in this volume, as well as in other sources.

1. *Role-Modeling.* Perhaps as potent as any of the direct advice and suggestions that the counselor may bring forth for the client's consideration is the therapeutic power that resides in the behavior of the counselor as he performs the informal activities of daily life under the client's observation. Almost all clients will tend to perceive their counselors as people worth observing and worth imitating. And whether we intend it or not, inevitably we find our clients emulating many of our behaviors, particularly in those areas in which they feel unsure how best to function. Counselors need to be aware of these

imitative tendencies, and being thus aware, to make it a point to model for their clients the types of behaviors that they hope to instill in clients.

A simple example: a client, like so many correctional clients, has for much of his life demonstrated a rather cavalier attitude toward punctuality—he is frequently late for work and misses appointments. In this situation, the counselor's attention to punctuality becomes immensely important in modeling appropriate social behavior. If he regularly arrives late for counseling sessions, he may be certain that the client will take with a large grain of salt any suggestion he may offer regarding the necessity of reporting on time for work, or for appointments. It is the classic instance of "Do as I say, not as I do." As any parent can testify, the latter is a sure-fire formula for failure. Again, if neatness, courtesy, proper language usage, upright posture, and eye contact are among the social skills that the client appears to lack in his interactions with the world, they are hardly likely to be acquired in working with a counselor who is unkempt, rude, ungrammatical, slouching, and whose gaze constantly wanders during his interactions with clients.

Examples of the type just presented are of the informal variety which are likely to arise spontaneously in the course of counselor-client encounters. This is not always the case, however. For some behaviors, it may become necessary for the counselor to *construct* situations in which appropriate behavior can be demonstrated.

Again, let us consider an example: a client becomes flustered and incoherent when his wife calls him at work, and then proceeds to become abusive toward her for provoking the situation. The counselor, assuming he views the relationship with the spouse as a potential source of problems, may actually encourage his own wife (or girl-friend) to call him during the counseling session, whereupon he may proceed to explain calmly, "I'm with a client, so I can't talk to you right now; but I'll call back in three quarters of an hour."

Many correctional clients become panicky in, and flee from, situations requiring that they fill out forms or application blanks, thus missing out on opportunities for employment, social services, tax refunds, veteran's benefits, and driver's licenses. Counselors employed in community-based correctional settings—e.g., half-way houses, work-release centers, alcohol and drug rehabilitation programs—are particularly well placed to model behaviors appropriate to such occasions. Simply put, it is a matter of arranging it so that one or several clients can be present—in the counselor's office or at the pertinent agency—when the counselor fills out such forms for him/herself. This is preferable to a more formal instructional session back at the correctional setting, since it allows the client to observe how the counselor deals with unanticipated complications in completing the form—a point at which, for many correctional clients, the panic peaks and is resolved by flight. It is helpful, additionally, if the counselor thinks out loud, enabling the client to see how the counselor arrived at the answers.

2. *Role-Rehearsal.* While the enactment of specific roles by the counselor is likely to have maximum impact on clients, there inevitably will arise in the lives of individual clients situations rather remote from the counselor-client interaction, or from the direct life experience of the counselor. In such instances, recourse may be had to role-modeling, involving invented situations, where the specific problem area is embedded in a fictionalized skit. This writer recalls one parolee-client who was being pressured by several of his fellow-employees to join them for drinks after quitting work. Besides being a violation of parole regulations, the client was aware of how heavy drinking had contributed to his previous criminal record. Still, he was running out of excuses for not joining in and came close to yielding on several occasions. What's more, he was afraid that his continued refusal was making him appear ridiculous—even less than manly—in the eyes of his co-workers. The counselor encouraged his client to sketch in the circumstances under which the pressure took place, including some of the actual words used by the co-workers. Counselor and client then reviewed a number of possible responses which the client might make, including: "My wife isn't feeling well"; "I've got a headache"; "I can't" (without further comment or explanation); "Alcohol and I don't get along . . . but thanks anyhow, I appreciate the invitation." We agreed that the last one might have the best prospect of permanently reducing the pressure, with minimum risk of alienating his co-workers. We then proceeded to "role-play" the situation right in the office, with the client taking the part of a fellow-employee attempting to persuade the former to go drinking, while the counselor played the client responding in the previously agreed-upon fashion. We then reversed roles, giving the client an opportunity to rehearse his own behavior. Typically in this procedure, several direct and reverse-role enactments would take place, each followed by discussion of both participants' feelings while going through the experience, how realistic it felt, and of modifications to be tried. With each repetition, clients gain greater mastery of the situation, hence greater confidence in their ability to handle it in real life.

A wide range of problem areas can be adapted for role-rehearsal—family interactions, on-the-job situations, handling criticism, and resisting pressure to engage in illegal activities, to name just a few. Some guidelines for the most effective use of the procedure would include the following:

a. It is most effective where the client takes an active role in developing and modifying the "script," so that it becomes increasingly his/her behavior style—including the client's own natural verbal style.
b. It is best to start with fairly short, simple units of behavior. Thus, if

the goal is to teach the client habits of social courtesy, one might begin with as limited an interaction as saying "Good morning" to a spouse on awakening in the morning (one is continually amazed at the absence of even such simple responses as this from the repertoire of many correctional clients). From the shorter and simpler behaviors, we can progress to increasingly complex interactions—e.g., responding to the complaint of the spouse (or boss).

c. Whenever possible, the appropriate behavior should first be enacted by the counselor, so that the impact of modeling can be brought into play and, at the same time, making certain that the client understands the salient aspects of the modeled response, even if the client decides to vary specific details in order to have them fit more comfortably into his/her personal style.

d. Rapid feedback in the form of discussion immediately following the role-rehearsal should be a constant feature of the procedure. Where there is the necessary equipment, the feedback is strengthened immeasurably through the use of tape recording—or even more powerful, video instant replay.

e. Feedback from the counselor should be liberally spiced with comments of approval and encouragement, and should contain a minimum amount of negative criticism. Instead of "That wasn't too good," it would be better to say "That was fine. I was wondering how it would work if you were to look at the foreman while telling him why you were late. Let's try it."

f. Role-rehearsal gains in effectiveness when it is carried out in a group setting, particularly where the group members are significantly related to one another and can provide feedback based on a realistic appreciation of each other's life circumstances. These would include members of the same family, as well as peer groups of offenders, alcoholics, gamblers, or drug addicts. Many clients, especially during the early phases of counseling, seem more willing to accept feedback, especially if it is negative, from people with whom they feel closeness or similarity. The counselor should view group members as therapeutic allies and be prepared to encourage their feedback by acknowledging their contributions freely and approvingly.

3. *Desensitization.* Role-modeling and role-rehearsal are of particular value in assisting clients to acquire new and more effective patterns to replace the less adaptive ones which they have used heretofore. For some correctional clients, the problem is not one of not *knowing* appropriate behavior, but rather that they become so anxious or aroused in certain social situations that they forget how to act, or else they avoid the situations completely, out of

anticipated failure. Typical is the ex-offender who avoids applying for better-paying jobs for which he/she possesses the necessary skills because of fear that others will learn of the past record and shun its possessor; consequently, this individual falls back on familiar sources of illegal income.

Desensitization procedures have been developed as a means of overcoming anxiety or avoidance responses in small graduated steps, so that feared situations become gradually more approachable. Let us consider the ex-offender who fears applying for jobs. Initially, we would review with him the range of behaviors called for in landing a job. These might include such things as checking want ads, visiting the state employment office, getting references, preparing resumes, filling out applications, telephoning for appointments, being interviewed, taking employment tests, and so forth. Once the main items have been identified, the client is asked to rank them with respect to the degree of anxiety they produce in the client. This ranking—sometimes referred to as an anxiety-hierarchy—should not be carried out mechanically or superficially, but instead should grow out of a thorough review, conducted jointly with the client, of actual past experiences with each, so that they are reliably differentiated with respect to the amount of fear accompanying each one. The ranking should start with the *most* anxiety-producing situations at the top, the second most anxiety-producing next, and so on down, in rank-order to the least anxiety-producing situation. In the case of one client, with respect to the items cited above, the anxiety hierarchy might look something like the following:

1. being interviewed (most anxiety-producing)
2. filling out application
3. taking employment test
4. asking for references
5. telephoning prospective employer for appointment
6. preparing resume
7. visiting the employment office
8. checking help-wanted ads (least anxiety-producing)

Having identified and ranked the items in the hierarchy of one hypothetical client, we now turn our attention to the lowest ranked item, in this case "checking help-wanted ads". (The reader is cautioned that an anxiety-hierarchy is a highly individualized thing, so that both the specific items as well as their rank-ordering will vary from person to person. The counselor cannot assume that what is anxiety-producing for one client will be similarly so for all clients. Thus, the initial review with the client, in order to identify items, should never be omitted or abbreviated). Our object, in other words, is to initiate the actual desensitization with the least anxiety-producing (or, to put it another way, most easily approachable) situation. This writer would then instruct the client to check the help-wanted ads each day between now and their next meeting, and to circle in red all those ads which could apply to the client; should the client, while carrying out the assignment, start to feel anxious, he should *immediately* stop the activity for that day, and start in on a fresh set of ads the next day, again quitting *as soon as he feels himself becoming uneasy*.

Some clients appear to need considerable reinforcement and support at this early point in the procedure, and with them this writer has found it useful to build some added elements into the procedure. These might include one or more of the following: (a) Have the client check the time at the beginning and end of the task each day; since we are dealing with the low-anxiety end of the hierarchy, the client should be able to see quick progress in the form of increasing periods of time at the task, free of anxiety; (b) Have the client phone the counselor upon completion of the assignment each day; this enables the counselor to express approval and/or encouragement of the client's efforts, and it is particularly useful for clients in need of immediate support or reinforcement in order to keep them on-task until the next session; (c) In a few extreme instances, the counselor might actually schedule brief daily sessions in which clients can report their experiences face-to-face, without having to wait until the next regularly-scheduled session.

Once the lowest item in the anxiety-hierarchy is desensitized, i.e., can be experienced without anxiety, we proceed to the next—in our illustration, "visiting the employment office." Again, together with the client, we prepare the assignment, including a schedule for carrying it out, as well as for offering reinforcing support for the client's efforts. Being higher on the anxiety hierarchy, the next item may require a longer time (more exposure trials) for the client to become desensitized to it than was the case with the one(s) preceding. Should it appear to be taking an inordinately long time, several possibilities need to be considered. One is that the item is too low on the hierarchy, relative to other items, so that the hierarchy requires revision, with the item in question being placed at a higher rank. Another possibility is that the item involves behavior of such complexity that it needs to be broken down into its parts, which should, in their own turn, be cast in a sub-hierarchy for the purposes of desensitization. A corollary to the last point is that the distance between steps in the hierarchy should not be so large as to demand undue speed of progression of the client. One should not expect an individual to progress from a bicycle to a Grand Prix racing car without covering any of the steps in between. The necessity for reviewing the rank-order of items, as well as for subdividing items into sub-hierarchies, increases the higher up we go. With most clients, therefore, it can be expected that lower (less anxiety-producing) items will undergo desensitization more rapidly than those higher up.

Desensitization can be expected to operate most effectively if the counselor keeps several principles in mind. In constructing the anxiety-hierarchy, the client should be an active collaborator, since it only has validity insofar as it reflects the client's own experience of feared and avoided situations.

The lowest item in the hierarchy should be one that the client can carry out with little or no anxiety almost from the very first exposure. Sometimes this may require that the counselor arbitrarily devise a first step just below the lowest one arrived at collaboratively with the client. This helps to ensure that the client's initial encounter with the desensitization procedure is a positive one, encouraging the client to proceed to the next level.

By keeping the distance between items relatively small, there is minimal danger of the client going too abruptly from a low-anxiety level to one of intolerably high anxiety, in which case the previously-learned avoidance behavior may be triggered and generalized to the entire counseling experience. The best indication that the distance between items is too great is likely to come directly from the client, taking the form of missed appointments, failure to call in, or to keep progress records (e.g., time of beginning and ending assignments), or of open verbalizations, such as "I'm not ready to go for an interview" or "I got scared and chickened out" or "I figured I better wait till next week."

The success of the desensitization method can be maximized if, before the client attempts to carry out real-life assignments related to the items on the hierarchy, the techniques of role-modeling and role-rehearsal are utilized during counseling sessions to prepare the client. In our hypothetical example, the counselor might circle likely sounding help-wanted notices. This might be followed by the client doing the same with the counselor looking on. Role-modeling and role-rehearsal should take place in preparation for real-life exposures at each level of the hierarchy.

Finally, the counselor is reminded of the inestimable desirability of *quick, positive feedback*. The client's smallest effort to carry out assignments should be greeted readily with approval and with recognition of the client's courage in confronting (or attempting to confront) a feared situation.

4. *The "Helper Principle."* Most readers of this chapter are familiar with the program of Alcoholics Anonymous. They will recall that a central element is the responsibility assumed by each A. A. member to come to the assistance of other alcoholics. This, in the view of the writer, represents one of the most powerful tools in the entire thrust of A.A., and is applicable to a large number of therapeutic efforts. To the extent that clients assume responsibility for helping other clients with similar problems, the client, as helper, is strengthened in the capacity to deal with the client's own life. Whenever possible, consequently, the counselor ought to be alert to opportunities to enlist the aid of clients (especially those with whom the counselor has been

working for some time) in working with other (especially newer) clients. The counselor will be amazed at how much more effectively the older client starts to absorb the lessons of counseling, once the client assumes a co-counselor role. Simultaneously, of course, the "junior" client finds a kindred soul, a role-model, who understands where the client is coming from, and with whom identification is possible.

5. *Analysis of Client Logic.* For most of this review of positive therapeutic intervention procedures, we have tended to ignore the thought processes of the client in favor of the client's action tendencies. We have taken as our working hypothesis the assumption that observable *behaviors* are, in general, more amenable to change than are internal experiences. This should not be interpreted, however, as a total lack of interest in the thought processes—cognitions—of clients. There is one type of thinking, especially common among correctional clients, which deserves attention even while the primary emphasis remains on changing behavior. Reference here is to the tendency of clients to interpret misfortunes or temporary setbacks as permanent disasters, sometimes called doomsday thinking or catastrophizing. It is seen in the statement "Nobody wants to hire an ex-con," based on having been turned down by one or two employers. In another context, the college campus, the same type of thinking is typified by the student who has failed a course, or even a single test; instead of the correct statement, "I failed math," such a student catastrophizes, "I am a failure (as a person)." As can be seen from these examples, a major problem here is the readiness of some individuals to draw broad negative generalizations about their personalities, or their future prospects, from a small number of negative events in their lives. In counseling, such thinking sometimes results in clients concluding, following some setbacks, that the counseling is a failure. The counselor who is aware of this potential pitfall will make it a point, at the outset of the relationship, to let the client know that setbacks—relapses, slips—are quite possible and quite normal, but that they need not be construed as disastrous failures. The counselor will be listening attentively, moreover, for evidences of doomsday logic, as the counseling proceeds and the client attempts to cope with increasingly difficult situations in his or her life. Besides providing ample encouragement and support, as described earlier, the alert counselor will share with the client the observation that such thinking is taking place, and point out the egregious consequences. The counselor may, for example, note the client's tendency to go from experiencing *a* failure to the judgment of *self* as a failure. Or the client's attention can be called to the unreasonableness of expecting that every attempt will result in success; some failures are to be expected when one is learning new (social) skills, and each individual is different and will learn at his own pace.

AFTERWORD

In this brief description of positive therapeutic intervention (PTI) the purpose has been to acquaint readers with a number of practical tools available to correctional practitioners. These were not invented by this writer, but they represent procedures culled from original sources. In this writer's judgment, these procedures can be learned and used by many correctional counseling practitioners.

However, readers are cautioned that *merely reading this chapter cannot, in any sense, be taken as sufficient preparation for the counseling of clients.* Indeed, to do so could be construed as a serious breach of professional ethics. At the very least, the would-be counselor should be prepared to spend time acquiring the necessary skills through enrollment in appropriate training workshops taught by experienced counselors. Even more desirable, if circumstances permit, would be enrollment in university-based courses in counseling, where not only the techniques but their underlying rationale are presented.

Having offered this cautionary note, the author would close with a word of encouragement to the student, the corrections professional, the paraprofessional, or the volunteer-in-corrections who may be contemplating becoming a correctional counselor. Do, by all means, read further about the various techniques discussed here (a short list of related readings appears below). While no one of the procedures described, or even all of them combined, are a cure-all for the problems of crime and corrections, they represent the best methodologies currently available to us. If you are willing to read about, and receive training in, the basic skills of listening and communicating, as well as the specifics of the procedures covered, then you have the chance to make a real contribution as a correctional counselor.

SOME SUGGESTED READING RELATED TO PTI

Carkhuff, R. R. *Helping and human relations.* Holt, Rinehart, & Winston: N.Y., 1969.

Ho, M. K. Application of helper principle in working with delinquents. *Federal Probation,* September 1972, 26–29.

Krumboltz, J. D. & Thoresen, C. E. *Behavioral counseling.* Holt, Rinehart, & Winston: N. Y., 1969.

Lazarus, A. A. *Behavior therapy & beyond.* McGraw-Hill: N. Y., 1971.

Phillips, E. L., et al. Achievement Place: behavior shaping works for delinquents. *Psychology Today,* June 1973, 75–79.

Sarason, I. G. & Ganzer, V. J. Modeling & group discussion in the rehabilitation of juvenile delinquents. *Journal of Counseling Psychology.* 1973, *20,* 442–49.

Part Seven

Rehabilitation and Modification—Adult Offenders

Rehabilitation and modification programs for adult offenders have appeared, disappeared, and reappeared for some time. Professional correctional workers responsible for the planning, development, and operational functioning of offender rehabilitation have been criticized for having too few or too many programs, too much or too little involvement, the right methods at the wrong time, and the wrong methods at the right time. Legal forces have asserted that offenders have the right to rehabilitative treatment, that they should be supplied rehabilitative treatment on demand and, conversely, that offenders cannot be forced into participation in treatment programs. All of these factors have contributed to the present state of confusion in which correctional rehabilitators are floundering as they attempt to resolve the conflict between punishment and rehabilitation for adult law violators.

One needs merely to peruse the professional literature to become aware that whether an author favors punishment or rehabilitation, the same bias against correctional rehabilitation emerges. For example, in the same issue of one professional journal, *Psychiatric Opinion*, two authors express opposing viewpoints about correctional rehabilitation. Coleman states that the rehabilitation of criminals in prisons "has become the foundation and rationale for a system of oppression undreamed of by its founders" (Coleman, 1974, p. 5). Coleman indicates that it is his belief that treatment in prison is just not effective. Rundle, on the other hand, states that the crime in prisons is the lack of treatment (Rundle, 1974, p. 17). Although Coleman and Rundle are presenting opposing viewpoints of correctional rehabilitation, both place the problem of too much or too little treatment squarely at the feet of the correctional rehabilitator.

Martinson (1974, p. 25) has stated in unequivocal terms that rehabilitation efforts for offenders between 1945–1967 have, except in a few isolated instances, resulted in no "appreciable" effect on recidivism. Wilke and Martinson (1976, p. 43) postulate that "perhaps the criminal justice system has reached the point of diminishing returns" as far as treatment of offenders is concerned. In this fashion the controversy continues over the effectiveness of the number and variety of rehabilitative programs for adult offenders.

From this state of affairs emerges the obvious question, What do we do now? The answers range from the alternative of doing nothing to a profusion of rehabilitative behavior change alternatives. It is logical to concentrate on the most workable correctional rehabilitative alternatives. By concentrating our efforts on successful behavior change programs, we decrease the risk of becoming mired in fruitless, nonproductive criticism of ineffective rehabilitation schemes. It is better to constructively criticize those methods and techniques which have been successful and which can be positively changed to increase their success, than to waste precious time and energy censuring those programs which have proven to be ineffective. We need only to stop using the ineffective methods and apply our efforts to those programs which have shown they can successfully accomplish our rehabilitative behavior change goals.

If the solution to the enigma of adult offender behavior change programs is to concentrate our energies on those programs which are effective, then before going further we must also consider the suitability of differential treatment. For in espousing this particular solution we are, indeed, espousing the value of differential treatment. There are many who extol the philosophy of the single, all-encompassing behavior change modality as the answer for all offender treatment programs. Others adhere to the opposite viewpoint of "different strokes for different folks," which describes the differential treatment approach. Arguments for and against the adoption of one philosophy over the other would fill several volumes. We have neither the time nor the space to present these viewpoints in a definitive manner. However, we can go so far as to state that, to date, no single rehabilitative approach has proven so effective as to be considered the only means of bringing about positive behavior change in offenders. On the other hand, there have been a number of different treatment programs which have proven successful with different types of offenders. Thus, it would appear that differential treatment holds the most promise for behavior change program development. If this is the case, concentration of our efforts on differential treatment programs which help different types of offenders is the wiser path to follow.

We begin this section with an article which makes direct reference to utilizing differential treatment with adult offenders. At the outset of this scholarly and thought-provoking work, Levinson adopted the position that the task of correctional rehabilitation is to develop different treatment programs to their fullest, and then determine which one will be of most benefit to a particular type of offender. If this is to be done, there must be some means of categorizing offenders into different treatment groups. A method which Levinson found to be effective is Quay's Adult Offender Typology. By using information collected from the offender's self-disclosure, life history records, and current behavior patterns, and also by applying factor analytic techniques, five dimensions of adult offender behavior have been isolated. The first dimension, labeled Aggressive-Psychopathic, reflects the degree of toughness, defiance, physical and verbal aggression, troublemaking, victimizing, and quick temperedness of an individual. Division two, which is called Neurotic-Anxious, concerns worry, tenseness, sadness, help-seeking, and fear of other offenders. The third dimension involves the individual's inability to follow directions, daydreaming, sluggishness, preoccupation, moodiness, incompetence, and social withdrawal. This dimension has been labeled Immature-Dependent. The fourth dimension "suggests an individual without a pattern" of deviant behavior but who probably committed his crime because of some precipitating environmental stress. This dimension is called Situational. Finally, the fifth dimension measures manipulativeness, which is reflected in an individual's conning behavior, distrust, accusation of "unfairness" and pitting one staff member against another. The offender is categorized based on the highest combined score he receives on these dimensions. In this manner, he can be classified by behavior type and placed in the treatment program which is most suited to his particular behavior change needs. As Levinson indicated, the objective is not to determine if a particular treatment modality is a good approach for use with offenders, but "to develop the best treatment programs we can and then ascertain what one helps which type of inmate."

Behavior modification techniques have been, and in many circles still are, popular offender rehabilitative treatment approaches. The second presentation in this section discusses behavior modification in general and also its specific application to offender rehabilitation through the START Program at the Medical Center for Federal Prisoners in Springfield, Missouri. Scheckenbach believes that many adult offenders lack acceptable "social skills and interpersonal relations." He indicates that many of these offenders need "their skills and motivations channeled in a more positive direction." Scheckenbach believes that the development of appropriate social skills and interpersonal relations and the channeling of existing skills and motivation in a more positive direction could be behavior change goals for adult offender treatment programs. These were the goals of the START Program. As Scheckenbach states, "The program's objective was to change those aspects of a man's behavior which are maladapted to living in a prison environment, as well as society." This program was designed for treatment of those inmates who were considered incorrigibles or severe management problems. The desired terminal behaviors, once a man had completed the program, were (1) to maintain appropriate personal hygiene, (2) to increase the frequency of positive social interaction, and (3) to learn productive work habits.

The behavior modification treatment procedure employed in Springfield was a "progressive level system" utilizing increasing behavioral requirements with each succeeding level attainment. Two types of positive behavioral rewards were used as reinforcers to behavior change. The first was a feedback system embodied in a "Good Day Concept." The inmate was rated on 12 behavior categories and if he showed acceptable behavior in these categories for the day, he was awarded a "Good Day." The attainment of a set number of Good Days allowed for movement from a lower level to a higher level that included more privileges. The second reward category was social reinforcement from the staff. The total program was able to demonstrate that behavior modification techniques could be adapted and applied to a treatment program with management problem inmates and be an effective means for positive behavior change and modification.

The third presentation in this section also deals with the treatment of

447

difficult-to-manage adult offenders. In his discussion, Kruschwitz indicates that professional correctional rehabilitators are increasingly adopting the position that criminal behavior is learned and as such can be modified. Thus, the task of corrections is to design more effective behavior change programs. He, too, reports on a program which utilizes treatment techniques derived from learning theory and behavior modification.

This behavior modification program was conducted with inmates in the Control Unit at the Federal Reformatory in El Reno, Oklahoma. The Control Unit housed repeatedly assaultive and disruptive inmates. Its goals were to isolate these inmates from the rest of the population and to provide "programming experiences" geared toward acceptable behavior change that would allow the inmates to return to successful compound living. This program, like that described by Scheckenbach, used the progressive level system. The rewards for successful behavior change consisted of a Good Day system and increased privileges at each successive plateau. A token reinforcement procedure consisting of points being earned was utilized. These points, which could be spent for various privileges, were stamped on cards for performance of the "target behavior." This program had positive results with the other incarcerated individuals. Kruschwitz concludes that the success of the program supports the "proposition that a treatment alternative to dealing with difficult-to-manage offenders is feasible."

Both Scheckenbach and Kruschwitz's program presentations lend support to the concept that behavior modification techniques hold much utility for gaining positive behavior changes in hard to handle prison inmates. As Kruschwitz reveals in his conclusion, however, his program may not necessarily be useful for all disruptive inmates. This statement also can be applied to the program reported by Scheckenbach. We see two programs which have been successful for a particular type of inmate. However, because these programs were not successful with one hundred percent of those inmates involved, it is clear they are not panaceas for the problem of correctional rehabilitation. One can conclude, though, that differential treatment may be of benefit to those inmates who have been categorized into particular groups. To reach those individuals who did not respond to these two particular treatment techniques, a different type of program needs to be developed which is more suitable to their behavior change problems.

Lantz and Ingram continue the study of behavior modification techniques in their paper concerning the treatment of psychopathic behavior. The problem in this area seems to be one of finding a method which will suppress and modify psychopathic behavior. Lantz and Ingram conclude that the "concept of the psychopathic personality can be considered a specific disorder, having certain characteristics common to all cases." However, even though these characteristics are found in common, the treatment of the psychopath is extremely difficult. This type of individual has no motivation for psychotherapy and when he is incarcerated, the problem is compounded because he holds the psychopathic view of the therapist as the enemy. Even with these disadvantages, behavior change through educational and psychological treatment is possible. Many workers are "turning to the use of behavior therapy" as a means of altering "human behavior and emotion in a beneficial manner according to the laws of modern learning theory." In utilizing these behavior modification techniques, the rehabilitator can regard the psychopathic offender as an individual who exhibits antisocial behavior which has been acquired through learning or improper conditioning. By using behavior modification, the therapist can bypass the lengthy, historical psychological data collection used by the more traditional therapies and concentrate on changing the maladaptive behavior of the psychopathic offender.

In the next selection, Kohlenberg describes a case study of the treatment of an adult male homosexual pedophiliac using in vivo desensitization. The subject had been arrested on previous occasions for child molestation and had requested that a therapy program be instituted to help him with his problem. The program used in treating this individual was taken from the Masters and Johnson desensitization model used with adult male-female couples who were experiencing difficulty relating sexually. It was adapted for use with a male homosexual who wished to eliminate his sexual interest in young boys but who did not desire heterosexual relationships. The approach of this program was the same as that of Masters and Johnson in orienting the individual toward increasing approach behavior and reducing the "aversive properties of the sexual interaction." Therefore, it concentrated on increasing the approach behavior toward other adult male homosexuals and reducing the aversive problems of engaging in sexual relations with these adult males. By increasing the attraction to adults, the attraction to children was decreased. An important feature of this program was that a "progression through a sequence of directed interaction" took place and that this sequence was presented in vivo (the client actually engaged in the behavior specified in the sequence). This, of course, demanded a partner who was willing to engage in the desired behavior with the client. This was done in a hierarchial arrangement progressing from very basic observation behavior and eventually culminating in an actual sexual relationship. This case study presents a unique approach to treatment of a unique category of adult offender, and is certainly an outstanding example of what can be done in treating a very difficult problem.

The final selection in this section concerns the treatment of male alcoholic felons who were incarcerated in the Federal Correctional Institution in Lexington, Kentucky. The rehabilitative approach used with this special group of offenders was Rational Behavior Training, developed by Maxie C.

Maultsby, Jr., M. D., at the University of Kentucky. This is a "highly directive method of teaching people how to increase their skill in reasoning so that they will be better able to deal with the problems and stresses of daily living" (Goodman and Maultsby, 1974, p. 8). This approach deals with the individual's perception, thought process, and emotions. An individual first perceives something through one of his five senses. After this perception, he has thoughts about what he has or is perceiving. These thoughts are then channeled through his belief system, which is composed of not only his beliefs but his attitudes, values, and morals. The individual finally chooses an emotion based on his beliefs about the original perception. After the emotion is chosen, the individual exhibits behavior relative to the chosen emotion. It is clear that Rational Behavior Training assumes that an individual's brain controls emotional and physical behavior. The brain is "directed by the individual's thoughts and beliefs about what he sees, hears and physically feels." In this manner, it is the individual who controls both emotional feelings and physical behavior. Once the individual learns this, he must take responsibility for his own actions and develop an independence which has no built-in crutch for placing the blame for his action on others, on situations, or both. The alcoholic offender was taught, through a variety of techniques included in this treatment program, that he was responsible for his excessive drinking behavior as well as his criminal behavior. He could change these behaviors and avoid incarceration again only if he chose to do so. If his choice was to change the behavior, he had to change his thinking to a more rational pattern and subsequently change some of his beliefs. By changing his thinking to a more rational pattern, he first had to perceive things in the real world as they really were and not as he wanted them to be. Then, he had to tell himself the truth about his world and himself. Once he reached this point, he was better able to choose an appropriate emotion and exhibit appropriate behavior. He could learn in this manner to control his excessive drinking and exhibition of criminal behavior.

This section contains descriptions of many varied rehabilitative behavior change approaches for different types of adult offenders. By placing different types of offenders in programs which have proven successful in helping individuals who have similar characteristics and problems, we increase the possibilities of behavior change that is conducive to productive rather than destructive societal living.

REFERENCES

Coleman, L. Prisons: The Crime of Treatment. *Psychiatric Opinion*, 1974, *11*, 5–16.
Goodman, D. and Maultsby, M. *Emotional well-being through rational behavior training.* Springfield, IL: Charles C. Thomas, 1974.

Martinson, R. What Works? Questions and Answers About Prison Reform. *The Public Interest*, 1974, 22–54.

Rundle, F. Prison: The Crime of No Treatment. *Psychiatric Opinion*, 1974, *11*, 17–21.

Wilke, J. and Martinson, R. Is the Treatment of Criminal Offenders Really Necessary? *Federal Probation*, 1976, *40*, 3–9.

27

Differential Treatment: An Adult Typology

Robert B. Levinson, Ph.D.

Reprinted from the proceedings of the 104th Congress of Corrections, American Correctional Association, 1974, Houston, Texas. Author's permission to reprint is gratefully acknowledged.

Let us assume that two individuals rob a bank. The first one has recently lost his job, is heavily in debt, has a seriously sick child, and has just learned that his wife will need an operation. In sheer desperation, he hands a bank teller a note asking for $7500 and is promptly caught while leaving the bank. The second individual is in the bank-robbing business. Since banks are where the money is, he very calculatingly plans and carries out a robbery; eventually, he too, gets caught.

While both individuals have committed the same felonious act, surely there are differences between the persons involved. A continuing research effort has been under way in several parts of the country to deal with the nature of these differences. Methodolgies have been developed to differentiate subgroups among offenders. The adult typology discussed in this paper has evolved from early work with delinquents in this area.

DEVELOPMENTAL BACKGROUND

The pioneering work was done by Hewitt and Jenkins (1945). Warren and her associates, working for a number of years with the California Youth Authority, have developed sub-types of delinquents based upon level of interpersonal maturity (1971). The types which emerged from what has come to be known as the I-level system were based on consistencies noted during extensive clinical interviews.

A different—empirical rather than clinical—tack in dealing with this question was taken by Quay and his associates (1972). Utilizing only those items which significantly differentiated between delinquents and non-delinquents, factor analysis was applied to information derived from past histories, present behavior, and responses to personality questionnaires. These analyses consistently revealed the presence of four underlying dimensions:

452

the first dimension is one of overt hostility, aggression, defiance of authority, alienation from close interpersonal relations with manipulation the goal of such contacts, and other manifestations of an unsocialized, psychopathic behavior syndrome.

the second dimension involves guilt, anxiety, social withdrawal, fearfulness, and conflict together with considerable subjective distress. These characteristics may be coupled with impulsiveness and flight behavior which leads to involvment with the law.

the third dimension involves preoccupation, dreaminess, behavioral ineptness, immaturity, and a tendency to be easily led and victimized by stronger and more forceful individuals.

the fourth dimension involves gang activities, loyalty to delinquent peers, a life style at odds with the law-abiding majority, but without what is generally considered to be personality maladjustment.

This scheme for classifying youthful offenders has been employed by a number of state and local correctional systems and quite extensively in the Federal Prison System (viz. "Differential Treatment: A Way to Begin. . ."). It has led to homogenous grouping of offenders along these personality dimensions. Different treatment modalities are then offered to the various groups, based on a theoretical and empirical analysis of which treatment approach would be more helpful to which type of offender. Thus, the research question is no longer: "Is group therapy effective with offenders?" Rather, it becomes: "For which subgroup of offenders is group therapy helpful?" For those groups which do not benefit from group therapy, other treatment modalities can be tried.

Research and development of Quay's typology for youthful offenders has been on-going for over ten years. Its successful implementation in several federal correctional facilities led to increasing interest in developing a similar conceptual framework for more efficient work with adult offenders. The 2½ year developmental process for Quay's Adult Offender Typology followed the methodology utilized with youthful offenders. In constructing the adult classification instruments, samples were drawn from federal institutions across the country to increase representativeness.

Three measuring instruments are under development: a personality questionnaire consisting of 204 true-false items; a checklist for the analysis of life history records, containing 50 items; and a 63-item correctional adjustment checklist. The questionnaire is filled out by the offender, the life history checklist is completed by the inmate's caseworker—based on available presentence information as well as an interview; and the adjustment checklist is completed by a correctional counselor or officer during the inmate's first two weeks at the institution—based on behavior observed during that time period.

Thus, information is collected from three different sources: what the individual himself is willing to reveal on a questionnaire; what the offender's past history reveals about him; and what type of behavior he currently displays as observed by institutional staff members. Factor analytic techniques applied to this adult data revealed the presence of five dimensions:

the first dimension reflects toughness, defiance, physical and verbal aggression, trouble-making, a history of thrill seeking, victimizing, and quick temperedness. This dimension was labeled Aggressive-Psychopathic.

the second dimension involves worry, tenseness, sadness, help-seeking, fear of other inmates, and emotional liability; it has been labeled Neurotic-Anxious.

a third dimension involved inability to follow directions, daydreaming, sluggishness, preoccupation, passivity, dullness, moodiness, incompetence and social withdrawal; it was labeled Immature-Dependent.

the fourth dimension suggests an individual without a pattern of aggression or inadequate behavior who very likely committed his offense out of some immediate precipitating environmental stress. This dimension was labeled Situational.

the fifth factoral dimension of Manipulativeness reflected such characteristics as trying to con staff, lack of trust, accusing staff of unfairness, and playing off one staff member against another.

INSTITUTIONAL UTILIZATION

Operationally, first, the three classification instruments are completed by the inmate and two different staff members; second, each instrument is scored and the obtained raw scores converted to normalized T scores; the T scores on like-named dimensions are combined; and lastly, the individual is categorized on the basis of his highest combined score. At this point crucial management decisions come into play.

Traditionally, institutions for juvenile delinquents have been organized on a cottage plan while facilities for older offenders have been conglomerate type prisons. The cottage—or small unit—approach permits subdividing large numbers of inmates into smaller, less anonymous groups. The Federal Prison system calls such entities Functional Units; it has embarked on a program of reorganizing its institutions along function unit lines.

A Functional Unit can be conceptualized as one of a number of small, self-contained "institutions" operating within the confines of a larger facility. The concept includes the idea of: (a) a relatively small number of offenders (50–100); (b) who are housed together (generally throughout the length of their institutional stay or as they near completion—12–18 months—of a long term); (c) who work in a close, intensive treatment relationship with a multidisciplinary, relatively permanent assigned team of staff members whose offices are located on the unit; (d) with this unit team having decision-making authority on all within-institution aspects of programming and institutional living arrangements; (e) and with the assignment of an offender to a particular unit being contingent upon his need for the specific type of treatment program offered in that unit (Levinson & Gerard, 1973).

While this type of institutional organization structure may or may not be present in a given facility, the critical management decision mentioned above remains: "What will be the practical consequences of the classification process?"

For far too long the standard operating procedure has been to spend a lot of valuable time and effort administering diagnostic instruments and then assigning a given inmate on a space-available basis. If any classification system is to be more than merely a paper program, then there need to be specific consequences; this means that an individual determined to be a type "A" is in a number of meaningful ways treated differently than an individual classified as a type "B." The cottage or unit system described above can facilitate this happening. It can also occur within the more traditional type institutional structure. However, if differential consequences do not result from the classification system—then there really isn't any such system!

SOME EXAMPLES

Two federal correctional institutions are currently implementing the Quay Adult Typology: one of our most recently acquired institutions in Oxford, Wisconsin, and the federal facility in Seagoville, Texas. The first is a medium security institution for long-term young adult offenders; the second is a minimum security facility for adult offenders. A third institution in Terminal Island, California, has recently expressed an interest in using Dr. Quay's system; this is a medium security institution for adult male and female offenders.

With the increase in the number of youthful and young adult offenders coming into the federal prison system for crimes of violence—they now represent the largest single category of offense in the federal system, almost 25% of the population—a pressing need developed for new type programming. The program for the typical youth or young offender was predicated on an institutional stay of approximately 18 months. We needed a program for this age group in which initial parole eligibility would be almost twice as long. Our experience with this type of individual was that he might go through a regular program fairly well but then would increasingly become involved in disciplinary problems resulting in his transfer to a more secure institution for an older age population. When we acquired the Oxford institution it was decided to develop a program there for this long-term young adult offender; it was further decided to utilize Quay's Adult Typology.

Four units have been established at Oxford. Each of these consists of two buildings housing 56 inmates—one of these having more security features than the other. Inmates start out in an admissions-diagnostic section—where they stay for two weeks—then, based upon their Type classification, they are transferred to one of three units. The fourth unit is a Transactional Analysis therapeutic community, which draws volunteers from the other three programs. Initially, the Quay "typed" inmate is assigned to the more secure of the unit's two buildings. As he shows progress he is moved to the less secure unit building, which is under the jurisdiction of the same staff members. From the less secure building he goes into a pre-release program and then out into the community.

The Oxford program design demonstrates some of the management flexibility which can be achieved with a typological approach. One unit—called MAPS—combines two of the dimensions in the Quay Typology—the manipulative with the aggressive-psychopathic type inmate. Its program was designed for inmates typified by a long, involved history of difficulties with the law; individuals who consciously or unconsciously attempt to manipulate the staff or other inmates to get their own way. They tend to develop shallow peer relationships and require more supervision than other types of inmates. They often have a difficult time following rules; many openly defy staff and other inmates who attempt to interfere with their activities. Typically, these individuals do not respond to direct group or individual counseling; they are quite concerned about maintaining an image of masculinity; and they may form cliques which function at cross-purposes to institutional goals. Unless thwarted, these people are quite pleasant and easy to get along with; however, those in authority positions frequently find them difficult to relate to.

Because of the demonstrated lack of success of "talk" therapies with the manipulative, aggressive-psychopathic type individual, the treatment focus of the MAPS unit is on limit-setting and establishing behavior controls. Staff assigned to this unit are selected for their ability to be consistent and firm in their dealings—the firm but fair staff member who "goes by the book." Conscious effort is required by the staff in this unit to avoid rewarding manipulative behavior; therefore, communication among staff members is open and frequent.

The Evergreen unit at Oxford houses inmates who receive high scores on the Neurotic-Anxious and Immature-Dependent dimensions of the Quay Adult Typology. These individuals generally have difficulty adjusting to an institution because of their anxiety. They easily become upset, depressed, and socially withdrawn. They get little pleasure from life and characteristically appear preoccupied and/or sad. Further, they have difficulty relaxing, have a low self-concept, are easily led, have few (if any) friends and may continually seek protective reassurances from staff regarding real (though frequently exaggerated) threats made against them by more aggressive individuals.

The primary treatment approach for the Evergreen unit is being supportive; the physical separation from offenders in the MAPS unit helps in this regard. Emphasis is on individual and group counseling or psychotherapy. In order to encourage emotional growth and avoid the development of excessive dependency on staff, considerable effort is made to develop self-governing features within this unit. Staff selected can work in close relationships with inmates, are knowledgeable about counseling, and will encourage these offenders to learn to manage their own affairs.

The Situational offender represents the final dimension in the Quay Adult Typology. These individuals are housed in Oxford's TOPS unit where the guiding principle is "do no harm." This type of offender tends to have few treatment needs which can be met in an institutional setting; generally, they recognize their own responsibility for the behavior which led to their incarceration, their legal difficulties are attributable, primarily, to family and/or financial problems. Their background typically shows stability, and some success in living and interacting with the outside world.

Treatment programs for the situational offender are being developed along vocational-industrial training lines. The main emphasis is to further develop and maintain the skills that this type individual brings with him where he is incarcerated. Situational offenders will be given academic, vocational, and general counseling, as needed; the intensive treatment programs of the other units are not seen as appropriate for this group.

The Oxford program has been operating for a relatively short time. As of July 1974, 218 inmates have been received and assigned; the distribution has been: MAPS—39%; Evergreen—31%; and TOPS—19%. The average length of sentence for these units is 10.8 years, 9.4 years, and 9.0 years. It has been of interest to note that the transfers to the TA unit have all come from either MAPS or Evergreen; and, further, that these two units are both showing a significantly greater number of disciplinary reports than is true of the situational offenders. An extensive program evaluation effort is being mounted to assess Oxford's approach as well as that underway at Seagoville.

Since new facilities are not acquired every day, Seagoville may be more representative of institutions which decide to develop an adult typology program. Their program emerged as a two-step sequence: first, decentralization, and second, differential treatment using the Quay Adult Typology.

Seagoville was functioning as a typical conglomerate minimum-security type correctional facility when its staff decided to restructure the institution. The first step was to decentralize its organizational structure. Functional units were established with random assignments to inmates to these units. Staff roles were changed in accordance with that required in a unitized institution. After this had been accomplished and in operation for about a year, and staff felt comfortable under the new organizational structure, they began to ask if more could not be done. They were aware that Quay's Adult Typology was being developed and asked if Seagoville could participate. When the development of the typology classification instruments was far enough along, Seagoville opted to set up part of their program utilizing this approach.

The Seagoville program consists of five units of approximately 90 inmates each. Three of these units have established specific treatment approaches: Transactional Analysis with a focus on intensive group interaction; a Human Resources Development program based on the writings of Robert Carkhuff; and facilitive counseling based on Carl Rogers' philosophy as operationalized by Sherman Day and others. The other two units operate with a more eclectic type treatment philosophy and program.

Inmates enter Seagoville's Admission and Diagnostic program and after two weeks are assigned to one of the other five units. Using the Quay Adult Typology "pure" Types are assigned in the following fashion—a "Pure Type" is an individual whose highest dimension score differs from his next highest score by five or more points. The Manipulative, Aggressive-Psychopathic types are assigned to the TA unit; the Neurotic-Anxious and Immature-Dependent types are assigned to the Facilitative counseling unit; the Situational types and the "indeterminates"—the 30% of the population whose primary and secondary/dimension scores differ by less than five points—are assigned on an odd-number/even-number basis to the two eclectic units. A proportionate number of all the "pure" types is assigned to the Human Development unit.

You will note that a program-evaluation design has been built into the Seagoville institutional plan. This arrangement will enable their staff to better assess which type of program works better with which type of offender. Further, by comparing Seagoville's results with minimum security inmates classified by the Quay Adult Typology with Oxford's results for long-term offenders, additional information with programmatic implications will become apparent. Terminal Island will offer further opportunities to add to the mix of offender types and treatment approaches; moreover, it will also bring in female offenders, for whom Quay is currently developing a set of classification instruments.

These program alternatives will be evaluated on a variety of Institutional

Performance Measures. Attempts will be made to assess intra-psychic changes as well as unit "climate" and other sociometric changes. MMPI, Rotter locus of control, State Trait Anxiety Inventory, Loevinger's Ego-Strength Measure, and Moos' Correctional Institution Environment Scale will be administered.

Conclusion

As stated at the outset, in all of this the intention has not been to determine "is X a good treatment approach for use with offenders?" Rather, it has been to develop the best treatment programs we can, and then ascertain which one helps which type inmate. This effort reflects the statement recently made by the Director of the Bureau of Prisons, Mr. Norman A. Carlson, before the House Committee on the Judiciary; Subcommittee on Courts, Civil Liberties, and the Administration of Justice (1974).

> We candidly admit that we know relatively little about how to assist offenders in changing their life-style so that when released from custody, they can live a law-abiding life in society. It is our hope, however, that through innovation we can significantly improve the effectiveness of the Federal Prison System.

Note

1. The author wishes to express his appreciation for the assistance he received in preparing this paper from Drs. W. Allen Smith and Myron Lazar, Coordinators of Mental Health Programs, respectively, at the Federal Correctional Institutions, Oxford, Wisconsin, and Seagoville, Texas.

References

Carlson, Norman A., "Behavior Modification"; and the Federal Center for Correctional Research, Butner, North Carolina, Statement before the House Committee on the Judiciary; Subcommittee on Courts, Civil Liberties, and the Administration of Justice, 2/27/74.

Differential Treatment: "A Way to Begin . . .", U.S. Bureau of Prisons, Washington, D.C., 1970.

Hewitt, L. E. & Jenkins, R. L., "Fundamental Patterns of Maladjustment; the Dynamics of Their Origin," State of Illinois, 1946.

Levinson, R. B. & Gerard, R. E., "Functional Units: a Different Correctional Approach," Federal Probation, 12/73.

Quay, H. C. & Wheery, J. S., "Psychopathological Disorders of Childhood," Wiley, N.Y., 1972.

Warren, Marguerite Q., "Classification of Offenders as an Aid to Efficient Management and Effective Treatment," *Journal of Criminal Law, Criminology and Police Science*, 62, pp. 239–58, 1971.

28

Behavior Modification and Adult Offenders

Albert F. Scheckenbach, Ph.D.

Reprinted from proceedings of the 104th Congress of Corrections, American Correctional Association, 1974, Houston, Texas. Author's permission to reprint is gratefully acknowledged.

A prolific area of behavioral technology application has been in the educational setting of penal environments. These initial thrusts with behavioral techniques have been extended in ever-increasing number to other areas of corrections ranging from the operation of an institution such as the Kennedy Youth Center in Morgantown, West Virginia, to major rehabilitative programs such as the Draper Project in Alabama. In general, reports have clearly demonstrated the applicability of behavior modification principles and techniques with every population. However, there is little information and only scattered reports on its use with adult offenders.

If behavior modification has been so successfully adapted to youth correctional settings, why then have the techniques and principles not found more acceptability in adult institutions? One possible explanation for this difference may stem from the type of inmate in question. Where a behavioral goal for youth offenders would include a stress on educational achievements, the adult offender is frequently uninterested in vocational and educational training. Age and lack of motivation to learn new skills are factors for this disinterest. The adult offender's interests lie formost in serving his time, exerting a minimum amount of energy, and returning to the streets. But in the course of serving his time, he needs something more than just maintaining a marginal existence. Many adult offenders are deficient in acceptable social skills and interpersonal relations. Some need their skills and motivation channeled in a more positive direction than has been evident from their past behavior which has resulted in incarceration.

The youth offender is frequently described as immature, lacking in methods of handling everyday problems, and impressionable. These same characteristics usually exist in the adult offender, but are camouflaged by "tough guy" images and social sophistication in dealing with others. Probably, the concept of sophistication best describes the difference between these two inmate groups. The adult is usually more mature, has experienced many more behavioral consequences and has learned to maliciously manipulate others. He projects blame for his shortcomings without realizing how vividly he is exhibiting and expressing his inadequacies and lack of self-confidence. He views prison as a power struggle between himself and the staff. This power struggle and sophistication can be best described by quoting briefly the observations and remarks of an inmate who has served almost twenty years in the Federal prison system.

> It would be thought that just anyone, including other people with anti-social behavior, could fulfill the inmate's function. Not so! Training, persistence, and ingenuity are required. Since clear rebellion or justifiable outrage against the institution provides instant and savage punishment—for his own good, the inmate must behave like a difficult person while indicating that it's not really the true him. This gives the impression to the staff that the inmate may be suffering from some mental illness. The administration is reluctant to give him the business, choosing often to place him on a "pay-him-no-mind-list." Once the inmate had managed to get on this list, almost anything short of physical violence is permitted. The whole thing is learning the trick to indict while disarming and thereby escape blame, all neatly in one maneuver. Another acceptable trick is to make caustic comments while acting silly—who can punish an idiot? One can also indict by actions without ever saying a word. When an inmate refuses to do anything whatsoever, work, play, talk, or take part in any of the organized activities, all the while assuming a passive position, the staff suspects that they are being told that they are crucifying the inmate, yet are told in a way that they cannot accept or deny the implied accusation, or blame the inmate—herein lies the true art of an inmate.

This description of the difference between the adult and youth offender is not meant to be all-inclusive but only a gross overview and possible explanation for the lack of studies in behavioral intervention.

Many of the factors which seem to be relevant to an understanding of youth offenders such as socio-economic conditions, cultural factors, educational experiences, and so on are in many respects totally irrelevant with the adult offender. In this respect, the goals or terminal behaviors must be established which are realistic in respect to the individual's eventual return to society. But what goals are relevant? One particular correctional goal which has proven to be somewhat an indicator of future community adjustment is institutional adjustment. Many adult offenders have long histories of not being able to maintain a job for an extended period of time because of absenteeism or poor work habits. Instead of placing major emphasis upon vocation and education, it is often more important to teach the adult offender the value of productive performance in a work situation, steady work attend-

ance, and how to deal with everyday problems. Likewise, social interaction
of a non-manipulative nature is usually lacking for fear of showing one's
weaknesses. No doubt there are many more areas of difference, but the lack
of study utilizing a functional analysis rather than a cognitive or guesswork
approach is needed. Most of us feel that we know the interactions of behavior
and environmental consequences within prisons, but little information in the
form of data has verified our convictions. Until these functional relationships
are demonstrated or better understood in objective definable terms, we will
continue to grope for answers.

A step in this direction would be to examine current programs, procedures, and methods to see what functional relationships exist and then how
we can systematically arrange prison environments to accomplish the institu-
tion-to-community goal. Even though behavior modification in the adult
correctional setting is currently being heavily criticized, the traditional use of
behavior techniques and principles is readily observable in any correctional
system. Most institutions have what has been termed a tier system, level
system, cell block division, and so on. This, in its basic form, is nothing more
than a graduated behavioral step system with corresponding increases in
privileges or tangible rewards in exchange for acceptable behavior. The increased use of half-way houses or Federal Community Treatment Centers is
clearly a systematic use of the behavioral technique called fading. The goal
behavior here is adjustment in the community through a gradual transition
from a prison to supervised living on the outside to total release. The earning
of statutory and extra good time and monetary rewards for performance in a
work area are also behavioral consequences used to reinforce current behavior and motivate the inmate to continue his present level of performance.
Inmate and staff peer pressure has its own set of techniques to shape, reinforce and punish behaviors.

The remainder of the paper will pay specific attention to one particular
adult program which was established at the Medical Center for Federal
Prisoners in Springfield, Missouri, in September, 1972, and terminated on
March 1, 1974. The program was named START, which stands for Special
Treatment and Rehabilitative Training.

The START program was designed as an initial step in providing training
and treatment for that segment of the prison population which is considered
incorrigible. The program's objective was to change those aspects of a man's
behavior which are maladapted to living in a prison environment, as well as
society. These maladaptive behaviors include aggressive, assaultive acts; disruptive influences to rehabilitative or treatment programs; excessive use of
verbally abusive language; inciting riotous conditions; agitation of others,
including staff; manipulative responses for self-gain only, and general disre-

gard for orders, rules, procedures, requests and/or suggestions. However, this does not mean that these individuals do not demonstrate some adaptive behaviors. It simply indicates that their maladaptive behaviors far exceed their appropriate responses. The task which was presented to the START staff was to develop a program to establish and/or increase what the institution and society deems as adaptive, appropriate behavior. Two basic questions were asked: (1) How to more effectively change behavior in a control unit environment, and (2) How to better generate high levels of adaptive performance.

The primary goal of START was to provide for the care, control, and correction of the long-term adult offender in a setting separated from the total institution, and to enable these offenders to be reintegrated into a general prison population and function at an optimal level of performance and achievement. It was designed to provide an alternative to long-term segregation, increase the level of adaptive participation, and influence in a positive manner the development of interpersonal relations. The desired terminal behaviors were:

1. Maintain an appropriate level of personal hygiene
2. Increased frequency of engaging in positive social interactions
3. Learn productive work habits

The selection procedure for START candidates entailed an examination of the inmate's prior history and level of institutional adjustment. All admissions to the program were selected from penitentiary type institutions with several being state prisoners housed within the federal system. They were heterogenous in respect to race, creed, age, type and number of offenses, area of residency, etc. Specifically, the inmates admitted into the START program had: an average of 5 intra-institutional transfers because of disciplinary problems; received an average of 21 disciplinary reports of which an average of 12 were for major incidents including: arson, assault, possession of a weapon, violence, etc.; spent an average of 49% of their institutional time in segregation status where they continued to be destructive of property, assaultive towards other inmates, and verbally and physically abusive towards staff, including throwing food, urine, and feces at them. While incarcerated, eleven additional sentences were given for offenses committed while in prison: Possession and Use of a Weapon (1), Assault (4), Murder (5), Escape and Kidnapping (1).

Clinically, each admission had demonstrated a long history of opposition to authority figures and lack of impulsive controls. In conjunction with these adversities, each had experienced environmental consequences which were primarily negative in nature. In order to cope with this type of environmental stress and consequence each man had developed an elaborate system of compensation by learning to manipulate his environment, but in ways unacceptable to normal standards of behavior adaptable to prison as well as in the community. He had learned to make life "miserable" for those who were forced to care and deal with him in everyday custodial situations. He sought immediate gratification of his wants, desires, and needs without regard for others around him. His repertoire of responses were manipulative in nature and often self-destructive.

Other means of dealing with these individuals had been fruitless because the problem had been attacked from the position of attempting to rationalize their behavior and verbally set up situations which were thought to be beneficial. However, this did nothing more than "feed" their continuing system of rationalizing and intellectualizing their behaviors and thus it reinforced an overcompensating defense mechanism. It was the usual course of events that they would promise or say one thing and react or respond in an entirely different manner. Talk and verbal therapy with this group is foolish and highly ineffective. In some respects talk therapy is nothing more than "playing in the man's own ball park" and not really influencing behavioral change for more than a short period of time. Thus, any form of treatment, therapy, training, or corrections had to deal directly with his overt or observable behaviors and not concentrate exclusively upon his verbal responses. In addition, several basic assumptions have been demonstrated to be credible in other areas of human behavior (Ullmann and Krasner, 1965) and should thus be applicable in a penal environment.

1. Deviant behavior is learned and can be altered. The development and maintenance of maladaptive behavior is no different from the development and maintenance of any other behavior.

2. Desirable behavior change can occur within an institution. This change occurs primarily in terms of interactions with other individuals, especially with correctional workers in realistic, action situations within the institutional environment.

3. Offenders are not mentally ill or psychotic. Their actions are not a result of a dysfunction of the psyche, but rather from a failure to learn adaptive responses, i.e., internalize the values, norms, and controls of the majority of American society.

With these assumptions accepted as feasible, a programmatic format was developed employing behavioral analysis leading to intervention and behavioral change. The treatment procedure was a progressive level system. It consisted of a number of levels requiring increasing acceptance of personal behavioral responsibilities in exchange for increasing privileges. Inmates began at the lowest level and progressed through successive levels as their behavior improved and demonstrated consistency. Each level had an increased behavioral requirement with the upper levels, including a consistency criterion for promotion. If the inmate failed to meet the behavioral criteria at any of the levels, he remained there until he had satisfactorily met the behavioral condition. Flagrant violation of operationally defined rules and procedures resulted in demotion to a lower level. When a participant reached the highest level, he had demonstrated consistent ability to maintain adaptive behavior which then permitted him to return to a regular institution.

The START program format went through a variety of modifications and changes in an effort to design an effective program. The graduated level system existed at the inception of the program with eventual changes resulting in a design of a one-week orientation period followed by eight levels. The number of levels was determined from personal experience in working with this type of population. A participant could successfully complete the program requirements in 8 to 9 months which I previously found to be the optimal period for demonstration of behavior change and continuation of this change.

The length of time in each level and between levels was governed by a "Good Day" concept. This concept involved a daily measure of behavior in twelve areas of adaptive behavior ranging from personal hygiene and personal conduct to work and recreational behaviors. Each individual was rated daily by the unit's staff on all twelve measures by simply indicating acceptable or unacceptable performance. Also on a graduated basis were the quantity and quality of tangible reinforcers exchanged for acceptable behavior.

During the orientation period of one week the new admission was allowed only basic personal articles, little time out of his cell, and limited exercise in accord with the Federal Bureau of Prison Policy on inmate discipline. These conditions differed very little from the lock-up condition from which the individual had been transferred. Following the Orientation period and the inmate's expressed desire to participate in the program a wide range of rewards were immediately available in the areas of personal property, increased time out of the cell, earning of extra Good Time and money, and opportunities for self-improvement courses. Participation and progress through the levels provided the opportunity for access to more tangible rewards, including restoration of all forfeited Good Time. An expressed desire not to participate meant remaining at the Orientation level in a nonparticipation status.

Within the START program two types of positive behavioral consequences or rewards were used. The first was the behavioral feedback system embodied in the Good Day concept. It provided daily communication to the inmate as to his progress in the program and the length of time required to meet predetermined goals. The second type of consequence or reward was social reinforcement. Tangible reinforcers and motivators were evident throughout the program, but it was the effects of social reinforcement that was the goal of achievement for the staff. Since the staff was considered little more than "pigs," it was necessary to establish the reinforcing value of social interaction with the staff, as this would be the major means of reinforcement in maintaining any behavior change in the other institutions. However, to attain this goal the inmates' behavior had to be weaned from doing something right only because of receiving a tangible reinforcer. It was necessary to establish social contact with staff as a potential reinforcer and modifier of behavior, just as the tangible rewards were. In behavioral terms, behaviors being strengthened by tangible rewards needed to come under the environmental control of social interaction with staff. To accomplish this goal the staff constantly strived to be models of acceptable behavior by always being reasonable in talking with inmates even in the face of extremely abusive language and constant threats of bodily harm to the staff member himself and frequently to his family. The staff used the technique of extinction or ignoring inappropriate verbal behavior to reduce the frequency of these remarks. Gradually, over a period of months each program participant came under the influence of social reinforcement. Likewise the power of social reinforcement gradually replaced the tangible reinforcers in daily importance. Where staff was constantly initiating conversation, the participants eventually initiated conversation with the natural course of any discussion between individuals evolving. Many lively discussions were evident with tempers flaring but respect on both sides for opinions without physical threats observed. This is the same condition that can be found in a regular institution, but prior to their admission the participants' frequency of this type of behavior was extremely low. The staff did not want to create mild, passive inmates, but to only channel the inmates' energies in an acceptable direction which can be found in an situation where people come together.

The goal of the START program of the internalizing of self-control and performing in an adaptive manner was observed in many participants but not everyone. Getting along with others in a work area, living area, and recreational area without the need for threats or aggressive actions was the ultimate objective. Through contingent use of tangible and social reinforcement, some success was observed. The best example was seen in the influence of peer pressure. Upon admission each inmate conformed to the group, right or wrong, without judging the situation for himself. Peer pressure controlled the unit, but slowly each participant eventually became more interested in his personal well-being. For those who completed the program and some who did not, the "we-ness" of the inmate group had been shattered with each man being more concerned with himself than others. It was a curious transition in that most reached the stage of "I am more important than the group" long before they let the group observe the behavior. The artificial fronts were quite noticeable. To demonstrate this collapse of the strong group feeling, mention of the hostage incident is important. Several months prior to the close of the program, an inmate took an officer hostage and held a piece of glass to his neck. Eight other inmates were recreating in the same area with two other staff present. Not one inmate joined the attacker, and in fact offered assistance to the staff in preventing harm from coming to the officer. It is hypothesized that one year earlier the incident would have resulted in serious injury and possibly even death. Thus much of the progress participants made and their corresponding growth in personal values was evident. In general, tangible and social reinforcers were needed to accomplish the goals of the program. Each was used to shape or develop the existing behaviors of the inmates in the appropriate direction. Each was used independently, but interrelated as to the final goal of the project.

There were 19 potential participant admissions to the START program. Ten of these admissions successfully completed the requirements of the program. Of the remaining nine admissions, three failed to complete the requirements and were returned to their sending institutions after one year of disruptive, non-participating behavior; three were in a non-participation status at the close of the program, two were removed for administrative reasons, and one was removed with federal charges pending as the result of the hostage incident.

A 50% success rate with a population of this nature has to be considered exceptional in the respect that almost every other traditional correctional technique had completely failed. However, the measure of success in addition to program completion was adjustment upon release from the program. Follow-up information as of August, 1974, indicated that six of the ten who successfully completed the program also adjusted acceptably to their new environments. Of this total success group, three were released from prison as a result of meeting their maximum release date under federal statutes and have made an acceptable adjustment to the outside community. The other three total success cases are functioning at an above-average level in regular institutions with one residing in a state institution following parole to a state detainer. The remaining four, who successfully completed the program, are all in a control unit status at this time, but two were able to function adequately for six months before reverting to earlier patterns. The original criterion of acceptable adjustment for three months following completion of the program was initially established as reasonable by the START Unit staff because of the large number of uncontrollable variables operating within an institution. Using the staff criterion the total success rate was 80% for those who completed the program.

Follow-up information on the 9 admissions who did not complete the program has only one individual outside a segregation status at this time. Of the remaining eight, one has been indicted for killing another inmate, one has stabbed another inmate, and the other six have continued their aggressive pattern of behavior in various federal institutions' segregation units. Only the one mentioned above has successfully met the three-month criterion following release from the program.

As previously indicated, each participant had a history of projecting blame for his shortcomings, disrupting standard institutional procedures, and finding his reinforcers in negative action. These factors also accounted for the program not having more success. There were existing reinforcers outside the program much stronger than any which could have been offered by the staff. One such reinforcer was federal court action. Each admission was well-versed prior to admission in legal action and steps to take in response to program and procedural requirements they did not like or want to do. Again they were able to find relief by projecting blame to others. At the same time solicited assistance was provided by the National Prison Project branch of the American Civil Liberties Union. Instead of encouraging more constructive behavior, they reportedly encouraged non-participation and alleged that any form of participation was brainwashing. With the promises of legal relief and back-door tactics the ACLU possessed a reinforcer for non-participation much greater than programmed reinforcers for participation. Nevertheless, the majority of the admissions did show behavior improvements, even with minimal participation.

The primary legal issue was involuntary admission to the program. The basic argument for involuntariness arises from the original idea of such a program as START.

> A voluntary program could be expected to be used by those prisoners who find themselves distressed by their situation, not by those who are causing extreme distress to others but are little inconvenienced themselves. To make the program so replete with privileges and so devoid of responsibility that all prisoners would volunteer, would invite the occurrence of persons seeking out imprisonment or disturbance in prisons, as a method of obtaining the substantial satisfactions without effort, as has happened with mental hospital patients. (Dr. Nathan Azrin, expert witness to the court, comments to the question of designing a voluntary program with START's goals that would reach the population that START attempted to reach.)

Nevertheless, a recent court order bans all future involuntary behavior modification programs under the issue of conditions of confinement without due process.

A second reinforcer for non-participating which eventually turned into a potential punisher for participation was publicity in the news media. Many exaggerated and false reports were aired and published about the START program. The use of psychosurgery, drug abuse, brainwashing techniques, and total disregard for the individual's rights eventually seemed to become synonymous with START. These were totally false, but for the participants it meant serious repercussion to their former "tough guy" images upon returning to a regular institution if they participated in the program. In fact there is a direct correlation between the hostage incident and slanderous news reporting.

Even though the START program had more than its share of difficulties, some promising results were indicated. The application of a structured system of graduated behavioral levels with corresponding tangible reinforcers was effective in modifying aggressive, maladaptive behaviors. The dependency on tangible reinforcers had to be shifted to more naturally occurring consequences as in social reinforcement to provide assurance of maintaining the behavior change in another environment. It also became evident that these adult offenders were not interested in academic achievement. Only three pursued educational goals, with two eventually earning their GED diplomas. However, most admissions were constant readers with material ranging from underground news journals and socialistic literature to cultural and positive attitude books. Each lacked positive social interaction skills and the constant reference to their reading material often strained discussions. Nevertheless, it did provide an arena for social reinforcement and the teaching of appropriate interpersonal relations skills. The most noteworthy result of the START program was the procedural interlace of tangible and social reinforcers within a behavioral feedback system.

Behavior modification principles and techniques with adult offenders has not received as much attention as with other groups. The START program did demonstrate the effectiveness of behavior modification with sophisticated, management problem individuals. However, influences outside the program prevented an examination of many variables which with further study could prove to be valuable techniques in meeting the goals and objectives of corrections.

I would like to conclude by stating another principle of behavior modification. Negative reinforcement is an event the occurrence of which decreases the probability that the behavior will occur again. Perhaps the application of behavior modification techniques with the adult offender offers promise in program design, but where will all the professional men be after receiving so much negative reinforcement and unjustified criticism for their efforts?

REFERENCE

Ullmann, L. P. & Krasner, L., *Case Studies in Behavior Modification*, "Introduction." Holt, Rinehart, and Winston, Inc., 1965.

29

Investigation of the Effectiveness of a Voluntary Token Reinforcement Procedure in Changing Behavior of Difficult-to-Manage Inmates[1]

Stanley V. Kruschwitz, Ph.D.

Reprinted from proceedings of the 104th Congress of Corrections, American Correctional Association, 1974, Houston, Texas. Author's permission to reprint is gratefully acknowledged.

The broad issues surrounding mandatory treatment programs in correctional institutions have recently been debated and redebated vociferously in the popular press, professional circles, and Congress. Whereas it is not possible to discuss these issues at length, the basic conflicts will be mentioned in order to provide a background for the present study.

One side of the conflict arises from what correctional administrators perceive as the very real need to deal with the behavior of inmates who are "a thorn" in their side. These individuals typically are those who are repeatedly involved in (or suspected of being involved in): assaults on staff or other inmates; pressuring other inmates for sex, commissary, etc.; planning and/or participating in disruptions in the institution; and escapes or attempted escapes. While inmates behaving in those kinds of ways may not pose as great an actual threat to an institution as imagined, action of some sort is deemed necessary by most administrators. Two common alternatives are to assign those inmates to long-term segregation status or to move them in and out of segregation status as each disruptive act occurs. Neither alternative typically results in substantial long-term behavior change. Another alternative has been the establishment of treatment programs designed to effect significant behavior change in difficult-to-manage individuals in units segregated from the general population.[2]

It is particularly on this latter alternative that the major conflict arises from critics of treatment programs in prisons.[3] Their concern has been focused in several areas: (1) There is concern that some individuals are assigned to these kinds of programs because they are politically active and are interested in changes in correctional systems. Mandatory treatment programs in segregation could become a convenient way of "disposing of" such individuals. (2) It is felt that the rights of inmates are not upheld when they are mandatorily assigned to treatment programs with no opportunity to choose what their "treatment" will be. (3) There is special reaction to the use of treatment techniques broadly categorized as "behavior modification." This term is often associated with the use of drugs, aversive therapy, psychosurgery, and stimulus deprivation, as well as positive reinforcement.

This conflict between the "treaters" and the "treated" brings into focus the difficulty of agreeing on the fundamental goal of corrections in our society. Briefly, the "liberals" seem to be saying that prisons and their programs are not necessary—the problems of crime stem from a corrupt and unjust society, most people commit crimes and do not get caught, and our efforts should be directed toward correction of that society. The "conservatives" take the stance that punishment for criminal behavior is good and necessary. The only trouble is that we should catch more criminals and punish them severely. Those taking the "rehabilitative" stance suggest that criminal behavior was learned, it can be modified, and the task in corrections is to design increasingly more effective treatment programs to change behavior.

Professional correctional workers increasingly are favoring the latter approach and, consequently, the treatment programs dealing with difficult-to-manage offenders have arisen. Programs using techniques derived from learning theory and behavior modification have been attractive to correctional workers, since results have been particularly promising. One of the dilemmas of the correctional worker, then, is that even though individuals have been sentenced to prison ostensibly to effect behavior change (this point is debatable), as effective techniques are developed, there are pressures not to make treatment too effective or mandatory.

Using a "rehabilitative" approach with difficult-to-manage offenders suggests that program experience can be provided in an attempt to shape behaviors that will increase the probabilities of successful living on an institution compound. The underlying assumption of a learning theory approach is that inappropriate behaviors are learned and that new, more acceptable, behaviors can be learned to replace them through programming.[4] Several projects indicate the potential efficacy of such an approach.

A research project conducted at the National Training School involved the use of an innovative, "fast-moving" program with "psychopathic" youthful offenders.[5] One of the components of their program was the use of a point system whereby students could earn money for positive behavior and for winning in organized game competition. The investigators found that youths in this program performed significantly better than a control group in various behavioral categories. One of their conclusions was that "action-oriented" programs where the consequences of behavior were immediately felt were more effective than were traditional verbal approaches.

Stayer and Jones reported the use of a token reinforcement program for soldiers who were labeled conduct disorders. Soldiers earned points for participation in various scheduled activities and work performance.[6] Follow-up assessment revealed a higher percentage of treated soldiers having completed a tour of duty or serving in good standing than a nontreated comparison group. Also, a token program with delinquent soldiers showed that token reinforcement increased attendance at meetings, verbal behavior, and discussions of personal as opposed to impersonal problems.[7]

This study was a research component of a treatment program implemented for difficult-to-manage inmates in a maximum security unit at a federal reformatory. The major objective of the study was to investigate the effectiveness of a token reinforcement procedure in increasing a variety of inmate behaviors in the unit. A preliminary follow-up of program "graduates" was made to determine whether inmates completing the program were successful on the compound. There was an attempt to address some of the aforementioned issues in the development of the program. Particular emphasis was placed on establishing a program which afforded as much freedom of choice regarding participation in treatment as possible. Whenever possible, activities were made available in such a way that inmates decided whether or not to participate. This feature of the program is considered somewhat unique in dealing with this population, is important in ethically and legally dealing with the issues of treatment, and provides some guidance for future developers of programming in this area.

METHOD

SUBJECTS, SETTING, AND BACKGROUND

This study was conducted in the Control Unit at the Federal Reformatory, El Reno, Oklahoma. The reformatory is a medium security facility housing approximately 1000 federal offenders ranging from 18 to 28 years of age. The Control Unit was located in one section of the maximum security cellhouse of the institution. The unit was established to achieve two goals with repeatedly assaultive, disruptive inmates in the reformatory: (1) to remove them from the compound for an extended period of time and, (2) to provide programming experiences in an attempt to change behavior sufficiently to allow return to successful compound living. The number of inmates in the Control Unit ranged from 17 to 28 and varying numbers of inmates were involved in the study in the different phases.

The first inmate was assigned to the Control Unit approximately four months before the initiation of this project. Approximately two months later, there was a take-over of the unit by inmates in which three hostages were taken for a brief period of time. There was a near complete turnover in staff subsequent to the incident, a reanalysis of the program was conducted, and planning for the implementation of the present program was revitalized. At the time of the incident, the progression system was partially in effect—the token reinforcement system was not.

PROGRESSION SYSTEM

The basic program consisted of a progression system. Inmates were assigned to the unit by the Warden's Advisory Committee on Treatment upon recommendation from their parent treatment team. The program consisted of four levels, Level I being the highest. Once assigned to the unit, the inmate entered Level IV, the program was explained to him, and he was promoted to Level III upon acceptance of the program. As individuals progressed through the levels, additional privileges were made available, e.g., more out-of-cell time, eligibility for radios, access to a TV, etc. A Good Day system determined when an individual was promoted from one level to the next.[8] Individuals earned Good Days by achieving daily acceptable ratings in six citizenship behavior areas (room and personal appearance, responsible behavior, cooperation, positive communication, and non-industrial work) and four formal program areas (education, counseling, industry, recreation). Movement from Level III to Level II, and from Level II to Level I, each required 45 Good Days. Once reaching Level I, short-term individualized goals were established for movement back to the compound. If an inmate earned all Good Days, movement through the complete program could be accomplished in three to four months.

PROCEDURE

EXCHANGE SYSTEM AND EXPERIMENTAL DESIGN

In an effort to supplement the progression system, a token reinforcement procedure (the exchange system) was initiated. This consisted of points stamped on cards for performance of the target behaviors. These points were punched out and spent for various privileges, e.g., additional out-of-cell time, rental of radios and guitars, etc. The exchange system served as the primary independent variable for the investigation.

Three dependent variables were studied: hygiene behaviors, educational accomplishments, and social interaction in group counseling. The intervention was applied to the three behaviors using a multiple baseline design, since a reversal of the behaviors was not desirable.[9] There was a three week baseline period in which data in each of the three areas were collected before the exchange system was initiated. At the end of this period, the exchange system was applied to hygiene for two weeks, to hygiene and education for two weeks, and to all three behavior areas for the final two weeks.

After the three week baseline period, input was solicited from inmates regarding the feasibility of an exchange system. In addition to contact on the galleries, the counseling groups were used as a forum for this discussion. Since the behaviors being emphasized in the exchange system were also part of the Good Day system, inmates were asked whether or not they would like to personally keep track of their progress (which the card would provide). At the same time, they were asked about the desirability of additional privileges and what privileges they would like. Through this process, inmate cooperation and support was procured for the exchange system, while potentially reinforcing items were identified. The exchange system was voluntary. Non-participation did not affect movement through the levels.

HYGIENE

The first target involved room and personal hygiene behaviors. These were considered basic citizenship behaviors, important to line staff, and improvement in them would provide good feedback for staff. Each morning, correctional officers conducted an inspection of each inmate's room and personal appearance. Seven inspection items were specified and communicated to inmates. Verbal feedback was given on their performance at all times and the points were dispensed by the officer for acceptable ratings after the third week. The dependent variable was the number of inspection items rated acceptable. Five inter-observer reliability checks averaged 98% agreement.

EDUCATION

The second target behavior involved performance in an individualized mathematics program. Since education levels were quite low for Control Unit inmates, developing study work skills and encouraging achievement in an academic area was considered a worthwhile program goal. A representative from the Education Department solicited volunteers for this program. Eight individuals were involved in the program throughout the study and are included in the results.

Material in three books (*Basic Essentials of Mathematics*, Parts I and II by James T. Shea, and *GED Preparation Course*) were divided into daily units. A placement test was given to determine the level of ability and a flow chart was developed to guide progression through the books. Daily contact was made with each participant to determine the number of units completed and to render assistance. One day each week was spent on testing individuals over the material they had covered. Beginning the sixth week, points were given for units completed and tests passed, with a considerably higher number of points given for passing tests. The number of units completed and tests passed were the dependent variables. Three inter-observer reliability checks averaged 96% agreement.

The unit counselor solicited volunteers for group counseling. Two groups of six each met for an hour two times a week with the counselor and another staff member. It was hypothesized that a major determinant of assignment to the Control Unit program, in many cases, was a deficit of skills in interpersonal relationships. One of the major goals of the meetings was to increase the degree of positive interaction with inmate and staff group members. Positive interaction was defined as the frequency of positively valenced statements to inmates and staff. Total interaction and negative interaction were also recorded. During the eighth and ninth weeks, points were given only for positive interaction. The group was behaviorally structured in that emphasis was placed on behavior in the unit and on the compound, and on determining the relationships between behaviors and consequences. The counselor's ratings of positive interaction with inmates and staff were the dependent variables. The other staff person present also made an independent rating of the variables. Since there were four possible ratings of positive and negative interaction (0 = none, 1 = 1 to 3 statements, 2 = 4 to 8 statements, and 3 = 9 or more statements) the following formula was devised to test for reliability:

$$1 - \left(\frac{\text{absolute value of difference between ratings (rating 1 } - \text{ rating 2)}}{\text{TOTAL POSSIBLE DISTANCE BETWEEN RATINGS (3)}} \right)$$

Reliability averaged 80%.

Results and Discussion

HYGIENE

Figure 29.1 shows the group multiple baseline data. The group data for hygiene behaviors showed an increase during baseline. This increase may have been due to the verbal feedback by officers initiated at the beginning of baseline. There was also an increase over baseline during intervention from a median of 6.3 to 6.9. It can be speculated that the hygiene behaviors would have increased without the intervention, however, it is unlikely they would have remained as consistently high without it.

Individual analysis of the hygiene data showed that with three individuals there was a large increase in the number of acceptable hygiene behaviors between the baseline and intervention phases. For three other individuals, the progression system appeared to influence their hygiene behaviors. They

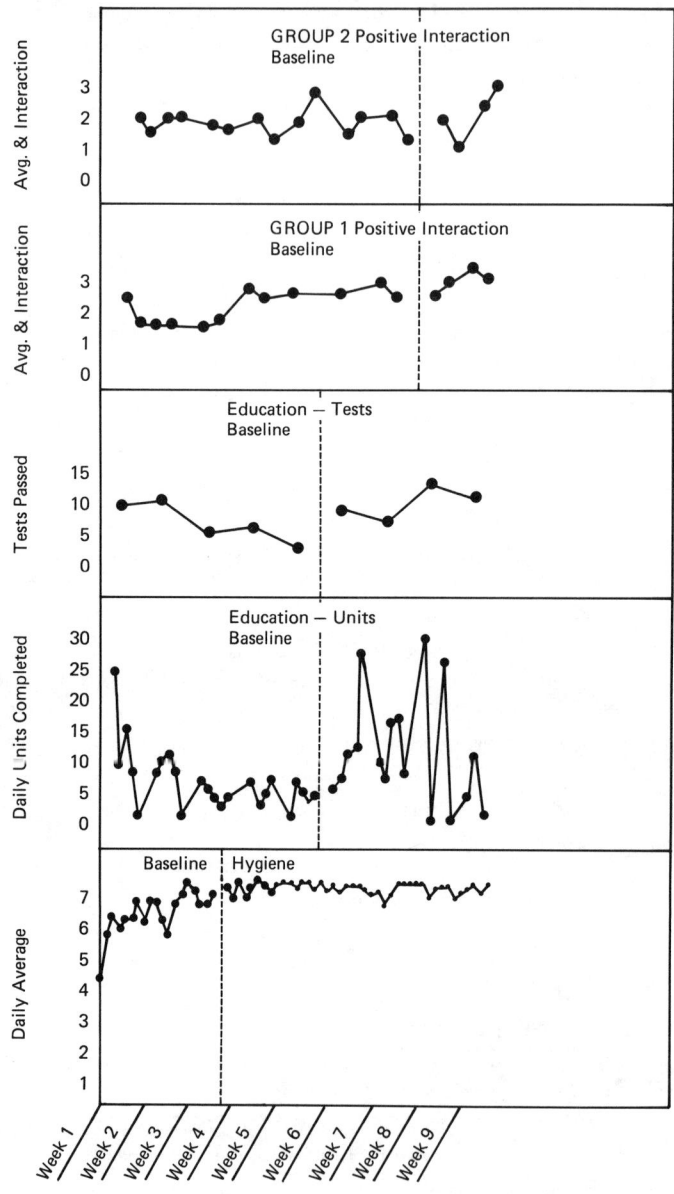

FIGURE 29.1.
EXCHANGE SYSTEM MULTIPLE BASELINE DATA

increased dramatically subsequent to promotion from Level III to Level II. In five instances, hygiene increased to near perfect during the baseline period, probably due to the feedback of daily inspections and the Good Day system. With four individuals, hygiene remained near perfect for both the baseline and intervention phases. During the data collection period, then, 11 individuals showed increases in acceptable hygiene behaviors and 4 remained near perfect for both the baseline and intervention phases. In three cases, hygiene behaviors remained low during both the baseline and intervention phases. This may have been due to ineffective reinforcers. In one case, hygiene behaviors were increased to perfect by requiring Good Days in that area to earn promotion from Level I to the general population.

EDUCATION

Units completed and tests passed showed a marked decrease during the baseline period. One explanation is that academic work was relatively difficult for this population, very few tangible rewards were forthcoming, and the novelty wore off. Daily math units showed an increase from a baseline median of 4.0 units per day to a median of 9.5 during the reinforcement phase (Figure 1). In four individual cases, the reinforcement phase increased the number of daily units completed by as much as 300%. There were less dramatic, but still evident, changes between baseline and reinforcement phases in two cases. In one instance, daily units completed remained at the same level during both phases. One important result of the reinforcement phase is that it apparently encouraged at least two individuals who had dropped out of the program to restart. One individual, however, did not restart after he failed a test near the end of the baseline period. It is interesting to note that during the reinforcement phase there was a large amount of variability in daily unit output. It appears that some individuals completed a large number of units one day and rested the next day. Also, few units were completed on test days since they were not expected on those days and time was normally used in studying for the tests. The number of daily units might have stabilized if points had been contingent upon a minimum number of units completed per day.

Data on the total number of unit tests passed (80% or more correct) are shown in Figure 29.1. During the reinforcement phase, four individuals increased the number of tests passed by as much as 700%. Less dramatic increases were shown by three others (200% increase), and one person maintained a high level of tests passed throughout both baseline and intervention phases. One person dropped the program near the end of the baseline condition and did not resume participation during the reinforcement phase. The results suggest that the intervention phase was instrumental in increasing the total number of tests passed per week.

GROUPS

Data for the group counseling phase of the project are shown at the top of Figure 29.1. Both groups show an increase in positive interaction during the reinforcement phase. Group 1 began increasing in positive interaction before the end of the baseline period. There may have been a generalization effect on Group 1 from the intervention on the hygiene behaviors. No other generalization effects appeared, suggesting the target behaviors were uncorrelated. For Group 1, positive interaction (reinforced) increased for both areas (interaction with staff and interaction with inmates) while negative interaction dropped considerably during the reinforcement phase. Low negative interaction was not reinforced, which indicates that the differential reinforcement of the incompatible behaviors (positive interaction vs. negative interaction) was effective in causing a change in both behaviors. Group 2 showed similar results near the end of the intervention phase. In Group 1, all three members increased their positive interaction and decreased negative interaction. In Group 2, three of the five members showed distinct improvement during the latter part of the intervention phase. One member maintained approximately the same interaction levels during both the baseline and intervention phases. One other member showed a decrease in positive interaction during the intervention phase. It should also be noted that, while total interaction was not reinforced, it increased during the intervention phase. Ideally, the reinforcement phase should have been extended to better determine experimental effects.

MOVEMENT TO COMPOUND

Due to the short time the Control Unit had been in operation, it was impossible to ascertain significant long-range effects. However, short-term results were encouraging: five inmates were transferred for disciplinary reasons prior to the implementation of this program, one individual was transferred for non-disciplinary reasons after completing the program, and eight individuals have completed the program and have returned to a unit on the compound. None have returned to the Control Unit, although one individual has received a minor disciplinary report and another has received three major disciplinary reports (the latter involved drugs, whereas his assignment to the Control Unit was for escape).

Subjective reports from inmates and staff on the compound indicate that it is a safer place to live now and that "graduates" typically are doing very well in their assigned duties. Further, more extensive follow-up is recommended.

CONCLUSIONS

This study lends support to the proposition that a "treatment" alternative to dealing with difficult-to-manage offenders is feasible. It must be emphasized that inmates exert considerable counter-controls over their keepers (indeed, the hostage incident was one form) and considerable effort was exerted to design the program in a manner to maximize individual choice regarding program participation. It was discovered that with it operated in this manner, inmates became experts in the mechanics of the program, were quick to point out staff mistakes in implementation, and continued to make constructive recommendations for improvement. It is possible that this element of choice was the single most important determinant of program success. While many of the issues mentioned earlier were not completely resolved in this program, it represents a beginning of their resolution.

Some inmates responded more dramatically to the intervention than others. The selection of reinforcers favored some individuals over others. Additional effort is being made to individualize reinforcers. Even so, it is doubtful that all individuals will respond to this kind of program. It is interesting to note that the initiation of the exchange system appeared to stimulate stronger interaction between staff and inmates. The exchange of points provided many occasions for communication to occur. The resulting intensive inmate-staff interactions were extremely important assets of the treatment program.

The results indicated that the progression system and the exchange system were complimentary. That is, the progression system seemed to be more influential with some inmates and the exchange system with others. This coincides with results obtained in other programs using these systems, e.g., the Kennedy Youth Center in West Virginia. It is noteworthy that the exchange system applied to one class of behaviors typically did not increase the other classes of behaviors. Whereas this provides assurance that the behaviors were uncorrelated, it also suggests that in order to effect an increase in a class of behaviors, reinforcing consequences may need to be directed specifically to that class.

Finally, the multiple baseline design seems particularly well-suited for the "real world" applied research situations found in corrections. This study was not viewed as a research project as much as a natural sequence in developing a treatment program. Rather than initiate the program at one time, the program component was applied slowly to one class of behaviors at a time. This allowed the system to be reviewed and modified, and provided staff and inmates time to become adjusted to the "new way of doing things."

NOTES

1. The author is indebted to Mr. Lynn Garst for aiding in the design and implementation of the project. Without his efforts, it would not have happened. Also, the efforts and cooperation of the Control Unit staff, Mr. E. O. Toft, Warden, and Mr. Eldon Jensen, Associate Warden (Programs) are greatly appreciated.
2. Programs at the Kennedy Youth Center and Marion, and the START Program in

Springfield, Missouri, have appeared in the Federal Bureau of Prisons. Various programs have also appeared in state systems, e.g., Maryland, Illinois, and California.

3. Mitford, Jessica, *Kind and Unusual Punishment*, Alfred A. Knopf, N.Y., 1973. Wicker, Tom, "A Bad Idea Persists," *The New York Times*, Friday, February 8, 1974.

4. Bandura, Albert, *Principles of Behavior Modification*, Holt, Rinehart, and Winston, N.Y., 1969.

5. Ingram, G. L., Gerard, R. E., Quay, H. C., and Levinson, R. B., "An experimental program for psychopathic delinquents: looking in the 'correctional wastebasket.'" *Journal of Research in Crime and Delinquency*, January, 1970 (pp. 24–30).

6. Boren, J. J., and Colman, A. D., "Some experiments on reinforcement principles within a psychiatric ward for delinquent soldiers." *Journal of Applied Behavior Analysis*, 3, 1970 (pp. 29–37).

7. Stayer, S. J., and Jones, F. Ward 108: *Behavior modification and the delinquent soldier*. Unpublished paper presented at Behavioral Engineering Conference, Walter Reed General Hospital, 1969.

8. The author is indebted to Dr. Albert Scheckenbach for the Good Day concept, from which this system evolved. He also suggested the card format used in the exchange system.

9. Baer, D. M., Wolf, M. M., and Risley, T. R., "Some current dimensions of applied behavior analysis." *Journal of Applied Behavior Analysis*, 1, 1968 (pp. 91–97).

30

The Psychopath and His Response to Behavior Modification Techniques

Helen Lantz and Gilbert Ingram

Appeared originally in *FCI Technical and Treatment Notes*, Vol. 2, No. 1, 1971. Published by the Federal Correctional Institution, Tallahassee, Florida.

In the light of the rapidly rising rate of crime and violence in America, this topic could well be one of the most relevant of our times. It seems to be of utmost importance that such problems as the psychopathic delinquent's behavior be not only suppressed, but modified. But how?

The sciences of behavior are left with the burden for understanding and solving these problems, and for finding new models to meet changing needs.

NATURE, ETIOLOGY, AND TREATMENT OF THE PSYCHOPATHIC PERSONALITY

Since Prichard first described the psychopathic personality[1] in 1835 as "moral imbecility," theories about the nature, etiology, and treatment of the disorder have had a wide range, reflecting a variety of psychodynamic and organically based interpretations. Despite continuing controversy about many facets of the psychopathic personality, certain central behavioral features have been described by a number of investigators (Cleckley, 1955; Millon, 1969; Peterson, Quay, & Tiffany, 1961; Quay, 1965; White, 1964). The psychopath is almost universally characterized as highly impulsive, with a diffuse and chronic incapacity for persistent ordered living of any kind. He has a marked absence of any sense of responsibility, and his penchant for creating excitement for the moment without regard for later consequences seems almost unlimited. His failure to learn from experience and his lack of ability to delay gratification are manifest in an inability to follow socially approved codes of behavior. A marked lack of ethical or moral development seems to indicate that the psychopath may be incapable of real love and attachment for others. He is unable to tolerate routine and boredom. While he may engage in asocial, highly aggressive behavior, his behavior frequently appears to be motivated by little more than a need for thrills and excitement. Together with an absence of emotional reactivity in the psychopath, there is present a seemingly self-destructive failure to modify this pattern of asocial immoral behavior in spite of repeated painful consequences.

In probably one of the most extensive psychiatric treatments of this condition, Cleckley (1955) writes:

> The opinion here maintained is that the psychopath fails to know all those more serious and deeply moving effective states which make up the tragedy and triumph of ordinary life, of life at the level of human personality—no normal person is so uninvolved, no ordinary criminal so generally unresponsive and distorted, but that he seems to experience satisfaction, love, hate, grief, a general participation in life at human personality level, much more intense and more substantial than the affective reactions of the psychopath.

It would appear, then, that a class of people have been identified who are characterized by chronic misbehavior and by marked emotional flatness. Other descriptions are considerably more precise. In a review of the literature from 1947 to 1953 (Albert, Brigante, & Chase, 1959), there was found to be decided agreement regarding the following psychopathic tendencies: antisocial faction, lack of ability to delay satisfaction, lack of insight, inadequacy of ego functioning, deficiency in planning ability, hyperactivity, callousness, and agreement with respect to many other characteristics. Gough (1948) combines all characteristics in his description of psychopathy in role-playing ability; for him, psychopathy is normlessness as a result of a failure of socialization. The problem thus becomes one of attempting to account for these and related features of the psychopathic disorder.

Lykken (1957) first tested the relationship of anxiety to criminal sociopathy. Assuming that sociopaths are defective in their ability to develop anxiety in the sense of an anticipatory emotional response to warning signals in the environment, Lykken postulated that they should be relatively incapable of avoidance learning where such learning can only be effected through the mediation of the anxiety response. Lykken convincingly demonstrated that psychopaths are relatively anxiety-free and virtually incapable of learning to avoid a painful stimulus. Other workers have shown that psychopaths, having once learned an avoidance response to an annoying stimulus, such as an air puff on the cornea, fail to develop good conditioned discrimination because they would continue to respond to a negative stimulus, thus avoiding possible discomfort (Warren & Grant, 1955).

Eysenck (1957, 1964) has proposed that criminal behavior represents a failure to learn and that the chronic offender is constitutionally inferior. He views the problem as a central nervous system defect which hinders classical conditioning necessary for the development of socially appropriate behavior.

Schacter and Latane (1964), in a replication of Lykken's work, demonstrated that while sociopaths and normals are equally capable of positively reinforced learning, normals can learn to avoid pain with facility, and sociopaths do not. Under the influence of injected adrenalin, however, sociopaths were found to show marked improvement in their avoidance conditioning, while normals performed more poorly, Schacter and Latane hypothesized that sociopaths are simply less sympathetically responsive, and that whatever the cause—endocrinological, neurological, or learning history—low autonomic responsiveness should lead to emotional flatness and low anxiety. They cited several independent studies which used GSR (galvanic skin response) and heart rate as indices of autonomic reactivity, to support their hypothesis that sociopaths are more reactive autonomically than are emotional subjects. Thus it appears that bodily conditions which for others are associated with emotionality are, for the sociopath, his "normal" state; and that only intense states of autonomic reaction, presumably stronger than and differentiable from his normal reactions, acquire emotional attributes for the sociopathic subject. Given a chronic history of autonomic reactivity, only a marked increase in activation (or a high level of stimulation) will be labeled as an emotional state, and perhaps even noticed.

Allen et al. (1969) did not support Lykken's and Schacter's results. They found that, although epinephrine elevated heart rate and skin resistance more in the sociopath than in the nonsociopath, both groups learned to avoid shock at the same rate under both epinephrine and saline conditions.

Quay (1965) postulated that psychopathic behavior may represent an extreme of stimulation-seeking behavior and that the psychopath's primary abnormality lies in the realm of basal reactivity and/or adaptation to sensory inputs of all types. It is this which accounts for the impulsivity and the lack of even minimal tolerance for sameness which appear to be the primary and distinctive features of the disorder. If the level and variability of sensory inputs which are necessary for the maintenance of pleasant affect are much greater for the psychopath than for the normal individual, it is possible that under ordinary life conditions, the psychopathic individual frequently suffers from the unpleasant affect which is produced by complete sensory deprivation or monotony (Berlyne, 1960). Thus, within this model, the psychopath's deficiencies in conditionability in terms of both avoidance and approach responses could be interpreted as failure of either the unconditioned (avoidance learning) or reinforcing (approach learning) stimuli to have aroused excitatory processes in the individual. The findings of Schacter and Latane could be interpreted within Quay's theory as supporting a lowered basal reactivity to stimuli. Other researchers (Fox & Lippert, 1963) have found that psychopaths exhibit significantly less spontaneous activity, or changes in GSR, than do normals; Mundy—Castle and McKiever (1953) had previously discovered that subjects with less spontaneous activity, of GSR, adapt more rapidly to a repetitive stimulus—these studies seem to point to a more rapid adaptation process in the psychopath. Thus if the psychopath, due to lowered reactivity and/or more rapid adaptation, frequently finds himself in a condition of stimulus deprivation which he is motivated to change by the seeking of stimulation, it may be this seeking of either added intensity or added variability of stimulation which leads to the psychopath's frequent transgressions of the law.

Several other workers have attempted to tie together the varied research which has been done on psychopaths in order to reach a general theory of the nature of the disorder. Hare (1965, 1966, 1970) has found that the psychopath's failure to avoid punishment may be related to his relative low level of emotional reactivity and poor fear conditionability; cues associated with response-produced punishment are incapable of generating sufficient fear in the psychopath for the response to be inhibited, particularly when punishment is anticipated in the future. For psychopaths, the amount of fear elicited by cues associated with punishment decreases as the temporal remoteness of anticipated punishment increases (i.e., Hare found that psychopaths fail to show an increased number of immediate vs. delayed shock choices over trials). He therefore suggests that the psychopath's impulsivity and repeated failure to inhibit antisocial behavior and hence to avoid punishment might be understood in these terms. Welch and Hayes (1957) support Hare's hypothesis that the psychopath has not been sufficiently fear-conditioned in pointing out that the psychopath manifests little or no psychogalvanic reaction to huge falsehoods and confabulations after even violent transgressions of the law.

Assuming that these conceptions of the psychopathic personality are at least partially explanatory of the behavioral manifestations of the disorder, one must then consider its possible origins. Little adequate work has been done concerning the etiology of the psychopathic disorder, and what has been done has failed to produce a variety of clear concrete findings.

Essentially two origins of psychopathic behavior are typically noted: constitutional and psychogenic. Thompson (1961) states unequivocally that "psychopathy is an organic disease." Karpman (1948), in a description perhaps closest to the traditional constitutional theory of an inborn but unknown defect, concludes that there is a small group of "primary psychopaths" who have no conscience; they are amoral and there appear to be no known psychogenic factors involved.

White (1964) hypothesizes that the psychopathic personality may be produced by generalized brain injury which weakens the capacity for inhibition and control, and he cites as evidence the fact that sometimes following a severe head injury, and sometimes following an attack of encephalitis (which is known to injure brain tissue), the behavior of a previously well–adjusted child may change in a delinquent direction: he becomes overactive and aggressive, is unable to postpone immediate satisfaction or to accept the restraints of the schoolroom. Also supporting this viewpoint is the fact that several different investigators have reported a much higher incidence of abnormal EEG's in persons classed as psychopaths (Ellingson, 1954; Jenkins & Pacella, 1943). Evidence of this kind suggests that brain abnormalities may contribute in some way to the psychopath's behavior. These abnormities may be acquired during childhood through infection or head injury; they might result from birth damage or injury during the fetal period; or they might be the product of hereditary influences (Nielsen & Thompson, 1947).

Thus the concept of the psychopathic personality can be considered a specific disorder, having certain characteristics common to all cases. There is evidence that it can be produced by generalized brain injury which weakens the capacity for inhibition and control. There is also evidence that it can be produced by severe privation of affectionate support in early childhood, leaving the child without adequate motive to identify with, or learn and interject restraints and social standards. Neither type of evidence is as yet by any means secure, and both types of explanation may ultimately be needed to understand the problem of the psychopathic personality (White, 1964; McCord & McCord, 1956).

In the meantime, the treatment of the psychopath is anything but an inviting task. He brings no motivation to psychotherapy, which is therefore very hard to initiate. In an institutional setting, the therapist is at a serious disadvantage because, to the delinquent, he is the enemy; he represents law and order and is presumed to be trying to convert his patient to the hated cause. Depth psychology schools in the Freudian, Adlerian, and Jungian traditions regard psychopathic delinquent behavior as an expression of frustration resulting from childhood conflicts; the Rogerian school approaches such delinquent problems in an accepting manner, apparently thus hoping to divert negative forces in the delinquent into positive channels (Vietor, 1967). However, in the therapeutic situation the psychopath meets the therapist with distrust; usually reacting to psychotherapeutic attempts with defiance. If he cooperates at all, it is with an air of playful grimness (Bromberg, 1964). Hetrick (1962) points out the underlying similarity between psychotherapy and verbal conditioning, since anxiety is related to both success in therapy and to conditionability; the low anxiety level characteristic of the psychopath seems to be detrimental to both. None of the traits of the adolescent psychopath seem to make him a suitable candidate for traditional modes of therapy.

This does not indicate, however, that change through educational or psychological treatment is impossible. Bender (1961), following a psychotherapeutic plan of treatment, suggests the placement of psychopathic children in a warm, protective, nonpunitive group during latency, where he may learn by imitation to pattern his behavior in more acceptable ways. The conventional approach to individual therapy with psychopaths has been for the therapist to establish such a warm, permissive environment in which the patient may express his hostility and aggressiveness to the fullest. Aichhorn (Lippman, 1951) has utilized a therapy situation consisting of repeatedly outsmarting the patient, pointing out his stupid mistakes and showing that the therapist, too, has all the skills to exploit but uses them differently. The result is narcissistic identification. Within this orientation, however, the most frequent approach to treatment has become a plea for prevention through research, especially into mother-child relationships.

Schmideberg (1961), on the other hand, asserts that a suitable approach to the treatment of psychopathy must be one that is different from that applicable to neurotics and psychotics. This treatment involves "largely in wearing him out, deflating, redramatizing, and out-maneuvering him. This is one reason why treatment within the community, cooperation with the court, and other team approaches are more successful than a one-to-one psychiatric office relation to the therapist. She views the goal of therapy as a process of trying to develop "the ego and orient it socially, rather than make the unconscious conscious, and develop values, ideals, sublimations, self-control, to educate, reeducate, and socialize."

Methods of overcoming resistance encountered by the lack of motivation for treatment found in the psychopathic personality are considered mandatory. The use of drugs such as sodium pentothal and hyponanalysis (Lindner, 1947) appear to overwhelm such resistance. A technique requiring the use of both LSD and hypnosis in a single extensive treatment has experienced success (Lyle, 1968b). Thus the drug and hypnotherapy methods are intended to overwhelm resistance, the individual treatment and milieu treatment may erode resistance, group methods are used to divert or rechannel resistance. But this is only part of the problem faced.

Craft, Stephenson, and Granger (1964) list the types of prognosis and treatment which have been and are being used with the psychopathic individual:

1. Physical (electroshock) or drug treatment has experienced only short-term success when used with psychopaths; although immediately effective, there does not appear to be a long-term effect.

2. Individual psychotherapy: as previously discussed, only short-term success, if any, is experienced with the adolescent psychopath in this type of setting.

3. Group therapy appears to have little success with psychopaths because

of their mistrustful and uncooperative approach to others (Bixenstine & Douglas, 1967). Group therapy has even been used as an "aversive" technique within an institutional setting (Levinson, Ingram, & Azcarate, 1967).

4. The effect of good leadership upon young delinquents has not experienced any long-term success at the present stage of research.

5. Authoritarian disciplinary treatment of psychopaths: the unsocialized delinquent is not relieved by punishment but is embittered by it. They are dominated, not by feelings of guilt, but by feelings of frustration and hatred (Jenkins, 1957), and thus any effects due to punishment have been without long-term success.

With reference to the seeming lack of applicability of such treatment methods which appear to be based on extremely nebulous foundation theory, Pierson and Kelly (1963) raise the question as to the adequacy of present treatment methods with psychopathic delinquents. At best, these treatment models have been mainly developed for use with neurotics, and such models are often simply superimposed over psychopathic delinquents whether they fit or not. A treatment method is needed for work with psychopaths which would provide therapeutic objectives applicable to the disorder, and show treatment responses through measurement. Penal measures alone are not sufficient to correct delinquent behavior, and psychotherapeutic measures aimed at changing the delinquent's personality structure have not been successful.

BEHAVIOR MODIFICATION

Many workers in this field today are increasingly turning to the use of behavior therapy, or the attempt to alter human behavior and emotion in a beneficial manner according to the laws of modern learning theory (Eysenck, 1964), in treating delinquency, and in particular, delinquents classified as psychopathic through behavioral diagnoses (Quay, 1960). Within such a model, the offender is regarded as an individual whose antisocial behavior has been acquired by learning or improper conditioning. Behavior therapy with adolescent psychopaths is gradually becoming the focal point in attempts to correct criminal behavior. This approach has the advantage of having a firm scientific basis in learning theory, and although there are as yet too few large research series to warrant a definite conclusion about the value of this form of therapy, promising results have been and are being obtained.

Thus, behavior therapy is one of the hotter items in the therapeutic market today. This very "simple" approach to human learning and problems has a great deal of appeal to common sense. With its appeal to common sense and its very pragmatic approach of treating the behavior problem immediately rather than seeking the underlying causes, as the more conventional

psychodynamically oriented therapies do, it has been finding increasing acceptance in this country. Behavior therapy has particular appeal to the
academically oriented psychologists because, in addition to speaking their
language, it apparently lends itself to experimental manipulation.

Behavior therapy or the use of behavior modification techniques is basically an attempt to apply the results of modern learning theory and experimental psychology to the problem of altering maladaptive behavior (Ullmann
& Krasner, 1965; Eysenck, 1964). Basic to all concepts of learning is the
acquisition of a functional connection between an environmental stimulus
and a subject response; supposedly, there are specific stimuli which will elicit
specific responses. By discovering which stimuli will elicit what response
(usually taken to be a symptom or some form of undesirable behavior), either
the stimuli can be eliminated or a new competing response can be conditioned to the old stimuli. Thus, in either event the undesirable behavior is
eliminated. In essence, this is the strategy of the behavior therapies.

There are two primary schools of behavior therapy. One is based on
Pavlovian or respondent conditioning (Wolpe–Eysenck school) in which a
stimulus elicits a response, with the pairing of the CS and UCS being reinforcement. If the UCS is repeatedly omitted, the CR gradually diminishes
and the repetition of the CS without reinforcement is called extinction—in
short, inhibition, or the tendency not to respond, is learned. The other
school of thought is based on the operant conditioning approach of Skinner:
the subject must emit a response to the situation prior to the environmental
event that becomes associated with and alters its frequency of occurrence in
the future, either by contiguity or reinforcement. Skinner's concepts are
based primarily on the frequency of emissions of overt behavior (Ullmann &
Krasner, 1965; Eysenck, 1964; Mowrer, 1950).

Maladaptive behaviors, with the exception of organic syndromes, are considered to be learned—any behavior that increases positive reinforcement or
helps reduce aversive stimuli is likely to be increased. In short, patterns of
behavior are increased, shaped, and maintained through reinforcement.
After a new behavior has been developed by various techniques, it is maintained because it pays off and is more likely to lead to reinforcement.

Therefore, the major emphasis of behavior modification is focused on overt
behavior and the application of concepts drawn from learning theory to attain
change. While there are many techniques, there are few concepts of principles involved. Techniques of extinction, discrimination learning; methods of
reward, punishment, social imitation; procedures of aversion; negative practice, positive conditioning reinforcement withdrawal, and desensitization all
boil down to utilizing systematic environmental contingencies to alter the
subject's response to a stimulus.

Assessment in behavior modification involves the identification of meaningful aspects of the environment that may be programmed to become contingent on behaviors that are to be increased or decreased in frequency (Ullmann & Krasner, 1965). For each personality UCS, and the response in question must be determined along with the way in which variables have become associated and the best method of achieving the particular treatment called for by theory (Eysenck, 1964). It is likely that different personality types will react differently to any proposed scheme of treatment, and diagnostic methods have to be developed geared to the problem at hand.

BEHAVIOR THERAPY WITH PSYCHOPATHIC DELINQUENTS

The psychopathic personality—undersocialized and asocial—may well be the group of disorders for which the greatest departure from traditional treatment is needed. Such antisocial personalities are likely to present learning deficits, and consequently, the goal of therapy is the acquisition of secondary motives and the development of internal restraint habits (Bandura, 1961). Mowrer (1950) asserts that the development of socially desirable behavior patterns in children can only be accounted for through the process of Pavlovian conditioning; whenever a maladaptive response becomes a habit, it is because the response (CS) has become associated with consequences immediately pleasurable to the patient although there may be socially undesirable and highly unpleasant for the individual in long-term consequences. Thus the goal of behavior therapy in such a situation is the inhibition of the maladaptive response or habit and the development of new positive habits.

Many studies have been performed in which systematic attempts have been made to apply certain principles of learning to the area of behavior therapy with psychopathic delinquents. Frequently, these studies do not differentiate between delinquents as a group and specific categories such as psychopathic delinquent. The applicability of research results from delinquent groups to psychopathic delinquent groups is questionable. Those studies failing to identify "types" of delinquents used as Ss should be considered suggestive at this point for purposes of this presentation. Stumphauzer (1970) has critically reviewed the literature on behavior modification with juvenile delinquents.

The following discussion of psychological processes through which changes in behavior can occur is not exhaustive, nor are they without overlap. The basic intended purpose is to apply an overview of many of the behavioral modification techniques which have been found to be useful in work with psychopaths.

Methods of Reinforcement. Most theories of psychotherapy are based on the assumption that the patient has a repertoire of previously learned positive habits available to him, but that these adaptive patterns are inhibited or blocked by competing responses motivated by guilt or anxiety. The goal of therapy, then, is to reduce the severity of the internal inhibitory controls, thus allowing the healthy patterns of behavior to emerge (Bandura, 1961). However, the undersocialized or sociopathic personality is likely to present learning deficits; consequently, the goal of therapy is the acquisition of secondary motives and the development of internal restraint habits. Primary and secondary rewards in the form of the therapist's interest and approval may play an important, if not indispensable, role in the treatment process.

Ferster (1958) has asserted that most human behavior is social, having its effects on other organisms, who in turn arrange the reinforcements; and that reinforcements from groups of people may have a larger order of magnitude of effect than those supplied by a single individual. The psychopath's behavior is maintained by avoiding aversive consequences rather than producing positive effects. A potentially reinforcing environment exists for every individual if he will only emit required performances on the proper occasions. Ferster assumes that the psychopath's deficient behavioral repertoire may arise because (1) of an inadequate reinforcement history, (2) schedules of reinforcement are inadequate, and (3) punishment may distort a performance which otherwise would be reinforced. Thus the therapist's task is to generate adequate behavior repertoires which will escape punishment and make contact with reinforcements potentially available to him in a wide variety of situations. Reinforcement is the most important process by which behavior is generated and maintained according to Ferster, and the therapist is in a position to "shape" the behavior in a patient by beginning with a performance already in his repertoire and exposing him to selected portions of his environment designed to generate the new more complex form.

A study by Wetzel (1966) demonstrates the use of such a behavioral principle in the modification of a deviant behavior. The study concerned Mike, a ten-year-old compulsive stealer, with "many qualities of a full-blown psychopath," little conscience, and a tendency to project faults to others. In treatment, Wetzel used as reinforcement Mike's customary visits with a motherly cook; when Mike stole, his visits with her were canceled. All of Mike's socially appropriate behavior was praised and reinforced when possible. Mike's stealing was thereby successfully eliminated over a 3½-month period (records indicated that his behavior had been the source of difficulty for five years). Wetzel emphasizes the necessity of reinforcing immediately and consistently. In situations where target behavior is maintained by recognizable and controllable reinforcers, extinction coupled with reinforcement of alternate behavior seems to be most desirable, with the use of naturally existing reinforcers in the environment of the target individual being advisable. Wetzel also notes that the reinforcing value of a stimulus may be a function of whether or not the subject perceives reinforcement to depend on his own behavior or on the whims of the environment.

Bijou and Baer (1961, 1965) speak of three types of reinforcers: a positive reinforcer is a stimulus event produced by a particular behavior which results in an increase in frequency of the behavior; negative reinforcers are stimulus events that are removed, avoided, or terminated by a behavior, thus yielding an increase in the frequency of the behavior. Those stimulus events, whether produced or removed by a response, which will fail to change the response from operant level or maintain it above or below operant level are neutral stimuli. Thus a particular behavior can have four consequences:

1. Produce + reinforcers ("reward")——————
                                                    ⎤—Strengthen response
2. Remove or avoid-reinforcers ("relief")——————⎦

3. Produce-reinforcers ("punishment by hurt")——————
                                                         ⎤—Weaken response
4. Remove or avoid + reinforcers ("punishment by loss")⎦

Thus, undesired behavior can be weakened by having a behavior (1) produce a negative reinforcer, (2) lose a positive reinforcer, or (3) produce a neutral stimulus when it previously had produced a positive reinforcer. Bijou and Baer also feel that no new responses are created by reinforcers; rather, strengthened or weakened old responses are put together in a new arrangement.

Punishment, as differentiable from negative reinforcement, involves aversive stimuli, but its nature is to suppress the operant response without allowing it to extinguish. Estes (1944) writes:

> . . . a response cannot be eliminated from an organism's repertoire more rapidly with the aid of punishment than without it. In fact, severe punishment may have precisely the opposite effect. A response can be permanently weakened only by a sufficient number of unreinforced elicitations and this process of extinction cannot proceed while a response is suppressed as a result of punishment. The punished response continues to exist in the organism's repertoire with most of its original latent strength.

Estes does feel punishment can be useful if: (1) the degree of punishment is adjusted so that responses still continue to occur, but at a lower rate; this saves time; (2) where reward cannot be controlled, a degree of punishment can hold the response low; (3) when a response needs to be kept low while another response is being strengthened.

All of this work appears to be quite relevant to behavior therapy with psychopathic delinquents, especially with respect to such procedures as "time out" which have been found to be an effective device in work with delinquents. For an example of this time-out procedure, Buchard and Tyler (1965) report work with a 13-year-old, institutionalized delinquent, Danny. The staff was instructed that all unacceptable behavior (behavior requiring a sanction) would result in time out, or removal and isolation from ongoing activities. If it did not warrant isolation, there should be no response. This is not "pure" punishment; further deviant behavior can receive no reinforcement while he is alone, thus it continues to extinguish. Once Danny's major behavior problems were under control, the staff reported noticing that they then worked on such behaviors as making too much noise, running in the cabin, and others that, although they too were against the rules, had paled earlier beside Danny's aggression and hostility.

Another such example, done by Wolf, Risley, and Mees (1964), demonstrates the combination of mild punishment and extinction to cure the temper tantrums of an institutionalized 3-year-old. The child was placed in his room contingent upon each tantrum, with the door remaining closed until tantrum behavior ceased. This eliminated the positive reinforcement throughout the undesired behavior and provided for differential reinforcement of non-tantrum behavior by the door being opened contingent on such behavior. Thus such a technique involves the removal of all social reinforcers, and resembles "time out" from positive reinforcement as an aversive stimulus. The child's tantrums decreased significantly in both frequency and severity.

Other studies (Cooper, Adams, and Gibby, 1962; Gewirtz and Baer, 1958) report that exposure to both social isolation and perceptual deprivation for a brief period leads to increases in ego strength and the effectiveness of certain social reinforcers. There has been some evidence (Johns and Quay, 1962) that psychopathic individuals are unresponsive to social reinforcement. However, if Quay's theory of psychopathic disorders as pathological stimulation seeking is correct, psychopaths should find perceptual deprivation even more distasteful than normals, and thus be more susceptible to the effects of social reinforcement as a behavioral modification device after such isolation. Even so, Gewirtz and Baer have shown this technique to be more effective for older children who have longer and better integrated histories of conditioning of these reinforcers; because of the psychopath's deficit in conditionability, this may hinder the use of social reinforcers.

However, Bernard and Eisenman (1967) have found that sociopathic subjects conditioned better than normal subjects for either immediate social or monetary reinforcement. These workers suggest that sociopaths have learned different values, imitate different models, and otherwise lead a different pattern of behavior than the normal population. They conclude that social rewards may or may not be effective with any given sociopathic person depending on the value of the social reward administered; for example, with Wetzel's Mike—the visits with the motherly cook were highly reinforcing for Mike. Thus conditioning is dependent on situational variables, and although psychopaths do fail to learn in a variety of situations, it would be a mistake to consider sociopaths as necessarily unable to learn or to otherwise respond to social stimuli.

Painting (1961) emphasizes the importance of immediacy of the reinforcer, especially for the psychopath. If the individual is not given reinforcement (knowledge of the consequences of his behavior) within a period of time, that reinforcement does not have the strength it could have, and may even have an aversive effect of reinforcing other wrong or inappropriate behaviors. In testing the contention that psychopaths are less capable of perceiving relationships between past events and consequences of present actions, Painting found that when stimulus and response were in close proximity, the psychopathic individual's performance is superior, but that it deteriorates more rapidly under more remote stimulus-response connections.

V. O. Tyler (1967), conjecturing that academic incompetence may contribute to delinquency, has attempted to apply operant token reinforcement to the academic performance of an institutionalized delinquent. Tyler asserts that the improvement of academic competence could be therapeutic in itself, because it should provide training in skills necessary for better school functioning on return to the community; it should produce social reinforcement, compete with antisocial behavior and reduce the "need" for getting into trouble. He cites the case of Nick, a severe discipline problem in the institution, whose attitudes could not be changed through group or milieu therapy. The treatment formulation was to use operant conditioning procedures to strengthen the limited class of behaviors—namely, academic performance in school—with the hope that strengthened academic functioning could serve as a first step toward socialization, since Nick had reported that he felt "dumb" in school and resisted the educational process. Nick rented the use of his mattress at night and the right to wear his own clothes instead of institution clothes, and purchase canteen items (cigarettes, candy, etc.)—these items were chosen as reinforcement because they were important to Nick—with tokens, which he earned with daily and weekly school grades. Over a period of 30 weeks, Nick's grades on the average improved somewhat, and Tyler concluded that token reinforcement had improved his academic performance. But at the end of the study, Nick was still a "con artist" and resistant to authorities, including those at school. Academic performance was chosen for this study because of the difficulty of attacking the presenting symptom (auto theft) directly; however, it was hypothesized that skill in reading, etc., would lead to social and tangible reinforcements which may lead to other behaviors competing with antisocial behavior.

Rickard and Dinoff (1965) report the establishment of therapeutic summer communities for problem boys, with the orientation rooted within the framework of learning principles. The ability to reinforce is partially dependent on the personality characteristics of the reinforcer, and the individual who reinforces subsequently becomes part of a stimulus complex which in itself elicits desired behavior. A specific behavior must be selected for modification for each individual and reinforcements must be used which will be meaningful for that individual. The verbal and non-verbal behavior of the staff often set the stage for adaptive behavior to emerge; when the individual refused to comply with regulations, alternate channels were pointed out to him, and the expected behavior was labeled clearly in a nonpunitive, non-judgmental manner. These workers also emphasize the important reinforcement parameter of immediacy.

Schwitzgebel (1967), in attempting the short-term operant conditioning of adolescent offenders on socially relevant variables, found that when hostile statements by delinquents in therapy were followed by a mild aversive consequence (disagreement or inattention) while the other selected operants were followed by a positive consequence (verbal praise or a small gift), the delinquents showed a significant increase in the frequency of behaviors followed by positive consequences. Attempted punishment, however, resulted in no decrease. Schwitzgebel suggests that the difficulty experienced with delinquents in therapy (i.e., missing of appointments, unpunctuality, uncooperativeness) could be modified in such a way without extreme difficulty.

Schwitzgebel has suggested that the characteristic impulsivity ascribed to juvenile delinquents is likely influenced or determined by the particular type and schedule of reinforcement in the individual's life history. The operant conditioning paradigm seems to provide a very useful framework for the manipulation of reinforcements for that individual. Since many of the psychopathic delinquent's problems seem to consist of behavior deficits, the question is how to teach the desired behavior and reinforce it so as to assure its occurrence. It is important to note that these operant techniques are effective only in highly structured, controlled situations; and the institution or delinquent cottage affords such an environment.

Hanson (1971) attacked a problem area that has bothered correctional personnel who attempt to work with youthful offenders; i.e., the failure of inmates to keep their appointments. He was successful in demonstrating a significant improvement in promptness and reliability of attendance for these inmates exposed to positive and negative contingencies. No such change occurred for the control group or the neutral contingency group. Hanson also found that positive reinforcement (approval) worked best for three times as many inmates as did negative reinforcement (disapproval of lateness). This study demonstrates the effectiveness of operant techniques, especially in highly structured, controlled situations.

Ingram et al. (1970) is another example of the advantages of using operant techniques (among other treatment approaches) with psychopathic offenders in a highly structured institutional environment.

Extinction. Closely related to operant conditioning through methods of reward, and already partially discussed with respect to punishment, is the technique of extinction. "When a learned response is repeated without reinforcement, the strength of the tendency to perform that response undergoes a progressive decrease" (Dollard & Miller, 1950). Extinction involves the development of inhibitory potential, which is composed of two components (Bandura, 1961). The evocation of any reaction generates reactive inhibition which presumably dissipates with time. When reactive inhibition (fatigue, etc.) reaches a high point, the cessation of activity alleviates this negative motivational state and any stimuli associated with the cessation of the response become conditioned inhibitors.

The use of extinction as a method for eliminating maladaptive behavior appears to have been limited mostly to anxiety-motivated behavior in recent research (i.e., tics, speech disorders, etc.), and therefore does not appear to be applicable to psychopathic delinquents. Williams (1959) has, however, been successful in eliminating tantrum behavior of a male child by extinction procedures. Consistent with the learning principle that behavior that is not reinforced will be extinguised the child was put to bed (the occasion setting off most of his tantrum behavior) and let scream and rage, but no attention was paid. The treatment did not involve aversive punishment; all that was done was to remove the reinforcement, and the extinction of the tyrant-like tantrum behavior then occurred.

The "time out" procedure, already discussed, has been found to be an effective technique for extinguishing undesirable behavior. Extinction of aggressive acting-out behavior in the institutional setting can be most effectively accomplished by quickly stopping the aggression and then not paying any more attention to it. Tyler and Brown (1967) have used this technique by placing the boy, at the onset of aggressive behavior, alone in a room for several minutes; when he quiets down he is allowed outside. Buchard and Tyler (1965) also describe how the more severe forms of acting-out behavior can be eliminated by the extensive use of isolation.

Therefore, it appears that extinction may be an effective way of getting rid of maladaptive behavior, and that some method of reinforcement might then be used in developing new positive habits.

Counterconditioning Methods. A wide variety of techniques using counterconditioning theory have been developed and are being used with numerous types of patients. Joseph Wolpe's (1958) reciprocal inhibition is probably the best recognized of these methods: "If a response antagonistic to anxiety can be made to occur in the presence of anxiety-evoking stimuli so that it is accompanied by a complete or partial suppression of the anxiety response, the bond between these stimuli and the anxiety responses will be weakened." Wolpe (1961) describes systematic desensitization (a form of reciprocal inhibition therapy) as a technique in which the therapist establishes a hierarchy of stimulus situations in terms of their anxiety-provoking potential. In a deeply relaxed state, the patient is called on to visualize a scene incorporating the mildest of anxiety-provoking situations. The deep relaxation which is anxiety inhibiting is thus paired with the anxiety-provoking stimulus situation, and after a series of presentation, anxiety ceases to dominate as a response to that situation. The next most provoking stimulus situation is dealt with in a similar manner, and the next in turn as the former ceases to become effective in provoking anxiety.

Although these methods have been employed most extensively in eliminating anxiety-motivated avoidance reactions and inhibitions, it has been used with some success in reducing maladaptive approach responses as well. In the latter case, the goal object is repeatedly associated with some form of aversive stimuli. Cautela (1967) reports an example of such therapy in the use of a technique which he calls "covert sensitization," which appears to be quite useful in work with delinquents in eliminating such maladaptive approach behavior as stealing. Neither the undesirable stimulus or aversive stimuli are actually presented; the purpose of the procedure is to build up avoidance responses to the undesirable stimulus. The subject is first taught to relax as in desensitization procedure, and the therapy then proceeds as follows:

> You are walking down a street—you notice a real sharp sports car—you walk toward it with the idea of stealing it—as you walk toward it you start to get a funny feeling in your stomach—you feel sick to your stomach and have a slight pain in your gut—as you keep walking you really start to feel sick and food starts coming up in your mouth—you're just about to reach for the handle of the door and you can't hold it any longer—you vomit all over your hand, car door, upholstery inside, all over your clothes—the smell starts to get to you and you keep puking from it—it's all over the place—it's dripping from your mouth—you turn around, run away, and then start to feel better.

Cautela emphasizes that such treatment should be explicitly applied to the individual's desire to steal, drink, etc. and not just to the object itself. The patient is told he is unable to stop his problem because it is a strong learned habit, which now gives him much pleasure: the way to eliminate his problem is to associate the pleasurable object with an unpleasant stimulus. Cautela reports that most juvenile offenders appear to respond well to these behavior therapy procedures.

Eysenck (1965) postulates that psychopathic behavior is the failure of the conditioning process to occur which would produce socially desirable habits. When the patient is suffering from a maladaptive habit where the conditioned stimulus has become associated with consequences immediately pleasurable to the patient, although they may be socially undesirable and highly unpleasant in long-term consequences for the individual himself, formal or informal punishment often provoked by socially unacceptable behavior is seldom successful in extinguishing the undesirable act. If the behavior pattern is immediately followed by reward and only much later by punishment, it can be expected to persist. Aversion therapy consists of pairing the stimulus in question with a strong aversive stimulus producing sympathetic reactions; the aversive stimulus should be supplied immediately after the conditioned stimulus in such a way that it eliminates or at least precedes positive reinforcement resulting from the act. In psychopathic disorders, treatment must take the form of reconditioning to change maladaptive patterns of behavior.

Nauseant drugs, especially emetine, have been utilized as the unconditioned stimulus in the aversion treatment of alcoholism, and may also be applicable to aversion therapy with psychopathic delinquents. Strong electric shock has also been used as the aversive stimulus in the treatment of such disorders. When such methods of aversion treatment are used with psychopaths, it is advisable to follow the elimination of the maladaptive behavior with some method of reinforcement in order to develop a more adaptive form of behavior to take its place.

Other forms of delinquent behavior can also react favorably to deconditioning psychotherapy. Schwitzgebel and Kolb (1964) used a deconditioning technique with forty juvenile delinquents. They were offered a part-time daily task of speaking into a tape recorder, allowed to speak about any subject they chose; simple reinforcement procedure increased the bond with "work" within 25 sessions. A follow-up over three years disclosed significant decreases in the frequency and seriousness of delinquency in the experimental group. With respect to this, Vietor (1967) emphasizes the importance of establishing an appropriate and adequate regimen of deconditioning.

Other Techniques. Numerous other techniques have been developed and lie within the behavior modification paradigm. A brief review of these techniques which may be found to be useful in work with psychopathic delinquents follows:

1. Social imitation: Bandura (1961) asserts that social imitation may serve as an effective vehicle for the transmission of prosocial behavior patterns in the treatment of antisocial patients. The treatment of older unsocialized delinquents is a difficult task, since they are relatively self-sufficient and do not readily seek involvement with a therapist. In many cases, socialization can be accomplished only through residential care and treatment. Bandura

suggests that treatment through social imitation may be a possible method for modifying antisocial patterns. In the treatment home, the therapist can personally administer many of the primary rewards and mediate between the boys' needs and gratifications. Through the repeated association with rewarding experiences for the boy, many of the therapist's attitudes and actions will acquire secondary reward value, and thus the patient will be motivated to reproduce these attitudes and actions in himself. Once these attitudes and values have been thus accepted, the boy's inhibition of antisocial tendencies will function independently of the therapist.

2. Rational Psychotherapy: Ullmann and Krasner (1965) suggest that Albert Ellis' rational psychotherapy techniques also fall in the realm of behavior modification. In brief, Ellis believes that the effective therapist is continually unmasking the client's past and present illogical thinking by (1) bringing them to his attention or consciousness, (2) showing him how they are causing and maintaining his disturbance and unhappiness, (3) demonstrating exactly what illogical links exist, and (4) teaching him how to rethink and reverbalize in a logical, more self-helping way. The therapist makes a forthright unequivocal attack on the client's specific irrational ideas and tries to induce him to adopt more rational ones in their place. In work with psychopaths, the therapist must show the individual that his pattern of criminal behavior is not merely immoral and antisocial (which he already knows) but, more important, that it is self-defeating. Psychopaths act in an irrational and self-defeating manner because they believe they are helping themselves. Ellis gives an account of Jim, who, after 31 sessions of this type of rational therapy, was able to admit self-defeatism and wrongness of his criminal behavior.

3. Sensory Deprivation Procedures: Sensory deprivation involves the prolonged exposure to extreme conditions involving drastic reduction in all forms of meaningfully patterned sensory stimuli. Individually prepared messages are presented during sensory deprivation and social isolation, with the purposes of reducing overall symptomatology and to convince the patient of the availability of more intensive individual psychotherapy. Adams (1965) describes the situation: the patient is placed in a bed in a quiet conference room, eyes covered, ears plugged with glycerin-soaked cotton, head wrapped in gauze. After two hours a prerecorded taped message is presented to him describing the unique patterns of maladaptive behaviors that led to his institutionalization and explaining how future contacts with the therapist might help him acquire new and more effective patterns, and that it would require a more sincere sustained effort on his own part to achieve these changes in himself and to consolidate them anew as enduring habits. The patient is removed after three hours. This type of therapy has been shown to

be successful with delinquents, resulting in more readiness on their part to enter actively into a working relationship with the therapist.

4. Negative Practice: Ullmann and Krasner (1965) suggest that practicing an undesirable habit leads to inhibition or fatigue associated with having made the response so often that performing the response may be painful and not performing it avoids an aversive situation and thus becomes a positively reinforced behavior. Although this technique appears to be feasible for work with psychopathic delinquents, no research seems to have been done on it to date.

5. Stimulus Deprivation and Satiation: Also seemingly applicable to work with psychopathic delinquents is the technique of stimulus satiation. There is a likelihood that a subject will change his behavior to alter the frequency of a presumed reinforcing stimulus, and this may be manipulated by depriving him of that stimulus, or making that stimulus so abundant that he becomes satiated thus reducing the reinforcing characteristics of the stimulus. There is also possibility in this technique for future research (Ullmann and Krasner, 1965).

There are many other behavior modification techniques. The foregoing discussion includes only those which have been found to be useful in behavior therapy with psychopathic delinquents, and those which appear to hold forth promise for future work in this field. The core of all these behavior modification techniques rests not on methods of application or techniques, however, but on the planned manipulation of the environment contingent on the individual's responses to stimuli.

EVALUATION OF BEHAVIOR MODIFICATION TECHNIQUES

It would be unfair not to report the many criticisms which have been leveled against behavior therapy or the other methods used to treat psychopathic delinquents which have been successful.

The deliberate use of the principles of learning in the modification of human behavior implies, for most psychotherapists, manipulation and control of the patient, and control is seen by them as antihumanistic and therefore bad. Thus advocates of a learning theory approach to psychotherapy are often charged with treating human beings as if they were rats or pigeons, and of leading on the road to Orwell's *1984* (as noted by Bandura, 1961). However, many of the changes that occur in traditional psychotherapy derive from the unwitting application of well-known principles of learning; perhaps a more deliberate application of knowledge of learning processes to psychotherapy would yield far more effective results. One important problem should be mentioned. If a person's behavior has become a burden to society and if his behavior can be changed, whether he wants it or not, would it be right and proper to change that behavior?

Breger and McGaugh (1965) have leveled some devastating criticisms at "learning theory" theory: their three major criticisms are (1) the fact that learning therapies explain things in terms of single units, generally S-R links, is a misapplication of methodology to how humans operate. While S-R units may be the simplest to analyze and measure, they don't account for generalization, acquiring new responses, or the fact that humans think in terms of whole strategies; (2) the application of "Conditioning laws" established in laboratories with animals to therapeutic situations involving humans is a break of logic. The conditions are just not the same and the only thing that is demonstrated is that the same types of apparatus are being used; (3) to assert that reinforcement is necessary for learning is incorrect in the light of evidence. To define reinforcement, as Skinner does, as anything which produces a behavior change, is to explain nothing.

While Breger and McGaugh's criticisms seem well taken, there is no denying that, for certain types of problems and in certain situations, behavior therapy is extremely effective and relatively rapid. Nowhere does this appear to be clearer than in work with such disorders as the psychopathic personality. Behavior therapy with such offenders has gradually come to be focal in attempts to correct such behavior, as other, more traditional methods have failed.

Changes in behavior brought about through such methods as counterconditioning are apt to be viewed by the dynamically oriented therapist as being not only superficial "symptomatic treatment," in that the basic underlying cause of the behavior remains unchanged, but also potentially dangerous, since the direct elimination of a symptom may precipitate more seriously disturbed behaviors. However, on the whole the evidence, while open to error, suggests that no matter what the origin of the maladaptive behavior may be, a change in behavior brought about through learning procedures may be all that is necessary for the alleviation of most forms of emotional disorders.

Stampfl and Levis (1967) highlight what they feel are four distinct assets of learning-oriented approaches to the study of behavior disorders: (1) The identification of psychotherapy with objective experimental disciplines that provide a model susceptible to generating testable hypotheses; (2) the establishment of a common language between basic research and applied area; (3) highlighting of vast amounts of human and subhuman research frequently overlooked by the clinician; (4) they provide a foundation for the development of new treatment techniques. These together with the basic ideas that behavior modification techniques have a firm scientific basis in learning theory, and that they work, seem to more than justify the use of such an approach.

This approach seems to be especially well suited to the treatment of the adolescent psychopath. None of the personality characteristics of the psychopathic delinquent appear to make him a suitable candidate for traditional modes of psychotherapy. This traditional psychotherapy has been mainly developed for use with neurotics and, more often than not, the application of such treatment formulations to the psychopath are quite inappropriate with a flat, unemotional, nonanxious personality structure such as the psychopath's. The three working questions of a behavior modification model—(1) What behaviors are maladaptive? (2) What environmental contingencies currently support the subject's behavior? (3) What environmental changes, usually reinforcing stimuli, may be manipulated to alter the subject's behavior?—all imply a therapy focused on overt subject responses and stimuli that control these responses. Ample research findings have documented the reasons for many of the psychopath's typical response patterns: by manipulating these "reasons" or environmental contingencies supporting the psychopath's behavior, the alteration of this behavior seems, for the first time, to be highly likely.

This is not to say that the use of behavior modification techniques with psychopathic delinquents constitutes a panacea or has no limitations. Here, too, a majority of the techniques thus far developed can be applied best to neurotics with high degrees of anxiety. Although promising results have been obtained, there are too few large series of research findings to warrant, as yet, a definite conclusion about the value of this form of therapy. Many studies suffer from obvious methodological problems; i.e., small N, a lack of an objective pre- or post-evaluation, and other typical weaknesses inherent in anecdotal and/or descriptive case studies (for example, lack of randomized assignment and an adequate control group). But the possibilities for future research in this field seem almost unlimited. Directions for the immediate as well as far–reaching future include the use of intermittent rather than continuous reinforcement in the use of aversion therapies to reduce the frequency of relapse; the application of concepts not now used; and the development of new techniques. For the psychopath, these new techniques may take the direction of the use of environmental stimulation as possible reinforcement; forms of role playing and psychodrama may be used to increase through practice and reinforcement the emission of adaptive behaviors; the concept of the audience as a therapeutic device, rather than as ingroup of inmates opposed to guards or treatment staffs, where fellow inmates carry on the role of therapists by responding negatively to inappropriate behavior (Ullmann and Krasner, 1965); and work on changing attitudes or expectancies of the psychopath to facilitate other forms of treatment. Thus there are innumerable new and improving techniques of behavior modification which could be put to use in the treatment of the psychopathic delinquent. And these behavior modification techniques are as strong (or as weak) as the research and theories on which they rest.

REFERENCES

Adams, H. B. "Case utilizing sensory deprivation procedures," in L. Ullmann & L. Krasner (Eds.), *Case studies in behavior modification*. New York: Holt, Rinehart & Winston, 1965.

Albert, R. S., Brigante, T. R., and Chase, M. "The psychopathic personality: A content analysis of the concept." *J. of General Psychology*, 1959, *60*, 17–28.

Allen, H. E., Lindner, L., Goldman, H., and Dinitz, S. "The social and bio-medical correlates of sociopathy." *Criminologica*, 1969, *4*, 68–75.

Bandura, A. "Psychotherapy as a learning process." *Psychological Bulletin*, 1961, *58*, 143–159.

Bandura, A., & Walters, A. H. *Adolescent aggression*. New York: Ronald Press, 1959.

Bender, L. "Psychopathic personality disorders in childhood and adolescence." *Archives of Criminal Psychodynamics*, 1961, 4, 412–415.

Berlyne, D. E. *Conflict, arousal, and curiosity*, New York: McGraw-Hill, 1960.

Berman, S. "The formation of antisocial character disorders: A reconstruction of early life experiences." *Archives of Criminal Psychodynamics*, 1961, *4*, 198–199.

Bernard, J. L., & Eiseman, R. "Verbal conditioning in sociopaths with social and monetary reinforcement." *Journal of Personality and Social Psychology*, 1967, *6*, 203–206.

Bijou, S. W., & Baer, D. M. *Child development: I. A systematic and empirical theory*. New York: Appleton-Century-Crofts, 1961.

Bijou, S. W., & Baer, D. M. *Child development: II. Universal stage of infancy*. New York: Appleton-Century-Crofts, 1965.

Bixenstine, V. E. & Douglas, J. "Effect of psychopathology on group consensus and cooperative choice in a six-person game." *Journal of Personality and Social Psychology*, 1967, *5*, 32–37.

Breger, L., & McGaugh, J. L. "Critique and reformulation of 'learning-theory' approaches to psychotherapy and neurosis." *Psychological Bulletin*, 1965, *63*, 338–358.

Bromberg W. "The treatability of the psychopath." *American Journal of Psychiatry*, 1954, *110*, 604–608.

Bryon, J. H., & Kopche, R. "Psychopathy and verbal conditioning." *Journal of Abnormal Psychology*, 1967, *72*, 71–73.

Buchard, J. O., & Tyler, V. O. "Modification of delinquent behavior through operant conditioning." *Behavior Research and Therapy*, 1965, *2*, 245–250.

Buehler, R. E., Patterson, G. R., & Furniss, J. M. "The reinforcement of behavior in institutional settings." *Behavior Research and Therapy*, 1966, *4*, 157–167.

Cason, H. "The attitudes of the psychopath." *Journal of Clinical Psychology*, 1948, *4*, 276–281.

Cautela, J. "Covert sensitization." *Psychological Reports*, 1967, *20*, 459–468.

Cleckley, H. *The mask of sanity*. St. Louis: Mosby, 1955.

Cline, V. B., & Wangrow, A. S. "Life history correlates of delinquents and psychopaths." *Journal of Clinical Psychology*, 1959, *15*, 266–270.

Cooper, G. D., Adams, H. B., & Gibby, R. G. "Ego strength changes following perceptual deprivation." *Archives of General Psychiatry*, 1962, *7*, 213–217.

Craft, M. J., Stephenson, G., & Granger, C. "Controlled trial of authoritarian and self-government regimes with adolescent psychopaths." *American Journal of Orthopsychiatry*, 1964, *24*, 543–554.

Darling, H. F. "Electroshock treatment in psychopathic personality." *Journal of Nervous and Mental Disease*, 1945, *101*, 247.

Denenberg, V. H. "Interactive effects of infantile and adult shock levels upon learning." *Psychological Reports*, 1959, *5*, 351–364.

Dollard, J., & Miller, N. *Personality and psychotherapy*. New York: McGraw-Hill, 1950.

Ellingson, R. H. "The incidence of EEG abnormality among patients with mental disorders of apparently nonorganic origin: A critical review." *American Journal of Psychiatry*, 1954, *111*, 263–275.

Ellis, A. "Rational psychotherapy." *Journal of General Psychology*, 1958, *59*, 35–49.

Ellis, A. "The treatment of a psychopath with rational psychotherapy." *Journal of Psychology*, 1961, *51*, 141–150.

Estes, W. K. "An experimental study of punishment." *Psychological Monographs*, 1944, *57* (3), Whole No. 263.

Eysenck, H. J. *The dynamics of anxiety and hysteria*. London: Routledge and Kegan Paul, 1957.

Eysenck, H. J. *Experiments in behavior therapy*. New York: Macmillan, 1964.

Eysenck, H. J. "Note on criticisms of Mowrer/Eysenck conditioning theory of conscience." *British Journal of Psychology*, 1965, *56*, 307–309.

Eysenck, H. J. & Claridge, G. "Position of hysterics and dysthymics in a two dimension framework of personality description." *Journal of Abnormal and Social Psychology*, 1962, *64*, 465.

Eysenck, H. J., & Rachman, S. *Causes and cures of neurosis*. San Diego: Robert R. Knapp, 1965.

Ferster, C. B. "Reinforcement and punishment in the control of human behavior by social agencies." *Psychiatric Research Reports*, 1958, *10*, 101–118.

Fox, R., & Lippert, W. "Spontaneous GSR and anxiety level in sociopathic delinquents." *Journal of Consulting Psychology*, 1963, *27*, 368.

Fox, V. "Psychopathy as viewed by a clinical psychologist." *Archives of Criminal Psychodynamics*, 1961, *4*, 472–479.

Gewirtz, J., & Baer, D. "The effect of brief social deprivation on behaviors for a social reinforcer." *Journal of Abnormal and Social Psychology*, 1958, *56*, 49–56.

Gewirtz, M. "The intelligence factor in psychopathic personality." *Journal of Clinical Psychology*, 1947, *3*, 194–196.

Goodkin, R. "Some neglected issues in the literature on behavior therapy." *Psychological Reports*, 1967, *20*, 415–420.

Gordon, S. A. "Psychotherapeutic approach to adolescents with character disorders." *American Journal of Orthopsychiatry*, 1960, *30*, 757–766.

Gough, H. G. "A sociological theory of psychopathy. *American Journal of Sociology,* 1948, *53,* 359–366.

Grossman, H. "Behavior directed against others as prognostic indicator for three types of psychopathology." *Dissertation Abstracts,* 1967, *28* (3-B) 1194–1195.

Gynther, M. B. "Crime and psychopathology." *Journal of Abnormal and Social Psychology,* 1962, *64,* 378–380.

Hanson, G. W. "Behavior modification of appointment attendance among youthful offenders." *FCI Research Reports,* 1971, *3* (2).

Hare, R. D. "Acquisition and generalization of conditioned-fear response in psychopathic and non-psychopathic criminals." *Journal of Psychology,* 1965, *59,* 367–370. (a)

Hare, R. D. "Psychopathy, fear arousal, and anticipated pain." *Psychological Reports,* 1965, *16,* 499–502. (b)

Hare, R. D. "Temporal gradient of fear arousal in psychopaths." *Journal of Abnormal Psychology,* 1965, *70,* 442–445. (c)

Hare, R. D. "Psychopathy and choice of immediate vs. delayed punishment." *Journal of Abnormal Psychology,* 1966, *71,* 25–29.

Hare, R. D. *Psychopathy: Theory and research.* New York: John Wiley & Sons, 1970.

Henderson, D. K. *Psychopathic states.* New York: W. W. Norton & Company, 1939.

Hetherington, E. M., & Klinger, K. "Psychopathy and punishment." *Journal of Abnormal and Social Psychology,* 1964, *69,* 113–115.

Hetrick, W. R., Hess, K. "Some personality correlates of verbal conditioning." *Journal of Psychology,* 1962, *53,* 409–415.

Ingram, G. L., Gerard, R. E., Quay, H. C., & Levinson, R. B. "An experimental program for the psychopathic delinquent: Looking in the 'correctional wastebasket.'" *Journal of Research in Crime and Delinquency,* 1970 (Jan.), 24–30.

Jenkins, R. L. "Motivation and frustration in delinquency." *American Journal of Orthopsychiatry,* 1957, *17,* 528–537.

Jenkins, R. L., & Pacella, B. L. "Electroencephalographic studies of delinquent boys." *American Journal of Orthopsychiatry,* 1943, *113,* 107–120.

Johns, J., & Quay, H. C. "The effect of social reward on verbal conditioning in psychopathic and neurotic military offenders." *Journal of Consulting Psychology,* 1962, *25,* 217–220.

Karpman, B. "Conscience in the psychopath: Another version." *American Journal of Orthopsychiatry,* 1948, *18,* 455–525.

Krasner, L. "Studies of the conditioning of verbal behavior." *Psychological Bulletin,* 1958, *55,* 148–170.

Levinson, R. B., Ingram, G. I., & Azcarate, E. "Aversive group therapy; Sometimes good medicine tasted bad." *Crime and Delinquency,* 1968, *14,* 336–339.

Levy, D. "The deprived and the indulged forms of psychopathic personality." *American Journal of Orthopsychiatry,* 1951, *21,* 223–272.

Lindner, R. M. "The hypnoanalytic technique with prisoners." In R. M. Lindner and R. V. Seliger (Eds.), *Handbook of correction psychology.* New York: Philosophical Library, 1947.

Lippman, H. S. "Psychopathic reactions in children." *American Journal of Orthopsychiatry,* 1951, *21,* 223–272.

Lippman, H. S. "Antisocial acting out." *American Journal of Orthopsychiatry*, 1954, *24*, 667–696.

Luebeck, R. M. "Sensory adaptation in psychopathic and neurotic delinquents." *Dissertation Abstracts*, 1967, *28* (1-B), 351.

Lykken, D. T. "A study of anxiety in the sociopathic personality." *Journal of Abnormal and Social Psychology*, 1957, *55*, 6 –10.

Lykken, D. T. "Black cats, red herring, and horses of another color." *Psychological Reports*, 1966, *18*, 621–622.

Lyle, W. H. "The psychotherapeutic technique for the sociopathic offender." *Correctional Psychologist*, 1968b (July–August), 6–9.

Lyle, W. H. "The psychopathic offender: Issues in treatment." *Correctional Psychologist*, 1968a (March–April), 3–8.

Mandler, G. "The interruption of behavior." In D. Levine (Ed.), *Nebraska symposium of motivation: 1964*. Lincoln, Nebraska: University of Nebraska Press, 1964.

Massimo, J., & Shore, M. "The effectiveness of a comprehensive vocationally-oriented psychotherapy program for adolescent delinquent boys." *American Journal of Orthopsychiatry*, 1963, *33*, 634–642.

McCord, W., & McCord, J. *Psychopathy and delinquency*. New York: Grune & Stratton, 1956.

Millon, T. *Modern psychopathology*. Philadelphia: W. B. Saunders, 1969.

Mowrer, O. H. *Learning theory and personality dynamics*. New York: Ronald Press, 1950.

Mundy-Castle, A. C., & McKiever, B. L. "The psychophysiological significance of the galvanic skin response." *Journal of Experimental Psychology*, 1953, *46*, 15–24.

Murphy, I. C. "Serial learning, conditionability, and choice of independent measure of anxiety." *Journal of Abnormal and Social Psychology*, 1964, *69*, 614–619.

Nielson, J. M., & Thompson, G. N. *The engrammes of psychiatry*. Springfield: Charles Thomas, 1947.

Painting, D. N. "Performance of psychopathic individuals under conditions of positive and negative partial reinforcement." *Journal of Abnormal and Social Psychology*, 1961, *62*, 352–355.

Persons, R. W. "Psychotherapy with sociopathic offenders: An empirical evaluation." *Journal of Clinical Psychology*, 1965, *21*, 204–207.

Persons, R. W. "Psychological and behavioral change in delinquents following psychotherapy." *Journal of Clinical Psychology*, 1966, *22*, 337–340.

Persons, R. W., & Bruning, J. L. "Instrumental learning with sociopaths: A test of clinical theory." *Journal of Abnormal Psychology*, 1966, *71*, 165–168.

Persons, R. W., & Persons, C. E. "Some experimental support of psychopathic theory: A critique." *Psychological Reports*, 1965, *16*, 745–749.

Peterson, D. R., Quay, H. C., & Cameron, G. R. "Personality and background factors in juvenile delinquency as inferred from questionnaire responses." *Journal of Consulting Psychology*, 1959, *23*, 395–399.

Peterson, D. R., Quay, H. C., & Tiffany, T. L. "Personality factors related to juvenile delinquency." *Child Development*, 1961, *32*, 355–372.

Pierson, G. R., & Kelley, R. F. "Anxiety, extraversion,and personality idiosyncrasy in delinquency." *Journal of Psychology*, 1963, *65*, 441–445.

Prichard, J. C. *Treatise on insanity.* London: Gilbert & Piper, 1835.

Quay, H. C. "Dimensions of personality in delinquent boys as inferred from the factor analysis of case history data." *Child Development,* 1964, *35,* 379–484.

Quay, H. C. "Psychopathic personality as pathological stimulation-seeking." *American Journal of Psychiatry,* 1965, *122,* 180–183.

Quay, H. C., & Hunt, W. A. "Psychopathy, neuroticism, and verbal conditioning: A replication and extension." *Journal of Consulting Psychology,* 1965, *29,* 283.

Quay, H. C., Peterson, D. R. & Consalvi, C. "The interpretation of three personality factors in juvenile delinquency." *Journal of Consulting Psychology,* 1960, *24,* 555.

Rabinovitch, R. "The concept of primary psychogenic acathexis." *American Journal of Orthopsychiatry.* 1951, *21,* 223–272.

Rachman, S. "Learning theory and child psychology: Therapeutic possibilities." *Psychological Reports,* 1963, *3,* 149–163.

Raymond, M. J. "The treatment of addiction in aversion conditioning with apomorphine." *Behavior Research and Therapy,* 1964, *1,* 287–291.

Rickard, H. C., & Dinoff, M. "Shaping adaptive behavior in a therapeutic summer camp." In L. P. Ullmann & L. Krasner (Eds.). *Case Studies in behavior modification.* New York: Holt, Rinehart & Winston, 1965.

Ricks, D., Umborges, C., & Mack, R. "Measures of increased temporal perspectives in successively treated adolescent delinquent boys." *Journal of Abnormal and Social Psychology,* 1964, *69,* 685–689.

Rosenberg, S. "The relationship of certain personality factors to prognosis in psychotherapy." *Journal of Clinical Psychology,* 1954, *10,* 341–345.

Schachter, S., & Latane, B. "Crime, cognition, and the autonomic nervous system." In D. Levine (Ed.), *Nebraska symposium on motivation: 1964.* Lincoln, Nebraska: University of Nebraska Press, 1964.

Schmideberg, M. "Psychotherapy of the criminal Psychopath." *Archives of Criminal Psychodynamics,* 1961, *4,* 724–735.

Schwitzgebel, R. L. "Short-term operant conditioning of adolescent offenders on socially relevant variables." *Journal of Abnormal Psychology,* 1967, *2,* 134–142.

Schwitzgebel, R., & Kolb, D. A. "Inducing behavior change in adolescent delinquents." *Behavior Research and Therapy,* 1964, *1,* 297–304.

Siegman, A. W. "Personality variables associated with admitted criminal behavior." *Journal of Consulting Psychology,* 1962, *26,* 199.

Stampfl, T. G., & Levis, D. J. "Essentials of implosive therapy: A learning-theory-based psychodynamic behavioral therapy." *Journal of Abnormal Psychology,* 1967, *72,* 496–503.

Stumphauzer, J. S. "Behavior modification with juvenile delinquents: A critical review." *FCI Technical and Treatment Notes,* 1970, *1* (2).

Thompson, G. "Psychopathy." *Archives of Criminal Psychodynamics,* 1961, *4,* 736–747.

Tyler, V. O., Jr. "Application of operant token reinforcement to academic performance of an institutionalized delinquent." *Psychological Reports,* 1967, *21,* 249–260.

Tyler, V. O., & Brown, G. D. "The use of swift brief isolation as a group control device for institutionalized delinquent." *Behavior Research and Therapy,* 1967, *5,* 1–9.

Ullmann, L. P., & Krasner, L. *Case studies in behavior modification.* New York: Holt, Rinehart & Winston, 1965.

Van Tassel, E. "Taking the role of the other in psychopathy." *Dissertation Abstracts,* 1966, *27* (3-B), 974.

Vietor, W. P. "Conditioning as a form of psychotherapy in treating delinquents: Some data from the literature." *Excerta Criminologica,* 1967, *7* (7), 3-6.

Vogel-Spritt, M. D. "Response generalization under verbal conditioning in alcoholics, delinquents and students." *Behavior Research and Therapy,* 1964, *2,* 135–141.

Walton, D. "The interaction effects of drive, reactive and conditioned inhibitions, their application to the remedial treatment of the adolescent psychopath." *Behavior Research and Therapy,* 1963, *1,* 35–43.

Warren, A. B., & Grant, D. A. "Relation of conditioned discrimination to the MMpi, Pd personality variable." *Journal of Experimental Psychology,* 1955, *49,* 23–27.

Weitzman, B. "Behavior therapy and psychotherapy." *Psychological Review,* 1967, *74,* 300–317.

Welch, L., & Hayes, R. F. "Elements of conditioning in normal and pathological human behavior." *Journal of Genetic Psychology,* 1957, *91,* 263–293.

Wetzel, R. "Use of behavioral techniques in a case of compulsive stealing." *Journal of Consulting Psychology,* 1966, *30,* 367–374.

White, R. W. *The abnormal personality.* New York: Ronald Press, 1964.

Williams, C. D. "The elimination of tantrum behavior by extinction procedures." *Journal of Abnormal and Social Psychology,* 1959, *59,* 269.

Wolf, M. M., Risely, T., & Mees, H. L. "Application of operant conditioning procedures to the behavior problems of an autistic child." *Behavior Research and Therapy,* 1964, *1,* 305–312.

Wolpe, J. *Psychotherapy by reciprocal inhibition.* Stanford, California: Stanford University Press, 1958.

Wolpe, J. "The Systematic desensitization treatment of neuroses." *J. of Nervous & Mental Disease,* 1961, *132,* 189–203.

31

Treatment of a Homosexual Pedophiliac Using In Vivo Desensitization: A Case Study

Robert J. Kohlenberg

Reprinted by permission from *Journal of Abnormal Psychology* 83 (1974): 192–95. Copyright 1974 by the American Psychological Association. Author permission to reprint is gratefully acknowledged.

An adult male who was sexually attracted to male children was treated with in vivo desensitization. The in vivo desensitization involved a sexual counseling program modeled after that of Masters and Johnson and resulted in decreased attraction to male children and increased attraction to adult males.

Behavior therapists have used two principal approaches in the treatment of sexual problems associated with the choice of sexual objects. The first approach involves building in an avoidance response to the inappropriate sexual stimulus. The second approach is based on the notion that appropriate sexual stimuli are aversive to the patient and are hence avoided. The second approach thus involves increasing approach behavior to the appropriate stimulus by using desensitization (Wolpe, 1958). Masters and Johnson (1970) have developed an extensive sexual counseling program which corresponds to the desensitization approach. The Masters and Johnson program is oriented toward increasing approach behavior and hence reducing the aversive properties of the sexual interaction. The essential components of this treatment plan include (a) a history-taking and feedback session in which the patient is given an explanation for his or her current sexual behavior, (b) a graded sequence or hierarchy of instructed sexual interactions that range from touching to intercourse (this sequence of directed interactions is prescribed by the therapist, and the couple practices these assignments at home), and (c) a progression through the sequence of directed interactions at a rate that results in minimal anxiety and discomfort. An important feature of the Masters and Johnson program is that the hierarchy is presented in vivo, that is, the patient actually engages in the behavior specified in the hierarchy. This in vivo approach necessitates the involvement of a sexual partner, and hence the Masters and Johnson treatment always involves a couple.

The sexual treatment program described above has been used with a wide variety of male and female sexual problems such as orgasmic dysfunction, premature ejaculation, impotency, etc. Although Masters and Johnson limit their program to male–female couples, it would seem that certain homosexual problems could be treated in a similar manner. That is, from a learning viewpoint, the nature of the sexual response is the same for all people and techniques that apply to the treatment of heterosexual problems would also apply to homosexual problems.

The present paper is about a male homosexual who stated he was unable to become sexually aroused with adult males or females but was sexually attracted to male children. At the patient's request, a therapy program was instituted to bring about increased sexual responsiveness to adult males. Adult males were chosen as the positive goal sex object because the patient's social contacts were homosexual, and heterosexual sex was not one of the therapeutic goals requested by the patient.

METHOD AND PROCEDURE

SUBJECT

The patient, Mr. M., was 34 years old and had been arrested twice for child molesting. The first arrest occurred eight years ago, and the second occurred three years ago. The patient considered his sexual orientation to be homosexual, but he became aroused only with young males of about 6–12 years of age. He claimed that he "prowled" or actively looked for sexual contacts with male children about twice each week by going to the playground or swimming pool where he would be likely to see children. Mr. M. reported that this "prowling" or active looking did not currently result in sexual contacts but did result in both sexual arousal and subsequent discomfort and stress. Another troublesome behavior for Mr. M. was what he referred to as "thinking about children," which occurred about two times per day. These "thoughts" were centered on male children who were sexually attractive to him. Fantasies during masturbation were also centered on male children and masturbation occurred several times a week.

Mr. M. stated that his desire for children was immoral and had ruined his life. He had sought treatment twice before and received three years of individual and one year of group therapy. Mr. M. felt this therapy had given him some understanding of his behavior but had not led to any changes in his desire for young males.

DATA COLLECTION

There were three dependent variables in this study. The first variable was the number of thoughts that were centered on young males. The second variable was the number of prowling incidents, and the third was the number of sexual encounters with adults who were sexually arousing. Mr. M. was instructed to keep a daily record of the occurrences and circumstances of these events. These daily records were to be turned in at the weekly therapy sessions, or if no session was scheduled the records were to be mailed in each week. The return and keeping of these records was required as a condition for treatment and for rebate of approximately one half of the fees charged. The patient paid a $20 fee for each treatment session and received a $5 rebate for each weekly report turned in. The total amount of rebated monies was to be paid at the completion of the six-month follow-up period.

THERAPY PLAN

Since Mr. M.'s attraction to children was a problem that could lead to harm and trauma to another person and serious legal consequences for Mr. M., the initial phase of treatment was directed at reducing the sexual arousal value of children by pairing imagined stimuli with electric shock.

The second phase of treatment was to be directed at increasing the arousal elicited by male adults and reducing apprehension and tension associated with sexual contacts involving adults. The second phase was to be accomplished by using a treatment plan modeled after Masters and Johnson.

BASELINE PERIOD

The first four weeks involved weekly interview sessions during which Mr. M.'s history was obtained and a treatment plan was developed. This phase also provided an opportunity to obtain pretreatment measures of sexual activities as discussed above. The rates of "thoughts," "prowling," and "adult" events are given in Figure 31.1. The first two weeks resulted in the lowest rate of prowling for this phase; the rate then increased during the last two weeks. Mr. M. indicated that the rate of prowling events during the last two weeks was more typical of his behavior. There were no sexual contacts with an adult male during this phase.

PHASE I: AVERSIVE CONDITIONING

Weeks five through eight involved the pairing of arousing stimuli with electric shock. The shock source was a Lehigh Valley 551-12 finger shocker. Shock intensity was set at a level judged to be painful to Mr. M. Shock duration was less than a second and consisted of a momentary depression of the operate button.

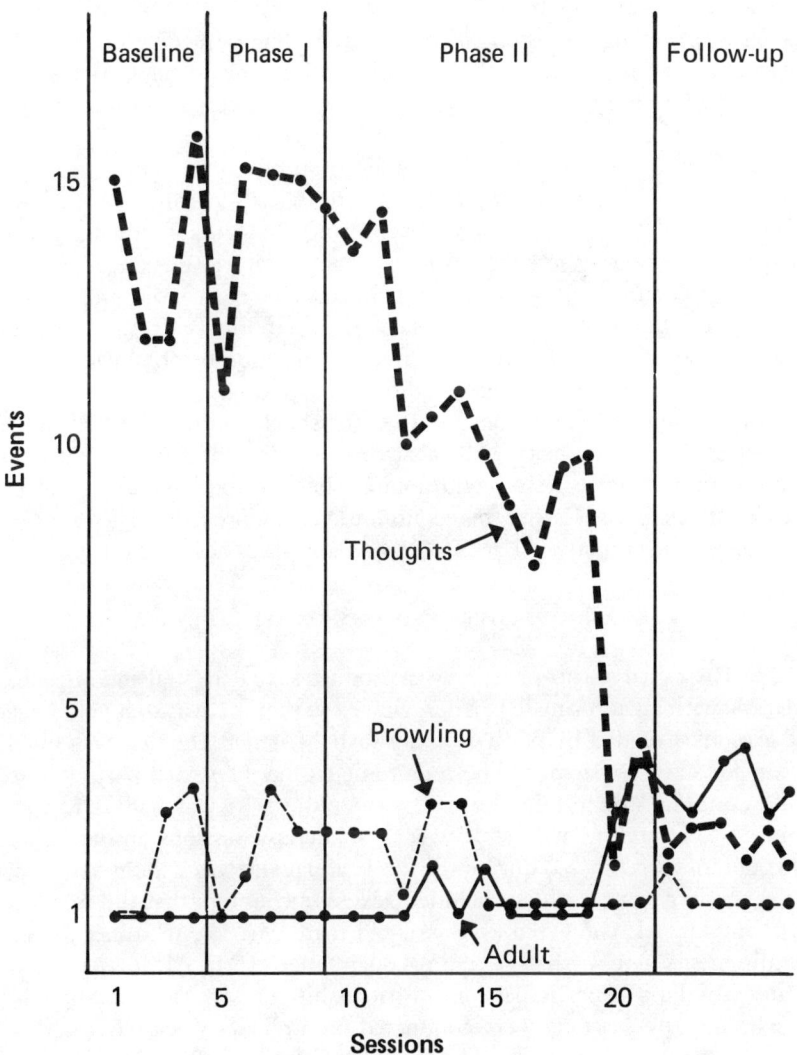

FIGURE 31.1.

Note: The number of "thoughts" and "prowling" incidents concerning children and "adult contacts" for three treatment phases and follow-up. The follow-up data are means for each of the six months following treatment.

The first session of this phase involved pairing the shock with imagined scenes of prowling and thoughts of children. The sequence was as follows: instructions were given by the therapist to imagine a scene; Mr. M. then signaled when the image was vivid; shock was delivered. Eleven such pairings occurred during the first session of aversive conditioning.

The second session involved six more pairings of imagined scenes and shock. Mr. M. reported that the previous week's pairings seemed to be effective, and the number of events during the week following the first aversive conditioning session was lower than previous values.

The procedures for the third and fourth aversive conditioning sessions were similar to the previous sessions. As shown in Figure 31.1, the shock did not, however, appear to have an effect on the number of incidents. The apparent failure of the aversive conditioning could have been due to both an insufficient number of pairings between the shock and imagined stimuli and inadequate shock intensity. Thus, at this point in the treatment program, continuation of the aversive conditioning phase would have necessitated increased shock levels. Rather than continue aversive procedure, it was decided to proceed with the in vivo desensitization approach described below.

PHASE 2: MASTERS AND JOHNSON TYPE THERAPY

The basic goal of this phase was to produce sexual arousal and orgasms for Mr. M. with an adult male partner. Since the therapy was to involve a series of sessions attended by Mr. M. and a sexual partner, the first task involved finding a suitable partner. The requirements for the sexual partner were as follows: (a) he was to be at least 30 years old; (b) he was willing to commit himself to attending at least 10 weeks of therapy sessions and at least two encounters with Mr. M. during the week; and (c) he was willing to follow the therapeutic regimen which included sexual encounters that did not lead to orgasm. Mr. M. contacted a 32-year-old man, Mr. C., who met the above requirements. Mr. C. had been an acquaintance of Mr. M. for several years and was willing to participate out of friendship for Mr. M.

The therapy sessions were conducted on a once a week basis with both Mr. M. and Mr. C. present. The therapist was the author. The first session of this phase included a discussion of learning principles as related to choice of sexual object. Instructions were given for Mr. M. and Mr. C. to engage in at least two encounters during the week. These first encounters were to take place with both men in bed without clothes. As described in Masters and Johnson for heterosexual couples, they were instructed to take turns giving each other sensate pleasure. Touching, caressing, etc., of any kind was permissible, but there was to be no touching of the genital or anal area and sexual arousal was not a goal.

During the second treatment session of this phase, Mr. M. reported that he was very tense and perspired profusely during the previous week's encounters with Mr. C. Mr. C. found the encounters pleasant and arousing.

According to Masters and Johnson, a primary source of inhibition to sexual arousal is that of performance anxiety wherein the patient acts as an "observer" of his own sexual behavior. In the present case, Mr. M. seemed to have been concerned about his performance during the previous week's encounters and was also concerned about Mr. C.'s negative evaluation of his own (Mr. M.'s) lack of sexual arousal. The importance of eliminating the observer role and its inhibitory effects was emphasized to Mr. M. and Mr. C. Mr. C. reassured Mr. M. that it was okay with him if Mr. M. did not become sexually aroused. A restatement of the goals for the coming week's encounter was made. The goal was to become relaxed and have pleasant feelings; sexual arousal was not a goal.

The second week of encounters was reported to be relaxing and pleasant by Mr. M. Mr. M., incidentally, reported that he also became sexually aroused.

The following steps were taken during the remainder of the program. Instructions to proceed to the next step were given only after the patient was completely relaxed at the preceding item: (a) touching for sensate pleasure, no genital involvement; (b) touching for sensate pleasure, some exploratory touching of genital area; (c) simultaneous genital touching, orgasm not permitted; (d) simultaneous genital touching and belly rubbing with genital contact, orgasm not permitted; (e) no restrictions, orgasm permitted.

The last step of treatment was reached during the thirteenth week of Phase 2. Mr. M. was seen six months later for a follow-up interview, at which time he turned in daily reports covering some of the previous six months' behavior.

RESULTS

The primary result of treatment was that Mr. M. became sexually aroused with Mr. C. as a partner. Reports of fantasy during masturbation also indicated that Mr. M.'s sexual object was becoming older. Mr. M. also reported that he found other adult men attractive and had sexual contacts with adults (other than Mr. C.) that were sexually arousing. Figure 31.1. also shows that the number of incidents involving children decreased as Mr. M. progressed through treatment and for the six-month period following termination.

Mr. M. reported that he had become less preoccupied and attracted to children. He ceased "prowling" for children after the sixth week of Phase 2 treatment, and at the six-month follow-up he reported that he had not actively sought any sexual contact with children since the termination of treatment.

DISCUSSION

This case seems to indicate that the acquisition of new, appropriate sexual behavior was effective in reducing child–related sexual behavior. The lack of effect of the aversive stimulus may have been due to several different factors including a lack of generalization, insufficient shock intensity, and an insufficient number of aversive conditioning trials. The difficulty of generalization is that the office situation with finger electrodes applied and imagined stimuli is no doubt highly discriminable from actually seeing a child at a playground in the natural environment.

It is not completely clear as to why the increase in attraction to adults would reduce attraction to children. Increasing the amount of appropriate sexual behavior toward adult males probably resulted in a repertoire of behavior that was incompatible with "prowling" for children. That is, those periods of times that normally would have been spent seeking contacts with children were now spent making contacts with adult males. The number of "thoughts" concerning children decreased as the amount of experience increased with the adult males. This could be accounted for by the respondent conditioning model in which successful sexual experience with adults produced pairings between adult males and sexual arousal (including orgasm). After a number of such pairings, adult males served as conditioned stimuli for sexual arousal; and thoughts that elicited sexual arousal were similarly changed.

It would also seem reasonable to suggest that in addition to the sexual attractiveness of children, there were also some aversive properties associated with children. In fact, Mr. M. sought treatment because of the aversiveness associated with his sexual desire for children. The effect of treatment, then, could have provided Mr. M. with the choice between children associated with approach-avoidance characteristics, and adults associated primarily with approach properties. The reduced rate of child-related sexual activities would thus reflect that Mr. M. selected the least aversive of the two types of sexual objects.

The results of this case also indicate that an in vivo treatment similar to Masters and Johnson type of treatment for heterosexual dysfunction can be used for homosexual dysfunction problems and holds promise as an effective means of changing sex object choice.

REFERENCES

Masters, W. and Johnson, V. *Human sexual inadequacy*. Boston: Little, Brown, 1970.
Wolpe, J. *Psychotherapy by reciprocal inhibition*. Stanford, Calif.: Stanford University Press, 1958.

32

Rational Behavior Training for Alcoholic Offenders

Steven G. Cox, Ph.D.

A paper presented at the 1976 APGA Convention, in Dallas, Texas, by Steven G. Cox, Ph.D., Associate Professor of Criminal Justice, Illinois State University

Many helping techniques have been applied with repeat offenders with varying amounts of success. A number of individuals seem to respond well while they are involved with the counseling strategy associated with the particular correctional setting. However, once the offenders terminate their affiliation with the correctional agency, it appears that very little carryover exists concerning their functioning productively in society. Evidence of this is the high rate of recidivism. It appears a counseling strategy which will allow offenders to understand and perceive, in a positive manner, the personal benefits of accomplishing long-range goals as opposed to the oftentimes negative aspects of immediate gratification would be most beneficial in helping to reduce the high recidivism rate. In addition, this strategy also needs to teach offenders those skills which help individuals make rational decisions which have practical implications for living within societal norms.

A method incorporating both these goals which was used with male alcoholic offenders at the Federal Correctional Institution at Lexington, Kentucky, is Rational Behavior Training structured by Maxie C. Maultsby, Jr., M.D., and based on the theoretical concepts of Albert Ellis' Rational-Emotive Therapy (Goodman & Maultsby, 1974). This counseling strategy, in the words of Dr. Maultsby, "is a highly directive method of teaching people how to increase their skill in reasoning so they will be better able to deal with the problems and stresses of daily living" (Goodman & Maultsby, 1974). To understand this strategy, one must first understand the definition of "rational thinking" as it is used in conjunction with the counseling theory. Rational thinking is defined as thinking or acting which (a) is based on objective facts, (b) is life-preserving, (c) helps a person achieve his or her self-defined goals, (d) enables a person to function with a minimum of significant internal conflict, and (e) enables a person to function with a minimum of significant conflict with his or her environment (Goodman & Maultsby,

1974). These comprise the five basic criteria for rational thinking. In this definition, *significant* means the degree of conflict that one is unwilling to accept or which proves to be objectively counterproductive (Goodman & Maultsby, 1974).

Rational Behavior Training has as its primary goal the teaching of the skills involved in rational thinking. In addition to the primary goal, RBT incorporates several other important secondary goals for its users: (1) maximum independence from neurotic needs, desires and support of others—including the helping person, (2) acceptance by the individual of full responsibility for achieving his or her desired behavior changes, (3) self-determination of goals and values in life, (4) freeing the person from poorly controlled reactions to environmental stresses, and (5) unqualified acceptance by each person of his unavoidable fallibility (Goodman & Maultsby, 1974).

Rational Behavior Training also follows the premise that an individual's brain controls emotional and physical behavior. The brain is directed by the individual's thoughts and beliefs about what he or she sees, hears and physically feels. In this manner, the individual controls both emotional feelings and physical behavior. In following this premise and its consequent subtenets, three basic insights to rational behavior are revealed. (1) What is rational behavior for one individual may not be rational behavior for another. (2) What is rational behavior for an individual at one time may not be rational for him or her for another time. (3) In each different situation, it's the individual's responsibility to decide for him or herself what seems to be the most rational manner of functioning (Goodman & Maultsby, 1974).

This was the counseling strategy chosen to be used with the residents of the Alcohol Rehabilitation Unit at the Federal Correctional Institution in Lexington, Kentucky. This unit consisted of 80 male alcoholic felons who had requested to join the Alcohol Rehabilitation Unit at FCI, Lexington, Kentucky, either by applying for admission and subsequently being recommended by institution staff of the federal institution in which they resided or by having their attorney petition the courts requesting they be allowed to fulfill their sentence at Lexington. The residents ranged in age from 21 to 62 and the race was overwhelmingly Caucasian. The average of the group was 39. All residents had had a history of criminal behavior and of heavy abuse of alcohol. None were first-time offenders and all had been incarcerated for at least one offense in a state or federal prison prior to their present offense.

Rational Behavior Training was adopted for use with the residents of the alcohol rehabilitation unit because its tenets could be understood and fairly quickly grasped cognitively by the residents. The residents readily understood that their behavior certainly did not help them achieve their goals since most of them had not started out with the goal of becoming a resident of an alcohol rehabilitation unit in a federal prison. They also readily understood that their excessive drinking and consequent criminal behavior were not "life-preserving," did not lend to their "functioning with a minimum of significant internal conflict," and most certainly were not conducive to functioning with a "minimum of significant environmental conflict." The only area which seemed difficult for the residents to adopt was that of basing their thinking on objective facts. The problem was not one of resistance to the idea but one of misperception. These residents, like many other individuals, found it difficult to base their perceptions of things and situations on objective reality. They therefore continued to respond in robot fashion to situations because (1) "They were taught to react that way by their parents and society," (2) "They have never used an effective method for stopping those reactions," and (3) "They believe that they can't stop them" (Maultsby, 1974a). With these particular residents, work began on helping them correct their misperceptions so they would be better able to base their thinking on objective reality. This was a necessity if these individuals were ever going to have a chance at ultimately exhibiting rational behavior based on rational thinking.

TECHNIQUES

The principle rational counseling methods utilized in this counseling program with these residents in helping them develop more rational thinking patterns consisted of the five following techniques.

1. *Teaching each resident the consequent goals of learning the skills involved in rational thinking in terms of what the accomplishment of these goals could mean to an individual once he has changed his thinking and behavior patterns.* (These goals were discussed earlier.) This process was accomplished by group discussion and lecture. The material was given out in handout form and then discussed by the residents with a trained correctional counselor in small group sessions. These materials were presented to the residents as attainable goals which they could achieve through learning to think and behave rationally. The residents were told that at this early stage of their contact with RB they need only learn and understand these goals and that they consider them as behaviors they might want to attain in the future. By approaching these goals and consequent behaviors in this manner, no pressure was placed on any resident to change his behavior automatically. The cognitive seeds had been planted, however, and the residents now had the opportunity to nurture and feed these seeds if they so desired.

2. *Teaching each resident the five basic criteria for rational thinking.* These criteria were introduced earlier. *Criteria for Thinking and Behaving Rationally* (Rational Behavior = Behaving in My Own Best Interest) Would my feeling or acting this way be:

1. Thinking objectively about the actual facts and considering real probabilities?
2. Life-preserving?
3. Likely to get me what I want? (Long-term goal producing)
4. Likely to let me feel the way I want to feel?
5. Likely to keep me out of trouble? (Maultsby, 1974b)

As with the goals discussed in number one above, these criteria were given to each resident in handout form and discussed in small groups with a correctional counselor. The residents were asked to accept these criteria, as they had the goals, on a cognitive basis. The counselors then went a step further. They asked the residents to begin evaluating their present behavior or potential behavior in terms of meeting these criteria. Thus, residents began to think about their behavior and even to make some minimal changes. Reinforcement for utilizing these criteria for positive behavior change was given in the groups or individually by the staff. No positive behavior change was too small to receive reinforcement and no behavior change of this type was treated minimally. For example, if an individual who usually stayed inebriated most of the time by clandestinely making "homebrew" or "jack" or by consuming the alcohol in cans of hair spray or alcohol from other sources stayed sober for one day, he was given reinforcement for his behavior and it was discussed with him how his behavior related to the five criteria for rational behavior.

3. *Teaching each resident the anatomy of an emotion.* This, again, was taught through handouts and group and individual discussion. The anatomy of an emotion was separated into five identifiable stages. First an individual perceives a situation through one or more of the five senses (seeing, hearing, touching, smelling, tasting). The individual then cognitatively describes the situation to himself, a process which is called self-talk. The third stage consists of pushing the description of the situation through the individual's belief system which is composed of attitudes, beliefs, habits and values. Next the individual chooses an emotion appropriate to his description of the situation. Finally the individual arrives at the consequent feelings and behavior based upon the emotion he has chosen (Maultsby, 1974a).

It was important for residents to understand the anatomy of an emotion so they could learn to base their perceptions and beliefs on objective reality (testable facts) and, therefore, choose and control emotions which were appropriate to situations. As the residents developed a cognitive understanding of this concept, they could incorporate it with the first two cognitive learning experiences. The residents were also taught the idea that individuals evaluate all perceived situations through thoughts which are relatively positive, relatively negative, relatively neutral, or some mixture of those three (Maultsby,

1964a). Residents thus could be asked to begin evaluating their own thoughts about their perceptions on the basis of these four criteria. This would allow them to gain insight and understanding about the emotions they were having.

4. *Teaching each resident the understanding and utilization of the Rational Self-Analysis* (Maultsby, 1971). The rational self-analysis (RSA) is made up of six parts each based on one of the three parts of an emotion previously discussed. The RSA format is as follows (Maultsby, 1974a):

Section A	*Section Da*
Facts and Events	Camera Check of Section A
(Perception)	
Section B	*Section Db*
Self-Talk	Rational Debate of Section B
(Evaluation thoughts)	
Section C	*Section E*
Emotional Consequences of	Emotional Goal of future
Section B	Section A
(Emotive Responses of feeling)	(More rational feeling about
	Section A)

Section A consisted of a resident writing down the facts of the event or situation that occurred and about which he upset himself. This section was to state only the objective facts completely devoid of any subjective or artibrary value judgments. In order to have a check of this section, the resident was told to reread his section as if he were actually recording the situation with a movie camera which, of course, would be recording the resident's situation without any value judgments. If his camera check was free of value judgments, the resident was to write "Section A is fact" in Section Da. If the camera check revealed that value judgments had been recorded, the resident was to write Section A over and go through the same camera check again. He continued to go through the process until he could record that Section A was indeed factual description.

The resident was asked to write down his thoughts about the event or situation in Section B of the RSA. Here the resident stated clearly the self-talk he had used to describe the situation to himself especially including any subjective value judgments and ideas which were a source of the negative emotions and undesired behavior he was exhibiting about the situation. The resident then challenged each of the statements in Section B by writing his challenges in Section Db. For example, a resident might write down in Section B, "If John hadn't made me take that first drink, I wouldn't have gotten drunk and been arrested." He could challenge that statement by writing in Section Db, "John didn't hold me down and force that drink down my throat. I picked up the glass, put it to my lips, and swallowed the alcohol on my own. I also picked up and swallowed the liquor in all of the other drinks that were placed in front of me. After drinking those drinks, I became drunk. I got loud and began to fight. The bartender called the police to stop the fight and I was arrested for breaking the law." The resident could even go into more detail with the challenges if he so desired. If the statement written in Section B was actual fact, then the resident wrote "fact" beside the statement in Section Db.

In Section C the resident was asked to write down the emotional label which accurately described the emotional response to the particular situation. This section assisted the resident in distinguishing between feelings and thoughts. For example, if the resident just discussed above had written in Section C, "I took those drinks because I felt I was cornered and the situation was hopeless," he would not be recording an emotional response but a thought about the situation. His statement would actually be better recorded in Section B, especially after the communication was made more accurate by changing the word "felt" to "thought." His accurate emotional response to be recorded in Section C might have been "I felt bad about it." Or the resident might just simply record one-word emotional responses such as "angry," "depressed," etc., in Section C.

The resident wrote in Section E a more appropriate, rational emotional response which he could have used and which he would concentrate on using the next time he found himself in a similar situation.

The five criteria for rational thinking were always written at the bottom of the RSA.

The Five Criteria for Rational Thinking
1. Based on objective reality
2. Protects my life
3. Gets me my goals
4. Eliminates significant emotional conflicts
5. Keeps me out of trouble with others

This enabled the resident to chose more rational emotional responses for Section E, helped the resident to evaluate the appropriateness of his emotional responses in Section C, and aided the resident in comparing his self-talk statements in Section B to the criteria in order to help him with his challenges to the Section B statements.

The RSA is the method which draws together all the other didactic, cognitive learnings of the first three techniques and allows them to be taken out of the cognitive realm and used in a practical manner to help individuals analyze their feelings and evaluate the appropriateness of their behavior. Once the residents on the unit used the RSA techniques for a period of time, they were able to understand their problems better, gain insights into practical, more rational ways to react to situations, perceive and think about situations objectively, control their emotional responses, and chose the appropriate behavior for which the situation called.

5. *Teaching each resident the use of imagery in rational self-conditioning.* This technique actually involved two forms of imagination utilization. The first, Rational Emotive Imagery, involved the individual doing repeated RSAs covering the problem-eliciting behavior (Goodman & Maultsby, 1974). While doing them, he was to determine his self-talk and to challenge thoroughly the irrational statements. After doing several RSAs, the resident was instructed to imagine himself in a situation which led to problem behavior such as becoming intoxicated. He was then instructed to picture himself in the same situation but this time behaving in the way he would like to behave (refusing the drink offered to him or walking by the bar without going in). While doing this imagery, he was to simultaneously review repeatedly the rational challenges he had written in his RSAs. The resident was asked to do this type of imagery for 10 minutes a day at the same time each day.

The second type of imagery which was utilized with the residents is called auto-aversive imagery (Goodman and Maultsby, 1974). Here the resident was instructed to pair an especially noxious image with the desired object, alcohol. He was asked to picture vomit floating in a drink. He then was instructed to picture himself consuming this drink. The resident was also asked to perform this task 10 minutes a day at the same time each day. Unless he was overweight, the resident was told to do this type of imagery at a time other than when meals were served.

It would be best, of course, to have been able to have the resident actually experience some of his imaginings concerning the consumption of alcohol. However, this was not possible inside the institution; therefore, only the use and practice of these two types of imagery was performed. It was hoped that the residents would learn a technique, which like the RSA, could be used once he left the institution.

The five techniques which have been described made up the basic program of Rational Self-Counseling used with the male alcoholic offenders at the federal prison in Lexington, Kentucky. The task of teaching and using these techniques was carried out primarily in two or three small group sessions per week. These group sessions were led by a correctional counselor and formal individual reinforcement was given each group member at least twice a week during individual counseling sessions with the correctional counselor.

EVALUATION

To evaluate the effectiveness of the counseling program, two areas of the residents' behavior change were examined; behavior change while residing in the institution and behavior change after leaving the institution on parole. Those residents who were released by accomplishing their mandatory release date were not followed up because of the difficulty of maintaining contact once the residents left the institution. Since the majority of residents were released from custody on parole status, the number leaving by mandatory release was quite small and their effect was negligible as far as obtaining program evaluation data.

The most obvious means of evaluating overall behavior change within the institution was to determine whether or not there had been an increase of positive rational behavior. This was done by keeping careful records of the number of discipline reports received by the residents when they were on the unit or in some other part of the institution. Two months prior to instituting this rational behavior counseling program the residents of the alcohol rehabilitation unit were receiving an average of 26 discipline reports a month. After having the counseling program, the number of discipline reports steadily declined until the number of discipline reports reached six during the third month of programming. The average number of discipline reports per month leveled off and fluctuated between six and eight per month. It should be noted here that the vast majority of discipline reports after the average was reached were received by new residents who had not been exposed to the program or who had only had initial contact with it.

It was found during the first six months of the following data collection that of fifteen residents released on parole who had completed the program, only two had had problems severe enough to have their parole revoked. All of the thirteen individuals who were still functioning normally six months after release had been incarcerated in federal institutions prior to their present incarceration and six of these people had previously had their parole revoked within two months after their release from incarceration.

REFERENCES

Goodman, D. S., & Maultsby, M. C. *Emotional well-being through rational behavior training*. Springfield, Illinois: Charles C. Thomas, 1974.

Maultsby, M. C. *Handbook of rational self-counseling*. Madison, Wisconsin: The Association for Rational Thinking, 1971.

Maultsby, M. C. *More personal happiness through rational self-counseling*. New York: Institute for Rational Living, 1974a.

Maultsby, M. C. *You and your emotions*. Lexington, Kentucky: Psychiatry Out-Patient Clinic, University of Kentucky Medical Center, 1974b.

Part Eight

Rehabilitation and Modification—Juvenile Offenders

The establishment of the first juvenile court in Cook County, Illinois, in 1899, was in all probability also the inauguration of juvenile offender re-habilitation in this country. This becomes evident when one is cognizant of the title of the law which established this court: "An Act to Regulate the Treatment and Control of Dependent, Neglected and Delinquent Children" (Johnson, 1975, p. 3). Even though this act utilized "treatment" in its title, it did not stipulate that treatment was to be used in place of punishment. It merely established the proviso that the court was to function as a surrogate parent and furnish the child with the "care," "custody," and "discipline" which the parents should have given him (Johnson, 1975). However, this in itself can be viewed as rehabilitative in nature, since it was an attempt to supply some direction for the child who was perceived as not receiving such direction in the home.

The problem that exists today is that little progress toward establishing rehabilitative programs for our juvenile offenders has resulted as an out-growth of the original intent of the law which established the first juvenile court. To verify this, one needs merely to scrutinize the continuous examples of the miscarriages of juvenile justice presented in the report by the National Council of Jewish Women entitled *Children Without Justice* (Wakis, 1975). This report vividly illustrates documented case upon case of the mistreat-ment of children who come in contact with our juvenile justice system. It is a graphic exposé illustrating the onerous attitude which has been historically rooted in juvenile justice and which is still adhered to tenaciously by many who are concerned with our neglected, misguided, mismanaged, and some-times recalcitrant youth. However, change is inevitable, and this report does conclude on a note of optimism when it indicates that change is beginning to take place in the form of a "new accountability" that is being "forced" upon the system. With this new accountability come searching questions concern-ing juvenile crime deterence, rehabilitation of juvenile offenders, and public protection (Wakis, 1975).

It is with the public mandate for accountability that we can see the need for sound, workable, and productive juvenile offender behavior change pro-grams. Not only is this demand for accountability appearing in reports such as the one discussed, but this injunction is also permeating much of the professional and popular literature on the subject of juvenile offenders. Per-haps at no time in the history of our country have we had a better opportu-nity to help children who have had negative experiences with the criminal justice system. With public awareness concerning our abused and troubled youth being greater than at any other time, it would seem most appropriate to plunge wholeheartedly into developing and instituting behavior change programs for our juvenile offenders.

These include programs which will allow troubled youth to develop skills beneficial to their growing into productive adults; programs which will help these youth modify their behavior in such a manner that they can see the personal benefits which accrue for them when they choose to make the necessary positive behavior modification; and finally, programs which will help them develop behavior beneficial to their flowering into constructive parental models. For most of these children will surely become parents—the archetypes for a large segment of our future population.

With all this increase in awareness, demand for accountability, and public clamor for juvenile crime reduction, little evidence exists which indicates a broad commitment to the development of juvenile behavior change programs. Perhaps this is due to the ingrained philosophy that spanking the child usually modifies the undesired behavior, at least for the moment. Of course, as research points out, this does little toward permanently inhibiting or extinguishing the unwanted behavior. So, we spank our juvenile offenders by putting them on probation with a paucity of supervision by our overworked probation officers or by placing them in our correctional closets commonly called youth homes, youth farms, industrial schools, or reform schools, where untrained staff, meager budgets, and an ever–changing administration generally provide warehousing services for our juvenile offenders.

This is not to say that positive change in the behavior of our juvenile offenders is not a sought-after goal, because it is. But our juvenile justice system, at least to this point, does not appear to have lent itself particularly well to establishing behavior change programs with the professional continuity needed for them to have made a significant contribution to helping youthful offenders. There have been many programs tried at diverse locations with varying amounts of success. These programs appear and disappear dependent on a number of factors: administrative changes, budget fluctuations, availability of consultants, and changes in political atmosphere. However, the lack of total commitment on the part of the personnel working in various correctional agencies seems to be one of the most common problems. This lack of commitment becomes evident as the programs falter once their originators no longer are present to keep them functioning.

This is just as true for those programs which do show positive results as for those which do not. Thus our youthful offenders often are pushed through the labyrinth of the juvenile justice system without being exposed to successful rehabilitative programs which help them learn new skills and behavior modifications fundamental to their maturing into productive adult citizens.

In order to transcend the boundaries presently inhibiting effective rehabilitation programs for our juvenile offenders, one must leave the philosophical commitment stage and enter the realm of practicality, which evolves and utilizes direct methods to encourage positive behavior change in our youthful offenders. The items presented in this section are a direct response to this construct. They are examples of what can be and is being done to help misdirected juveniles modify their behavior before they develop ingrained patterns.

The paper by Miller, Mayer, and Whitworth presents a study that utilizes a special treatment method with mentally retarded offenders. They attack the dual problem of delinquent behavior and mental retardation. As anyone who has worked in the area of mental retardation knows, commitment is a prerequisite to any type of program development. This also holds true for the area of offender behavior modification, be it juvenile or adult. Thus, commitment is a given when one launches an onslaught against both problem areas.

A number of studies have shown that the incidence of mental retardation among our juvenile offenders is significant. This incidence of mental retardation is likely to be much greater than these studies would indicate, since the deficient diagnostic procedures in most agencies and institutions are not sophisticated enough to single out juvenile offenders who are mentally retarded. However, as this study indicates, when mentally retarded juvenile offenders are professionally diagnosed and rehabilitative treatment programs are designed for them, positive results can accrue. The authors report findings which indicate that for these positive results to happen, the two most important aspects "needed in treatment of the retarded offender are constant supervision and repetition of expectations." These aspects demand close involvement with the retarded offender and a relationship where the case-worker is looked on as a benefactor by the client.

Sarazen and Ganzer offer the reader a choice of two rehabilitative methods for changing behavior of juvenile delinquents. In this study, they present findings which yielded positive results when either a "modeling" or "structured discussion" approach was utilized in a behavior change program. This positive change was apparent in both institutional and post-institutional behavior. In the modeling rehabilitative program, the juvenile offenders became intricately involved in actual role-playing sequences that dealt with problem situations which had been designed as being particularly difficult for the juvenile to handle. These problem areas included how to apply for a job, how to resist temptations by peers to engage in antisocial acts, and how to take problems to a teacher or a parole counselor. The structural discussion groups were similar to the modeling groups in sequence and content of the meetings, except that "all references to role-playing were omitted." Sarazen and Ganzer's findings suggest that very few differences exist between the two approaches in encouraging positive behavior changes among the juvenile delinquents in the two groups. They did find, however, that modeling and structured discussion had "greater concurrent and long-term effects on adolescent delinquents" than did the institution's regularly used rehabilitative program.

In summarizing the findings of the Preston Typology Study, Jesness makes a case for the utilization of differential treatment with institutionalized juvenile offenders. The development of differential treatment programs based upon the different personality typologies of the male juveniles sent to the Preston School of Industry in California seems to hold the most utility for effecting behavior changes that allow for better institutional management of the offenders. However, as the author himself points out, there seems to be little carryover of these changes, at least as far as parole performance is concerned. These results could be viewed as an indictment of differential treatment methods based upon personality typologies. However, should we be discouraged because programs are not 100 percent successful? If these methods had a beneficial effect on positive offender behavior change inside the institution, should the blame for post-institutional failure be born totally by the treatment program?

The answer to these questions would appear to be an unqualified no. We need to look at the many factors which inhibit a complete behavior change carryover once an individual has left the institution. Superficial commitment of institution staff to the program, limited staff training, lack of reinforcement progress in the community, and the vast differences in the array of skills needed to cope with institutional life as compared to life in the free society are a few of the problems besetting institutional treatment programs. These problems are not insurmountable, but they must first be recognized as problems so that public and governmental agencies may share a commitment to finding solutions to them. When this occurs, the effects of differential treatment programs and the effect of other programs will have an adequate opportunity to be tested for carryover in the community. This is a must if help is to be forthcoming for our juvenile offenders.

The final selection for this section discusses developing and using behavioral contracts with delinquent adolescents. As a technique for helping these adolescents modify their behavior toward more socially acceptable standards, the behavior contract can be a most effective tool. Rutherford stresses the necessary negotiation which must take place between the contractor and client and the applied behavior analysis model on which the contract is based. The four examples of behavioral contracts presented in this paper emphasize the pre-planning, behavior programming, and skill development during the modification of the various behaviors which take place once individuals enter into a contract. This method appears to be an excellent and effective "intervention strategy" for use with delinquent adolescents. It allows the adolescent to take responsibility for his or her behavior while at the same time being supplied direction and guidance by the contract mediator. In this manner, behavior change can occur with more socially appropriate skills being developed simultaneously. It is toward this goal that the establishment of rehabilitative programs for our juvenile offenders needs to progress.

REFERENCES

Johnson, T. *Introduction to the juvenile justice system*. St. Paul, Minnesota: West Publishing Co., 1975.

Wakis, E. *Children without justice*. New York: National Council of Jewish Women, Inc., 1975.

33

A Study of Mentally Retarded Juvenile Offenders in Corpus Christi, Texas

Clark J. Miller, Deborah Mayer, and Wallace E. Whitworth, Jr.

Reprinted from *Federal Probation* (June 1973) pp. 54–61 by permission of the publisher, the Administrative Office of the United States Courts.

There are very few specialized treatment programs for retarded offenders in this country. Historically, there has been no special judicial treatment accorded the mentally retarded juvenile offender. This younster is normally subjected to the same judicial and therapeutic procedures as is the offender who has higher intelligence. Misconceptions about the mentally retarded person have created an enigma within the judicial system about which very few answers have been elicited. It is estimated that there are over 125,000 mentally retarded children born each year in the United States.[1] Many of these children later become offenders in either adolescent or adult life, partially because of a lack of resources available to them to aid normal social development.

There are very little data available about the number of retarded offenders who appear in juvenile courts each year, or who are committed to juvenile institutions. However, studies show that there are a relatively large number of these offenders who have gone through the penal system. Merrill[2] found in a study of Los Angeles Juvenile Courts that 23 percent of those younsters taken through the court were retarded. Sheldon and Eleanor Glueck[3] reported that 13.1 percent of a sample of children referred to their clinic by the Boston Juvenile Court were retarded. Brown and Courtless[4] conducted a very extensive study of prisons and training schools in 1963 and found that 9.5 percent of these inmates had IQ's under 70. A study done by Allen[5] in 1968 indicated that 74 percent of inmates of the penal systems in six states were retarded. Other states have not compiled sufficient data from which to gather information. Because of this, there is still a great lack of data about the number of retarded persons who flow through our courts each year.

One of the reasons for this lack of information is the deficiency in diagnostic procedures in most agencies and institutions. The number of public agencies who are able to afford either the equipment or the necessary staff to have a diagnostic program are few. Some mentally retarded younsters pass through the developmental years of school without being identified as to their intellectual potential. This problem is evident in the Southwest, where many children from the Chicano culture enter public school with a deficient ability to speak English. Thus, the retarded child who speaks limited English may never be identified as being retarded, having simply been recognized as being deficient in English. Many of these youngsters will become academic casualties before they reach high school. On the other hand, there are children who somehow become identified as mentally retarded who are later found to be of higher intelligence. That there has been a social injustice in each of these cases can hardly be argued.

The early years of the child appear to be a definite factor in the development of the child's IQ. This is especially pertinent to the deprived child and the retarded child. In many cases these two syndromes are found in the same child. Mackie[6] indicates that there is a large number of children who have been handicapped by cultural factors, which causes them to function as mentally retarded, when in essence they are not limited in this manner. The lack of cultural and educational stimulation has prevented a proper level of intellectual maturity in these children. Professor S. A. Kirk[7] at the University of Illinois has demonstrated the effect of a child's early school experience with retarded children. A group of retarded children were given preschool training and later were compared to a control group of retarded children who had not received preschool training. The children who had received the earlier education tended to retain the additional growth rate, while the children in the latter group continued to fall behind in their subsequent experience.

Psychologist and author Frank Reissman[8] described the hidden IQ in his book on cultural deprivation. In one chapter he lists several assumptions that are held regarding the IQ which may serve to penalize the deprived child. Among these points is the idea that intelligence is best demonstrated in a school environment. Therefore, IQ tests may tend to reflect scholastic aptitude and do not reflect the kind of problem–solving abilities that deprived children may have. A number of the deprived children in the Southwest are from Chicano homes, where the deprivation is related to an educational lag supported largely by a linguistic handicap. Radin[9] indicates that difficulties in the education of children of low social and economic status involve several different factors. These factors include cultural elements; organizational factors (for example, the school systems with which the child has to contend); family group practices (including maternal inadequacies and lack of intellectual stimulation); and the child's abilities and desire to achieve.

Mental retardation is a concept also to be understood within a social and cultural context. This is a very important idea for corrections. Many of the factors which are found to be prevalent in delinquency are the same factors which are seen to have contributed to intellectual deprivation. A characteristic which stands foremost among these factors is social incompetency. Many times a diagnosis of retardation is made after some form of social incompetence has been demonstrated. In a recently published book about retardation, one author emphasizes the social and cultural implications as she writes, "The sociological significance of a retardation lies in the fact that the existence of this disability on a large scale is essentially a phenomenon of societies which have evolved to a high level of complex social functioning and organization. First, societies with a more complex pattern of organization call for a higher level of adaptive ability than what passes as average in earlier states, so more people fall below the norm of behavior and functioning which is expected and needed for survival. As with the Darwinian process of natural selection, the people of above-average intelligence by previous standards become the norm in the next evolutionary phase, and the slow ones drop back to become the social casualties of the new order."[10]

In the field of corrections, very little effort has been made to differentiate the retarded delinquent from the non-retarded delinquent. While there are certainly many counselors who are professionally astute enough to recognize the retardate, most counselors are not sufficiently trained to identify this youngster readily. More often than this is the lack of training on the part of correctional workers to effectively deal with the retarded adolescent once he is identified. The tendency, in corrections, is to treat the retarded offender in the same manner as the offender who has higher intelligence.

RETARDED OFFENDER STUDY

A study conducted at Martineau Juvenile Hall in Corpus Christi, Texas, utilized a specialized treatment approach with a caseload of retarded offenders. Supported by funds from the Texas Criminal Justice Council, a consultant and counselor were employed to work with these adolescents. During the first year of the grant, 28 male youngsters were placed on this special caseload. These offenders fell within the juvenile court ages of 10 to 17, with a median age of 14.5. The IQ range established by the staff for this project was 50 to 83. The staff felt that a child below the lower limit of 50 should probably be institutionalized, while 83 is set by the American Psychiatric Association as the upper limit for borderline retardation. Characteristics of the families and offenders selected for the caseload were relatively homogeneous. The IQ's ranged from 51 to 83, with a median IQ of 67.5. Thirteen of the boys lived with both natural parents, while 10 lived with the natural mother only. Two others lived with guardians, and three lived with a natural parent and step-parent. The families were relatively large, the largest being 16 in number and the smallest four, with a median of 6.5 children. Sixty-eight percent of the families had other children who had been referred to the department at some time. These boys had been on probation an average of 9.7 months prior to being selected for this special program.

Besides the level of intelligence, selection of clients for this caseload was based on seriousness of family problems, individual dynamics of the adolescent, seriousness of acting–out behavior, and school problems. The grant was proposed because of the relatively large number of low IQ youngsters who are referred to the court each year. This program was funded for a 2-year period, during which time it was hoped to fulfill the goals of the project. Evaluation of the program was based on (a) recidivism, (b) school progress, (c) family dynamics, and (d) the individual adolescent's personality reintegration. The purpose of the program was to develop techniques and methods with which to more effectively aid the offender in becoming a more productive member of society. One of the goals of the project staff was to produce an evaluation of this program and utilize this information for inservice training for the casework staff of Martineau Hall.

RETARDED OFFENDER'S PERSONALITY

The personality structure of a retarded offender may be described as passive-dependent. He is usually the compliant type of person whose problem-solving approach is to let someone else do it. The apparent contradiction of these youngsters is that they sometimes use ingenious methods to pass for normal and yet they become very compliant with their counselor–friend. These youngsters will lie or cheat to claim a place in a normal world but not as a means of trying to deviate from it. On first appearance this seems antisocial, thus the irony of their acting-out behavior.

The life style of the retarded offender is to expect defeat and consequently much of their behavior is motivated to accomplish such failure. The retarded offender was discovered to utilize such defense mechanism as denial of his referral behavior, projection of the blame for his behavior outside himself, and avoidance of working through the causes of his problems. Without exception, the retarded offenders tended to either minimize or deny their participation in the referral behavior. Frequently, attempts were made to sidetrack the counselor by projecting the blame on to something outside themselves, such as, "The other boys at school tease me," or, "My father beats on my mother." It is very difficult for them to admit to their own part in the behavior.

They exhibit very poor impulse control in their behavior, normally acting out without regard to the consequences of their behavior. They exercise very little discipline in postponing gratification. Below the surface of their behavior, there is an underlying depression which characterizes the retarded offender, brought on partially by the life-style of continued failure. Their life-style of failure is so complete in most cases that they are generally not conscious that there is a difference between success and failure. When they become overtly conscious of a failure, there is generally an excessive amount of anxiety and frustration. The anxiety stems partially from the fact that they do not know how to analyze their behavior to achieve success in the future. On the other hand, when they do infrequently achieve some sort of success, there is frequently a type of "success anxiety" brought on because they are uncertain as to how to deal with this success.

Passivity has become a polished trait in their personality. It is an important tool in their defense from the intrusion of the outer world. This passivity was an unmistakable obstacle to the development of a therapeutic relationship. Perhaps because of their status of "being retarded," they evidenced a poverty of experience in communication with other people. Their self-image of stupidity and dumbness are usually highly supported unwittingly by family members. They have not learned to elicit relationships with people, or to respond to the attempts of communication with them. This passivity is as much an example of poor ability to interrelate with other people as it is a mistrust of these people. The treatment techniques of restructuring personality dynamics focused on dependency, passivity, impulse control, depression, anxiety about failure, sexual identity, and the dynamics of being a loser.

TREATMENT CONSIDERATIONS

Various treatment considerations were used with these children. It was discovered that intensive supervision was a vital aspect of the total counseling situation. The counselor had some type of contact with the offender as much as three and four times per week. The importance of this is recognized because the retarded offender with his image of a loser needs constant support and encouragement. A form of behavior modification was utilized with these youngsters by giving positive reinforcement to the child's progress for success in any area, no matter how small the accomplishment. On the other hand negative reinforcement was given for any type of poor or unacceptable behavior such as truancy, misbehavior in the classroom, or runaway from home. This program of reinforcement proved to be quite effective in building a better self-image on the part of these youngsters.

It was also discovered that repetition is an extremely good technique to use with these youngsters. The level of understanding of these children is on a much lower degree than a normal child and the expectations and demands made upon the retarded offender must be continually outlined to him. In doing so, it is important to communicate with him on a very simple level common to their degree of comprehension. It is generally necessary to use simple clear language for them to comprehend. Casework goals must be on a very short-term basis with these youngsters. Most of them cannot see more than a few weeks in advance and are unable to work toward distant goals.

During the first few months of the grant, it was discovered that the majority of these offenders were not in the appropriate classroom. Therefore, during the summer months prior to the beginning of the school year, a great deal of effort was expended to have the children placed in the proper environment in school. The largest percentage of them were not in any type of special education class. These children had suffered many educational disappointments in the past and very few had a positive attachment to the classroom. In most cases, the parents would not allow their children to be placed in special education, as they did not recognize their child as being retarded. This seemed to fit quite well into their scheme of denying the reality of the child's situation. Numerous conferences were held with school authorities and parents during the first half year of the grant. The success of these conferences was shown by improvement in the child's behavior and grades in nearly every case.

At the school, the probation counselor's role was primarily to provide some support for the retarded delinquent. She would give information to the teacher and the counselor, to help them in understanding and gaining knowledge in dealing with these adolescents. She would notify the school of attendance problems, and they would return similar information to her through telephone calls. The probation counselor would offer suggestions on how to simplify instructions and explanations to the school authorities. She would discuss complaints to the school authorities, and help them deal with personality conflicts in the classroom. Frequent visits were made to the school to increase the accountability of the school to the probation counselor and the retarded delinquent to his probation counselor. The approach used with the school personnel was a cooperative approach which attempted to focus on problem areas with the retarded delinquent in the classroom.

FAMILY DYNAMICS

The dynamics within these families generally include a pseudo-stoic mother, who is overly protective and constantly serving as a buffer for her child's behavior. In almost every family involved in this program, the mother was the dominant parental figure. The father, when present, avoided any real involvement with the family life. In most cases, the father limited his activities to supporting the family financially, leaving the supervision and disciplining of the children to the mother. When forced to confront problems in the family, the father had a "give up" attitude. This avoidance of reality was similar to that exhibited by the retarded child offender. The adolescent developed a similar attitude of noninvolvement. The father's weakness or inability to handle the marriage relationship in many of these cases stirred up resentment and hostility in the child. So the adolescent who is striving for a strong masculine figure with whom to identify was frustrated. The mother was then left with her martyred role of almost completely raising the child by herself.

Diagnosis of the dynamics in the family was the goal of family and group therapy. Identification of the power structure in the family or the alignments and alliances between family members was a primary goal. The use of the single family approach helped to identify the power figures, the scapegoats in the family, those members who use sneaky power, and the specific relationship complex between family members. It was also helpful to use the single family approach to negotiate agreements between members of the family.

Several families were selected for group therapy. The group selection process and the screening of the family group members considered their availability to make appointments, at least one parent in the home, and an IQ of the child no lower than the milder retardation range. Preparation of the members for the group was done individually with each family. The normal rules for group therapy were laid down, such as each member being expected to use his share of the group time and confidentiality of group activities. It was discovered that the parents of most of these offenders were almost similarly passive as were the offenders themselves. For the first several sessions there was a great deal of resistance towards being verbal among the members of the group. After about four sessions, the members seemed to become more relaxed and socialized more in the waiting room prior to the group meeting.

The group therapy sessions utilized group games to stimulate verbal communication. One of these was called insult and compliment, where each group member would be asked to compliment the person on his right and insult the person on his left and in this way it was hoped that each member would learn to express both his positive and his negative feelings. A second game was called the sponge game, where a sponge was thrown between members and when it landed in a member's lap, the other group members, as a whole, gave this person feedback about his behavior and the impressions he makes on other people. When the individual feels that he has had enough criticism, he throws the sponge to another member. It was discovered that the group therapist had to be generally more active than usual in these group therapy sessions.

The groups consisted of either the therapist introducing subjects to talk about, or utilizing the sessions for the members to criticize each other as a whole. The success of the group therapy sessions can be considered to be only marginal due to the great amount of passivity and reluctance of the members to handle criticism and be verbal. The group therapy did help at least two of the five families involved as there appeared to be some significant progress in family relationships.

Causes of Retardation

The project staff found that there were a number of factors to be considered about the causation of mental retardation. There are of course numerous causative elements that can be discussed, including physiological factors. The staff considered it important to discuss primarily the psychological and educational factors. These are outlined below:

1. Failure to acquire a motivational structure.—Somewhere in the developmental period, these youngsters had not internalized the value system which enables them to compete in a normal world. They lack the motivation to become involved in activities which bring them into contact with nonoffenders. They cannot, for example, comprehend the relationship between the structure of homework and exams and their future. Later on, they are unable to acquire a job or if they do obtain employment, they are unable to stick with it. It is simply not within their value system to do this.

2. The use of a system to get around achievement.—The passivity of these youngsters has been a good defense against having to compete or achieve. They play dumb even when they have the ability to do something. They cannot cope with the anxiety of achievement and do not want the responsibilities inherent in completing a task or learning a skill. Many of them have become quite successful in hiding behind a shield of retardedness in order that they should not have to achieve. Thus they utilize a minimum of self-survival techniques to get around achievement.

3. Restriction of learning opportunities.—A lack of stimuli in the preschool environment has caused a restriction of the chances for most of these children to advance normally in an academic setting. The lack of encouragement and support from parental figures keeps a child from achieving his maximum potential.

4. Self-defeating techniques.—The behavior of a retarded offender seems to be geared toward failure. Where the normal person strives for success, it seems to be the opposite for the retarded offender. Since he has known only minimal success, he does not comprehend the rewards of such. His behavior in the classroom is frequently disruptive. This is a method of being involved in the classroom for the retarded offender. He does not see this as antisocial.

On the contrary he sees this as a means of gaining attention from the normal world.

5. Expectations of behavior.—The retarded offender is normally expected to act dumb. The expectations are commmunicated to him in numerous ways throughout the developmental period by parental figures, school authorities, and peers. He soon learns to fit into these expectations in order to effect some sort of stability for himself. These expectations soon become a convenient cover for the offender to hide behind to avoid a responsible position more compatible with his potential.

6. A lack of belief in essential self-worth.—The retarded offender has failed to acquire a self-concept which sustains a positive psychological growth. His sense of self-worth is essentially poor or negative. His self-concept has little room for achievement or productivity. There is a very little self-sustaining sense of confidence in his abilities.

7. Social humiliation.—The attempts of the retarded offender to gain recognition in the normal world often meet with defeat or rejection. Gradually, this becomes a lifestyle to the point that he becomes extremely sensitive to becoming involved socially with other persons. Soon a void develops in his life and he has very few interrelationships. He then protects himself from the social world by his passivity and lack of gregariousness. His attempts to become involved in a normal world become more and more traumatic to him and he thus begins to shut out people. His world is generally limited to some type of family relationships or a few peers, most of whom are retarded themselves. Frequently, he is used by peers of higher intelligence to do their dirty work for them, such as breaking into a building or stealing.

8. Parental abandonment or indifference.—In the majority of these cases there are indications of either or both of these syndromes. Several of the parents of these youngsters have long since abandoned the family. The large percentage of the parents who remain in the home demonstrate an air of emotional indifference to the child. Most of them are so involved with their own problems that they are unaware that the child has any of his own. They set very few limitations for their children and use few disciplinary measures with them. This can be quite frustrating to these children who normally would require strict supervision. Thus the support and confidence that these children need from an adult figure is lost.

9. Bareness of the home.—There is a great lack of stimuli in the homes of most of these youngsters. The poor social-economic nature of many of these homes is conducive to an attitude in a child where he cannot visualize a future for himself amidst this lack of even the bare necessities of life. They are not subjected to most of the normal conveniences of life, only occasionally coming into contact with such.

10. Language difficulty.—Several of these youngsters evidenced extreme

language difficulties. Most of the families in this project were Chicano and several of the children spoke very little English upon entering school. This lack of knowledge of the English language is perpetuated frequently when the child is not encouraged to learn English within the first several years of school. Therefore, he does not learn to communicate verbally and does not gain the same intake that the normal child would in the classroom. Secondly, if the classroom is geared too high for the retardate, he will not learn to communicate verbally. In most cases, these children are passed from one grade to another for "social" reasons and generally become dropouts sometime within the junior high level.

Considerations for Therapy

During the progress of the grant's first year, the project staff found a number of factors which it felt to be important in counseling with the retarded offender. The staff narrowed these down to the following 14 points which it felt were most pertinent:

1. Intensive supervision.—The retarded offender needs much more supervision and counseling time made available to him than the normal delinquent. During the first several weeks of supervision, the counselor made from three to five contacts per week in either a direct or indirect manner regarding each child. Following this, the frequency of contacts was determined by the behavioral progress of the child. It is suggested that a minimum of two contacts a week is necessary in any event. It is extremely important for the retardate to develop a mutual trust relationship with his counselor. It is important for the retarded offender to know that someone is interested in him and this is expressed largely by the frequency and quality of the contact made with him.

2. Repetition is important.—With most of these clients it is important to continually repeat the expectations placed on him. While the youngster with a normal IQ would find this a boring and irritable aspect of probation, the retarded offender needs this repetition for a more solid foundation in his relationship with the counselor.

3. It is important to establish short-term goals for these youngsters.—The retarded offender's history of impulsiveness and lack of self-discipline requires that a different value system be established for him in the counseling relationship. In most cases it is necessary to start out with day-to-day goals. Gradually, as the offender begins to experience success in meeting short-term goals, the counselor should set longer-range goals. The offender will then learn to postpone immediate gratification in turn for more complete satisfaction later.

4. The use of simple, clear language is necessary.—It is incumbent on the

counselor to discover at which level he can best communicate with each youngster. In general, it is necessary to use simple language with a minimum of extravagant words. This is one of the most difficult areas in which the counselor had to operate, because of the verbal passivity of these youngsters.

5. Nourish improvement skills.—Once the retarded offender begins to realize his potential in some area, it is necessary to follow up on this by continual encouragement for him to develop this skill to a greater degree. This is in reference to various types of skills ranging from verbal communication, academic development, social development, or to some type of job training.

6. Avoid categorizing the client as retarded.—The retarded offender has already learned a self-concept of retardation and has thus stereotyped himself to fit this role. This should not be encouraged or reinforced by the counselor in any way. This, of course, does not mean that one encourages a retardate to become a medical doctor. It simply means that he is encouraged to develop the potential that he has.

7. Avoid being tricked into a defeatist relationship with the retarded offender.—These youngsters have manipulated people within their environment to fit within their scheme of defeat and failure. They are very skillful at this and while it is not a conscious manipulative act, their whole behavior pattern is directed towards the development of a similar relationship with other people. They have learned to expect defeat in interpersonal relationships and will attempt to manipulate the counselor into a similar relationship which in turn will simply substantiate their past experience.

8. Expect a minimum feedback.—The passivity exhibited by the majority of these youngsters in their relationship with people, as well as their verbal communication, is a result of several years of poor intercommunication. It will take many counseling sessions to develop good feedback.

9. Be positive in the counseling approach.—Feedback and reinforcement from these younsters is minimal, making the rewards of counseling minimal. It is vital that an optimistic and positive outlook be realized in a treatment approach of these youngsters. They have become accustomed to years of neglect and mistrust of other people. They are extremely sensitive to any type of rejection and become especially sensitive to this in the counseling relationship.

10. The use of visual aids is helpful.—This is extremely important with some of these youngsters in the lower ranges of intelligence. These individuals, whose verbal communication is minimal, are very susceptible to visual cues. They are able to incorporate visual cues into their world of passivity much easier than verbal language, which they may or may not understand.

11. The passivity may be threatening to the counselor.—It is especially difficult for a counselor to develop communication with a passive client, and

the counselor may become impatient or angry if the client pursued this passive course. It is important for the counselor to particularly examine his own areas of defensiveness and dependency needs so that these areas may not confuse the development of a good relationship with the retarded offender. If the counselor has not reconciled his own dependency needs, he may quite likely projecthis own feelings of frustration into this relationship.

12. Family counseling is necessary with these youngsters.—When there are parental figures in the home, it is important to involve them in the counseling process. They spend many more hours with the offender than does the counselor and may undo any therapeutic progress if they are not included in therapy. Normally there are strengths within these parents which can be drawn out by a competent counselor and utilized for the benefit of the retarded offender.

13. The retarded offender tends to hide behind his retardation.—While this is not a conscious act, the behavior pattern developed by most of these offenders is such that they expect a minimum of responsibility to be placed upon them. If it appears that too much is being demanded from them, they may quietly retreat into their own world of retardation.

14. The IQ deception.—It is important to keep in mind that the IQ, as measured by most intelligence instruments, is basically an examination of scholastic aptitude and should not be viewed in terms of a set score. This avoids the trap of sterotyping the youngster by his IQ score. The IQ points of most of these youngsters can be raised, some significantly, by academic training. Sterotyping them with a set IQ score may also prevent further imaginative counseling or treatment techniques.

SUMMARY AND CONSIDERATIONS

The two most important aspects needed in treatment of the retarded offender are constant supervision and repetition of expectations. It is vital that the caseworker demonstrate his interest in the retardate by frequent involvement with him. The retardate will respond by becoming more dependent on his therapist than does the usual client. But this is important for the retarded person, who is in need of a benefactor. It is also necessary to frequently repeat casework expectations and probation rules, expecially to those in the lower range. This serves to refresh the memory and reinforce these rules in the mind. To the youngster with a normal IQ, this would be irritating, but the retarded offender needs and accepts this type of reinforcement. He is much more comfortable when he knows what is expected from him.

The first year of the project proved to be a success in most areas of therapy. Progress was noted in the areas of school achievement and attendance and family dynamics. The one form of treatment that met with only minimal success was group therapy, which did not prove profitable because of the tremendous passivity of those clients involved. It is important to recognize that the IQ can be a limiting factor in treatment if the therapist accepts it at face value. It should not, however, sterotype and limit creative efforts in therapy. The vast majority of retarded offenders can be helped to become more socialized through educational training and behavior modification techniques.

NOTES

1. Meyer Schreibner (ed.), *Social Work and Mental Retardation*. New York, 1970, p. 220.
2. Harry M. Shulman, *Juvenile Delinquency in American Society*. New York and Evanston: Harper & Row, 1961, p. 362.
3. Ibid.
4. The President's Commission on Law Enforcement and Administration of Justice, Task Force Report: *Corrections*, pp. 29–30.
5. Richard C. Allen, "The Retarded Offender: Unrecognized in Court and Untreated in Prison," *Federal Probation*, *32* (3): 1968, p. 27.
6. Romaine Mackie, "Functional Handicaps Among School Children Due to Cultural or Economic Deprivation," *Special Education*, *42* (1): 1967, pp. 8–12.
7. Nancy Faber, *The Retarded Child*. New York: Crown Publishers, Inc., 1968, p. 185.
8. Frank Reissman, *The Culturally Deprived Child*. New York, Evanston, and London: Harper & Row, 1962, pp. 49–62.
9. Norma Radin, "Some Impediments to the Education of Disadvantaged Children," *Children*, *15* (5): 1968, pp. 170–176.
10. Margaret Adams, *Mental Retardation and Its Social Dimensions*. New York and London, 1971, pp. 1–15.

34

Modeling and Group Discussion in the Rehabilitation of Juvenile Delinquents[1]

Irwin G. Sarason[2] and Victor J. Ganzer[3]

Reprinted by permission from *Journal of Counseling Psychology* 20 (1973): 442–49. Copyright 1973 *by the American Psychological Association.* Authors' permission to reprint is gratefully acknowledged.

This investigation compared the relative effectiveness of two group methods of communicating information relevant to the social, vocational, and educational adjustment of institutionalized male juvenile delinquents. One method relied on modeling procedures and required subjects to imitate roles which they had observed models perform. The other method employed structured discussions of the same material but without modeling or imitation. Both groups were attended by two models or discussion leaders and four or five subjects. A control group did not participate in any meetings and received no special condition. Treatment effectiveness was evaluated through changes on a number of attitude, self-concept, and behavior ratings that were obtained on a repeated-measures basis and through follow-up interviews and indices of recidivism. Both treatment conditions prompted more positive attitudes, behavior change, and less recidivism among participants than did the control condition.

This study represents an experimental exploration of the means by which delinquents' awareness of what constitutes socially acceptable and effective behavior can be heightened. Implicit in the research was the assumption that social behavior, both conventional and deviant, is explainable in terms of the information available to and salient for individuals. The experimental manipulation consisted of the manner by which information was made available to persons. One third of the subjects were exposed to a sequence of social modeling, a technique used with increasing frequency by counselors and clinicians (Krumboltz & Thoresen, 1969). A second group participated in discussions with an intent similar to that of subjects in the modeling

program. The third group of comparable subjects constituted a control condition.

The modeling treatment was derived from social learning theory. For a
wide variety of purposes, demonstrations in the form of modeled behavior
are effective instructional techniques (Bandura, 1969; LaFleur & Johnson,
1972). Some evidence suggests that institutionalized delinquent boys become
more socially adaptive as a function of observational learning opportunities
(Sarason, 1968; Sarason & Ganzer, 1969). Modeling, however, is not the
only or necessarily the best way of conveying information. The second experimental approach consisted of providing information about, but not demonstration of, prosocial ways of responding to environmental problems.
Delinquent boys under this condition received information about social behavior within a structured discussion or counseling format. In the course of a
series of discussions, subjects were given examples of desirable and undesirable ways of coping with social, vocational, and educational situations. Boys
in a control group experienced only the normal program offered by a well-
staffed institution with a relatively low resident–staff ratio. The control boys
received as many contacts with caseworkers and counselors as did experimental group boys.

METHOD

SUBJECTS

The research was conducted at the Cascadia Juvenile Reception-
Diagnostic Center in Tacoma, Washington. This institution, which was
described in an earlier article (Sarason, 1968), receives all delinquent children
committed by Juvenile Court judges to the State's Division of Institutions.
The length of stay is approximately six weeks for new commitments. Approximately 12% of the children are paroled directly to their home communities, the majority being transferred to another state facility.

The subjects were 192 male first offenders who at admission were between
15½ and 18 years of age (mean = 16 years, 7 months). The average IQ
estimated from the Lorge–Thorndike (Lorge, Thorndike, & Hagen, 1966)
Nonverbal Intelligence Scale was 95.3. The three groups were comparable in
age, IQ, diagnostic classification made by the Cascadia staff, and type and
severity of delinquent behavior prior to institutionalization. There were 64
subjects in each of the modeling, discussion, and control groups. Half of the
subjects in the modeling and discussion groups received either audio- or
videotaped feedback of their group behavior. Conditions and feedback media
were counterbalanced for the two cottages used. Assignment of subjects to
conditions was essentially random but was occasionally influenced by weekly
admission rates; that is, if too few boys were admitted during a week when a

new experimental group was needed, those admissions were all designated as controls.

Sarason (1968) has described the general procedure used in modeling sessions. In this study modeling was oriented toward a practical approach to the problems of adolescent boys. Each session was attended by four or five subjects and two models. The models were psychology graduate students trained to lead the groups. Each modeling session had a particular theme, such as how to apply for a job, how to resist temptations by peers to engage in antisocial acts, how to take problems to a teacher or a parole counselor, and how to pass up immediate gratification in order to lay the groundwork for achieving more significant goals in the future. Emphasis was placed on the generality of the appropriate behaviors being modeled and on their potential usefulness in different interpersonal situations. Each situation was written to illustrate topics or problem situations that had been nominated frequently by boys in a pilot study as presenting difficulty to them.[4]

One of the models began each session by introducing and describing the scene to be enacted that day. The introduction oriented the subjects to the topic for the day and provided a rationale for the particular scene. After the boys had been briefed concerning points to which they should pay special attention, the models role-played the particular situation for the day while the boys observed. Most of the situations were divided into parts. In some cases the first part depicted an undesirable way of coping with a problem and the second a more desirable way. Following the models' enactment of the situation, one boy was called upon to summarize and explain the content and outcome of what had just been modeled. Each meeting was either audio- or video-tape recorded.

Recorded segments of the modeled behavior then were played, after which pairs of boys or a boy and a model imitated as closely as possible the behavior that they had just observed. A short break ensued during which soft drinks were served and an audio or video role-playing tape was played. Then the remaining subjects enacted the situation so that each boy participated in each session. The audio- or videotape replay of this enactment was followed by comments and critiques by the boys of their role playing. Each meeting ended with a summary of the session, its most salient aspects, and its generalizability.

Comments and questions by the models were focused on sustaining the group's interest in and attention to the scenes being role played. Remarks made by the models were brief and to the point. Lengthy discussions by group members were not encouraged. The models attempted to get the boys to think about related and similar situations in which the modeled contents of the scene could be applied to their lives. An example is provided by the "Job Interview" scene in which boys observed and imitated appropriate interviewee behaviors and then verbally were given an enumeration of situations in which boys would be required to make a good impression on somebody in authority.

A different topic or situation was modeled for each of the 14 hour-long sessions. Pairs of subjects in the groups formed and enacted their own scenes during the fifteenth session. These scenes subsequently were role played by the other boys. The final session, the sixteenth, served as a review and summary of the work conducted during the previous 15 meetings. This was done through either a video or audio master tape upon which selected aspects of previous scenes had been condensed and recorded.

DISCUSSION CONDITION

Every effort was made to keep the sequence and content of the discussion group meetings as similar as possible to the modeling sessions. The orientation given to the discussion groups presented the same rationale and purposes as that given to the modeling groups, except that all references to role playing were omitted. Each meeting also was either audio- or videotape recorded. An example of how these meetings were conducted is provided by the "Job Interview" discussion. One of the leaders introduced the topic by indicating the importance of jobs as a means of getting money for things that we need. He also emphasized that employment is a way to earn something through one's own effort and to achieve independence. He commented that getting a job isn't easy and that knowledge and skill are relevant to getting jobs. The job interview was described as a key step in this process. One of the two group leaders then asked the boys what interviews they had experienced, what questions had been asked of them, and how they had handled the situations. Interventions of the group leaders were analogous to those used in modeling groups. Audio- and videotape feedback for the discussion group was employed in a manner similar to the modeling situations.

During the fifteenth session the subjects were asked to present topics that they themselves felt should be discussed and to give reasons why these topics were important. The sixteenth meeting was a summary session. While the manner in which the modeling and discussion groups were conducted differed, their content and sequential characteristics were comparable.

DEPENDENT VARIABLES

Three types of dependent variables were premeasures, repeated measures, and postmeasures.

Premeasures. Shortly after admission to Cascadia, subjects were administered a short true-false personality inventory that included Sarason's (Sarason & Ganzer, 1962) Test Anxiety Scale (TAS), the Pd scale of the Minnesota Multiphasic Personality Inventory (MMPI) (Dahlstrom & Welsh, 1960), the Gough (1957) Impulsivity Scale, and Navran's (1954) Dependency Scale.

Repeated measures. Additional self-report data and staff behavior ratings were obtained on subjects at the time of the premeasures and again just prior to their release from Cascadia. The interval between pre- and post-testing was approximately five weeks. Self-report measures yielded scores on 10 variables: (a) Wahler's (1969) Self-Description Inventory, which contains descriptions of favorable and unfavorable personal characteristics rated on a scale from "very much like me" to "not at all like me"; (b) the Word Rating Scale, which consists of 12 bipolar semantic differential items designed to measure five aspects of the self-concept (e.g., "Me as I am now," "Me as my parents see me"); (c) a goal scale on which subjects estimated the likelihood that they would achieve various future goals (e.g., "Finish high school"); (d) Lykken's (1957) Activity Preference Questionnaire; and (e) Rotter's (1966) Internalization-Externalization (I-E) Scale.

Cottage counselors completed two kinds of reliability ratings (e.g., interrater rs ranged from .75 to 1.00 on each subject: (a) a Behavior Rating Scale which contained 10 bipolar behavior descriptions (e.g., "Never hits and pushes—Often hits and pushes"), each rated on a 7-point scale, and (b) a Weekly Behavior Summary which included a seven-category behavior checklist dealing with peer and staff relationships, work detail performances, personal habits, and general cottage adjustment.

Postmeasures. Each subject's disposition was rank ordered from most favorable (e.g. parole) to least favorable (e.g., transfer to a high security institution). Placement in any given institution was objectively rated by clinical staff as reflecting degrees of maladjustment and need for control. Measures obtained during the postparole follow-up included retesting on several of the previously described measures, interview material, and indices of recidivism. Since the recidivism data were gathered almost three years after administration of the experimental treatments, they were the most significant indices of long-term treatment effects. An initial expectation was that since the treatments were only four weeks in duration, their effects would be more detectable before than after parole.

RESULTS

In spite of some cottage differences, the three treatment groups were comparable across all premeasures. Significant (p<.05) positive changes were found from pre- to post-testing for 10 of the 12 repeated dependent variables for the pooled groups. Analyses of variance changes in their attitudes, self–concepts, and their rated overt behavior during the five-week interval between pre- and post-assessment. Comparisons of changes among the three treatment groups revealed two significant differences for the 12 measures. Modeling subjects showed a reduction in emotional reactivity on the Activity Preference Questionnaire that was significantly greater (p<.05) than that for the other subjects. Both discussion and modeling subjects showed a greater (p<.05) shift toward internalization on the I-E scale than did the control subjects. The difference between modeling and discussion conditions was not significant.

Analyses of variance of the repeated self-reports and staff ratings showed that the televised feedback had different effects on modeling and discussion groups (p<.01). The differences were small between the discussion groups that did and did not receive televised feedback. The televised and non-televised modeling groups differed widely. The latter showed the most and the former the least overall positive change.

One variable, case disposition, was analyzed by nonparametric comparisons because of the range and distribution of this measure, suggesting that it did not meet the assumptions required for parametric analyses. Table 34.1 shows the distribution of case disposition scores for all subjects according to group membership. The eight possible dispositions were combined and reduced to four categories to permit chi-square comparisons. Categories 1–2 represent favorable case dispositions (i.e., 1 = diagnostic parole) and Categories 7–8 represent placement in the more structured, higher security institutions that generally receive more chronically delinquent and maladaptive boys. Approximately three times as many boys in the nontelevised modeling groups received favorable placements as compared with other groups. A chi-square comparison among boys receiving Category 1–2 placements revealed a significant difference (p<.05). The number of subjects in the nontelevised modeling group (n = 14) was also significantly greater (p<.01) than the number of boys in the televised discussion (n = 5) or televised modeling (n = 4) and nontelevised discussion (n = 4). Comparisons across groups within each of the remaining three placement categories did not reveal significant differences. Nontelevised modeling subjects clearly received more favorable case dispositions than did subjects in other groups.

Many factors interact to determine the Cascadia Review Board's decision to place a boy in another institution or to return him directly to the community. Other things being equal, his behavior in the cottage significantly influences his case disposition. It cannot be said with certainty that participation in a modeling group was the major determinant of favorable placement; however, since most boys were comparable across the dimensions measured in this investigation at the time of their admission to Cascadia, the modeling treatment probably did influence boys' attitudes and behaviors for

TABLE 34.1.
COMPARISONS OF PLACEMENT RATINGS FOR MAIN EXPERIMENTAL
AND CONTROL GROUPS

Group	Combined placement rating			
	1–2 favorable	3–4	5–6	7–8 unfavorable
Televised modeling	4	9	6	13
Nontelevised modeling	14	7	2	9
Televised discussion	5	8	9	10
Nontelevised discussion	4	11	8	9
Cottage A control	4	12	4	2
Cottage B control	5	7	5	15
Total	36	54	34	68

Note: n = 32 for each group.

the better, and this difference was to some degree reflected in the favorable decisions made by the Review Board.

The intermediate term data consisted of behavior ratings made by counselors after the subjects had spent approximately four months in the institutions to which they had been sent from Cascadia. Independent and reliable Behavior Rating Scale and Weekly Behavior Summary ratings were obtained from pairs of counselors for each subject. Counselors were not told which boys had been in groups while at Cascadia. Mean behavior rating scores among experimental and control subgroups did not differ significantly. The large differences previously associated with the feedback variable had completely "washed out" by the time the four-month ratings were made.

Further comparisons were made for the behavior rating data of whether subjects showed positive, no further, or negative change from the Cascadia post-rating to the subsequent four-month institution rating. The criterion for determining direction of change was based on a one standard deviation of the mean Cascadia post-rating. These comparisons are summarized in Table 34.2.

Between- and within-group comparisons of positive and negative behavior changes were performed by chi-square tests. The proportion of subjects who continued to show positive change did not differ significantly among the three groups. However, a significantly greater proportion of control subjects changed negatively than did either modeling (p<.01) or discussion (p<.07) subjects. Significantly greater numbers of subjects within both the modeling

TABLE 34.2.
SUBJECTS SHOWING POSITIVE, NO FURTHER, OR NEGATIVE RATED
BEHAVIOR CHANGE FROM CASCADIA POST-RATING TO SUBSE-
QUENT
INSTITUTION RATING

			Behavior change			
Subject	n	Positive	No further	Negative	% positive	% negative
Modeling	44	17	23	4	38.6	9.1
Discussion	51	20	23	8	39.2	15.8
Control	57	15	26	16	26.3	28.1

(p<.01) and discussion (p<.05) conditions showed positive as opposed to negative behavior changes. This was not the case for the control group.

Follow-up interviews and self-report data were obtained for 53 subjects subsequent to their discharge from parole. Of this sample, 20 had been in the modeling, 18 in the discussion, and 15 in the control groups. The sample is biased by (a) early parole discharges given to some boys (the majority of these were in the modeling group), (b) voluntary participation of the interviewees (however, only 7 boys or their parents out of 60 boys who were contacted refused to participate), and (c) urban residence of most subjects.

Three kinds of data were obtained from each follow-up contact: (a) descriptions by subjects of their experiences following release, (b) reports by subjects of their recall, application of, and rated usefulness of their Cascadia experiences, and (c) readministration of several self-report measures including a specially devised checklist on which subjects compared their current adjustment in several areas to that prior to institutionalization.

Blind ratings were made of interview typescripts in order to determine subjects' evaluations of their experiences during institutionalization and parole. Interviews were rated as reflecting positive, neutral, or negative response to these experiences. Only in the case of the modeling group did any absolute majority of the subjects indicate an overall positive response to the state's programs for young offenders (p<.01).

Another type of follow-up data was derived from subjects' recollections of their participation in the modeling and discussion groups. Recall of content, procedure, and the group's goals was rated as adequate to good or as poor. A higher percentage of subjects in the modeling group (79%) recalled the content and purpose of the groups than was the case for the discussion group (38%; p<.05). Although it was expected that recall of the content would be superior for modeling group boys because of the greater specificity and repetition involved in the imitative procedures, their better recall of the purposes of the groups might not have been anticipated, since approximately the same amount of time was taken by models or leaders in describing this aspect of the group sessions. The subjects also were asked to remember as many of the different topics or scenes as they could without prompting from the interviewer. A subject was considered to have recalled a topic or scene if he was able to describe adequately the concept which had been dealt with and to illustrate that concept (e.g., relating to people in authority—the job problem situation). Fifteen out of 19 boys in the modeling group spontaneously recalled at least two topics ($p < .02$, binomial test). Only 7 of the boys in the discussion group recalled two or more topics.

The interviewer sought to elicit from subjects examples of applications of the concepts and topics to their subsequent lives. This was done to determine if the subjects could make meaningful connections between the topics presented in the group sessions and actual events they had subsequently experienced. They were considered to have applied a topic if they clearly stated that their behavior in the example situation had been a direct function of what had been learned in the group. Sixteen of the 19 subjects in the modeling group applied at least one topic ($p < .01$, binomial test). Seven of these subjects applied three or more. Six of the 13 discussion group subjects applied one topic and 2 made three or more applications. Two subjects in the modeling group stated that they had not understood the concepts and topics and 6 discussion group boys had not understood the material.

Complete records of each subject's movements were obtained, such as leaves, escapes, transfers, discharges, and readmissions. Recidivism was defined as (a) return of a boy to a juvenile institution because of unsatisfactory behavior, (b) conviction in Superior Court resulting in adult status probation, or (c) confinement in an adult correctional institution. A covariate of the recidivism rate is the period at risk, the time elapsed since institutionalization. The cumulative recidivism rate for juvenile offenders in Washington ranges from 22% to over 30%, depending on the period at risk and on yearly fluctuations in the population. The period at risk for the subjects was at least 18 months, which is sufficiently long to warrant confidence in the assumption that the number of recidivists identified closely approximated the maximum number that would eventually occur, because a risk period of this length is estimated to identify over 80% of the maximum expected number.

At a time almost three years after their arrival at Cascadia, 43 of the 192 boys in the sample, or 22.4%, had become recidivists. More recidivists were in the control group (n = 22) than in the modeling (n = 12) and discussion (n = 9) groups ($p < .06$, chi-square test). The recidivism rate for the control group (34%) was consistent with the then current cumulative recidivism rate for the male population in the state. Comparisons were made of the proportion of recidivists to nonrecidivists in each of four samples: (a) modeling group, (b) discussion group, (c) control group, and (d) the cumulative Cascadia male population (n = 1,242). The Z-score comparisons of differences among proportions indicated that fewer modeling (p.<.06) and discussion (p.<.009) subjects became recidivists than did controls. Compared to the base rate of recidivism in the population, these differences are more highly significant (modeling vs. population, p.<.02; discussion vs. population, p.<.001).

An additional set of findings merits reporting because it demonstrates the significant interaction that may take place between the personal characteristics of subjects and the treatments to which they may be subjected. Sarason's (Sarason & Ganzer, 1962) TAS was one of the premeasures obtained on all subjects. Evidence gathered in laboratory studies of college students has suggested that highly anxious subjects scan the environment especially intently for cues and information which might be of assistance in problem solving (Sarason, 1968, 1972; Wine, 1971). High-TAS subjects have been found to show a stronger response to reinforcement than do their lower scoring counterparts (Sarason & Ganzer, 1962). High-TAS scorers have also been found to be more responsive to modeled cues than have low scorers (Sarason, Pederson, & Nyman, 1968). Might test anxiety interact significantly with the conditions of the present investigation?

To answer this question it seemed important to take account of the feedback factor, whether or not a subject viewed videotapes of his own role playing or group discussion behavior. Most of the subjects reported that receiving televised feedback of their own behavior was upsetting because of the contrast between the polished role playing of the models and their own less expert performance. Since highly anxious persons typically do not respond favorable to stress, it was of interest to compare high- and low-TAS groups under televised and nontelevised conditions. For modeling groups in the present study, only 1 out of 15 high-TAS subjects (scores≤ 6) whose role playing was televised and later replayed for them received favorable behavioral ratings (i.e., in a socially desirable direction). Fourteen out of 19 high-TAS subjects who did not receive televised feedback showed positive behavior change (p<.05).

Comparison of the relative efficacy of the modeling and discussion techniques for subjects differing in TAS scores yielded one significant result. For nontelevised high-TAS groups, a greater proportion of modeling subjects (14 of the 19) than discussion subjects (6 of the 20) received positive behavior ratings (p<.02). Comparisons were also made in which the magnitude as well as the direction of behavior change was taken into account. High- and low-TAS subjects who changed either plus or minus one standard deviation of the sample score mean were compared. For modeling, 6 out of 7 high-TAS subjects who received the televised feedback condition were rated as changing in a negative direction, whereas 7 out of 9 high-TAS boys in the nontelevised condition changed favorably (p = .05, Fisher's test). Significant differences did not emerge in other comparisons, and a similar pattern of relationships was not found for televised and nontelevised high-TAS subjects in the discussion groups nor for subjects in the control group.

Discussion

The results of this research suggest that the modeling and the structured discussion approaches had greater concurrent and long-term effects on adolescent delinquents than did the normal program of a high-quality institution. (During the time periods when the modeling and discussion boys were in the experiment, the control boys were participating in a variety of educational, recreational, and vocational activities.) There were no strong, consistent differences between the two experimental groups. Both the modeling and discussion treatments provided personally relevant information to subjects in an interesting and meaningful way, and both treatments were highly structured. They lacked "depth" in that they did not focus on psychodynamic factors. Informal comments by the subjects suggested that they were impressed with and responded favorably to the well-ordered, informational, and no-nonsense approach of both experimental treatments.

As part of the standard routine at Cascadia, most youngsters are diagnosed in accord with a classification system. After completion of our experiment, we examined the diagnosis of boys who had responded differentially to the treatment conditions. Of the boys receiving the modeling sequence and showing improvement on our dependent measures, a disproportionate number bore such diagnoses as "neurosis" and "passive-dependent personality." Case reports tended to describe these types of boys as benign, passive, and markedly deficient in verbal skills. Of the boys who improved while receiving the discussion treatment, a disproportionate number bore such diagnoses as "passive-aggressive personality" and "sociopathic personality." Case reports tended to describe these types of boys as socially active, hostile, and verbally aggressive. These differences suggest the possibility that social modeling and group discussion regimes have different effects on identifiable, relatively homogeneous groups. Future research aimed at systematically evaluating this differential responsiveness would be helpful both from a practical treatment and a theoretical standpoint.

Another issue arising from the present investigation which merits further study concerns the similarities and differences between the modeling and discussion formats and their psychological impacts on the subjects. The treatments were similar in that they were high structured, but they differed in their amounts of physical and social activity. Recently, several attempts have been made to increase adaptive behavior through highly structured informational and counseling programs similar to our modeling and discussion conditions. These attempts have been directed toward behavior in a variety of educational and vocational settings: reclaiming high school dropouts, strengthening work-related behaviors in unemployed persons, and providing therapeutic avenues for disturbed individuals (Krumboltz & Thoresen, 1969; Sarason & Ganzer, 1969; Vriend, 1969). Further inquiry into these types of questions will advance both theory and practice. What are the desirable personal qualities of an effective model? How similar should a model or discussion leader be to the persons with whom he works (e.g., with regard to age, socioeconomic status, and level of adjustment)? To what degree are modeling and discussion effects separable?

A question arises from the fact that both experimental groups showed greater increases in adaptive behavior than did the control group. Could this have happened because these groups received more attention at Cascadia than did the control group? While a positive answer to this question cannot be completely ruled out, it seems unlikely that extra attention is a sufficient explanation of the results presented here. Of several reasons for this conclusion, the most obvious is the long-term effects. It is difficult to imagine that simply giving attention to boys for a few hours a week over a period of 1 month would bring about significant differences in recidivism almost three years after treatment. Furthermore, as was mentioned earlier, the Cascadia environment is not the impoverished one in which one would expect attention effects to flourish. Finally, the relative recidivism rates for the modeling, discussion, and control groups have remained relatively stable over the entire follow-up period. If anything, the differences in recidivism between the experimental and the control groups have been somewhat greater for the last 12 than for the first 12 follow-up months.

The findings related to subjects' TAS scores suggested the hypothesis that high-anxiety persons are more sensitive to cues provided by the behavior of others (models) than are low–anxiety persons. However, the salutory effects of this sensitivity were found only when a stressful element (television) was omitted from the situation. It would thus seem important to minimize and control stressful elements in situations designed to be therapeutic for high-anxiety individuals but which do not focus on the reduction of anxiety per se. Modeling appeared to be superior to discussion as a means of effecting behavior change among high-anxiety persons. Research is needed to clarify the interactions among treatments and personal characteristics for the gamut of psychological therapies.

NOTES

1. This investigation was supported in part by a grant from the Social and Rehabilita-

tion Service, Department of Health, Education, and Welfare. Robert Trojan, William Callahan, and the staff of the Cascadia Juvenile Reception-Diagnostic Center made important contributions, as did Ralph Sherfey, Sarah Sloat, Theodore Sterling, V. M. Tye, H. J. Wahler, Lloyd Bates, and Cameron Dightman. We gratefully acknowledge the contributions of the superintendents and staffs of Washington's juvenile institutions and of these assistants: David Barrett, Peter Carlson, Duane Dahlum, Douglas Denney, Richard Erickson, Robert Howenstine, Robert Kirk, and David Snow.

2. Requests for reprints should be sent to Irwin G. Sarason, Department of Psychology, Center for Psychological Services and Research, NI-15 University of Washington, Seattle, Washington 98105.

3. Now at the Child Study and Treatment Center, Steilacom, Washington.

4. A limited number of sets of the modeling scripts as well as the discussion format to be described are available from Irwin G. Sarason.

REFERENCES

Bandura, A. *Principles of behavior modification.* New York: Holt, Rinehart & Winston, 1969.

Dahlstrom, W. G. & Welsh, G. S. (Eds.) *An MMPI handbook.* Minneapolis: University of Minnesota Press, 1960.

Gough, H. G. *California Psychological Inventory manual.* Palo Alto, Calif.: Consulting Psychologists Press, 1957.

Krumboltz, J. D., & Thoresen, C. E. (Eds.) *Behavioral counseling: Cases and techniques.* New York: Holt, Rinehart & Winston, 1969.

La Fleur, N. K., & Johnson, R. G. "Separate effects of social modeling and reinforcement in counseling adolescents." *Journal of Counseling Psychology,* 1972, *19,* 292–95.

Lorge, I., Thorndike, R. L., & Hagen, E. *Technical manual: Lorge-Thorndike Intelligence Test.* Boston: Houghton-Mifflin, 1966.

Lykken, D. T. "A study of anxiety in the sociopathic personality." *Journal of Abnormal and Social Psychology,* 1957, *55,* 6–10.

Navran, L. A. "A rationally derived MMPI scale to measure dependence." *Journal of Consulting Psychology,* 1954, *18,* 192.

Rotter, J. B. "Generalized expectancies for internal versus external control of reinforcement." *Psychological Monographs,* 1966, *80,* (1, Whole No. 609).

Sarason, I. G. "Verbal learning, modeling, and juvenile delinquency." *American Psychologist,* 1968, *23,* 254–66.

Sarason, I. G. "Experimental approaches to test anxiety: Attention and the uses of information." In C. D. Spielberger (Ed.), *Anxiety: Current trends in research and theory.* Vol. 2. New York: Academic Press, 1972.

Sarason, I. G. & Ganzer, V. J. "Anxiety, reinforcement, and experimental instructions in a free verbalization situation." *Journal of Abnormal and Social Psychology,* 1962, *65,* 300–307.

Sarason, I. G., & Ganzer, V. J. "Social influence techniques in clinical and community psychology." In C. D. Spielberger (Ed.), *Current topics in clinical and community psychology.* Vol. 1. New York: Academic Press, 1969.

Sarason, I. G., Pederson, A. M., & Nyman, B. "Test anxiety and the observation of models." *Journal of Personality,* 1968, *36,* 493–511.

Vriend, T. J. "High performing inner-city adolescents assist low-performing peers in counseling groups." *Personnel and Guidance Journal*, 1969, *47*, 897–904.

Wahler, H. J. *Wahler Self-Description Inventory*. Los Angeles, Calif: Western Psychological Services, 1969.

Wine, J. "Test anxiety and direction of attention." *Psychological Bulletin*, 1971, *76*, 92–104.

35

The Preston Typology Study: An Experiment with Differential Treatment in an Institution[1]

Carl F. Jesness

Reprinted from *Crime and Delinquency* 8 (January 1971): 38–52 by permission of the author and publisher, National Council on Crime and Delinquency.

The Interpersonal Maturity Level (I-level) classification system subdivides delinquents into types hypothesized as having clear-cut implications for the kinds of treatment intervention strategies required. The present study investigated the feasibility and effectiveness of applying the system in an institutional setting. Subjects were randomly assigned to a control or experimental group. Experimental subjects of a particular subtype were assigned to one of six living halls where unique treatment programs were developed.

Immediate effects on institution operation were noted, including a significant reduction in management problems in the experimental units. Evaluation of pre- and post-psychological and behavioral measures also showed that significantly greater gains were made by the experimental subjects. Parole data, however, revealed no significant differences in the violation rates of experimental and control subjects. The fact that after two years of possible exposure to parole more than three out of five (62 percent) of the 1,607 wards had violated parole and been returned to an institution suggests that whatever rehabilitation is accomplished in an institution must be complemented by supportive community services.

This paper summarizes the findings of the Preston Typology Study and discusses the theoretical and practical implications of these findings. The Preston Typology Study was a two and one-half year research-demonstration project concerned with the classification and treatment of delinquent adolescents. The purpose of the study was to explore the usefulness of the Interpersonal Maturity Level (I-level) classification system in the differential treatment of delinquents in an institutional setting. The specific objectives were:

1. To develop an efficient and reliable procedure for the classification of delinquent youth into one of nine I-level subtypes.

2. To train institutional staff in the Interpersonal Maturity Level system.

3. To develop, for each of the major I-level subtypes, differential treatment programs applicable to institutional settings.

4. To evaluate the effects of differential assignment and treatment on the operation of the institution and on the behavior of the subjects.

BACKGROUND

For several years the California Youth Authority has been engaged in research efforts designed to improve the effectiveness of its treatment programs. Generally, the approach taken to increasing the effectiveness of its rehabilitation program has been to focus on the introduction of new elements into an existing treatment program. Several of these treatment components such as group counseling, psychiatric treatment, intensified vocational training, and large group community meetings have been evaluated—generally without very impressive results.[2] Probably the most important of these innovative projects has been the Community Treatment Project,[3] in which treatment in the community was substituted for incarceration. Delinquents classified into one of nine I-level subtypes are assigned to a treatment agent and a treatment modality in the community hypothesized as optimally effective for wards of each particular type. Although the research findings are not without ambiguity, feasibility of substituting treatment in the community for incarceration with no worse outcomes is being clearly demonstrated. The most emphatic findings relate to the greater success where the treater's personality or natural behavior style has been judged to be congruent with the treatment strategy. Limited data from one institutional study[4] indicated that certain types of subjects, primarily those labeled or diagnosed as neurotic, responded more to an intensified treatment program involving higher staff-to-boy ratios. These studies suggest that even where gross categories are used, some differential outcomes can be expected and that each class of subjects may be more responsive to one kind of intervention strategy than another.

The theory that forms the basis of the I-level classification system first presented in a paper written by Sullivan, Grant, and Grant (now Warren)[5] in 1957, described a "basic core structure personality" comprised of a relatively consistent set of expectations in regard to the external world. As a child develops, new discriminations are made and assimilated. Seven successive levels of integrations (hence I-level) are postulated, each stage of which is defined by crucial interpersonal problems that must be resolved before further maturity can occur. The level of integration is manifested primarily through the individual's perception of self and others, that is, his ability to understand intra- and interpersonal events. Although the authors originally described seven levels of integration, more recent elaborations have concentrated on levels two, three, and four, for these include the vast majority of delinquent subjects.[6] Within each of these three maturity levels, subtypes are distinguished according to the characteristic manner in which the individual responds to interpersonal events. Thus, nine delinquent subtypes are identified (two I_2 subtypes, three I_3 subtypes, and four I_4 subtypes). These are listed below [in Figure 35.1] with their symbol (code name) and the proportion of the subjects classified into each subtype during the Preston Study.

THE SETTING

Preston School of Industry is a large California Youth Authority institution housing approximately 900 wards in 16 living units. The boys sent to Preston ranged in age from 16 to 20 (median 17.6) and remained in the institution for an average of 8.4 months. Most boys sent to Preston had more lengthy and serious records than those sent to other facilities, and 45 percent had previously been committed to a Youth Authority institution. Of the 16 housing units at Preston, five were assigned work meeting special criteria in that they had been cleared for work outside the confines of the institution or had been assigned to one of two psychiatric units on the basis of their amenability and motivation for individual psychotherapy and/or on the basis of a special recommendation made by the Youth Authority.

SUBJECTS

The study sample consisted of boys who arrived at Preston during a 13-month period (February, 1966, to March, 1967). All subjects who were not preselected for special programs, such as for work outside the institution or for the Psychiatric Treatment Program, were placed in a pool of eligibles who were then assigned by random methods to either the experimental or control group. Experimental subjects were subsequently placed in one of six living units according to their I-level subtype classification (with infrequently diagnosed I_2 Aa together with Ap subjects, and Se and Ci subjects in the Na or Nx units). Subjects designated as controls were assigned to one of five living units according to previously established institutional procedures that did not take account of personality type. A total of 655 experimental subjects and 518 control subjects remained in the study sample after losses resulting from transfer or failure to meet the eligibility criteria (more than three months in the program during the project period). Four hundred and thirty-four were assigned to special programs.

FIGURE 35.1.
CODE NAME-SUBTYPE

I-level	Code Name	Subtype	Proportion in Preston Sample
I₂	Aa	Unsocialized Aggressive	2.6%
	Ap	Unsocialized, Passive	9.5%
I₃	Cfc	Conformist, Immature	23.8%
	Cfm	Conformist, Cultural	13.6%
	Mp	Manipulator	18.6%
I₄	Na	Neurotic, Acting-Out	13.8%
	Nx	Neurotic, Anxious	15.2%
	Se	Situational Emotional Reaction	1.9%
	Ci	Cultural Identifier	1.0%

STAFF TRAINING AND ASSIGNMENT

Because the development of differential treatment programs in the institution was so highly dependent upon the creative efforts of Preston staff, the training program for the experimental unit treatment personnel took the form of problem-solving sessions rather than formal didactic instruction. Management personnel received approximately 70 hours of training, and the group supervisors and youth counselors received 34. In addition, monthly training seminars were held throughout the project's operational period. Most of the training centered on discussions of the characteristics and treatment of the particular subtype that was the responsibility of each treatment team. The responses of staff to a questionnaire, administered before and after the training period, indicated that during the course of training the attitudes of staff had become more congruent with those points of view believed to be best suited for working with subjects assigned to their treatment unit.

To further implement differential treatment, an attempt was made to match treaters to treated in accordance with behavior predilections inherent in each staff member's personality, interests, and natural working style. While there was much resistance to reassignment, some transfers were accomplished during the course of the project, transfers that were in part guided by the staff's response to the questionnaire designed for this purpose. By the end of the study the majority of treatment staff were working in experimental units where the desired treater-stance was compatible with staff's stated preferences. The Mp, Cfc, and Na experimental lodges began and finished the study with the highest percentage of compatible staff assigned. This point is worth noting since, by the end of the training period, these three units appeared to have moved furthest toward establishing unique differential treatment strategies that most closely approximated the desired models.

CLASSIFICATION

Classification of subjects into one of nine I-level subtypes was based on the integration of data from three sources: an interview, an inventory, and a sentence completion test. The initial guidelines to the interpretation of these data came from the responses of a previously diagnosed sample of cases from the Community Treatment Project. The characteristic responses of wards of each subtype to the interview and sentence completion test, administered to a larger sample, were compiled in a manual (Manual on Sequential I-level Classification, 1970).[7] The computer technology developed for classification based on the Jesness Inventory is also described in the Manual.[8]

Extensive data were presented showing the agreement of each of these measures with one another and with a final staff subtype diagnosis. Overall, the interviewer's impression agreed with the final staff diagnosis in 56 percent of the cases, the sentence completion test diagnosis agreed in 35 percent of the cases, and the classification based on the inventory in 49 percent of the cases. Agreement among independent interviews occurred in 55 percent of the cases, and agreement in diagnosis between independent staffing teams was 60 percent.

Data reporting the relationships among the three independent measures indicated there was significant agreement among these measures and, therefore, evidence of convergent validity for all subtypes except for the I_2 Aa subjects.

SUBTYPE CHARACTERISTICS

Mean scores obtained by subjects of the nine subtypes on a variety of psychological and behavioral measures presented few surprises, with most of the subjects responding as could have been predicted from Warren's original description of the subtypes.[9] The fact that these classes of subjects differed significantly in their responses to a wide variety of measures was regarded as additional evidence of the usefulness and coherence of the classification system. It was noted that, though many of the measures discriminated among the subtypes, the behavioral deficits and/or psychological problems of certain subtypes were amplified on certain measures and were not clearly evident on others.

DESCRIPTION OF EXPERIMENTAL TREATMENT PROGRAMS

Descriptions of the experimental treatment programs were obtained through periodic meetings with each treatment team and with panels of selected wards from each of the six experimental units. Members of the research staff also spent several hours observing each program. There was considerable congruence between the observations of staff, wards, and researchers. Highlights of each program are as follows:

I_2—Juniper Lodge. Staff style: patient, protective, tolerant, not demanding, able to give yet willing to set clear limits. Establish supportive, nonthreatening, nonpunitive, clearly structured environment; build confidence through work and school accomplishment; extinguish (ignore) bizarre behavior, but attend to and reinforce positive behaviors; assign two special teachers for remedial reading; all wards to work one-half day in laundry, starting with the simplest job, working up to the more complex jobs.

I_3Cfm—Ironwood Lodge. Staff style: willing and able to offer support and positive encouragement for small accomplishment with low expectation of verbal insight. Insulate from more delinquently oriented peers; build up self-esteem and autonomy at every opportunity; establish nonconfrontive milieu and positive educational experience; attempt to establish positive attitude toward school by assigning a selected three-man teaching staff with special skills in arts and crafts and athletics.

I_3Cfc—Greenbrier Lodge. Staff style: preference for group rather than individual counseling, sufficiently secure and confident to confront residents, yet able to interact comfortably and honestly. Use power of group to confront wards with nonpayoff for delinquent behavior and attempt to establish trust of adults working in an authoritarian role. Large group (community meetings) held at least three times each week.

I_3Mp—Hawthorne Lodge. Staff style: comfortable with tight limits, confident, skeptical, able to discriminate manipulation from serious efforts to communicate. A main goal is to extinguish manipulative behavior and reinforce honest, "straight," interpersonal behavior. During most of the operational period a micro (token) economy was established to give staff greater control of wards' behavior.

I₄Na—Fir Lodge. Staff style: able to tolerate hostility and verbalized anti-authoritarian statements; open, honest, and equalitarian; willing to allow and encourage wards to assume major responsibility for hall operation; nondefensive and able to acknowledge personal inadequacies. A main goal is to increase anger and acting-out threshold, establish a trusting relationship with adults; emphasis on individual counseling using concepts of transactional analysis to help wards understand and deal with family hang-ups.

I₄Nx—Evergreen Lodge. Staff style: preference for permissive, loosely structured settings; desirous of becoming involved in serious discussions of wards' personal problems; supportive and equalitarian. Goals include increasing self–respect and confidence and gaining insight into the reasons behind their delinquent acts through group counseling.

In actuality, could one discern clear differences in the behavior of staff and wards in each of the six living units? The research staff's impression was that differences were apparent, but that most of the uniqueness in living unit milieu came from individual difference in the interpersonal behavior of the wards. The quiet relaxed atmosphere of the Nx and Cfm units; the often hostile, tense climate in the Na unit; the perambulating, attention-seeking behavior apparent in the I₂ unit—all seemed primarily related to the individual differences among the subtypes.

It was apparent that some treatment teams had moved along considerably faster and further in developing unique treatment programs. The Mp and Cfc experimental programs, in particular, seemed to have made more progress than others in developing appropriate strategies. There were probably several reasons for this, including the fact that these more structured and confrontive treatment strategies appeared to be more readily adapted to the institutional setting and staffing pattern. The Nx, Na, and I₂ programs, emphasizing as they did the need for one-to-one individual contacts, seemed to demand a much higher staff-to-ward ratio than was present in the Preston institution. With the Cfm subjects, whose behavior was inconspicuous and seemingly innocuous in the institution and whose problems were not clearly evident, staff were presented with a difficult problem both in formulating specific treatment objectives and in developing programs to achieve these objectives.

DIMENSIONS OF TREATMENT

The experimental programs were compared, both with one another and with the control units, through the application of a common set of dimensions. Estimations of lodge climate and interpersonal events were obtained from three sources: (1) wards' perceptions of their institutional experience, gained through use of a questionnaire; (2) ratings made by outside experts who had read and evaluated typed scripts of program descriptions obtained by means of interviews with the senior group supervisors of each of the 16 living units; and (3) Moos Social Climate Scale.[10]

Predictably, subjects of the various subtypes differed in their perceptions of treatment conditions and relationships with staff. Generally, I_4 subjects tended to evaluate their institutional experiences more positively than did I_2 subjects. A comparison of scores obtained by experimental and control subjects showed that Na and Nx experimental subjects perceived their treatment programs as more permissive and equalitarian than did Na and Nx subjects assigned to the control units, whereas the Mp and Cfc experimental subjects viewed their treatment programs as less permissive than did their control counterparts. These differences, though small, were significant and in the expected direction.

There was considerable agreement between the ratings of experts and the wards' perceptions of treatment on those dimensions common to both (permissiveness, involvement, equalitarianism). Experimental and control units, however, were most clearly distinguished on the dimension of treatment orientation. Ratings of experts indicated that the treatment team supervisors of the experimental units were better able to articulate rational treatment programs. Although a nonexperimental psychiatric treatment unit was ranked first, the Mp, Na, and I_2 experimental units were ranked second, third, and fourth on this dimension compared with all 16 units.

Regarding the question of the relationships between perceived treatment and measured change, significant correlations were found between the wards' perceptions of staff as involved and fair and change scores on several Inventory and behavior variables. Although it is easy to take for granted that such basic ingredients as trust, involvement, and fairness in the interpersonal relationships of wards and staff are prerequisite to change, it is reassuring that such relationships can actually be demonstrated. Some of the more enlightening outcomes of this particular analysis were the appearance of contradictory correlations in the experimental and control groups. Although the evidence was sketchy, the data suggested the possibility that certain basic qualities in the interpersonal behavior of staff may be necessary but not sufficient conditions for change. Perhaps only when such process variables or intervention strategies as adversive stimulation, selective reinforcement, or confrontation are also present can change with some kinds of subjects be predicted.

PROGRAM IMPACT ON UNIT MANAGEMENT, GROUP COUNSELING, AND GROUP COHESION

Data on the immediate impact of the experimental program on the institution indicated fairly consistently that the introduction of the I-level system tended to decrease unit management problems. During the operational phase of the study, significantly fewer reports of serious rule infractions and peer problems were reported in the experimental units. Paralleling the decrease in serious incident reports in these units was a significant reduction in the use of confinement. The decrease in incidence of behavioral problems was particularly dramatic in the Nx and Cfm units, where reductions of 63 percent and 43 percent occurred. In only one unit, the I_2 lodge, was an increase in problems reported. This was believed to be more related to the unique characteristics of this subtype than to homogeneous assignment per se, since a corresponding increase in problems was also reported in the control unit to which a large number of I_2 subjects had been assigned.

An analysis of the content of the small-group-counseling meetings held before and during the operational period of the study did not reveal any consistent patterns of change. The expectation that the I_4 Nx subjects and, to a lesser extent, the I_4 Na subjects would spend more time discussing personal problems in these meetings was not substantiated. The issue was confounded, however, by the fact that a reduction in staff during the operational period of the study resulted in an overall drop in the number of small-group-counseling meetings held during that period. The subjective impression gained from reading the counseling notes was that the variation in content of small-group-counseling meetings was primarily a function of staff willingness (or lack of willingness) to lead the boys into and keep them focused on discussions of difficult personal subject matter and, only secondarily, a function of ward characteristic or classification.

Sociometric data revealed few important differences in the choice—rejection patterns among the experimental and control lodges—but several trends specific to subtype. As expected, the I_2 subjects assigned to the mixed control lodges were underchosen and over-rejected in relation to their number in the total population (ration of choices to rejections was .79), whereas the more socialized subjects such as Cfc's and Nx's attained much higher social status (ratios of choices to rejections of 2.51 and 1.93, respectively). Analysis of choice patterns also showed that except for I_2 subjects, proportionately more choices and fewer rejections were directed toward subjects of like subtype.

EVALUATION OF OUTCOMES

The impact of the experimental program on the study subjects was evaluated through psychometrics, behavior ratings, and parole follow-up data. Most of the evidence regarding the development of treatment programs indicated that the Mp, Cfc, Na, and I_2 experimental units had been more successful in developing unique treatment strategies than other units; and, consequently, differential outcomes could be most confidently predicted for these subtypes.

The results of the analysis of pretest to post-test change scores generally substantiated these expectations. On psychological measures, the Mp experimental subjects showed the most unambiguous change in the desired and expected direction. Compared with the Mp control subjects, Inventory data showed the experimental group as having become less autistic and alienated and, at the same time, more aware of problems in interpersonal relationships. The Cfc and Na experimental groups showed the greatest improvement on behavioral criteria. Compared with their controls, the experimental Cfc and Na subjects at the time of release were rated as significantly less aggressive and alienated and as more responsible and conforming. The expectation of differential changes favoring the experimental I_2 program was not verified.

In spite of the fact that violation of parole is a crude measure that may be of questionable value as a criterion of treatment effectiveness, any analysis of treatment outcomes with delinquents seems incomplete unless recidivism data are examined. Thus, a detailed analysis of the comparative success or failure on parole of E and C subjects was made. (Failure was defined as a suspension leading to revocation of parole within a 15-month postrelease period.)

Although almost all the evidence of behavioral and psychological changes favored the experimental groups, parole data shown in Table 35.1 indicate the performance of these two groups to be the same. Overall, 54 percent of the controls and 54 percent of the experimental subjects had violated parole on or before the 15th month after their release to parole.

The first step in refining the analysis was to compare violation rates as broken down by I-level subtypes. As shown in Table 35.2, revocation rates of the nine experimental and control subtype groups were remarkably similar. A Chi-square analysis failed to show statistically significant differences between E and C groups for any of the subtypes. Data based on a 24-month exposure period also showed no significant difference.

Because certain background variables are known to be related to parole outcome, a further refinement in the analysis was carried out by classifying wards as good, average, or poor parole risks (base expectancy categories) according to scores derived from weighted background variables.[11] Of Preston wards, 43.6 percent fell in the poor-risk category, 30.9 percent in the medium category, and 25.5 percent in the good-risk category.

As shown in Table 35.3, the percent of violators for experimental and control groups at 15 and 24 months were remarkably similar within each base expectancy category. This applies to the special control groups as well. No noticeable treatment effects were apparent for wards assigned to the psychiatric program, or to the special vocational programs then in effect for boys cleared for work outside the institution.

Those classified into each risk category behaved much as predicted. Of the total group, 66.0 percent of the poor risks; 50.5 percent of the medium risks, and 38.6 percent of the good risks had violated parole on or before 15 months

TABLE 35.1.
PAROLE VIOLATION RATES BY LIVING UNIT AT
15 MONTHS AND 24 MONTHS OF POSTRELEASE EXPOSURE

Living Unit	N	15 Months		24 Months	
		n fail	% fail	n fail	% fail
Experimental					
Evergreen (Nx)	116	58	50.0	70	60.3
Fir (Na)	128	69	53.9	82	64.1
Greenbrier (Cfc)	103	61	59.2	73	70.9
Hawthorne (Mp)	100	53	53.0	60	60.0
Ironwood (Cfm)	121	67	55.4	82	67.8
Juniper (I_2)	87	46	52.9	56	64.4
Total	655	354	54.0	423	64.6
Control					
Arbor	92	46	50.0	60	65.2
Buckeye	94	54	57.4	65	69.1
Cedar	114	57	50.0	68	59.6
Douglas	107	65	60.8	74	69.2
Linden	111	58	52.2	68	61.3
Total	518	280	54.0	335	64.7
SC-Outside Assignment					
Ponderosa	95	40	42.1	50	52.6
Tamarack	108	57	52.8	67	62.0
Manzanita	129	62	48.1	69	53.5
Total	332	159	47.9	186	56.0
SC-PTP Psychiatric Treatment					
Oak	51	26	50.0	30	60.0
Sequoia	51	21	41.2	27	52.9
Total	102	47	46.0	57	55.9
Total Institution	1607	840	52.3	1001	62.3

Table 35.2.
Number and Percent of Violators for Experimental and Control Groups by I-level Subtype at 15 Months Postrelease Exposure*

Subjects	Subtype									Total
	Aa	Ap	Cfm	Cfc	Mp	Na	Nx	Se	Ci	
Experimental n	14	55	89	84	78	90	84	11	5	510
n Violators	8	29	49	50	42	55	46	1	1	281
15 Mo. % Violators	57.1	52.7	55.1	59.5	53.8	61.1	54.8	9.1	20.0	55.1
Control n	8	43	109	55	103	50	45	3	1	417
n Violators	4	25	60	33	52	29	26	1	1	231
15 Mo. % Violators	50.0	58.1	55.0	60.0	50.5	58.0	57.8	33.3	100.0	55.4

*Excludes subjects on whom base expectancy scores were not available, and those whose length of stay in the institution was less than three months.

568

TABLE 35.3.
PAROLE VIOLATION RATES AT 15 AND 24 MONTHS PAROLE
EXPOSURE ACCORDING TO BASE EXPECTANCY CLASSIFICATION

Group	Base Expectancy Score		
	Low (Poor Prognosis)	Medium	High (Good Prognosis)
15 Mo. Exposure			
Experimental	66.8%	52.4%	39.2%
Control	65.7%	50.8%	43.6%
SC (Outside Assignment)	66.6%	44.1%	31.6%
SC (Psychiatric Treatment)	57.7%	51.4%	34.3%
Total	66.0%	50.5%	38.6%
24 Mo. Exposure			
Experimental	75.7%	63.3%	50.0%
Control	77.3%	60.5%	54.5%
SC (Outside Assignment)	70.8%	59.3%	43.4%
SC (Psychiatric Treatment)	63.2%	62.2%	49.7%
Total	74.8%	61.7%	49.7%

of postrelease exposure to parole. These differences in violation rates between high and low risk groups were approximately the same at 24 months.

There were significant differences in the violation rates for subjects of the various subtypes, with the highest (poorest) 15-month violation rate (57 percent) being obtained by the Na group, and the lowest (24 percent) by the Se group. As shown in Table 35.4, the Se, Ci, and Nx subtypes were doing best at 24 months, with Cfc and Na subjects doing worst.

IMPLICATIONS

It seems almost incredible that when this study began in 1965, the idea of classifying delinquent subjects and assigning them to unique institutional treatment programs according to their I-level subtype was regarded as a radically innovative procedure. The fact that the system has now been accepted as standard procedure at Preston, as well as at two other California Youth Authority institutions which have opened since the project began, is evidence of its feasibility in the institutional treatment and management of

TABLE 35.4.
PAROLE VIOLATION RATES BY I-LEVEL SUBTYPES AT 15 AND 24
MONTHS EXPOSURE PERIODS FOR TOTAL PRESTON SAMPLE

	Aa	Ap	Cfm	Cfc	Mp	Na	Nx	Se	Ci	Total
Total Number	35	150	393	216	293	228	244	33	15	1,607
Percent Violators										
at 15 Mo.	45.7	54.0	49.6	56.9	54.6	57.0	49.6	24.2	40.0	52.3
at 24 Mo.	60.0	63.3	62.8	67.6	62.4	67.1	56.4	36.4	46.7	62.3

delinquents. The data indicate that assignment and program planning based on the system can lead to a significant reduction in management problems.

The data presented in this report do not fully convey the impact of the experimental program on the institution, for its effects were most apparent in the changed attitudes and behavior of Preston staff. The introduction of the I-level classification system contributed to increased professionalism and enthusiasm on the part of treatment personnel, some of whom had the reputation of being "old line" supervisors, not noted for their openness to change. Providing a rational classification and treatment approach made it possible for these staff members to become increasingly knowledgeable about the behavior and treatment of one or more classes of delinquents. In addition, the involvement of middle-management personnel in the diagnostic process stimulated the exchange of ideas and experimentation in new ways of treatment, which have continued beyond the end of the project.

Although there can be little argument with regard to the feasibility of introducing the system into an institutional setting, the success of the programs in leading to desired change was not emphatic, and the greater success of its graduates on parole was not established. While the test and behavioral data tended to substantiate the hypotheses of differential outcomes favoring the experimental programs, it would not be difficult to argue that these results were quite trivial. The behavior and psychological changes that appeared to be associated with differential treatment need to be substantiated, and preferably in situations where alternative treatment programs can be compared. Two weaknesses of the present study were the failure to more clearly specify the "control" treatment conditions and to provide stimulation (training, interviews, etc.) to the control staff to balance out any possible "Hawthorne" effect.

The use of the I-level classification system can be expected to increase the amount of useful information resulting from research conducted with different populations of delinquents in a variety of settings, for there seems little question that the classification can be done efficiently and reliably, even after a relatively short period of training. Compared with data reported about other classification systems, the reliability and validity of the present system appeared to be satisfactory.[12] There are, of course, some problems in using the classification system—problems that may become increasingly apparent as persons outside the immediate influence of those who have developed the system begin to adapt procedures for their own use. The "core personality" is a theoretical construct inferred from qualitatively different characteristics and responses. It was found that an individual might place a greater or lesser emphasis on any particular characteristic, depending upon his idiosyncratic interpretation of subtype definition, or might infer the presence or absence of a particular characteristic using a quite different rationale.

At other times in the diagnostic process some staff members tended to overemphasize the subject's behavior in a group-living situation, as opposed to his perceptual frame of reference. If group-living behavior were viewed as especially central to the diagnosis, a more direct route to classification could, of course, be attempted through such devices as behavioral ratings. Fortunately for the system, the various heteromethod characteristics usually did fit together in a coherent gestalt.

The integration-level theory itself did not seem to play an important role in the establishment of treatment goals. Most of the treaters at Preston soon became skeptical over the likelihood of helping subjects change from one I-level to a higher level within the time limits of the existing institutional program. In the classification decisions, the theory of developmental levels sometimes appeared to be a help and at other times a hindrance. It usually proved helpful for the staffing team to decide first whether the individual satisfied the general criteria for subjects functioning at a particular level. At other times, the concept of levels seemed a deterrent to clear thinking. There was a noticeable tendency for some staff to conceptualize the I-levels in a concrete manner and exaggerate the discreteness of the categories so that if a subject manifested any one characteristic of the next higher I-level step, he was somehow considered to have "made it" all the way. Warren (1966) has stated that

> . . . interpersonal development is viewed as a continuum . . . individuals are not classified at the level which reflects their maximum capabilities under conditions of extreme comfort, but rather are categorized at the level which represents their typical level of functioning or their capacity to function under conditions of stress.[13]

Nevertheless, the tendency to regard the levels or the subtypes as discrete, nonoverlapping categories is a hazard of which staff need to be aware.

The question may be asked if it is necessary to accept the theory of integration levels in order to use the system; probably not. Some may prefer to conceptualize the subtypes as convenient syndromes or combinations of traits and attributes without reference to a theory of developmental levels. Others might prefer to apply the concepts of social learning theory in theorizing about subtype patterns. Such differences in point of view could add impetus to future research, particularly if the defining parameters of the subtype as presently conceived could be retained. The present I-level classification system seems to provide a functional system for the integration of traits and characteristics that enables a variety of statements to be made concerning the individual. These statements include material relevant to the probable origin or explanation of the subject's delinquency; his perceptions of himself, his family, his peers; his attitude toward adults; his probable response to certain treatment intervention strategies, and so forth. Further familiarity with this system, together with experimentation with new approaches to treatment, could lead to the eventual development of more rational and truly individualized treatment programs. Furthermore, and probably most important, the adoption of this system could immediately make possible the exchange of more meaningful data from researchers using different populations in different parts of the country. It would probably be generally agreed that the usefulness of a classification system such as that of I-level is related to its power in enabling the greatest number of useful predictions to be made regarding a subject's response to a variety of critical situations. At our present state of knowledge, however, it is not always clear what these most useful predictions might be. One can easily imagine that in the future the responses of subjects to various clearly defined intervention strategies will play a more prominent role in determining a system's utility and in defining classes of delinquents. This task should probably be one with high research priority in the next few years.

The most discomforting findings of this study were that the experimental program had no noticeable effect on parole performance, and that on or before two years of exposure to parole more than three out of five (62 percent) of all 1,607 subjects had failed on parole and had been returned to an institution. Evaluating the study with this long-range parole data in hand, the brief staff training and moderate changes in the institution treatment program implemented by the research project seem rather feeble and inadequate to the task. To effect a change in traditional procedures takes time, and the amount of time and training involved must be considerable to compete with the resistance to change that can be anticipated. Staff in the usual institution are in turn severely limited in their capacity to function as change agents by low staff-to-ward ratios, the small proportion of staff time available for treatment-related activity, and the intractibility of the delinquent subjects themselves. These realities almost demand that program innovations be evaluated by the extent to which they achieve limited but clearly defined intermediate goals, rather than by differential recidivism rates.

In addition, the parole data reiterate the generalization that no institutional treatment program can stand alone. It appears unlikely that behavior changes accomplished in an institutional treatment setting can be maintained in the community without some change in the home environment having occurred and some extension of supportive programs into the community. Returning a boy to an unchanged setting that will systematically reinforce the same problem behaviors that brought him to the institution in the first place approximates an exercise in futility. To quote from a recent summary on the effectiveness of behavior therapy, "All the social arrangements that conspired to produce and to sustain this behavior remain waiting, with some probability, to recapture him as he emerges. . . ."[14]

NOTES

1. This study was supported by a grant from the National Institute of Mental Health, United States Public Health Service, made to the Institute for the Study of Crime and Delinquency (now the American Justice Institute).
2. Evelyn S. Guttman, "Effects of Short-Term Psychiatric Treatment," Research Report No. 36, (Sacramento: California Youth Authority, December, 1963); J. P. Seckel, "Experiments in Group Counseling at Two Youth Authority Institutions," Research Report No. 46, (Sacramento: California Youth Authority, 1965).
3. Marguerite Q. Warren, "Classification of Offenders As an Aid to Efficient Management and Effective Treatment," paper prepared for the President's Commission on Law Enforcement and Administration of Justice, Task Force on Corrections, 1966; T. B. Palmer, "Types of Treaters and Types of Juvenile Offender," *Youth Authority Quarterly*, 18:14–23, (1965); T. B. Palmer, Community Treatment Project: An Evaluation of Community Treatment for Delinquents, Ninth Progress Report, Part 1, (Sacramento, California, 1968).
4. C. F. Jesness, The Fricot Ranch Study, Research Report No. 47, (Sacramento: California Youth Authority, 1965).
5. C. E. Sullivan, M. Q. Grant, and J. D. Grant, "The Development of Interpersonal Maturity: Applications to Delinquency", *Psychiatry*, 20:373–385, (1957).
6. Warren, op. cit., supra note 3.
7. C. F. Jesness and R. F. Wedge. Sequential I-level Classification Manual, (Sacramento: California Youth Authority, 1970).
8. Work on the classification system and on more systematic procedures for its application continues, and it is anticipated that a more clearly specified, economical, and more reliable procedure will be developed in the near future.
9. Warren, op. cit., supra note 3.
10. R. H. Moos, "A Situational Analysis of a Therapeutic Community Milieu," *Journal of Abnormal Psychology*, 73:49–61, (1968).
11. R. F. Beverly, "An Analysis of Parole Performance by Institution of Release,"

(1959–1962), Research Report Number 40, (Sacramento: California Youth Authority, March 1965).

12. Data on the reliability of psychiatric classification have generally been unimpressive. In one of the more adequate studies only 24 percent agreement was found between initial interview-based diagnoses of four characterological types and final staffing diagnoses; H. O. Schmidt and C. P. Fonda, "The Reliability of Psychiatric Diagnosis: A New Look," *Journal of Abnormal and Social Psychology*, 48:67–77, (1956).

13. M. Q. Warren, "Interpersonal Maturity Level Classification: Juvenile; Diagnosis and Treatment of Low, Middle, and High Maturity Delinquents," (Sacramento: California Youth Authority, 1966).

14. H. F. Hunt and J. E. Dyrud, "Commentary: Perspective in Behavior Therapy," see J. M. Shlien, H. F. Hunt, J. D. Matarazzo, and C. Salvage (Eds.), Research in Psychotherapy, Vol. III, (Washington D.C.: American Psychological Association, 1968).

36

Establishing Behavior Contracts with Delinquent Adolescents

Robert B. Rutherford, Jr., Ph.D.

Reprinted from *Federal Probation* (March 1975) pp. 28–32 by permission of the publisher, the Administrative Office of the United States Courts.

The effectiveness of behavior modification (applied behavioral analysis) principles and techniques has been demonstrated repeatedly with children and adults in a variety of learning environments. Some behavioral techniques are more effective than others, depending upon the environment where intervention is to take place. The custodial or institutional setting has the potential for controlling the widest range of variables competing with the intervention strategy. Intervention strategies which originate in the home, school, or community, on the other hand, may be limited in their behavioral influence because the individual will have access to many other sources of reinforcement. Older subjects such as delinquents may be more adept at developing alternate strategies for obtaining reinforcers and avoiding manager- or mediator-imposed interventions. It appears, especially with the more sophisticated adolescent, that in order to maximize the effectiveness of the behavioral intervention, and to bridge the gap between the institutional setting and real life, the adolescent must be given the power to negotiate various aspects of the tasks and reinforcers included in the intervention strategy. The strategy which lends itself most appropriately to the adolescent's involvement is behavioral contracting.

BEHAVIORAL CONTRACTING

Behavioral contracting involves the systematic negotiation between mediator (parent, teacher, probation officer, social worker, unit counselor, or supervisor) and a target (delinquent adolescent) of the behaviors to be performed within a given environment, and the specific reinforcing consequences or "payoffs" to be provided when performance requirements are met.

Behavioral contracting is based upon an applied behavior analysis model

575

whereby the environmental dynamics which maintain behavior are assessed. In behavioral contracting, a behavioral analysis involves specifying: (A) the antecedents which will cue the contract behavior, (B) the contract behavior to be developed, and (C) the consequences which will maintain the contract behavior (see figure below).

A   B   C

ANTECEDENTS   CONTRACT BEHAVIOR   CONSEQUENCES

FIGURE: BEHAVIORAL ANALYSIS OF CONTRACT BEHAVIOR

The "antecedents" are events which are present in the environment to cue behaviors. They include those stimuli, cues, directions, or prompts that set the occasion for a given behavior and a specific, predictable consequence. The antecedent cues for doing 20 arithmetic word problems at home may be a math book, a sharp pencil, 3 sheets of paper, directions at the top of the page, and a quiet, well-lighted room. These cues may signal that the "consequences" of completing the "contract behavior," e.g., math problems done correctly by 9:00 A.M. the following morning, will be positive. The positive consequences may be a higher letter grade, praise from teacher and parents, and/or a specifically contracted item or event such as a Coke or 20 minutes of free time at midday. Behavioral analysis makes the assumption that consequences which are positive will result in an increase in the frequency of the desired behavior.

In summary, behavioral analysis involves planning before the fact and behavioral programming after the fact of a given behavior. Sound behavioral contracts specify systematically each of the three steps of the behavioral analysis model.

RULES FOR ESTABLISHING BEHAVIORAL CONTRACTS

The following are steps which appear to be most crucial for the development of sound behavioral contracts:

1. A behavioral analysis must be made of the behavior to be contracted. As mentioned earlier, analysis must be made of the antecedents and consequences of the contracted behavior, as well as of the behavior itself.

2. The behavioral contract must be precise and systematic. Each condition of the contract must be specified. Dates, times, criterion behaviors, amounts and/or range of consequences, names of contractor and contractee, and names of others involved in the contract should all be included. The

terms of the contract must be adhered to strictly and systematically at all times.

3. The behavioral contract must be fair to both the contractor and the contractee. A contract implies the power of both parties to negotiate terms. If the terms are unfair, the contract will fail. The contracted behaviors and the consequences must be balanced to the satisfaction of both parties.

4. The terms of the behavioral contract must stress the positive. A behavioral contract which implies positive reinforcement for appropriate behavior rather than punishment for inappropriate behavior will be more readily adhered to by the contractee. Positive reinforcement strengthens the behavior which it follows; punishment only temporarily suppresses behavior.

5. The concept of "shaping" may be used when establishing behavioral contracts. If a behavior initially does not exist or exists at only a minimal level, the contract must reinforce approximations of a final specified behavior. Opportunities for easy initial success must be enhanced. It should be emphasized that behaviors that are already in the contractee's behavioral repertoire *must* be built into the contract.

6. A consultant or arbitrator may be helpful at first in the negotiation of behavioral contracts between the contractor and the contractee. In many contracts, both the contractor and the contractee must change their behaviors; under these circumstances a consultant or arbitrator permits the terms of the contract to be fair to both parties.

7. The behavioral contract should be a formal written document which specifies all privileges and responsibilities of the parties involved. It should be signed by both parties. The behavioral contract is a negotiated agreement between two people which allows the contractor and the contractee to predict the consequences of the contracted behaviors. Signatures enhance the formality and commitment of the contract.

8. Both the consequences which follow the completion of the contracted behavior (*the* A *clause*), and the consequences which follow the noncompletion of the contracted behavior (*the* B *clause*), must be specified. By specifying the consequences for completing and not completing the contract, the possibilities for misinterpretation of the contract are reduced. Inclusion of both the A and B clauses reduces the chances of error.

9. Reinforcing consequences must always follow the completion of the contracted behavior and must be delivered immediately. In establishing a behavioral contract, the opportunity should be available to receive some portion of the reinforcing consequence immediately upon completion of the contracted behavior. Contracts are often negotiated which allow for small but continuous payoffs for daily behaviors, while at the same time making a large payoff contingent upon completion of a whole series of daily behaviors.

10. Behavioral contracts should progress from contractor-initiated to contractee-initiated as rapidly as possible. While behavioral contracts are negotiated documents, it is generally true that the terms of the initial contracts are designated and controlled by the contractor (parent, teacher, probation officer, unit supervisor, etc.). Behavioral contracting will have more generalized results when the contractee (adolescent) proposes the privileges and responsibilities to be included in the contract.

CASE STUDIES AND SAMPLE BEHAVIORAL CONTRACTS IN FOUR SETTINGS

In order to demonstrate the diversity of the environmental settings where behavioral contracts may be negotiated with delinquent adolescents, four cases are presented along with sample behavioral contracts. The contracts described include a family contract (between mother and son); a school contract (between teacher, counselor, and student); a community contract (between probation officer and probationer); and an institutional contract (between unit supervisor and inmate).

FAMILY CONTRACT

John is a 15-year-old boy. His parents have been separated for several years and he lives with his mother and younger brother and sister. John's mother is concerned that John has been suspended from school because of his poor attendance record. His mother has been trying to reason with him because the school counselor has told her that unless he attends for the rest of the semester and turns in all work assignments, John will not be readmitted to that school. His work assignments consist of two take-home assignments per week. Only 4 weeks remain until the end of the semester. As a last resort, John's mother has threatened to withhold enrollment in a driver's education course unless he can stay in school. John has expressed a strong interest in the driver's education course and in getting his driver's permit in August.

Several other problems exist in the home. John has been going out on weekends without permission and staying out past curfew, a situation which worries his mother because he has been picked up twice by the police and brought home. In order to try to gain John's confidence, his mother has started buying him cigarettes by the carton. She has discovered John is selling unused cigarettes to his friends.

When John is not at home, he frequently visits his mother's friend, Rick Blackley, who lives a few houses away. Rick has a garage full of tools and an old car on which John has worked since his suspension from school. However, the work that John was doing on the car was completed several weeks ago.

Contract

Date_____

1A For each day that John attends all classes, he will earn the privilege of ten (10) cigarettes per day or one (1) package of cigarettes every other day.

1B For each day that John does not attend all classes, ten (10) cigarettes per day will not be earned.

2A If John attends 90 percent of the *full* school days between Monday, May 21, 1973, and Friday, June 14, 1973 (20 days), he will earn one (1) driver's education course. The driver's education course will begin on June 18, 1973.

2B If John does not attend school for 90 percent of all classes between May 21, 1973, and June 15, 1973 (20 days), the privilege of the driver's education course will be withdrawn.

3A For each take-home assignment that John turns in to his teachers between Monday, May 21, 1973, and Friday, June 15, 1973, John will earn one evening out on the weekend, provided his mother knows his whereabouts and the time that he will return home.

3B For each take-home assignment that John does not turn in to his teachers between Monday, May 21, 1973, and Friday, June 15, 1973, John will stay in one evening during the weekend.

* * * * * * * * *

As negotiator and overseer of this contract, Mr. Rick Blackley will see that all sections of this contract are followed and that said consequences will be paid.

As a representative of the Central High School, Mr. Tom Anderson, counselor, will act as the monitor of the behaviors in the school (i.e., attending classes and turning in assignments).

* * * * * * * * *

_____   _____

Mr. John Wright, Student   Mrs. Judy Wright, Mother

_____   _____

Mr. Rich Blackley, Negotiator   Mr. Tom Anderson, Counselor

SCHOOL CONTRACT

Ron is a 16-year-old boy of above average intelligence who is quite disruptive in all of his 10th grade classes except math. His grades, in all but the math class, have been D's and F's for the last two 6-week periods. He is currently maintaining an A in math. He enjoys being with his math teacher, Mr. Leigh, as demonstrated by his appearances in Mr. Leigh's classroom before and after school to discuss math problems and backpacking (a hobby both he and Mr. Leigh have in common). When Ron is not actively disrupting his other classes, he is usually doing math problems rather than the assigned task.

Ron was arrested twice in the last 4 months for selling pills after school near the high school. In addition, he was accused of beating a 14-year-old boy for allegedly failing to make good a debt related to his drug sales. The charges were eventually dropped. However, Ron is still on probation for the drug arrests and his probation officer has stated that if he does not pass all of his courses at the end of the school year, Ron will remain on probation.

Ron's disruptive classroom behavior includes being verbally abusive to his teachers and his peers, making loud noises when others are speaking, walking around the classroom and poking constantly at his classmates. Presently he is excluded from English and machine shop classes due to his behavior. His counselor, Mr. Quinlin, and his math teacher, Mr. Leigh, have discussed establishing a contract with Ron to facilitate his getting back into English and machine shop classes and raising all of his grades to passing level.

Contract

1A   If Ron returns to both his English and machine shop classes and attends at least 4 days out of 5 days each week, he will be allowed to spend his last period (formerly a study hall) in Mr. Leigh's intermediate math class as a math assistant and tutor.

1B   If Ron either fails to return to his English and machine shop classes or fails to attend at least 4 out of 5 days, he will not be allowed to be Mr. Leigh's math assistant and tutor.

2A   If Ron's behavior in both his English class and his machine shop class is judged appropriate by the teachers (criteria of appropriateness to be determined before this contract is to be initiated), he will earn one chit per class per day to be turned in to Mr. Quinlin, the school counselor. Thus a maximum of 10 chits per week can be earned for attendance.

Ron will earn one chit per letter grade on the math, the social studies, the English and the machine shop tests each Friday. An F = 0 chits, a D = 1 chit, a C = 2 chits, a B = 3 chits, and an A = 4 chits. These chits will also be turned in to Mr. Quinlin. Thus a maximum of 16 chits per week can be earned for grades.

For each week that Ron earns at least 18 chits, Mr. Quinlin will issue Ron a pass to spend one half hour a day for three days of the following week with Mr. Leigh, after school. These three ½-hour periods will be spent discussing any topic Ron wishes.

2B   If Ron does not earn a total of 18 chits per week, he cannot spend the ½-hour periods after school with Mr. Leigh.

* * * * * * * * * *

All terms of this contract have been negotiated freely between me, *Ron Chan*, and Mr. Leigh, my math teacher, and Mr. Quinlin, my counselor. I also understand that Mr. Mock, my machine shop teacher, and Mrs. McGlothlin, my English teacher, will assist in this contract.

* * * * * * * * * *

_____	_____
Ron Chan	Mrs. McGlothlin
_____	_____
Mr. Leigh	Mr. Mock
_____	_____
Mr. Quinlin	Date

COMMUNITY CONTRACT

Pamela is 14 years old. She has a record of being a runaway for periods of up to 1 year. When she leaves, it is usually to be with older men. When she was 9 years old she had her first sexual experience with a 19 year old. She now has a 4-month-old baby, fathered by her 21-year-old ex-boyfriend. She has also been treated a number of times for venereal disease.

Pamela's mother is mainly concerned with two of Pamela's problems. The first of these problems is her constant running away from home. Pamela says that the argument that usually precedes her running away deals with the mother's placing too much responsibility for household chores on Pamela. She has three sisters in the home, but she is expected to do the major portion of the work. The second problem area that the mother identifies deals with the $96.00 which Pamela receives every 2 weeks from the County for her baby. Pamela thinks that she should have control of it. Currently the County is making the check payable to the mother.

Pamela enjoys parties with her friends, watching television, and listening to music. She has shown a great deal of interest in going to Disneyland and going out to a nice dinner. She also greatly enjoys the peer group activities that are periodically provided by the County Probation Department, i.e., trips to the mountains, beaches, sports events, museums, and movies.

Contract

Date_____

1A   Pamela receives $96.00 every 2 weeks. Of that $96.00 she will pay her mother, every two weeks:

Food	$30.00
Board	20.83
Utilities	3.00
Total	$53.83 Every 2 weeks

2A   For following the chore chart each week (which divides the household chores evenly between Pamela and her sisters), Pamela will be able to attend any and all group activities provided by the Probation Department that week.

2B   For not following the chore chart each week, Pamela will not be able to attend group activities provided by the Probation Department that week.

3A   For each Friday or Saturday night that Pamela goes out and is home by 1:00 A.M. her mother will provide free baby sitting for the baby that evening.

3B   For each Friday and Saturday night that Pamela is not home by 1:00 A.M., she will pay her mother fifty cents (50¢) per hour for the time that she is gone past 1:00 A.M.

4A   PAMELA WILL RECEIVE FREE BABY SITTING FROM 9:00 A.M. to 1:00 P.M. from her mother on weekdays when Pamela is attending summer school.

4B   Pamela will pay fifty cents (50¢) per hour to her mother for baby sitting if she does not attend summer school.

* * * * * * * * * *

As negotiator and overseer of this contract, Mr. Glen Hamilton, County Probation Officer, will see that all sections of this contract are followed and that said consequences will be paid. Mr. Hamilton will see that both Pamela and her mother are treated fairly by the contract.

* * * * * * * * * *

_____
Ms. Pamela Brooke, Student

                         _____
                         Mr. Glen Hamilton,
                         Probation Officer

_____
Ms. Sue Brooke, Mother

INSTITUTION CONTRACT

Unit III of the County Detention Facility contains 20 girls whose ages range from 13 to 17 years. The average length of confinement is 13 months. The major reasons for confinement include drug use, incorrigibility, theft, assault, and prostitution.

Problem behaviors on the Unit include fighting, refusal to obey staff orders, attempts to run away, refusal to go to school, refusal to work on Unit projects such as group behavioral counseling sessions and Unit cleaning and decorating activities, destroying property in the dayroom and in the dormitory, and stealing from the staff and the other girls.

Possible positive reinforcers available include shortened sentences, having one's own room, weekend passes home, staying up late, special materials to decorate rooms, radios and televisions in one's room, and items from the token economy store.

A token economy system has been established in order to reinforce the girls systematically for performance of appropriate behavior. All of the girls earn tokens for specific behaviors: 5 points for being at breakfast at 7:30 A.M., 3 points for each 20 minutes on-task in the school classroom, 5 points for brushing teeth and hair in the evening, etc. Each girl can also negotiate individual contracts to deal with behaviors unique to herself.

Barbara is a 13-year-old who was placed in the County Detention Facility for being an accomplice to an armed robbery committed by her 19-year-old boyfriend. Barbara, who has lived in nine foster homes since she was 18 months old, was at the County Detention Facility 5 weeks when the first contract was negotiated with her. She participated in the basic token economy of Unit III, but she refused to take part in either the school program or the daily group counseling sessions on the Unit. When she was forced by the staff to attend these activities, she did not speak or in any way acknowledge the other participants.

Barbara has expressed a great deal of interest in visiting her current foster parents. She has been with them over a year and they seem to be as attached to Barbara as she is to them. Also, Barbara has beautiful long black hair which she spends a great deal of time brushing and combing. Barbara's hair is very important to her as she has received many compliments on it both before she entered the Detention Facility and in the Facility itself.

BEHAVIORAL CONTRACT

Date:_____

1A I, _____, agree to attend the school from 9:00 A.M. to 12:00 noon for at least 4 out of the 5 days of the week contingent upon receiving 25 *bonus* points per day and being allowed to stay up until 9:30 to watch TV or play cards with staff.

1B I, _____, agree that if I do not attend school from 9:00 A.M. to 12:00 noon for at least 4 out of 5 days of the week, I will not receive 25 *bonus* points per day and I will have to go to bed at 8:30.

2A When I, _____, am in school, I will complete, 80 percent correctly, 5 of 6 lessons per day contingent upon 5 *bonus* points per lesson and the use of the hairdryer for 30 minutes each evening.

2B When I, _____, am not in school or do not complete, 80 percent correctly, 5 of 6 lessons per day, I will not receive 5 *bonus* points per lesson nor will I be allowed to use the hairdryer that evening.

3A When I, _____, attend each behavioral counseling session, I will receive 5 *bonus* points and the use of all of the hair conditioner, shampoo, curlers, hairnets, bobby pins, and scotchtape I need to do my hair that evening.

3B When I, _____, do not attend a behavioral counseling session, I will not receive 5 *bonus* points and I will not get to use the hairsetting materials.

4A If I, _____, contribute to the behavioral counseling sessions (as judged by Mr. Denison, the behavioral counselor, and the other girls on a scale of 1 to 15) with an average score of 10 or above, I will receive 10 *bonus* points.

4B If I, _____, receive a score below 10 on my contribution to the behavioral counseling session, I will not receive 10 *bonus* points.

5. When I, _____, receive 3150 points, I can visit my foster parents at home from 4:00 P.M. Friday until 4:00 P.M. Sunday of the weekend following my earning the 3150 *bonus* points.

* * * * * * * * * *

_____   _____
Ms. Barbara Russell   Teacher

_____   _____
Unit Supervisor   Behavioral Counselor

CONCLUSION

Applied behavioral analysis, in the form of written behavioral contracts, can be an effective intervention strategy with delinquent adolescents. The contract provides the adolescent with: (1) maximum negotiation power,

(2) directly observable contractor responsibilities, and (3) a system for predicting the behavior of the contractor. The contract provides the contractor or mediator with: (1) the power to negotiate change in the adolescent's behavior, (2) observable contractee behaviors and contingencies, and (3) a system for predicting contractee behavior.